Destruction and Its Impact on Ancient Societies at the End of the Bronze Age

Destruction and Its Impact on Ancient Societies at the End of the Bronze Age

Jesse Millek

LOCKWOOD PRESS
Columbus, Georgia • 2023

Destruction and Its Impact on Ancient Societies at the End of the Bronze Age

Copyright © 2023 by Lockwood Press

All rights reserved. No part of this work may be reproduced or transmitted in any form or by any means, electronic or mechanical, including photocopying and recording, or by means of any information storage or retrieval system, except as may be expressly permitted by the 1976 Copyright Act or in writing from the publisher. Requests for permission should be addressed in writing to Lockwood Press, PO Box 1080, Columbus, GA 31901 USA, admin@lockwoodpress.com.

ISBN: 978-1-948488-83-9

Cover design by Susanne Wilhelm
Cover image: Akrotiri. Jan M, CC BY-SA 3.0, via Wikimedia Commons

Library of Congress Cataloging-in-Publication Data

Names: Millek, Jesse, author.
Title: Destruction and its impact on ancient societies at the end of the Bronze Age / Jesse Millek.
Description: Columbus, Georgia : Lockwood Press, 2022. | Includes bibliographical references and index.
Identifiers: LCCN 2022045705 (print) | LCCN 2022045706 (ebook) | ISBN 9781948488839 (hardcover) | ISBN 9781948488846 (pdf) | ISBN 9781957454016 (epub)
Subjects: LCSH: Bronze age–Mediterranean Region. | Natural disasters–Mediterranean Region–History–To 476. | Mediterranean Region–History–To 476. | Archaeology and natural disasters.
Classification: LCC GN778.25 .M55 2022 (print) | LCC GN778.25 (ebook) | DDC 937–dc23/eng/20221201
LC record available at https://lccn.loc.gov/2022045705
LC ebook record available at https://lccn.loc.gov/2022045706

Printed in the United States of America on acid-free paper.

Contents

List of Figures	vii
Abbreviations	ix
Acknowledgments	xiii
Chapter 1: Destruction and the End of the Bronze Age	1
Chapter 2: The Archaeology of Destruction: Denoting, Describing, and Classifying	23
Chapter 3: The Destruction That Wasn't	53
Chapter 4: Destruction in Mycenean Greece and the Wider Aegean World	131
Chapter 5: Destruction in Anatolia and the Fall of the Hittite Empire	171
Chapter 6: Cyprus and the Absence of Destruction at the End of the Late Bronze Age	199
Chapter 7: The Levant: A Mixed Bag of Destruction	219
Chapter 8: Destruction and 1200 BCE: Overview and Impact on Mediterranean Societies	271
Appendix: Overview of Destruction ca. 1200 BCE	289
References	303
Index	381

v

Figures

Fig. 1.1. Comparative chronology chart of regions in the Eastern Mediterranean. 2

Fig. 1.2. Map after Drews's 1993 map of the "Catastrophe" ca. 1200 BCE. (For sites in italics destruction was assumed probable but not certain.) 5

Fig. 3.1. Misdated destructions in the Eastern Mediterranean excluding the southern Levant. 57

Fig. 3.2. Misdated destructions in the southern Levant. 66

Fig. 3.3. Assumed destructions in the Eastern Mediterranean excluding the southern Levant. 75

Fig. 3.4. Assumed destructions in the southern Levant. 94

Fig. 3.5. False Citations in the Eastern Mediterranean excluding the southern Levant. 106

Fig. 3.6. False Citations in the southern Levant. 121

Fig. 4.1. Map of sites with a destruction event ca. 1200 BCE on mainland Greece (Kastanas not pictured). 132

Fig. 4.2. Plan of the central enclosure at Gla. Iakovidis 2001, 23 fig. 7. Courtesy of the Library of the Archaeological Society at Athens. 139

Fig. 4.3. Plan of the Melathron with traces of fire. Iakovidis 2001, 41 fig. 15. Courtesy of the Library of the Archaeological Society at Athens. 141

Fig. 4.4. Plan of Tiryns. Courtesy of Joseph Maran. 155

Fig. 4.5. Map of sites with a destruction event ca. 1200 BCE on Crete. 161

Fig. 5.1. Map of sites with a destruction event ca. 1200 BCE in Anatolia. 172

Fig. 5.2. Plan of the central temple district noting which buildings were burnt and which were abandoned. For unmarked buildings, the situation is not clear. From Seeher 2001, 629 Abb 1. Courtesy of Jürgen Seeher. 178

Fig. 6.1. Map of sites with a destruction event ca. 1200 BCE on Cyprus. 200

Fig. 6.2. Modified plan of Enkomi Area III Level IIB detailing where possible traces of destruction were uncovered. Dikaios 1969, pl. 252. 202

Fig. 6.3. Modified plan of Enkomi Area I Level IIB detailing where possible traces of destruction were uncovered. Dikaios 1969, pl. 272.   203

Fig. 7.1. Map of sites with a destruction event ca. 1200 BCE in the northern Levant.   220
Fig. 7.2. Plan of the *Ville Sud* noting where weapons were uncovered. Courtesy of Olivier Callot.   222
Fig. 7.3. Plan of Tell Afis Area E4 Phase Vb. Courtesy of Fabrizio Venturi.   228
Fig. 7.4. Map of sites with a destruction event ca. 1200 BCE in the southern Levant.   232
Fig. 7.5. Tel Mor, Strata VIII–VII. Courtesy of Tristen Barako.   242

Tables

Table 4.1. Weapons of war uncovered in the destruction of Midea.   151

Abbreviations

General

LC   Late Cypriot
LH   Late Helladic
LM   Late Minoan

Bibliographic

AA   *Archäologischer Anzeiger*
AAA   *Annals of Archaeology and Anthropology*
AAAS   *Annales archéologiques arabes syriennes*
AASOR   Annual of the American Schools of Oriental Research
ÄAT   Ägypten und Altes Testament
ABRL   Anchor Bible Reference Library
ABS   Archaeology and Biblical Studies
ABSA   *Annual of the British School at Athens*
ADAJ   *Annual of the Department of Antiquities of Jordan*
ADOG   Abhandlungen der Deutschen Orient-Gesellschaft
ADPV   Abhandlungen des Deutschen Palästina-Vereins
AeL   *Ägypten und Levante/Egypt and the Levant*
AfO   *Archiv für Orientforschung*
AfOB   Archiv für Orientforschung, Beiheft
AHL   *Archaeology and History in the Lebanon*
AJA   *American Journal of Archaeology*
AJASup   American Journal of Archaeology Supplement
AJSL   *American Journal of Semitic Languages and Literatures*
AmJT   *American Journal of Theology*
AnAnt   *Anatolia Antiqua*
ANESSup   Ancient Near Eastern Studies Supplement
AnSt   *Anatolian Studies*
AOAT   Alter Orient und Altes Testament
AoF   *Altorientalische Forschungen*
ArchDelt   *Archaiologikon Deltion*
ArRep   *Archaeological Reports*
ASORAR   American Schools of Oriental Research Archaeological Reports

AuOrSup	Aula Orientalis Supplementa
AW	*Antike Welt*
BA	*Biblical Archaeologist*
BAAL	Bulletin d'archéologie et d'architecture libanaises
BaM	*Baghdader Mitteilungen*
BAR	*Biblical Archaeology Report*
BARIS	British Archaeological Reports International Series
BArte	*Bollettino d'Arte*
BASOR	*Bulletin of the American Schools of Oriental Research* (from 2020 *Bulletin of ASOR*)
BCAW	Blackwell Companions to the Ancient World
BCH	*Bulletin de Correspondance Hellénique*
BCHSup	Bulletin de Correspondance Hellénique Supplément
BICS	*Bulletin of the Institute of Classical Studies*
BZAW	Beihefte zur Zeitschrift für die alttestamentliche Wissenschaft
CA	*Current Anthropology*
CAH	Cambridge Ancient History
CCEM	Contributions to the Chronology of the Eastern Mediterranean
CHANE	Culture and History of the Ancient Near East
COS	Hallo, William W., and K. Lawson Younger Jr., eds. *The Context of Scripture.* 4 vols. Leiden: Brill, 1997–2016.
CRAI	*Comptes rendus des séances de l'Académie des Inscriptions et Belles-Lettres*
DamM	*Damaszener Mitteilungen*
DMOA	Documenta et Monumenta Orientis Antiqui
EAEHL	*Encyclopedia of Archaeological Excavations in the Holy Land.* Edited by Michael Avi-Yonah. 4 vols. London: Oxford University Press, 1975–1978.
ESI	*Excavations and Survey in Israel*
HANEM	History of the Ancient Near East, Monographs
IAAR	Israel Antiquities Authority Reports
IEJ	*Israel Exploration Journal*
JArS	*Journal of Archaeological Science*
JCS	*Journal of Cuneiform Studies*
JHS	*Journal of Hellenic Studies*
JNES	*Journal of Near Eastern Studies*
JSOTSup	Journal for the Study of the Old Testament Supplement Series
KUB	Keilschrifturkunden aus Boghazköi
MDOG	*Mitteilungen der Deutschen Orient-Gesellschaft*
MRS	Mission de Ras Shamra

ABBREVIATIONS

NABU	*Nouvelles Assyriologiques Breves et Utilitaires*
NEA	*Near Eastern Archaeology*
NEAEHL	Stern, Ephraim, ed. *The New Encyclopedia of Archaeological Excavations in the Holy Land.* 5 vols. Jerusalem: Israel Exploration Society, 1993, 2008.
NS	new series
OBO	Orbis Biblicus et Orientalis
OEANE	*The Oxford Encyclopedia of Archaeology in the Near East.* Edited by Eric M. Meyers. 5 vols. Oxford: Oxford University Press, 1997.
OIP	Oriental Institute Publications
OJA	*Oxford Journal of Archaeology*
OLA	Orientalia Lovaniensia Analecta
OpAth	*Opuscula Atheniensia*
OpAthRom	*Opuscula*
Or	*Orientalia* NS
ORA	Orientalische Religionen in der Antike
PAe	Probleme der Ägyptologie
ΠΑΕ	*Praktika tēs en Athēnais Archaiologikēs Hetairias apo ... mechri*
PEQ	*Palestine Exploration Quarterly*
pl(s).	plate(s)
QDAP	*Quarterly of the Department of Antiquities in Palestine*
RA	*Revue d'Assyriologie et d'archéologie orientale*
RAr	*Revue Archéologique*
RB	*Revue biblique*
RDAC	*Report of the Department of Antiquities, Cyprus*
RSFSup	Rivista di studi fenici Supplemento
RSO	Ras Shamra-Ougarit
SAHL	Studies in the Archaeology and History of the Levant
SAOC	Studies in Ancient Oriental Civilization
SCAn	Smithsonian Contributions to Anthropology
Sem	*Semitica*
SHAJ	*Studies in the History and Archaeology of Jordan*
SJOT	*Scandinavian Journal of the Old Testament*
SMEA	*Studi Micenei ed Egeo-Anatolici*
SMNIA	Tel Aviv University Soia and Marco Nadler Institute of Archaeology Monograph Series
StBoT	Studien zu den Boğazköy-Texten
StMed	Studia Mediterranea
StPhoe	Studia Phoenicia
TA	*Tel Aviv*

TAPA	*Transactions of the American Philosophical Society*
TMO	Travaux de la Maison de l'Orient
UF	*Ugarit-Forschungen*
WAW	Writings of the Ancient World
WAWSup	Writings of the Ancient World Supplement Series
ZÄS	*Zeitschrift für Ägyptische Sprache und Altertumskunde*
ZDPV	*Zeitschrift des Deutschen Palästina-Vereins*

Acknowledgments

For any work of this magnitude, while a single name is attached as author, it simply would not have been possible without the help and contributions of so many unnamed individuals. While I cannot express my gratitude to all of them here, I would like to thank at least some of those who made this work possible and helped see it through to fruition. First and foremost, I thank and am tremendously grateful to my wife Anna. She helped me in every step of this project back when I had begun it as a PhD student, while supporting, encouraging, and keeping me sane through to its end. She has listened to enough talk on destruction that she deserves an honorary degree in archaeology, and it is to her that I dedicate this work, as without her it simply would not have been possible. I would also like to thank my mother, Linda Millek, who helped us out for months during the pandemic taking our two rambunctious boys so that I could have a quiet place to work at home when there were no offices to go to.

I also owe a debt of gratitude to Brian Schmidt of the Department of Middle East Studies at the University of Michigan for acting as my mentor during this project. His advice was invaluable, and I am sure he heard more about destruction ca. 1200 BC than he cared to know. I am also grateful to the department as a whole for hosting me during this time. I would also like to thank Kim Larrow the department's administrative assistant for all of her help in getting me situated, helping me with paperwork, and for all of the tremendous support she gave throughout my time in the department. Since library research was the major component for this work, I would like to say thank you to Evyn Kropf and Zachary Quint, who helped me find a number of volumes or journals that I could not track down myself. Then there are the many people who work in the library system at the University of Michigan and in the interlibrary loan office, who tracked down, scanned, or delivered countless books and articles for me. If it were not for their unseen work and the amount of time they saved me, this project would not have been completed for many more years.

There are also a number of individuals including but not limited to Gary Beckman, Philipp Stockhammer, Marlies Heinz, Hanan Charaf, Artemis Georgiou, Zsolt Simon, Peter James, Joseph Maran, Michael Galaty, and Ido Koch who either read or discussed portions of this book with me and gave their valuable feedback. I am also extremely grateful to the many people who shared unpublished information with me, answered what must have seemed at times to be inane questions, or who gave me articles, book chapters, dissertations, or even whole books. Without their contributions, many of which are listed as "pers. comm." in the text, this project would not have been possible.

I would like to thank the Deutsche Forschungsgemeinschaft (German Research Foundation), who funded my project, "Destruction and the End of the Late Bronze Age in the Eastern Mediterranean." Without their support I would not have been able to undertake this project and they were generous enough to extend my fellowship due to the turbulences brought on by the Covid-19 pandemic. Finally, I would like to thank Billie Jean Collins and Lockwood Press for taking on this project. As always, any errors or omissions in the text are solely my own.

CHAPTER ONE

Destruction and the End of the Bronze Age

Collapse, Crisis, and the Year 1200 BCE

Throughout the Eastern Mediterranean from the Mycenean palaces of Greece to the shores of the Nile, the years surrounding 1200 BCE are often described as ones of crisis, collapse, transition, and change. The description given as part of this introduction of the possible causes and consequence of the end of the Late Bronze Age do not reflect my personal opinions on these matters. As will be seen throughout the body of this text, I will disagree with many of these suppositions, or, in some cases, demonstrate them to be fallacious. The following unnuanced opening narration is meant to give a brief overview of many of the commonly held assumptions, theories, and in some cases canonic explanations for the changes and transformations that took place at the end of the Late Bronze Age ca. 1200 BCE.

While the Late Bronze Age world was one of trade between the great kings, empires vying for power, and the construction of historic monuments, after the events of the years encircling 1200 BCE all was changed, many would say for the worse (fig. 1.1). Populations were displaced and moved freely about the Eastern Mediterranean causing havoc in their wake. Writing was abandoned in the Aegean, Ugarit, and parts of but not all of Anatolia and the Levant, as was the construction of monumental architecture throughout the entire Eastern Mediterranean. The trade that had flourished during the Late Bronze Age ground to a halt with the collapse of the world system that fed the coffers of the rich and elite. The palatial system that had constructed some of the greatest ancient monuments in Greece was dissolved with the destruction of those palaces, while the empire of the Hittites was broken. Egypt's hold on part of the Levant lasted through the reign of one last great pharaoh, Ramesses III, but even this empire, which had stood for nearly three hundred years, could not stand against the tide of change, a wave brought on by the movement of the "Sea Peoples," who themselves were only the victims of a corrupt system and a devastating drought that had gripped the Eastern Mediterranean.

This admittedly rather dramatic description of the end of the Late Bronze Age mirrors the kind of grandiose narration that permeates the scholarly literature. The year 1200 BCE in particular holds a prominent place in historical commentaries relating to the ancient Near East and classical world—though other dates, in particular 1177 BCE and 1184 BCE, are also put forward. The

1

Period	Egyptian Dynasties	Egyptian Kings	Hittite Kings	Southern Levant	Cyprus	Aegean
mid- to late LBA 1450–1200	mid- to late Eighteenth Dynasty 1475–1295	Thutmose III 1479–1425		LB IB 1450–1400	LC IIA 1450–1375	LH IIB 1450–1400
		Amenhotep III 1390–1352	Suppiluliuma I 1350–1322	LB IIA 1400–1300	LC IIB 1375–1340/25	LH IIIA:1 1400–1375
	Nineteenth Dynasty 1295–1186	Ramesses II 1279–1213	Hattusili III 1267–1237	LB IIB 1300–1200	LC IIC 1340/1325–1200	LH IIIA:2 1375–1300
		Merneptah 1213–1203	Suppiluliuma II 1207–unknown			LH IIIB 1300–1190
LBA transitional / Iron I	Twentieth Dynasty 1186–1070	Ramesses III 1186–1155		Iron IA 1200–1150	LC IIIA 1200–1100	LH IIIC 1190–1030
				Iron IB 1150–1000	LC IIIB 1100–1050	

Figure 1.1. Comparative chronology chart of regions in the Eastern Mediterranean.

DESTRUCTION AND THE END OF THE BRONZE AGE

year 1177 BCE is one date given for the arrival of the Sea Peoples on the shores of the Nile Delta during the eighth year of Ramesses III's reign, while 1184 is one of the traditional dates suggested for the Trojan War.[1] The year 1200 BCE however serves as a fulcrum in the reconstructed narrative of history, the before and after of which are viewed in such stark contrast—great empires before and collapse after—even if that particular calendrical year has no special significance.[2] Because of the assumed significance surrounding 1200 BCE, a great deal of scholarly effort has gone into trying to piece together the series of events that led to the crisis, collapse, and transition and to the changes and transformations that transpired afterwards.[3]

This discourse around the end of the Late Bronze Age has waged for more than 150 years, as Gaston Maspero (1873, 1886, 1896) laid the foundation for many of the still current ideas of the end of the Late Bronze Age. He based his ideas on Greek myth and the then recently translated texts from Ramesses III's mortuary temple at Medinet Habu in West Thebes with a particular focus on one story from Ramesses's eighth regnal year. These texts, and their associated reliefs purportedly told the story of several mobile groups who had "made a conspiracy in their islands" to ransack the great kingdoms of the Eastern Mediterranean, with a final plan to attack Egypt itself. However, they were stopped by the valiant efforts of Ramesses III in both a great sea battle and a land battle. These groups were given the name the *Peuples de la mer*, or the Sea Peoples, even though the term was never used in any ancient text. It was these texts from Medinet Habu describing the movements of the "Sea Peoples," combined with the mythology, that gave way to the idea that moving people groups placed pressure on other groups, such as the Dorians, who in turn displaced the populations in Greece turning them into the Sea Peoples, who then went on to attack the remainder of the Eastern Mediterranean.[4]

---

1. For 1177 see Cline 2014, 2021. For the Trojan War, this date was calculated by Eratosthenes; see Forsdyke 1957; Mylonas 1964; Blegen 1975, 163.

2. See discussion in Knauf 2008, 78, as well as the discussion later in this chapter.

3. I offer here a selected list of the books from the last forty years covering the topic of end of the Late Bronze Age in the Eastern Mediterranean ca. 1200 BCE: Dothan 1982; Sandars 1985; Karageorghis 1990; Dothan and Dothan 1992; Ward and Joukowsky 1992; Drews 1993; Gitin, Mazar, and Stern 1998; Oren 2000; Fischer 2003; T. Harrison 2008; Bachhuber and Roberts 2009; Middleton 2010, 2020b; Yasur-Landau 2010; Galil et al. 2012; Killebrew and Lehmann 2013b; Yener 2013b; Cline 2014, 2021; Garbati and Pedrazzi 2015; Kopanias, Maner, and Stampolidis 2015; Sommer 2016; Cunningham and Driessen 2017; Fischer and Bürge 2017b; Driessen 2018; Niesiołowski-Spanò and Węcowski 2018; Charaf and Welton 2019, 2020; Millek 2019c; and de Martino and Devecchi 2020. There are of course a legion of other articles, book chapters, dissertations, and excavation reports that analyze the end of Late Bronze Age but they are too numerous to mention here—though many will be referenced throughout the volume.

4. See discussion in Dothan and Dothan 1992, 26–28; Drews 1993, 55–59; Silberman 1998, 269–70.

The monocausal explanation for the end of the Late Bronze Age featuring the onslaught of the Sea Peoples, oftentimes accompanied by the Dorians and the Phrygians, persisted through the end of the nineteenth century and into the mid-twentieth century. However, this initial idea based on Greek myth and Egyptian "history" was fleshed out and seemingly confirmed by the archaeological excavations that began in earnest in the latter part of the nineteenth century. This trend began with Heinrich Schliemann's excavations at Troy, Mycenae, and Tiryns, while excavations throughout the remainder of the Eastern Mediterranean uncovered corroborating evidence of the demise of the Late Bronze Age, as many sites yielded evidence of massive conflagrations. However, over the course of the past sixty years other ideas that diverged from the Sea Peoples and Dorians as the main causal factors in the collapse have been put forward, though the Sea Peoples themselves have not yet been laid to scholarly rest—they have merely been transformed.

Climate change represented by the cooling and drying of the environment throughout the Eastern Mediterranean has been attributed with bringing about the end of the Late Bronze Age.[5] Drought over the course of a hundred years or more supposedly placed stress on the centralized and rigid economic system of the palaces throughout the Eastern Mediterranean. Cities and nations began to starve, as vividly illustrated in several texts and eventually, as many of the theories propose, climate change induced a revolt among the populations, turning starving peasants into ravaging Sea Peoples, eventually leading to the downfall of nations and states.[6] Others, while invoking climate change as a factor, place the collapse at the feet of revolutions and peasant uprisings against a cruel and unjust ruling class, who forced their populations into debt and eventually into debt slavery without periodic forgiveness.[7] The empires and polities already under stress were then pushed over the edge to ruin by the coming of the Sea Peoples (Liverani 1987; 2003, 27–29; 2020, 21).

Another theory was championed by Robert Drews (fig. 1.2), who dubbed the end of the Late Bronze Age the "catastrophe," believed that the years surrounding 1200 BCE represented "arguably the worst disaster in ancient history, even more calamitous than the collapse of the western Roman Empire" (1993, 3). Drews went into great detail to dismiss the major theories proposed up to that point (1993, 33–96), and instead posited that all of the destruction wrought at the end of the Late Bronze Age throughout the Eastern Mediterranean was due to

---

5. See Carpenter 1966; Weiss 1982; Gallet et al. 2006; Issar and Zohar 2007, 163–66; Kaniewski et al. 2010, 2011, 2013, 2019; Drake 2012; Langgut, Finkelstein, and Litt 2013; Kaniewski, Guiot, and Van Campo 2015; Kaniewski and Van Campo 2017a, 2017b; and Finkelstein et al. 2017b.

6. For responses countering the environmental models for the collapse, see Middleton 2012; Knapp and Manning 2016; Karakaya and Riehl 2019.

7. Liverani 1987; 2003, 27–29; 2020, 21; Zuckerman 2007; Van de Mieroop 2008, 332–37; Klengel 2013; Jung 2016.

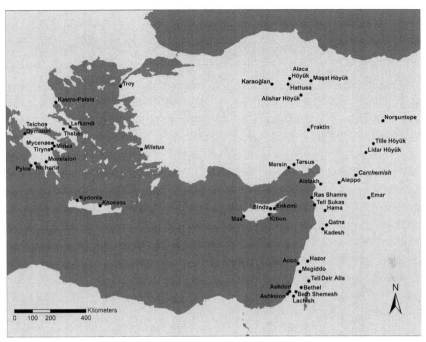

Figure 1.2. Map after Drews's 1993 map of the Catastrophe ca. 1200 BCE. (For sites in italics destruction was assumed probable but not certain.)

raiders equipped with advanced weapons and military techniques that the elite nations' chariot forces could not withstand (1993, 97–226). Others, however, preferred a more nature-based solution, looking to earthquakes and repeated seismic events as the catalyst that helped to bring about the end of the world as it was known ca. 1200 BCE.[8] According to this theory, these earthquakes, in what Amos Nur and Eric Cline (2000) dubbed an "earthquake storm" where one seismic event was followed by another further down the fault line, helped to bring ruin to already struggling nations. Systems collapse and similar theories, such as complexity theory, admixtures of all the above, have also been widely adopted. Earthquakes, climate change, peasant revolts, warfare, Sea Peoples, destruction, and the failure of trade all coalesced in the years surrounding 1200 BCE to bring about the end of an age, ushering in a new world.[9] Trade relations, gift exchanges, international marriages, and the exchange of goods, ideas, and people all came to a halt once this "perfect storm" (per the title of ch. 5 from

---

8. Schaeffer 1948, 565–66; 1968; Kilian 1983, 1988, 1996; Nur and Cline 2000; Nur and Burgess 2008; Cline 2014, 140–42.

9. See, e.g., Dever 1992; Frank 1993, 389–97; Betancourt 2000; Killebrew 2005, 24–42; Monroe 2009, 284–98; Cline 2014, 160–63; 2021, 167–80; Knapp and Manning 2016.

6   CHAPTER ONE

Cline 2014, 139) of circumstances broke apart the system that had upheld the empires, kingdoms, and powerful polities of the Late Bronze Age.

There are of course many more theories pertaining to the end of the Late Bronze Age, both for the Eastern Mediterranean as a whole and for specific regions or even individual sites.[10] Nevertheless, despite the variety of these theories and the various causal factors that have been proposed, there is one nearly universal baseline shared by all of them: destruction. For some theories, the role of destruction is more overt, as it is in Drews's reconstruction. His book *The End of the Bronze Age* begins with a survey of the sites destroyed ca. 1200 BCE, and it was the destruction wrought by his technologically advanced raiders that brought about the end of the Late Bronze Age. He stated that, "Within a period of forty to fifty years at the end of the thirteenth and the beginning of the twelfth century almost every significant city in the eastern Mediterranean world was destroyed, many of them never to be occupied again" (1993, 4).

The Sea Peoples, no matter the form they take in the literature, be they Aegeans, impoverished peasants, or a famine-driven populace, helped to bring ruin to healthy or limping societies through the physical destruction they caused throughout the Eastern Mediterranean. The "earthquake storm" also aided in ushering in the end of the Late Bronze Age via destruction, even if the theory does not state that all sites were destroyed or even that all sites with destruction were destroyed by an earthquake (Nur and Cline 2000, 61; Nur and Burgess 2008, 244). The Late Bronze Age system connecting the elites, while hampered by piratical activates and ailing from drought and internal and external stresses, was finally broken with the destruction brought on by any number of supposed causes. Destruction too was supposedly a major factor in the abandonment of prestigious and once central sites such as Pylos, Hattusa, Sarissa, Ras Shamra, Emar, Hala Sultan Tekke, Hazor, and Lachish, to name just a few.

In many ways, destruction stands as the physical manifestation of the end of the Late Bronze Age. Before Hattusa was destroyed, the Hittite Empire ruled much of Anatolia and Syria and was one of the great powers in the ancient world. After its destruction, the empire was in ruins. Before Ras Shamra was burned, it was a great trading hub bustling with international activity. After its destruction, trade ceased, and its palace was replaced by stables for local herdsmen. Indeed, destruction, often in the form of massive burning events, is the tangible and visible metaphor for the catastrophe that is so often associated with the years

---

10. See discussion in Drews 1993, 33–96; Middleton 2010; 2017, 129–81; Cline 2014; Millek 2019c, 29–88, 140–44. One such theory is the privatization of trade that was championed separately by Artzy (1985, 1997, 1998), and Sherratt (1994, 1998, 1999, 2000, 2003, 2010; see also Sherratt and Sherratt 1991, 1993, 1998) whereby the centralized palace economy was gradually replaced and subverted by private entrepreneurial actives. However, this theory has been refuted in the literature; see Manning and Hulin 2005; Routledge and McGeough 2009; Zuckerman 2010; Cline 2014, 152–54; Janeway 2017, 118–19; Millek 2019c, 140–44.

surrounding 1200 BCE. Thus, destruction acts as a symbol in the archaeological and historical narratives not only for the physical destruction of sites or empires and the end of the Late Bronze Age, but also for other less materially observable tragedies. William Dever (2017, 105) has so aptly articulated this point saying, "Archaeologists and historians speak somewhat cavalierly of destructions.... But it was not just sites that were destroyed ... it was people, their lives lost or shattered. Thousands might have been slaughtered, thousands of others made refugees or homeless." Destruction at the end of the Late Bronze Age was not just the burning of some palaces or the collapse of some walls. In the literature and the popular imagination, destruction represents the loss of complexity, the loss of writing, the loss of trade connections, and perhaps more tragically the loss of house and home, the loss of life, the dislocation of entire populations, forced migrations, and famine and starvation that led once innocent peoples to turn to violence to feed themselves. Destruction ca. 1200 BCE is then far more than just ash, burning, mud-brick collapse, and crushed pottery; it is devastation and desolation manifest.

It is for this reason that in nearly all discussions of the end of the Late Bronze Age, destruction is at least mentioned, if not deeply deliberated upon, as there is no end of the Late Bronze Age in the scholarly narrative without destruction. The two have been intertwined into a tapestry that is so tightly woven together that it is nearly impossible to separate the end of the Late Bronze Age from the concept of destruction. Since destruction plays such a strong role not only in the theories for what brought about the end of the Late Bronze Age, but also embodies its end, the question must be asked, How did destruction come to play such a crucial role in the narratives for every region in the Eastern Mediterranean ca. 1200 BCE?

A Brief History of Destruction ca. 1200 BCE

How destruction became intertwined with investigations into the end of the Late Bronze Age is to some degree a moot question, as there was never a time when destruction and the end of the Late Bronze Age were not connected. This association has its roots in Greek mythology, specifically with Homer's account of the fall and subsequent destruction of Troy. As far back as 1838, in Philip Alexander Prince's *Parallel Universal History: Being an Outline of the History and Biography of the World, Divided into Periods*, an early overview of the complete understanding of human history, the author (1838, 1) subdivided history into seventeen periods, the first beginning with the creation of the world in 4004 BCE as calculated by Bishop James Usher. His Period II began with Moses, but importantly ended with the fall and destruction of Troy in 1184 BCE (8–20). We must recall that this was before Schliemann had ever

8   CHAPTER ONE

set a shovel into the dirt of Hisarlık, Mycenae, or Tiryns; before Maspero ever
wrote on the *peuples de la mer*; before Emmanuel de Rouge (1855, 1867) had
translated Ramesses III's year 8 inscriptions; and even before the existence of
a Hittite kingdom was acknowledged (see discussion in Sayce 1888). In sum,
before there was even a Late Bronze Age as we now understand it, Prince's
historical reconstruction ended with the destruction of Troy.[11] This intellectual
concept steeped in Greek mythology took shape over the next decades of the
nineteenth century beginning with the work of de Rouge and Maspero, and
was fed by the evidence being revealed by the burgeoning field of archaeology
with the discovery of destruction at Tiryns, Mycenae, and Troy.

These events were laid at the feet of either the Dorian invasion or Homer's
Greek invasion (Schliemann 1880, 343–44; Tsountas and Manatt 1897, 341;
Dörpfeld 1902, 184–92). During the first half of the twentieth century, excavations
at Pylos, Mycenae, Krisa, Troy, Hattusa, Karaoğlan, Yumuktepe, Tarsus, Ras
Shamra, Carchemish, Megiddo, Tell Beit Mirsim, Beth-Shemesh, Bethel, and
Tel Gerisa, among others, all yielded "evidence of destruction," which was then
dated to ca. 1200 BCE based on the ceramic sequences and synchronies that had
been developed during the same period. This "destruction" was associated not
only with the Sea Peoples and the Dorians, but also the Phrygians, Philistines,
and Joshua's conquest of the promise land.[12] It was beginning to appear to
the scholarly community that a pattern of destruction was emerging that only
solidified the "truth" of the historical narratives found in the Greek poets, the
biblical writers, and the Egyptian scribes.

By the second half of the twentieth century, lists of sites destroyed began
to appear, and it was simply the assumption going forward that there was a
massive wave of destruction ca. 1200 BCE. The general works by Per Ålin (1962,
148–50), John Hooker (1976, 148–52, 166–80), and R. Hope Simpson and Oliver
Dickinson (1979) provided many of the now standard destructions we think of
for Mycenean Greece, such as Krisa, Pylos, Mycenae, Tiryns, Gla, Orchomenos,
the Menelaion in Sparta, Nichoria, Kastro-Palaia in Volos, which at the time
was assumed to be Iolkos, as well as Mycenean sites further afield such as
Miletus.[13] As Carl Blegen (1962) described the end of the LH IIIB in the early

---

11. Chapman (1989, 92) found that the earliest use of the three ages terminology for Levantine
archaeology dates to a letter written in 1902 by Macalister, who used this periodization to explain
the seven strata he had uncovered at Gezer.

12. Woolley 1921; Wace et al. 1923; Albright 1926, 1930, 1932, 1939; Grant 1929, 1939; Vincent
1929; Arik 1939a, 1939b, 1939c; Loud 1948; Schaeffer 1948; Blegen et al. 1950; Garstang 1953; Goldman et al. 1956; Blegen and Rawson 1966; Bittel 1970, 132; 1977, 41. Each of these will be discussed
in further detail in the subsequent chapters. Also, while some of these publications date after the
first half of the twentieth century, the excavations were conducted during this period and the material was only published after 1950.

13. See also Barnett 1975, 370; Desborough 1975, 659.

1960s, it "was marked almost everywhere on the Greek mainland by a trail of calamity and disaster."

By 1975, the four destruction events most commonly associated with the end of the LC IIC on Cyprus, Enkomi, Sinda, Kition, and Maa *Paleokastro* were put into print by Hector Catling (1975, 209; see also Desborough 1975, 660 who only omits Maa), while Paul Åström (1985, 8) added Hala Sultan Tekke to the list a decade later. In the Levant, again many of the sites commonly associated with the end of the Late Bronze Age were already on lists of destruction by 1975 including Ras Shamra, Alalakh, Tell Sukas, Carchemish, Hama, Hazor, Tell Abu Hawam, Tel Dor, Megiddo, Beth Shean, Tell Deir Alla, Ashkelon, Lachish, Bethel, and Tell Beit Mirsim (Katzenstein 1973, 59; Barnett 1975, 370; Franken 1975, 334–35). For Anatolia the proper list of destructions did not come into being until 1983 with Kurt Bittel's article "Die archäologische Situation in Kleinasien um 1200 v.Chr. und während nachfolgenden vier Jahrhunderte." While there was already the assumption that, "Wherever excavations have been made they indicate that the Hittite country was ravaged, its cities burned down" (Goetze 1975, 266), it was Bittel's 1983 article that we have to thank for most of the commonly cited destructions in Anatolia, such as Hattusa, Karaoğlan, Alaca Höyük, Maşat Höyük, Fraktin, Yumuktepe, Tarsus, and Norşuntepe. Importantly, Bittel (1983, 32 Abb. 2) included a map of destructions ca. 1200 BCE in Anatolia, which represented an advance in the presentation of destructions at the end of the Late Bronze Age by adding a visual dimension.

For the Aegean, Klaus Kilian, in the 1980s, expanded upon the previous lists of destruction adding sites such as Midea, Prophetis Elias, Thebes, Athens, Lefkandi, and Kastanas in a chart of destructions ca. 1200 BCE, many of which he assumed had been caused by earthquakes (1983, 56–57 fig. 1). In the early 1990s, Amihai Mazar (1990, 290), William Dever (1992, 110 fig. 13.1), Marguerite Yon (1992), and Anne Caubet (1992) added other sites to the ever-growing list of destruction in the Levant with Ras el-Bassit, Ras Ibn Hani, Emar, Tell Keisan, Ashdod, Tel Zeror, 'Afula, Aphek, Gezer, Tel Sera', Tel Batash, Tel Zippor, and Tel Haror. Indeed, the idea had by now been cemented that destruction was rampant ca. 1200 BCE in the Eastern Mediterranean and beyond, an idea epitomized by Åström (1985, 3) who wrote,

> Around 1200 B.C., we may ... note widespread destructions in the Mediterranean region and the Near East from Italy in the west to Iran in the east. Inhabited sites which did not suffer from conflagrations at that time are few. Per Alin has written a whole book about the destructions in Greece at the end of the Late Helladic IIIB period. The Hittite Empire fell. The major cities of Cyprus were destroyed. Ugarit was abandoned. Cities in Palestine were covered with ash layers.

10   CHAPTER ONE

Up until this point in the late 1980s and early 1990s, while lists of sites destroyed abounded and many of the common destruction events had been set into scholarly stone, it was in 1993 that destruction at the end of the Late Bronze Age went beyond lists of regional destruction and the concept that destruction was rampant throughout the Eastern Mediterranean. The widespread nature of destruction ca. 1200 BCE was visually solidified with the publication of Drews's 1993 book, *The End of the Bronze Age: Changes in Warfare and the Catastrophe ca. 1200 BC*. Drews spent the first thirty-three pages of his book discussing the destructions that he placed ca. 1200 BCE, beginning with Anatolia and moving throughout the Eastern Mediterranean from Cyprus, to Syria, the southern Levant, Mesopotamia, Egypt, Greece, the Aegean islands, and Crete. This marked the first time such effort had been put into categorically demonstrating the breath and width of destruction throughout the Eastern Mediterranean and beyond ca. 1200 BCE.

While Drews's theory for what caused the end of the Late Bronze Age was never widely adopted, his influence on the perceived amount of destruction and which sites were destroyed has persisted to this day. In particular it was his map, "The Eastern Mediterranean: Major sites destroyed in the Catastrophe" (1993, 9 fig. 1) that had the most lasting affect. This is most evident in the maps of destruction that were produced after Drews, such as that in Nur and Cline (2000, 44 fig. 1), Carol Bell (2006, 137 map 1), and Cline (2014, 110–11 fig. 10) that either explicitly or implicitly copied Drews's map.[14] Moreover, for the general public, Drews's map of destruction, and by extension Cline's facsimile of this map, have become the common source in the nonscholarly domain for what sites were destroyed ca. 1200 BCE.[15] What is particularly important to note about this map is that in his chapter on destruction ca. 1200 BCE, Drews describes several other sites as having been destroyed, such as Tell Jemmeh,

---

14. In Cline's recently revised and updated version of 1177 BCE (2021, 104–5), he has slightly altered the figure heading for his map to "Sites destroyed or affected ca. 1200 BCE" (see Cline 2021, 211 n. 62 for the reason behind this change). However, this slight alteration only makes the map more confusing, as there were no changes to the sites listed on the map. Thus, there is now a great deal of ambiguity as to which sites Cline assumes were destroyed and which were merely affected. There is also no definition of what "affected" entails. E.g., neither Tille Höyük nor Lidar Höyük experienced any major changes ca. 1200 BCE. Carchemish and Kition flourished without any evidence of destruction and if they were "affected" it was only in the positive. After the ca. 1250 BCE multibuilding destruction, Hazor was uninhabited ca. 1200 BCE and could not be affected, as there was nothing to affect. Likewise, there is no evidence of any destruction or real affects dating to ca. 1200 BCE at Hama, Qatna, and Tell Nebi Mend (see discussion of all of these sites in ch. 3). Moreover, sites such as Hama or Qatna, while listed on the map, are not discussed in the text, and there is no clear message on whether or not Cline assumes these sites are destroyed or affected, given the lack of discussion. Thus, rather than helping to clear up any misconceptions, this slight alteration to the figure heading has only created more confusion.

15. This is clear from the Wikipedia page on the end of the Late Bronze Age where both are widely cited; https://en.wikipedia.org/wiki/Late_Bronze_Age_collapse.

Khirbet Rabud, or Koukounaries of Paros but, for whatever reason, he did not display these sites on his map of destructions. Yet, these very sites have subsequently not appeared as destroyed in later publications or maps. Drews's impact and influence on our understanding of just how perversive destruction was and what sites were destroyed ca. 1200 BCE is attested to in some of the reviews of his book from the 1990s. One such reviewer went on to say that, "Chapter Two, 'The Catastrophe Surveyed,' is a laundry list of the devastation by archaeological site, treating Anatolia, Cyprus, Syria, the southern Levant, Mesopotamia, Egypt, Greece and the Aegean Islands, and Crete each in turn. For anyone who has wondered where to go for a comprehensive survey of the destruction, these pages will serve admirably" (Collins 1996: 129).

It was with Drews's book, in combination with Bittel 1983, Kilian 1988, Caubet 1992, and a 1997 article by Cynthia Shelmerdine, who added several sites destroyed in Greece, that the now standard list of destructions for the end of the Late Bronze Age came into being.[16] While of course other sites have been listed as destroyed in various books or articles either from old or new excavations, nevertheless, one will find that most any destruction mentioned from a list of destructions ca. 1200 BCE is likely a reference to one of these works, or a further derivative of these works.[17] Thus, by the end of the 1990s, destruction had taken its seat on the throne as a major cause or contributor of the end of the Late Bronze Age throughout the Eastern Mediterranean.

Herein lies one of the major issues with the current scholarship on the end of the Late Bronze Age. Over the course of 150 years of research and excavations, the body of references has grown exceedingly large, and more often than not, when discussing Late Bronze Age destruction, these modern lists or maps are referenced rather than going back to the original source material. For example, rather than read through the numerous books and articles that describe the end of the Late Bronze Age at Alaca Höyük in Anatolia, it is easier to simply cite Bittel (1983), who says the site was destroyed, as he was a respected authority on the subject. The same could be said for Iria, a small village in the Argolid. It is easier to cite Shelmerdine, who says that the site was destroyed, than it is to go back to the single report written about the site by Hartmut Döhl (1973), who actually reported the findings from Iria in an article that Shelmerdine herself did not even reference.

---

16. Shelmerdine 1997, 581 n. 275. She lists, "Sites destroyed: Argolid: Mycenae, Tiryns, Midea, and Iria; Laconia: Menelaion; Messenia: Pylos; Achaea: Teichos Dymaion; Boeotia and Phocis: Thebes, Orchomenos, and Krisa." This article was republished in 2001, which is the more widely cited version.

17. E.g., Knapp and Manning 2016 completely rely on Bittel for their list of sites destroyed in Anatolia, while they utilize Shelmerdine 2001 and Deger-Jalkotzy 2008 for the Aegean. However, Deger-Jalkotzy 2008 is only a reference to Shelmerdine 2001; see discussion in ch. 3.

12 CHAPTER ONE

In many ways, the current discourse on destruction at the end of the Late Bronze Age has become disconnected from the actual archaeological material that the discussion is supposedly based on. This is only compounded by the fact that there is no consensus on what is or is not evidence for destruction. The word of the excavator is taken as supreme, and if a site's excavator says the site was destroyed ca. 1200 BCE, then this is taken at face value without considering whether the archaeological evidence actually shows that the site suffered a destruction event.[18] This situation is only magnified as there is a clear lack of any standard theory or method to interpret destruction events—or even how to define what constitutes a destruction (see ch. 2). It thus falls to every excavator, archaeologist, and historian to decide for him or herself what is or is not destruction or what sites were in fact destroyed.

There are no commonly accepted guidelines for identifying destruction, something that is standard in almost every other area of archaeology, from ceramic sequences to temple typologies. Almost everything is classified and categorized, often down to the minutiae of whether not something is a wavy line or a chevron or whether a rim is flared or not. Yet, with destruction this is simply not the case, and has resulted in an interpretive free-for-all, with each individual scholar applying his or her own standard for what a destruction is, how to describe it, and defining what was the cause of said destruction. Additionally, there is another major issue outside of exactly what was or was not destroyed at the end of the Late Bronze Age or what materials have been cited that plague the scholarship on this transitional period. This is of course, When exactly did the Late Bronze Age actually end?

1200 BCE and the End of Late Bronze Age:
Consensus, Misnomer, or Shorthand

To understand how 1200 BCE came to be the consensus answer to the question, "When was the end of the Late Bronze Age?" it is worthwhile to explain briefly the history and origin of this date as a significant one in Eastern Mediterranean history.[19] The first meaningful use of 1200 BCE came from the work of the German historian Arnold Heeren, who, in 1817, dated the fall of Troy to "about B.C. 1200" (135). Heeren went on in 1826 to use his established "approximate" date for the destruction of Troy to also mark the end for the Egyptian Nineteenth Dynasty. He employed the king list of the third-century Egyptian priest Manetho, in which the last pharaoh of the Nineteenth Dynasty was Thuoris, who was known in Homer's account of history as Polybus, the husband of Alkandra, who was also the pharaoh when Troy fell (Heeren 1826,

---

18. Many examples of this will be discussed in ch. 3.
19. For a lengthier discussion, see: Millek 2021a, forthcoming b.

324; 1838, 449–50). Combined with Heeren's previous dating of the Trojan war, the Nineteenth Dynasty then had to have ended at 1200 BCE. Therefore, already two hundred years ago, Heeren dated two crucial events, the fall of Troy and the end of the Egyptian Nineteenth Dynasty, to 1200 BCE, setting it up as a pivotal date in ancient Eastern Mediterranean history.

From there, during the remainder of the nineteenth century, other crucial events were dated to 1200 BCE.[20] John Anderson in 1881 (48, 92) ended Egypt's New Kingdom glory at 1200 BCE, while also noting that this was when the "Migration of the Hellenic races" began. The emergence of Sea Peoples was added to 1200 BCE in 1882 by W. M. Ramsay (258), an event that was again mentioned by W. M. Flinders Petrie in 1890 (277) and by Harry Reginald Hall in 1902 (158). In 1892, it was confirmed that the Mycenean civilization fell in 1200 BCE (Smith 1892, 466), while the attack by the Dorians was placed at 1200 BCE in 1897 (Dawkins 1897, 392). Only a few short years later, in 1910, John Garstang (1910, 211, 391) claimed that the Hittite Empire had fallen to the first invasion of the Phrygians in 1200 BCE. Thus, by the beginning of the twentieth century, 1200 BCE had become an absolutely essential year for the entire early history of the Eastern Mediterranean.

An important matter needs to be addressed here. It seems there is a misconception concerning the year 1200 BCE as the date related to the biblical exodus and conquest, and that this supposed connection is where 1200 BCE derived its reputation. For example, as Ernst Axel Knauf (2008, 74) has articulated, "'1200 B.C.E.' is based on two Egyptological biblicisms: the assumption that the Israelites were employed building the 'City of Rameses' under Ramses II, and that Merneptah's mention of Israel in Canaan ... refers to the 'post-exodus' Israel of the Bible." However, this simply cannot be the case. This is because, as noted above, 1200 BCE was already a year of significance in Eastern Mediterranean history for some seventy to eighty years prior to Flinders Petrie's discovery of the Israel Stele in 1896.[21] It was only after this discovery that Israel was connected with 1200 BCE, when Flinders Petrie made the argument against the exodus occurring during the Eighteenth Dynasty favoring a later date (1896, 623–26). Flinders Petrie though, when discussing the Israel Stele, only mentioned 1200 BCE in association with the reign of Merenptah, not Israel (1896, 626). However, in the same year that Flinders Petrie found the stele, William Hayes Ward (1896, 409) made the claim and association between 1200 BCE and Israel stating, "All that can now be said is that about 1200 B.C., Merneptah found Israelites in Palestine." Indeed, looking at prior histories of the ancient world, Israel, the exodus, and the conquest, had nothing

---

20. The fall of Troy was also dated to about 1200 BCE by Maunder (1850, 383) and Bell et al. (1859, 478), while Reinisch (1864, 1) too placed the end of the nineteenth Dynasty at 1200 BCE.

21. Petrie 1896. See also the discussion in Drower 1985, 221.

14   CHAPTER ONE

to do with 1200 BCE. Prince, in 1838 (8–11), utilized the traditional biblical chronology that placed the conquest at the end of the fifteenth century BCE during the Eighteenth Dynasty, while Anderson in 1881 placed the exodus at 1652 BCE, a date well before either the fall of Troy or the end of the Nineteenth Dynasty, which he himself placed at 1184 BCE and 1200 BCE respectively (1881, 48, 90, 92, 291). Thus, Israel was a latecomer to the 1200 BCE party as, prior to 1896, the fall of Troy, the end of the Egyptian Nineteenth Dynasty, the attacks by the Sea Peoples, and the fall of the Mycenean civilization had all been placed at ca. 1200 BCE. Israel's connection with the year 1200 BCE occurred only after the date had already been elevated as a year of significance in eastern Mediterranean history.

After its establishment in the nineteenth century, during the twentieth century, the year 1200 BCE became synonymous with the end of the Late Bronze Age and vice versa. Yet, now, in the general literature, the term "circa" has been stretched beyond any reasonable meaning of the word. As has been noted in a number of instances, some of which will be discussed below and others throughout the remainder of this volume, the Late Bronze Age did not end in all regions or all sites at the same time. Certain sites lost or maintained their Late Bronze Age material culture or their Late Bronze Age administrative systems decades or centuries before and after 1200 BCE. For example, at Zeyve Höyük-Porsuk, in Anatolia, the site's Late Bronze Age character ended between 1514 and 1430 BCE (Beyer 2010, 100–101), while at Arslantepe it ended at the beginning of the thirteenth century BCE (Manuelli et al. 2021) and at Tille Höyük only after 1090 BCE (Griggs and Manning 2009). In the southern Levant, the Late Bronze Age at Hazor ended ca. 1250 BCE (Ben-Tor and Zuckerman 2008), while other sites such as Azekah, Lachish, and Megiddo have a so-called LB III phase, as does Sarepta in the central Levant, extending the Bronze Age into the late twelfth century BCE.[22] In Greece, Iklaina was destroyed and lost its palatial character in the mid-thirteenth century BCE, while nearby Pylos persisted until the beginning of the LH IIIC Early (ca. 1180 BCE), some seventy years or so later. For Cyprus, the Bronze Age in general persisted until the end of the LC IIIA at 1100 BCE (Steel 2004, 185; Iacovou 2008, 635–37; 2014, 662–63, 667) except, that is, for sites such as Kalavasos-*Ayios Dhimitrios*, Maroni-*Vournes*, and Alassa, all of which were abandoned between 1200 BCE and 1150 BCE, prior to the end of the Late Bronze Age at other sites on the island.

This phenomenon can be seen throughout the entire Eastern Mediterranean, as there was not a single radical shift, but a period of change lasting decades, if not longer. However, in the literature this unspecified time frame is generally referred to as the end of the Late Bronze Age or as "ca. 1200 BCE," even if its

---

22. Anderson 1988, 390; Kleiman, Gadot, and Lipschits 2016, 110; Finkelstein et al. 2017a, 264; Garfinkel et al. 2021, 422. Garfinkel et al. 2021 utilize both Iron IA and LB III as a label for Level VI.

duration is stretched out to as long as 150 years or more. For example, Israel Finkelstein's (2016, 113) offers the following definition of this period: "The end of the Late Bronze Age commenced in the middle or second half of the thirteenth century [that is the destruction of Hazor] and continued until about 1100 B.C. [the recent date for the destruction of Megiddo Stratum VIIA]." This inflation of the term "circa" to encompasses more than a century is apparent on maps of destruction, as Drews lists Hazor's mid-thirteenth century BCE destruction event along with Lefkandi, which suffered a destruction in the mid-twelfth century BCE; yet both are listed as ca. 1200 BCE.[23] In Nur and Cline 2000, 56–57, the authors explicitly state that they are focusing on destructions that took place between 1225–1175 BCE, and yet one of the major destruction events discussed in the article is Troy VIh, which even at the time was still dated to 1250 BCE and was later pushed back to 1300 BCE.

Taking destruction events from such a broad chronological window and collapsing them into a single date like "1200 BCE" to create a hypothetical momentously chaotic moment is a perfect example of what Dario Puglisi (2013, 177) has dubbed the Atlantis Premise, which is "an unconscious premise according to which destructions related to a radical historical change or, more specifically, to the disappearance of a highly developed 'civilization,' like mythical Atlantis, have to be put in a very short, archaeologically undetectable, time span." However, often in the case of the end of the Late Bronze Age this is not an unconscious premise but a blatantly accepted practice. Temporally displaced events have been lumped together to create a crisis or wave of destruction at one time or over a compressed period of time, even though these events chronologically have nothing to do with each other.[24]

In the course of history, there will never be a time without major destruction, particularly given such a broad geographic area, and one could easily expand the borders of the end of the Late Bronze Age to destructions in the fourteenth century BCE, claiming them all to be part of the same process of disintegration.[25] Stretching out what constitutes the end of the Late Bronze Age essentially makes the term functionally useless. If we applied the same sort of chronological gymnastics to historical periods by tying together events spanning 150 years as causally linked, not as separate phenomena that followed one after another, the scholarly response would likely be less than accepting.[26]

---

23. Drews 1993, 9 fig. 1; a problem that was carried over to Cline's map; Cline 2014, 110–11 fig. 10.

24. See my discussion on the destruction of Hazor and Lachish during the Late Bronze Age and Lachish and Ashkelon in the Iron II in Millek 2018b: 256–58.

25. As Bonacossi 2013, 127–28 has already suggested doing for the northern Levant, or Kreimerman 2017, 191 has done, reaching back to textual evidence from the Amarna tablets to elucidate the situation in the southern Levant ca. 1200 BCE.

26. As I have mentioned elsewhere, the city of Hamburg Germany suffered massive destruc-

16   CHAPTER ONE

Thus, while the past obviously affects the future in one way or another, events in the past need not be causally connected to events in the future, nor do they need to be part of some greater overarching process.

Since it is the case that the Late Bronze Age ended at different times in different regions and with different outcomes, what should constitute the end of the Late Bronze Age as a functional date range that defines a set of events that can be reasonably placed together chronologically?[27] That is, what span of time should mark the end of the Late Bronze Age? Quite simply it should be defined as the years between 1225–1175 BCE or ca. 1200 BCE, as we have known it for nearly two centuries. The reason for this is that many of the hallmarks of the end of the Late Bronze Age are encompassed cross-regionally within this fifty-year period. Linear B, Ugaritic, and writing in much—though not all—of Anatolia and the Levant are abandoned; most of the major palaces in Greece suffered some kind of destruction and the palatial system largely dissolved; the Hittite Empire as it was known in the Late Bronze Age collapsed; Ugarit was destroyed; various subregions suffered apparent depopulation; locally made LH IIIC pottery appears throughout the Levant and Cyprus; and there are of course Merenptah's and Ramesses III's infamous run-ins with the Sea Peoples. All of this transpired, as far as we currently understand it, between 1225 and 1175 BCE. Even this "narrow" temporal period of fifty years is more than a generation, likely blurring together events that are not connected, since they could be dispersed through time and space. However, since we cannot be more precise than this, we must allow for some wiggle room in the temporal span that encompasses the end of the Late Bronze Age.

The reason for selecting 1200 BCE is not merely to continue a two-century-long tradition, but because it acts as a natural midpoint between these two dates that do contain many of the major events typically considered to be characteristics of the end of the Late Bronze Age. If the date was ca. 1175 BCE, covering the time between 1200 through 1150 BCE, this would leave out major destruction events, such as those at Gla, Lachish Level VII, Aphek, Tarsus, and Mersin, among others. Moreover, it would exclude the first incursion by the Sea Peoples during the time of Merenptah, and the initial appearance of locally made LH IIIC pottery, typically defined as evidence of the arrival of the Philistines in the southern Levant (Asscher et al. 2015a). Likewise, even if the date for the "end of the Late Bronze Age" was extended to 1150 BCE, this

---

tion both in 1842 and 1942. The first began as an accidental fire, while the latter was the result of bombing campaigns during World War II (Millek 2018b, 257). Or as another example, the American Civil War did not result in the election of Donald Trump, two events that are separated by the same amount of time that separated the destruction of Qatna in 1340 BCE and Ras Shamra in 1185 BCE (Millek 2019a, 170).

27. But not causally, as that is an entirely different question.

still would not incorporate the end of Egypt's hegemony over the southern Levant, the site-wide and multibuilding destructions uncovered at Azekah, Lachish Level VI, Beth-Shean, and Tell Deir Alla, nor the end of the Bronze Age on Cyprus, all of which occurred after 1150 BCE. The year 1199 BCE would be just as good a date, but historians and archaeologists tend to prefer rounding dates when there is no secure calendrical year for a historic event, and the same is true in this case (Millek 2021a; forthcoming b). Thus, 1200 BCE, as a specific year, has no special meaning or significance other than that it is a readily known natural midpoint between two dates that contain many of the typical markers of the end of the Late Bronze Age. This conclusion is in many ways similar to the one reached by Sturt Manning (2007, 78), who stated that,

> In turn, considering the Sea Peoples phenomena and the changes associated with the end of the Late Cypriot IIC period, or the close of the Late Helladic IIIB period, the collapse of the Hittite Empire, and so forth, a date range ca. 1200 BCE can still be used as a suitable "textbook" round number approximation, so long as we are mindful that the relevant time period might in fact have been a few decades earlier or later (and need not have been contemporary across the relevant cultures/areas), and that the processes involved covered periods of time rather than point events.

It also needs to be clarified that the "end of the Late Bronze Age," as defined here, is more of a scholarly tool demarcating a period of time containing a set of events that might be correlated chronologically and, in some cases, possibly causally. The "end of the Late Bronze Age"—that is, the time between 1225–1175 BCE—is not meant to encapsulate every instance where Late Bronze Age cultural traits ended prior to these dates or persisted after them. To do this would include numerous microregional events that are neither chronologically, geographically, nor causally connected to one another.

To have any meaningful discussion concerning the aspects that are typically associated with the end of the Late Bronze Age, such as those listed above, this discussion must be chronologically limited. To add in all sites or regions where the Late Bronze Age phase ended or persevered into one overarching mega "end of the Late Bronze Age process(es)" would only create confusion or, worse yet, succumb to the Atlantis Premise by putting these events all as "ca. 1200 BCE" when they are in fact separated by a century or more. Therefore, when speaking of the "end of the Late Bronze Age," I am not considering the physical end of Late Bronze Age traits at all sites in all regions. Rather, the "end of the Late Bronze Age" or "ca. 1200 BCE" are both meant to be scholarly or academic shorthand for the above-mentioned timeframe containing a set of events and processes that are commonly understood to constitute the end of the Late Bronze Age (see Millek forthcoming b).

Purpose, Scope, and Organization of the Work

From the above discussion we can draw out several issues with the perceived volume of destruction and destruction's affects on causing or facilitating the end of the Late Bronze Age throughout the Eastern Mediterranean that must be addressed. The three primary issues are as follows. (1) The more than a century of research on the end of the Late Bronze Age has produced ever-growing lists and maps of destruction, but over time the lists and maps have become unquestioned and there has been no thorough review to see if all of the cited sites actually were destroyed ca. 1200 BCE. (2) The first problem is only compounded by the fact that there are no widely used interpretive tools to determine first, if a site has evidence of destruction; second, if there is evidence of destruction, how much of the site was affected; and third, what might have caused the destruction. It is now the situation that one archeologist's ash is another's conflagration. Thus, in the absence of any standards for what constitutes a destruction and how to define and describe destruction events, we are left in a position whereby if any given scholar states that "X site was destroyed ca. 1200 BCE," then it was destroyed, with very few questions asked, and the site then appears in later lists or maps of destruction. (3) The chronological conflation of the end of the Late Bronze Age has become a catchall for destructions that are separated in time by more than most subperiods in the Late Bronze Age or the Iron Age lasted, such as the LB IIA or LH IIIB. This has led to the problem that chronologically disparate events have been placed on maps of destruction ca. 1200 BCE, even if the events themselves are separated by decades—if not by a century or more.

These three factors combined have created a situation where numerous sites have been listed as destroyed when they were never destroyed, or in some cases at least not ca. 1200 BCE. In other instances, while certain sites certainly did suffer destruction ca. 1200 BCE throughout the Eastern Mediterranean, often the severity of those destructions has been blown out proportion, as only a single building from the whole site was found burnt or ruined. Nevertheless, generally in the summary and conclusion sections from site and excavation reports, archaeologists tend to report again that, "X site was destroyed in a conflagration ca. 1200 BCE" without nuance as to how much was actually destroyed. Or in other cases there is blatant fudging of the data to make it appear that more of the site was destroyed than what was uncovered in the excavation.[28] At times, more attention has been paid to what might have caused some of the destructions, but even here there is often an interpretive rift where certain scholars believe all destructions were manmade and the result of warfare or violent human action, while others prefer natural causes, such as earthquakes, as the primary

---

28. See the discussion on Enkomi in ch. 6.

DESTRUCTION AND THE END OF THE BRONZE AGE 19

bringer of destruction. Very few assume that an accidental tabun fire could have burnt the house down, that building a fortress on a literal foundation of sand might have led to a structural engineering failure, and often there is not a detailed examination of all available evidence for what might have caused the destruction, if a cause can even be determined at all.

In order to address these issues and come to a clearer understanding of what transpired ca. 1200 BCE, this volume pursues two main objectives. The first is to set out an interpretive framework for the systematic classification and interpretation of destruction events. This system will be applicable to sites throughout the Near East and the Aegean, regardless of the period under study. It is meant to be a general method of classifying what a destruction event is, how to describe the destruction, the scale of destruction, and to lay out criteria to assess the possible cause of the destruction, if one can be ascertained at all, while also cutting out unneeded verbiage that only confuses rather than aids our understanding of the nature of the destruction. If there is not reasonable evidence based on these criteria, then no cause can or should be assigned to the destruction event.

The second purpose of this volume is to systematically apply this interpretive method and analysis to the destructions at the end of the Late Bronze Age throughout the Eastern Mediterranean by providing a singular assessment to determine how many sites were actually destroyed ca. 1200 BCE, and where there is reasonable evidence, what caused those destructions. This will help test certain theories for the end of the Late Bronze Age that rely on massive numbers of destruction, be that by warfare or by earthquake. Part of this analysis is also to asses the degree to which destruction ca. 1200 BCE plays a role in the scholarly literature. While lists and maps abound, and there are lengthy discussions on destruction at the end of the Late Bronze Age, not every list or every map is equal, and there are a number of sites referenced as destroyed in some publications that are left out in others. Or, as is often the case, many sites have been cited as destroyed ca. 1200 BCE, but these sites have not gained the same level of publicity as others and exist as singular references of destruction ca. 1200 BCE. Thus, one of the primary aspects of this work is to gather these references, lists, and maps of destruction into one cohesive whole to properly ascertain how many cities, towns, and villages have been cited as destroyed ca. 1200 BCE.

By applying a rigorous method to the destruction events throughout the Eastern Mediterranean, all following the same rubric, this study aims to challenge several assumptions about destruction at the end of the Late Bronze Age. While I will discuss various theories for the end of the Late Bronze Age as a whole and for individual regions, the purpose of this volume is not to answer what caused every change, transition, crisis, or collapse from the Late

20   CHAPTER ONE

Bronze Age to the Iron Age. Rather it is to examine what affect destruction had on the societies at end of the Late Bronze Age, either as a widespread or localized phenomenon. For example, I will not try to answer the question, What sociopolitical, geopolitical, environmental, governmental, and economic situations could have brought down the Hittite Empire? Rather, I seek to answer the question, Is there evidence that destruction by any cause helped to exacerbate or directly caused the downfall of the Hittite Empire? These other factors certainly played a role to one degree or another, but taking all of these into account and trying to answer "What caused the end of the Late Bronze Age?" is another book entirely. This is especially true when examining as wide a geographic area as this volume considers.

This brings up the geographic scope of the volume. The focus is on Greece, Crete, the Aegean Islands, Anatolia, Cyprus, and the entirety of the Levant. There are of course other regions that one could include, as there is much discussion on the events in Italy ca. 1200 BCE, with destruction being one of the components (see Kilian 1983; Jung 2009, 2012b, 2018b). There are also references to destruction closer to Egypt in the Sinai (see Oren 1984; Hoffmeier 2018), and one could also expand the search inland to Mesopotamia (see Brown 2013) or even to Central Europe (see Kristiansen and Suchowska-Ducke 2015). However, to enlarge this study beyond the borders of the Eastern Mediterranean would become a never-ending quest for more destruction. In any given fifty-year period some site in any given region will suffer destruction, and one could increase the geographic scope without bounds. There will always be another site over the next hill that was burnt, suffered structural failure, collapse from winter rains, or burned because of a careless oil lamp. The geographic area under study already encompasses 153 cited destruction events, and, regrettably, the other regions must wait for a separate study.

Chapter two presents the theory and method for interpreting destruction events and will serve as the basis for the remainder of the book. Chapter three focuses on the 61 percent of all sites claimed to have been destroyed ca. 1200 BCE that either were not destroyed ca. 1200 BCE, or do not meet the criteria for a destruction event, or that have simply been falsely identified as destroyed even though there is no evidence or claim by the excavators that the site under question was destroyed ca. 1200 BCE. Chapters four, five, six, and seven each focuses on destruction in a specific region beginning with Greece and Crete, followed by Anatolia, Cyprus, and finally the Levant. Each chapter will offer an extensive examination of the evidence for destruction, the scale, and the possible cause for each destruction, as well as how this information when taken together affects the various theories for the end of the Late Bronze Age in each region, and what affect, if any, destruction might have had on it.

Throughout chapters three through seven, each site will be discussed individually, even if at times that discussion is brief. While it may seem that some of this information could simply be displayed on a chart, graph, or map, this would only perpetuate the current problems that plague the study of destruction at the end of the Late Bronze Age, namely, that more often than not, most sites are simply listed as having been destroyed without explanation. Thus, while it may appear long-winded at times, we must examine the actual archeological evidence before coming to any conclusion.

Chapter 8 concludes this study with a presentation of the wider picture of exactly how much destruction took place ca. 1200 BCE and what the scale of that destruction was, as well as a discussion as to whether there are any broader, widespread tendencies in the pattern of destruction. This final chapter seeks to answer the question what effect destruction itself had on the various societies of the Eastern Mediterranean ca. 1200 BCE, as well as to lay a path for the future study of destruction ca. 1200 BCE and beyond.

CHAPTER TWO

The Archaeology of Destruction: Denoting, Describing, and Classifying

The Problem with Destruction

Destructions abound in the archaeological record and often are featured in site reports as important time capsules or chronological markers; yet, despite their importance in constructing archeological narratives, there is no systematic method of describing and interpreting these events. Moreover, and more importantly, there is not even a consensus as to what is or is not a destruction. As the late Sharon Zuckerman (2007, 4) so aptly stated over a decade ago, "Given the ubiquity and prevalence of destruction layers in ancient Near Eastern tell sites, it is surprising that a systematic treatment of this phenomenon is largely neglected and that there is no conceptual paradigm for dealing with it," and the situation remains largely unchanged today. Consequently, while ancient destructions are replete throughout the archaeological record and have been featured numerous times in site reports, there has unfortunately been little study of destruction as a phenomenon, how to interpret it, describe it, or even what it is. There is no overarching theory or method that can be brought to the fore to compare adequately one destruction with another, whether that is from the same site but different levels, a neighboring site from the same period, or from different regions, to see if there are differences in regional patterns of destruction from so-called destruction horizons.

Under the current paradigm each archaeologist and historian employs his or her own criteria and interpretive standards for destruction. The presently accepted approach to analyzing destruction in the archaeological record could be compared to a hypothetical scenario where all Late Helladic pottery was cataloged with a unique typology, chronology, and nomenclature invented by each individual excavator throughout Greece and the Mediterranean wherever the pottery was uncovered. The result of this type of approach would only create utter confusion and would essentially make much of the information about the pottery useless. If any scholar attempted to discuss pottery styles regionally during a set period of time, unless that scholar examined the drawings and plates from every excavation and created their own set of standards, the resulting study would be a hopeless mishmash of terms, dates, and definitions. It is for this very reason that so much effort has gone into creating ceramic typologies in every region of the world where ceramics were produced. In general, no matter where Late Helladic pottery is uncovered it can be placed

23

into a neat typology, if there is enough information. Sometimes it will be quite clear that the sherd belongs to a LH IIIB2 flask, at other times the sherd may be so small that it is only clear that it is a body sherd from a vessel from some time in the LH IIIA–B. Nevertheless, this is possible since there is a method to categorize each sherd, which allows for intersite and interregional comparison.

However, for destruction the exact opposite approach is taken, as every archaeologist utilizes his or her own definition of what constitutes a destruction, as well as a unique method of analysis for each individual destruction. Every independently defined destruction is then incorporated into larger regional and superregional discussions, even though the criteria that each excavator applies to its own destruction vary widely. So, much as with the muddled outlook that would come without a standard for Late Helladic pottery, this is currently the situation for destruction, both in general, and particularly for the end of the Late Bronze Age. There is a great deal of uncertainty around exactly what sites were destroyed ca. 1200 BCE because there is no standard to judge the "destructions." Moreover, as mentioned in chapter 1, while at times the original excavation reports are referenced in broader articles on the end of the Late Bronze Age, there is rarely an in-depth analysis of the evidence for destruction from each site that is reported as destroyed, since many discussions on the end of the Late Bronze Age rely upon secondary or tertiary sources for their information.

This is of course not to say that destruction has been left out of the scholarly discussion or that there are not excellent examples of scholarship that examine destruction events for some sites ca. 1200 BCE.[1] Moreover, there have already been attempts at categorizing destruction. Israel Finkelstein, more than a decade ago, came to same conclusion as Zuckerman that there needs to be a standard in the study of destruction. He (2009, 113) stated that, "The exact nature and meaning of 'destruction' has never been fully deliberated on in the archaeology of the Levant. The word is used quite freely to describe ashy layers found in a dig. The fact of the matter is that not every ashy layer represents destruction, that not all destructions entail heavy conflagration, and that not all destructions are of the same nature." Finkelstein went on to define what a destruction is, a definition that we will return to shortly, as well as proposing a "Megiddo Destruction Scale which may then be used to scale most cases of destruction layers in other sites" (120). His scale comprised three levels of severity and impact on the site.[2] However, within the archeological community

---

1. See, e.g., Iakovidis 1986; Seeher 2000; Lagarce and Lagarce 2006. Others of course will be mentioned throughout the course of the text. For a discussion of destruction in general and some theoretical considerations, see Rakoczy 2008; Driessen 2013.

2. Scale 1: "Partial destruction of a city with no occupational gap following it." Scale 2: "A more severe destruction, with evidence for conflagration and/or collapse, sometimes followed by a short abandonment." Scale 3: "Complete annihilation of a settlement with evidence for a heavy

as a whole there does not appear to be an appetite for any sort of scale or classification of destruction, for as to my knowledge this scale system was never utilized outside of the article where it was presented, even by Finkelstein himself. Others have since presented methods of interpreting and classifying destruction, but apparently to no avail, as we remain in a sea of ideas for what is or is not a destruction and what might or might not have caused them (see, e.g., Hasel 2016; Kreimerman 2017; Millek 2017, 2018b, 2019c). Nevertheless, to try to make sense of destruction in a way where we can determine patterns of scale and cause across sites and regions, we must adopt a definition for destruction, a universal set of terms that are employed to describe destruction, a scale of destruction, as well as distinct criteria to determine what might have caused the destruction.

What Is a Destruction?

Perhaps the most vital component to this discussion is to clarify what should be the definitive evidence to determine if a building was destroyed, as at the moment there is no consensus on precisely what material remains, and in what quantities, constitute a destruction.[3] This lack of an agreed-upon definition inherently leads to complications in how we interpret and understand the past, as destruction events are often key markers for chronologies, transitions, or collapse at individual sites or regionally. To illustrate this problem, let us assume there is scholar A who deems that destruction is typified by a mass of burnt mud brick and rubble that crushed whole vessels. On the other hand, scholar B assumes that an ashy layer of a couple of centimeters on a floor from one room in a structure could also be evidence of destruction. Both scholar A and B go on to their own independent excavations and uncover a "destruction." Scholar A excavates a building that had been burnt to a pile of baked mud bricks filled with pottery and weapons of war, while scholar B uncovers some burnt material in a pit, which he assumes represents a destruction that affected the entire site even though no further evidence of burning or collapse were uncovered. In most cases, these two hypothetical scholars will publish evidence for their "destruction," and in the end they will summarize the finds in an article or chapter by saying, "Site X was destroyed by fire ca. 1200 BCE."

---

conflagration, wall and roof collapse, and large assemblages of finds on the floors. An occupational gap of some sort follows" (Finkelstein 2009, 120).

3. One could take the philosophical approach to this question, as indeed every building that we excavate has been destroyed by later building activities, weathering, plowing, time, or by the act of excavation itself. However, for the purposes here, destruction is viewed in the narrower sense: a specific instance in time where one or more buildings were destroyed by a natural disaster, structural failure, accidental fire, or was directly destroyed by human agency during the period of occupation and use of the structure(s).

26   CHAPTER TWO

These two references will then be combined by a third party, scholar C, who will then summarize both into a single statement saying, "Sites X and Y were both destroyed by intense conflagrations" even though the actual evidence for destruction from both sites could not be further apart. Furthermore, scholar D will then go on to reference scholar C perhaps adding in sites W and Z, which each have their own set of criteria for destruction and in this way the web of confusion only grows.

This is not a hypothetical illustration but a very real situation in the scholarship surrounding destruction and the end of the Late Bronze Age. For example, Pylos suffered a site-wide destruction event that Carl Blegen vividly detailed in his report, and in this case, Blegen would be scholar A. Meanwhile, at the small coastal site of Iria, Hartmut Döhl, or scholar B, assumed that the site was destroyed even though there was no evidence of destruction in the architectural remains. Some burnt material was only uncovered in a nearby *bothros* or pit, but this is not sufficient evidence that the site was destroyed or that even a single building was destroyed.[4] Both stated that their sites had been destroyed and this was combined by Cynthia Shelmerdine (2001, 373), or scholar C, into a list of Mycenean destructions ca. 1200 BCE with no differentiation between the two. Shelmerdine was referenced by Bernard Knapp and Sturt Manning (2016), scholar D, who added her list into a discussion of over fifty sites throughout the Eastern Mediterranean that were "destroyed" at the end of the Late Bronze Age. The sites that Knapp and Manning reference include a host of false destructions as well as a wide variety of scales and causes that have all fallen under the undefined rubric of "destroyed."

It is for this very reason that there is the pressing need for a strict definition of what constitutes a destruction. However, it is not necessary to invent a new definition, as Finkelstein's set of criteria is already a suitable description of what should constitute a destruction, only requiring a few minor additions. Finkelstein (2009, 113) states that:

> A real destruction of a settlement should be defined by the presence of at least two of the following features: 1. A black layer with charcoal, representing burnt beams, on the floor, usually overlaid with a thick ashy layer. 2. A thick accumulation of collapse—of bricks or stones—on the floor. This accumulation can at times be as much as one meter or more deep. In the case of bricks and a strong fire, the bricks may turn red or even white. 3. In most cases, an accumulation of finds, mainly broken pottery vessels, on the floors.

There are of course some minor additions that need to be taken into consideration. Ash in and of itself in association with pottery is not evidence

---

4. See discussion of both sites in chs. 3 and 4.

of destruction. This is particularly true if the ash or charcoal is uncovered in areas of industry or food preparation where we would expect there to be ash (Finkelstein 2009, 120; Kreimerman 2017, 176). For example, at Enkomi in the Area III structure, while there is evidence of action by fire in the western half of the structure, this was related to the copper smelting industry in that sector of the building. Given the absence of any structural collapse, there is no evidence that this section of the building was destroyed, as the ashes and burning resulted from smelting not destruction (see full discussion in ch. 6). Therefore, when ash is present, we must examine what the function of the area was. Was there any sort of industry that could account for the ash; is there a nearby hearth or tabun; or was it an area of food preparation? If there is a reasonable nondestruction explanation for the presence of ash, it should not be considered evidence of a fire or destruction. Likewise, small lenses of ash or ash accumulation on certain floors without other evidence of destruction should not be used as evidence for a destruction. Burning can occur without the physical destruction of the architecture or wind can blow ash from areas with the controlled use of fire to other rooms or spaces.

Another factor that must be taken into deliberation is the timing of the destruction. If, for instance, a building was abandoned with some of its contents remaining and after some time the structure simply collapsed due to a lack of maintenance, one could call this a destruction even by the above definition, as it would yield two of the criteria listed by Finkelstein.[5] If this is taken as the case, then essentially every building from every period was destroyed and the definition becomes functionally meaningless. Therefore, to be considered a destruction under this definition, there would need to be a direct impact on the inhabitants of the site. The destruction event must be contemporaneous with the building or settlement period of occupation or use. If there is evidence that a site was abandoned, and decayed mud bricks are found fallen on the floors along with other rubble, this evidence must be taken with caution, as it is likely that after the buildings were no longer maintained they simply crumbled and collapsed on whatever remained in the structure (Millek 2019a, 159; 2019b, 120).

Finally, for a structure to be defined as destroyed, more than one or two rooms from a building must show signs of destruction. Thus, even if there is evidence of a fire that raged in one room, if the building in general was spared, then it was not destroyed. For example, the Pithos Magazine from Building II at Alassa burned with such intensity that it cracked some of the ashlar blocks

---

5. The two criteria being collapsed walls and some crushed pottery. For example, a small settlement on the southern beach of Ashdod was abandoned at some time toward the end of the Late Bronze Age. After this, the mud-brick walls collapsed, covering over some pottery and other finds (Nahshoni 2013, 119). However, this is not destruction, but merely the fate of all abandoned buildings that are brought to ruin by time and entropy.

in the walls. However, outside of some burning on the floor of the adjoining Room P, there is no other evidence that the rest of the building was burnt (see full discussion in ch. 3). In this case, even though there was damage by fire in one wing, the building was not destroyed. In other words, localized damage does not equal building-wide destruction. To put this into perspective, if your modern-day kitchen caught on fire but the fire did not spread to the rest of the house, you would likely say that your kitchen burned, not that your house burned to the ground. The severity of the damage between the two statements is entirely different, as would be the impact on your life. The same could be said in the past, as obviously a fire that burned one or two rooms would certainly not have been a "good thing," but it does not mean that it would end the life cycle of the structure or that it destroyed the building. This is to say, there is a difference between a damaged building and a destroyed building.

The Description of Destruction

As with any endeavor in archaeology, there is a set of generally agreed upon terms that we utilize to describe the past.[6] Yet, for destruction there is no set of agreed-upon nomenclature. One will find such descriptors as: violent, fiery, severe, intense, conflagration, and mixtures of those, such as violent fire, severe conflagration, or a violent destruction resulting in an intense conflagration. However, each of these terms either has no scientific meaning or has been misused. There are no criteria for what makes a destruction or a fire "violent" nor are there any for a fire to be intense. Is a violent destruction only one caused by human agency or can a natural disaster also violently destroy a building? Is an intense fire only one that burns above 900 degrees Celsius, which is the beginning for calcination and vitrification, or does it also apply to fires that did not burn as hot? The answer to these questions is that there is no difference and these terms are only used to be graphic, catching the reader's eye, not to add any scientific value. It would be comparable to saying that a vessel was explosively carinated or that someone uncovered an extreme cooking pot. These descriptors would only hinder our understanding of the vessels under discussion rather than enhancing it. Much the same, the terms that are often added onto destruction events can create more confusion, as the reader will assume a violent conflagration is more than just an ash layer on a floor, even if that is all that was excavated.

Conflagration as a label is at times appropriate, but the word is more often than not misapplied. The English word "conflagration" literally means, "An

---

6. For another discussion of the problems of the terms employed to describe destruction events, see Millek 2017, 135.

THE ARCHAEOLOGY OF DESTRUCTION 29

extensive fire which destroys a great deal of land and property."[7] If there is evidence that a large portion of a site or a whole site was destroyed by fire, this would be a conflagration. Yet, any other application of the term, "conflagration" describing a fire or ash deposits smaller than this, would be misplaced, denoting a greater degree of damage than what was uncovered in the archaeological record. This is not only a problem in the English-language literature, as each language has its own particular descriptors and terms that have no agreed upon meaning and thus no real scientific value. In German, there is no substantial differentiation between a *Brandkatastrophe* ("fire disaster"), a *Brandzerstörung* ("fiery destruction"), or a *Zerstörung* ("destruction"), as each is applied by the individual archaeologist under his or her own preconized understanding of how to describe destruction. This is despite the fact that a *Brandkatastrophe* appears more deadly and destructive than a simple *Zerstörung*.

One of the most widely used, misleading, and obstructive turns of phrase to describe destruction is to simply say, in whatever language, "X site was destroyed." To illustrate why this is so problematic we must go back to our modern kitchen-fire mentioned above. If after the fire, you call your insurance agency and say, "My house burned down," when the agent arrives to inspect the damage and finds that only the kitchen was burnt, they might assume you were attempting insurance fraud, as obviously your house did not burn down. Likewise, if a mayor said publicly that their city had been destroyed by an earthquake but in fact only one building collapsed due to a faulty foundation, the public at large would likely assume that the mayor was exaggerating beyond what is reasonable. Yet, while these examples might seem silly, this is the exact situation for nearly every single site that suffered destruction in the entire ancient world. Very rarely were sites destroyed as a whole in what I will describe below as a site-wide destruction. More often than not, only a single structure or a set of structures was destroyed in any given destruction event, and many, if not most, buildings were left intact to be reused in the following phase or were abandoned without destruction. Nonchalantly stating that "X site was destroyed," often gives an impression of a far worse scenario than what was in fact uncovered. This problem is only magnified if any of the above destruction descriptors are added to this overly generic statement.[8]

As another way to illustrate this problem, when the phrase, "X site was destroyed" is employed in the scholarly literature, it would be much the same as saying at the end of a season of excavation that, "We found a lot of pottery this

---

7. Oxford Dictionaries; http://www.oxforddictionaries.com/definition/english/conflagration.

8. Snodgrass (1987, 41) made a similar observation when he stated that, "If an archaeologist reports that a settlement site that he is excavating was burned and then abandoned, the historian and the layman in general will understand him to mean the settlement as a whole, or at least very substantial parts of it. In fact, of course, such an inference is only secure when the settlement has been entirely, or very largely, excavated."

year," or "We found some pots and a couple of small finds," without providing any further details, images, or drawings. While this gives the most basic of information about what was uncovered in that year's excavation, this statement is essentially useless, as there is not enough detail about the pots or small finds to be subsequently utilized by other researchers. Yet, this is again the case for destruction in the scholarly literature. Over time, crucial information has been masked, details smoothed over, and patterns made invisible due to this unnuanced approach to describing destruction.

What then is the way out of this terminological and phraseological conundrum? For the most part the answer is simple. Abandon using the majority of these descriptors and enlist plain language and rigorous descriptions of the destruction, detailing the evidence room by room and building by building. While it might be less exciting if we no longer had violent destructions or intense conflagrations, it would be more scientific. There might at times be certain instances where the term conflagration is appropriate, but it should be seldomly employed. At other times, these descriptors might be better suited in less generalized statements. If in a destruction one finds victims who were bludgeoned to death, someone else with a lance in their side, or masses of victims in associations with evidence for warfare, one could rightly say that the people were violently killed or that the destruction was an act of violence.[9] Likewise, if there is evidence that the fire in a building burned so hot that it caused vitrification or calcination, then one could say that the fire was intense in that building or often in that specific room. It is frequently the case that if there is evidence of an intense fire, this is not uniform throughout a single structure—and certainly not across several structures. High heat fires are often uncovered in specific contexts and rooms based on the contents of that room or how well it contained the heat. Nevertheless, in general, these terms are neither helpful nor necessary when describing a destruction event and should be abandoned all together in general settings, or at least sparingly utilized for more detailed statements.

The main issue is to replace the adage, "X site was destroyed." This phrase can be substituted in two ways. The first is to replace it by stating that a site suffered or was affected by a "destruction event." The phrase "destruction event" simply indicates that at the site under discussion there is evidence of destruction based on the criteria listed above. It does not signal the scale or cause of the destruction, as that information is to follow. The second is to denote the scale of the destruction at the beginning of the description, which I will discuss in more detail below. Nevertheless, the most suitable way to describe a destruction is to be as plain as possible, noting what rooms had what type of destruction debris, which buildings were or were not destroyed,

---

9. Such as at Beycesultan or Kaman-Kalehöyük; see Omura 2011; Boz 2016.

and critically analyzing probable cause based on what was uncovered in the destruction and what was destroyed. Again, avoiding obtuse verbiage is common practice when describing pottery, and it should become common practice when describing destruction.

The Scale of Destruction

In addition to the general issues with the vernacular encompassing the descriptions of destruction events, there is the lack of a clear scale denoting exactly how much of any given site was in fact destroyed. Nevertheless, ensuring a consistent scale of destruction can illuminate details that are otherwise lost without intense inspection of each individual destruction event. For example, there is a difference between saying that "Ras Ibn Hani was destroyed," and "Ras Ibn Hani suffered a single-building destruction event, as only the *Palais Nord* had any signs of destruction." With the former, one assumes the site was destroyed wholesale, while in the latter it is evident that only a single building was in fact destroyed.[10] Therefore, it is essential that we utilize a universal and direct system to easily relate how much of any given site was destroyed. The scale system proposed here is divided into four categories: partial, single-building, multibuilding, and site-wide (see also Millek 2018b). This method of organizing the magnitude of each destruction documents the number of buildings uncovered from a single stratum, level, or phase that have evidence of destruction.[11]

The smallest destruction event falls into the partial destruction classification. This category is generally reserved for excavations where there is apparent evidence of destruction based on the criteria set out above, but the published descriptions are too vague or the archaeological record too sparse or disturbed to say exactly how much of the site was destroyed. Examples of this would be Soli Höyük in Anatolia or Teichos Dymaion in Greece. In both cases, evidence of destruction has been uncovered dating to the end of the Late Bronze Age, but for Soli Höyük the material was highly disturbed, and for Teichos Dymaion, the currently published information is not detailed enough to say what was destroyed. Certain partial destructions may in turn be no destruction at all if further excavations uncover that the patch of burnt debris was a localized phenomenon, or it may be that a partial destruction masks a larger destruction event once the materials have been properly published or more excavations uncover more damage. Thus, the partial destruction designation may under

---

10. Which is in fact the case, as the remainder of the site was found without evidence of destruction; see discussion in ch. 7.

11. This is unlike other scale or classification systems such as in Finkelstein 2009; Hasel 2016; and Kreimerman 2017, which are based on how severely a site was damaged in combination with what occurred after the destruction, i.e., reoccupation, short hiatus, or abandonment.

or oversell the scale of destruction, but this is to err on the side of caution, as we should not assume that more of a site was destroyed if there is no physical evidence to back this claim.

The second scale is a single-building destruction. This is when only a single building from a stratum, level, or phase yielded any evidence of a destruction event. Additionally, when only a single building from a period has been uncovered, the rule in this system is not to magnify the destruction event based on this one building to the site as a whole. This is the minimalist approach, as when only a single building is excavated from any given stratum, it does not rule out that there might be more evidence of destruction waiting to be uncovered elsewhere in the site. However, in the same way, further excavation might demonstrate that no further structures have any evidence of destruction, as both possibilities are as equally likely. Thus, to not inflate a destruction beyond what can be archaeologically verified, in these cases, the site will be categorized as a single-building destruction, acknowledging that any further excavation can always alter the scale attribution, much the same as with the partial destruction.

Kastro-Palaia in Volos in Greece is an excellent example of a single-building destruction, as only the main public building has any evidence of destruction, while the surrounding domestic structures were uncovered without evidence of destruction. For Tel Miqne-Ekron in the southern Levant only a single storage building dating to the end of the Late Bronze Age has so far been unearthed and this building was destroyed. However, this single-building destruction does not indicate the site as a whole was destroyed until further evidence of such an event is uncovered. Therefore, Tel Miqne-Ekron is attributed to a single-building destruction unless additional evidence of a more widespread event is unearthed.

Following a single-building destruction is naturally a multibuilding destruction, where several structures suffered a destruction event in the same stratum while other buildings were left untouched. Several of the more infamous end of the Late Bronze Age destruction events fall into this category, such as Tiryns, Hattusa, or Emar. While several structures were indeed destroyed at each site, many buildings were left unscathed prior to the eventual abandonment or subsequent phase of occupation.

Finally, there is the site-wide destruction. This is reserved only for sites that yielded evidence of a contemporaneous destruction event found in all areas of excavation at the site. Examples of this would be Troy VIIa, Pylos, and Maa *Paleokastro*, where destruction was uncovered in every structure excavated. This scale of destruction is often what would be imagined when one reads, "Pylos was destroyed in a conflagration," as in general the site truly was destroyed by a conflagration.

There are of course several caveats to this scale system, as not every destruction will fit neatly into one of these designations. Moreover, as with all things in archaeology, there is still a measure of interpretation that goes into determining the scale of any given destruction. This is particularly true when the information about the destruction is sparse due to the age of the excavation where all relevant information might not have been recorded, or because the archaeological record is incomplete due to later building activates, erosion, or modern agriculture and construction activities. It is possible that more destruction lies unexcavated or that buildings that had been destroyed were simply removed by the builders in the following phase or that the early excavators were not interested in recording or describing evidence of the destruction they uncovered. Thus, depending on how one approaches destruction, either from the minimalist perspective or the maximalist perspective, one could expand or contract the scale of destruction when the information is not clear enough to make an easy judgment.

For this system the rule is not to assume that there is more destruction than can be empirically demonstrated. It is in times such as this that the old archaeological adage might be brought up, that absence of evidence is not evidence of absence. However, what is oftentimes forgotten is that it is also true that the absence of evidence *is* the absence of evidence. It is good to exercise a degree of caution and allow for some margin of error, as there may be more destruction in the ground or evidence of destruction that existed in the past may no longer exist. Nevertheless, if taken too far, this line of thinking also leads to wild speculation that is no longer grounded in empirical data. It is because of this that the scale attribution is then not a permanent fixture, as future excavations or publications can change it based on the discovery of more evidence.

A connected issue is what to do with well-excavated sites that do not fit neatly into this scale system. For example, when Aphek Stratum X12 suffered a destruction event toward the end of the LB IIB there was only a single building (Palace VI) at the site. Given this, it could be classified as a single-building destruction, seeing as only a single building was destroyed. However, being the only building at the site at the time and since it was destroyed, all excavation areas yielded evidence of destruction and it could be classified as a site-wide destruction. Ras Shamra too falls into a scale classification gray area. A tremendous amount of the site has been excavated and destruction has been uncovered nearly everywhere and it would not be a stretch to say that Ras Shamra was destroyed in a site-wide destruction. Yet, destruction was not uncovered in every area of excavation, as the *Ville Sud* yielded no evidence that it was destroyed, meaning that the destruction could be classified as a multibuilding destruction. In both cases, the destruction could rightly be placed

34 CHAPTER TWO

into two separate scale categories, and it is incumbent on the researcher to decide which designation fits best with the destruction. In both cases, I have opted for the site-wide destruction, as this scale reflects the true devastation both sites suffered, even though the amount of destruction differs greatly between the two. For Aphek, the entire site was destroyed, and for Ras Shamra, only a handful of buildings were not burnt; yet, there is enough evidence for destruction throughout the site to grant it the site-wide designation in my opinion.

Another issue when determining the scale of a destruction comes with the multibuilding and site-wide destructions, as there is the assumption that the destruction uncovered in various structures occurred at the same time. However, as Anthony Snodgrass (1987, 41) noted more than thirty years ago, "the conclusion that [a] destruction was synchronous [throughout a site], that it was all a single episode, is likely to be based on common sense inference rather than on demonstration: the degree of precision, in even the best dated pottery series, is unlikely to justify a distinction between one day and, say, ten years." Jürgen Seeher (2001, 626, 634) too has noted this problem with the destruction uncovered at Hattusa. In many of the buildings that were destroyed there were few chronological markers to create a connected stratigraphy between buildings, some of which are separated by several hundred meters. Thus, one must always consider that not every structure was destroyed at the same time as all others if there is no stratigraphical correlation between the destroyed buildings. This again brings up the need to thoroughly and individually scrutinize each building that was destroyed to ascertain if there might be any indication that there were different causes to the destructions, particularly if the buildings are widely separated from each other.[12]

Another important point to bring up is what impact the scale of destruction has on interpreting the cause or affect of the destruction. In other systems of classifying the scale of destruction the scale is also tied to certain outcomes, such as reoccupation of the site for more minor destructions or the total abandonment of the site after a major destruction.[13] However, the scale of the destruction is only a single data point among many and there is not a one-to-one correlation with more severe destructions resulting in abandonment. For example, the end of the Late Bronze Age destruction event at Tiryns would likely fall into the most severe categories of destruction for both Finkelstein and Kreimerman; however, despite suffering a multibuilding destruction, the site was not abandoned. The same could be said for Troy VIh, which appears

---

12. See, e.g., Lachish Level VII in ch. 7, which could be an example of this.

13. E.g., Finkelstein's (2009, 120) Scale 3, his most severe destruction, which is followed by an occupational gap, versus Kreimerman's (2017, 182) Type 1, which is that the complete destruction of the city is also followed by a hiatus lasting decades or centuries.

to have suffered from a site-wide destruction, but it too was not abandoned afterward.[14]

While there are cases where multibuilding and site-wide destructions are followed by a hiatus or abandonment, this may not even be related to the destruction event per se. Sites such as Emar, Hazor, and Lachish VI all suffered either a multibuilding or site-wide destruction and were abandoned after the destruction event. However, importantly, each site was also under a period of crisis or had already been partially abandoned prior to the destruction.[15] In these cases, the destruction was only the archaeological capstone on an already ongoing process of abandonment. Therefore, while a site may be abandoned or experience a hiatus after a multibuilding or site-wide destruction, this will not always be the case, and there may be preexisting conditions that affected this outcome more than the scale of the destruction itself. In the same way, the scale of destruction also does not determine the cause of the destruction. The scale is a data point, but there is nothing to say that site-wide destructions are only brought on by X cause. In this way, the scale designations are not meant to elucidate on the possible cause of the destruction nor to signal what occurred after the destruction. Rather, the scale is meant to indicate how much of any given site was destroyed in a destruction event, nothing more.

The Cause of Destruction

There are four basic categories for the possible cause of any given destruction event, which follow the same types applied in current forensic fire investigations. According to David Redsicker and John O'Connor (1997, 91–93, 121), these possible causes are in a modern setting: undetermined, natural, accidental, and incendiary, that is, intentionally set. The nomenclature in this classification system is slightly modified, as "undetermined" has been changed to "unknown," "incendiary" has been changed to "human activity," while "accidental" and "natural" remain the same (see also Millek 2018b, 243). If there is insufficient evidence to determine the cause of the destruction, then the cause must be classified as unknown following in line with modern forensics fire investigation. As Redsicker and O'Connor describe it, unless all possible origins and causes for a fire have been eliminated, other than that proposed by the investigator, then, "the cause of the fire/explosion must be listed as undetermined or unknown until such a time as a logical, scientifically acceptable cause can be determined" (93). Therefore, if modern forensic investigators cannot determine the cause of every recent fire and must list the cause as unknown, how much

---

14. Having not examined the material firsthand, I hesitate to state exactly what the scale category for the VIh destruction should be.

15. Zuckerman 2007; Millek 2017, 2018b, 2019a; see also chs. 5 and 7 in this volume.

more caution must we take when attempting to determine and assign the cause of a fire that occurred thousands of years ago with far less existing evidence. Unless there is a reasonable burden of proof based on a set of criteria, the cause of a destruction must remain unknown. Likewise, all possible options must be taken into consideration based on the available evidence. The lack of sufficient evidence to determine cause is true for most partial destructions or for many older excavations where information was not kept, recorded, or published. However, it is also the case for site-wide destructions that have been well excavated or published, as at times there is simply not enough convincing evidence to favor any one cause over another. This does not mean one cannot discuss a hypothetical possible cause, but in terms of the final classification, rather than assuming the cause of the destruction based on too little evidence, it is better to classify these destructions as unknown, even if this necessitates that many destruction events may fall into this category.

Despite the modern precedent whereby not all fires can be categorized with a known cause, it is frequently the case that the cause of a destruction event in the archaeological record is assumed based on presuppositions held by the archeologist or historian. For example, if a site is in a region of intense seismic activity, one will tend to find more references to earthquakes as the cause of destruction. In other cases, there is the assumption that buildings were too difficult to burn, as there simply were not enough incendiary materials in the structure and the architecture did not allow for the easy combustion of mud-brick buildings. Thus, for those who hold to this assumption, the majority of destructions featuring fire are assigned to the hand of man in an act of war or aggression who added the fuel needed to feed the flames of destruction (e.g., Jung 2016, 557–58; Kreimerman 2017, 178, 191). However, we cannot assume the cause of any destruction based on the general seismic activity of the region or because we presume that nature and accidents did not catch buildings on fire in the past.

A modern example can help illustrate how taking preconceived notions on how and why a destruction took place based on presupposition rather than the physical evidence can lead to faulty results. On January 19th, 1917 during the height of World War I, in Silvertown of London, England, an important military instillation was destroyed, which resulted in the death of seventy-three individuals and an additional four hundred who were injured.[16] At the time, London was undergoing the first great aerial bombing campaign by Germany, which lasted from December 1914 to August 1918 (Morris 1925). One might assume that, because this building was an important element to the British war effort, and since it was destroyed during the time of German

---

16. "Remembering the Silvertown Explosion 100 Years on." European Union News 2 Feb. 2017; Business Insights: Global 25 July 2019. http://bi.galegroup.com/global/article/GALE|A480632064.

aerial raids in the exact location where those raids were concentrated, that the building was destroyed in an act of war. However, this would ignore the fact that the building, the Brunner Mond Munitions Factory, manufactured TNT. An accidental fire broke out in the building, setting off approximately fifty tons of TNT, resulting in the explosion that destroyed the building and killed the seventy-three individuals. This example demonstrates that while warfare might have seemed like a plausible cause of the destruction at first glance, further scrutiny demonstrates that the assertion was unfounded.

Accidental and natural destructions happen even during times of war and will be conglomerated together in the archaeological record. Therefore, one cannot assume what the cause of a destruction might be based solely on the regional seismic activity, historical accounts, the supposed difficulty of burning down a mud-brick structure, or if a region was at war based on historical documents. Each destruction event must be examined critically without preconceived notions of the cause, which can lead to false conclusions not adhering to the physical evidence. Furthermore, to avoid this presuppositional pitfall, there must be a system to define certain criteria one should look for in a destruction event to determine what caused the destruction; I will describe these criteria below.

Natural Destruction

When discussing natural destructions as a possible cause, the most commonly sought-after explanation is a seismic event such as an earthquake.[17] Typical evidence for earthquakes includes: faulting, rupturing, or cracking of floors and walls; falling, folded, leaning, deformed, or tilted walls; crushed victims or skeletons in situ; crushed pottery; fallen objects from a second story; objects or columns fallen in the same orientation; and evidence that the event was sudden.[18] However, the major issue with the majority of the common markers for destruction by earthquake is that many of them are simply general aspects of any type of destruction or they can also be produced through nonseismic events. Vertical cracks in walls can form naturally due to a tilt in the structure, weathering, erosion, or water leaching into the mud bricks and foundations, while walls may lean if the mud bricks become compromised over time (Ambraseys 2006, 1010; Nur and Burgess 2008, 94). In other cases, it is well

---

17. For a more technical discussion of the possible traces earthquakes leave in the archaeological record, see Rapp 1986; Stiros 1996; Nur and Ron 1997; Nur and Cline 2000; Ambraseys 2006; Marco 2008; Nur and Burgess 2008; Jusseret, Langohr, and Sintubin 2013; Hinzen et al. 2018.

18. See specifically Stiros 1996; Nur and Ron 1997; Nur and Cline 2000; Marco 2008; Jusseret, Langohr, and Sintubin 2013, with each providing either a list or a chart of possible earthquake damage. Jusseret, Langohr, and Sintubin 2013 list "potential earthquake archaeological effects (PEAEs)" that are seen as primary and secondary effects on both the structures and the stratigraphy.

known that if mud-brick structures are not maintained, even for one season, they will collapse partially or completely.[19] Moreover, fallen walls are common in most destruction events, as are crushed pottery, or even objects from a second story and these are not key markers for earthquake-related damage, as they are general-destruction-related damage.

Likewise, suddenness is not an indication of an earthquake; it is merely a sign that the event was sudden, that is, that there was no time to remove objects, and it appears as if it the event was a "snapshot" of time when the destruction occurred. However, there are several ways a building could be destroyed suddenly that are not earthquake related. Structural failure due to floods, heavy rains, or even the lack of proper maintenance would likely be sudden and would create an archaeological feature that may appear to be an earthquake. Likewise, the appropriately named "surprise attack" would by its very nature take a city or town without warning and the destruction could appear sudden. What this suggests is that while an earthquake would likely have characteristics of being sudden, suddenness by itself is not a clear indication that the damage was caused by a seismic event. The same can be said for skeletons or crushed victims.

Skeletons are a staple in assigning destructions to earthquakes, as it is presumed that the inhabitants may have been sleeping at the time of the tremor or were trapped inside the house or temple when the walls came tumbling down.[20] However, skeletons are again not an indication of destruction by earthquake, as people can be trapped in a burning or collapsing building for any number of reasons. If a city is raided, it would be reasonable that the inhabitants might shelter indoors hoping to avoid being seen, but if that house or building is caught ablaze this would be the prime opportunity for a skeleton to enter the archaeological record through nonseismic means.[21] Therefore, the presence of skeletons in a destruction only indicates that some poor person or group of people were unable to escape death and were either killed by attackers, were crushed by falling walls when a poorly made foundation finally gave way, or died from smoke inhalation when trapped in a burning building; corpses might have been thrown into a building after a raid on a city, or they might have been crushed to death by an earthquake-induced destruction. Consequently,

---

19. See, e.g., modern Egyptian mud-brick houses that collapsed due to lack of maintenance (Amador 2013, 72 fig. 4). Müller-Karpe (2017, 55) also notes that during their time excavating Sarissa, every winter in the nearby village of Başören, one or two houses partially collapsed due to the harsh climate and the need for upkeep.

20. See also the discussion in Ambraseys 2006, 1011, who notes that during the 1960s through the 1970s in more remote parts of the Middle East where constructions techniques are in many ways similar to those found in the archaeological record, if individuals were killed in an earthquake, their remains were almost certainly recovered after the event was over.

21. See several examples in Boz 2016 where this is exactly the case.

the presence of skeletons does not indicate the cause of the destruction, let alone that it was triggered by an earthquake.

Given all of these interpretive caveats, What evidence should determine if a destruction was caused by an earthquake or not? The answer ought to be a preponderance of evidence pointing to an earthquake in conjunction with the lack of certain other types of evidence. A destruction by earthquake should appear sudden and there should be evidence of faulting or cracking in the walls or floors. Parts of buildings may have been sheared off, falling down the side of the tel or mound. The pottery should be examined to see if there are joins between sherds that were found spread throughout a room or perhaps between pottery uncovered on the floor and in a crack (as was the case at Tell Deir Alla; see Franken 1992; Millek 2019b). Walls may also be tilted, but there must be more than one slanted wall. In particular, one ought to look for walls skewed in the same orientation from more than one building. It is unlikely that several walls from different buildings would all tilt in one direction just from seasonal weather changes. In this case it is also important to examine the structure's foundation. Was it built on bedrock or on top of accumulated settlement debris? If the underlying soil matrix is itself unstable or faulty, this might make the building more prone to an earthquake or simple structural failure. One example of this would be building a fortress on a foundation layer of sand that collapsed without evidence of burning or warfare. In the absence of typical earthquake damage, the structural collapse would be the likely result from this engineering oversight.[22]

In addition to this, a destruction by earthquake should lack certain types of evidence. For example, earthquakes should be random in what they destroy. Not all buildings will suffer destruction during an earthquake, though this is certainly a possibility, and the buildings that were destroyed should not follow a pattern appearing random. If in a destruction event only monumental structures, temples, or defensive structures were destroyed, the lack of randomness should be taken as evidence against an earthquake. Additionally, if weapons of war are scattered throughout the site in open-air spaces, on streets, in domestic structures and the like, this should be taken as evidence against an earthquake.[23] Likewise, while earthquakes certainly can cause buildings to catch on fire, there needs to be a source for that fire, as there is no active agent setting buildings alight. Thus, there may be a differentiation in the pattern of destruction as some rooms or buildings might have been burned, while others

---

22. See the discussion of Tel Mor in Millek 2018a and ch. 7, where two separate Egyptian-style fortresses collapsed due to the fact that they had foundations of sand in the wet and rainy environment of the southern Levantine coast.

23. See discussion of Midea in ch. 4 where this is indeed the case. The site has been often touted as destroyed by an earthquake, but the preponderance of evidence points to an act of war.

40 CHAPTER TWO

only had their walls collapse without burning (which was the case for Beth-Shean; see Millek 2018a). To assign a destruction to an earthquake, it should be readily apparent that the destruction was caused by an earthquake and not by some other means. Even structural collapse without burning while also lacking evidence for warfare should not be assigned to an earthquake unless there is a preponderance of evidence. Structural failure or storm damage are more than likely causes for a building to collapse without needing to resort to a seismic catastrophe. Moreover, earthquakes are not the only seismically induced event that might cause destruction, as tsunamis or seiches might leave similar markers along with alluvial deposits in the destruction.[24]

There are, of course, more advance methods of analyzing the physical debris, architecture, and the surrounding geology to help determine if earthquakes influenced the destruction or not.[25] However, this approach requires enlisting the help of at least one geologist or archaeoseismologist, which will oftentimes be out of reach for most excavations. In other cases, the materials from many older excavations do not even exist anymore to be put under this type of scrutiny, or the sites are in parts of the world that are no longer accessible due to modern political upheavals and the surrounding geology cannot be physically examined. Thus, the litmus test for earthquakes needs to be exhaustive, as there need to be clear signs of earthquake damage without evidence of other types of destruction. Not every building or wall that collapsed without a fire was brought down by an earthquake, as there are other natural causes that could bring this type of destruction about.[26]

Accidental Destruction

Accidental destructions by fire are likely to be the most difficult to determine with any degree of certainty given our current ability to examine destruction events, particularly if one cannot physically examine the remains in situ (see discussion in Millek 2017, 117–18). However, even though it is likely a difficult task to identify these destructions, it certainly does not mean that we rule out accidental fires brought on by the slip of a hand that resulted in a destruction

---

24. For a discussion on the archaeological approach to identifying damage caused by tsunamis or seiches, see Salamon et al. 2007, 2011; Morhange et al. 2014; Shtienberg et al. 2020.

25. See, e.g., Marco et al. 2006; Ferry et al. 2011; Hinzen et al. 2018; Lazar et al. 2020.

26. I should also not forget to mention the more spectacular though less frequent natural destructions such as volcanic eruptions that blanket sites in ash (Bruins, Van Der Plicht, and MacGilli 2009; Driessen 2019) or a Tunguska-like aerial burst where a meteorite or comet explodes in the atmosphere, sending a superheated pressure wave toward the surface of the earth obliterating everything within a wide radius. See the discussion in Moore et al. 2020 on possible aerial burst at Tell Abu Hureyra. Steven Collins has also proposed a destruction by a cosmic burst for Tall al-Hammam in Jordan (https://phys.org/news/2018-12-meteor-air-years-obliterating-dead.html). The proposed scientific evidence for this was recently published in Bunch et al. 2021.

preserved in the archaeological record. One possible method to determine if a destruction was accidental is to determine the origin of the fire. As Redsicker and O'Connor (1997, 98) point out, one clear indication that a fire was arson is if there are multiple points of origin. Thus, if one is trained in forensic fire investigation techniques, it may be possible to examine the physical archaeological remains to determine if there are hints of multiple origins of a fire, which would point to arson and thus not an accident.[27] On the other hand, if there is evidence that the fire originated near the tabun, it might indicate that this was the accidental source of the fire.

There may at times be some destructions that could be classified as accidental based on the circumstances of what occurred before and after the destruction, though this classification may not be certain. For example, if a domestic structure burns down and is then quickly rebuilt without any other indication that other buildings were destroyed at the same time, an accidental fire would be a likely cause.[28] Additionally, if a site is abandoned and one of the structures is reinhabited by squatters, if that building burns down, providing there are no signs of warfare or seismic activity, an accidental fire would also be a likely solution for the cause. Since the town had been abandoned and only a handful of people were squatting in a dilapidated building, if a fire got out of hand there would be no way for them to control it.[29] However, outside of these possible signals of accidental destruction, we are currently limited in assigning destruction to accidental fires and this area requires further research.

In this context, I must address the supposition that mud-brick structures could not burn down in an accidental fire, as allegedly there was not enough fuel in these mud-brick buildings to burn them, whether that be by accident or even in a natural disaster.[30] However, what is oftentimes ignored in these discussions is the abundance of incendiary materials that were stored in, on, and around these buildings. Fuel would need to be kept close at hand, particularly during the winter months, for tabuns, tannurs, hearths, or for any sort of industrial activity that involved the controlled use of fire. Whether the fuel was brushwood, dung cakes, or the remains from threshing and the stalks of

---

27. For a discussion of the forensic methods that can be applied to fires in the archeological record, see K. Harrison 2004, 2008, 2013; Lagarce and Lagarce 2006; LaFayette-Hogue 2011, 2016; Taylor et al. 2015; Shahack-Gross et al. 2018; Kreimerman and Shahack-Gross 2019; D'Agostino 2020.

28. See discussion of Lachish Level VII Area S domestic structure in ch. 7.

29. See discussion of Kalavasos-*Ayios Dhimitrios* Building X in ch. 6.

30. Which has been argued by Gordon 1953; Jung 2016, 557–58; Kreimerman 2017, 178, 191. Based on Douglas H. Gordon's experience of military actions in Waziristan against the Mahsuds and Wazirs during the winter of 1919–1920 he states that, "A house with mud and rubble walls and a flat mud-covered roof has to be prepared for burning or it will not burn at all: the two essentials being extra fuel and a good draught. These houses will not burn by the simple application of a torch to such woodwork as forms part of their fabric; elaborate preparation must be made if they are to be even rendered uninhabitable" (Gordon 1953, 149).

harvested grains, these fuels would have likely been stored in or near the house or perhaps on the roof along with other agricultural products.[31] For example, in the book of Joshua, when the two spies are sent to investigate Jericho, the local authorities attempt to find them, but the spies are aided by Rahab who, "hid [the spies] in the stalks of flax which she had laid in order on the roof" (Josh 2:6 NASB). No matter when exactly this story was written, it reflects a tradition of storing agricultural products on the roof of a house, a practice that continues in the Middle East to this day, as agricultural products and plant fuels are stockpiled near or on the homes of modern villages.[32] Thus, it is safe to assume that the Late Bronze Age residents of the Eastern Mediterranean likely kept fuel or agricultural products close at hand, revealing that there would have been an abundant supply of fuel for accidental or natural fires to burn. Moreover, there would have been a plethora of other flammable materials housed in these ancient structures, including but not limited to, bedding, feed for animals, bedding for animals, furniture, materials to produce textiles, and foodstuffs, all of which would have been close to active fires, along with the flammable components of the structure itself.

It is perhaps for this very reason that many storerooms burned in the past, as they would have been replete with flammable materials and would have provided an easy source for an accidental fire to take place. It is more than possible that the Pithos Magazine from Building II at Alassa, which showed traces of intense burning, was an accidental fire that was kept from getting out of hand and destroying the entire structure. This is also the probable though not the definitive case for the storage building at Tel Zippor, as it was the only structure that burned at the end of the Late Bronze Age, while the nearby temple remained unscathed (see Millek 2017 as well as the discussion in ch. 7). Per Ålin (1962, 12–13, 15, 24, 150), nearly sixty years ago, too suggested that the "granary destruction" at Mycenae from the LH IIIC was possibly caused by an accidental fire, and it is more than probable that many destructions that have been assigned to warfare were in fact the result of carelessness, negligence, or a misplaced oil lamp.

In our modern world, it is often forgotten the dangers that our predecessors faced, as flour and dust are also highly combustible and can cause explosions from a static spark or the flame of an oil lamp if there is enough material suspended in the air.[33] Moreover, grain, hay, and straw if not stored properly

---

31. For a discussion of the possible fuels used in tabuns and tannurs, see Gur-Arieh et al. 2014; Rova 2014; Budka et al. 2019.

32. See the discussion and images in Cappers and Neef 2012, 423–34.

33. See discussion in Van Leuven 1979. While I certainly would not agree, nor did I find any evidence that grain explosions destroyed the Mycenean palaces; nevertheless, it is at least worth remembering the danger of what we consider commonplace products.

can spontaneously combust.[34] Oil, whether it be for cosmetic purposes, rituals, or cooking would also have been a ready source of a highly combustible substance. Igor Kreimerman and Ruth Shahack-Gross in their experimental burning of a miniature single-story mud-brick house, deduced that oil is not a significant contributor to the heat of a fire.[35] Their experiment, though, only placed a small jar of oil in the mud-brick house. However, if we look in the archaeological record, we must place oil in its proper context, such as the pithoi in the administrate complex at Hazor that could store more than 3,500 L of oil (Ben-Tor 2013) or the large pithoi in the Pithos Magazine from Alassa Building II (Hadjisavvas 2017, 272–73). The combustion of the oil, or perhaps wine, in these huge storage vessels would have contributed to the intense heat at least in the rooms where they were stored when they burned. Accordingly, it is unlikely that a jar of oil from a house would be an extra danger or contributor to a fire, as Kreimerman and Shahack-Gross deduced. However, if greater quantities of it were stored, particularly if this was near any other sort of combustible materials, such as wood for heating the tabun where the oil was used for cooking, it would have provided a more ready source for the fire to grow in intensity.

There is even a precedent from a Late Bronze Age textual source that notes both the types of flammable materials stored in a guard tower and the possible dangers of storing that material. As Andreas Müller-Karpe has pointed out, in a text from Hattusa that gives guidance to a "Bei Madgalti" or "Lord of the Watch(tower)," who was an overseer of a border or rural province, this official was instructed to, "store firewood in the fortresses as follows: Each log should be twelve fingers thick, but the length should be one cubit and four spans ... the log should be three fingers thick.... It should be sealed, and he should check it year after year" (Müller-Karpe 2017, 39; citing Schuler 1957, 44).[36] Müller-Karpe also notes that in another section of the text it mentions the risk of an accidental fire in these fortresses because of the stored firewood. The Bei Madgalti was warned to let, "no one take a torch into it.... No one lights a fire in the fortress" (Müller-Karpe 2017, 39; citing Schuler 1957, 44). Thus, given the lengths of time and humanity's propensity to make mistakes, it is more than plausible that in any given fifty to one hundred years several buildings would have caught on fire because of an accidental mishap with stored fuel and that these accidents would be preserved in the archaeological record.[37]

---

34. See, e.g., Rothbaum 1963. The US Fire Administration lists spontaneous fires as a leading cause in agricultural storage facilities, such as barns, silos, and stables. https://www.nps.gov/articles/fire-prevention-52-spontaneous-combustion.htm.

35. They state that, "Ignition of olive oil within burning structures is not expected to cause a significant elevation in the conflagration's temperature" (2019, 2927).

36. Unless otherwise noted, all translations throughout the book are by the author.

37. The text instructing the Bei Madgalti also goes on to give directions on how to properly

44 CHAPTER TWO

Another consideration when assessing the possibility of accidental fires is environmental factors, such as long periods of aridity, regional high-winds, and the combination of the two. A simple spark could easily start a forest fire that, pushed by winds, could threaten a site. This was the very case in August of 2020 when a wildfire broke out near the tomb of Agamemnon at Mycenae and it required two planes, several fire engines, and more than twenty firefighters to put out the blaze before it damaged the ancient structures.[38] The same occurred at Lachish before excavations began in the 1970s. The tel was covered with brush and, as David Ussishkin (2004a, 5) recounts the story, "On one hot, windy *hamsin* day one of the workers threw a cigarette butt aside, and in a short time the entire mound was ablaze. The fire brigade was called to prevent the fire from spreading to the nearby forest.... All the vegetation had disappeared, and suddenly, the entire surface of the mound was visible!" Since we know little to nothing of ancient fire prevention or how they handled fires such as this, it is quite possible that sites could have suffered greatly from wildfires with few ways of combatting them.

Furthermore, in the Hittite votive text KUB 15.1 the text most likely references either an accidental fire or a forest fire that was burning part of the city of Ankuwa. In KUB 15.1, the queen, most likely Puduhepa the wife of Hattusili III, dedicates several offerings to the gods pleading for the city of Ankuwa, "(So that) it shall not burn down completely" (de Roos 2007, 103). The text does not explicitly state how the fire started, but given that there are no named enemies and only that the city needs saving from fire, it is reasonable that this records an accidental or forest fire that was threatening the city. It is improbable that the text refers to any enemy attacking Ankuwa, since an adversary is neither named, vaguely mentioned, nor is an attack referenced. Moreover, as Ankuwa was situated to the south of Hattusa in the Hittite heartland it is unlikely that an enemy, even the Kaska, could have attacked the city during the time of Hattusili III. Thus, it is most likely that the fire mentioned in KUB 15.1 was either an accidental or forest fire that threated to destroy the city.[39] Therefore, from a practical level and from a historical perspective, there would have been enough fuel in buildings to burn them; accidental fires were a known hazard, and likely even threatened cities when they got out of hand. Accidental fires cannot be categorically ruled out as a possible cause for major or minor fires and if a destruction by fire cannot be

---

maintain and care for the structures and what to do in the case of a leaking roof because of the danger of structural collapse; see Schuler 1957, 41–52.

38. https://www.theguardian.com/world/2020/aug/30/wildfire-breaks-out-near-tomb-of-agamemnon-greece.

39. I owe a great deal of thanks to Zsolt Simon for discussing the particulars of this text with me and the idea of an accidental or forest fire as the likely cause of the fire mentioned in the text.

safely ruled as human activity, one cannot assume that it was not an accidental fire and it must be categorized with an unknown cause.[40]

Anthropogenic Destruction

Destruction brought on by humans is not only warfare induced but can manifest in a multitude of forms. This can be the deliberate destruction in an act of war where a battle raged in a city while buildings were being burned, the purposeful desecration of temples or monumental structures after they have been looted, or the reverential decommissioning of a temple.[41] However, to assign a destruction to human hands, there must be a burden of proof, which again demonstrates it was likely caused by humans and not by nature or accident. For warfare this should be the physical presence of weapons of war found within the destruction debris in contexts that do not indicate that they were being stored or manufactured.[42] Thus, weapons found in domestic structures, on streets, in open spaces, or simply scattered throughout a site in a random fashion in association with a destruction event are a probable indicator of warfare.[43] If, however, the weapons are found piled together within a destruction event, this is likely an indicator of weapon storage rather than of warfare. For example, over five hundred bronze arrowheads were uncovered in Room 100 of the North Eastern building from the "Palace of Nestor" at Pylos (Blegen and Rawson1966, 318–24).[44] These weapons are clearly evidence of weapon storage. Likewise, if weapons of war are found in association with the manufacture of bronze objects, they cannot be readily identified as weapons that were deposited during an act of war, as they may have simply been a product of that industry or were being recycled.[45] Moreover, there must be multiple weapons in several nonstorage or industrial contexts to assign the destruction to warfare. A single arrowhead or knife can have any number of nonwarfare-related reasons for their context, but thirty-two arrowheads along with several other weapons scattered throughout domestic structures, open-air spaces, and on streets do point to an act of aggression.[46]

---

40. This is more forgiving than the system employed in modern forensic investigation where, "Unless all relevant accidental causes can be eliminated, the fire must be declared accidental" (Redsicker and O'Connor 1997, 121.).

41. For a discussion of termination rituals, see Zuckerman 2007.

42. For an overview of investigating warfare via archaeological means, see Zuckerman 2007; Paz 2011; James 2013; Selover 2015; Gottlieb 2016; Millek 2017, 2020.

43. Not to mention the occasional projectile point found lodged in a mud-brick wall. See discussion of Hala Sulten Tekke below, as well as Aphek in ch. 7.

44. Though as I will discuss in ch. 4, other weapons uncovered in the destruction point to warfare and it happens to be the case that there is evidence for storage of weapons and warfare at the same time.

45. See Tell Kazel in ch. 7 and in Millek 2019a, 2020.

46. Which was the case for the *Ville Sud* in Ras Shamra (see Millek 2019a, 2020, and ch. 7), and

46   CHAPTER TWO

The physical presence of weapons of war is again only one piece of evidence and no single weapon is proof of conflict; there must be an accumulation of evidence suggesting warfare over some other cause. If a building that was filled with rubble has weapons of war in it but there are no signs of fire or burning, the destruction is more likely the result of a natural disaster or faulty construction techniques, and it should not automatically be assumed that the cause was anthropogenic solely because weapons were found in the structure. The pattern of destruction can also be a clue to the possible cause of the destruction itself. If only certain buildings were destroyed such as the monumental structures, public buildings, or parts of the fortifications, while others such as domestic structures were not destroyed, this would be an indicator that the destruction was manmade rather than being a natural or accidental fire. Nature and happenstance are not so selective to only destroy the most magnificent structures at any given site and the lack of randomness suggests a guiding human hand.

In this way, destruction by warfare and arson can be differentiated. Warfare being a destruction with the visible presence of weapons and arson being those that do not have the physical evidence of weapons in the destruction. This may seem to be a question of semantics, as a battle may have occurred outside of the city's walls with the invading army eventually defeating the defenders only to go on to pillage and burn the city. However, in creating a historical reconstruction of events, it does matter whether or not one is arguing that physical combat occurred within the city and that defenders remained as a battle ensued within the confines of the settlement. Or, if the defenders were defeated outside of the city and the populace had already abandoned the settlement leaving it open for the purposeful desecration and termination of the site's public and monumental structures. Furthermore, evidence of burning only in a temple structure may be evidence of a termination ritual and not of violent human action at all. The termination ritual can include, "defacement, mutilation, breaking, burning or alteration of portable objects (such as pottery ... or stone tools), sculptures, stelae or buildings. They may involve the alteration, destruction, or obliteration of specific parts; the moving of objects such as stelae or the scattering of their broken pieces; and even the razing and burial of a monumental structure before new construction" (Zuckerman 2007, 8, citing Mock 1998, 5).

Sharon Zuckerman, who brought the concept of termination rituals to Near Eastern archaeology, notes that, while it may be impossible to clearly distinguish a reverential from a desecratory termination ritual, "If the remains of such rituals are identified in a phase of alterations and crisis architecture,

---

as I (2020, 108) have said before, "It is highly doubtful to me that the citizens of Ras Shamra would leave a lance, sword, dagger, or arrowhead simply lying on the street for a child to pick up."

and precede the abandonment or destruction of the monumental temple, they should probably be understood as desecratory termination acts rather than reverential decommissioning of the superseded structure" (2007, 7). A temple may be ritually terminated to end its use, keeping it from being desecrated, and instances of arson against religious structures may be viewed as termination rituals, though which of the two types may not be clear. Consequently, warfare and arson should be differentiated within the archaeological record, as arson may not even represent an act of violence.

An important point that needs to be discussed in the context of destruction and warfare is the, at this point, clichéd acceptance that weapons would have been collected after a battle, and thus one should not seek them out as proof positive for destruction by warfare (e.g., Jung 2016, 559; Müller-Karpe 2017, 147). However, this seemingly dogmatic supposition is not based on the actual archaeological record. Weapons would have been collected to be reused and there are likely cases where every weapon was collected after a battle. However, there will be other cases where not all weapons were collected after the battle, particularly if the city that was being attacked was ablaze. Deadly fires and collapsing buildings tend to make it difficult to go around collecting arrowheads. Moreover, there is abundant evidence of weapons left behind in destructions in the aforementioned nonstorage contexts. This is the case for Midea in Greece, Maa *Paleokastro* on Cyprus, Ras Shamra and Tell Kazel in the northern Levant, as well as Aphek in the southern Levant, among others (see discussion in chs. 4–7). Yes, certainly some weapons would have been retrieved if there was the time, but this would not have been the case for every destruction by warfare. This would have also been the case for open-air combat, as not every weapon could be or would be recovered, which was indeed the case for the massive battle that took place during the thirteenth century BCE in the Tollense River Valley, Germany, where weapons, belongings, and skeletons alike were left behind, only to end up a part of the archaeological record (see Jantzen et al. 2011; Uhlig et al. 2019).

Another assumption that needs to be removed is that every attack on every city resulted in its destruction by fire and conflagration. However, this is only an assumption and it is doubtful that every or even most attacks would result in the total destruction of a city. Moreover, there is historical evidence to back this point. As Michael Hasel (1998, 241–54; 2016, 221) notes, in the entirety of the Ramesside period there is very little evidence that the Egyptians, when attacking or sieging a city, had much interest in the physical destruction of the city. There are only a few instances from the textual and iconographic perceptive where a couple of gates were destroyed by the Egyptian army; however, it does not seem to have extended far beyond this. Or as Kenneth Kitchen (2009, 135) also summarized the situation from the Egyptological perspective,

48 CHAPTER TWO

The appearance of town names in these lists (even highly original, up-to-date ones) does NOT necessarily imply that the places concerned had been wiped off the map by a warring pharaoh. That could happen on occasion; Tuthmosis III once mentions reducing settlements to "reddened mounds." But normally, the astute pharaohs preferred to *defeat* foreign/hostile places, and leave them alive, more profitably to become tribute paying vassals. To vanquish a foe or town does not automatically mean kill/destroy, unless explicitly stated. So, a place might indeed suffer damage, or partial destruction, then, be allowed to rebuild and get on with becoming Pharaoh's profitable vassal. Thus, all of us, including archaeologists, need to be careful in interpreting Egyptian written data and site destruction levels alike. (emphasis original)

Consequently, one should not assume that every text that mentions a battle resulted in destruction and it is likely that many battles that took place in city limits did not result in destruction.[47]

This appears to be the case for Hala Sultan Tekke, which was abandoned in the mid-twelfth century BCE without destruction;[48] however, there is significant evidence that it was attacked prior to being abandoned. In the recent excavations, two bronze arrowheads and eleven lead sling bullets were uncovered scattered throughout the domestic quarters (Fischer 2011, 79; 2013, 49; Fischer and Bürge 2015, 32–33). In the original excavations at the site, forty-two lead sling bullets were uncovered, though it is unclear if they derived from the final phase of the site's habitation (Fischer and Bürge 2017a, 78–80; Fischer 2017, 193). However, one key piece of evidence that likely indicates that the site was attacked without a destruction was uncovered in the original excavations conducted by Paul Åström. He discovered an arrowhead stuck in a wall dating to the city's final phase (Åström 1998, 83; 2001, 120–21). Moreover, aside from the arrowhead that was stuck in a wall, Åström (1986, 11–12) went on to mention other arrowheads from the final phase of the city that were found alongside walls, or he describes it as "if they had been shot from a distance." Given that the sling bullets and arrowheads were found scattered throughout the site in domestic areas, as well as the arrowhead discovered stuck in a wall, this cumulative evidence indicates that Hala Sultan Tekke was attacked prior

---

47. See the discussion of the Sea Peoples in ch. 7, who have been blamed for massive amounts of destruction throughout the Eastern Mediterranean even though there are no textual sources that ever state that they destroyed anything. This was an assumption and overinterpretation of the text.

48. While Fischer (2017) maintains that the city was destroyed, there is little evidence that the city was destroyed. Ashy layers or deposits that were uncovered were generally associated with cooking areas or near hearths. E.g., in City Quarter 1 (CQ1) Room 5 ash intermixed with bones was found in a context interpreted as a kitchen. In Room 58, the courtyard in CQ1, the soil was described as very ashy in appearance, but it was found in association with several hearths. Likewise, in CQ2 Room 42, an open space had an area covered in ash. However, this area too has been interpreted by the excavators as a place where food was prepared. Moreover, only four rooms were described with fallen walls or roofing materials found on the floors (Fischer 2011, 79; 2017, 188; Fischer and Bürge 2014, 67; 2015, 33; 2017a, 54).

to abandonment but, significantly, without a destruction.[49] Thus, as Hala Sultan Tekke exemplifies from the archaeological record, attacks on a settlement need not result in the destruction of said settlement, which is in concert with the historical evidence from Egypt.[50]

Another important aspect when interpreting anthropogenic destruction are the inventories of the structures destroyed (see Seeher 2000, 624–25). If natural disasters and structural failures should appear "sudden" in the archaeological record, the opposite may be true for anthropogenic destruction. During live combat certainly many of the most valuable and easily movable objects would have been retrieved by the inhabitants as they fled or by the attacking force while looting. However, the systematic clearing of buildings prior to destruction suggests a much more methodical and planned process. This was the case at Gla in Greece, where throughout all the excavated structures not a single fragment of gold or silver has been recovered, nor any precious stones. In the main building, the Melathron, pottery was scarcely found, suggesting that the building had been thoroughly cleared out without haste prior to the burning of the monumental and defensive structures at the site (see discussion in ch. 4). Seeher (2001) too has argued the same for many of the buildings at Hattusa that were seemingly emptied of all objects prior to burning.

For these two destruction events, and others like them, the systemic removal of nearly all movable objects, including larger pithoi and storage vessels, indicates that the destruction was not sudden and was likely planned. It might also suggest that those who removed the objects were not the enemies but the inhabitants, as it would be unusual for an attacking army to carry off every single pot, which would have been impractical and unnecessary. One could also argue then that in these cases, the buildings may have been purposefully destroyed by the inhabitants rather than by an aggressive force, perhaps to keep the buildings or site from being reused or desecrated by invaders.

Conclusion: An Archaeology of Destruction

Destruction as a phenomenon in the archaeological record has languished in a state of understudy for more than a century. When Zuckerman (2007, 4) stated that, "it is surprising that a systematic treatment of this phenomenon is largely neglected and that there is no conceptual paradigm for dealing with it," at the time there was no way of approaching destruction under a single interpretive rubric. However, this situation needs to change, and destruction must become its own area of specialization. There ought to be an archaeology of destruction,

---

49. Consequently, if one argues that these weapons found in domestic structures do not indicate an attack, then one must present a persuasive explanation for why they are found in these contexts, particularly how an arrowhead became lodged in a wall.

50. This may have also been the case for Kamid el-Loz; see discussion in ch. 3.

one that is applicable from region to region and period to period, as I have laid out. Nevertheless, what needs to be recalled is that even though I have listed criteria for various causes of destruction, when examining a destruction one must come at it without a preconceived idea of the cause, scale, or even if there was or was not a destruction. Each site and each level must be vetted building by building, room by room to see what the cumulative evidence brings to the fore. There could be evidence of a site-wide destruction by warfare, structural failure in one building, or that some ash in a courtyard with some pottery is not evidence of destruction at all. Preconceived notions about any given "destruction," whether that is based on what has been published before or texts from the period that might mention the site or the region, must be put aside to see what the physical archaeological evidence reveals.

When examining a destruction, everything must be taken into consideration, from the building's construction, the location of objects in or outside the structure, the amount and types of objects in each room, the function of each room and building, where evidence of destruction was uncovered room by room, along with all of the factors mentioned in the discussion above. Moreover, we must not only examine the level of the destruction itself, but we must also inspect what occurred before it (Zuckerman 2007), and what happened after it (Millek 2017). For example, one can look for evidence of crisis architecture prior to the destruction.[51] In many cases where there is evidence of crisis, if the site is abandoned after a destruction, it is most likely that the prior crisis affected the site's ability to respond to negative situations more so than the destruction itself. The destruction event may have had little to do with the site's overall outlook and well-being, as monumental structures might have already lost their function, becoming the abode of squatters, as the site was already in the process of abandonment.[52] Furthermore, we must also take into account what occurred after the destruction. Were there any major changes

---

51. Originally proposed by Driessen (1995) and applied to the Near East by Zuckerman (2007) is the concept of crisis architecture. Driessen (66) defined a crisis as, "Situations that may be seen as specific, sudden, unannounced short term changes in normal socio-cultural conditions." These changes may be witnessed in alterations to the architecture of a settlement including, "A decrease of energy input in construction and maintenance (disrepair, repair with inferior materials), a change in original plan (restriction of access and circulation, changes in the permeability of the buildings) and a change in the original function of the structures (blocking of functional spaces or their partial abandonment)" (Zuckerman 2007, 4). The changes in architecture that might indicate a period of crisis are more readily apparent in monumental structures where the symbolic value is more pronounced, such as in temples or cultic installations. It is easier to perceive a cultic structure with once-fine building materials that was turned into a domestic structure with crudely made interior partition walls than it is to notice a domestic structure with moderately good building materials that had been turned into a domestic structure with slightly worse building materials (Millek 2019b, 121).

52. See Millek 2019b for several examples of this, as well as the discussion of Kalavasos-Ayios Dhimitrios in ch. 6.

or alterations to the site? Or was the building or city rebuilt on the same lines with the same material culture? Was there actually an improvement to the architecture after the destruction event (see examples in chs. 6 and 7). Was a burnt temple left alone with no further rebuilding nor was there any evidence of digging to search for valuables (perhaps indicating that the remnants remained sacred to some degree)? Was the rebuilding quick or was there a period of hiatus and was this the case for the site as a whole or only for one building?

There will, of course, be differing levels of information available to study depending on the state of publication, the age of the publication, the amount of any given phase that has been uncovered, and other factors that might have affected the remains uncovered in the archeological record. Likewise, having access to the original fieldnotes or the actual materials in situ will greatly enhance what one might be able to piece together about the destruction, as oftentimes not all relevant information about destruction events is published.[53] However, not having access to the excavated materials or the fieldnotes is not a hinderance to the study of destruction, as most archaeologists and historians will never have access to that material, and the published information is sufficient in many if not most cases. It is then with a system in place to analyze, describe, and interpret destruction, that I will begin to go through the 153 "destructions" from the end of the Late Bronze Age beginning with the 94 "destruction events" that in fact have no evidence of destruction or, at least, not at the end of the Late Bronze Age ca. 1200 BCE.

---

53. With again a great many thanks to the many excavators who shared information with me on unpublished material or from their firsthand knowledge.

CHAPTER THREE

The Destruction That Wasn't

False Destructions

Over time, errors are bound to occur and the need for correction arises. This is true in any scholarly endeavor, as most progress in science and the humanities is made either by the discovery of something new, or by revealing that old assumptions about the nature of reality, the past, or the present are in fact incorrect. A classic example of this is the famous Albert Michelson and Edward Morley luminiferous aether experiment. Michelson and Morley were two late-nineteenth-century physicists, and their experiment was meant to prove once and for all the already assumed existence of the "aether," the medium through which light propagated. However, instead of verifying its existence, the experiment demonstrated that there was no such thing, and their research helped to pave the way for the physics revolution in the early twentieth century allowing room for Einstein's theory of relativity to emerge (Swenson 2013).

While Michelson and Morley were inadvertently disproving a major tenet of physics, at the same time in the late nineteenth century a major precept for the end of the Late Bronze Age was being established. Through the excavations at Troy, Mycenae, Tiryns, and Tell el-Ḥesi the tale of destruction at the end of the Late Bronze Age was in the process of being made into a historical certainty. Moreover, much as the aether had its origins with the Greeks, so too did the destruction narrative for the end of the Late Bronze Age. Then, over the course of more than a century of research, assumptions about the destructive nature of the end of the Late Bronze Age were set in proverbial scholarly stone through more excavations and the discovery of more tablets detailing the conditions ca. 1200 BCE. However, much like physics at the end of the nineteenth century, recent discoveries combined with testing old assumed realties sheds a very different light on the end of the Late Bronze Age, particularly on just how much destruction took place and when it took place.

With the passage of time, errors have crept into the literature on the end of the Late Bronze Age. As discussed in chapter 1, when the lists and maps of sites destroyed at the end of the Late Bronze Age began to grow during the 1970s and through to the modern day, more often than not once a site made it onto a list or map there was no double check to see if there was in fact a destruction or if more recent evidence had shed new light on the date of the destruction. This was only compounded by the lack of a decisive definition for what constitutes a destruction, as discussed in chapter 2. Thus, these factors combined over more than one hundred years of accumulation has created a situation where the margin of error has grown to egregious proportions. This is woefully obvious when examining the 153 cited destruction events at the end of the Late Bronze Age. Of these 153 destruction events, 94 are false destruction events, which is a 61 percent error rate. Much as there are different possible causes for actual destruction events, there are also different types of false destructions, which fall into three general types, that plague the scholarly literature on the end of the Late Bronze Age. These are: misdated destructions, assumed destructions, and false citations.

1. Misdated destructions. Misdated destructions are destruction events that have been cited as occurring ca. 1200 BCE, or at the end of the Late Bronze Age, when in fact the destruction occurred either well before or well after the end of the Late Bronze Age. In the case of the misdated destruction events oftentimes the term "end of the Late Bronze Age" or "ca. 1200 BCE" are employed rather liberally, stretching these generalized terms to encompasses destruction events that took place over the course of centuries. These destruction events have been chronologically compressed to fit into a 1200 BCE mold despite the fact that they occurred well outside of what is typically considered the end of the Late Bronze Age. To be fair, some of these misdated destructions were cited when, at the time of writing, the current scholarly literature did indeed place some of these destruction events at ca. 1200 BCE. However, after further excavations or reevaluations of the stratigraphy, the ceramics, or C14 dates, the destruction was found to fall outside of the years surrounding 1200 BCE.

2. Assumed destructions. Over the past century and more, numerous sites throughout the Eastern Mediterranean have been cited as destroyed based on an assumption that the site should have been destroyed, as the layer or phase ended ca. 1200 BCE, even though there was a lack of convincing archaeological evidence of said destruction event or the evidence was negligible. These assumed destructions can be subcategorized into one of two subsets. The first is that certain sites were assumed destroyed because there was a theoretical model that dictated that massive amounts of destruction took place at the end of the Late Bronze Age. It might involve a massive wave of destruction brought on by the Sea Peoples in the Levant, or the mythical Dorians in Mycenean Greece, or even simply that the years surrounding 1200 BCE are assumed to have been teeming with destruction. Thus, even if no evidence of destruction was found at the site, a destruction was still assumed, as the presupposition was that all sites had been destroyed. The second of these two types of assumed destructions are those where minimal evidence of destruction was maximally interpreted, that is, where some ash in one small part of a site was then blown out of proportion,

being transformed into a site-wide destruction. These assumed destruction events fall outside the range of what is defined as a destruction and thus are not destructions at all.

3. False citations. The third and final type of false destructions are false citations. These false destructions are the most pernicious of the group, as sites have been added to lists or maps as destroyed to act as evidence of the supposed vast destruction horizon ca. 1200 BCE; yet, there is no evidence of destruction at the site nor is there any claim by the excavators that the site was destroyed. Often these sites appear inexplicably on maps, charts, or lists of sites destroyed ca. 1200 BCE without any citations to even back the claim. They are simply listed or displayed as destroyed without any reason or rationale.

Together these three types of false destructions have created an image of the end of the Late Bronze Age that is not reflected in the archaeological reality. In the following pages, I will present each false destruction event and why these destruction events are in fact misdated, assumed, or false citations. Often, chains of citations have been created over time where one author reported that a site was destroyed ca. 1200 BCE, and this was cited by others, and then by others still, until finally the destruction became an unquestioned fact about the end of the Late Bronze Age. However, because of the time and intensive labor it takes to fact check every destruction event, these false destructions were never weeded out, as authors simply cited other authorities on the subject and did not go back to the original excavation reports to see if the destruction actually took place and if it happened when the general reference work claimed it did.

In many ways, certain false destructions became a scholarly reality in a similar fashion to the way a message is distorted in the childhood game of telephone. In the game, one person at the end of a line of people whispers a phrase to the next person in line such as "Alaca Höyük was not destroyed at the end of the Late Bronze Age." This second person then whispers the phrase to the next in line and so it goes until the phrase finally reaches the end of the line where the last person says out loud what they were told the phrase was. In this case, they would say, "Alaca Höyük was destroyed in a massive conflagration!" as the message was distorted with each person until finally it came to the opposite of what was initially said. It has functioned much the same way for many of the end of the Late Bronze Age destructions in the scholarly literature through repeated citations. The original author stated one thing, others cited that author stating something slightly different, and those were then cited by others who changed the "facts" even more. By going through each of these false destruction events, I will attempt in many cases to demonstrate not only why they are false destructions, but also, how they came to be cited as false destructions wherever the trail is clear enough to follow. Within each of the

56 CHAPTER THREE

three categories, I will present the false destructions by region. We begin with the misdated destructions.

Misdated Destructions

Greece (fig. 3.1)

Lefkandi

On the coast of Euboea, about halfway between Chalkis and Eretria, lies Lefkandi. A destruction event has been ascribed to the site ca. 1200 BCE and it is one of the commonly cited destruction events at the end of the Late Bronze Age.[1] However, little LH IIIB material was uncovered at Lefkandi, as it appears the LH IIIC inhabitants cleared most of the LH IIIB remains away. Consequently, there can be no evidence of an end of the LH IIIB destruction, as the settlement no longer exists to be excavated (Evely 2006, 304). Yet, even in the following LH IIIC Phase 1a no clear evidence of destruction was uncovered.[2] In the South House, some mud bricks appear to have fallen from the house onto the yard to the north with no evidence of burning or extensive damage, and from the remains of the West and East Houses there is no indication that they were destroyed at the end of the Phase 1a. Rather, the South House was simply rebuilt while the East and West Houses were cleared and reused in the following Phase 1b without any indication that they were destroyed (Evely 2006, 10–13). Thus, there is no evidence that Lefkandi was destroyed either at the end of the LH IIIB or at the beginning of the LH IIIC. A destruction event did occur at the end of Phase 1b during the LH IIIC (Evely 2006, 1, 305). However, given that it occurred at the end of the second phase of the settlement already in the LH IIIC, this destruction event cannot be included in those commonly associated with the end of the Late Bronze Age ca. 1225 to 1175 BCE. And yet, this likely mid-twelfth century BCE destruction event was misdated by Robert Drews (1993, 9, 22 fig. 1) who placed it at ca. 1200 BCE, even though he himself notes that there was no LH IIIB material uncovered at the site.

Kynos

Kynos is situated on a cape at the northern extremity of the Opuntian Gulf, and it first appeared as an end of the Late Bronze Age destruction in Amos Nur's and Eric Cline's 2000 (55–56) earthquake article citing a 1996 article by Fanouria Dakoronia (1996, 41), who claimed that storerooms uncovered at the site were struck and destroyed by an earthquake. This ca. 1200 BCE destruction by earthquake was then repeated by Nur and Dawn Burgess (2008, 243), and

---

1. Drews 1993, 9, 22 fig. 1; Nur and Cline 2000, 56; Nur and Burgess 2008, 225 fig. 8.1; Middleton 2010, 15; Cline 2014, 110–11, 128 fig. 10; Knapp and Manning 2016, 123.

2. Middleton 2010, 15 states that there was a destruction at the end of Phase 1a.

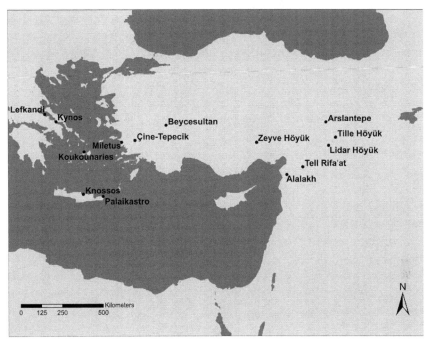

Figure 3.1. Misdated destructions in the Eastern Mediterranean excluding the southern Levant.

this destruction also made an appearance in the "The Encyclopedia of Ancient History" where Antonia Livieratou (2012, 3842) stated that the storerooms were destroyed, possibly by "an earthquake at the end of Late Helladic IIIB (ca. 1200)." However, in the original 1996 article by Dakoronia (1996, 41), she made clear that the destruction of the storerooms took place during the mid-twelfth century BCE in the LH IIIC Middle, meaning this destruction falls well outside of the end of the Late Bronze Age (see also Dakoronia 1993, 125; Kounouklas 2011, 15–19).

Crete (fig. 3.1)

Knossos

Knossos is located just south of modern-day Heraklion, near the northern coast of Crete. The supposed ca. 1200 BCE destruction of the site is part of a long-running debate for when exactly the final palace was destroyed. One camp places the destruction toward the end of the fourteenth century BCE, which was followed by a postpalatial occupational phase. The other camp places the destruction at ca. 1200 BCE to put it in line with the destruction of the palaces on the Greek mainland, arguing that the evidence of the postpalatial

58 CHAPTER THREE

occupation was in fact part of the destruction.[3] However, from the current state of the debate, it appears that the final destruction of the Palace at Knossos was indeed in the fourteenth century BCE, and moreover, there is no evidence of a destruction in the postpalatial occupational phase ca. 1200 BCE (Hatzaki 2004, 2005, 2017; MacDonald 2010, 540; Hatzaki and Kotsonas 2020, 1031–35). The doubt over the date of the destruction was known to Drews in 1993 (p. 9 fig. 1), and it was for this very reason that on his map of destruction, he italicized Knossos stating that, "sites in italics destruction in the Catastrophe is *probable but not certain*" (emphasis added). This ambiguity about this destruction was carried on in the maps of destruction in Nur and Cline (2000, 56) and Nur and Burgess (2008, 225 fig. 8.1). However, in Cline 2014 (110–11 fig. 10), which is largely a copy of Drews's 1993 map, Cline removed the italics, simply stating that Knossos was destroyed ca. 1200 BCE while never discussing the problem of the date and why even Drews had not been completely confidant in the destruction ca. 1200 BCE.[4] David Kaniewski et al. (2011, fig. 1); and Kaniewski, Joël Guiot, and Elise Van Campo (2015, 370 fig. 1) also simply list Knossos as destroyed without any evidence or a discussion of the possible problems with the date of the destruction, all of which have helped to carry on the incorrect date for the destruction.

An interesting aside was Drews's vehement belief that a major site on Crete had to have been destroyed ca. 1200 BCE. He states, that if Knossos had been destroyed earlier in the LM III, that there must have been another site that took over its administrative role, and, "That when this other palace is discovered ... it will prove to have been destroyed in the early twelfth century" (1993, 29). Such was the strength of Drews's conviction in the catastrophic nature and widespread destruction in the years surrounding 1200 BCE, which was not based on the archaeological evidence, that he assumed a palace was destroyed that was never found or is even known to have ever existed.

Palaikastro Kastri

Palaikastro Kastri is situated at Rousolakkos two kilometers from the village of Palaikastro on the east side of Crete. A ca. 1200 BCE destruction at Palaikastro Kastri was first reported by L. Hugh Sackett in 1965 (Sackett, Popham, and Warren 1965) from area KA at the end of Floor 2, a destruction that has remained in the scholarly literature, being recently reiterated by Krzystof Nowicki (2018, 132).[5] However, after reviewing the material from Sackett's

---

3. See discussion and references in MacDonald 2010, 540; Hatzaki 2017, 71; Hatzaki and Kotsonas 2020, 1031–35.

4. See also Bell 2006, 137 map 1, who made the same change to her map of destruction.

5. Nowicki (2018, 132), citing Sackett, states, "The settlement continued to be occupied throughout the first decades of the twelfth c. BCE, although with two phases separated by a destruction episode, probably around or shortly after 1200 BCE."

original excavation, Timothy Cunningham (2017, 358–90) has demonstrated that Floor 2 ended during the mid-thirteenth century BCE and not ca. 1200 BCE. Thus, there is no end of the Late Bronze Age destruction at Palaikastro Kastri on Crete.

Cycladic Islands (fig. 3.1)

Koukounaries of Paros

Situated on the island of Paros within the rocky Koukounaries hill was the Mycenean citadel Koukounaries of Paros. The citadel was destroyed, and in the debris were animals and humans buried by burnt remains of the monumental structure. This destruction was first associated with the end of the LH IIIB ca. 1200 BCE in 1980 by the excavator Demetrius Schilardi and this date was repeated by Drews in 1993 (26). However, as early as 1981, the date of this destruction was put into doubt as Robin Barber (1981, 11) noted that LH IIIC ceramics had been recovered in the destruction debris. Subsequent reviews of the material firmly place the date of the destruction to the mid-twelfth century BCE around 1150 BCE (Mountjoy 2008, 473–74; Schilardi 2012, 90; 2016, 28–47; see also references therein). Despite the horrific nature of the destruction at Koukounaries of Paros, it was not a result of the events taking place at the end of the Late Bronze Age.

Anatolia (fig. 3.1)

Çine-Tepecik

Çine Tepecik is located five kilometers west of the town Çine in the province of Aydın in western Anatolia. A destruction event of ambiguous date was reported for the end of the Late Bronze Age at Çine-Tepecik (Günel 2010, 2015a, 2016). This destruction by fire was uncovered at the end of Level II la throughout the settlement but it is not an end of the Late Bronze Age destruction event. Mycenean style pottery dates the destruction to the LH IIIC Middle or the mid- to late twelfth century BCE and there was no destruction ca. 1200 BCE (Günel 2015b, 637–38).

Miletus

Miletus is situated on the western coast of Anatolia near the mouth of the Maeander River.[6] The excavation of Miletus began in the early twentieth century during the infancy of archaeology, which has severely complicated the picture of exactly when the end of the Mycenaean city came about and what

---

6. Miletus is also spelled Miletos; in the German excavation reports, the spelling is Milet.

60 CHAPTER THREE

happened to it.[7] Nevertheless, Miletus is a mainstay for the maps of destruction ca. 1200 BCE.[8] The end of the Third Building Period, or Miletos VI after the renewed excavation's terminology, has presented a complicated archaeological problem owing to the lack of material and the early date when much of it was excavated. This was already noted by Vincent Robin d'Arba Desborough in 1964 (162) who, based on the available evidence at the time, put the supposed destruction at some time during the LH IIIC but mentioned no specific dates or times within the LH IIIC.[9] However, Desborough (1964, 162) did make clear that there was no destruction uncovered at the site dating to the end of the LH IIIB. Penelope Mountjoy (2004, 198–200), after analyzing the ceramics from Miletus, concluded that the date of the possible destruction and the end of the Third Building Period occurred in the LH IIIC Early based on a comparison of the pottery from Miletus with that from Ugarit. However, as she noted, "it must be borne in mind that at the moment this date is based on pottery from Ugarit; there is as yet no stratigraphy for this phase from Miletos; it is to be hoped that further excavation will clarify this picture" (2004, 200). Indeed, it appears that further excavations at Miletus have answered this problem at least for the moment (see Niemeier and Niemeier 1997; Niemeier 2007). Based on the more recent excavations at Miletus, Wolf-Dietrich Niemeier (2007, 16) has concluded that the end of the Third Building Period, or their Miletus VI, came to an end at some time between 1130–1060 BCE, though as he notes, the exact date has still not been established.[10] Thus, while the matter is not entirely settled, it appears that Miletus too was not destroyed ca. 1200 BCE, despite it constantly reappearing as destroyed ca. 1200 BCE in works that were written after Niemeier published the results of the renewed excavation and the corrected date.

---

7. See Gorman 2001, 25 n. 29; Greaves 2002, 39–64 for an overview of the original excavations at Miletus and references to these excavations.

8. Drews 1993, 9 fig. 1; Nur and Cline 2000, 44 fig. 1; Bell 2006, 137 map 1; Nur and Burgess 2008, 225 fig. 8.1; Kaniewski et al. 2011, fig. 1; Cline 2014, 110–11 fig. 10; Kaniewski, Guiot, and Van Campo 2015, 370 fig. 1.

9. Desborough 1964, 162. It should be noted that Drews cites Desborough as evidence of a ca. 1200 BCE destruction at Miletus even though Desborough never made the claim that the city was destroyed ca. 1200 BCE. Drews thus misquoted Desborough as evidence to support a ca. 1200 BCE destruction. Both maps in Nur and Cline 2000 and Nur and Burgess 2008 are direct copies of Drews's 1993 and therefore repeat this error, as the authors never fact checked Drews's work. Cline's 2014 is also a slightly altered version of Drews's 1993 map and again repeats Drews's misquotation. For Kaniewski et al. 2011 and Kaniewski, Guiot, and Van Campo 2015 both maps simply list Miletus as destroyed ca. 1200 BCE, by the Sea Peoples no less, without any citation whatsoever as outside of the map, the site is never mentioned in either article. Thus, likely because of one misquotation by Drews, Miletus has become a common feature of destruction ca. 1200 BCE in the Eastern Mediterranean.

10. Niemeier also notes that no evidence of a destruction ca. 1200 BCE was uncovered in the original excavations.

THE DESTRUCTION THAT WASN'T 61

Beycesultan

Beycesultan is located about five kilometers southwest of the modern-day city of Çivril in the Denizli Province. The site's Level II (Layer 5b of the new excavation) came to a tragic end, as corpses were found tossed into buildings; several people had been bludgeoned to death as they tried to hide from their attackers; and nine other individuals were crushed and burnt to death by a collapsed ceiling as they hid in the basement of a building. Weapons were found strewn throughout this destruction event, testifying to the devastation wrought on the inhabitants of Beycesultan by their fellow humans.[11] In the original excavations, Seton Lloyd and James Mellaart (Lloyd and Mellaart 1955, 1956; Mellaart and Murray 1995, 93, 96) assumed that the destruction of Level II took place at the end of the Late Bronze Age ca. 1200 BCE. This assertation has recently been repeated by Bernard Knapp and Sturt Manning (2016, 126) who claim that Beycesultan was destroyed at the end of the Late Bronze Age and K. Lawson Younger Jr. (2016, 113 n. 8) who also claims the site was destroyed ca. 1200 BCE. However, following the recent excavations at Beycesultan, based on the ceramics and C14 dates, it appears that Level II is far older than Lloyd and Mellaart first proposed (Dedeoğlu 2014; Dedeoğlu and Konakçı 2015; Fulya Dedeoğlu pers. comm. 09/30/2019). Layer 5b of the recent excavations, which corresponds to Level II of Lloyd and Mellaart, is at least 250–300 years older, dating to 1530–1410 BCE at the earliest (Dedeoğlu 2014; Dedeoğlu and Konakçı 2015; Fulya Dedeoğlu pers. comm. 09/30/2019). Thus, despite the truly tragic nature of the end of the Level II at Beycesultan, which could easily fuel images of the supposed violence at the end of the Late Bronze Age, the destruction of Level II was in fact already ancient history by the time the Bronze Age came to an end.[12]

Zeyve Höyük/Porsuk

Zeyve Höyük, also known as Porsuk Höyük, is located near the town of Ulukışla in the province of Niğde. A fortification system was uncovered at the

---

11. Lloyd and Mellaart 1955, 1956; Mellaart 1970; Lloyd 1972; Dedeoğlu 2014; Boz 2016.

12. One further question that must be taken up here is exactly how Beycesultan ended up on a list of end of the Late Bronze Age destructions for Anatolia in Knapp and Manning 2016. Knapp and Manning never cited the original excavation reports from Beycesultan or any of the recent excavations reports that specifically dealt with the chronology of Level II and were available prior to the publication of the 2016 article. What is even more curious is that the article Knapp and Manning cite for their list of destructions in Anatolia at the end of the Late Bronze Age is Kurt Bittel's 1983 treatise on the end of the Bronze Age in Anatolia. This is the common reference article, one that has been the basis for most maps for destruction featuring Anatolia, and it is not surprising that Knapp and Manning based their assessment of how much destruction took place in Anatolia on this article. However, in Bittel's article, he specifically states that in his assessment Beycesultan was *not* destroyed at the end of the Late Bronze Age (Bittel 1983, 31). Therefore, Drews 1993 and Cline 2014 do not claim that Beycesultan was destroyed, even though they also referenced the same article by Bittel. It is then unclear exactly how Beycesultan became featured as an end of the Late Bronze Age destruction in Knapp and Manning's article.

site, dubbed Level V, that was initially assumed to be dated to the end of the Late Bronze Age at the end of the thirteenth century BCE. On the floor of a possible gate system were masses of burnt debris from the superstructure, blackened raw bricks, charred beams, rubble, stones, and a half-burnt skeleton that had been crushed by a falling wall. The hands of the individual were frozen in place near their face as they appear to have attempted to shield themselves from their eventual doom (Dupré 1983, 42; Pelon 1992, 340; 1993, 16). In another section of the site, the so-called Hittite room was uncovered and on its floor were twenty smashed storage jars while in "Casemate 2" more evidence of destruction by fire was uncovered (Beyer 2005, 305–14; 2008, 315–25; 2010, 100; Beyer et al. 2006, 229). This was initially assumed to have been the fate for Level V and the end of the Late Bronze Age, and this ca. 1200 BCE destruction has been touted as recently as 2020 by Drews.[13] However, a dendrochronological analysis of timber from the destruction at Porsuk in 2005 revealed that the destruction likely dated to the mid-sixteenth century BCE (Kuniholm et al. 2005, 45; Mielke 2006a, 87–88), and C14 samples taken from the destruction have narrowed the date of the destruction to 1514–1430 BCE (Beyer 2010, 100–101; 2015; Beyer and Laroche-Traunecker 2017). As Dominique Beyer (2010, 101), who originally held that this was an end of the Late Bronze Age destruction, clarified, "The new date for the destruction of the Level V seems to indicate that the end of the Late Bronze Age-Hittite period occupation occurred much earlier than the end of the thirteenth century BCE." Therefore, there is no end of the Late Bronze Age destruction at Zeyve Höyük, as it likely took place more than two hundred years prior to ca. 1200 BCE.

Arslantepe

Arslantepe is located in the Malatya plain fifteen kilometers away from the Euphrates's right bank. The so-called Imperial Gate and the surrounding defensive wall at Arslantepe were initially assumed to have been destroyed at the end of the Late Bronze Age, which Mario Liverani dated to ca. 1180 BCE.[14] Liverani (2012, 336) proposed that the gate was possibly burned by the Mushki people who were, "assumed to be the vanguard of the Phrygian incomers." However, a recent project led by Federico Manuelli (Manuelli et al. 2021) aimed at a reanalysis for the Iron Age sequence at Arslantepe, has cast doubt on the original date for the destruction. Based on recent C14 measurements and the lack of certain ceramic forms, they place the beginning of the Iron Age back into the thirteenth century BCE. As Manuelli et al. (2021, 898–99) describe it,

---

13. Dupré 1983, 42; Pelon 1993, 16; Yakar 1993, 12–13; Beyer et al. 2006, 229; Beyer 2010, 100; Lehmann 2017, 237; Drews 2020, 229.

14. Pecorella 1975, 3–6, 65–68; Frangipane 2011, 986; Liverani 2012; Manuelli and Mori 2016, 217; Younger 2016, 120. For a discussion of the Late Bronze Age period at Arslantepe, see Pecorella 1975 and Manuelli 2013.

"The new chronology of Arslantepe IIIA.1 here proposed necessarily pushes back the final Late Bronze Age destruction, which was a uniform, widespread, and intense episode, to the first half of the thirteenth century BCE ... [though] a high dating of the Late Bronze Age gateway destruction between the fourteenth and the beginning of the thirteenth century BCE is plausible." Therefore, while the "Imperial Gate" was destroyed this had nothing to do with the Phrygians or the end of the Hittite Empire.

Tille Höyük

Tille Höyük is located on the west bank of the Euphrates River approximately sixty kilometers east of Adıyaman. An end of the Late Bronze Age destruction of a gate complex at Tille Höyük has been in the scholarly literature for over thirty years.[15] It was originally assumed that the massive burning event that destroyed the gate took place at the same time as the dissolution of the Hittite Empire in the first decades of the twelfth century BCE, and this ca. 1200 BCE date for the destruction has been repeated over the decades since.[16] However, in 2009, a revised analysis of the dendrochronology and the C14 samples taken from the gate complex placed the date of the burning event to sometime after 1090 BCE (Griggs and Manning 2009; see also Summers 2010, 2013). Thus, while again there is a destruction event at Tille Höyük, from the current evidence, it appears that it took place well after the end of the Late Bronze Age.

Lidar Höyük

Lidar Höyük was situated on the east bank of the Euphrates River, about fifty kilometers northwest of the provincial capital Şanlıurfa prior to the flooding caused by the Atatürk Dam. Much like nearby Tille Höyük, an end of the Late Bronze Age destruction of Lidar Höyük has been in the literature for nearly forty years.[17] However, as early as 1991, in the same article that stated that the destruction was ca. 1200 BCE, the authors noted that the material could also date much later, to the end of the twelfth or beginning of the eleventh century BCE.[18] Several years after this report was published, Uwe Müller (1999, 2003, 2005) did indeed demonstrate, based on an analysis of the ceramics, that

---

15. Summers et al. 1989, 6–7; Blaylock et al. 1991, 4–5; Drews 1993, 11; Summers 1993; Nur and Cline 2000, 44 fig. 1; Bell 2006, 137 map 1; Nur and Burgess 2008, 225 fig. 8.1; Cline 2014, 110–11 fig. 10.

16. Summers 1993; see also discussion of the history of the excavation in Summers 2010.

17. Hauptmann 1981, 198; 1987, 204; Littaver, Crouwel, and Hauptmann 1991; Drews 1993, 11; Nur and Cline 2000, 44 fig. 1; Nur and Burgess 2008, 225 fig. 8.1; Cline 2014, 110–11 fig. 10. Descriptions of this destruction event are unfortunately sparse, as there exists no final report and the initial field reports lack critical details.

18. Littaver, Crouwel, and Hauptmann 1991, 351. It should be noted here that this is the reference that Drews cited as evidence for the ca. 1200 BCE destruction at Lidar Höyük. However, he failed to mention that it was entirely possible that the date of the destruction could have been much later than 1200 BCE.

64　　　　　　　　　　　　　　　Chapter Three

the Lidar Höyük layer <7> and the Late Bronze Age cultural affinities at the site did not come to an end until late in the twelfth century BCE. This has been further verified, as grain taken from the destruction event was C14 dated to ca. 1130–990 BCE (Görsdorf, Hauptmann, and Kaschau 2002, 66; sample Bln-5129). Once again, there was no evidence of a ca. 1200 BCE destruction at Lidar Höyük.

Northern Levant (fig. 3.1)

Tell Rifaʿat

Tell Rifaʿat is located roughly forty kilometers north of Aleppo. An end of the Late Bronze Age destruction was assigned to the end of Level III dating to ca. 1200 BCE by Marjory Veronica Seton-Williams. She uncovered a red burnt layer and mud-brick collapse with crushed and broken pottery. Seton-Williams (1961, 82) notes that the pottery dated to the Late Bronze Age and assigned the partial destruction to ca. 1200 BCE.[19] However, based on the currently available evidence there is no clear date for this destruction. This was already mentioned by Thomas McClellan in 1992 (167), who notes that the ceramics were not well dated, and the destruction event cannot be reasonably placed at the end of the Late Bronze Age based on the current evidence. Thus, for the time being there is no direct chronological evidence that this destruction event occurred ca. 1200 BCE, though this certainly may change with further examination of the pottery uncovered in the destruction debris.

Alalakh (Tell Atchana)

Situated some thirty kilometers east of modern Antakya in Turkey, Tell Atchana, or Alalakh, has been appearing in the scholarly literature as destroyed at the end of the Late Bronze Age for nearly seventy years.[20] Leonard Woolley (1955, 375), the original excavator at Alalakh, believed that its Level I was destroyed by the Sea Peoples ca. 1194 BCE. However, based on the recent excavations led by K. Aslihan Yener, along with a reevaluation of the site's stratigraphy and ceramics, there does not appear to have been a destruction at the end of the Late Bronze Age. The new end date for Level I based on these recent finds is ca. 1300–1295 BCE, a hundred years before the end of the Late Bronze Age.[21] Moreover, based on the finds from the renewed excavation, there

---

19. This destruction was also cited in Sader 1992, 162.

20. Woolley 1955, 375; Drews 1993, 9 fig. 1; Nur and Cline 2000, 44 fig. 1; Bell 2006, 137 map 1; Nur and Burgess 2008, 225 fig. 8.1; Kaniewski et al. 2011, fig. 1; Kaniewski, Guiot, and Van Campo 2015, 370 fig. 1.

21. Yener 2013, 17–24; Yener and Akar 2013, 269–70; see also discussion in Millek 2019a. This new dating is based on the continued abundance of Nuzi and LH IIIA2 pottery, while LH IIIB pottery is completely absent, all in conjunction with radiocarbon dates that fall within the same range.

may not even have been a destruction at the end of Level I at all ca. 1300 BCE prior to when most of the site was abandoned.[22] Thus, the destruction that Woolley assumed was brought on by the Sea Peoples at the end of the Late Bronze Age is not borne out by the recent developments uncovered at Alalakh.

Southern Levant (fig. 3.2)

Tel Dan

Tel Dan is located in northern Israel near the modern Lebanese border. An end of the Late Bronze Age destruction of Level VIIA1 was originally assigned to the beginning of the twelfth century BCE based on the association with the ceramics from Beth-Shean Stratum S-5.[23] However, a more recent investigation examining the ceramics and C14 dates from Level VIIA1 indicates that this possible destruction took place closer to 1150–1130 BCE and it is not an end of the Late Bronze Age destruction.[24]

Hazor

Hazor is situated in the upper Galilee on the northern Korazim Plateau. The final destruction of the Late Bronze Age Canaanite Hazor is a staple for any map or list depicting the end of the Late Bronze Age in the southern Levant ca. 1200 BCE.[25] This destruction has oftentimes been associated with the biblical narrative of Joshua's conquest of Hazor (see discussion in Ben-Tor 2013). Within the destruction, statues of the gods were beheaded, had their hands cutoff, and were smashed in an act of desecration, while the Ceremonial Precinct was laid

---

22. Yener and Akar 2013, 269–70. New evidence has also indicated that Alalakh was not abandoned at the end of the Late Bronze Age and there was a small Early Iron Age occupation; see the discussion in Yener 2017; Montesanto and Pucci 2019; Montesanto 2020.

23. Ben-Dov 2009, 377; see also Kreimerman 2017, 188; Millek 2019c, 256, who based their dates for the destruction in Ben-Dov 2009.

24. Ilan 2019, 605–11, 635. It is not clear based on the archaeological evidence how much of Level VIIA1 was actually destroyed, as it was highly disturbed by later pitting activity and much of the stonework and lumber had been salvaged and reused up until Level V (Ilan 2019, 617). As Ilan (617) describes it, "The next level up, Stratum VIIA1, shows possible signs of destruction: burnt brick debris and charcoal on plaster or tamped earth floors, but here, too, the architectural remains are not well preserved; the horizon is not always discernible. Since the charcoal samples from Strata V and VI yielded consistent calibrated dates in the thirteenth to twelfth centuries BCE, I have suggested that the wood originates in the structures of Stratum VIIA. If beams and posts were salvaged, it stands to reason that stones were salvaged too. This is probably the reason that Stratum VIIA1 is so poorly preserved (in addition to the damage done by the pits of Stratum VI)." Thus, if there were at least beams to salvage that had not been burnt, this demonstrates that the destruction had not ravaged every building. Indeed, as Ilan has demonstrated, there is much continuation between the Level VIIA1 and the following levels; see the discussion in Ilan 2019, 617–19, 635–38.

25. Dever 1992, 100 fig. 13.1; Drews 1993, 9 fig. 1; Nur and Cline 2000, 44 fig. 1; Bell 2006, 137 map 1; Nur and Burgess 2008, 225 fig. 8.1; Kaniewski et al. 2011, fig. 1; Cline 2014, 110–11 fig. 10; Kaniewski, Guiot, and Van Campo 2015, 370 fig. 1; Knapp and Manning 2016, 130. Kaniewski et al. 2011 places the date even later to 1185 BCE.

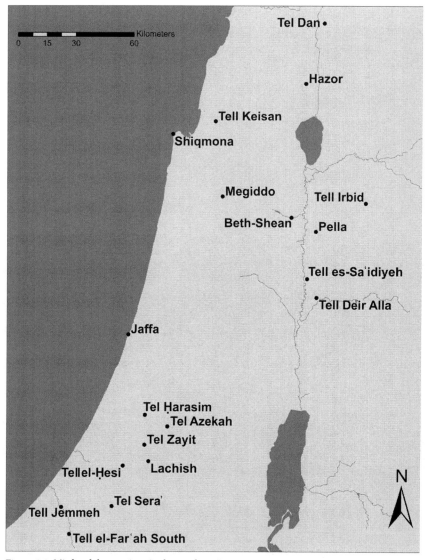

Figure 3.2. Misdated destructions in the southern Levant.

waste in a fire where the temperature reached 1300°C, triggering mud bricks to vitrify, basalt to crack, and clay vessels to melt. However, despite the violent nature and the possible biblical connections, both of which lend a certain mystery of mythic proportions to this multibuilding destruction that brought about the end of the Late Bronze Age at the site, it has been known for some time that destruction of Late Bronze Age Canaanite Hazor took place ca. 1250

BCE, fifty years or more before 1200 BCE.[26] Thus, despite it being a common placeholder for the tragedies at the end of the Late Bronze Age, and while the Late Bronze Age culture at Hazor did come to an end with this destruction event, it occurred in the mid-LB IIB and is not an end of the Late Bronze Age destruction.

Tell Keisan

Tell Keisan is located fourteen kilometers north of Haifa and eight kilometers from the Mediterranean coast. In Tell Keisan's Stratum 13, two rooms belonging to what was likely a storage unit were found burnt and filled with burnt mud bricks. The original excavator Jean-Baptiste Humbert believed that this destruction dated to the end of the Late Bronze Age and attributed it to the Sea Peoples ca. 1200 BCE, as have other scholars following him (Humbert 1981, 386–89; 1993, 864; Dever 1992, 100; Stern 2012, 506; 2013, 5). However, Mariusz Burdajewicz (pers. comm. 04/16/2020), who is preparing the pottery from the final two years of excavations at Tell Keisan, informed me that the date for end of Stratum 13 is likely much lower, occurring sometime around 1150 BCE. Thus, while there is indeed evidence of a destruction at Tell Keisan, it appears that it does not belong to the end of the Late Bronze Age or the Sea Peoples but rather to the mid-twelfth century BCE.

Shiqmona

Shiqmona is situated on Israel's Mediterranean coast some seven kilometers west of Haifa's city center. Joseph Elgavish (1993), the original excavator at Shiqmona, mentioned one time that a public building was destroyed at the end of the thirteenth century BCE, a destruction that was later cited by Ephraim Stern (2012, 506; 2013, 5) in his attempts of defining the "northern Sea Peoples," who supposedly laid waste to the Carmel region before replacing the local population. Nevertheless, Shay Bar (pers. comm. 04/13/2020), who conducted recent excavations at Shiqmona and who has been reevaluating the material from Elgavish's original excavation, has informed me that this LB II public building dates to the fourteenth century BCE rather than the thirteenth century BCE. The recent excavations have also uncovered remains that do date to the thirteenth and twelfth century BCE, but no evidence of an end of the Late Bronze Age destruction was uncovered. Based on this new information, there is no evidence that Shiqmona was destroyed ca. 1200 BCE.

---

26. Ben-Tor 1998, 2002, 2006, 2013; Ben-Tor and Rubiato 1999; Ben-Tor and Zuckerman 2008; Zuckerman 2007, 2009, 2013; Ben-Tor et al. 2017. For a more recent discussion, see Bechar et al. 2021 who place the destruction in the first half of the thirteenth century BCE.

68   CHAPTER THREE

Megiddo Stratum VIIA

Megiddo is located at an important crossroads in the Jezreel Valley some thirty kilometers southeast of Haifa. An end of the Late Bronze Age or ca. 1200 BCE destruction was originally attributed to Megiddo Stratum VIIA, which is one of the benchmark destructions of the southern Levant, closing out the Late Bronze Age cultural affinities at this once powerful and influential site.[27] However, Israel Finkelstein et al. (2017a, 274–75) and Mario Martin (2017, 279–84) have recently argued that the date for the destruction of Stratum VIIA appears to fall in the middle decades of the eleventh century BCE based on radiocarbon measurements and correlations with recent finds in Area H. It should be mentioned, however, that this drastically lowered date is uncertain as the correlation between the finds in Area H and the Palace in Area AA are not secure. It may well be that the date for the destruction should remain in the middle to latter twelfth century BCE (Ussishkin 2021). Nevertheless, whichever date is accurate, this destruction is well outside of the transition from the LBA to the Iron Age.

Beth-Shean

Beth-Shean is situated in the southeastern corner of the Galilee toward the end of the Jezreel Valley and lies close to the Jordan River, which is five kilometers to the east of the site. The destruction of the residential buildings at Egyptian Beth-Shean at the end of Stratum S-3a has oftentimes been accredited with ending the Egyptian presence at the site (Morris 2005, 709; Mazar 2010) and has been listed as an end of the Late Bronze Age or ca. 1200 BCE destruction (Cline 2014, 114; 2021, 110; Knapp and Manning 2016, 130). However, the destruction, most likely by earthquake (Millek 2018a), took place in the mid-twelfth century BCE ca. 1150 BCE and was not part of the events occurring at the end of the Late Bronze Age.[28]

Jaffa

The ancient port of Jaffa is situated in the southern section of modern Tel Aviv. Excavations revealed a destruction of Jaffa's Level IVA Egyptian gate complex that Jacob Kaplan (1967, 116; 1972, 79–84; see also discussion in Burke

---

27. Drews 1993, 9 fig. 1; Nur and Cline 2000, 44 fig. 1; Bell 2006, 137 map 1; Nur and Burgess 2008, 225 fig. 8.1; Cline 2014, 110–11 fig. 10. Both Drews and Cline state in their text that the destruction occurred in the mid- to late-twelfth century BCE (Drews 1993, 16; Cline 2014, 116). However, the maps from both books showcasing the destructions throughout the Eastern Mediterranean give a date of ca. 1200 BCE (Drews 1993, 9 fig. 1; Cline 2014, 110–11 fig. 10).

28. Mazar 2009a, 2009b, 2010; Panitz-Cohen and Mazar 2009. In addition, the destruction was unlikely the cause for the end of the Egyptian presence at the site, as unrest in Egypt rather than destruction in the southern Levant is the more likely culprit for the dissolution of Egyptian hegemony and physical presence of Egypt rather than a wave of destructions; see discussion in Millek 2017, 132–35; 2018a; and in ch. 7 below.

et al. 2017) originally dated to the beginning of the twelfth century BCE, which he accredited to the Sea Peoples. The date for the Level IVA destruction was originally adopted by the renewed excavations of Jaffa's gate complex prior to an analysis of the finds uncovered during the recent excavations and the C14 dates derived from the destruction debris.[29] However, after the renewed excavations were completed and the data examined, it was apparent that the initial date set out by Kaplan was incorrect by nearly a century. Under the naming convention of the renewed excavations, the destruction of the gate complex from Phase RG-3a likely took place between 1134–1115 BCE, placing the destruction well outside of the end of the Late Bronze Age (Burke et al. 2017, 120; see also Burke and Peilstöcker 2017).

Tel Ḥarasim

Tel Ḥarasim lies between the southern Coastal Plain and the Shephelah, and it has been assigned a destruction by Avraham Faust (2017, 23), "during the transition to the Iron Age I." A destruction event was indeed uncovered at Tel Ḥarasim, as ash, collapsed mud bricks, sherds, and other artifacts were uncovered in Areas D and E (Givon 2008, 1766–67). However, this too appears to be a case where the limits of what constitutes the period of transition to the Iron I have been stretched beyond reason, as the destruction occurred in the mid-thirteenth century BCE and cannot be associated with the end of the Late Bronze Age and the beginning of the Iron I (Givon 2008, 1767).

Tel Azekah

Tel Azekah is located twenty-six kilometers northwest of Hebron in the Shephelah. Like Tel Ḥarasim, Tel Azekah has also been assigned a destruction by Faust (2017, 23) during the transition to the Iron Age, and similar to Tel Ḥarasim, the destruction took place well outside any period of transition. A site-wide destruction event was uncovered at Tel Azekah that included several victims who had been trapped in burning buildings. However, this destruction occurred close to the end of the twelfth century BCE and not during the transition to the Iron Age ca. 1200 BCE (Kleiman, Gadot, and Lipschits 2016; Lipschits, Gadot, and Oeming 2017; Webster et al. 2017).

Tel Zayit

Tel Zayit is situated as well in the Shephelah about thirty kilometers east of Ashkelon. Much like the two sites above, Tel Zayit has also been assigned a destruction by Faust (2017, 23) during the transition to the Iron Age. Much like the two prior sites, the date for this destruction was not during this transitional period. As Ron Tappy (2008, 2082) states, the destruction event at Tel Zayit took

---

29. Burke and Lord 2010; Burke 2011; Zwickel 2011; see also Gadot 2010, 61 who states that Jaffa was destroyed ca. 1200 BCE.

place at some point during the early to mid-LB IIB, and while it did suffer a destruction, this event was not part of those at the end of the Late Bronze Age and the transition to the Iron Age.

Lachish Level VI

Lachish is located some forty kilometers southeast of Jerusalem. The site-wide destruction event that obliterated the Level VI city at Lachish has often been a focal point for destruction at the end of the Late Bronze Age.[30] And while the destruction itself was widespread and brutal, resulting in the death of at least four individuals, including children, it was not part of the end of the Late Bronze Age (Ussishkin 1985, 1993, 2004b, 2004d, 2004e, 2007, 2008; Smith 2004; Millek 2017). The destruction of Lachish Level VI, for all of the devastation that it wrought, took place ca. 1130 BCE (Ussishkin 1993, 2004b, 2007, 2008). While this destruction may have ended the Late Bronze Age Canaanite culture at the site, the destruction occurred well after the end of the Late Bronze Age.

Tell el-Ḥesi: Pilaster Building

Tell el-Ḥesi is some seventeen kilometers west of Lachish and ten kilometers south of Kiryat Gat. The Pilaster building, likely an Egyptian administration center (Morris 2005, 549–50), was uncovered by Flinders Petrie in the late nineteenth century during the first systematic excavations in Israel. The destruction of the Pilaster building has commonly been associated with the end of the Late Bronze Age (Oren 1992, 118; Drews 1993, 16; Morris 2005, 550), as Flinders Petrie (1891, 22–25) had uncovered evidence that the structure had been destroyed by fire. However, the date of the building and the destruction are likely to be much later than the end of the Late Bronze Age. The renewed Joint Expedition that excavated Tell el-Ḥesi in the mid-twentieth century uncovered part of the Pilaster building Petrie had missed. Based on these new data, and the material that had been recorded and kept by Flinders Petrie, the Pilaster building was destroyed after 1150 BCE, if not around 1130 BCE, in association with Lachish Level VI (Blakely 2000; 2018, 279–80). Thus, once again, while there was a destruction, it dates well after the end of the Late Bronze Age.[31]

---

30. Drews 1993, 9, 15 fig. 1; Nur and Cline 2000, 44, 60 fig. 1; Nur and Burgess 2008, 225 fig. 8.1; Knapp and Manning 2016, 130; Faust 2017, 23. Drews places the destruction at ca. 1200 BCE while Nur and Cline, Cline, and Knapp and Manning all place the destruction at 1150 to 1130 BCE, though they still discuss the destruction at length as an end of the Late Bronze Age destruction. For a complete discussion of this destruction see Millek 2017.

31. My discussion of Tell el-Ḥesi in Millek 2018a; 2018b; and 2019c, 170 was wrong. While I would still ascribe no end of the Late Bronze Age destruction to the site, there is a clear destruction of the Pilaster building. Thus, my previous writings claiming no destruction whatsoever was simply inaccurate and an error on my part. However, as noted below, I would argue against there being evidence of destruction of the City Sub-IV Egyptian governor's residence.

Tel Sera'

Tel Sera' is located in the Negev twenty kilometers northwest of Beer-Sheba.[32] A destruction of the Stratum IX Egyptian garrison at Tel Sera' was initially associated with the incursion of the Sea Peoples at the end of the thirteenth or beginning of the twelfth century BCE (Oren and Netzer 1974, 265; Oren 1982, 166; 1984, 41; Mazar 1990, 290). However, the date of the destruction was in actuality later, in the middle or third quarter of the twelfth century BCE (Oren 1993a, 1330; 1997a, 2048; Reade, Barag, and Oren 2017, 14), indicating that the destruction had nothing to do either with the Sea Peoples or with the end of the Late Bronze Age.

Tell Jemmeh

Tell Jemmeh is situated in the northwestern Negev about twelve kilometers south of Gaza. In another early twentieth-century excavation conducted by Petrie (published as Gerar), evidence of a destruction was uncovered in his Phase G–H, and Petrie (1928, 6) assumed the Philistines had destroyed the site ca. 1194 BCE. This destruction was later cited by Drews (1993, 16; see also Wood 1991) as one of the many destruction events he claimed took place in the southern Levant ca. 1200 BCE. However, already in the 1930s, William Foxwell Albright (1932, 74) and G. Ernest Wright (1939, 460) both argued that this burnt layer could not be associated with the Philistines, as the archaeological evidence indicated that the possible destruction dated to the middle of the tenth century BCE. This suggestion was corroborated by the recent Gus Van Beek excavations at Tell Jemmeh, as they uncovered no evidence for destruction at the site during the transition from Late Bronze Age to the Iron I. Moreover, the burnt layer in Petrie's Phase G–H has been shown to date to later in the Iron I or after by more recent investigations.[33]

Tell el-Far'ah (South)

Tell el-Far'ah (South) is some twenty-two kilometers south of Gaza and twenty-six kilometers west of Beer-Sheba. It is yet another site that was excavated by Flinders Petrie (1930, 17–19) during the early twentieth century, where he uncovered the destruction of Building Y-R. This destruction has been associated with the influx of the Sea Peoples during the first half of the twelfth century BCE based on a reworking of the site's stratigraphy proposed by Bryant Wood (1991, 52). However, prior to this suggested reworking of the site's chronology the accepted date for the destruction was put at the end of

---

32. It may also be found under the Arabic name of Tell esh-Shariah or by the ancient name of Ziklag though there is no definitive evidence that this was biblical Ziklag, as the exact location for this site is still debated.

33. Van Beek 1993, 668–69; Ben-Shlomo 2012; 2014a; 2014b, 1056; David Ben-Shlomo pers. comm. 08/18/2015; see also Millek 2019c, 177–78.

72 CHAPTER THREE

the twelfth century BCE, and given that after thirty years this chronological overhaul has not been accepted, it appears that the date of the destruction of Building Y-R at Tell el Far'ah (South) far outdates the end of the Late Bronze Age.[34]

Tell Irbid

Tell Irbid is located about seventy kilometers north of Amman on the northern ridge of the Gilead. A Late Bronze Age public complex titled Structure I was uncovered at Tell Irbid that had been completely destroyed by fire. The excavators dated the fire that destroyed Structure I to ca. 1200 BCE and attributed it to some natural cause.[35] However, while the end of the thirteenth century BCE was given as the date for this destruction event, C14 dates derived from grain unearthed in the destruction place the date of the event between 1395–1260 BCE. The grain cache likely dates to within one year of the destruction of the building and the C14 date firmly places the destruction of Structure I well before the end of the Late Bronze Age (Ambers, Matthews, and Bowman 1989, 28).

Pella

Pella is located on the eastern foothills of the Jordan Valley close to the modern village of Tabaqat Fahl. An end of the Late Bronze Age destruction ca. 1200 BCE for the Late Bronze Age temple at Pella was initially proposed by the excavators and was reiterated by Eveline van der Steen.[36] However, the date of the destruction based on a reanalysis of the ceramics is likely after the mid-twelfth century BCE if not even later.[37]

Tell Deir Alla

Tell Deir Alla is situated in western Jordan, about eight kilometers east of the River Jordan, and about one kilometer north of the Jabbok River. The site-wide destruction of Tell Deir Alla is another standard end of the Late Bronze

---

34. Yisraeli 1993, 441; Yannai 2002; Morris 2005, 745–52; Blakely 2018, 279–80. Moreover, it appears that the Egyptian presence at the site had ended prior to this destruction event (Blakely 2018, 273 and references therein). Thus, much as with many other Egyptian sites in the southern Levant as discussed in Millek 2018a, destruction was not the cause for the disappearance of the Egyptian presence at the site.

35. Lenzen, Gorden, and McQuitty 1985, 153–55; Lenzen and McQuitty 1988, 268; Lenzen 1997, 181; Strange 2008, 283.

36. Smith and Potts 1992; Van Der Steen 1996, 58. Fischer (2014, 570) states the destruction of Late Bronze Age temple at Pella occurred at the end of the Late Bronze Age, though he does specifically state that the date of destruction is ca. 1150 BCE. Here the confusion is again exactly what constitutes the end of the Late Bronze Age.

37. Bourke 2012a, 184–86. The destruction at Pella may be correlated with that uncovered at Beth-Shean mentioned above and Tell Deir Alla discussed below. However, it is currently unclear both from a chronological and evidential standpoint if the destruction was by earthquake and if it can be correlated with that found at nearby Beth-Shean and Tell Deir Alla.

Age destruction event for the southern Levant. It can be found destroyed ca. 1200 BCE on most maps and lists of destruction for the end of the Late Bronze Age in the Eastern Mediterranean.[38] A site-wide destruction event was uncovered at the end Phase E, as the temple was burnt, one victim was discovered crushed and burnt under a falling wall, massive cracks were found throughout the site, and even part of the cella had broken off and slid down the tell in a clear destruction by earthquake.[39] Originally this destruction was dated to ca. 1200 BCE based on a faience vase with a cartouche of Pharaoh Tawosret that was uncovered in the temple's cella (Franken 1992, 31, 187; Van der Kooij 2006, 221). However, the excavators have recently lowered the likely date for the destruction to ca. 1150 BCE based on the ceramics (Kafafi and Van der Kooij 2013, 123, 126). Thus, despite the fact that this destruction is commonly associated with the end of the Late Bronze Age ca. 1200 BCE, the earthquake that destroyed Tell Deir Alla occurred well into the Iron Age.

Tell es-Saʿidiyeh

Tell es-Saʿidiyeh lies roughly midway between the Sea of Galilee and the Dead Sea some two kilometers east of the Jordan River. The site suffered a site-wide destruction that was caused by the same earthquake that destroyed nearby Tell Deir Alla.[40] Jonathan Tubb (1990, 29; 1993, 1298; 1998, 86) asserted that the material remains from Tell es-Saʿidiyeh date the destruction to the mid-twelfth century BCE or even as late as 1120 BCE. Cline (2021, 110) has recently claimed that Tell es-Saʿidiyeh was destroyed possibly between 1187–1185 BCE, basing this assertion on the now erroneous date for the destruction of Tell Deir Alla's Phase E that was derived from the cartouche of Pharaoh Tawosret. As mentioned above, this date for the Tell Deir Alla destruction has been shown to be inaccurate, as the destruction was later in the mid-twelfth century BCE. Currently, Tubb (1990: 29; 1993: 1298; 1998: 86) places the date of the destruction between 1150 and 1120 BCE, while Ferry et al. (2011: 56) have correlated the damage uncovered in Stratum XII to the earthquake that also affected Tell Deir Alla ca. 1150 BCE. However, Amihai Mazar (1990: 401 n. 21) has argued that the pottery associated with the Stratum XII buildings appears to be late Iron IIA (late tenth–ninth centuries BCE). This is a suggestion that John Green (2006: 416–18 and references therein), who examined the burials at Tell es-Saʿidiyeh, agrees with, as he also suggests redating Stratum XII to the tenth or ninth century BCE. If this is the case, then the destruction is even

---

38. Drews 1993, 9 fig. 1; Nur and Cline 2000, 44 fig. 1; Nur and Burgess 2008, 225 fig. 8.1; Cline 2014, 110–11 fig. 10; 2021, 110; Knapp and Manning 2016, 130.

39. Franken 1992, 17–38; Van der Kooij 2006; Kafafi and Van der Kooij 2013; see also Millek 2019a, 127–29.

40. Tubb 1986, 1988a, 1988b, 1990, 1993, 1998; Tubb and Dorrell 1991, 1993; Tubb, Dorrell, and Cobbing 1996, 1997; Ferry et al. 2011; Millek 2019b, 125–27.

74   CHAPTER THREE

further removed from the end of the Late Bronze Age than Tubb's assertion. Moreover, it should go without saying that if this destruction does indeed date to the Iron IIA, then it is not associated with the Tell Deir Alla Phase E earthquake destruction. It would also give pause in assuming that the cause of the destruction of Stratum XII was by earthquake as, at the moment, one of the main points in favor of the earthquake determination is its proximity to Tell Deir Alla and the fact that the Stratum XII destruction is also site-wide (Millek 2019b, 127). The exact date for the destruction will not be settled until a final publication of the findings is made available; nevertheless, it is clear that this destruction occurred well after the end of the Late Bronze Age either during the mid- to late twelfth century BCE or later in the Iron IIA.[41]

Assumed Destructions

Greece (fig. 3.3)

Orchomenos

The first of the assumed destruction to be discussed here is the widely cited destruction of the LH IIIB2 palace at Orchomenos known as Minyan in the *Iliad* and the *Odyssey*. Much like Hazor in the southern Levant, the destruction of Orchomenos has appeared in most discussions of the end of the Late Bronze Age in the Eastern Mediterranean as a classic example of a destruction of a Mycenean palace ca. 1200 BCE.[42] However, unlike Hazor's misdated destruction, there is no actual archaeological evidence suggesting that Orchomenos was destroyed at all.

At Orchomenos, a possible Mycenaean palace made up of three parallel wings was uncovered during the 1970s adjacent to the Byzantine church of Skripou.[43] The excavator, Theodoros Spyropoulos (1973; 1975; 2015, 358), claimed that the structures were destroyed at the end of the LH IIIB2 in a fire. However, despite the claim, there is no published evidence that there was any kind of destruction. The only reported possible evidence that might possibly indicate there was minor evidence of destruction was that some broken pottery, fragments of fallen plaster, and some pieces of melted lead were recovered

---

41. In my previous discussion of this destruction event, I followed the dates provided by Tubb as I was unaware of the work done by Mazar and Green (Millek 2019b, 125–27). Thanks are due to Amihai Mazar for bringing this to my attention.

42. Shelmerdine 1997, 581 n. 275; 2001, 373 n. 275; Deger-Jalkotzy 2008, 390; Middleton 2010, 14; 2020a, 11; Cline 2014, 128; Knapp and Manning 2016, 123. Hooker (1976, 149) mentions that there was a destruction of Orchomenos; however, he states that it was of an unknown date and does not readily associate it with the end of the Late Bronze Age.

43. The claim that the three structures uncovered by Spyropoulos were wings of a palace has been debated with respect to whether they are indeed a palace or more akin to the Mycenae House of the Oil Merchant; see the discussion in Iakovidis 1995, 73; Boulotis 2000.

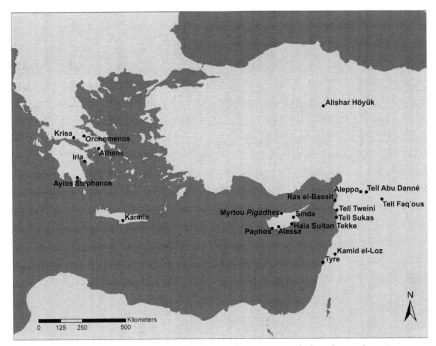

Figure 3.3. Assumed destructions in the Eastern Mediterranean excluding the southern Levant.

from the floor of the courtyard (Spyropoulos 2015, 358). However, based on the criteria for what constitutes a destruction, this evidence does not represent a destruction event.[44] Therefore, until such time as conclusive physical evidence of a destruction has been described and published, there is no physical evidence that Orchomenos suffered a destruction at the end of the LH IIIB2. This lack of archaeological evidence of a destruction is perhaps the reason why R. Hope Simpson and Oliver Dickinson (1979, 237) did not claim that the site was destroyed in their oft-cited *Gazetteer*. Rather they too only state that it *might* have been destroyed, not that it *was* destroyed.[45]

---

44. Maggidis (2020, 116) too has recently noted that there is no evidence of destruction at Orchomenos but rather that the site was abandoned.

45. The reoccurring assertion that Orchomenos was destroyed even though there is a lack of evidence is simply owing to the fact that the original excavations reports were not consulted. Rather, the Simpson and Dickinson *Gazetteer*, which does not specifically say Orchomenos was destroyed, was cited by Shelmerdine (1997, 581 n. 275; 2001, 373 n. 275). The Shelmerdine reference was then cited by Deger-Jalkotzy (2008) and by Middleton (2010). Both Cline (2014) and Middleton (2020) cite Middleton (2010). Knapp and Manning (2016) cite Shelmerdine (2001), Deger-Jalkotzy (2008), Middleton (2010), and Cline (2014) as evidence for the destruction of Orchomenos, even though these are all derivative citations of a work that never even claimed that Orchomenos was destroyed in the first place. In all of these cases, outside of the Simpson and Dickinson *Gazetteer*, the actual archaeological evidence from the excavation reports was never cited or examined.

76 CHAPTER THREE

Krisa

Krisa is located on the promontory of Mount Parnassos, and the assumption that the Mycenean settlement at the site was destroyed at the end of the Late Bronze Age is predicated on the long-disproven theory that the Dorians caused a massive wave of destruction ca. 1200 BCE.[46] Moreover, like Orchomenos, Krisa is a typical example of a destruction ca. 1200 BCE.[47] However, the only evidence for this supposed destruction is a statement by Lucien Lerat and Jean Jannoray (1936, 145), along with Henri van Effenterre and Jean Jannoray (1937, 301) that Krisa was destroyed by the Dorians at the end of the LH IIIB, without providing any archaeological evidence for their claim.[48] Nevertheless, based on the archaeological reports that they wrote, there is no evidence that Krisa was destroyed, by Dorians or otherwise. While not all of the Mycenaean buildings were described in Van Effenterre and Jannoray's (1937, 315) original report, the three structures dating to the LH IIIB period that they do describe have no signs of destruction. Nowhere in the description of Buildings E, F, and G, with Building F being the megaron, is there ever any report of fallen mud bricks or stones, crushed pottery, or any traces of fire, burning, or ash (Van Effenterre and Jannoray 1937, 316–23; 1938, 147). Thus, there is no published or verifiable evidence that Krisa was destroyed at the end of the LH IIIB. This is perhaps the reason that in Edward Kase's (1970, 24) reexamination of Krisa, never does he mention that the site was destroyed, as there is no evidence of such an event. It appears at this time that Lerat, Jannoray, and Van Effenterre believed Krisa was destroyed by the Dorians without any archeological evidence to back this claim, and this false assumption has gone unquestioned and has been readily cited as fact for nearly one hundred years.

Iria

Iria is situated some forty-two kilometers southeast of Mycenae in the Argolid. The destruction of the small Mycenean village at Iria too is often cited in the literature as evidence of the catastrophe ca. 1200 BCE, acting as a witness to the widespread nature of the catastrophe as it spread to smaller

---

46. See Hooker 1976, 171–75 for a comprehensive and early overview of why the mythical Dorians were not responsible for any of the destruction ca. 1200 BCE in Mycenean Greece.

47. Simpson and Dickinson 1979, 257; Shelmerdine 1997, 581 n. 275; 2001, 373 n. 275; Nur and Cline 2000, 56; Dickenson 2010, 486; Middleton 2010, 14; 2020, 11; Cline 2014, 128; Knapp and Manning 2016, 123; Livieratou 2020, 818. The citation chain for Krisa follows the same pattern as Orchomenos. In this case, however, Simpson and Dickinson do state in their *Gazetteer* that Krisa was destroyed. This statement was then cited by Shelmerdine (1997, 2001), who was then cited by Middleton (2010), who was then cited by Cline (2014) all of which were cited by Knapp and Manning (2016). And much as with Orchomenos, no one reviewed the actual archaeological reports with respect to what was found, or in this case what was not found at Krisa.

48. Van Effenterre and Jannoray (1937, 301) state, "[Krisa shone] with supreme brilliance at the time of the Trojan War, before succumbing to the Dorians who reduced it to ashes."

rural settlements outside of the palatial centers.[49] However, as mentioned in chapter 2, Iria was not destroyed. A short ten-day excavation was undertaken in 1939, the remains of which were no longer visible when Hartmut Döhl (1973, 128) summarized the unpublished finds in 1973. Döhl believed and stated that the site was destroyed at the beginning of the LH IIIC. Yet, his claim of destruction was based only on the partial contents of a pit, called a *bothros*, not on any evidence from the architecture. In addition to ashes and lumps of clay, the *bothros* contained a large number of almost complete vessels; remnants of figs, seeds, and fruits; a number of partly burnt, partly unburnt animal bones; and one of the smaller vases also contained the charred remains of its original contents. Döhl (1973, 142–43, 151–52, 168, 192) suggested that because the *bothros* filling appeared to be a closed group from a single depositional event, that this was evidence for the complete destruction of the site at the beginning of the LH IIIC. While the finds in the *bothros* suggest a minor fire, there is no evidence that this affected the entire site, and more than likely it did not affect much more than a single room. Given the contents of the *bothros*, it would likely have been a kitchen or food preparation area where an accidental fire would be likely to break out, given that the fuel for the fire and other combustible materials would have been stored near active flames. However, it is unlikely that it extended much beyond this. From the architectural remains, which were disturbed by later Byzantine activity, there is no evidence of destruction by fire at the beginning of the LH IIIC (Döhl 1973, 136–39). Given this, the burnt pottery found in the *bothros* likely indicates a minor fire that was quickly cleaned up and disposed of. What it does not represent is the destruction of the site, either in total or even partially, and yet, despite the lack of evidence, the destruction of Iria has gone unquestioned in the scholarly literature for fifty years.[50]

Athens

The supposed destruction of Athens at the beginning of the LH IIIC is one of the classic examples of the telephone game-esque citation exaggerations. There exists virtually no evidence of the Mycenean habitation on the acropolis other than perhaps a single limestone column-base, as the remains were removed

---

49. Shelmerdine 1997, 581 n. 275; 2001, 373 n. 275; Middleton 2010, 14–15; Cline 2014, 128; Knapp and Manning 2016, 123.

50. Much like Orchomenos and Krisa, the citation chain for the destruction of Iria stems largely from Shelmerdine who cited the Simpson and Dickinson *Gazetteer*, which was then again cited by Middleton, who was then cited by Cline, who was then cited by Knapp and Manning. However, in the 1979 brief overview from the *Gazetteer*, Simpson and Dickinson (1979, 50) never state that Iria was destroyed. Rather they only report that some burnt material was uncovered in the *bothros*. Thus, much like for Orchomenos, Shelmerdine misquoted the Simpson and Dickinson *Gazetteer* and from there, after repeated citation without any fact checking of the original excavation report or the *Gazetteer*, Iria became a common destruction at the end of the Late Bronze Age.

78   CHAPTER THREE

during subsequent building activities, particularly during the classical period (Hurwit 1999, 73; Lemos 2006). In 1933, excavations on the north slope of the Athenian acropolis did uncover a staircase with a floor overlaying several of those stairs, and on the floor were some complete vessels covered by debris. This floor was dated, at the time, to a brief habitation at the beginning of the LH IIIC, which Oscar Broneer (1933, 352–55; 1939, 319, 424–25) assumed was a squatter's dwelling. In his original reports, Broneer never said that the "Houses on the North-Slope" were destroyed. Rather, he assumed, because the vessels were left behind, that the inhabits had simply fled some approaching danger, leaving their wares behind only to be covered over time by erosion from the acropolis (Broneer 1939, 424–25). However, in 1976, Jens Andreas Bundgaard (1976, 29–30) argued that Broneer had misinterpreted the archeological evidence, suggesting that there was no way the debris covering the floor could have come from simple abandonment and erosion. Rather he suggested that this was indeed a destruction caused by an earthquake that made it impossible for the inhabitants to come back and retrieve their pots. Klaus Kilian (1983, 57 fig. 1) also listed Athens as destroyed in his 1983 article on destruction without discussing the evidence. However, in general, Athens remained undestroyed in the scholarly literature.[51] That is, until 1993 when Mountjoy (1993, 20) mentioned in passing that the houses on the north slope of Athens were destroyed along with a number of other sites in Greece. However, Mountjoy did not cite Broneer, Bundgaard, Kilian, or any other reference for why or how these houses might have been destroyed. In fact, later in the same book, Mountjoy (1993, 132), while citing Broneer, states that the houses on the north slope of Athens were abandoned and made no reference to the destruction she had mentioned earlier in the book. Then in 2010, Guy Middleton (2010, 14), citing Mountjoy, stated that these houses were destroyed. However, nearly ten years later in 2020, Middleton (2020, 11), citing himself from 2010, posited that, "The collapse is marked by fiery destruction at major palace sites ... and probably Athens (a palace?)."

The chain of citation goes from the original excavator stating that these houses were not destroyed but were abandoned. Forty years later another archaeologist disagreed and said the houses were destroyed by an earthquake. Twenty years after that, another archaeologist, citing no references, states the houses were destroyed, but, later in the same monograph, while citing the original excavation reports, said the houses were abandoned. Some twenty years after that, the houses then reappear as destroyed with no citation to the original excavation reports or to the one claim based on those excavation reports

---

51. Hooker 1976, 149. Athens does not appear as destroyed in other common works on the end of the Late Bronze Age in Greece such as Drews 1993; Shelmerdine 1997, 2001; Nur and Cline 2000; Deger-Jalkotzy 2008; Cline 2014; Knapp and Manning 2016.

stating the houses were destroyed. Then ten years later, the "destruction" of these houses became the destruction of a possible palace. This is the citation chain that explains how some pots on a floor on a staircase became the possible destruction of a possible palace ca. 1200 BCE.

All that aside, there is still Bundgaard's claim that these houses were destroyed by an earthquake. From the archeological evidence, and based on the original excavation reports, the meager finds can neither prove nor disprove a destruction (Broneer 1933, 1939). However, a reexamination of those finds and Broneer's original notebooks can, which is exactly what Walter Gauss and Jeremy Rutter (Gauss 2003) have done. They uncovered that the houses on the north slope of Athens were never houses at all. Rather, the pottery on the Northeast Ascent was debris that, "was either dumped after the stairway had gone out of use, or alternatively, which was dumped and therefore caused [the stairway's] abandonment" (Gauss 2003, 98). Thus, there were never even houses to destroy in the first place. However, despite the fact that Gauss and Rutter demonstrated nearly two decades ago that there were no houses to destroy, Drews (2020, 230) too has recently asserted that Athens was destroyed while at the same time circumventing all of the above references to its "destruction." In this 2020 article, Drews (2020, 230) claims that Gauss in an article from 2000 in fact suggested that the citadel of Athens was destroyed. However, in Gauss's (2000, 175–76) article, he never even mentions destruction, or anything that would suggest that Athens suffered a destruction event at the end of the Late Bronze Age. This is another instance where Drews misconstrued Gauss's 2000 article and overlooked his 2003 article that clearly states there was no destruction of Athens at the beginning of the LH IIIC.

Ayios Stephanos

Drews (2020, 229) has recently claimed that Ayios Stephanos, situated on the southern coast of Lakonia, was destroyed at the end of the Late Bronze Age. However, Drews overestimated the extent of the destruction, as the excavators (Taylour and Janko 2008, 605) note that while burning was uncovered in one room of an LH IIIC early structure from Trench Beta 11, no other damage was recorded in any other area. Thus, while there was some minor evidence of burning, the excavators have made it clear that the site was not destroyed at the end of the Late Bronze Age.[52]

---

52. The excavators do claim that the site was attacked prior to its abandonment, as the site was emptied of valuables, three sling bullets were uncovered in nonstorage locations, a dog was uncovered dead in a room, and most importantly, in the one room that was burnt, four severed heads were discovered in a pit (Taylour and Janko 2008, 605, 610). Thus, it is likely, as Janko argues, that the site was attacked prior to its abandonment, even if this did not lead to the destruction of Ayios Stephanos.

Crete (fig. 3.3)

Khania (Kydonia)

Situated in the modern city of Khania, Crete, a ca. 1200 BCE destruction of ancient Kydonia is another commonly cited destruction event for the end of the Late Bronze Age.[53] The destruction has been alternatively described by the excavators as a thorough destruction by fire of the entire site (Hallager and Hallager 2003, 286) and as at least a partial destruction of the site by fire (Hallager 2017, 38). The destruction is dated to ca. 1225 BCE, closer to the end of the LM IIIB2, placing it at the very beginning of the "end of the Late Bronze Age" as it is defined here (Hallager 2017). However, there is not enough substantial evidence that the site suffered even a partial destruction. In Room A of Building 1, an almost forty-centimeter-thick layer of burnt debris was discovered in the northeastern third of the room covering over some complete vessels (Hallager and Hallager 2003, 65–66). Room P, which was connected to Room A, had some evidence of burning on part of the floor; however, other rooms connected to or adjacent to Room A, such as Rooms E, H, K, Space D, and Courtyard F were all devoid of any evidence of destruction or action by fire (Hallager and Hallager 2003, 24, 30, 49, 56, 58, 81). The excavators assume that this destruction affected more of Building 1 than the debris found in part of Room A evokes, but that this material was completely cleared out leaving no other evidence of this burning event (Hallager and Hallager 2003, 256; Hallager 2017, 38). Nevertheless, the evidence of burning in Room A is not enough to conclude that Building 1, let alone the site as a whole, was destroyed by fire.

The excavators suggested that the burnt material was cleared out of the entirety of Building 1; yet, this burnt debris was nowhere to be found. Even the Rubbish Area North to the northeast of Building 1, which consisted of alternating dumps and pits, was not filled with any of the supposed destruction debris.[54] Likewise, if such a fire had raged in Building 1, we might assume that some evidence of calcination or cracking of the stones might be found in some of the other rooms. Stone was the primary construction material for Building 1 rather than mud brick, and if they had been exposed to high temperatures, given their placement in the walls of the structure, they would have been difficult to remove other than by completely demolishing the building.[55] Nevertheless, there is no evidence of the stone in the building suffering any kind of intense heating event. Therefore, the more likely scenario is that at some time ca. 1225 BCE a fire broke out in Room A of Building 1 slightly affecting Room P, which

---

53. Drews 1993, 9, 28 fig. 1; Nur and Cline 2000, 44 fig. 1; Hallager and Hallager 2003, 286; Nur and Burgess 2008, 225 fig. 8.1; Cline 2014, 110–11 fig. 10; Hallager 2017, 38.

54. Hallager and Hallager 2003, 128–59. Only in Pit E was there a high percentage of burnt pottery at 26 percent of the assemblage (2003, 140).

55. Hallager and Hallager 2003, 286; see, e.g., Alassa Building II below.

shared an opening with Room A. The debris from this minor and eventually controlled fire was cleaned up and the rubble was left in Room A, only to be walled off during the construction of Room M in the following phase of the LM IIIC (Hallager and Hallager 2003, 66). There is insufficient evidence of a destruction event to qualify Building 1 even as a partial destruction.

The general lack of evidence for a massive destruction event is likely the reason why Maria Andreadaki-Vlazaki (2010), another excavator at the site, never even mentioned this destruction in her overview of Khania. Rather she makes the point that the site was not destroyed as part of the typical events surrounding the end of the Late Bronze Age at the beginning of the LM IIIC. She (2010, 527) states, "It is worth stressing that the city of Khania was not destroyed but simply deserted. This is clear from the almost empty rooms and the complete absence of signs of destruction."

Anatolia (fig. 3.3)

Alishar Höyük

Alishar Höyük is situated in Yozgat Province near the modern village of Alişar. The common appearance of Alishar Höyük on maps of destruction ca. 1200 BCE is most likely due to Drews's reference to the destruction of the city.[56] In 1993, Drews (1993, 8) reported that the city had been "destroyed by fire." This was based on a passing line from 1937 in the original excavations reports where Hans Henning von der Osten (1937, 287) simply stated that, "After the destruction of the fortified city of the Hittite Empire, the settlement on the Alishar mound lost its importance." To begin, von der Osten never claimed that Alishar Höyük was destroyed by fire, this was a misquotation by Drews. Second, von der Osten (1937, 1–24) had already noted the remains dated to the Hittite Empire were virtually nonexistent on the citadel due to the later construction by the Phrygians, making any assessment of the city at the end of the Late Bronze Age a difficult task. Third, von der Osten clearly indicated that it was his assumption that the site from the Hittite Empire had been destroyed and leveled by a conquering force and there was no clear archeological evidence for this assumption.[57] Despite these problems, Drews's claim that Alishar Höyük was destroyed by fire ca. 1200 BCE has been cited repeatedly in the decades since. However, already in 1990, Ronald Gorny, in his dissertation on Alishar Höyük, demonstrated that while there are likely remains from the LB II at Alishar Höyük, the Hittite city was abandoned ca. 1250 BCE.[58] Thus, based on

---

56. See Drews 1993, 8–9 fig. 1; Nur and Cline 2000, 44 fig. 1; Nur and Burgess 2008, 225 fig. 8.1; Cline 2014, 110–11, 126 fig. 10; Knapp and Manning 2016, 216.

57. Von der Osten 1937, 3, "I think it probable that the fortress of that period [Hittite Empire] was destroyed completely and the area leveled by the conquerors in order that they might rebuild."

58. For a discussion of the LB II remains from Alishar Höyük, see Gorny 1990, 366–91, 421–

82   CHAPTER THREE

the decades-old evidence, there was no end of the Late Bronze Age settlement
at Alishar Höyük to destroy, as it had already been abandoned well before
this.[59] The assumption that the site had been destroyed and the misquotation
that this destruction was wrought by fire are unfounded.

Cyprus (fig. 3.3)

Kouklia Palaepaphos

Located some sixteen kilometers from the city of Paphos, what is known
about Kouklia *Palaepaphos* from the LC IIC, apart from the poorly preserved
Sanctuary I, is largely derived from tombs and the two well fillings at Evreti
that were excavated by Franz Maier in the 1960s.[60] When Maier (1969, 42)
excavated them, he uncovered some burnt pottery and assumed that this burnt
pottery was the result of a destruction of the site by the Sea Peoples. This
meagre evidence of destruction from a site that was never found in excavations
was recited in the decades following, creating a destruction at *Palaepaphos*,
even though the end of the Late Bronze Age site remains archaeologically
unknown.[61] Given that little is known of the actual settlement, some burnt
pottery in a well filling is hardly sufficient evidence to conclude that Kouklia
Palaepaphos was destroyed, let alone by the Sea Peoples. Moreover, the recent
examination of this pottery, mainly pithoi sherds, demonstrates that only
a few examples had traces of burning and it was not clear if this happened
pre- or post-firing of the vessels (Keswani 2016, 217–34). To his credit, Maier
(Maier and Karageorghis 1984, 79) later acknowledged that the burnt pottery
was not enough evidence to conclude there had been a destruction event at
Palaepaphos. Therefore, unless evidence from a clearly stratified section of the
site dating to the LC IIC with evidence of destruction is uncovered, Kouklia
Palaepaphos shows no signs it was destroyed in the transition from the LC IIC
to the LC IIIA ca. 1200 BCE.

34; see also Gorny 1994, 1995a, 1995b. For the date of abandonment, see Gorny 1990, 378, 434–
35. Gorny (1990, 434–35) does state that the terminus post quem for the Alishar Höyük's LB II
settlement could be pushed as low as ca. 1225 BCE but that the date is almost certainly higher.

59. Gorny (1990, 434; 1995b, 89) does propose that if Alishar Höyük is equated with Ankuwa,
then it is possible that it was devastated by the fire mentioned in the Hittite votive text KUB 15.1
dating to ca. 1260 BCE during the reign of Hattusili III, discussed in ch. 2 as a likely accidental fire
or a wildfire. However, it is still unclear which site is ancient Ankuwa.

60. Maier and Karageorghis 1984, 52; Maier and von Wartburg 1985, 146. For a full discussion
of the wells and their contents see von Rüden et al. 2016. For a discussion of Sanctuary I, see Maier
and Karageorghis 1984, 91–102

61. Knapp 1997, 54–55 table 2; 2009, 54; 2013, 474; Voskos and Knapp 2008, 664; Kaniewski et
al. 2011, fig. 1; Kaniewski, Guiot, and Van Campo 2015, 370 fig. 1; Knapp and Manning 2016, 132.
Fischer also suggests a possible destruction at Palaepaphos; see Fischer 2017, 198 table 1.

Myrtou-Pigadhes

Myrtou-*Pigadhes* is located near the modern village of Myrtou on the southern foothills of the western end of the Kyrenia range. A destruction of the sanctuary uncovered at Myrtou-*Pigadhes* was originally proposed by the excavator Joan Du Plat Taylor (1957, 20, 115) in 1957 but was not regularly mentioned in the scholarly literature.[62] This destruction has been brought back into scholarly light recently through Knapp's (Knapp 1997, 54–55 table 2; 2009, 54; Knapp and Manning 2016, 132) reference to the site's destruction ca. 1200 BCE. However, Du Plat Taylor (1957, 115) noted in 1957 that there was no actual evidence that the building had been destroyed nor was there any evidence of burning. Rather her reasoning for assuming that the sanctuary had been destroyed was that it appeared to her that the main horned altar was torn apart, and that the objects in the sanctuary had been smashed. Indeed, going through the remains uncovered in each room, there is no evidence that the sanctuary, that is, the building itself, was destroyed by human hands or by a natural disaster. While it remains a possibility that the objects in the sanctuary had been destroyed by humans, which is a reasonable assumption given the lack of evidence for an earthquake and the distributions of the piece of the altar in the Court, there is no evidence to suggest that these humans destroyed the building itself (Du Plat Taylor 1957, 18–20). Thus, given this, the sanctuary at Myrtou-*Pigadhes* was not destroyed, even if it might have been ransacked ca. 1200 BCE.

Alassa (Pano Mandilaris and Paliotaverna)

Situated on a triangular plateau in the Troodos foothills of southwestern Cyprus, Alassa-*Pano Mandilaris* and Alassa *Paliotaverna*, which are separated by only 250 m, together formed a major urban center in the Kouris River Valley. The destruction of these settlements has been widely cited (Knapp 1997, 54–55 table 2; 2009, 54; 2013, 474; Voskos and Knapp 2008, 664; Knapp and Manning 2016, 132); however, no evidence of destruction ca. 1200 BCE has been recorded at either site. The lower residential site Alassa-*Pano Mandilaris* has yielded no evidence of a destruction event in the transition from the LC IIC to the LC IIIA. No signs of burning or wall collapse were uncovered, and it remained occupied until it was abandoned in the LC IIIA without a destruction (Hadjisavvas 1986, 66–67; 1989, 41; 1991, 173; 2017, 9–68). The upper site Alassa *Paliotaverna* has yielded the remains of three ashlar buildings damaged by deep plowing, with the last phase dating to the LC IIIA. Here too, no LC IIC to LC IIIA destruction has been uncovered in Buildings I, II, and III. All three buildings were continuously occupied through the LC IIIA without a break in

---

62. See Webb 1999, 44–53 for an overview of the sanctuary's architecture. The destruction was mentioned in passing by Karageorghis 1992, 80.

84 CHAPTER THREE

the transition from the LC IIC to the LC IIIA (Hadjisavvas 1994; 1996; 2000; 2007; 2009; 2017, 129–214, 256–73; Hadjisavvas and Hadjisavva 1997). Given this, there is no indication that either Alassa-*Pano Mandilaris* or Alassa *Paliotaverna* suffered a destruction event at the end of the thirteenth century BCE or the beginning of the twelfth century BCE.

Sophocles Hadjisavvas (1994, 110; 2017, 472, 474), the excavator, has proposed that Building II and Building III suffered a destruction during LC IIIA prior to being rebuilt and abandoned later in the same period. Even so, based on the criteria for a destruction employed here, there is not enough physical evidence that either building suffered a destruction. To begin, no evidence of a destruction event has been noted for Building I, as it appears to have been simply abandoned, much as Alassa-*Pano Mandilaris* was abandoned without destruction (Hadjisavvas 1994; 1996; 2000; 2007; 2009; 2017, 134–37, 256–73; Hadjisavvas and Hadjisavva 1997). For Building III, there is not enough physical evidence that this building was destroyed. Traces of fire were extremely limited, as small patches of ash were exposed in Rooms 4, 5, and 6.[63] The building was badly preserved and there were no undisturbed contexts (Hadjisavvas 2017, 472). Nonetheless, what remains does not suggest a fire burned the structure and there is not enough physical evidence to consider Building III as destroyed.

A destruction event has also been ascribed to Building II; however, the extent of this burning event(s) was limited. In the recent final publication of Alassa, Hadjisavvas (2017, 472) has demonstrated that the structure underwent several phases of construction with a fire destroying Building II at the end of Phase 1. He describes it as an extensive fire that struck the Pithos Magazine in Building II, burning at such extreme temperatures that the inner faces of several of the ashlar blocks of the north wall were cracked. Hadjisavvas (2017, 471–72) assumes the intensity of the fire might have been owing to olive oil possibly stored in some of the pithoi found in the room. He (2017, 156–57, 168–69, 182, 207) goes on to describe other traces of burnt floors unearthed in the adjoining Room P, as well as in the South Wing from the Hearth Room and Rooms D, E, F and G. Burnt pottery, ashes, and burnt logs were found discarded in the North Corridor, likely from when the burnt debris was cleared before rebuilding (225, 473). Hadjisavvas does not suggest that this was accidental, as evidence of fire was uncovered in disconnected wings of Building II and, as he suggests, in Building III. Nevertheless, he (2017, 472–74) also does not believe it to be the result of invaders and maintains that Building II was rebuilt and abandoned during the LC IIIA without evidence of a destruction. On the contrary, based on the multiphase construction of Building II, it is unlikely that the structure ever suffered a serious destruction by fire.

---

63. See Hadjisavvas 2017, 257 fig. 4.142. "Plan of Building III."

The Destruction That Wasn't

Evidence for ash and fire were found at two opposite ends of Building II, leading Hadjisavvas to conclude that an accidental fire could not be the cause. Yet, because the building has multiple construction phases, this leads to the conclusion that there were likely two separate fires, neither of which resulted in the destruction of Building II. The fire uncovered in the Pithos Magazine and Room P was the initial event and the material from this fire was then thrown into the North Corridor once this section of the structure was rebuilt during Phase 2. However, the burnt floors and ash found in the Hearth Room, and Rooms D, E, F, and G derived from a subsequent event.

In the South Wing during Phase 2, the final phase prior to abandonment, its interior plan was remodeled, as the two lateral entrances were blocked up and only the central entrance remained in use until the final abandonment of the building. It is in this final phase, after the burning of the Pithos Magazine, that both the East and West Units along with the Hearth Room at the center the South Wing were remodeled. As Hadjisavvas describes it, the square pillar base, assumed to be the hearth in the Hearth Room, was reused from the previous phase when a pillar would have stood on it holding up a roof. Yet, in the final phase, the room was reconfigured to be an open space. The shell walls, which separate the East and West Units from the Hearth Room, are not bonded to the original walls and were placed directly on the floor of Building II (Hadjisavvas 2017, 142, 154–55, 473). Thus, as Hadjisavvas (155) argues, "it is obvious that these walls and, therefore, the subdivision of the South Wing are chronologically later than the original floor, belonging to the final occupation phase." However, if these subdivisions are from the final phase of construction, this would indicate that the ash and burnt floors found in the Hearth Room and West Unit derived from Phase 2 and not from the fire found in the Pithos Magazine and Room P dating to Phase 1. Given this, the two burning events would be separated chronologically and causally.

Ashes were uncovered in the Hearth Room, and the floors in Rooms D, E, and G were described as burnt. Room F was disturbed by a mechanical excavator and its *havara* floor was mixed with ashes, which may or may not be from this possible fire (Hadjisavvas 2017, 168–69, 182). This indicates that while there may have been a fire in the South Wing of Building II during its final phase of use before its abandonment, it does not appear to have been severe as, again, there is a lack of burnt pottery, burnt mud bricks, or a large quantity of fallen mud bricks and stones. Moreover, the ashes found in the Hearth Room may have derived from the aforementioned hearth from which the room derived its name. The decayed mud bricks found in Building II along with the decayed mud bricks found in the buildings from Alassa-*Pano Mandilaris* most likely originated from the gradual disintegration of the buildings after their abandonment as Hadjisavvas (2017, 211, 474) has suggested.

86 CHAPTER THREE

Given all of this, it does not seem as if there was any destruction event during the LC IIIA at Alassa *Paliotaverna*. Much like its sister site, Alassa-*Pano Mandilaris*, it was abandoned without a destruction event. The two separate fires were likely accidental, as there is no indication the site was attacked. Moreover, it appears that neither fire affected the majority of Building II or any of the surrounding buildings. Both were localized events with the more severe event engulfing the Pithos Magazine during Phase 1 but no other part of the structure. Moreover, the small patches of ash found in Building III do not amount to evidence for a destruction event. In sum, neither Alassa *Paliotaverna* nor Alassa-*Pano Mandilaris* demonstrates convincing evidence of a destruction event, either at the transition from the LC IIC to the LC IIIA or during the beginning of the LC IIIA.

Hala Sultan Tekke

Hala Sultan Tekke is situated near the Larnaca Salt Lake and it has been assigned a massive destruction to its Stratum 2 ca. 1200 BCE by the excavators Peter Fischer and Teresa Bürge (Fischer 2017, 2019, 2020; Fischer and Bürge 2018, 72, 151, 616–17). However, the only possible evidence for destruction came from City Quarter 2, the Northwestern Structure, Room 44, where some silver jewelry had been melted into a lump together with some unmelted gold, indicating that there was a fire that reached temperatures around 1,000 degrees Celsius based on the melting point of both metals (Fischer and Bürge 2018, 151). No evidence of action by fire was uncovered in any other space in both City Quarters 1 and 2 that could be attributed to a destruction, nor was there any debris typically associated with a destruction (Fischer and Bürge 2018, 37–72, 134–51). Interestingly, while the melted silver has been provided as evidence of a high heat intensity destruction by fire with a known temperature of around 1000 degrees Celsius, there is no evidence of any vitrification or calcination, both processes which begin to occur after 900 degrees Celsius (Stevanović 1997, 366). Given that pottery was found in the same area as the melted silver, this heating event must not have been extensive or even a fire at all, as one might expect this high heat to have affected other artifacts outside of one lump of silver. It was likely a contained event. Therefore, while a small area may have experienced high heat, which could have been related to any number of processes, there is no evidence that suggests that Hala Sultan Tekke was destroyed ca. 1200 BCE.[64]

Sinda

Sinda lies in the hinterlands of Enkomi some twenty-three kilometers from Salamis. The destruction of Sinda ca. 1200 BCE is one of the commonly cited

---

64. See discussion in Millek 2021b for the supposed final destruction and abandonment of Hala Sultan Tekke, which is also not borne out by the archaeological evidence.

destructions for Cyprus.[65] A small exposure was excavated in a short single season in the late 1940s by Arne Furumark, with the final publication coming out more than fifty years later (Furumark and Adelman 2003). Because of this, while commonly cited as destroyed at the end of the LC IIC, the empirical evidence from the short season of excavation is too limited, and based on the existing evidence, it does not fulfill the criteria for a destruction.

Finds related to the Sinda I period dating to the end of the LC IIC were only uncovered in the North West Area and the Gate Area; no remains dated to this period were found in the South Area. The results from the limited exposure in the North West Area record only two trenches that exposed material dating to Sinda I. Both the West–East Trench and the South East Part Trench revealed traces of ash but no other signs of burning or destruction debris (Furumark and Adelman 2003, 29–33). In the Gate Area, the Gate House's floor is described as burnt with no further detailed information (42–46). No wall collapse is mentioned, and no weapons of war were recovered from Sinda I (110). The site was then rebuilt during the Sinda II period.

Given the lack of excavated material from Sinda dating to the end of the LC IIC, there is insufficient evidence that Sinda was destroyed, as the traces of ash or burning are not concrete proof that the site suffered a destruction by fire. Unfortunately, we will not know whether or not there is actual evidence of destruction until such time as the site can be reexcavated, but given the modern political situation this is unlikely to occur at this time.

Northern Levant (fig. 3.3)

Aleppo: Temple of the Storm God

The Temple of the Storm God found beneath the citadel in Aleppo has been assigned a destruction at the end of the Late Bronze Age by the site's excavator Kay Kohlmeyer.[66] However, despite the numerous publications on the temple, never is this event described nor the evidence for it presented (see Kohlmeyer and Kai-Browne 2020; Kohlmeyer 2000, 2009, 2012, 2013, 2016; Gonnella, Khayyata, and Kohlmeyer 2005). It is only mentioned in a chart by Kohlmeyer (2009, 197), which states the temple was destroyed by fire at some uncertain time after 1200 BCE. However, in a later chart from 2016 (Kohlmeyer 2016, 297), this supposed burning event is placed before 1200 BCE. The fire that burned the Middle Bronze Age temple and the fire that burned the last phase of the

---

65. Drews 1993, 9 fig. 1; Nur and Cline 2000, 56; Nur and Burgess 2008, 225 fig. 8.1; Kaniewski et al. 2011, fig. 1; Cline 2014, 110–11, 128 fig. 10; Kaniewski, Guiot, and Van Campo 2015, 370 fig. 1; Knapp and Manning 2016, 130.

66. Kohlmeyer 2009, 197; 2016, 297; see also Sader 2014, 610, who states the temple was destroyed at the end of the Late Bronze Age, as well as de Martino 2018, 26; Matthiae 2018, 314; Emanuel 2015, 16.

88   CHAPTER THREE

temple ca. 900 BCE are both described by Kohlmeyer (2009, 194; 2013, 514–15, 523); however, this is not the case for the supposed ca. 1200 BCE fire. What little can be said is where Kohlmeyer describes the beginning of the Iron Age phase of the temple ca. 1100 BCE stating that, "The severely damaged temple was rebuilt again after being abandoned for some time."[67] Thus, at this time, it is impossible to tell if the temple was destroyed, how much of the temple was affected, or even at what time this event might have occurred. Given that there is no description of this supposed destruction event, it must be assumed for the time being that no such event ever occurred until a report of said destruction event and the evidence for it is published (see Millek 2019a, 166).

Tell Abu Danné

Tell Abu Danné is located some twenty-five kilometers east of Aleppo. A possible end of the Late Bronze Age destruction was uncovered at the end of Level V, which Roland Tefnin (1980, 190) described as, "layers of ash and collapsed and burnt bricks, [which] seem to indicate the violent destruction of small houses." However, as Tefnin (1978/1979, 147; 1980, 190–91) notes, the remains from Level V were sparse, there were few finds, and the architectural remains were meager. In the brief two-page description of the remains from Level V, this statement is the only mention of a "destruction," as Tefnin does not offer any other written or photographic evidence of the event in question. In the description of the Level V remains there is no indication of a destruction, as the only ash likely originated from the use of a terracotta brazier (Tefnin 1980, 190–91). Moreover, in two other articles where Tefnin (1978/1979, 1979) discusses Level V, he never mentions a destruction nor does he provide a description of any evidence related to this supposed destruction event. Furthermore, as McClellan (1992, 187) has pointed out, the ceramics that were recovered from Level V do not clearly date the remains to the end of the Late Bronze Age. No imported Mycenean or Cypriot ceramics were uncovered in the excavations (Tefnin 1978/1979, 67; 1980, 191), and there is no clear chronological marker that would place the end of Level V at ca. 1200 BCE. Thus, for the time being, there is neither substantial evidence that Tell Abu Danné suffered even a partial destruction, nor that Level V ended ca. 1200 BCE, and it cannot be counted as an end of the Late Bronze Age destruction based on the currently published information.

Tell Faq'ous

The small site of Tell Faq'ous, which is some twelve kilometers southeast of Emar, was briefly excavated in a single season. Jean-Claude Margueron (1980,

---

67. Kohlmeyer 2016, 303; see also Kohlmeyer 2012, 64; 2013, 202; Kohlmeyer and Kai-Browne 2020, 35, where the same basic statement is made.

54–62) who excavated both Tell Faq'ous and Emar uncovered some possible evidence of destruction, which he associated with the destruction of Emar ca. 1187 BCE. However, while it may be possible that the site suffered a destruction event, the date of the destruction is purely an assumption.[68] Margueron (1980, 62) plainly states that the material uncovered at Tell Faq'ous could only be dated to the Late Bronze Age, but it was his hypothesis that if there was a destruction at Tell Faq'ous that it should be associated with the destruction that was clearly evident at nearby Emar. However, if there is no clear reason to date this destruction to ca. 1200 BCE, it should not be dated ca. 1200 BCE, as destruction events are not exclusive to the end of the Late Bronze Age. Just because a nearby site suffered a destruction event at some point in time is no reason to assume that another site was also destroyed at the same time. Therefore, until a clear archaeological date can be given to the material from Tell Faq'ous, there is no reason to place this possible destruction at ca. 1200 BCE, as it cannot be reasonably associated with the multibuilding destruction of Emar.

Ras el-Bassit

To the north of the capital of Ugarit lies Ras el-Bassit, likely a northern outpost for the kingdom of Ugarit, and the site's supposed destruction is a commonly cited destruction at the end of the Late Bronze Age for the northern Levant.[69] Paul Courbin (1990, 504), the excavator, assumed that the site had been destroyed by the Sea Peoples ca. 1200 BCE. However, there is not enough archeological evidence to presume a destruction ruined Ras el-Bassit at the end of the Late Bronze Age, despite its common appearance in the literature as destroyed. A large building, the *grand bâtiment*, along with a street separating it from a house, were uncovered in the excavations and dated to the Late Bronze II. What it is clear is that the *grand bâtiment* was largely emptied of its contents as if it was abandoned without destruction.[70] The only possible evidence of destruction came from the house next to the *grand bâtiment*. Traces of fire and a carbonized wooden joist were discovered near the west wall of the house, and this is the only published evidence of burning (Courbin 1986, 186–87). From the currently available archaeological evidence, there is not enough reasonable proof to conclude that Ras el-Bassit was destroyed. There is no recorded evidence of action by fire in the *grand bâtiment*, and the

---

68. This is not clear based on the very preliminary results of the single season of excavation.

69. Courbin 1990, 504; 1992, 127; Bretschneider and Van Lerberghe 2008, 33; 2010, 138; 2014, 151; Sader 2014, 610; Cline 2014, 110–10, 112 fig. 10; 2021, 108; Knapp and Manning 2016, 128; Vacek 2020, 1171.

70. Courbin, 1975, 60; 1976, 64; 1983, 290. The only ash mentioned was in association with a hearth and thus is not an indicator of a destruction event, but rather the day-to-day use of the building (Courbin, 1976, 64).

minor evidence of burning found in the adjacent building is not enough to be considered a destruction. Rather it appears to have been abandoned, which resulted in the gradual collapse of the buildings (see also Millek 2019a, 159).

Tell Tweini

Tell Tweini is located one kilometer east of the modern city of Jableh, and much like Ras el-Bassit, Tell Tweini has become a commonly cited destruction on the northern Levantine coast at the end of the Late Bronze Age, which is often associated with the destruction supposedly wrought by the Sea People.[71] The destruction has been described in the wider scholarly literature as, "Perhaps the best ... evidence for widespread destruction at this time [ca. 1200 BCE] has been found at Tell Tweini" (Cline 2021, 108). Kaniewski et al. 2011 (1), which included members of the excavation team, described the destruction as follows: "The destruction layer contains remains of conflicts (bronze arrowheads scattered around the town, fallen walls, burnt houses), ash from the conflagration of houses, and chronologically well-constrained ceramic assemblages fragmented by the collapse of the town." However, this assessment of the damage from the 2011 article was preliminary, and after further review of the excavated remains from Level 7A, the actual evidence for a destruction is minimal.

In Area A Level 7A, in the loci where ash was present (as it was not uncovered everywhere), it ranged in thickness from two to fifteen centimeters with no evidence of vitrification, indicating that whatever burning produced the ash was not intense. There was also an absence of other signs of destruction, such as fallen walls or crushed debris. Much of the early debris that was assumed to be the result of a massive destruction was later determined to be the remains of heavy construction activity during the Iron Age II that left fill layers resembling destruction debris.[72] Thus, Bretschneider et al. (2019, 6) have redescribed the "destruction" as follows: "Around 1200 BCE ... some parts of the site of Tweini seem to have been damaged by fire. Stratigraphic evidence from Field A shows hints of unrest with a layer of ashes superimposing the ruins of various Late Bronze Age buildings."[73] This is a far cry from the earlier assessment of the remains mentioned in Kaniewski et al. 2011.

The lack of severe burning, the general thin and intermittent layer of ashes, and the lack of typical signs of destruction (e.g., fallen stones, mud brick, burnt

---

71. Bretschneider and Van Lerberghe 2008, 2010, 2014; Kaniewski et al. 2011 fig. 1; Kaniewski, Guiot, and Van Campo 2015, 370 fig. 1; Bretschneider, Jans, and Van Vyve 2014; Cline 2014, 110–11, 113 fig. 10; Knapp and Manning 2016, 129; Bretschneider et al. 2019, 6–7; Emanuel 2020, 101.

72. Joachim Bretschneider pers. comm. 06/07/2018. In a recent publication by Bretschneider et al. (2019, 6), the ash is reported as ca. five to twenty-five centimeters thick where it was uncovered; see also discussion in Millek 2020, 111–12.

73. They go on to say, "This may have been valid for other areas of the tell as well but heavy construction activities during the Iron Age II have generated fill layers resembling destruction layers and often obliterating older evidence."

pottery) suggest that Tell Tweini was not destroyed at the end of the Late Bronze Age (see also Millek 2019a, 161–62; 2020, 111–12). The ash could have come from any number of sources, such as cooking and industrial activities or a minor fire, and it is not immediately evident that it was caused by an act of war or a part of a destruction in general.[74] Indeed, Michel Al-Maqdissi (Al-Magdissi et al. 2008, 344) reported that evidence of fire was only encountered in a limited number of loci from Level 7A, while the majority of the structures appear to have been abandoned without destruction.[75] Of course, further investigation at the site may very well change this interpretation. However, from the currently available evidence, it does not appear that Tell Tweini was destroyed at the end of the Late Bronze Age.[76]

Tell Sukas

To the south of Tell Tweini and six kilometers south of Jableh lies Tell Sukas, which too is one of the commonly cited string of destructions on the northern Levantine coast ca. 1200 BCE, with Knapp and Manning (2016, 128) recently describing the destruction as a major conflagration.[77] The supposed destruction was originally associated again with the Sea Peoples ca. 1200 BCE (Lund 1986, 186); yet, much like its neighbor Tell Tweini, Tell Sukas has limited evidence of a destruction event. In Area G 13, two buildings, Complexes I and II, were uncovered. Signs of severe destruction were lacking in both, as only some small patches of red-burnt earth, some charcoal, and ashes were uncovered,

---

74. Three arrowheads were found in Level 7A (Joachim Bretschneider pers. comm. 07/06/2018). However, their context is not clear and these three arrowheads are not an indication of warfare.

75. He states, "The transition between the Late Bronze Age and Iron Age I at Tell Tweini is well preserved in Houses 2 and 3. Destruction by fire has been attested in only a limited number of loci and most structures seem simply to have been abandoned."

76. Recently, Cline (2021, 209 n. 30), when discussing the supposed destruction of Tell Tweini, stated that, "Rather surprisingly, Millek ... downplays all of this and suggests that the site was not destroyed, which seems to fly in the face of the evidence published by the excavators." The evidence that Cline is referring to is the above quote from Kaniewski et al. 2011, 1. However, the evidence Cline cited is outdated, as the revised interpretation of the "destruction" was published by Bretschneider et al. in 2019. Even though Bretschneider et al. still assume the site was destroyed, they at least have corrected that essentially only ash was found in some loci, an assessment that was already in the literature as reported by Al-Maqdissi et al. in 2008. However, as the excavators have demonstrated, there is currently no evidence of a major fire or collapsed walls, as much of this "evidence" was Iron II fill that resembled destruction. Moreover, in my 2019 article as well as in the more recently published 2020 article, the information that I presented on Tell Tweini Level 7A was given to me through personal communication with the lead excavator Joachim Bretschneider, as well as through my review of all of the reports made by the excavation team outside of the climate articles by Kaniewski et al. Thus, my analysis of the material remains from Tell Tweini Level 7A, rather than flying in the face of the evidence, fits in well with the up-to-date published information as reported by the excavators.

77. Listings include Caubet 1992, 127; Drews 1993, 9 fig. 1; Nur and Cline 2000, 44 fig. 1; Nur and Burgess 2008, 225 fig. 8.1; Bretschneider and Van Lerberghe 2008, 33; 2010, 138; 2014, 151; Sader 2014, 610; Cline 2014, 110–11 fig. 10; Vacek 2020, 1171.

92 CHAPTER THREE

and evidence of this burning was not witnessed in all areas, nor were other signs of destruction uncovered, let alone a major conflagration (Riis 1970, 24, 26, 29, 34, 38; Lund 1986, 15–16, 19–22, 24–43). Again, based on the criteria set out for what constitutes a destruction, this likely minor and limited burning episode was not a destruction event (see also Millek 2019a, 162; 2020, 112–13).

Central Levant (fig. 3.3)

Tyre

A destruction of Tyre was mentioned by H. Jacob Katzenstein (1973, 59) in 1973 before any excavations had even uncovered the Late Bronze Age to Iron Age transition at the site. Katzenstein simply assumed the site along with several others on the Levantine coast had been destroyed.[78] However, the small-scale excavation at Tyre conducted later in the 1970s that yielded remains dating to the end of the Late Bronze Age, dubbed Stratum XV, showed no signs of destruction. This small area was covered with a black ashy layer (Bikai 1978, 7–8, 72–76); however, in the absence of any other signs of destruction, such as fallen or burnt mud bricks, and burnt pottery, this black layer is not reasonable enough evidence to conclude that Tyre was destroyed at the end of the Late Bronze Age. This was also the opinion of the excavator Patricia Maynor Bikai (1992, 133), who stated, "Over much of the excavation area between Strata XV and XIV, a black floor was found. The round fire pit in the center of the room in area 2 and a tannur oven on the floor in area 1 suggest that the blackness is the result of domestic cooking activity and not of destruction" (1978, 8). Therefore, Katzenstein's assumption of destruction was just that, an assumption.

Kamid el-Loz

Kamid el-Loz is located in the Beqa'a plain fifty kilometers southeast of Beirut. In the scholarly literature, Kamid el-Loz has generally been explicitly mentioned as having witnessed no destruction at the end of the Late Bronze Age.[79] Yet, there are claims from some members of the excavation team that at least the Temple T1 and several houses were destroyed (Metzger 1991, 217; 1993, 121; Adler and Penner 2001, 350; Wagner-Durand 2020, 75), an opinion that is not shared by all who have worked at the site (Heinz 2016, 153–85). However, upon review of the material, there is insufficient evidence that Kamid el-Loz experienced any destruction prior to its abandonment toward the end of the Late Bronze Age.

The Palace P1/2 had no evidence of burning or destruction prior to its abandonment (Adler and Penner 2001, 311–40, 349–50). For the Temple T1,

---

78. The possibility of a destruction without fire was also briefly mentioned by Elayi 2018, 95.

79. Bikai 1992; Bell 2006, 110, 137; 2009, 32; Charaf 2008; Heinz 2016, 153–85; Núñez 2018.

evidence of burning was only recorded in three rooms, Rooms F, H, and L, all of which are on the western side of the structure. Room F had a black fire layer with burnt debris, Room H's floor was covered with white ash, while Room L was covered with gray ash (Metzger 1993, 96, 105, 112). However, while it does appear that Room F suffered a minor burning event and ash seems to have been scattered in Rooms H and L though without evidence of action by fire, Rooms G, H, and K, which are also situated in the western half of the structure, show no signs of ash or damage by fire (Metzger 1993, 103–11). Thus, there is no reason to assume that the building as a whole was destroyed by a fire, as the evidence for action by fire is minimal at best. On the east slope of the tell, in Area II-e-5 two structures dubbed House 4 and 5 were uncovered and it was initially assumed that they had been burnt at the end of the Late Bronze Age (Heinz et al. 2010a, 42; 2010b, 30, 35; Wagner-Durand 2020, 70, 82 table 3). Marlies Heinz (2016, 181) later stated that these houses were not destroyed, though Elisabeth Wagner-Durand (2020, 70, 82, table 3) maintains that they suffered some kind of destruction. However, the only evidence for a possible destruction was that the wall foundations were covered over by a layer of grayish-white ash, with no other signs of destruction (Heinz et al. 2010a, 42; 2010b, 30). Thus, taking all of this together, there is not enough reasonable evidence suggesting that Kamid el-Loz suffered any kind of destruction at the end of the Late Bronze Age.[80]

Southern Levant (fig. 3.4)

Achzib

Achzib is located thirteen kilometers north of Acco on the Mediterranean coast. It, along with a number of other sites, which will be discussed below, are part of a supposed string of destructions proposed by Stern. Stern (2012, 506; 2013, 5) has described the situation at the end of the Late Bronze Age as follows: "All sites on the Canaanite coast of the Hefer Valley, in the Sharon, and on the Carmel coast—without exception—were laid waste at the end of the thirteenth century BCE in a total destruction that put an end to the Canaanite culture and Egyptian domination. This destruction has been attributed by the excavators of all the settlements in these areas to the Sea Peoples." Outside of Stern's claim, there is only one reference that there was an end of the Late

---

80. The site might have suffered from an attack prior to its abandonment. In the Palace P1/2 an arrowhead was uncovered in Courtyard H (Adler and Penner 2001, 339), while in Temple T1 three arrowheads were found in Room M/T1, two in Room J, one arrowhead was discovered in each Room B and Shrine D. Four arrowheads were located in Room K one of which was found resting on the threshold between rooms, while in Courtyard G three additional arrowheads were uncovered (Metzger 1993, 35 40, 57 65, 104, 111, 122). This scattering of weaponry in courtyards, rooms, and on a threshold between rooms may be an indication that Kamid el-Loz was not abandoned peacefully, but was a forced abandonment after a battle was waged in the city, even if this battle did not result in the ultimate destruction of the buildings.

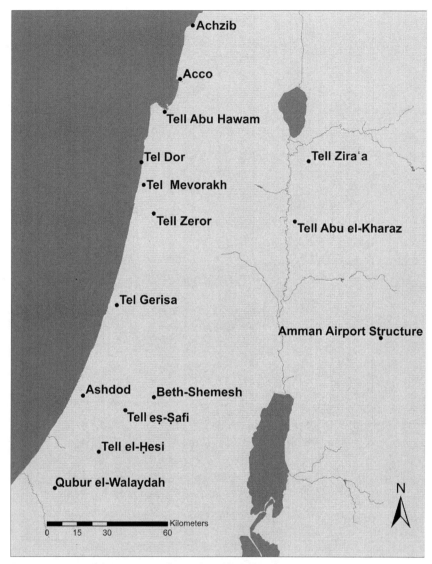

Figure 3.4. Assumed destructions in the southern Levant.

Bronze Age destruction at Achzib, in a 1993 article by Moshe Prausnitz (1993, 32) the original excavator. In it he simply stated that, "By the end of the Late Bronze Age, the [Middle Bronze Age] defenses were again destroyed." Outside of this offhand comment, nowhere in any of the preliminary reports does Prausnitz (1963, 1965, 1993) ever even mention this supposed destruction of the defenses. Moreover, in his excavation he never uncovered any remains of a settlement dated to the end of the Late Bronze Age that could have been

THE DESTRUCTION THAT WASN'T

95

destroyed by the Sea Peoples. The recent excavations at Achzib led by Philippe Abrahami, who excavated not far from Prausnitz's original excavation area, provides further evidence against an end of the Late Bronze Age destruction. The renewed excavation only uncovered a destruction event at the end of the MB IIB, and the final phase of occupation at Achzib ended during the LB I without destruction.[81] Because there is only a single unclarified and unsubstantiated claim that there was an end of the Late Bronze Age destruction of the Middle Bronze Age defenses with no physical evidence of habitation at the site dating to ca. 1200 BCE, we must conclude for the moment that Achzib was not destroyed.[82]

Acco

The destruction of Acco ca. 1200 BCE is another listed by Stern (2012, 506; 2013, 5); the supposed destruction of the site is common on most lists or maps of destruction in the southern Levant ca. 1200 BCE.[83] Drews goes so far to say that the well-datable scarab of the Egyptian queen Twosret helps to place the destruction firmly ca. 1200 BCE, as the scarab was found in an ash layer from the destruction.[84] However, what Drews failed to mention is that this ash was not from a destruction at all. Rather, the ash layer was uncovered next to a kiln in an industrial area of the site and was refuse from the industrial activity, and there is in fact no evidence of an end of the Late Bronze Age destruction at Acco, despite the common claim it was destroyed ca. 1200 BCE.[85] Drews cited his information from Trude Dothan 1983 (103–4) who claimed that Acco had been destroyed at the end of the Late Bronze Age. T. Dothan cited Moshe Dothan 1981 as her source of information. However, the 1981 report on Acco by M. Dothan (1981, 111), that T. Dothan cited, never mentioned a destruction, and it appears that T. Dothan is the originator of this false destruction. M. Dothan never claimed that Acco was destroyed, and this lack of destruction should have been apparent to Drews, as M. Dothan had already made it clear in several articles prior to Drews's 1993 book that there was no destruction, and that the

---

81. Philippe Abrahami pers. comm. 04/14/2020; see also Thareani, Jasmin, and Abrahami 2016, 2017.

82. This is contrary to what I reported in Millek 2018b and 2019c where I state there was a partial destruction of an unknown cause. At the time I was unaware of the recent work conducted by Abrahami, which helped to clarify the situation.

83. Dothan 1983, 103–4. Drews 1993, 9, 16 fig. 1; Nur and Cline 2000, 44 fig. 1; Nur and Burgess 2008, 225 fig. 8.1; Cline 2014, 110–11, 114 fig. 10; 2021, 110; Knapp and Manning 2016, 130.

84. Drews 1993, 16; Cline 2021, 110. Knapp and Manning also make a similar claim about the well-dated nature of the destruction of Acco.

85. Dothan 1981, 111; 1988, 297–99; Dothan and Dothan 1992, 212; Artzy and Beeri 2010, 18; Yasur-Landau 2010, 170. While listed as "no destruction" in Millek 2018b and Millek 2019c, I mistakenly stated there that the destruction was misdated when in fact it is an assumed destruction. This was an error on my part and should be corrected to there being no physical evidence of a destruction ca. 1200 BCE.

96   CHAPTER THREE

ash was from industrial activities.[86] Moreover, the refutation of the destruction
at Acco presented here is not even the first time it has been demonstrated
that there was no end of the Late Bronze Age destruction at the site. Carol
Bell (2006, 137) noted in 2006 that there was no destruction at Acco, Assaf
Yasur-Landau (2010, 170) went into greater detail in demonstrating the lack of
destruction in 2010, while Michel Artzy (Artzy and Beeri 2010, 18), who also
excavated the site, clearly stated in 2010 that there was no destruction.[87] For
those recent citations claiming that Acco was destroyed (Cline 2014, 110–11,
114 fig. 10; 2021, 110; Knapp and Manning 2016, 130), there was already ample
evidence both from the excavators and other archaeologists demonstrating that
Acco was not destroyed ca. 1200 BCE.

Tell Abu Hawam

Tell Abu Hawam, which is situated in modern-day Haifa, has had a
destruction of the site in the scholarly literature since the 1950s.[88] However,
while various scholars have claimed that the site was destroyed ca. 1200
BCE at the end of the Stratum VC, there is never any mention of what this
destruction supposedly looked like or entailed. Indeed, when looking over the
archaeological evidence there is no evidence of a destruction in any areas of
habitation ca. 1200 BCE.[89] This was a fact that Jacqueline Balensi (2004, 162),
one of the excavators at Tell Abu Hawam, made clear as she mentioned that
the only possible evidence of destruction was of the site's fortifications, but
this was not due to a destruction event. Rather, this "destruction" was actually
a degradation over time as the defenses were not maintained and simply fell
apart. This is a fact further emphasized by Artzy, the current leader of the Tell
Abu Hawam excavation, who has also made it clear that there is, at the moment,
no evidence of an end of the Late Bronze Age destruction at Tell Abu Hawam.[90]

Tel Dor

Tel Dor, which is located some thirty kilometers south of Haifa on the
Mediterranean coast, is another of the supposed sites caught up in a massive
wave of destruction brought on by the Sea Peoples that Stern assumed had
devastated the region.[91] What should be noted first is that only a small portion

---

86. Dothan 1981, 111; 1988, 297–99; 1993a, 21; Dothan and Dothan 1992, 212.

87. They (2010, 18) state, "Akko's adaptation to the Iron IA period seems to have taken place
with little disruption. No signs of destructions by the 'Sea Peoples' or others were noted. The site
continued to function and slowly bolstered habitation on its eastern side, closer to the agricultural
area, as the maritime network weakened."

88. Maisler 1951, 22; Anati 1963, 142; 1975, 11; Dever 1992, 100 fig. 13.1; Stern 2013, 5; Manolova
2020, 1199.

89. Hamilton 1935; Anati 1963; 1975; Gershuny 1981; Balensi 2004; Artzy 2006, 2013.

90. Michal Artzy pers. comm. 07/04/2016; see also the discussion in Millek 2017, 118–20.

91. Stern 1992; 2000, 85–101; 2012, 506; 2013, 5; see also Stager 1995, 338; Kaniewski et al. 2011

of the thirteenth to twelfth century BCE transition was uncovered at Tel Dor in Area G Phase 11. In this area, no evidence of destruction was found, a fact that has been noted by Ayelet Gilboa and Ilan Sharon (Gilboa and Sharon 2003; 2017; Sharon and Gilboa 2013; Gilboa et al. 2018, 28–35), who continued the excavations at Dor after Stern. However, the fact that no destruction was found at Dor did not escape Stern, even though he claimed the site was destroyed and has propagated this destruction in the literature for decades. Stern reasoned that Dor had to have been destroyed based on his theoretical assumption that all sites in the region were destroyed by the Sea Peoples, who later replaced the local culture. Yet, Stern (2013, 5) himself clearly states that, "The Bronze Age stratum of destruction at [Tel Dor] *has not yet been reached*" (emphasis added). Therefore, Tel Dor was not destroyed at the end of the Late Bronze Age, as the destruction was only an assumption that is not borne out in the archaeological record.

Tel Mevorakh

Tel Mevorakh is located on the southern bank of Nahal Taninim some thirty kilometers south of Haifa, and it too was excavated by Stern. Much like Tel Dor, Stern (1978, 76; 1984, 9; 2000, 53, 61 2012; 2013, 5) too claimed that the site was destroyed ca. 1200 BCE by the Sea Peoples. However, while Stern excavated the site, in the report of the excavation of the Stratum IX Temple there is no mention or described physical evidence of destruction debris or burning (Stern 1984, 8). Rather than a destruction, it is more likely that the temple simply disintegrated, as the site was abandoned for two hundred years. As Stern (1984, 8) himself states, "We may assume that the upper part of the wall was made of mud-brick, and it was totally demolished during the 200 years of abandonment, i.e., from the end of the thirteenth century to the late eleventh century B.C." Thus, much as at Tel Dor, it appears that Stern's theoretical assumption that the Sea Peoples conquered the area through violent destruction created a destruction at Tel Mevorakh when there is in fact no archaeological evidence of said destruction (see also Millek 2019c, 166).

Tel Zeror

Tel Zeror is located in the northern Sharon Plain four kilometers east of Hadera. It appears as one of the many sites supposedly destroyed at the end of the thirteenth century BCE listed by Amihai Mazar (1990, 290), or by the Sea Peoples, which Dever (1992, 100 fig. 13.1) claimed in 1992, and more recently by Stern (2012, 506; 2013, 5). Nevertheless, there is no significant evidence that either the north or south mound suffered any kind of destruction ca. 1200 BCE (Millek 2017, 131–32). The only possible evidence of destruction comes from

---

fig. 1, who state Dor was destroyed.

98   CHAPTER THREE

the northern mound stratum XII where a building with a limestone floor was uncovered, and on top of this floor were some burnt beams; however, there was no other evidence of destruction, such as fallen mud bricks, large amounts of ashes, fallen walls, or crushed and burnt pottery (Ohata 1966, 22, 25, 29). Moreover, on the southern mound, which was the site's acropolis, the Stratum 9 "palace" was deserted and emptied of most of its contents. As Kiyoshi Ohata (1966, 29) describes it, a "desertion of the palace is indicated by the absence of ashes and debris and the paucity of finds." Most interestingly, while the criteria set out in this volume for what constitutes a destruction are not met at Tel Zeror, it appears as well that the excavators themselves generally believed there was no destruction. In the original report, they (Ohata and Kochavi 1964, 284) stated, "At the end of the Late Bronze Age (thirteenth century BCE) the city was abandoned. Only the remains of the brick walls, standing sometimes to a height of 1.5 m. or more, were found in this stratum. Grinding stones and other stone vessels were too heavy to carry, a golden earring, and sherds of pottery are the only testimony left of the culture of the last Canaanite city." While in their 1993 entry into *The New Encyclopedia of Archaeological Excavations in the Holy Land* they never even mention the possibility of a destruction at the end of the Late Bronze Age (Kochavi 1993, 1525). Thus, outside of one mention from 1966 that some beams had been burnt, there was never any indication that Tel Zeror was destroyed, and archaeologically speaking, there is no evidence that Tel Zeror was destroyed ca. 1200 BCE, by Sea Peoples or anyone else.

Tel Gerisa

Tel Gerisa (also called Tell el Jerishe or Tell Jerishe) is located on the southern bank of the Yarkon River. The "destruction" of Tel Gerisa could be considered one of the original end of the Late Bronze Age destructions in the southern Levant, as the origins of the "destruction" can be traced back to 1927, though it has persisted in the literature until modern times.[92] Yet, the supposed destruction of Tel Gerisa is based on one report from 1929 not even written by the excavator. E. L. Sukenik, the original excavator, began excavation at Tel Gerisa in 1927 with a trial sounding. The results of the first season of excavation were reported in the French journal *Revue Biblique* by L. H. Vincent (1929, 113–14) in 1929 who stated that the last Bronze Age city was covered in a thick bed of ashes, which he says was, according to Sukenik, evidence of a destruction by the Philistines.[93] Vincent's French summary was then repeated for the English-speaking world by Arthur Cook (1929, 114–15), who then transformed the

---

92. Vincent 1929, 113–14; Cook 1929, 114–15; Avigad 1976, 578; Drews 1993, 16; Herzog 1993a, 481; Gadot 2010, 61; Stern 2012, 501; 2013, 5.

93. Vincent (1929, 113) states, "They [the Iron I remains] are isolated from the characteristic ruins of Bronze III by a very thick bed of ash: a poignant witness to a cataclysm for which the Philistine invasion could be held responsible."

ashes into a "conflagration at the close of Bronze Age III." It appears Cook overtranslated Vincent's original statement, adding to the severity of the evidence in an early example of the telephone game-esque exaggeration of destruction. Nevertheless, not once in any of the preliminary reports written by Sukenik (1935, 1938, 1944) was this destruction ever mentioned nor was any other evidence of this destruction ever reported, even when Late Bronze Age material was excavated. The only major destruction event that Sukenik described affected the Iron I Philistine settlement (Sukenik 1935, 209; 1944, 198; Albright 1935, 142; Breasted and Engberg 1935, 263). Therefore, solely based on this information, there is no evidence of a destruction.

Excavation began again at Tel Gerisa in the 1980s headed by Ze'ev Herzog (1982; 1983; 1988; 1989; 1990; 1991; 1993a; 1997, 183; Herzog and Tsuk 1996). In his excavation, Herzog uncovered two large LB II buildings in Area A and C and given their size and construction it appeared that they were palaces or at least monumental public buildings. Yet, at the end of the Late Bronze Age, both buildings were found abandoned. The structure in Area A appears to have been abandoned first followed by the "palace" in Area C (Herzog 1982, 30–31; 1991, 121–22; 1997, 183; Herzog and Tsuk 1996, 60–62). As Herzog (Herzog and Tsuk 1996, 62) states about the building in Area C, "The floors were generally cleared of finds, suggesting that movable objects had been removed before the building was abandoned." Moreover, in Area D, which mainly had evidence of Iron Age occupation, there was one level of end of the Late Bronze Age occupation, but, "It was found that the latest LB stratum was abandoned, as there are no traces of destruction by fire" (Herzog 1990, 52). Thus, from the modern excavations there is no evidence of an end of the Late Bronze Age destruction, which matches the reports given by Sukenik in the 1930s. It is unclear exactly what the reason was for Vincent's original statement that ashes were found at the end of the Late Bronze Age, as there is no way to know what Sukenik told him. Nevertheless, based on both the old and renewed excavations, there is no evidence that Tel Gerisa was destroyed ca. 1200 BCE.

Beth-Shemesh

Beth-Shemesh is located thirty kilometers west of Jerusalem. An end of the Late Bronze Age destruction was illustrated with a literary flair by Elihu Grant, who excavated the site in the early twentieth century. Grant (1929, 34), taking on the character of a local Canaanite, described the destruction as, "Fire had done its destructive worst on the buildings of our city, or many of them. Roof timbers and clay upper stories had come crashing down on good masonry of the first floor, and charcoal and ash showed where the dwellings had smouldered for days." However, the destruction event at the end of Stratum IVB is only described as an ash layer found under Stratum III's *Herrenhaus* and

100   Chapter Three

in some other sections of Stratum IV and Grant (1939, 11–12, 39–41) gave no other details of this supposed horrific event. The renewed excavations at the site have not unearthed any substantial evidence of destruction of their Level 8, which corresponds to the end of Grant's Stratum VIB (Ashkenazi, Bunimovitz, and Stern 2016, 171; Shlomo Bunimovitz pers. comm. 08/22/2015). For the time being, it does not appear that Beth-Shemesh was destroyed ca. 1200 BCE.[94]

Tell Ziraʿa

Tell Ziraʿa is located four kilometers southwest of the ancient Decapolis city of Gadara in northern Jordan. A destruction event was assigned by the excavators of Tell Ziraʿa to the end of Phase 14a, which supposedly brought the Late Bronze Age to a close ca. 1200 BCE.[95] However, there is minimal evidence that would suggest Tell Ziraʿa suffered any kind of destruction at the end of the Late Bronze Age. In Complexes D, E, G, H, P, and O there is little evidence of any substantial signs of destruction, as only occasional patches of ashes or a fallen wall were uncovered at the end of Phase 14a (Soennecken pers. comm. 02/08/2018). This, however, does not equate to a destruction event based on the criteria listed above. Perhaps the final publication of the Late Bronze Age remains will help to illuminate what happened at the end of Phase 14a at Tell Ziraʿa, if indeed there is more substantial evidence of a destruction event. Until then there is insufficient evidence to conclude that the site was destroyed. Perhaps an explanation for the occasional fallen wall is Katja Soennecken's (2017, 257–313, 462) suggestion that the site was abandoned for a brief period of time. This period of abandonment would also result in the occasional fallen wall as the buildings fell out of use and were not maintained.[96]

Tell Abu al-Kharaz

Tell Abu al-Kharaz is located four kilometers east of the Jordan River and six kilometers southwest of Pella, and a destruction of the site's Phase VIII has been assigned by the excavator Fischer.[97] However, the remains of Phase

---

94. In Millek 2017, 2018b, 2019c Beth-Shemesh is attributed a partial destruction. However, given the criteria for what constitutes a destruction that have been adopted here, there is not enough evidence of even a partial destruction of the site. This mistake then is my own and it should be rectified in the future.

95. Vieweger 2011, 2013; Soennecken 2017, 40; Häser, Soennecken, and Vieweger 2016, 126. Some references place the possible destruction at 1300 BCE; however, this has been corrected to 1200 BCE (Katja Soennecken pers. comm. 02/08/2018).

96. The patches of ash could have resulted from any number of controlled uses of fires, such as hearths, tabuns, and industrial activities, or they could have been the result of ash being dumped. If there was a period of abandonment, wind would have certainly moved any ash remaining in the buildings creating small patches of ash. Thus, as mentioned above, the patches of ash are not a sign of destruction without further corroborating evidence of such an event; see Millek 2019b, 122.

97. Fischer 2006, 374; Fischer 2014, 570; see discussion in Millek 2019b, 124–25. Fischer (2006, 347), even though he assumes that the site was destroyed at the end of the Late Bronze Age, does

VIII at Tell Abu al-Kharaz are sparse at best and were affected by later Iron Age construction activities and erosion (Fischer 2006, 158, 347). In Area 2, only scanty remains of stone walls were uncovered, and it appears to have been a short-lived settlement. Some of the stone walls, along with stone slabs that were used to support a roof, appear to have collapsed (Fischer 2006, 158); however, there was no evidence of burning or any other indictors of a destruction, and the collapse of the walls was most likely caused by natural degeneration once the site was abandoned. Similarly, in Area 3, there were again scanty remains, as only some partial walls were uncovered in association with a possible courtyard and the remains of either a pit or silo, with no evidence of destruction found in the area (Fischer 2006, 175–76). Little is known of this final Late Bronze Age phase, and it was apparently abandoned at some time in the thirteenth century BCE until ca. 1150 BCE. With that in mind, the most likely answer to what happened to Phase VIII at Tell Abu al-Kharaz is that a few walls collapsed, most likely owing to the natural deterioration of architecture after the site was abandoned. Thus, until further information can be obtained about the end of the Late Bronze Age at Tell Abu al-Kharaz, the finds from Phase VIII do not indicate the site was destroyed at the end of the thirteenth century BCE.

Amman Airport Structure

Located at the former Amman Civil Airport in Markeh, Jordan, the Amman Airport Structure is a most unusual building of contested function— ranging from different types of temples, possibly involving human sacrifice, a cultic structure, a watch tower, and a fortified trading post, among others.[98] A destruction of the site ca. 1200 BCE was suggested by Gregory Mumford (2015, 109) who recently revised the structures stratigraphy at the end of his Phase 4b (Level 1). Mumford (2015, 110) suggested that the destruction was perhaps caused by Merenptah's or Ramesses III's actions in the region, or as he states, the destruction was caused "More likely, [by] the turmoil surrounding the widespread Sea People raids and overland migrations and invasions by refugees and others in year 8 of Ramesses III." However, the only evidence of a possible destruction event was uncovered in Room VII, where a layer of ash covered over a burnt pavement and contained burnt pottery. Yet, the evidence for destruction is not convincing, as outside of Room VII no other rooms were burnt and the burning in Room VII can likely be attributed to the hearth found in the same room. Thus, the only possible evidence for burning was most likely a result of the day-to-day use of the hearth and not a destruction event at all (Millek 2019b, 130–31).

---

acknowledge that due to erosion and later building in the Iron Age, it is difficult to say if Phase VIII came to a violent end or not.

98. Hennessy 1966, 1985; Herr 1983; McGovern 1989; Mumford 2015, 90; see also references therein.

102 CHAPTER THREE

Ashdod

Ashdod has been subject to perhaps one of the most commonly cited destruction events for the southern Levant, as a widespread or partial destruction of Stratum XIV, that is, the LB IIB to Iron I transition, has been widely reported in the scholarly literature.[99] However, of the four excavated areas where Stratum XIV was uncovered, evidence of destruction was minimal. Only Area A had any possible evidence of a destruction as a "thick" layer of ash was discovered in a very small portion of the area.[100] In Area G no evidence of destruction was uncovered, and in Area H where the thirteenth century "Canaanite" or "Egyptian governor's residence" was located, no evidence of a destruction was detected.[101] Based on this, the small area of ash in Area A does not equate to a destruction and there was no destruction at Ashdod ca. 1200 BCE. The lack of evidence for destruction led David Ben-Shlomo (2011, 202), who researched the material from Ashdod and published the material from Areas H and K, to state that "Sites like Ashdod display no evidence for destruction in the Early Iron Age levels."

In the past, I have reported a partial destruction at Ashdod (Millek 2017, 122; 2018b, 149; 2019c, 246). However, this was before I had implemented a more rigorous standard for what constitutes a destruction; nevertheless, this too was a false destruction on my part. No one is immune to creating or propagating false destructions at the end of the Late Bronze Age—not even the present author.

Tell eṣ-Ṣafi/Gath

Tell eṣ-Ṣafi/Gath is located thirty-five kilometers northwest of Hebron. An end of the Late Bronze Age destruction at the site was originally reported by the excavator Aren Maeir (2012, 18; 2013, 204), who stated that there was evidence of a *possible* violent destruction ca. 1200 BCE at least in Area E. This assessment was cited by Knapp and Manning (2016, 131) who stated that Tell eṣ-Ṣafi was "*at least* partially destroyed" (emphasis added) suggesting that the destruction was even more widespread beyond Area E. Nevertheless, the "destruction" in Area E Stratum 4a was some well-preserved and restorable pottery found on the floor the Late Bronze Age building (Maeir 2012, 18; 2013, 204; Shai, Uziel, and Maier 2012, 229–30). There was no wall collapse, burning,

---

99. Dothan and Freedman 1967, 81; M. Dothan 1971, 25–26; T. Dothan. 1983, 103–4; Dever 1992, 100 fig. 13.1; Drews 1993, 9, 16 fig. 1; Nur and Cline 2000, 44 fig. 1; Nur and Burgess 2008, 225 fig. 8.1; Yasur-Landau 2010, 220–21; Cline 2014, 110–11, 122 fig. 10; Knapp and Manning 2016, 130; Kreimerman 2017, 187 table 9.3; Millek 2017, 122; 2018b, 249; 2019c, 149.

100. Dothan, and Freedman 1967, 81; Dothan 1971, 25–26; Yasur-Landau 2010, 220–21. Area B also yielded evidence of burning; however, this area was seemingly joined with Area A, leaving Area A with the only possible evidence of destruction.

101. Dothan 1971, 155; Dothan and Porath 1993, 47; Dothan and Ben-Shlomo 2005, 3, 63; Yasur-Landau 2010, 220–21.

THE DESTRUCTION THAT WASN'T 103

or anything of the sort, and there is thus no evidence of destruction at all, let alone a violent one. Maeir (pers. comm. 06/11/2014; published in Millek 2017, 126) reported in 2014 that after subsequent seasons of excavation, there was indeed no evidence of destruction in Areas E, A, P, and F. Recently, however, Maeir et al. (2019, 13) have again suggested that there was a destruction at Tell es-Safi/Gath. They state that,

> An interesting question is whether or not the site was destroyed during this transition. Previously (Maeir 2012), it was suggested that there was evidence of a destruction of the last LB phase in Area E, perhaps indicating a general destruction of the site at this point. Since then, continued excavations in other areas (Area A, D, F and P), present a more complex picture. In Areas A and P, there is no evidence of a destruction in the late LB, while in Area F, there might be some evidence in some squares, but not in others. Thus, it would appear that if in fact the end of the LB at Tell es-Safi/Gath was a complex process—some parts of the site (perhaps the elite zones in Area E and F) were partially destroyed, while other parts of the site were not.

But there remains no evidential backing that Tell es-Safi/Gath was destroyed at the end of the Late Bronze Age. As Maeir et al. note, there is no evidence of destruction in either Areas A and P. Additionally, in the brief overview of the finds from Area F there is no mention or description of any evidence of destruction (Shai et al. 2017, 294–95). All that is said of the end of the Late Bronze Age in Area F is that a small cultic shrine was deliberately covered with fifty centimeters of fill soil that covered a bench and a massebah (Shai et al. 2017, 294). However, this fill layer does not constitute a destruction. Likewise, what we must again recall is that the cited evidence for the "destruction" in Area E was some restorable pottery on a part of a floor, which Maeir (2020, 13) still maintains is evidence of destruction. However, even in the recently published final report from Tell es-Safi/Gath, which included additional material from Area E Stratum 4a, there is no evidence of a destruction, as once again no wall collapse, no burning, and no general piles of debris were in evidence.[102] Given all this, the conclusion must be that there was no destruction at Tell es-Safi/Gath at the end of the Late Bronze Age.[103]

---

102. Shai, Uziel, and Maier 2020a, 386–87; 2020b, 499–500. In the Area E Loci List found in Shai, Uziel, and Maier 2020b there are several instances where a locus from Stratum 4a is described as having "destruction debris." However, the "destruction debris" is typically decayed mud bricks or gray sediment, often not in association with any architecture or the locus was without any pottery. Moreover, most loci were without any "destruction debris" (Shai, Uziel, and Maier 2020b, 502–18). This is however not evidence of destruction and is more likely an indication of abandonment that led to the degradation of some of the superstructure. It should be noted though that in Shai et al. 2017; Shai, Uziel, and Maier 2012, 2020a, and 2020b, Shai, the lead author, never states that there was a destruction in Area E Stratum 4a.

103. In the introductory chapter of the second final report from Tell es-Safi/Gath, Maeir (2020, 17) has likely accidentally published a typo or at worst has contradicted himself. He states concern-

104 CHAPTER THREE

Qubur el-Walaydah

Qubur el-Walaydah is situated on the right bank of the Nahal Besor between Tell Jemmeh and Tell el-Far'ah (South). The assumption that Qubur el-Walaydah was destroyed ca. 1200 BCE can be attributed to the excavators themselves, despite the complete lack of evidence of destruction, which they clearly state is the case.[104] As the excavators (Asscher et al. 2015b, 79) describe it, "Stratum 1-5d was abandoned with complete pottery vessels in situ left behind. There are no signs of burning, but a violent destruction of Stratum 1-5d is possible. The walls of Stratum 1-5d did not collapse and were still standing after Stratum 1-5d was abandoned." As there is no evidence of burning or even wall collapse, a destruction cannot be assumed even if some pottery was left behind.

Tell el-Ḥesi: City Sub-IV Egyptian Governor's Residence

Jeffrey Blakely (2018, 276–77) has recently asserted that the Egyptian governor's residence, excavated by Frederick Jones Bliss in 1894, was destroyed ca. 1200 BCE. However, there is a lack of evidence suggesting that the Egyptian governor's residence was in fact destroyed. One must first remember that the building was excavated when archaeology was in its embryonic state, and the record of the excavation is vague at best. That said, from Bliss's (1894, 71–73) excavation report, he never mentions any sort of burning, masses of pottery, ash, or any other evidence of destruction. Bliss describes the walls of the building as being largely removed, and in some sections a single course of bricks was still visible above the foundation layer of sand. The interior of the building was said to have been filled with "general debris" (71). The only possible indication of destruction is where Bliss (73) states that, "We have cleared other rooms which at first seemed one mass of indistinguishable brick, owing to the falling inward of the upper part of the walls." But wall collapse by itself is not certain proof of a destruction, as the walls could have fallen naturally if the building had been abandoned. Given that Bliss does not report finding anything of worth under the mass of bricks, this might suggest that the building was largely empty when the

---

ing the end of the Late Bronze Age at Gath that, "I believe that all these finds indicate that during the final stage of the LB, the city of Gath was quite large. This phase seems to have ended in some areas in destruction *(Areas E and P)*, and perhaps abandonment *(Area F and maybe A)*" (emphasis added). The acute reader will notice that here Maier states that Areas E and P were destroyed while *Areas F and A* were abandoned. However, in his 2019 article he explicitly stated that *Areas E and F* were partially destroyed while *Areas P and A* had no evidence of destruction (Maeir et al. 2019, 13; see quotation above). To give Maier the benefit of the doubt, this is likely an oversight and the area letters were simply confused. If it is not, then it is in blatant contradiction to his previous statement from just a year prior without any evidential backing.

104. Asscher et al. 2015b, 79; see also Kreimerman 2017, 189, who, citing Asscher et al. 2015b, places a destruction at the site at the end of the Late Bronze Age.

THE DESTRUCTION THAT WASN'T

walls fell inward. Moreover, given that Bliss uncovered the mass of bricks still in place, it suggests that no one tried to dig into the rooms in search of valuable objects, again being another indication that the building was simply abandoned. There is currently no evidence that the City Sub-IV Egyptian governor's residence was destroyed ca. 1200 BCE.

False Citations

Greece (fig. 3.5)

Pefkakia

Pefkakia is located to the south of Volos on the Pagasitikos Gulf. There are several references to the supposed destruction of Pefkakia, which has largely been recounted by Vassiliki Adrimi-Sismani the excavator of nearby Dimini. She has stated on several occasions that the three major sites in the Volos region, Dimini, Kastro-Palaia, and Pefkakia were all destroyed ca. 1200 BCE (Adrimi-Sismani 2007a, 168; 2007b, 29; 2011, 317; 2020, 23). Or as she (2020, 23) describes it, "All three of them suffered in the same destruction, which in excavations was detected as an extensive layer of fire." However, the supposed destruction of Pefkakia is a false citation by Adrimi-Sismani. In all of the excavation reports from Pefkakia, the excavators have made it clear that Pefkakia was *abandoned* and not destroyed. In 1972, Vladimir Milojcic (1972, 66), one of the original excavators, stated, "The remains of the building and household items are less important than the fact that this settlement [Pefkakia] is not like most other Mycenaean settlements from Thessaly to the Peloponnese that were destroyed in a conflagration, but it [Pefkakia] was abandoned." In the recent excavations carried out by Anthi Batziou-Efstathiou (2012, 184), the excavators too have found no evidence of destruction. Batziou-Efstathiou stated in 2012 that the site was abandoned, and in 2016 she (2016, 139) summarized the situation at Pefkakia ca. 1200 BCE by saying, "The abrupt and definitive abandonment of [Pefkakia] occurred at the end of LH IIIB2 to LH IIIC Early.... There are no signs of generalized fire." It is unclear exactly how Adrimi-Sismani concluded that Pefkakia was destroyed ca. 1200 BCE when the excavators have gone to great lengths to state the opposite. By looking at the chain of citation both Adrimi-Sismani 2020 and 2011 reference Adrimi-Sismani 2007a as the source citation for the destruction of Pefkakia. In this 2007 article, Adrimi-Sismani (2007a, 168; see also 2007b, 29), when citing an excavation report from Pefkakia, states that it was indeed abandoned, but a paragraph later, she simply states, without any citation, that Pefkakia was destroyed. However, there is no evidence that the site was destroyed ca. 1200 BCE, and its "destruction" is only the figment of a chain of false citations.

106   CHAPTER THREE

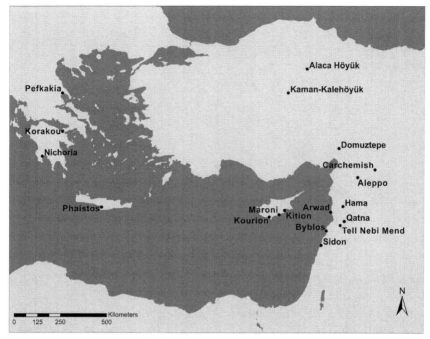

Figure 3.5. False Citations in the Eastern Mediterranean excluding the southern Levant.

Korakou

Korakou, located on the Corinthian Gulf, is one of the typically cited destructions ca. 1200 BCE on the Greek mainland.[105] However, this false citation appears to have originated with Drews. In his 1993 book, Drews (1993, 23) simply states that Korakou was destroyed, even though he notes that Carl Blegen never mentioned a destruction, and that Rutter, in his dissertation, pointed out that there was no evidence of destruction ca. 1200 BCE. However, Drews (1993, 23) goes on to broadly state that, "The argument *ex silentio* has little significance since the site provides no stratigraphic record of the transition from the [LH] IIIB to IIIC." To put this quotation another way, "The lack of any evidence of a destruction is no reason not to assume that the site was destroyed." Therefore, the question is then, Is there any evidence of destruction at Korakou from the end of the Late Bronze Age? The answer is no.

The original excavation report by Blegen (1921) offers no substantial description of the end of the LH IIIB remains from Korakou, while the more detailed analysis offered by Rutter demonstrates that there is no evidence of a destruction event at the end of the LH IIIB2. Of the several houses uncovered by Blegen, none appear to have been destroyed in this transitional period. House L

---

105. Drews 1993, 23; Nur and Cline 2000, 56; Nur and Burgess 2008, 225 fig. 8.1; Middleton 2010, 14; Galanakis 2013a, 3810–11; Cline 2014, 128; Knapp and Manning 2016, 123.

was abandoned without destruction sometime toward the end of the LH IIIB (Rutter 1974, 131–32). All other structures date to the LH IIIC Early 2 with this phase ending ca. 1150 BCE, and even here, Houses H and P were abandoned without destruction (Rutter 1974, 314, 349, 380–81, 546–48; 2015). Thus, if there is no physical evidence of destruction, then a destruction event cannot be assumed to be the case. Despite Drews's opinion to the contrary, destruction is not the inevitable end for all sites during transitional periods. The repeated propagation of the false destruction of Korakou appears to be the blind citation of Drews's false citation, again creating a destruction where none ever existed.

Nichoria

Situated on a ridgetop near modern Rizomylos, Nichoria's false destruction ca. 1200 BCE originated from the initial assessment of a small-scale trial excavation led by Nicholas Yalouris and William McDonald in 1959. McDonald and Simpson reported on the finds from the trial excavations stating that, "Like Blegen's palace site [Pylos], this town appears to have been destroyed by fire about 1200 B.C. and was never rebuilt."[106] Despite the claim of a ca. 1200 BCE destruction, no description or evidence was provided to substantiate this claim. Nevertheless, the "destruction" of Nichoria was reported by Per Ålin (1962, 91, 149) and by Desborough (1964, 94) who stated that the site was, "destroyed probably at the same time as the Palace of Nestor." Drews went on to cite Desborough, repeating the destruction of Nichoria ca. 1200 BCE. Subsequently, Drews was then cited by Nur and Cline, Nur and Burgess, and Cline on their maps of destruction ca. 1200 BCE.[107] However, even prior to Drews's 1993 book there was ample evidence that Nichoria was not destroyed ca. 1200 BCE.

During the full-scale excavations, no evidence of destruction was ever mentioned in the initial reports (McDonald 1972; McDonald et al. 1975). In fact, McDonald (McDonald et al. 1975, 139) noted in 1975 that, "There is very little evidence to suggest that the L.H. IIIB buildings suffered a general conflagration." This was followed by Simpson and Dickinson (1979, 152) who in their 1979 *Gazetteer* again noted that there was no evidence of a destruction at the site at the end of the LH IIIB. Moreover, in the 1992 final excavation report, McDonald and Wilkie (1992, 336–414, 764–67) clearly describe how all of the structures in Areas II West and East, Area III, and Area IV displayed no signs that they

---

106. McDonald and Simpson 1960, 740. Simpson (1965, 60) later reported that, "Trial excavations made by Yalouris and McDonald in 1959 revealed that the settlement of importance, and that it had been destroyed at the end of the LH IIIB period." Notice that in this quote there is no mention of burning.

107. Drews 1993, 9 fig. 1; Nur and Cline 2000, 56; Nur and Burgess 2008, 225 fig. 8.1; Cline 2014, 110 fig. 10. Cline's map, which clearly states that Nichoria was destroyed ca. 1200 BCE, appears in this case not to match the contents of his chapter on destruction. Cline on p. 128 quotes Middleton, who stated that Nichoria was abandoned and not destroyed, creating a conflict between his map and his written word.

108   CHAPTER THREE

underwent any kind of destruction ca. 1200 BCE. Rather, the excavation reports are quite clear that all of the structures were simply abandoned. Indeed, in all of the areas very few movable objects were discovered in the houses, suggesting to the excavators that the houses were not even abandoned in any sort of panic (McDonald and Wilkie 1992, 764–67). Thus, there has been ample time and evidence to weed out the original 1960 claim that Nichoria was destroyed. Initially, this false destruction could have been categorized as an assumed destruction that was later shown to be incorrect by further excavations. However, for all citations after 1975, when it was clear that site had not suffered a destruction, all further claims that Nichoria was destroyed ca. 1200 BCE are simply false citations.

Crete (fig. 3.5)

Phaistos

Phaistos is located nearly six kilometers from the Mediterranean in south-central Crete. The inexplicable false citation that Phaistos was destroyed ca. 1200 BCE can be found on both maps of destruction by the Sea Peoples in Kaniewski et al. 2011 (fig. 1) and Kaniewsk, Guiot, and Van Campo 2015 (370 fig. 1).[108] However, in both articles, there is never a reference to any of the excavation reports from Phaistos, nor even a mention of the site in the articles outside of the maps on which the authors claim that Phaistos was destroyed. Yet, from the excavations, never has any evidence of a destruction been uncovered nor was there ever a claim that the site was destroyed (Borgna 1997, 2003, 2007, 2011, 2017; Elisabetta Borgna pers. comm. 03/03/2020). It is a complete mystery exactly why Kaniewski et al. and Kaniewsk, Guiot, and Van Campo have twice claimed Phaistos was destroyed ca. 1200 BCE when all evidence points to the contrary.

Anatolia (fig. 3.5)

Alaca Höyük

Alaca Höyük is situated some twenty kilometers northeast of Boğazkale.[109] Its supposed destruction is one of the standard end of the Late Bronze Age destruction events for Anatolia, and it has been widely cited as destroyed by

---

108. The subtitle for fig. 1 from Kaniewski, Guiot, and Van Campo 2015 is, "Map of the sea-land invasions in the Aegean Sea and Eastern Mediterranean at the end of the Late Bronze Age. Some of the main cities destroyed during the raids of the Sea Peoples are displayed with a fire logo." Phaistos is given a tiny flame clearly indicating the authors assumed the site was destroyed.

109. For an overview of the early excavations from 1935 until 1978, see Gursan-Salzmann 1992, 11–33.

THE DESTRUCTION THAT WASN'T   109

fire.[110] All citations for Alaca Höyük's supposed fiery demise can be linked back to Kurt Bittel who in 1983 stated that "at Alaca Höyük ... only part of the monumental Hittite architecture has been definitively destroyed by fire."[111] Bittel cited the first excavation report published by Remzi Oğuz Arık (Arık 1937a),which detailed the first season of excavation at Alaca Höyük conducted in 1935, an excavation that has continued off and on for nearly a century. This report was published before the stratigraphy at the site had been firmly established, and during this initial excavation, Arık encountered evidence of a destruction belonging to the Hittite period. He describes it as follows: "The walls seemed to have been the target of a great fire and the object of a great destruction. Throughout the survey area, the ground was covered with ash and large red or black spots. Most of the walls had changed direction and were winding, which led us to conclude that they had suffered great tremors and that the period was ended following a fire."[112] Yet, Arık himself never stated that this was a destruction dated to ca. 1200 BCE, and, aside from this brief description, he does not mention this destruction again elsewhere in the report, not even in the summary and conclusions (Arık 1937a, 39–40, 117; 1937b, 224, 230). Moreover, in the excavation from 1936, which expanded the 1935 sounding to the east, south, and west, Hâmit Zübeyr Koşay, who led the excavations beginning in 1936, never encountered destruction debris or evidence of burning from Level II or the end of the Hittite period.[113] Furthermore, in the following ninety years of excavation reports and summaries written by the excavators, no evidence of a destruction at the end of Level II is ever described, nor was it ever claimed that Alaca Höyük was destroyed.[114]

---

110. Drews 1993, 8–9, fig. 1; Nur and Cline 2000, 56; Nur and Burgess 2008, 225, fig 8.1; Cline 2014, 110–11, 126, fig. 10; Knapp and Manning 2016, 126.

111. Bittel 1983, 31. Translation my own. As an aside, from Drews onward, even though all cite Bittel 1983, Drews, Cline, and Knapp and Manning extend the reach of this supposed destruction saying that it was far more massive than what even Bittel had stated. Drews (1993, 8) says that the ashy area extended over the entire excavation, while Cline (2014, 126) and Knapp and Manning (Knapp and Manning 2016, 126) simply state that the site had been destroyed by fire, implying a site-wide destruction. This is, even by itself, a stretch of Bittel's original claim and is another example of how the extent and supposed damage caused by a destruction tends to be amplified with repeated citations.

112. Arık 1937a, 39. Translation my own. See also Arık 1937b, 224 where a similar description is given, as this article summarizes the finds reported in Arık 1937a. He states: "3m. 50 to 4m., the ground was covered by a thick layer of fire and by sections of overturned walls."

113. Kosay 1944, 15–17; Gursan-Salzmann 1992, 20. See the plan in Kosay 1944, 17.

114. Kosay 1939–1940, 1940, 1944, 1951, 1954, 1973; Koşay and Akok 1966; Gursan-Salzmann 1992, 14–18; Ozgüç 2002; Baltacıoğlu 2008; Çelik 2008; Çinaroğlu and Çelik 2010. There is only one entry that comes close to a mention of destruction in the following ninety years of excavation reports. Koşay (1940, 10), stated in the report on the 1940 excavation season that after the Hittite empire had been destroyed, the Phrygians settled at Alaca Höyük and that "unfortunately, they destroyed the Hittite temple." He (1940, 11) went further to say when describing the temple that "this facade, and especially the northern part of the vestibule, were destroyed by the Phrygians,

110   CHAPTER THREE

It appears that this false destruction originated with Bittel, who apparently
dated the destruction debris uncovered by Arık to the end of the Late Bronze
Age despite Arık himself never stating that it dated to ca. 1200 BCE. The debris
that Bittel dated to ca. 1200 BCE may very well have originated in a previous
Hittite layer dating to well before the fall of the Hittite empire. A possible
point in favor of this interpretation is that the upper 2.50 m of excavated soil
from the 1935 season was a mixed layer of Ottoman, Byzantine, Roman, and
Phrygian remains, and Hittite material culture began to be unearthed below
this (Arık 1937a, 117; 1937b, 221; Gursan-Salzmann 1992, 18). Yet, the supposed
end of the Late Bronze Age destruction debris was only encountered at a depth
of 3.50 m to 4 m (Arık 1937b, 224). In the following seasons from 1936 to 1939,
which surrounded the original 1935 sounding, the depth of Level II, the final
Hittite phase, was between 3.25 m to 3.50 m, while Level III, an earlier phase
of the Hittite settlement, started at a depth of 3.50 m (Koşay 1944, 176; 1951,
156). During the 1936 season, directly surrounding the 1935 sounding, Koşay
uncovered a layer of burnt debris and ashes between Level IIIb and Level
IV, both of which were earlier Hittite levels (Koşay 1944, 25), and it may be
possible that Arık's Hittite layer, which Bittel took to be the end of the Late
Bronze Age, belonged to an earlier phase of the Hittite settlement based on
the depth measurements. This suggestion, while a possible solution, requires
further investigation as the depth measurements taken during the first years of
the excavation were not systematic in their presentation, and this is certainly
far from conclusive.[115]

Unfortunately, the single mention of an undated Hittite-era destruction
from 1937 was picked up by Bittel to generate a ca. 1200 BCE destruction
even though he had a wealth of archaeological data indicating that there
was no such destruction at Alaca Höyük. From Bittel onward, the supposed
destruction was blown out of proportion until it was positioned as one of the
key destruction events of the end of the Late Bronze Age; yet all the while

---

who added new buildings to it." In all of the reports detailing the excavation of the Level II temple,
beginning in 1936, Koşay never makes any mention of evidence of fire, burning, debris, or that
the walls had fallen, and he made no other statements that the temple had been destroyed (Kosay
1939–1940, 20–21; 1940, 11; 1944, 15–16; 1951, 111–13; Koşay and Akok 1966, 121–27). What is most
likely is that by "destroyed" Koşay meant that the Phrygians altered the temple, adding partitions to
it, dismantling it in part, and in the process "destroyed" it. This is indeed a point he mentioned in the
report on the 1937–1939 excavation seasons, as he notes that the Phrygian builders utilized stones
from the Hittite buildings for their own construction and refurbished Hittite buildings with interior
partition walls to suit their own needs (Koşay 1951, 111; see also Koşay 1939–1940, 21; Koşay and
Akok 1966, 120). Therefore, from the available evidence, there is no reasonable proof that the Level
II Hittite temple was destroyed, and most likely Koşay meant that the temple had been "destroyed"
by the alterations made to it, which does not count as a destruction as it is defined here.
    115. See the discussion in Gursan-Salzmann 1992, 14–16.

THE DESTRUCTION THAT WASN'T   111

the archaeological evidence has been clear. There was no destruction at Alaca Höyük ca. 1200 BCE.

Kaman-Kalehöyük

Kaman-Kalehöyük is located one hundred kilometers southeast of Ankara and six kilometers east of the town of Kaman. Drews (2020, 229) has recently claimed that Kaman-Kalehöyük was destroyed at the end of the Late Bronze Age. Drews cited as supporting evidence a 1996 article by Marie-Henriette Gates (1996, 297) that gave a brief update on the progress of the Japanese-led excavations at the site. In this article, there is a mention of a destruction of Level III, but importantly no date is given for the destruction and it appears that Drews simply assumed that the destruction was ca. 1200 BCE, as the following Level II is early Iron Age. However, the destruction of Level IIIc, which Sachihiro Omura (2011, 1102–8) excavated at Kaman-Kalehöyük, in fact dated to the Assyrian Colony period in the middle of the eighteenth century BCE. Never did the excavators claim that the site was destroyed ca. 1200 BCE, as little is even known of the end of the Late Bronze Age period at the site since the remains from Level IIIa were poorly preserved (Omura 2011, 1102).

Domuztepe near Karatepe-Aslantaş

Domuztepe near Karatepe-Aslantaş (not to be confused with the famous Neolithic Domuztepe) is situated on the left bank of the Ceyhan River some twenty-three kilometers from Kadirli. The "destruction" of Domuztepe is again another classic example of the telephone game-esque citation exaggeration, though this time with the date of the destruction rather than the evidence for a destruction. In a small-scale excavation in 1951 U. Bahadir Alkim, the excavator at Domuztepe at the time, uncovered a burnt stratum twenty to thirty centimeters thick, which he dubbed Level C. He noted that the pottery shared a resemblance to the Late Bronze Age pottery from Tarsus, and because of the lack of information, he only dated Level C to before the ninth century BCE (Alkim 1952a, 20; 1952b 135–36; 1952c, 249). Sixty-two years later in 2013, Gates (2013, 100), citing Alkim, states that a destruction affected Domuztepe at some point during the LB II. Four years after this, Gunner Lehmann (2017, 237), citing Gates, then goes on to say that Domuztepe was destroyed at the *end of the Late Bronze Age*. Thus, over the course of nearly seventy years, the date of the destruction went from some nebulous time before the ninth century BCE, to the LB II, to the end of the Late Bronze Age, all the while citing the same information. There is no way to know the exact date of the possible destruction event based on the material from Alkim's original excavation, and there is no reason to assume that the site suffered an end of the Late Bronze Age destruction based on this information. Further, Alkim was not the only

112 CHAPTER THREE

one to excavate at Domuztepe and in all of the following excavations carried out by Halet Çambel, no evidence of an end of the Late Bronze Age destruction ca. 1200 BCE was discovered.[116]

Cyprus (fig. 3.5)

Kourion (Episkopi)-Bamboula

Positioned on the southwest coast of Cyprus, Kourion (*Episkopi)-Bamboula* was assigned an end of the LC IIC destruction by A. Bernard Knapp in 1997.[117] Nevertheless, no signs of a destruction event were found in the transition from the LC IIC to the LC IIIA (Benson 1970, 35). No evidence of a destruction was uncovered in Area A Stratum C, though much of what had remained from the LC IIC was cleared out during the construction activity during the following Stratum D (Benson 1969, 7; Weinberg 1983, 9). Some house tumble was uncovered in Area B; however, it is uncertain whether this material dates to the end of the LC IIC or not (Benson 1969, 16; Weinberg 1983, 33). No evidence of fire or wall collapse was found in Areas C, D and E and neither Jack Leonard Benson (1969, 19–21) nor Saul Weinberg (1983, 37–52) ever claimed that the site was destroyed.

Maroni-Vournes

Maroni-*Vournes*, situated halfway between Limassol and Larnaca on the south coast of Cyprus, is another falsely cited destruction at the end of the Late Bronze Age (Knapp 2013, 474; Knapp and Manning, 132). The site was excavated by Gerald Cadogan who uncovered two buildings dating to the *Vournes* III period or the LC IIC.[118] These two buildings were named the Ashlar Building and the West Building. However, the only mention of any possible traces of a destruction were found in the Ashlar Building during the early phases of the excavation. Originally, Cadogan (1985, 196; 1986, 43; Cadogan and Domurad 1989, 77) assumed that a black layer found in Room 4, the Room of the Olive Press, was evidence of an accidental fire restricted to this room and not the building as a whole. However, it was later pointed out that this material

---

116. Çambel 1984; 1986; Çambel and Özdoğan 1985; Çambel, Ism, and Sadler 1987; Çambel, Ism, and Knudstad 1996.

117. Knapp 1997, 54–55 table 2. It should be noted that this was the only time Knapp claims that the site was destroyed, as in his other lists of destruction from 2008, 2009, 2013; and from Knapp and Manning 2016 he does not mention Kourion as destroyed.

118. Recent pedestrian survey and geophysical studies of Maroni-*Vournes* have expanded our understanding of the site. No grid plan for the site was uncovered in the survey. Nevertheless, the survey did indicate that the site was more expansive than originally thought (Manning et al. 2014). Manning et al. (25) state, "there is likely more of an urban settlement and habitus at Late Bronze Age Maroni than many previous scholars perhaps imagined, and a likely larger Late Bronze Age city-scale population." However, from this survey there is no evidence of any destruction at the site seen in the geophysical studies.

THE DESTRUCTION THAT WASN'T 113

was simply the pressing debris from the olive press found in Room 4 (Cadogan et al. 2001, 84). No other signs of a destructive event were seen in the Ashlar Building and none were found in the West Building. Both buildings and the site as a whole appear to have been peacefully abandoned at the end of the LC IIC and remained unoccupied for some 450 years (Cadogan 1996, 16–19; 2011, 401).

Kition

Kition, located on the southern coast of Cyprus in present day Larnaca, is one of the benchmark destructions on Cyprus at the end of the Late Bronze Age, as it appears on most lists and maps of destruction ca. 1200 BCE.[119] Nevertheless, in the final excavation report that covered the end of the LC IIC, both Vassos Karageorghis and Martha Demas, the excavators of Kition, made it clear that no evidence of destruction was uncovered. They (Karageorghis and Demas 1985, 92, 273–75; Karageorghis 1992, 80) state that Floor IV found in both Areas I and II ended peacefully and that the dismantling and reconstruction of the buildings and temples in both areas is not evidence of destruction but a deliberate effort to expand and remodel, especially in the temple precinct, where ashlar masonry was utilized in the remodeling process. Judging from the excavation reports there is no reason to disagree with Karageorghis's and Demas's interpretation.

In Area I Floor IV, a copper workshop, no traces of destruction were uncovered. There were no fallen walls and the only signs of ash or burning were found in Rooms 40 and 41. However, the ash in Room 40 likely came from Furnace B, which is where the ashes were the thickest. In Room 41, the floor was burnt; yet, here too this was in association with Furnace A (Karageorghis and Demas 1985, 6–11). No other rooms in this area yielded traces of burning. Therefore, industrial activity in the copper workshops of Area I account for any ash found in association with Floor IV at the end of the LC IIC.

The temples in Area II also yielded few if any hints of destruction. Temple 3 was found devoid of any finds on the patches of floor that survived the remodeling during Floor IIIA. The walls had collapsed onto the floors and the rubble was used as a base for the temple of Floor IIIA.[120] For Temple 2, the only possible evidence of destruction were bits of mud brick, charcoal, and ash found in Room 24, the main hall, where the temple's hearth was situated

---

119. Catling 1975, 209; Desborough 1975, 660; Åström 1985, 8; Drews 1993, 9, 11 fig. 1; Knapp 1997, 54–55 table 2; 2009, 54; 2013, 474; Nur and Cline 2000, 56; Bell 2006, 137 map 1; Nur and Burgess 2008, 225 fig. 8.1; Voskos and Knapp 2008, 664; Kaniewski et al. 2011 fig. 1; Kaniewski, Guiot, and Van Campo 2015, 370 fig. 1; Cline 2014, 110–11, 133 fig. 10; 2021, 127; Knapp and Manning 2016, 132. Fischer 2017, 198 table 1, places a destruction as possible but not definite.

120. Karageorghis and Demas 1985, 25–6. Interestingly, Karageorghis and Demas (26) mention a thin layer of alluvium on the floor of Temple 3 below the demolished walls. This may suggest a short hiatus or perhaps a brief period of abandonment before it was rebuilt during Floor IIIA.

114   CHAPTER THREE

(Karageorghis and Demas 1985, 26–29). Because this room held the hearth, the day-to-day use of fire in the main hall is the most likely explanation for the charcoal and ash, given the lack of other signs of destruction.

In the southwest of Area II, a single complex of rooms was uncovered that was poorly preserved and its function unclear, though the excavators assumed it to be an industrial area. A room had some marks of burning; however, no other signs of destruction were found in the complex (Karageorghis and Demas 1985, 32–33). Like the other structures of Area II, the fortifications, including Towers A and B show no evidence of a destruction. There are no traces of burning, and it appears that they were dismantled, their mud bricks used as a fill and built on top of by the conglomerate blocks used in the Floor IIIA walls and towers. The only possible signs of structural collapse were unearthed on Street A north of Tower A where a thick layer of mud brick was discovered (34–37). Given all of this, for Kition, there is no substantial evidence that it suffered a destruction event in the transition from the LC IIC to the LC IIIA, as Karageorghis and Demas noted in their report. Moreover, all the walls from Floor IV in Area I were reused in Floor IIIA. Temples 2 and 3 maintained the same basic plan, though they were rebuilt on a grander scale, while the possible industrial unit in Area II was rebuilt during Floor IIIA along the same basic plan found in Floor IV. The fortifications and towers were rebuilt and indeed it seems as if the city underwent a period of flourish rather than regression during the LC IIIA (Karageorghis and Demas 1985, 92, 273–75; Georgiou 2011, 117; 2015, 133; Iacovou 2013a, 599).

The repeated false citation that Kition was destroyed ca. 1200 BCE does not have a single origin, as multiple authors took different routes to this false citation. Drews (1993, 11) when stating that Kition was destroyed ca. 1200 BCE along with Enkomi and Sinda, cites Karageorghis 1992 as his supporting evidence. However, in this article, Karageorghis (1992, 80) clearly states, "At Kition, major rebuilding was carried out in both excavated Areas I and II, but *there is no evidence of violent destruction*; on the contrary, we observe a cultural continuity" (emphasis added). Thus, Drews's assertation that the site was destroyed was based on a reference that states the opposite to the claim he was making. Cline (2014, 133 n. 117) reached further back referencing a 1982 book by Karageorghis that offered a preliminary examination of Kition at the end of the LC IIC prior to the publication of the final excavation report. In Karageorghis 1982, he does indeed say in passing that Kition was destroyed along with Enkomi.[121] However, this mistake was corrected in the 1985 final publication as well as in Karageorghis 1990 and 1992 (Karageorghis and Demas

---

121. Karageorghis 1982, 82–83. He states, "It is proposed here, in agreement with Desborough and others, to associate the events which preceded the destruction of major coastal towns of Cyprus—such as Enkomi and Kition—with the activities of these wanderers, who are usually known

1985, 92, 273–75; Karageorghis 1990, 20; 1992, 80). In all cases, the actual final excavation report was never referenced, and outdated citations were employed over the final report and further articles that clarified the situation at Kition, which is clearly one lacking destruction.

The origins for the false citation appears to be with Karageorghis's early understanding of the excavated material before he and Demas analyzed what had been unearthed at Kition. This is clearly seen in the earliest excavation reports, where Karageorghis states several times that Kition suffered some major disaster much like Enkomi, which was brought on by the Peoples of the Sea. However, even in these early reports, Karageorghis (1962, 169; 1963a, 365–67; 1963b, 9–10) never makes any mention of evidence of destruction other than some patches of ash and a green layer of soil that covered the excavation area.

Northern Levant (fig. 3.5)

Carchemish

Carchemish is located on the east bank of Euphrates River about sixty kilometers southeast of Gaziantep, Turkey; its supposed ca. 1200 BCE destruction has appeared in several major works on the end of the Late Bronze Age (Nur and Cline 2000, 56; Nur and Burgess 2008, 225 fig. 8.1; Cline 2014, 110–11 fig. 10). While Woolley (1921, 48) proposed in 1921 that Carchemish was destroyed by the Sea Peoples, the modern accusation that the site was destroyed can be traced back to Drews. In his 1993 book, Drews (1993, 9 fig. 1) placed Carchemish on his map of the catastrophe, but much like Knossos, Carchemish is italicized indicating the destruction was probable but not certain, and Drews (1993, 14–15) goes on to state explicitly that no destruction was found in Wooley's excavation. In both Nur and Cline (2000, 56) and Nur and Burgess (2008, 225 fig. 8.1), who reused Drews's map, the italics remained, again indicating that they assumed a destruction was probable but not definite. However, on Cline's 2014 (110–11 fig. 10) map of destruction ca. 1200 BCE, which is again largely a copy of Drews's 1993 map, the italics are gone, indicating Carchemish was destroyed ca. 1200 BCE as the figure caption states.[122] Nevertheless, no evidence of destruction has ever been uncovered at Carchemish in both the original and renewed excavations, and Carchemish in fact went on to be the seat of a Neo-Hittite Great King.[123]

---

as the People of the Sea or the Sea Peoples." Much like Drews, Cline (2014, 132 n. 116) too cites Karageorghis 1992, which clearly states that Kition was not destroyed.

122. The figure caption is "Sites destroyed ca. 1200 BCE."

123. Marchetti 2012, 2013, 2014, 2015a, 2015b; Peker 2017, 2020; Hawkins 1988; Nicolò Marchetti pers. comm. 07/08/2018; see also discussion in Millek 2019a, 167.

Aleppo

Outside of the false destruction of the Temple of the Storm God in Aleppo, there is another false citation that Aleppo was destroyed prior to the temple's discovery. Again, in Drews 1993 (9, 14 fig. 1) book, he states that Aleppo was destroyed and sacked ca. 1200 BCE, an assumption that was again refenced in Nur and Cline (200, 56), Nur and Burgess (2008, 225 fig. 8.1), and Cline (2014, 110–11 fig. 10) that Aleppo itself, not the Temple of the Storm God, was destroyed at the end of the Late Bronze Age. Drews's cited a single reference from Woolley 1959 (164), who had simply stated that, "Carchemish was taken, and Aleppo." Woolley neither explicitly states that Aleppo was destroyed nor that it was sacked. Thus, Drews can be credited with this false destruction event, as he misquoted Wooley who did not claim that the site was destroyed, nor was there any reference to any archaeological excavation that could have uncovered said destruction.

Hama

Hama is situated on the banks of the Orontes River in west-central Syria some two hundred kilometers north of Damascus. The supposed destruction of Hama at the end of the Late Bronze Age is part of a string of false destructions that Drews popularized in 1993, where he (14, 221) states that "Hama, Qatna, and Kadesh [Tell Nebi Mend] [were] sacked and burned." This was then recited by Nur and Cline (2000, 56), Nur and Burgess (2008, 225 fig. 8.1), and Cline (2014, 110–11 fig. 10). However, Ejnar Fugmann, who excavated Hama, never mentioned a destruction at the end of Level G1, the last Late Bronze Age phase, nor can any evidence of destruction be seen in the excavation reports. He (1958, 126, 134, 141–43, 146–47) describes the transition from the Late Bronze Age Level G1 to the Early Iron Age Level F2 as continuing with almost no change.[124] Thus, the supposed destruction of Hama at the end of the Late Bronze Age is simply a false citation.[125] It appears that Drews overinterpreted a statement by Richard David Barnett whom Drews cited. However, Barnett (1975, 360) only states that, "Hamath was captured and occupied by the newcomers"; he never claims that Hama was destroyed.

---

124. Sader (1992, 167; 2014, 610) has also claimed that Hama was destroyed ca. 1200 BCE. However, for Sader, her claim of destruction would be a misdated destruction, as she does note that no destruction took place between Level G1 and F2, but cites the destruction event at the end of Level F2 (Sader 1992, 167). Fugmann (1958, 141–43) does report a destruction event at the end of Level F2; however, in the chronological overview of the site's stratigraphy, he (149, 275) clearly states that this destruction took place at ca. 1075 BCE and was not part of the general changes seen at Hama in the Early Iron Age; see also Millek 2019a, 165.

125. To their credit, Knapp and Manning 2016, 130 do state that there is no ca. 1200 BCE destruction at Hama.

Qatna

Much like Hama, Qatna, which is located eighteen kilometers northeast of Homs, too has an associated destruction event at the end of the Late Bronze Age, which is part of Drews's (1993, 9 fig. 1) string of destruction events in the region, and it has been recited in several publications.[126] However, this is simply not the case, as the major destruction event at Qatna took place ca. 1340 BCE and what followed was a scanty impoverished reuse of the site that is still poorly understood, with no evidence of a destruction ca. 1200 BCE (Pfälzner 2007, 42–43; 2012, 774, 778–79; Bonacossi 2013, 119–21; see also Millek 2019a, 165). Again, this was a false citation that Qatna was destroyed, not based on any archaeological evidence, one that has unfortunately been repeatedly cited and propagated. The origin of this false destruction, however, reaches further back to 1965 when Michael Astour listed the site as part of a string of destructions affecting the entire Levant without citing any archaeological reports to support his claim.[127] It is unclear exactly why Astour listed Qatna as destroyed, since no evidence of a ca. 1200 BCE destruction was uncovered in the original excavations from the 1920s nor did Robert Du Mesnil du Buisson (1935, 36) ever claim the site was destroyed at the end of the Late Bronze Age.[128]

Tell Nebi Mend (Kadesh)

A supposed destruction of Tell Nebi Mend (Kadesh), which is located some thirty kilometers southwest of Homs, is the third in Drews's (1993, 9 fig. 1) string of destructions in the Orontes River Valley that has been repeatedly cited.[129] Yet, much like Hama and Qatna, there was never a destruction at Tell Nebi Mend ca. 1200 BCE, nor did any of the excavators claim that there was. Some Late Bronze Age structures have been uncovered at Tell Nebi Mend (Parr 1983, 1991, 1997; Bourke 1993; Grigson 2015); yet, the archaeological material relating to the end of the Late Bronze Age is, as Stephen Bourke (2012b, 51) describes, "A challenging mix of discontinuous and badly disturbed strata, drawn from small exposures above the more substantial Late Bronze Age horizons." In sum, there is currently no evidence of a destruction event at the end of the

---

126. Nur and Cline 2000, 44 fig. 1; Nur and Burgess 2008, 225 fig. 8.1; Kaniewski et al. 2011, 2 fig. 1; Cline 2014, 110–11 fig. 10; Kaniewski, Guiot, and Van Campo 2015, 2 fig. 1.

127. Astour 1965, 254. He states, "The city [Ras Shamra] fell at the height vitality, suddenly, as the result of a terrible catastrophe the more terrible because it was not a natural disaster, but was wrought by human hands, the more colossal because Ugarit shared its doom with Hattushash, Tarsus, Carchemish, Alalah, Qatna, Qadesh, Hazor, Lachish, and many other ancient cities. Stratigraphical data prove that the Bronze Age in Syria and Anatolia came to an end in a single historical catastrophe."

128. Du Mesnil du Buisson never states that the site was destroyed, though he (1935, 36) does mention that Qatna, Tunip, and the region in general were likely affected by the Peuples de la Mer.

129. Nur and Cline 2000, 44 fig. 1; Nur and Burgess 2008, 225 fig. 8.1; Kaniewski et al. 2011, 2 fig. 1; Cline 2014, 110–11 fig. 10; Kaniewski, Guiot, and Van Campo 2015, 2 fig. 1.

118 CHAPTER THREE

Late Bronze Age at Tell Nebi Mend. In Trench III (Area 207) three phases of the Early Iron Age were discovered on top of an end of the Late Bronze Age stratum, and in between these two, there was no evidence of a destruction.[130] Therefore, of Drews's (1993, 221) supposed string of sites that were "sacked and burned" in the Orontes, none ever had any evidence of destruction, and despite this they have been frequently cited as destroyed, based solely on Drews's false accusation rather than the archaeological evidence. Much like Qatna, the original reference for this false destruction stems from Astour's 1965 (254) list of destruction in Levant, which was "corroborated" by Gustav Lehmann in 1985 (14), who stated that the site was part of a *Zerstörungshorizont* or destruction horizon. It is again unclear why Astour cited a destruction at Kadesh, as in the original excavations there is no mention of the *Peuples de la Mer* or a destruction at the end of the Late Bronze Age ca. 1200 BCE (Pezard 1930). Moreover, Astour's article was written prior to the excavations led by Peter Parr.

Arwad

The Phoenician city of Arwad, which is three kilometers from Tartus, Syria, has been cited as destroyed both by Katzenstein in 1973 (59) and Josette Elayi in 2018 (95). However, nothing is known about the physical Late Bronze Age site at Arwad nor what happened to it ca. 1200 BCE, as all remains except for those belonging to the Roman period have been removed by the continuous occupation of the island (Badre 1997, 218; Sader 2019, 36–37). The only information that we have on the site comes from texts mainly dating to the fifteenth and fourteenth centuries BCE (Astour 1959). Thus, there was no destruction at Arwad as neither the Late Bronze Age nor the Iron I site has been found and may very well be lost to history.

Central Levant (fig. 3.5)

Byblos

A destruction of Byblos by the Sea Peoples appears on maps in both Kaniewski et al. 2011 (fig. 1) and Kaniewski, Guiot, and Van Campo 2015 (fig. 1) neither providing a reason why they assume the site was destroyed ca. 1200 BCE or a citation to back their claim. The archaeological picture of Late Bronze Age Byblos has been complicated due to the excavation method employed by Maurice Dunand in the early twentieth century. Dunand excavated through artificial levels each consisting of twenty centimeters, which unfortunately lumped together objects that would have been separated by following the

---

130. Bourke 2012b, 51; Stephen Bourke pers. comm. 10/08/2018. For a recent publication clarifying the situation at Tell Nebi Mend, see Bourke 2020.

The Destruction That Wasn't

natural stratigraphy of the site (see Kilani 2016, 12–13; 2020, 6–23). However, even with this limitation in mind, a painstaking recent reinvestigation of the Late Bronze Age material from Byblos by Marwan Kilani (2016, 291; 2020, 241), has demonstrated that there is no evidence that would indicate Byblos suffered a destruction event at the end of the Late Bronze Age. As Kilani states, "No destruction level that could be associated with the end of the Late Bronze Age was identified in Byblos" (Kilani 2020: 241). Thus, it appears that Kaniewski et al. and Kaniewsk, Guiot, and Van Campo created a destruction when there is no evidence that Byblos was destroyed ca. 1200 BCE.

Sidon: College Site

Hélène Sader (2014, 610) suggested that the temple uncovered at the college site in Sidon was destroyed at the end of the thirteenth century BCE.[131] However, Doumet-Serhal has informed me that after further review of the material, there is no evidence that the temple was destroyed ca. 1200 BCE and it appears that there was a smooth transition from Late Bronze Age to the Iron Age.[132] It should be noted though that more recently, Sader (2019, 39–40) no longer makes any mention that Sidon was destroyed at the end of the Late Bronze Age.[133]

Southern Levant (fig. 3.6)

'Afula

Situated some twelve kilometers south of Nazareth, 'Afula appeared on William Dever's 1992 (100) list of sites destroyed by the Sea Peoples. He claimed that 'Afula Stratum IV had been destroyed, a destruction that was independently reiterated by Stern (2012, 506; 2013, 5). However, the only issue is that according to the excavators, Stratum IV or the LB II stratum is only attested to by graves, and the Late Bronze settlement has not been discovered (M. Dothan 1993b, 37). Thus, there cannot have been a destruction of a site that has not been found.

---

131. Katzenstein 1973, 59; and Barnett 1975, 360 both claim that Sidon was destroyed at the end of the Late Bronze Age based on the tradition of its destruction; however, this was long before the excavations had uncovered the Late Bronze Age temple mentioned by Sader. Regardless, Katzenstein and Barnett were incorrect in their assessment of the situation.

132. Núñez 2018, 120. Claude Doumet-Serhal pers. comm. 04/10/2018; see also the recently published volume on the temple, Doumet-Serhal 2021–2022.

133. In her 2014 article Sader (620) also proposes that there was a possible destruction at Beirut in the Late Bronze Age to Iron Age transition. However, no habitation levels from the end of the Late Bronze Age have been uncovered; Glacis II, which was excavated in Bey 03, 13, 20, and 32, was refurbished sometime between the second half of the thirteenth and the first half of the twelfth century BCE. Suffice it to say, no evidence of destruction of Glacis II has been found at Beirut dating to the end of the Late Bronze Age (Núñez 2018, 120).

120   CHAPTER THREE

Tel Michal

Tel Michal is located four kilometers south of Arsuf-Appolonia on the Mediterranean coast, and is another site attributed with a destruction event by Stern. Not only did Stern (2012, 506; 2013, 5) claim that Tel Michal was destroyed ca. 1200 BCE, in addition he claimed that the excavators of Tel Michal assumed the destruction was brought on by the Sea Peoples. However, much as at Achzib, Acco, Tell Abu Hawam, Tell Keisan, Shiqmona Tel Dor, 'Afula, and Tel Mevorakh, all of which were part of Stern's list of sites that were completely "destroyed," there is no evidence of destruction at Tel Michal, as the site had already been abandoned for one hundred years prior to 1200 BCE. As Herzog (1993b, 1037), clearly states, "The settlement remained unchanged in plan and continued to exist until its abandonment in *the fourteenth or early thirteenth century BCE*" (emphasis added). Moreover, in the excavation reports, there is no mentioned evidence that the LB IIA site suffered a destruction event either (Herzog 1989, 39–41; 2001, 28; Negbi 1989, 43–63). Tel Michal is thus another site that has been listed as destroyed with no evidence of destruction— even though there was not a settlement ca. 1200 BCE to destroy.

Tel Batash (Timnah)

Tel Batash is located in the lower Shephelah eight kilometers south of Gezer. Stratum VI has oftentimes been cited as destroyed at the end of the Late Bronze Age as recently as 2019.[134] However, there was no destruction ca. 1200 BCE at Tel Batash, a fact that has been apparent in the literature on the site for decades. George Kelm and Amihai Mazar stated as early as 1982 (14) that, "This stratum [VI] provides no signs of violent destruction." Moreover, in several subsequent publications, Mazar and Kelm (Mazar and Kelm 1993, 153; 1995, 67–72; Mazar 1997, 76; Mazar and Panitz-Cohen 2019, 103) clearly state that, "The debris of Phase VIA [the end of the Late Bronze Age] did not show any evidence of violent destruction." Or that, "Stratum VIA, and thus the Late Bronze phase, appears to end peacefully" (Kelm and Mazar 1995, 69). There was no destruction at Tel Batash ca. 1200 BCE, as the site was simply abandoned.[135] This apparent misattribution of destruction appears to have originated with a single passing comment in 1990 by Mazar (290) that the site suffered a destruction at the end of the Late Bronze Age. Nevertheless, the archaeological evidence is clear: the site was not destroyed ca. 1200 BCE.

---

134. Mazar 1990, 290; Dever 1992, 100; Dagan 2004, 2679; Yasur-Landau 2010, 216; Greenberg 2019, 322.

135. See also discussion in Millek 2017, 123. Additionally, there is no evidence of a destruction in the previous Phase VIB. As Mazar (1997, 75) states, "[There is] no indication of a violent destruction of this level, except at the southern end of Squares K-33–34, where a thin layer of reddish burnt debris was found." The thin layer of burnt debris in a corner is not evidence of a destruction event.

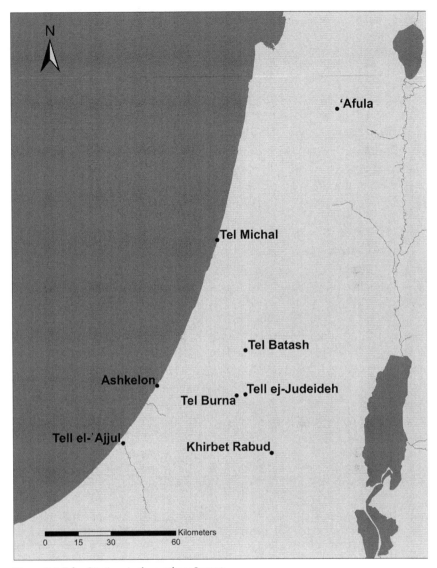

Figure 3.6. False Citations in the southern Levant.

Tell ej-Judeideh

Tell ej-Judeideh (also known as Tel Goded) is situated nearly ten kilometers southeast of Tell eṣ-Ṣafi/Gath and its "destruction" is one of several sites supposedly destroyed in the Shephelah mentioned by Faust in 2017 (23).[136] However, as Shimon Gibson (1994, 230) clearly notes, "There was a settlement

---

136. I have already demonstrated above that Tel Zayit, Tel Ḥarasim, and Tel Azekah were not destroyed ca. 1200 BCE.

122   CHAPTER THREE

gap at the site between EB III and Iron II."[137] Thus, much like 'Afula and Tel
Michal, there was no site to destroy ca. 1200 BCE and there was thus no end of
the Late Bronze Age destruction.

Tel Burna

Tel Burna, also roughly ten kilometers south of Tell eṣ-Ṣafi/Gath, is
another site listed by Faust (2017, 23) as destroyed at the end of the Late Bronze
Age. However much like Tell ej-Judeideh, this is another false citation, as no
evidence of an end of the Late Bronze Age destruction has been excavated,
and the nature of the end of the Late Bronze Age at the site remains unclear.[138]
However, for the time being there is no evidence that the site was destroyed
ca. 1200 BCE.[139]

Khirbet Rabud

The destruction of Khirbet Rabud, which is thirteen kilometers southwest
of Hebron, is another false destruction that can be attributed to Drews's
1993 (16) book. However, of the very little evidence of the Late Bronze Age
uncovered at the site, there is no evidence that Khirbet Rabud was destroyed
ca. 1200 BCE (Kochavi 1974; Kochavi, Greenberg, and Keinan 1975). The path
that brought Drews to the conclusion that Khirbet Rabud was destroyed is
convoluted at best. Drews drew his claim of destruction from a 1967 article by
Paul Lapp (285) which in turn was only a derivative reference of another work
by Albright (1963, 30) neither of which even mentioned Khirbet Rabud. Rather
Albright (1963, 30), and then subsequently Lapp (1967, 285), claimed that the
biblical town of Debir had been destroyed by the Israelites, a destruction that
he assumed was mentioned in the book of Joshua.[140] However, this supposed

---

137. It should be noted that this is the exact article that Faust sites as evidence for a ca. 1200
BCE destruction.

138. McKinny, Cassuto, and Shai 2015; Shai, McKinny, and Uziel 2015; Greenfield, McKinny, and
Shai 2017; McKinney, Tavger, and Shai 2019, 166.

139. In a recent article on the site, the excavators do claim in a footnote that there is "one sign
of possible destruction—the presence of human remains (a few bones) in the excavation area"
(McKinney, Tavger, and Shai 2019, 166 n. 26). However, much as some restorable pottery at Tell eṣ-
Ṣafi/Gath is not evidence of destruction, some human remains are not evidence of destruction. In
another more recent article, this possible destruction is omitted (McKinny et al. 2020, 7–9).

140. It should be noted, however, that Albright's assumption that Joshua and the Israelites destroyed Debir is in fact an overinterpretation of the text. Joshua 10: 38–39 states, "[38]Then Joshua
and all Israel with him returned to Debir, and they fought against it. [39]He captured it and its king
and all its cities, and they struck them with the edge of the sword, and utterly destroyed every
person who was in it. He left no survivor. Just as he had done to Hebron, so he did to Debir and its
king, as he had also done to Libnah and its king" (NASB). In the textual tradition there is never any
mention that Joshua destroyed Debir. He supposedly killed all of its inhabitants, but unlike Hazor,
Ai, and Jericho, which are explicitly listed as burned by the Israelites during the conquest, there is
no such statement made about Debir. Thus, Albright's assumption that Debir was destroyed by the
Israelites does not stand on textual ground even if one accepts the book of Joshua as having some
degree of historical truth to it.

destruction based on the biblical tradition had nothing to do with Khirbet Rabud, since Albright believed that Debir was Tell Beit Mirsim where he had excavated, and in fact, he rejected the identification of Khirbet Rabud with biblical Debir.[141] Thus, when Drews cited Lapp to make the claim that Khirbet Rabud had been destroyed ca. 1200 BCE, he misidentified the site that both Lapp and Albright were speaking of, as both meant Debir to be Tell Beit Mirsim. It appears that Drews was following the subsequent line of thinking after the excavation had taken place at Khirbet Rabud during the 1970s, which supported its identification with biblical Debir (Kochavi 1974; Kochavi, Greenberg, and Keinan 1975), though he did not reference any of the excavation reports on Khirbet Rabud. Thus, Drews created this false destruction by citing an article that referenced the purported destruction of a biblical site that the author did not even identify with Khirbet Rabud.

Ashkelon

The destruction of Ashkelon ca. 1200 BCE is one of the most widely cited end of the Late Bronze Age destruction events.[142] In 1923, W. J. Phythian-Adams (63–64; see also Schloen 2008, 156) reported that in his excavation, the Late Bronze Age material was clearly separated from the Iron Age Philistine material by a "thick line of ashes and black earth" though interestingly, at the time, Phythian-Adams (63–65) does not say that this was a direct result of a destruction.[143] Nevertheless, this black layer of earth and ashes was taken as evidence of destruction wrought either by Merenptah or the Sea Peoples (see Schloen 2008, 156). For those who cited this destruction prior to the 2008

---

141. Albright 1926; 1967, 207–9. Galling had suggested in 1954 that Khirbet Rabud be identified with biblical Debir.

142. Avi-Yonah and Eph'al 1975; Dever 1992, 100; Drews 1993, 9, 16 fig. 1; Stager 1993, 1995; Nur and Cline 2000, 44 fig. 1; Bell 2006, 137 map 1; Nur and Burgess 2008, 225 fig. 8.1; Kaniewski et al. 2011, 2 fig. 1; Cline 2014, 110–11 fig. 10; Kaniewski, Guiot, and Van Campo 2015, 2 fig. 1; Knapp and Manning 2016, 130. Ashkelon is another instance where Cline's map disagrees with his written statement. While the map clearly states that Ashkelon was destroyed ca. 1200 BCE, on p. 122 Cline writes that, "In Ashkelon, however, the transition appears to have been peaceful." However, much as with Drew's map, it is likely that given the power of the visual representation, Cline's map, which does indicate Ashkelon was destroyed ca. 1200 BCE, will continue to propagate the false destruction. This confusion can be seen in Knapp and Manning 2016, 130, which cites Cline's 2014 book, which appears to have caused the authors to claim that, "When we reach the southern Levant, however, there are a series of destruction levels in sites dated to the period ca. 1200 B.C.E.: for example, Tel Akko, Beth Shean, Megiddo, Lachish, Hazor, Ekron, Ashdod, *Ashkelon*" (emphasis added). They go on to state again, "Ashdod, Ekron (Tel Miqne), Gath (Tell eṣ-Ṣafi), and Ashkelon—were at least partially destroyed at the end of the Late Bronze Age *(more "peaceful" change at Ashkelon?)*" (2016, 131; emphasis added). In both instances Knapp and Manning cite Cline, and the contradiction between his map and statement appears to have caused some misunderstanding.

143. Phythian-Adams (1923, 65) summarizes the stratigraphy by saying, "[Stage] (V), ends only with the advent of the Philistines, and may be roughly dated from 1400 to 1190 B.C. (Late Bronze Age)."

124   CHAPTER THREE

publication of the renewed excavations at Ashkelon, the destruction could have been considered an assumed destruction, as there is insufficient evidence that Ashkelon was destroyed. However, in the 2008 final report Stager et al. make it clear that there was no destruction at Ashkelon, as no evidence of burning or general destruction debris were encountered in Grids 38 and 50 of the modern excavation. Rather, in Grid 38 they uncovered an Egyptian style fortress that had been abandoned before it was even completed, while in Grid 50 a courtyard building remained in use until the beginning of the twelfth century BCE, when it was apparently abandoned (Stager et al. 2008, 251, 256). As Stager et al. point out, the ash and blackened earth that Phythian-Adams excavated was likely localized patches of burnt debris and not a destruction at all, as no evidence of this destruction was encountered elsewhere even in Grid 50, which was near where Phythian-Adams had excavated his ash and black earth (Schloen 2008, 156; Stager et al. 2008, 306). Thus, for the more recent citations, the accusation that Ashkelon was destroyed ca. 1200 BCE is simply a false citation.

Tell el-'Ajjul

Tell el-'Ajjul is some seven kilometers southwest of Gaza city, and it is listed as destroyed on Bell's 2006 (137 map 1) map of destruction. However, much like Phaistos on the Kaniewski, Guiot, and Van Campo map, there is no explanation nor any rational why Bell listed Tell el-'Ajjul as destroyed, as there is no evidence of an occupation at the site ca. 1200 BCE to destroy (Tufnell and Kempinski 1993; Fischer and Sadeq 2000, 2008; Fischer at al. 2002). This is another inexplicable false citation of a destruction ca. 1200 BCE.

Conclusion: What Destruction?

This survey of the ninety-four false destruction events presents a radically different image of the end of the Late Bronze Age than is traditionally seen in the scholarly literature. Much as Michelson and Morley's experiment demonstrated the absence of the "aether," this review of destruction at the end of the Late Bronze Age too demonstrates that it was far less of a factor than previously believed. Certain regions such as the Cycladic Islands and the central Levant have no evidence of destruction ca. 1200 BCE, as 100 percent of the cited destructions are false.[144] In the northern Levant, of the twenty cited destruction events, fourteen are false representing a 70 percent error rate, a figure that is not any better for the southern Levant's sixty-three cited destruction events, as forty-two or 67 percent are false destructions. Other regions such as Crete and Cyprus were far less affected by destruction than the literature would

---

144. Despite the references to several destructions in the central Levant, it has been known for decades that there is at the moment no evidence of destruction in the entire region; see Bikai 1992; Bell 2006, 110, 137; 2009, 32; Charaf 2008; Núñez 2018.

lead one to believe, as out of the six possible destruction events on Crete, four were false destructions, and on Cyprus, of the thirteen destruction events, eight are false for a 66 percent and 63 percent error rate respectively. In both Anatolia and Greece, the figures are slightly "better." Greece has twenty-two cited destruction events and only ten or 45 percent are false destructions, while Anatolia has twenty-four cited destruction events and eleven or 46 percent are false destructions. Despite such claims that, "Within a period of forty to fifty years at the end of the thirteenth and the beginning of the twelfth century almost every significant city in the eastern Mediterranean world was destroyed, many of them never to be occupied again" (Drews 1993, 4), this was simply not the case. Drews (2020, 230) has recently stated that, "Although, there is little controversy about which cities were destroyed [ca. 1200 BCE], who did the sacking and burning is not yet agreed upon." This could not be further from the truth as there is clearly much controversy as to which sites were and were not destroyed ca. 1200 BCE. Moreover, this review demonstrates that destruction was not nearly as rampant as is oftentimes depicted ca. 1200 BCE. This is not to mention that of the destructions that did indeed occur at the end of the Late Bronze Age, most were minor events, a subject that will be taken up in the chapters to follow.

These ninety-four false destruction events representing in total a 61 percent error rate, reflects the egregious oversights that plague the current scholarship on the end of the Late Bronze Age in the Eastern Mediterranean. At any given moment, no matter the seniority of the scholar, the prestige of the journal or publishing house, whether or not the article or book was peer reviewed, or any other factor, there is a strong likelihood that 50 percent or more of the cited destructions mentioned for the end of the Late Bronze Age are false destructions. Now, some could claim that this figure is inflated, as I have included false destruction events that appear once in the literature, and that this has in some way overstated the percentage of false destructions.[145] However, this is not the case, as across the board, on average, the rate of false citations is generally more than 50 percent. This point is unmistakable is one examines several major works on the end of the Late Bronze Age where indeed the error rate does come out to 50 percent or more. In Drews 1993, of the more than fifty sites depicted on his map of the catastrophe and discussed in the chapter on destruction, thirty-one or 52 percent are false destructions.[146] Given that Nur and Cline 2000 and Nur and Burgess 2008 are roughly a copy of Drews, their error rates also come out to more than 50 percent. For Cline

---

145. In the following chapters I will also include destructions that only appear once in the literature as a counterbalance to this.

146. This figure grows worse with the recent addition of several other false destructions in Drews 2020 discussed above.

2014, of the more than fifty sites that he maps and discusses as destroyed ca. 1200 BCE, thirty-two or 53 percent are false destructions.[147] The overlap with Drews is not complete, as Cline omits certain destructions that Drews discussed and added others that Drews had omitted or from sites that had not been excavated prior to 1993. Thus, even though the percentage of false destructions are virtually the same between the two books, they are not a copy of one another. Knapp and Manning (2016) list nearly fifty destruction events, and of these twenty-six or 51 percent are false destructions. Kaniewski, Guiot, and Van Campo (2015) have one of the worst error rates, as of the twenty-three sites they map as destroyed by the Sea Peoples, fourteen or 61 percent are false destructions. These errors have become so ingrained in the zeitgeist that it is almost impossible to escape them, as in many cases the research already existed that demonstrated that some of the destructions were false, and yet, they have persisted in the literature as factual destruction events that struck the Eastern Mediterranean ca. 1200 BCE (e.g., Acco and Ashkelon).

The obvious question that arises from this overview is, exactly how did we get into this situation in the first place, where 61 percent of end of the Late Bronze Age destruction never occurred or at least not ca. 1200 BCE? There are of course some especially bad actors at play who helped to exaggerate the problem to the extent that it currently exists, with Drews and his 1993 book standing at the front of the line. However, as with any complex problem, there is no single answer, and I cannot pretend to know the exact reasons behind all of these errors and why certain scholars made the statements or maps that they did. Nevertheless, I can offer some observations of some of the problems that led us to this point.

To begin, as discussed in chapter 2, there is the persistent problem that for decades there has been no theoretical or methodological approach to interpreting destruction events in the archaeological record, and that even though in the past fifteen years there has been some progress, most researchers still approach destruction from the traditional point of view. That is, anything, everything, and nothing can be evidence of destruction, whether that is some pottery on a floor at Tell eṣ-Ṣafi/Gath as evidence of a possible violent destruction, one piece of melted silver from Hala Sultan Tekke, some ash in some loci at Tell Tweini, a pit filled with burnt debris from Iria, some destruction debris in part of one room from Khania, or even the complete lack of any signs of destruction from Qubur el-Walaydah. Each of these cases represent an instance where if there had been a strict and accepted definition of what constitutes a destruction, they may not have been cited as destroyed

---

147. This also factors in sites such as Nichoria and Ashkelon, which Cline presents as destroyed ca. 1200 BCE on his map of destruction but which he states in writing were not destroyed, as there remains a false reference to the destruction of both sites.

in the first place. The lack of a theory and methodology for the archaeology of destruction means that any and all can have their own standard for what constitutes a destruction. While some archaeologists would not consider the meagre evidence from many of these sites as evidence of a destruction, others do and will report scanty evidence as the remains of a massive conflagration. This problem is again compounded by the fact that there is also a general lack of a vocabulary for describing destruction events, and because of this, the inadequate evidence of destruction is simply summarized as "X site was violently destroyed." If a stricter definition of what constitutes a destruction can be widely adopted, such as the one presented here, along with clearer terminology and descriptions of the "destruction," this would help to alleviate some of these false destruction events appearing in the future.

The second issue is a compound set of problems involving the overcitation of secondary sources rather than seeking out the original excavation reports with a definition for destruction in hand. Certain standard works listing the known destruction events ca. 1200 BCE have been repeatedly cited rather than investigating the actual excavation reports, be that the final publication or preliminary results in the absence of final publication of the excavations. For the Aegean this largely involves the overcitation of Simpson and Dickinson 1979 and more recently Cynthia Shelmerdine 2001, who based her list of destruction on the former and Guy Middleton 2010, who based his list on Shelmerdine. In Anatolia, the go-to reference is Bittel 1983. For Cyprus and the Levant, Karageorghis 1992 and Caubet 1992 are commonly referenced, though in general the common reference point is Drews 1993, who too cited largely secondary literature that was decades old in 1993 rather than seeking out the original excavation reports (see again discussion in ch. 1).

Any errors that were made or overestimations of the amount of destruction in the secondary citations have carried over into further literature. Orchomenos is the perfect example of this. Knapp and Manning 2016 cite Shelmerdine 2001, Deger-Jalkotzy 2008, Middleton 2010, and Cline 2014, even though the latter three were further permutations of Shelmerdine 2001, who had cited Simpson and Dickinson 1979, who never said that Orchomenos was destroyed in the first place. Thus, the overuse of secondary and tertiary sources that have been blindly cited for decades has perpetuated many false destruction events, some of which have been in the scholarly literature for more than half a century.

A corollary to this same issue is that often subsequent excavations, reevaluations of stratigraphy, the ceramics, or C14 samples have changed the picture of when or if a destruction took place ca. 1200 BCE. However, again, a common secondary citation, such as Drews 1993, is referenced rather than searching out newer results and interpretations. For example, Knapp and Manning state that Beycesultan was destroyed ca. 1200 BCE, even though

128   Chapter Three

results from the renewed excavations had appeared several years prior to their
2016 article, results that unambiguously demonstrated that the destruction was
several hundred years older than originally assumed. The same can be said for
Tille Höyük and Lidar Höyük, both of which still appear as destroyed in Cline
2014, as he based his map on Drews's 1993 map of destruction. To Drews's
credit, in 1993, a ca. 1200 BCE destruction for both sites was based on the
current interpretation of the evidence at the time.[148] But both sites had their
chronology revised during the 2000s, and the literature was available to allow
for correcting the dates for these destructions in the subsequent literature.

     Another issue is how time is approached for the end of the Late Bronze
Age, which (as discussed in ch. 1) has been extended well beyond any sort of
meaningful parameters. This can be explicit, such as in Finkelstein's (2016, 113,
115) statement that "The wave of destructions in the Levant at the end of the
Late Bronze Age commenced in the middle or second half of the thirteenth
century [with the destruction of Hazor] and continued until about 1100 B.C.
[with the destruction of Megiddo]."[149] Or it can be implicit, such as Drews's,
Cline's, or Kaniewski, Guiot, and Van Campo maps of destruction that place
all of the destruction events at ca. 1200 BCE stretching "ca." to unreasonable
proportions, as Hazor's destruction event was fifty years prior to 1200 BCE
and Lefkandi's was likely more than fifty years after it. This is again all an
example of Puglisi's "Atlantis premise," where temporally displaced events
are artificially constricted together into one cataclysmic event; ergo, what
happened to mythical Atlantis (Puglisi 2013, 178). Destruction occurring over
the course of 150 years can hardly be called a wave or horizon. Moreover, there
is the implied notion that there were no major destructions before 1250 BCE
or after 1100 BCE, which is demonstrably inaccurate (see Garfinkel 2017, 156;
Kreimerman 2017, 184–87; Millek 2018b, 254). Even confining the "end of the
Late Bronze Age" to 1225–1175 BCE is not without its own problems, as fifty
years is a long time on a human scale.

     In many of these cases, the origin of the false destruction can be pieced
together by following the chain of citations. However, for some false
destructions it is entirely unclear how these sites came to be cited as destroyed
ca. 1200 BCE. This is true for Kaniewski, Guiot, and Van Campo (2015), who

---

148. This is similar for myself as well, as previously I have cited sites such as Tell Keisan or Tel
Dan as having an end of the Late Bronze Age destruction, which was accurate at the time based on
the then-published or known dates for the destructions (Millek 2017, 2018b). However more recent
research has demonstrated the original dates ca. 1200 BCE were inaccurate, as both occurred later
in the twelfth century BCE and the dates have been corrected here. That said, this correction takes
the necessary next step of checking for newer references for sites that I researched only a couple
of years prior to the preparation of this book.

149. Finkelstein (2016) in note 17 cites Hazor as the beginning of this wave of destruction and
in note 18 sites Megiddo as the end of the wave; see also Langgut, Finkelstein, and Litt 2013, 150.

state that Phaistos and Byblos were destroyed without offering any references to back this claim, nor are there any reference that make these claims. There is Bell's 2006 claim that Tell el-ʿAjjul was destroyed, when it has been clear for nearly a century of research and excavation that no settlement has been found dating to the end of the Late Bronze Age. Stern's claim that Tel Michal was destroyed ca. 1200 BCE, along with the assertion that the excavators stated that Tel Michal was destroyed by the Sea Peoples, is an enigma. In all of the reports on the site, the excavators make it patently clear that the site was abandoned one hundred years prior to 1200 BCE. In cases such as these, only a corrective work can hopefully weed out these false destruction events, however, as Acco exemplifies, even when a destruction is refuted, this may not stop the continued citation of that false destruction. Hopefully works such as this and others will enable future researchers to take a closer look at supposed destruction events, whether that is ca. 1200 BCE or in another time in the ancient past, as it seems highly unlikely to this author that only the end of the Late Bronze Age is plagued by false destruction events.

CHAPTER FOUR

Destruction in Mycenean Greece and the Wider Aegean

Destruction and the Fall of the Palatial System

The theories on the causes for the breakdown and abandonment of the palatial system in Mycenean Greece are too numerous to mention here. These theories call on a wide range of natural and manmade disasters to explain the collapse, including but not limited to bubonic plague, earthquakes, system collapse, environmental degradation, economic overspecialization, the breakup of trade, and even explosions caused by combustible flour.[1] However, as with all theories that purport to explain the end of the Late Bronze Age, destruction is a crucial factor, particularly the destruction of monumental structures and the palaces.[2] Certain explanations for these destructions have largely been abandoned, such as the Dorian invasion, which has not received any scholarly support for decades.[3]

Currently, the main candidates for the destruction of the palaces largely fall into one of three categories: "foreign attack, internal strife, or natural disaster" (Shelmerdine 1997, 582). For the natural disasters, this essentially means earthquakes, a theory that was championed by Klaus Kilian (1983, 1988, 1996) until his death, but has been further advocated for by Amos Nur (Nur and Cline 2000; Nur and Burgess 2008); Paul Åström and Katie Demakopoulou (Åström and Demakopoulou 1996; Demakopoulou 1995, 2003, 2007, 2015); Jacques Vanschoonwinkel (2002); and for a time Joseph Maran (2008, 2009, 2010, 2015), though his opinion has recently changed to the contrary (Hinzen et al. 2018; see the discussion of Tiryns below); as well as various excavators

---

1. For discussion of these theories and the inherent problems in them see, Dickinson 2010; Middleton 2010, 31–53; 2020a. For combustible flour, see Van Leuven 1979; this particular theory seems to have gone largely unnoticed, as it was missed in the general discussions on the end of the Late Bronze Age in Greece.

2. See, e.g., Ålin 1962; Barnett 1975, 370; Desborough 1975, 659; Betancourt 1976; Hooker 1976, 148–80; Kilian 1988; Shelmerdine 2001, 373; Deger-Jalkotzy 2008; Dickinson 2010; Jung 2010, 2016; Maran 2010; Middleton 2010, 14–15; Hinzen et al. 2018 and references therein.

3. The Dorian invasion was the common explanation during the beginning of the archaeological exploration into Mycenean Greece; see, e.g., Schliemann 1880, 343–44; Tsountas and Manatt, 1897, 341; Hall 1901, 41–43; Casson 1921; 1922, 13–15; Daniel, Broneer, and Wade-Gery 1948. For the decline of the Dorian invasion theory, see Hooker 1976, 171–75. See also Vermeule (1960, 66) who sixteen years prior had already noted that the Dorian invasion was questionable, though six years later Blegen (1966, 419–23) still utilized the Dorian invasion as an explanatory mechanism for the end of the palatial system, as did Stubbings (1975, 354) nine years after Blegen.

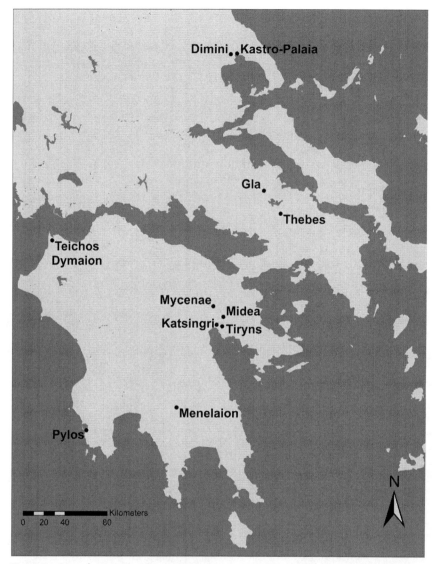

Figure 4.1. Map of sites with a destruction event ca. 1200 BCE on mainland Greece (Kastanas not pictured).

at Mycenae.[4] Yet, often humans still loom large as the agents of destruction for the palaces of Mycenean Greece. Destructive agents from outside of Greece are present in certain theories (largely Drews 1993), while intersite warfare within Greece is preferred by others, while still others claim that uprisings by the

---

4. Iakovidis 1986, 2013; French and Iakovidis 2003; French 2010; http://mycenae-excavations.org/citadel.html.

DESTRUCTION IN GREECE AND THE WIDER AEGEAN WORLD 133

lower-class brought on the destruction.[5] In all, either anthropogenic destruction or destruction by earthquakes are the main contenders for the end of—and destruction of—the palaces in Mycenean Greece. But before even getting into the scale of the destructions and the possible causes, we must remember that already there is less destruction than commonly reported, as 43 percent of all cited destructions on Greece and 66 percent for Crete never occurred, including the "destruction" of "palaces" such as Orchomenos and Mycenean Athens. Thus, prior to examining the archeological evidence from the destructions that did occur, it is apparent that destruction was not as rampant as is commonly assumed. Nevertheless, as I will demonstrate below, even for those sites that did suffer a destruction event ca. 1200 BCE (fig. 4.1), not all palatial destructions were equal in their extent, severity, or in the situation leading up to the destruction. With that reminder, we begin the investigation into the causes and extent of destruction in the far north at Kastanas in Macedonia, moving south from there all the way through to the two destructions on Crete ca. 1200 BCE.

Greece

Kastanas — Scale: Multibuilding — Cause: Unknown

Kastanas is located on the left bank of the Axios River in central Macedonia. A destruction ca. 1200 BCE was originally attributed to an earthquake, based on the assumption that Layer 16 dated to the end of the LH IIIB2, an assumption later brought up by Amos Nur and Eric Cline (Hänsel 1979, 1989 Kilian 1983; Nur and Cline 2000, 56). However, as Reinhard Jung (2002, 2003) pointed out in his reassessment of the pottery, and thus the site's chronology, it was in fact Layer 15 that dated to the end of the LH IIIB not Layer 16 as initially thought. Nevertheless, at the end of Layer 15, there too was a destruction event, as Kastanas appears to have been prone to destruction. Both Bernhard Hänsel (1989, 328–43) and Jung (2003, 131; 2012a, 3705) have pointed out that nearly every layer or phase ended with some amount of destruction.

Layer 15 at Kastanas suffered a multibuilding destruction, as action by fire was uncovered in two of the structures, though evidence of destruction was absent in others (already noted by Hänsel 1989, 109, 118, 332–33). Most of the buildings from Layer 15 were deeply affected by the reconstruction activities in the following Layer 14, making it impossible to determine whether or not certain buildings, such as the Ellipsenhaus, were destroyed in a destruction event or simply by the reoccupation in Layer 14. Some ash had been uncovered in the building, but as Hänsel noted, the leveling activities in the following

---

5. See Shelmerdine 1997, 582–85 for the various refences and theories on cause of the destruction; see also Deger-Jalkotzy 2008; Dickinson 2010; Jung 2010; Middleton 2010. For the uprising of the lower class see Jung 2016.

134 CHAPTER FOUR

phase was so thorough that there was no clear evidence of destruction rather than demolition and remodeling, nor any way of knowing where the ash had originated. Other structures, such as the Kantenhaus and the Profilhaus, as well as the open space and street, had no evidence of destruction by fire (Hänsel 1989, 109, 113). Only the Trapezhaus and the Antenbau appear to have been destroyed. The Trapezhaus was filled with scattered rubble, marks of burning, and refuse, while the Antenbau was filled with a layer of burnt rubble that had been leveled for the construction activities in Layer 14 (Hänsel 1989, 112, 117). As Hänsel (109) noted, the fire appears only to have affected two of the buildings in the eastern sector of the site, and it appears then that the fire was contained. There is no evidence of warfare, nor is there typical earthquake damage or any apparent targeted destruction. The remains are so fragmented that it is impossible to say what caused the destruction beyond making an assumption. Given that Kastanas suffered frequent destruction events by fire, and that life continued on after Layer 15 along the same developmental path (Hänsel 1989, 332–33), the destruction was likely accidental, or the result of a natural fire. This, however, is simply a guess and the cause of the destruction remains unknown.

Dimini — Scale: Single-Building — Cause: Arson/Termination Ritual

Dimini is situated on an inlet of the Pagasetic Gulf, in Thessaly. Reports on the extent of the destruction at Dimini vary and there are some claims that the site as a whole was destroyed.[6] However, it has generally been argued that only the two Megara, Megaron A and B, were destroyed at the close of the LH IIIB2 or the end of the thirteenth century BCE (Adrimi-Sismani 2004; 2006, 465).

---

6. Adrimi-Sismani 1994a, 1994b, 2004, 2006, 2007a, 2011, 2013. The reports on the destruction of the houses at Dimini outside of Megaron A and B are mixed. In one initial publication, Adrimi-Sismani (1994a, 36) claims that the houses were destroyed by an earthquake, though no evidence of said destruction was presented. However, in two publications from the early 2000s Adrimi-Sismani (2003, 73; 2004, 7) states that no evidence of destruction was uncovered in these dwellings at the time of the destruction found in Megaron B. Yet again, in later publications she (2011, 313) claims that destruction affected the site as a whole, which she describes as an extensive destruction. In the final publication she (2013, 84–125) reports that Houses A, K, Z, and the North House all were destroyed at the end of the LH IIIB2. Nevertheless, for Houses A and K, no destruction debris is ever described, nor is any evidence of burning visible in the photographs, and the early publications of these buildings too do not describe any evidence of destruction (Adrimi-Sismani 1994a; 1994b; 2013, 104). For Building Z, traces of fire were only uncovered in one room, Room 3, and thus the building was not destroyed according to the criteria set out above (Adrimi-Sismani 2013, 109, 111). The description of the North House is the only other possible evidence of destruction in the domestic dwellings; however, based on the description of the house, it is unclear if it was destroyed or not (Adrimi-Sismani 2013, 116–17). Nevertheless, the East and South Houses both show no signs of having been destroyed (Adrimi-Sismani 2013, 120–22). Thus, based on the general lack of evidence, it does not appear that the domestic dwellings were destroyed at the end of the LH IIIB2. Galanakis (2013b) claims the site as a whole was destroyed.

DESTRUCTION IN GREECE AND THE WIDER AEGEAN WORLD   135

However, the evidence clearly indicates that this destruction was targeted, as only Megaron B was burned.

Megaron A has been cited repeatedly as destroyed, though, importantly, without any evidence of fire (Adrimi-Sismani 2004, 2006, 2007a, 2007b, 2011, 2013). Yet, there is no physical evidence that would indicate that the building was destroyed at all. The assumed destruction of Megaron A was based on the idea that fallen plaster uncovered on some floors of the building was evidence of a destruction event. Most rooms of the building were without any fallen plaster and it was assumed that the plaster had been cleaned up by the residents of Dimini at the beginning of the LH IIIC. No evidence of burning or wall collapse was witnessed in the structure (Adrimi-Sismani 2004, 13–33), and given this, the small amount of fallen plaster on some of the floors does not equate to a destruction event, despite the fact that the building is often cited as destroyed.[7] Thus, rather than having been destroyed, it is likely that Megaron A was temporarily abandoned, which led to some disintegration of the wall plaster, and was briefly reused at the beginning of the LH IIIC only finally to be abandoned without destruction.

On the other hand, Megaron B was indeed destroyed, though the exact extent of this destruction is unclear. It has been reported that burning was seen throughout all of Megaron B and that every room was covered by a thick layer of destruction, while in Rooms 4 and 5 debris covered over a number of crushed vessels, some of which had traces of burning (Adrimi-Sismani 2004, 38–51; 2016, 55–56). All vessels from beneath this destruction debris clearly date the final phase of the structure to the end of the LH IIIB2, and after this the building was abandoned and not built over or reused by the following LH IIIC inhabitants (Adrimi-Sismani 2007a, 166). What then might have caused the destruction of Megaron B? The answer may lie in the use of the structure and the pattern of destruction and reuse in the LH IIIC.

A natural disaster such as an earthquake does not appear to be a likely cause, as there is no direct evidence of such based on typical earthquake damage, nor does it appear that the site as a whole suffered any damage in this event outside of Megaron B.[8] An earthquake, accidental fire, or natural fire would not be so selective to only destroy the most well-built structure at the site. The likely culprit behind this destruction were humans. The question is then, what

---

7. Oddly, in one recent article, Adrimi-Sismani (2016, 48) claims that Megaron A was destroyed by fire, completely contradicting herself and the evidence she had published, without providing any new evidence suggesting that the building had been burned. This situation seems to be akin to Adrimi-Sismani's false claim that Pefkakia was destroyed by fire at the same time, as there has been a gradual increase in the amount, severity, and type of destruction over time and through subsequent publications, even though the evidence has remained the same.

8. Adrimi-Sismani (2020, 25) has also recently stated that she does not believe that Dimini was destroyed by an earthquake.

group of humans might have done the destroying. For a possible answer, we must look at part of the function of Megaron B. In Megaron B, at the center of Room 1 directly in front of the main entrance to the structure, a large H-shaped altar was discovered (Adrimi-Sismani 2006, 473). The room was devoid of most artifacts, and it appears that it was cleared out before the building was burnt, and indeed it appears as if most objects of value were removed from the building as a whole prior to the fire. This indicates that the building did not simply catch on fire, as some group removed those objects before it was put to the torch (Adrimi-Sismani 2004, 41; 2020, 25). Likewise, in Room 3, four large storage vessels were also removed prior to the destruction of the building, which likely rules out an accidental fire, as one cannot anticipate an accidental fire in advance, giving enough time to remove large pithoi or most objects of value.

This destruction was premeditated, and since it appears that Megaron B acted as a sacred space and given that this was the only building that was burned at the end of the LH IIIB2, this destruction was likely a termination ritual. This is further highlighted by the fact that in the following LH IIIC habitation, while part of Megaron A was reused as a domestic structure along with other sections of the site, Megaron B was left alone (Adrimi-Sismani 2007a, 166). It appears that the ground where Megaron B once stood remained sacred after it was destroyed and was avoided to maintain the space's sacred past. The question then remains what group of people burned Megaron B?

Some possible evidence points to the possibility that the site was attacked, as one arrowhead was uncovered in Building Z and two others were found in the North House; however, this is not conclusive proof of an act of war (Adrimi-Sismani 2013, 312). It is my opinion that Megaron B was ritually terminated by the inhabitants of Dimini before the site was largely abandoned at the end of the LH IIIB2 and before the brief reuse of the site in the early LH IIIC. This would help to explain why all of the sacred objects were removed beforehand and the fact that the building appears to have remained sacred even after it was destroyed. If the site was attacked, then all of the public buildings likely would have been destroyed, including Megaron A. However, as Megaron A was not destroyed or desecrated, this leads me to the conclusion that this was a sacred termination ritual performed by the inhabitants prior to abandoning the site.

Moreover, there is no indication that the altar was smashed or desecrated in anyway prior to the burning of Megaron B, which might have been the case if attackers were seeking to sully the building. But this is an assumption and there is no definitive proof that Megaron B was destroyed in a sacred termination ritual rather than being torched in an act of arson or a desecratory termination ritual. However, that aside, what is clear is that far less of Dinimi was actually destroyed ca. 1200 BCE than has been commonly reported, as it is only a single-building destruction.

DESTRUCTION IN GREECE AND THE WIDER AEGEAN WORLD 137

Kastro-Palaia in Volos — Scale: Single-Building — Cause: Unknown

Not far from Dimini, Kastro-Palaia, located in the modern city of Volos, suffered a single-building destruction event by fire ca. 1200 BCE. In the general literature, it is assumed that the site as a whole was destroyed (Adrimi-Sismani 2007a, 168; 2007b, 29; 2011, 317; 2020, 23; Galanakis 2013c), however, as the original excavator Demtrios Theochares (1961, 46) already noted in 1961, the end of the Late Bronze Age destruction was limited to the monumental structure excavated in Trench III and no evidence of destruction was uncovered in the settlement at large.[9] This monumental structure was excavated in the 1950s and it consisted of seven rooms along with a courtyard, though unfortunately this is all that we know of the building, as much of it is still covered by more modern architecture.[10] Theochares (1956, 48; 1958, 18) assumed that the forty-meter-long building was a palace based on its size, the remnants of painted plaster, as well as hundreds of kylikes uncovered in the destruction; however, the exact function of the building is not known. As no more of the building could be uncovered after the initial excavation in 1956 or in the current work at the site owing to modern structures covering the remainder of the building (Skafida et al. 2015, 56–58) it is unlikely at this time that we will know the exact function of the monumental building from Kastro-Palaia and if it was indeed a palace or if it had a religious function like Megaron B from Dimini.

Much as for the function of the building itself, there is little tangible published evidence for the destruction. While it is clear that the building was destroyed in a fire, as ash, burnt rubble, and charred beams filled the structure, there is currently no highly detailed description of what was and was not found in the building other than hundreds of aforementioned kylikes.[11] Presumably, if there had been any gold, silver, or other precious objects in the destruction debris, Theochares would have mentioned it, and the absence of any mention of precious materials might indicate that the building was at least partially emptied. This would correlate with nearby Dimini, where the main public building was mostly emptied prior to destruction by termination ritual or arson. Given the lack of destruction elsewhere in the site, and the possible

---

9. See also Daux 1962, 792. This was confirmed in the "Stratigraphic Section," where Theochares uncovered a number of houses dating to the Mycenean period. While some ash was uncovered in the excavation it was clear that there was no actual evidence of destruction, indicating the targeted nature of the destruction. As Karouzou (2018, 34) has also recently pointed out, the ashes were most likely the product of household hearths rather than destruction.

10. Theochares 1956, 1957, 1958, 1960, 1961; Daux 1960, 1962; Skafida, Karnava, and Olivier 2012; Skafida et al. 2015; Karouzou 2018, 28. Skafida, Karnava, and Olivier among others are still working on analyzing the original notes and materials from Theochares's excavations and will publish them in the future (Artemis Karnava pers. comm. 02/11/2020).

11. Theochares 1956, 48; 1957, 593; 1958, 18; 1960, 50. See Skafida et al. 2020, 58–59 for a brief recent discussion of these vessels and the other pottery found in Theochares's excavation.

138   CHAPTER FOUR

emptying of the building of valuable objects, arson may have been the cause for
the destruction at Kastro-Palaia. However, this is again purely an assumption,
and until more evidence from the site is published, the cause of the destruction
must remain unknown, though it is clear that this was only a single-building
destruction.

Gla — Scale: Multibuilding — Cause: Arson

The Mycenean citadel of Gla (also spelled Glas; fig. 4.2) sits on a pear-shaped
island in the now-drained Kopias Basin in Boeotia. The site was surrounded by
a cyclopean fortification wall that had four gates leading into the settlement at
various points along its length. While it was originally believed that outside
of the central enclosure, but within the cyclopean fortification wall, the site
was devoid of habitation (Iakovidis 1989, 1992, 1998, 2001), recent surveys
and excavations have demonstrated that the site was filled with structures,
"including several large, well-built complexes, extensive residential quarters
and clusters of buildings stretching between these complexes, circular
structures (silos?), a cistern, sally ports, staircases, retaining walls and terraces"
(Maggidis 2020, 115). That said, both Spyros Iakovidis (1992, 615; 1998, 271, 278)
and Christofilis Maggidis (2020, 116) have stated that the Gla was violently and
completely destroyed by fire close to 1200 BCE when the LH IIIB2 pottery was
already common. After this destruction event, the site was abandoned never
to be reoccupied, and at the same time the drainage works that had created
the dry land surrounding Gla fell into ruin, filling the basin with water until
modern times. However, the destruction and abandonment of Gla is a much
more complicated tale than what is commonly presented.

To begin with, the majority of the excavated buildings at Gla were not
destroyed prior to the site's abandonment. Within the two building complexes
in the south of the central enclosure, only two structures were damaged prior to
abandonment. In the west complex, Building B's Rooms 1 and 2 were discovered
with their pillar bases burnt at times to the point that they had cracked in the
fire. However, no other rooms within Building B had any evidence of damage
or action by fire (Iakovidis 1989, 302). Moreover, no evidence of any sort of fire
or destruction was seen in Buildings A, E, and Wing Z (Iakovidis 1989, 301–6).
A similar story is true for the east building complex. Here only Building H
was destroyed. It was filled with fire-hardened mud-brick fragments, calcined
stones in the walls especially near the doorways, traces of burnt wood on
the thresholds, and ashy layers on the floors. Room H1 was found filled with
some five thousand pieces of broken pottery along with fourteen piles of
carbonized wheat that were likely stored in sacks, which indicates that the
room was used for storage or acted as a granary (Iakovidis 1998, 228–29). In

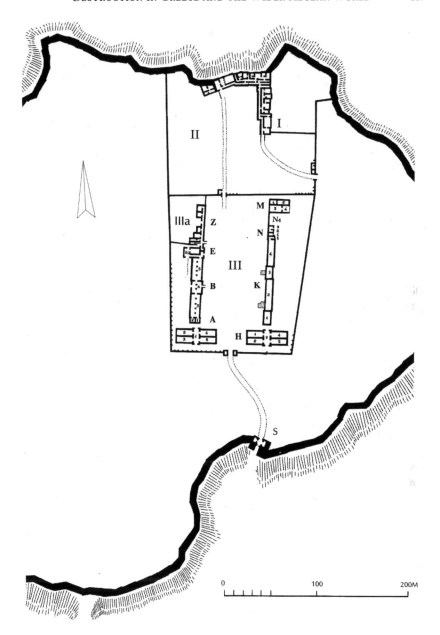

Figure 4.2. Plan of the central enclosure at Gla. Iakovidis 2001, 23 fig. 7. Courtesy of the Library of the Archaeological Society at Athens.

Corridor H3 one piece of pottery was burnt to the point of vitrification (230). Nevertheless, much like in the west building complex, no other buildings in this complex were destroyed. Buildings K, N, and M were all devoid of any

140   CHAPTER FOUR

signs of destruction and they appear to have simply decayed after having been abandoned (Iakovidis 1998, 234–42). In the recent survey and excavation work outside of the central enclosure headed by Maggidis (2020, 114–15), from the preliminary reports there is no mentioned evidence of any destruction by fire in any of the structures and complexes outside of the central enclosure.

The focus of destruction at Gla appears to have been on the four gates and the main residential building, the Melathron (fig. 4.3). Traces of fire, burning, and ash covered by unburnt stones were discovered on the floor of the guard room in the West Gate. The North Gate's floor was covered with burnt mud bricks and blackened pot sherds, all covered by the collapsed and dissolved mud-brick superstructure. In the Southeast Double Gate, both entrances were filled with dissolved mud brick and fallen stones, while traces of fire overlaid a layer of ashes and blackened earth. Burning was also discovered in the west and east bastions, as well as in the central tower. The South Gate too was destroyed, as the entrance to the outer court had its steps covered in calcined stones, bricks hardened by fire, burnt wood, and white ash (Iakovidis 1989, 280–84).

In the Melathron, evidence of destruction too was uncovered; however, exactly how extensive this destruction was is unclear. The structure was originally excavated by André de Ridder in the late nineteenth century. In his excavation, he explored the majority of the building, leaving little behind for future archaeologist (Iakovidis 1989, 288). De Ridder (1894, 285, 304, 307) states that he discovered fire-stained walls in all parts of the building; however, this could not be verified by more recent investigation, and damage by fire was only confirmed on the threshold blocks of the doors between Rooms 2 and 3, N1 and N2, P1 and P2, P2 and P3, P2 and 20, 21 and 22, and on the floors of Corridors I, N, and 14 (Iakovidis 1989, 300). However, while it may be the case that the building was at least partially burnt, the fire does not appear to have affected every part of the structure or at least not to a significant degree. A number of lead strips were found throughout the Melathron, some of which were still attached to walls, and many retained their original shape (Iakovidis 1989, 297). Given that lead has a relatively low melting point of 327.5 degrees Celsius the fire in general does not appear to have had enough fuel to reach very high temperatures.[12]

What is clear from the destruction of Gla is that the site as a whole was not destroyed. Indeed, the destruction appears to have been focused on the defensive structures, the storage facility in Building H, and the Melathron.

---

12. For comparisons sake, vitrification occurs at temperatures above 900 degrees Celsius, nearly three times the melting point of lead (Stevanović 1997, 366). Thus, the fire that affected Building H reached these high temperatures at least in corridor H3, testifying to the intensity of the fire in part of Building H building, which was likely fed by the structure's contents, such as the grain that was stored in the building and the constriction of the fire in the hallway, which would have produced higher temperatures than in a more open space.

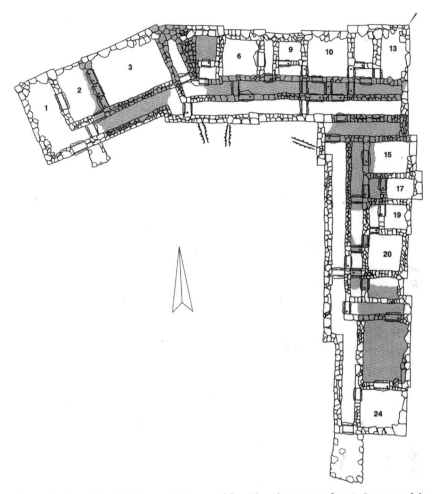

Figure 4.3. Plan of the Melathron with traces of fire. Iakovidis 2001, 41 fig. 15. Courtesy of the Library of the Archaeological Society at Athens.

However, the destruction was not nearly as extensive as is typically depicted, nor was it as intense. The question then remains, What caused this destruction? Natural or accidental causes are unlikely, as natural disasters and accidental fires are not so selective as to only affect defensive and administrative structures while leaving the more poorly built structures alone. Moreover, much of Gla was built on an artificial terrace of stone fill (Iakovidis 1992, 607–10), which would have made the buildings more susceptible to an earthquake, given the lack of a sure footing for the foundations. Yet, there is no apparent shifting of the buildings, nor any other damage that could be earthquake related, contrary to the claims of Nur and Cline (2000, 56).

142 CHAPTER FOUR

Much as Iakovidis originally argued, the destroyer appears to be man; however, much as at Dimini, the question remains, Who did it? To answer this, we must look at what was not found in the excavations at Gla. These are: gold, silver, and precious stones. In none of the three published excavations carried out at Gla have any gold or silver artifacts been uncovered, and only one object made from a precious stone was found.[13] This is a conspicuous absence and it is not merely the affect of simple looting, as even when a building appears to be looted at least some precious objects are left behind—as will be seen in the destruction of Pylos. Moreover, this does not appear to be a collection error by de Ridder, for although one can fault excavations at the end of the nineteenth century for many shortcomings, not reporting gold and silver finds is not one of them, and none of the modern excavations has uncovered any gold or silver either. Another interesting find in the Melathron, or rather the lack thereof, is that de Ridder only uncovered some thirty pieces of pottery in the whole of the structure (Iakovidis 1989, 309). Likewise, neither did Threpsiades, in his reinvestigation of the building, uncover much pottery, though no exact records of how many sherds were found exist (295). Much like gold, silver, and precious stones, no weapons of war were unearthed in any of the excavations at Gla (Iakovidis 1989, 315–18; 1998, 261–62).

All of this evidence points to Gla having been systematically emptied of items with great value prior to its being abandoned, and this is particularly true of the Melathron, which appears to have been almost completely emptied even of pottery. After this, only selected structures were burnt, and the site was abandoned, never to be reoccupied. Given this, it appears to me that the likely answer to who destroyed Gla is the residents of Gla themselves. The emptying of the structures took time: if it was carried by a hostile force, the site was already abandoned and there would have been no combatants left in or near the site to slow their progress. Moreover, it is unlikely that looters would take seemingly worthless pottery out of the Melathron. Rather, it appears that the site was a planned abandonment and with this abandonment came the purposeful destruction of the defensive and administrative structures, leaving the fortified settlement unusable or at least without a great deal of effort. Thus, Gla was not destroyed wholesale, as the vast majority of buildings were left untouched, the structures that were destroyed were not burnt in intense fires, and the likely perpetrators were the fleeing inhabitants of the site who left it and allowed the surrounding drainage works to fall into ruin.

---

13. De Ridder 1894; Iakovidis 1989, 277–316; 1998, 228–68. An agate seal stone was found in Building K Room K1 (Iakovidis 1998, 262).

DESTRUCTION IN GREECE AND THE WIDER AEGEAN WORLD   143

Thebes — Scale: Multibuilding — Cause: Unknown

The citadel of Thebes, known also as the Kadmeia, is a large yet relatively low pear-shaped plateau. A destruction event has been assigned to the end of the LH IIIB2 at Thebes; however, the difficulty with assessing this destruction is the date of the various buildings where destruction debris has been uncovered.[14] Anastasia Dakouri-Hild (2001, 106–7; 2010, 698) and Vassilis Aravantinos, Louis Godart, and Anna Sacconi (2001, 14–19) maintain that the destruction found in the Arsenal, the nearby Loukou plot, and the Linear B archive found on Pelopidou Street are evidence of one and the same destruction event, all occurring at the end of the LH IIIB2, including as well the destruction at the Soteriou-Dougekou plot. However, others place the destruction of the Arsenal, and the nearby Loukou plot at the end of the LH IIIB1, with the destruction of the archive on Pelopidhou Street taking place at the end of the LH IIIB2 (Symeonoglou 1985, 49; Sampson 1985, 25; Andrikou 1999, 86–87; Jung 2016, 555). Which side of this debate one takes will greatly influence how the evidence of destruction is interpreted. I cannot give an answer to which interpretation of the site's chronology is correct, and thus to err on the side of caution I will present the evidence of destruction from all of these debated plots and the relevant interpretation for both chronological perspectives.

In the Soteriou-Dougekou plot, evidence of a destruction was noted in four of the five sectors uncovered in Area 5, as Sector Alpha has no described evidence of destruction (Spyropoulos and Chadwick 1975, 11). In Sector Beta, melted lead, burnt animal bones, and burnt pottery were all found on the floor, along with calcined stones fragments of wall paintings, which had been damaged by fire, and a black layer of soil that contained pieces of burnt wood (11–13). Sector Gamma, the so-called Room of the Bath, had much the same type of destruction debris and the bath, the room's namesake, was found filled with burnt wood, melted lead, and stones (13–14). In Sector Delta, vessels were found on the floor as if they had fallen from above and landed upside down on the floor, along with the same type of destruction debris uncovered in the two previous sectors (15). Finally, in Sector Epsilon, the same type of destruction debris was uncovered along with the tablets, which were found in association with melted lead and many fragments of burnt wood (16–17). Theodoros Spyropoulos and John Chadwick (1975, 24) note that no objects of value were uncovered in the destruction and that either all of the objects were removed prior to destruction or that, given the function of the area as a workshop, there were no objects of great value in the area to begin with. They propose that the

---

14. Due to the fragmented nature of the Thebes excavations and the fact that many ceramic assemblages from these excavations remain unpublished, there is no standard Theben chronology that can be applied to all excavated plots (Dakouri-Hild 2010, 696–98).

144   CHAPTER FOUR

cause of the destruction was an earthquake or a natural phenomenon rather than an invasion (55).

The published information related to the destruction of the Arsenal is limited. It describes the building as having been burnt and filled with many weapons (hence its name), objects made of ivory, and many other finds (Platon and Touploupa 1965, 233; Spyropoulos 1971, 209). Unfortunately, this is the extent of the description of the destruction. At the nearby Loukou plot, the building was burnt to such a degree that the walls had been baked, causing difficulties for the excavators during its excavation (Sampson 1980, 218). The building was found filled with burnt material, a thick layer of ash, and many pieces of broken pottery. Parts of a human skeleton were uncovered 0.70 m above the floor of Room 1, suggesting that the individual had been in the second floor of the structure when the building was destroyed. The skeleton likely belonged to an adult female and the skull bore traces of wounds that have been ascribed to the destruction of the building as she was crushed by the fallen roof (Sampson 1980, 218–19; 1985, 226–27). The excavators believe that because of the seeming sudden nature of the destruction, which caught the victim by surprise, that it was caused by an earthquake (Sampson 1985, 29).

In the archive on Pelopidhou Street, again evidence of burning and debris were uncovered. However, in this case a number of Linear B tablets were discovered in the structure, many of which had fallen on the ground facedown from where they had been stored. The tablets were partially baked by the fire, which helped preserve them. Moreover, balls of clay still with fingerprints on them were uncovered, as though they were being prepared to be turned into tablets. The excavators assume that the time it would take to inscribe a fresh tablet was no longer than fifteen minutes, indicating the sudden nature of this destruction (Aravantinos, Godart, and Sacconi 2001, 14–17). The scribes appear to have been working just prior to the burning of the building, which the excavators assume is a line of evidence against warfare as a cause, as the scribes would not be working while the streets were raging with fighting just outside their door (18–19). Thus, they presume that the destruction was caused by an accidental event or an earthquake, though they lean toward an earthquake based on the assumed destruction of other Mycenaean cities by earthquakes at the same time.[15]

With all of this evidence, there is no clear answer that can be given for either the extent of the destruction or the cause of the destruction(s). Because

---

15. Aravantinos, Godart, and Sacconi 2001, 18–19. Andrikou et al. 2006, 55. They cite Pylos, the Menelaion, Mycenae, Tiryns, Midea, and Thebes as sites with evidence of earthquake destruction based on the theories proposed by Iakovidis and Kilian (Aravantinos, Godart, and Sacconi 2001, 19). I will present below why recent research and the present study demonstrate that none of these sites offer any conclusive evidence that they were destroyed by an earthquake at the end of the LH IIIB2 and thus are not strong supporting evidence for a destruction by earthquake at Thebes.

there is no clear chronological framework for all of these excavated areas and because much of the Mycenean city remains under more than three thousand years of further occupation, one cannot say with any confidence how much of the city was truly affected by a destruction event at the end of the LH IIIB2. This is not even including the absence of a description of the destruction for some areas like the Arsenal, which further hinders our understanding of this event(s).

What can be said with some certainty is that the event was sudden. However, there is no physical evidence that would suggest a natural disaster was the cause over human conflict or vice versa. Aravantinos, Godart, and Sacconi have argued that warfare is not a possible cause, given that the scribes would not have been working during an attack. Nevertheless, this would not take into account a surprise attack, which could cause a similar situation. Moreover, even if one includes the crushed skeleton of a possible LH IIIB1 date from the Loukou plot, there is still no direct evidence of an earthquake. Fallen walls, human victims, crushed pottery, and sudden destruction can all be caused by humans. If there was a fight going on in the street, it is very likely that the person could have been trapped or hiding on the second floor of the building, which then caught fire and collapsed around her. At the same time, there is no reasonable evidence that this destruction was caused by humans, as all of the above evidence could have been caused by an earthquake. In both cases telltale evidence of earthquake damage or warfare is not present. Thus, the cause of the multibuilding destruction uncovered at Thebes dating to the end of the LH IIIB2, no matter its extent or the exact date of the various structures, must be left as unknown.

Teichos Dymaion — Scale: Partial — Cause: Unknown

Situated in the western most part of Achaia, a destruction event at Teichos Dymaion has been ascribed to the late LH IIIB or LH IIIC Early.[16] However, due to the state of publication of the work conducted by Efthymios Mastrokostas, there is no certainty about what was destroyed at Teichos Dymaion or how. Burnt or ashy deposits with some traces of burnt mud bricks along with some fire-blackened pottery were uncovered dating to the late LH IIIB or LH IIIC, but no further details describing this possible destruction event are available (Mastrokostas 1962, 1963, 1964, 1965, 1966; Papadopoulos 1979, 47; Michalis Gazis pers. comm. 03/29/2019). Based on this, while it is still possible that the site suffered a destruction event, its extent and cause cannot be known until the unpublished material from the excavations has been examined in full.

---

16. Mastrokostas 1962, 1963, 1964, 1965, 1966; Papadopoulos 1979, 47; Kolonas 2009, 20; Gazis 2010, 247–48.

146   CHAPTER FOUR

Mycenae — Scale: Multibuilding — Cause: Unknown

Of the several destruction events typically ascribed to Mycenae during the LH IIIB (Iakovidis 1986), I will focus on the one attributed to the end of the LH IIIB2. However, this examination comes with several caveats and restrictions. Large parts of Mycenae were excavated at the end of the nineteenth and the beginning of the twentieth century, first by Chrestos Tsountas and followed by Alan Lohn Bayard Wace. Unfortunately, despite the large amount of excavation that was carried out in these early years, often information was simply not recorded at all, or what was recorded is not nearly detailed enough for this type of analysis.[17] Given these limitations, there is little that can actually be said about the end of the LH IIIB2 destruction at Mycenae; however, I will present the evidence as best as can be.

Iakovidis (1986, 259), in his detailed summary of the destruction events that affected Mycenae, described one such event at the end of the LH IIIB2, which was uncovered in "the Cult Centre, Tsountas' House, part of the Southwest Building, Panagia House II (but not III) and perhaps the palace."[18] In recent excavations at Mycenae further evidence of an end of the LH IIIB2 destruction was uncovered in Building K.[19] While burning has been noted in both the Southwest Building and Tsountas's House, both were excavated almost entirely by Tsountas, who left no record of the finds (Iakovidis 1986, 246, 248). The Palace too is described by Wace (Wace et al. 1923, 192, 233–38) as destroyed by fire, and additional traces of this fire were uncovered by George Mylonas (1966, 426) in the East Wing of the Palace. Nevertheless, these basic descriptions do not lend themselves to a critical analysis of possible cause. For the Cult Center, what has been published again does not provide enough detailed information for a critical analysis of the destruction. For the Temple, burnt debris was found on the floors of all four rooms, with the debris in Room XI varying in thickness from 2.5 m to 1 m (Taylour, French, and Wardle 1999, 1–2), while there is no description of the destruction debris uncovered in the Service Areas of the Cult Centre (French and Taylour 2007, 12). The most detailed records come from the Panagia House II and the recently excavated Building K.

The evidence of destruction from the Panagia House II varies from room to room. Rooms 8, 13, 14, 19, and 21 have no recorded evidence of destruction, though Ione Mylonas Shear (1987, 28–42) states that the destruction debris could have been washed down the hill due to erosion. Ash, melted lead, carbonized seeds, and broken pottery were found on the floor of Room 9, while burnt debris

---

17. Tsountas and Manatt 1897; Wace et al. 1923; Wace 1964; 1980; see discussion in Iakovidis 1986; French 2002; French and Iakovidis 2003.

18. Though he does note that it is not clear if these destruction events were contemporaneous with one another.

19. http://mycenae-excavations.org/citadel.html.

was uncovered in Rooms 16, 17, and 20 (37–38, 44). Room 15 too was found with its floor burnt and filled with burnt debris. A hydria was uncovered in Room 15 that was filled with burnt lentils (40–41). Thus, part of the Panagia House II was burnt in a fire at the end of the LH IIIB2; however, this destruction did not affect the entire structure. In Building K, a possible temporary extension or addition to the storerooms of Megaron M, was destroyed at the end of the LH IIIB2. Room 1 was filled with an ash layer 0.5 m thick, containing a variety of objects, crushed pottery, and burnt wood. Part of the destruction debris was sealed by the collapsed roof or parts of the mud-brick superstructure. The assumed cause of the destruction of Building K is an earthquake, based on the wavy outline of the long western wall, which is assumed to be evidence of seismic activity.[20]

It should come as no surprise that both the extent and cause of this destruction event cannot be classified with any certainty. The majority of the relevant information from structures such as the Palace, the Temple Complex, the Southwest Building, and Tsountas's House does not exist due to the early date of their excavation or state of publication. The one possible hint of an earthquake uncovered in Building K is not sufficient evidence that this destruction was caused by earthquake. For what it is worth, Tsountas (Tsountas and Manatt 1897, 341) reported in the late nineteenth century that for Tiryns and Mycenae, "The palaces of both were destroyed by fire after being so thoroughly pillaged that scarcely a single bit of metal was left in the ruins." If this is the case, it may indicate a human hand in the destruction, as several other sites were apparently looted or had their precious metals recovered prior to destruction in the region. However, given the very early nature of these excavations, the truthfulness of this statement must be taken with no more than a grain of salt. Unless additional evidence from other parts of the site is uncovered, it is unlikely that there will ever be a clear answer to what caused the multibuilding destruction witnessed in several areas of Mycenae toward the end of the LH IIIB2.

Midea — Scale: Site-Wide — Cause: Warfare

Midea, located some thirteen kilometers southeast of Mycenae, sits on the summit and the northern and northwestern slopes of the Palaiokastro Hill. The destruction of Midea has traditionally been assumed to be the work of an earthquake, based on fallen and tilted walls and the possibility that some victims may have been crushed in such a seismic event (Åström and Demakopoulou 1996; Demakopoulou 2003, 2007, 2015). However, a recent archaeological and seismological investigation of the region surrounding Tiryns and Midea has cast some doubt about the validity of the earthquake hypothesis as a causal

---

20. http://mycenae-excavations.org/citadel.html.

148   Chapter Four

explanation for the destruction witnessed at the site at the end of the LH IIIB2 (Hinzen et al. 2018). Fortunately, Midea was excavated in the modern era. Thus, unlike several other sites in Greece, the majority of the excavated information was recorded in a scientific manner. Unfortunately, this information is scattered over thirty years of publications, and no final synthesis yet exists. Nevertheless, an examination of this information does provide a likely answer for the cause of the destruction event at the end of the LH IIIB2.

For both the East Gate and the Inner Gate, which is located to the east of the East Gate, evidence of burning, mud-brick collapse, and an ashy layer were uncovered (Åström et al. 1990, 9; 1992, 11). Inside of the East Gate, the excavators report that the fire burned hot enough to warp some of the vases found on the floor of the gate (Åström et al. 1992, 11). The West Gate too was destroyed, as the gate chamber was filled with burnt debris and the remains of the living quarters that were situated in the second floor of the gate house that had collapsed into it.[21]

To the left of the West Gate, situated next to the fortification wall a building complex that is assumed to be a workshop was uncovered. However, the pattern of destruction varied from room to room within the structure. In Rooms I, III, IV, V, VIIIa, IX, X, XI, XII, XIII, and XIV numerous objects were on their floors covered by fallen debris and stones; however, there is no mention that these rooms were burnt.[22] Other rooms associated with this building complex found further away from the fortification wall too had no evidence of fire, though their floors were covered with fallen stones (Demakopoulou et al. 2002, 29). Traces of fire, ash, and burnt material were uncovered in Rooms II, VIa, VIb, VII, and VIIIb (Demakopoulou. Divari-Valakou and Walberg 1994, 23; Demakopoulou et al. 1998, 59, 72; 2001, 38). In the various R Trenches, much the same type of destruction was found, as some rooms were more severely affected by the destruction than others, much like in the building complex near the West Gate, though traces of fire are more prominent throughout the structure (Demakopoulou et al. 2001, 48–50; 2002, 48–54; 2003, 11–20; 2004, 9–20; 2005, 11–20; 2006–2007, 7–16). Likewise, the Megaron and Shrine area suffered from differentiated destruction. While stone collapse, mainly believed to have come from the citadel wall, was found in the structures, burning was limited (Walberg 1998, 24–28, 31–37, 39–45, 90–92, 176; 2007, 62–66, 70, 87, 198). What is clear is that all areas of Midea dating to the end of the LH IIIB2 were affected by a destruction event, though evidence of damage by fire was

---

21. Åström and Demakopoulou 1986, 20–25; Åström, Demakopoulou, and Walberg 1988, 10–11; Åström et al. 1990, 13; Demakopoulou 1995, 155–57; 2007, 66–67.

22. Åström et al. 1992, 13–14. Demakopoulou, Divari-Valakou and Walberg 1994, 20; Demakopoulou et al. 1996, 15–17; Demakopoulou et al. 2001, 46; 2002, 29, 45; 2008, 17–18; 2009, 7.

DESTRUCTION IN GREECE AND THE WIDER AEGEAN WORLD 149

not pronounced in every building. The question that remains is of course, What might have caused this site-wide destruction?

As mentioned above, the various excavators at Midea have maintained that the site was destroyed ca. 1200 BCE by an earthquake. They point to several lines of evidence to support this interpretation. The first is that wherever fallen stones or boulders were uncovered or traces of burning found, an earthquake was assumed to be the cause.[23] Tilted walls were the next assumed indicator of earthquake damage. The excavators state that titled walls were found in Trenches B, C, E, and F, though which walls they mean are not specified (Åström and Demakopoulou 1986, 19). A wall in Trench Ya was reported as tilting strongly to the northwest (Demakopoulou, Divari-Valakou and Walberg 1994, 38–39). Wall 8 of the building complex near the West Gate is described as, "out of alignment and tilting" (Demakopoulou et al. 1996, 16). Also, in the building complex, Wall 11 is reported as having a "tilted appearance," and Walls 15 and 25 are described as tilting toward the interior of rooms VIIIa and VIIIb.[24] In the Megaron Complex and Shrine area, Wall 5 of Room VI, Wall 11 of Room 7, and Wall 3 of the Megaron are reported as tilted (Walberg 1998, 92, 176), and some unspecified walls of Terrace 9 are described as tilted (Walberg 2007, 198). Finally, the walls of the Syrinx are described as distorted and tilted (Demakopoulou et al. 2010, 12).

The final piece of evidence that the excavators cite as an indicator that Midea was destroyed by an earthquake is the skeletons of several individuals that are believed to have been killed by fallen walls. One skeleton, possibly of a young girl, was crushed under fallen debris in one of the rooms of the East Gate (Åström and Demakopoulou 1996, 39). The scattered remains of an adolescent and a child were in the building complex in Room XIV. The bones were discovered among smashed pithoi and other vessels and it is believed that they represent two victims of the earthquake (Demakopoulou et al. 2008, 18). Finally, in Trench C of the lower west terrace, two human skulls with no other skeletal remains were discovered in association with fallen debris in front of Wall 3 and these are assumed to be other victims of the assumed earthquake (Demakopoulou et al. 2009, 19).

At first glance, the reported evidence for a destruction by earthquake at Midea appears to make a strong case. However, upon closer examination, an earthquake does not seem to be the likely cause for the destruction witnessed toward the end of the LH IIIB2 at the site. The first issue is that fallen rubble

---

23. See, e.g., Demakopoulou, Divari-Valakou and Walberg 1994, 34; Åström and Demakopoulou 1996, 38; Demakopoulou et al. 1996, 24; Walberg 1998, 26, 37, 39; Demakopoulou et al. 2002, 29, 39, 48; 2009, 19.

24. For Wall 11, see Demakopoulou et al. 1998, 59. Also, in the same article it is stated that other tilted walls were found in this building complex, but no walls are specified (73). For Walls 15 and 25, see Demakopoulou et al. 2001, 37.

150   CHAPTER FOUR

and stones along with burning is simply a marker of destruction in general, not solely of an earthquake. Thus, wherever this is mentioned as an indicator for destruction by earthquake it is only evidence that the site suffered a destruction event, and not of the exact type of destruction. The second issue concerns the tilted walls. Examining the photographs of the walls that have been clearly identified as tilted, it is not entirely evident that these walls show any signs of pronounced tilting. Furthermore, in the recent archaeological and seismological investigation of both Tiryns and Midea, while there is evidence that these sites were struck by earthquakes within the past 3500 years, no evidence indicates that they were struck by a devastating earthquake at the end of the LH IIIB (Hinzen et al. 2018, 1066). As Klaus-G. Hinzen et al. (1057) note, the destruction uncovered in the West Gate does not align with the damage that would have been caused in a coseismic event, as burning was found underneath the collapsed rubble. If the damage had been caused by an earthquake, then the walls should have collapsed first followed by burning, not the other way around. Thus, if any of the walls are tilted, the likely cause would be natural settling or a lack of maintenance rather than a seismic event.

While several skeletons at Tiryns have been assumed to be the victims of an earthquake, examination of the skeletal material has shown that there is no clear evidence that any of the individuals were killed in an earthquake. Rather, other causes such as infectious disease like meningitis or nonearthquake-related trauma were diagnosed as the cause of death (Hinzen et al. 2018, 1065). While no study has yet been carried out on the skeletal materials from Midia, the presence of skeletons in a destruction event is not an indicator of any specific cause of destruction. That is, if the five individuals were killed in the destruction event, this only indicates they were unable to escape death, and does not reveal the manner of their death. As burning was found in the East Gate and in the building complex, rather than being crushed to death, asphyxiation is just as likely to have killed the individuals, who were later buried under the collapsing buildings. Given all of this, there is a great deal of doubt that an earthquake caused the destruction at Midea.

However, there is one final piece of evidence that most likely indicates the cause of destruction. This is the pronounced quantity of weaponry spread throughout the site in the destruction debris. At least fifty weapons of war and one armor plate have been uncovered from the end of the LH IIIB2 destruction at Midea (table 4.1). Unfortunately, the exact find location for each of these weapons is not specified, as only the trench is given, meaning a full spatial analysis cannot be provided as of yet. Nevertheless, what is clear is that weapons of war were found scattered throughout the site. They were not stored in stockpiles and have been found in every context. Half of the arrowheads are made of bronze, while the other half are mainly made of obsidian, with

Table 4.1. Weapons of war uncovered in the destruction of Midea

Weapon	Amount	Material	Area	Citation
Arrowhead	1	Bronze	West Gate	Åström, Demakopoulou, and Walberg 1988, 9
Arrowhead	1	Flint	Inside West Gate	Åström et al. 1992, 13
Arrowhead	4	Bronze	Trench T	Divari-Valakou and Walberg 1994, 31–32, fig. 41
Arrowhead	1	Bronze	Building Complex	Demakopoulou et al. 1996, 23
Arrowhead	2	Obsidian	Building Complex	Demakopoulou et al. 1996, 23
Arrowhead	2	Bronze	Building Complex Room VIIIb	Demakopoulou et al. 2001, 41
Arrowhead	1	Bronze	Building Complex east of Room IX	Demakopoulou et al. 2001, 46
Arrowhead	1	Obsidian	West of the Building Complex	Demakopoulou et al. 2002, 32
Arrowhead	1	Bronze	West of the Building Complex	Demakopoulou et al. 2003, 11
Arrowhead	1	Obsidian	Building Complex Room XIII	Demakopoulou et al. 2009, 17
Arrowhead	1	Unspecified	Trench Ra	Demakopoulou et al. 2001, 49
Clay ball (Missile)	1	Clay	Trench Ra	Demakopoulou et al. 2001, 49
Arrowhead	2	Bronze	Trench Rb-d	Demakopoulou et al. 2002, 35
Arrowhead	3	Obsidian/ Flint	Trench Re-f	Demakopoulou et al. 2002, 52
Arrowhead	1	Bronze	Trench Re-f	Demakopoulou et al. 2002, 52

152   CHAPTER FOUR

Table 4.1, *continued*

Weapon	Amount	Material	Area	Citation
Arrowhead	3	Bronze	Trenches Rg, i, j Rooms IV and V	Demakopoulou et al. 2003, 14.
Arrowhead	4	Obsidian	Trenches Rg, i, j Rooms IV and V	Demakopoulou et al. 2003, 14.
Arrowhead	5	Obsidian/ Flint	Trench Rh Room IX	Demakopoulou et al. 2004, 12, 15, fig. 14.
Arrowhead	1	Bronze	Trench Rh Room XI	Demakopoulou et al. 2004, 15
Arrowhead	1	Bronze	Trench Rk	Demakopoulou et al. 2004, 20
Arrowhead	1	Flint	Trench Rk	Demakopoulou et al. 2004, 20
Arrowhead	1	Bronze	Trenches Ra–m Room VII or VIII	Demakopoulou et al. 2005, 11
Arrowhead	2	Bronze	Trench Rk Room XI	Demakopoulou et al. 2005, 17
Arrowhead	1	Obsidian	Trench Rk Room XI	Demakopoulou et al. 2005, 17
Arrowhead	1	Bronze	Trench Rk3 Room XIV	Demakopoulou 2006– 2007, 11
Arrowhead	1	Obsidian	Trench Rk4 NW of Room XIV	Demakopoulou et al. 2006–2007, 14
Arrowhead	1	Bronze	Street near East Gate found on top of ash	Åström et al. 1992, 11
Arrowhead	1	Bronze	Northeastern Sector of the Citadel	Demakopoulou et al. 1998, 74
Arrowhead	1	Obsidian	Trench Aa	Demakopoulou et al. 2009, 13

Weapon	Amount	Material	Area	Citation
Arrowhead	1	Obsidian	SW of Åström's Room 6 on upper step	Demakopoulou 2006–2007, 27
Armor plate	1	Bronze	Trench Nb Stratum 5	Walberg 1998, 37
Mace head	1	Stone	Trench Yb Stratum 5	Walberg 1998, 42
Arrowhead	1	Obsidian	Trench Na Stratum 5 South	Walberg 1998, 45

some made of flint. Several of these objects also came from unusual contexts, for example, one arrowhead that was found atop an ashy layer on a street near the East Gate (Åström, et al. 1992, 11). Another was found atop a step near Åström's Room 6, which led Ann-Louise Schallin to speculate that this might indicate another causal explanation for the destruction other than by earthquake.[25] The sheer number of weapons found in this destruction layer is only surpassed by the number uncovered at Pylos.[26] These weapons were scattered throughout the site, on a street, on a step, and in multiple different contexts none of which suggests they were being stored, but rather imply they were deposited by military action. Combined with the recent investigation that indicates that an earthquake is not the likely culprit for the destruction, this puts the cause squarely at the feet of humans.[27] The excavations also reveal a virtual absence of items of value, or at least the gold and silver, indicating that they were probably removed prior to destruction. To date, only one gold object from Trench 14, a plaque with argonaut decoration, has been unearthed in the Greek-Swedish excavations of Midea (Demakopoulou et al. 2006–2007, 28). However, foodstuffs and, relativity speaking, worthless pottery were found in abundance. This suggests that Midea was looted prior to being—at

---

25. Demakopoulou et al. 2006–2007, 27. In an update on Midea for the Swedish Institute at Athens, Schallin states that the cause of the destruction could be either earthquake or an invading enemy. This appears to be the only instance in which one of the excavators has proposed that an earthquake may not be the only possible cause of the destruction.

26. See below for a discussion of these weapons.

27. The fallen debris not associated with fire likely resulted from the disuse and abandonment of the majority of the site postdestruction, as the buildings simply crumbled. Another possibility is the natural defects in the Cyclopean wall, which likely resulted in most of the damage witnessed in the fortification walls (Hinzen et al. 2018, 1061).

154 CHAPTER FOUR

least mostly—burned in an act of war. As the gold and silver were removed but pottery was left behind, this was not a systematic abandonment, as appears was the case at Gla and Dimini.[28] The assailants took the majority of the precious metals out of Midea and the defeat of the city is witnessed by the weapons strewn throughout it. Thus, it no longer appears that Midea was destroyed by a natural disaster, but by a human-made disaster.

Tiryns — Scale: Multibuilding — Cause: Arson/Warfare

Situated on a low rocky outcrop on the east side of the Argive Plain, Tiryns (fig. 4.4), much like Mycenae, suffers from the fact that much of the relevant information from the destruction of its monumental structures was uncovered at the end of the nineteenth century by Heinrich Schliemann and was not recorded in a way that can be utilized in this type of analysis. The only record of the destruction that Schliemann (1886, 8) described is that one factor in the preservation of the palace was the fact that it was baked in the fire that destroyed it. Thus, much of the relevant information for the cause of this destruction too was not recorded. Further excavations undertaken by Kilian (1996) purported to find evidence that the site had been destroyed in an earthquake, a claim that he extended to most of the Mycenaean world at the end of the LH IIIB2 (1988, 134). However, two recent articles have thoroughly reexamined the details of the destruction uncovered at Tiryns at the end of the LH IIIB2 and the extent and likely cause of the destruction.

In a recent article by Hinzen et al. (2018, 1064), after an intensive archaeological and seismological investigation, the researchers found that none of the supposed indicators for an earthquake uncovered by Kilian could be attributed to an earthquake. Moreover, aside from the now-disproven evidence presented by Kilian, no other evidence of earthquake damage has been uncovered in any other excavations at the site. The Lower Town, which should have been greatly affected by a seismic event, has to date not yielded any evidence that it was struck by an earthquake at the end of the LH IIIB2 (1066–67). This has led the team to conclude that the majority of the destruction was likely caused by humans or, in some cases of wall collapse, was owing to poor building techniques (1061–67). Likewise, Jung in his analysis of the LH IIIB2 destruction at Tiryns has also noted that destruction by fire was generally restricted to the palace and adjacent wealthy buildings on the Upper Citadel,

---

28. Of course, it is also reasonable to assume the precious metals were sought out after the destruction and collected, which could account for their absence. However, given that no precious metals were found in the structures and the gates, which appear to have collapsed at least some time close to the destruction, and that there is no evidence that these buildings were searched postdestruction by the local people digging for treasure, it is likely that the metals were removed prior to destruction, likely during or after the attack, but before the site was burned.

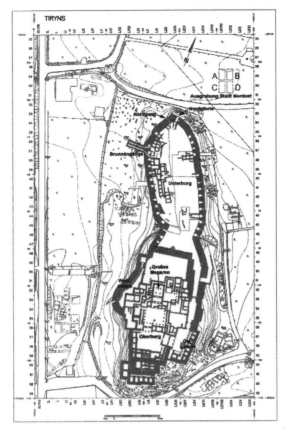

Figure 4.4. Plan of Tiryns. Courtesy of Joseph Maran.

while there was not a consistent burning of the houses in the Lower Citadel. This specific focus on the destruction of the monumental and public structures led Jung (2016, 556–60) to conclude that Tiryns had been destroyed by human hands and, in his assessment, it was caused by a revolution or civil war rather than an invasion by outside forces.[29]

The combination of both of these studies leads to the conclusion that the end of the LH IIIB2 destruction at Tiryns was brought on by human hands. Whether or not this was a civil war, revolution, or an attack by outside forces is not apparent in the archaeological record. However, some further evidence from the Lower Citadel might provide direct evidence of warfare. In a publication by Ursula Damm-Meinhardt (2015, 91, 94, 100), several arrowheads, darts, and a spearhead were seen to be scattered throughout the domestic structures in the Lower Citadel. In Building Complex A, Building 1, one bronze arrowhead and

---

29. See Marzolff 2004, 86 for an earlier dissent from the earthquake hypothesis proposed by Kilian.

156   CHAPTER FOUR

one obsidian arrowhead were discovered in the debris of Room 9. Likewise, in Room 8 a bronze spearhead was uncovered, while a bronze dart was found in Room 10. More conspicuously, to the south of this structure, in the North Corridor, under a layer of debris, lay a fragmented bronze arrowhead, while another bronze arrowhead was uncovered nearby in Room 192 (164, 180). Damm-Meinhardt (2015, 182) notes that these two finds in particular are rather unusual, given the that they were found in a domestic area. These finds may very well be the remnants of a battle that took place in the city, which would help to corroborate the evidence already presented by Hinzen et al. and Jung that Tiryns was indeed mostly destroyed in an act of war and not by natural causes at the end of the LH IIIB2. However, once again, due to the fragmented nature of the finds from the early excavations, whether or not this is direct evidence of warfare cannot be said with any certainty, though at the least arson is certainly likely.

Prophetis Elias/Katsingri — Scale: Partial — Cause: Unknown

Near Tiryns lies the small and briefly excavated site of Katsingri also known in the literature as Prophetis Elias. Kilian (1983, 70; 1988), while excavating at Tiryns, conducted a brief excavation of the hilltop settlement at Katsingri and reported that it too was destroyed by an earthquake.[30] However, despite the claim that the site was destroyed, no information from the excavations was ever published and the material has lain unstudied for nearly four decades. The excavated material is currently being studied by Daniel Frank, a PhD candidate at Heidelberg University. He (pers. comm. 11/02/21) has informed me, that based on his preliminary assessment, it is clear that both the summit and the architectural remains on the east slope were abandoned, possibly during the LH IIIB2 Early, though this date is still preliminary. Hence, the evidence for destruction is currently ambiguous at best. From the house complex on the eastern slope, some floors were partially burnt, but it is unclear if this represents a destruction or not. The situation on the acropolis is even more abstruse, as the area was highly disturbed by later buildings activities in the Archaic period, though Frank (pers. comm. 02/11/20) believes there may still be evidence of destruction. From the preliminary data shared with me by Frank, it is unclear if there was or was not a destruction. Much the same as with Teichos Dymaion, to err on the side of caution, a partial destruction of unknown cause can be attributed to the site. However, once the material from Katsingri has been published, this designation may be revoked depending on the final analysis of the material. However, if the partial destruction event did occur during the LH

---

30. See also Nur and Cline 2000, 56; Cline 2014, 141 who also state that the site was destroyed by an earthquake.

IIIB2 Early, as a preliminary assessment of the ceramics might suggest, then this event and the subsequent abandonment of the site occurred prior to the destruction at Tiryns described above.

Pylos — Scale: Site-Wide — Cause: Warfare

Overlooking the Bay of Navarino at Ano Englianos lies the "Palace of Nestor" at Pylos. The finds uncovered from the excavations carried out by Carl Blegen and Marion Rawson (1966) have already been presented in a number of dissertations, focusing on the finds in general (Hofstra 2000), the pottery (Hruby 2006), the architecture (Nelson 2001), as well as specifically on the destruction of the palace and the evidence for a postdestruction partial reuse of the structure (LaFayette-Hogue 2011, 2016).

These works have already challenged several of the traditional notions about the destruction of the palace at Pylos at the end of the LH IIIB ca. 1180 BCE.[31] As Michael Nelson, Julie Hruby, and Shannon LaFayette-Hogue have demonstrated, the fire that destroyed the building was less intense than Blegen and Rawson claimed. There was less evidence of vitrified pottery than what was reported by Blegen and Rawson (Hruby 2006, 31, 195). The so-called migma that Blegen and Rawson believed to be evidence of intense heat causing the partial melting of some of the architecture is more likely a construction material made of rubble and mortar used in the construction of the pier walls (Nelson 2001, 159).

Moreover, LaFayette-Hogue (2011, 266–67) has demonstrated that not all rooms of the palace suffered from the destruction; some were left unburnt. Indeed, it appears that some areas were entered after the destruction, as Room 18 could be accessed through Room 20, and Rooms 38, 40, Porch 41, and Court 42 too appear to have been reused after the destruction of the palace (LaFayette-Hogue 2011, 283; 2016, 154–55). As LaFayette-Hogue (2011, 285) has described the situation, "It is clear that the Palace of Nestor did not collapse immediately after the fire. The ruins were reentered and reused sporadically, but no cult sanctuary was established on the site. Therefore, reuse of the palace was short-term, small-scale, and non-ritual."

The proposed cause of this destruction ranges from uncertainty (Davis 2010, 687; Cline 2014, 129), to a certainty that it was humans (Bendall 2013, 5677), to it being the result of an earthquake (Kilian 1988, 134; Nur and Cline 2000, 56). Nevertheless, the archaeological evidence is quite clear. The "Palace of Nestor" was destroyed in an act of war, as evidenced by the distribution of weapons within the palace itself. Numerous arrowheads were uncovered

---

31. See discussion in Mountjoy 1997 for the date of the destruction event.

158   CHAPTER FOUR

scattered throughout the palace, appearing in nonstorage locations.[32] Indeed, Pylos is a prime example both of weapons likely deposited in an act of war and of weapons that were being stored at the time of the destruction. In the North Eastern Building, more than five hundred bronze arrowheads were uncovered in Room 100 in a pile, as if they had been stored in a basket at the time of destruction with another forty-five bronze arrowheads discovered in the adjacent Room 99 (Blegen and Rawson 1966, 318–24; Hofstra 2000, 97). These weapons are clearly in a storage context and do not represent a depositional context, which would suggest they were left there in an act of war. However, there are a number of other finds that, based on their context, do suggest they were deposited during armed conflict.

In Room 5 the Vestibule of the Megaron, one bronze arrow or javelin point was found near the doorway to the throne room (Blegen and Rawson 1966, 76). Toward the front of the palace, in Room 7, the first of the two archive rooms, a complete sword was uncovered in association with a bronze spearhead, while a bronze barbed arrowhead was uncovered in the adjacent Room 8, the second of the two archive rooms (94, 100). Furthermore, the fragment of a bronze dagger or spear head was uncovered in Room 10 along with part of a sword, and a bronze arrowhead was uncovered in Room 18 as well as part of a sword (Blegen and Rawson 1966, 105, 121. Hofstra 2000, 100–101). In the Northeast corridor section 35, part of a barbed arrowhead was uncovered, and in the Southeast corridor section 52 a bronze javelin head was found (Blegen and Rawson 1966, 167, 218). Two other bronze arrowheads were discovered in Room 60 (240).[33] These weapons all have unusual depositional contexts, as they were found in corridors, in front of the throne room door, in an archive, a waiting room (Room 10 according to Blegen and Rawson 1966, 103), and in a storage room for pots (239). As the major weapons storage area for Pylos is already known, these weapons of war were most likely deposited during the building's final hours before parts of it were put to the torch.

Moreover, it also appears that the building was looted or emptied of most, though, importantly, not all, of its precious goods. Gold, silver, and ivory were still present in the building when it was destroyed. Ten silver cups were uncovered in the Propylon, which suggests these cups were being taken out of

---

32. Hofstra (2000, 266) has posited that the chipped stone projectile points uncovered in the destruction may have originated from a previous period but were incorporated into the building material for the Palace. However, a thorough analysis of the chipped stone projectiles points is yet to be conducted and they cannot be entirely ruled as evidence of warfare. Moreover, if the stone projectile points did originate from the construction materials, Pylos still stands out among the Mycenean sites discussed here, as chipped stone arrowheads were found throughout all the structures of the Palace and in the Lower Town (Blegen and Rawson 1973; Hofstra 2000, 266; Bendall 2003, 198, fig 10.).

33. At least eleven other bronze arrowheads were found in the drain associated with this room, leading to Court 3 (Hofstra 2000, 97).

the building while the fire had already begun to burn the structure and were dropped in the entryway in the confusion (Blegen and Rawson 1966, 57–62. Hofstra 2000). This is in combination with the fact that no actual evidence for an earthquake has ever been described, nor is there any physical evidence that would suggest the building was destroyed in an earthquake.[34]

Given all the evidence together, this was not a natural disaster. The widespread nature of the fire and the thorough but incomplete looting of precious objects from the palace further suggests this was not an accidental fire. Finally, the presence of weapons of war in what would appear to be nonstorage contexts leads to the conclusion that Pylos was indeed destroyed during an act of war. Once again, who it was that destroyed the buildings is not discernable from the archaeological record, but what is clear is that a natural or accidental cause is not a reasonable explanation for the evidence from the destruction of Pylos.

Menelaion — Scale: Single-Building — Cause: Unknown

Located to the east of Sparta in the plain of the Eurotas River, the Menelaion suffered a single-building destruction at the end of the LH IIIB when Mansion 3, formally known as "Dawkins House," was burned. Unfortunately, much like many excavations at the beginning of the twentieth century, very little information about this destruction event was actually recorded by Boyd Dawkins, and after the excavation almost all of the remaining floor material from the end of the LH IIIB eroded away.[35] What Dawkins (Dawkins and Woodward 1910, 6–7) did record is that within the structure traces of fire and destruction were on every floor of the building.

In the renewed excavations carried out by Hector Catling in the 1970s, excavators uncovered a very small portion of Mansion 3 that Dawkins had not excavated. Within this small area, they discovered evidence of burning (Catling 1976–77, 33; 2009, 38). It again should come as no surprise that there is no clear cause for this destruction, though also importantly, there is no other evidence of destruction outside of Mansion 3, which may indicate that the destruction was targeted.[36] Whether it was manmade, accidental, or a natural disaster, there is

---

34. Both Kilian 1988 and Nur and Cline 2000, 56 state that Pylos either was or was possibly destroyed by an earthquake.

35. Catling 1976–1977, 33; 2009, 38. See also the discussion in appendix 1 from Catling 2009.

36. Catling 2009, 453. Also, at the Menelaion, the Great Terrace Wall on the Aetos South Slope collapsed, covering over the road in front of it, burying a victim dubbed Skeleton 1, and crashed against Building A rendering the structure unusable. Nur and Cline (2000, 55) have suggested that the collapse of this massive terrace wall was caused by an earthquake. However, Catling has ruled out an earthquake as a likely cause, as no evidence whatsoever of earthquake damage was detected in Building A adjacent to the Great Terrace Wall. If an earthquake was powerful enough to bring down the terrace wall, it should have at least damaged Building A, but this was not the case.

160 CHAPTER FOUR

simply no way to determine what caused Mansion 3 to burn and subsequently to be abandoned given the lack of records from the early twentieth-century excavations.

Crete

Kannia — Scale: Partial — Cause: Natural

Kannia is located at the foot of the Asterusi chain about one kilometer southwest of the village of Mitropolis and two kilometers from the top of the acropolis of Gortina (fig. 4.5). The excavations of a LM I Minoan Villa in the 1950s by Doro Levi (1959) revealed that, while much of the structure was in disuse at the end of the LM IIIB, three rooms, I, V, and XV, in the eastern half of the building functioned as a sanctuary in the second half of the thirteenth century BCE. These rooms housed several "Goddess with Upraised Arms" along with other objects likely associated with ritual activities (Levi 1959; Cucuzza 2009, 2015a, 2015b, 2017, 2018). Nicola Cucuzza (2009, 2015a, 2015b, 2017, 2018, pers. comm. 03/10/2020), who is currently studying the materials from Kannia, believes that the rooms were destroyed in an earthquake or some other form of destruction ca. 1200 BCE, though not necessarily as part of any chain of cataclysms at the end of the LM IIIB. He (pers. comm. 03/10/2020) notes that there is no evidence of burning, it does not appear that any objects were removed prior to the rooms being filled with debris, and the objects were in a good state of preservation under the debris. Much like several other sites, this may or may not be evidence of a destruction event, as we cannot say with any certainty if the rooms were actually in use at the time of the structural collapse or if it had been abandoned with the contents left behind, which were then simply buried due to natural structural collapse, a storm, minor earthquake, or any other variety of natural causes. Nevertheless, a natural cause of some kind is the most likely explanation for the partial destruction of Kannia.

Kato Gouves — Scale: Partial — Cause: Unknown

A LM III settlement was excavated in Kato Gouves, fifteen kilometers east of Knossos (fig. 4.5). The excavator Despina Chatzi-Vallianou (Vallianou 1995, 1057–58; 1996) has suggested that the site was destroyed due to a volcanic eruption and tsunami, or, more recently, by an earthquake whose submarine

---

The most reasonable explanation for the collapse of the terrace wall is, as Catling (2009, 215–18, 453, 461) suggests, structural failure due to poor design choices and inadequate drainage, which weakened the structure causing it to collapse suddenly, killing one victim who was unaware of the impending danger.

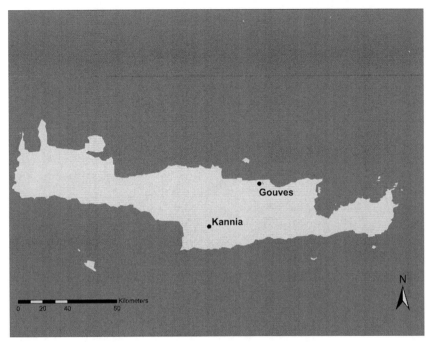

Figure 4.5. Map of sites with a destruction event ca. 1200 BCE on Crete.

epicenter was to the north of the site, which resulted in a tsunami at the end of the LM IIIB ca. 1200 BCE (Chatzi-Vallianou 2017, 140). Unfortunately, as Chatzi-Vallianou (Vallianou 1997, 333–35) has already pointed out, much of the site itself was destroyed by construction activities, particularly in the modern era, making a full assessment complicated. Three building complexes, A, B, and C, were excavated consisting of a number of rooms, a possible megaron, as well as potters' workshops. The evidence for the supposed destruction is sparse based on the condition of the material, but also due to the state of publication. Chatzi-Vallianou notes that throughout the site pumice was uncovered, sometimes reaching thicknesses of ten to twenty centimeters. A large mass of pumice was discovered on the northern exterior wall of Complex B and pumice was also on other walls that were in line with the sea (Vallianou 1996, 161; Chatzi-Vallianou 2017, 140). Particularly in Room XI, one of the potter's workshops, utilitarian objects, and tools for the pottery workshop, including a stone base for the potter's wheel, were buried under a layer of debris and pumice (Vallianou 1996, 161). She (2017, 140) also notes that the floor of Room XXIII was covered with a thick layer of sea pebbles, which she sees as evidence for the tidal wave.

Simon Jusseret (2017, 233) and Jusseret, Charlotte Langohr, Manuel Sintubin (2013) have already demonstrated that there is no reasonable evidence that the destruction was caused by an earthquake. Moreover, Jusseret has noted that

162 CHAPTER FOUR

the pumice may have been a structural component, or the pumice could have been utilized in industry that has been demonstrated at other sites on Crete. Thus, as he notes, there is likely an anthropogenic reason for the appearance of pumice at the site.[37] The pumice then may simply have been from a collapsing roof and the pumice could have been used for kiln activities, which would be particularly fitting given the number of potters' workshops uncovered at the site (Jusseret 2017, 233).

Unfortunately, the published descriptions of this destruction are such that it is not even clear how much of any one building was destroyed, and it must be classified as a partial destruction, even though the destruction may have affected more of the site. It does not appear that there is any evidence of action by fire, and there is no indication that there was any human involvement in the destruction. While a natural cause is most likely, there is no burden of proof to say what caused the damage. If there was a tsunami, then this should have affected and at least produced a layer of sediment or stones at other coastal sites on the northern coast of Crete, a layer that has not been reported. There is nothing to say the damage was caused by an earthquake, as a storm or faulty construction could have also produced the same type of damage. However, the main issue is the simple lack of a clear and definitive description of the destruction, plans of the structures, find locations, profiles, or pictures of the debris that would aid our understanding of the destruction. While the potters' workshops were a spectacular find, for the purposes here, they unfortunately have been the center of published attention by the excavators and the supposed destruction has generally been a side note.

How Did Destruction Affect the End of the LH IIIB?

Where then does this leave the end of the Late Bronze Age in the Aegean and how destruction might have affected it? To begin, destruction was less rampant than previously proposed and where there was destruction it was less destructive than traditionally claimed. Rather, in general, the destruction was far more targeted and deliberate, at least for most sites on mainland Greece that actually suffered a destruction event. For the Aegean as a whole, large areas went mostly unaffected by destruction ca. 1200 BCE. This includes the Cycladic Islands, where there are no reported cases of a destruction occurring ca. 1200 BCE, as the destruction of Koukounaries of Paros was well within the mid-twelfth century BCE.

Likewise, on Crete, the majority of the supposed destructions are false citations, misdated, or did not qualify as a destruction event. For both Kannia and Gouves, which, for the benefit of the doubt, can be ascribed a destruction event

---

37. Jusseret 2017, 233. See also references there in on the use of pumice in industry and roof construction in Minoan Crete.

ca. 1200 BCE, neither appear to have experienced a tragic or truly tremendous destruction, based on the currently published evidence. Both likely suffered some kind of natural destruction, though not necessarily from an earthquake, as there is no evidence of earthquake-related damage at either site. Indeed, on the whole of Crete, there is no evidence of any damage by earthquakes ca. 1200 BCE (Jusseret, Langohr, and Sintubin 2013). Rather, storms, settling, or faulty construction seem to be the most likely reason for these two partial destruction events. Therefore, in neither the Cycladic Islands nor on Crete did destruction play any role in the changes after 1200 BCE.

On the other hand, for Mycenean Greece there were several multibuilding and site-wide destruction events at Thebes, Tiryns, Midea, Mycenae, and Pylos, and targeted destructions at Gla, Dimini, Kastro-Palaia, and possibly the Menelaion. However, not all sites endured horrific destruction events. For both Teichos Dymaion and Prophetis Elias/Katsingri there is no clear evidence that either site was destroyed ca. 1200 BCE, as the remains were so fragmentary and have yet to be fully studied and published, and we cannot be certain whether the ash and debris uncovered at both sites is evidence of a destruction or not.

At Kastanas in Macedonia, the village endured some kind of destruction that only affected two buildings, and given its propensity for destruction, this was likely a regular occurrence at the site and was not part of any cataclysmic end of the Late Bronze Age scenario, as life went on at Kastanas.

At Dimini, Kastro-Palaia in Volos, and the Menelaion, the destruction was hardly widespread, as Megaron B at Dimini, the "palace" at Kastro-Palaia, and Mansion 3 at the Menelaion were the only buildings destroyed at these three sites. While the situation prior to the destruction at the latter two is currently unknown, for Dimini, Megaron B was mostly emptied before being terminated. Whether this was a sacred or desecratory termination is unknown, but given that the following LH IIIC inhabitants left the building alone, it may well have been a sacred termination ritual. Suffice it to say though that these sites were not destroyed; only a single building was destroyed.

The situation is similar for Gla, where only the defensive structures and the main structure, the Melathron, were destroyed. However, prior to destruction they were emptied of any valuable objects and the Melathron of most any object, and this premeditated and directed destruction left the majority of the site unscathed ca. 1200 BCE. After the destruction, Gla was rendered useless as a defensive site to any others who might try to take it over, at least without a tremendous amount of effort to rebuild the crucial structures that had been burned.

None of these sites can truly be called destroyed, as the destruction was relatively minimal. Rather, given the emptying of objects prior to the destruction at Dimini and Gla, there were other, as of yet unknown, outstanding factors that affected these sites prior to the destructions that would have had a

164   CHAPTER FOUR

greater toll on them than the destruction itself. Thus, while destruction was widespread at some sites, for most sites that suffered a destruction ca. 1200 BCE on Greece the destruction was contained and not cataclysmic.

But the lingering question remains: What brought about these destructions? Was it earthquakes, raiders, internal conflict, or a rebellion by the lower classes? This survey of the archaeological evidence cannot give a definite answer, but it can eliminate at least one main contender for the destructions. Based on the available evidence, much like for Crete, there is no evidence that earthquakes were a factor in the destruction of the palaces ca. 1200 BCE.

Both Midea and Tiryns were destroyed by acts of arson and warfare, and given the proximity to these two sites, it is unlikely that Mycenae was destroyed by an earthquake. While one wall from Building K in Mycenae might imply a destruction by earthquake, there is not enough physical evidence to conclude that there was an earthquake over structural failure or settling. Moreover, there is no evidence at any another other site on mainland Greece that they were damaged and destroyed by an earthquake or earthquakes ca. 1200 BCE. At Gla, Dimini, and Kastro-Palaia, buildings were targeted for destruction, and even despite the lack of any typical signs of earthquake damage, this targeted destruction is a clear clue that the destruction was by humans rather than random natural destruction. For Pylos, which Kilian (1988) also assumed was destroyed by earthquake, there is clear evidence that the site was destroyed in an act of warfare and there is no evidence of earthquake damage.

Nothing from any of these destructions suggests a string of devastating earthquakes striking the region, which is in line with the recent work by Jusseret, Langohr, and Sintubin (2013) who found that there is no clear evidence of a massive earthquake horizon ca. 1200 BCE on Crete. While it still remains a possibility that earthquakes struck the seismically active region, it no longer appears that these would have been the cause for any major disruptions or destructions at the end of the LH IIIB or beginning of the LH IIIC. This then leaves anthropogenic destruction, which is apparent at many of these sites, where it is evident that the fires were started by arson or acts of war. However, the question still remains: Who caused the destruction at those sites where it is relatively clear that the agent of destruction was human?

Unfortunately, archaeologically does not offer any quick and easy answers as to the identity the perpetrators. In some instances, such as at Dimini and Gla, I prefer to think that the destructions were brought on by the residents themselves, not as part of a coup, but to terminate the structures. However, I understand that this is a suggestion, one that cannot be verified either archaeologically or historically. The same can be said for other explanations for who brought on the destruction. For example, Jung's (2016, 556–60) argument that the destruction of Tiryns was by internal rebellion, civil war, or revolution cites the specific focus on the destruction of the monumental and public structures as evidence for a targeted practice of destroying the symbols of the elites. This line of thinking was similarly argued by Sharon Zuckerman (2007) as she hypothesized that Hazor in the southern Levant was destroyed by a revolution of the inhabitants of the Lower Town based on the lack of destruction seen in the domestic structures. However, as Amnon Ben-Tor (2013) noted, while these buildings may not have been destroyed, common dwellings were not generally the target of destruction in military campaigns, as was, for example, the case in the 732 BCE destruction of Hazor at the hands of Tiglath-pileser III, where only one of six private houses were found destroyed.

Thus the argument for an uprising over that of an invasion is not so easily solved by the broad absence of destruction in domestic structures, as, in general, domestic dwellings appear to have been avoided as targets of destruction. This is clearly seen at Gla, Dimini, and Kastro-Palaia, as well as at other sites in the Eastern Mediterranean, such as Hattusa, Ras Shamra, and Emar, all of which were affected by acts of war or arson. It seems that if the intent is to destroy symbols of power, no group, be it a revolutionary force or an invading army, generally goes to the trouble to destroy domestic structures. Nevertheless, some houses may still end up being caught in the destruction, as was the case at Tiryns, as several domestic structures in the Lower Citadel do show evidence of burning.

In general, attempting to answer who did the destroying is not a clear-cut quest, as even employing other archaeological and historical evidence to imply that there was fear of warfare prior to 1200 BCE is not without its problems. During the mid-thirteenth century in the Argolid, defensive structures were built or expanded at Mycenae, Tiryns, and Midea, along with the construction of massive silos, leading some scholars to believe that an air of impending doom and the threat of constant warfare prompted the rulers of these cities to construct them.[38] However, at least for Tiryns, the picture is more complicated. As Maran (2009, 255) describes the situation, "Shortly after the defensive architectural measures had been taken, some of them were undone and replaced by new concepts suggesting rather a consolidation of the political situation and more peaceful circumstances. I would therefore doubt that on the eve of the catastrophe the political dignitaries felt they were living under the shadow of a crisis." Indeed, even after the destruction of the Mycenean palace at Tiryns, a narrow megaron, called Building T was constructed on top of the ruin of the Great Megaron and the population of the Lower Citadel increased rather than decreasing (Maran 2008). As Maran (2008, 73) has put it, Tiryns fought against the tide of history, briefly keeping its legitimacy and likely becoming a center of power for a short period after 1200 BCE.

---

38. Müller 1930, 57–61, 65–66; Iakovidis 1983, 29–37; Kilian 1988, 134; Shelmerdine 1997, 280.

166 CHAPTER FOUR

A state of panic and emergency have also been extracted from Linear B tablets uncovered in the ruins of the palace of Pylos, which may have been without a defensive wall at the time of its destruction.[39] Four of the five so-called oka-tablets contain the line "Thus the watchers are guarding the coast," and this in conjunction with other tablets discussing military provisions led to the idea that Pylos was in a state of emergency prior to its destruction (Baumbach 1983). However, as Cynthia Shelmerdine (1999, 405) has noted, since many of these tablets were in storage, it is unclear when the tablets were written, as it could have been, "a day, a week or several months before the destruction." Moreover, as Maran (2009, 245; 2010, 729–31) has pointed out, "The main problem in assessing these texts and using them to gain historical insights consists in the fact that almost all Linear B documents derive from the latest phase of the palace. Accordingly, we have no means of comparing the evidence with previous periods, in order to assess how normal or exceptional this military planning really was." Thus, while the tablets do point to a state of weariness and a defensive posture, as Shelmerdine (1999, 409) has clearly demonstrated, there was no immediate crisis or state of emergency prior to the destruction of the palace at Pylos.

From the existing archeological evidence, while there is clear anthropogenic destruction at several palaces and monumental structures throughout Greece, there is no telling who actually destroyed them outside of informed inferences. This situation in Greece is in many ways best summed up by the excavators of the Cypriot site Maa *Paleokastro*, who, having the same problem of assigning who the human agents were behind Maa's destruction, said succinctly, "We might suggest that they were 'pirates,' 'adventures' or remnants of the 'Sea Peoples,' but this is simply another way of saying that we do not know" (Karageorghis and Demas 1988, 266). Nevertheless, even if we cannot determine who did do the destroying, we can ask what effect, if any, did these destructions have on ending the palatial system?

One proposed victim of the destructions in Greece and destruction in general was interregional exchange. Knapp and Manning have suggested that the destruction and devastation of the ports of trade at the end of the Late Bronze Age was a critical break in the link of international trade connections. As they state, "Once ports and harbors were devastated, there would have been no place left for traders (and thus for pirates) to conduct their business" (2016, 135). Meanwhile, Iakovidis (1993, 318–19) suggested that the destruction and loss of the Levantine ports ca. 1200 BCE proved to be a disastrous blow to the Achaean rulers, permanently breaking off trade connections. He (1990, 319) stated that owing to the destructions, "The capacity of coordinated commercial

---

39. No wall was excavated by Blegen; however, a recent geophysical survey has identified an underground feature that may be the remains of a wall (Shelmerdine 2001, 338–39, 378).

and economic planning on a large scale and under a unified control was lost."[40] However, destruction played no role in the perceived loss of trade at the end of the Late Bronze Age for Greece. For one, the destruction of the palaces in the Argolid, the region where most imported Mycenaean pottery was produced, did not prevent them from exporting their wares across the Eastern Mediterranean.[41] The reason is that the importation of Mycenaean pottery had largely come to an end in the Levant by the mid-thirteenth century BCE, some fifty years or more before these destructions ever even took place.[42]

Moreover, Iakovidis's supposed destruction of Levantine ports simply never happened. The only major port that was destroyed was Ras Shamra, while on Cyprus only Enkomi may have suffered a partial destruction, which as I will detail in chapter 6 may not be a destruction at all. Even so, destruction or not, Enkomi was quickly rebuilt on a grander scale than before 1200 BCE (see chs. 3, 6, and 7). Thus, there remained plenty of ports, such as Tell Abu Hawam, Sidon, Tyre, and Sarepta to continue the trade if there had been the need or want to trade. Moreover, as Maran (2009, 245–47) has demonstrated for Tiryns and Sarah Murray (2013, 312–17) for the whole of Mycenaean Greece, during the LH IIIC period, interregional trade did not stop, and indeed imported objects may have been more widespread after 1200 BCE than during the palatial period, when imported objects were largely concentrated in the Argolid.[43] Destruction could not then have been an active part in ending trade, as the exportation of Mycenaean vessels largely ceased well before the destructions ca. 1200 BCE; moreover, not all trade ended after these destructions.

In attempting to answer what effect these destructions might have had on the end of the palatial system, Maran (2015, 280) has asked the poignant question, "Why this particular [destruction] should have had much more devastating and enduring consequences than all the others which had occurred earlier in the Palatial period." Indeed, for many of these sites, the question can be asked if the destruction had any effect at all on the disappearance of the palatial system or if it was just the capstone on a set of varied preexisting conditions. This appears to be the case for settlements such as Dimini, Gla, and Tiryns. For Dimini and Gla it is clear that the destruction was far from unexpected and may very well have been part of the purposeful abandonment either of the site as a whole at Gla or of the administrative center at Dimini,

---

40. This suggestion also places an emphasis on the need for trade in the Mycenaean economy. However, there is little evidence that interregional trade and exchange was a vital part of the economy for any Mycenaean site; see Millek 2019c, 122–40.

41. Van Wijngaarden 2002, 13; Artzy 2006, 52; 2007, 364; Zuckerman et al. 2010, 410; Artzy and Zagorski 2012; Stockhammer 2019.

42. Bushnell 2013; Stockhammer 2019. See Millek forthcoming a for why destruction in the Argolid during the mid-thirteenth century BCE was also not a factor in the cessation of trade.

43. For a discussion of the imported exotica in LH IIIC period see Murray 2018.

168   CHAPTER FOUR

while for Tiryns, the rebuilding of the megaron indicates that the destruction did not end the palatial system ca. 1200 BCE.

Moreover, destruction was not limited to the end of the LH IIIB2. Mycenae suffered a more devastating destruction in the mid-thirteenth century BCE (Iakovidis 1986) as did nearby Tiryns (French, Stockhammer, and Damm-Meinhardt 2009; Maran 2010), while the Old Kadmeion of Thebes was burned at the end of the LH IIIA2 (Dakouri-Hild 2001), and as Middleton (2010, 14) has noted, there were numerous other destructions prior to the end of the LH IIIB2 throughout Greece.[44] In each case, the destruction did not bring about the end of the palatial system at any site and more than likely for all of the major destruction events in Greece that brought about the abandonment of the palaces, the destruction itself likely took a secondary role to the preexisting socioeconomic and cultural conditions, which largely remain shrouded in mystery. This was a point brought up already in 1960 when Emily Townsend Vermeule (1960, 71) noted, "that it was not the 'destructions' which hurt Mycenaean centers so much as economic deprivation which made it impossible for them to maintain and rebuild in the old manner."

These factors were likely regional or even site specific. While climate change and famine have been assumed to be a factor in the fall of the palatial system for decades, this was apparently not the case for Pylos, as a regional climatic study demonstrates that prior to the destruction, the region showed generally wetter conditions, meaning there would not have been a climate-induced famine to cause social distress (Finné et al. 2017).[45] Moreover, if there had been a famine that fueled the destructions across Greece, we must then ask why at Gla were the food stores the one thing that was not taken out prior to being burned, when even pottery was largely removed? The same can be said for Dimini, where grain was burnt in Megaron B, while at Midea foodstuffs were found throughout the burned and fallen debris, as it was in some parts of Mycenae.[46] If a famine had been caused by climate change that led to social unrest brought on in part by the search for food that the elites had horded, why burn the food? This is an issue for the famine theory throughout the whole of the Eastern Mediterranean, as we will see in the following chapters.

Another issue is the timing of the destruction events. As John Hooker already noted in 1976 (180), "As we sum up the events described and the

---

44. Though, as with any broad list of destructions, it is unclear to what extent each site was destroyed or indeed if there are not the errors and false destructions that tend to plague these lists.

45. For climate change and famine, see, e.g., Carpenter 1966; Weiss 1982; Drake 2012; Kaniewski et al. 2010, 2011, 2013, 2019; Kaniewski, Guiot, and van Campo 2015; Kaniewski and van Campo 2017a, 2017b; Weiberg and Finné 2018. For an argument against the climate devastation theory, see Middleton 2012.

46. Famine causing a shortage was proposed as part of the fall of Dimini; see Adrimi-Sismani 2020, 25.

conclusions reached ... we see that changes which affected the Greek mainland between 1200 and 1050 BCE are so diverse in character and are felt at such widely differing times that no one origin can be postulated for all of them. Nor are we justified in saying that all the destroyed sites met their end at the same time." This sentiment has more recently been echoed by Oliver T. P. K. Dickenson (2010, 487) stating,

> Although some, as in the Argolid, are agreed to fall very closely together, there is no reason why the whole group should not have been spread over twenty or thirty years, and, as already noted, the process of abandonment of sites may have taken much longer. Such points are bound to undermine all theories that rely on the idea of a single intolerable shock, whether natural or human-delivered.

Indeed, the first center in Greece to lose its palatial characteristics was Iklaina just east of Pylos. The palace and much of the site was destroyed, likely in an act of arson in the mid-thirteenth century BCE and was replaced by an impoverished industrial complex until it was abandoned without destruction several decades later (Cosmopoulos 2018, 2019; Cosmopoulos et al. 2019). This destruction is separated from the burning of the palace at Pylos by some seventy years, or nearly two generations. It is likely that for many of the destruction events, they were separated by years and decades and the abandonment of the palaces was a gradual process rather than one brought on by a string of destructions. While in archaeology and history thirty years is essentially no time at all, on a human scale it is nearly an entire generation. Thus, even trying to connect these chronologically dispersed destructions to the fall of the palatial system is questionable, as there was no wave of destruction.

As many have noted before, Mycenaean Greece did not collapse suddenly and neither did a single factor drive the collapse (e.g., Hooker 1976, 180; Dickenson 2010; Middleton 2010). By examining the destructions across the Aegean, we can however, come closer to an answer. For Crete and the Cycladic Islands, the absence of destruction testifies to the fact that destruction simply was not a factor, and the quest for a cause therefore moot. Likewise, when considering theories for the end of Mycenaean Greece we must consider that there was in fact less destruction than previously assumed to cause such a disruption, as demonstrated in chapter 3. What is also evident based on the archaeological evidence is that an earthquake or series of earthquakes did not destroy the palaces on Greece, nor did they affect Crete ca. 1200 BCE. The fact that many, though not all, of the monumental structures and palaces were destroyed is more than likely a symptom rather than a cause in the abandonment of the palatial system. Indeed, at Tiryns this was the case, as the destruction did not bring about the end of the palace, which was able to hold on for a little while longer. Larger and likely regional specific cultural changes led to this transition over time, not in one fell swoop.

CHAPTER FIVE

Destruction in Anatolia and the Fall of the Hittite Empire

Felling an Empire

The end of the Late Bronze Age in Anatolia is marked by the downfall and dissolution of the Hittite Empire when the once glorious capital of Hattusa was supposedly burned and abandoned, while other sites throughout Anatolia suffered a similar fate. In the infancy of Hittite studies, the destruction and the breakup of the Hittite Empire was placed squarely at the feet of the Sea Peoples, often in combination with the Phrygians.[1] However, as time wore on the Phrygians and Sea Peoples were largely abandoned as a means of explaining the destruction and were replaced by the hostile and seminomadic Kaska in the Hittite heartland, though the Sea Peoples still loom large as the possible agents of destruction for the coastal centers in Cilicia.[2] Earthquakes have also been an assumed bringer of ruin for Anatolia, as they have for the rest of the eastern Mediterranean (Nougayrol et al. 1968, 753–68; Nur and Cline 2000; Nur and Burgess 2008). Indeed, as Albrecht Goetze (1975, 266) described the situation in Anatolia ca. 1200 BCE, "The archaeological evidence proves that a catastrophe overtook Anatolia and Syria. Wherever excavations have been made they indicate that the Hittite country was ravaged, its cities burned down."[3] However, with that rather intentionally verbose introduction aside, nearly two decades ago Trevor Bryce already cast doubt on the amount of

---

1. Sayce 1909, 376–77; Garstang 1910, 53; Luckenbill 1914, 54–55; Bury et al. 1924, 16; Forrer 1936, 194–95. For an overview of the history of research on the Phrygians see Woodhouse 2009.

2. For the Kaska, see Müller-Karpe 2009, 9; 2017, 154; Bryce 2012, 12; Beal 2011, 595; Cline 2014, 125–26. For an overview of history and archaeology of the Kaska see Singer 2007; Yakar 2007. For the Sea Peoples, see Singer 2000, 27; Yakar 2006, 8; Collins 2007, 78; Beal 2011, 595; Genz 2013, 477.

3. For an excellent review of the history of the research surrounding the end of the Hittite Empire, see Alaura 2020. She (2020, 11) describes the scholarly research on the end of the Hittite Empire as, "Over the years, the political, social and cultural aspects of the end of the Hittite Empire have been defined or characterized as, for example: collapse, fall, destruction, disintegration, dissolution, disruption, conflagration, catastrophe, demise, crisis, decline, deterioration, decay, abandonment, with much consideration and speculation, and with major reorientations of, and changes to, previous theories and interpretations. In regard to interpretations, the key terms that are generally used to discuss the causes of the end of the Hittite Empire include: migrations and invasions, cultural and political incapacities to face new problems, conflicts with neighbouring peoples, environmental circumstances, climate change, depopulation. As for the aftermath of the end of the Hittite Empire, some of the terms that have been employed are: dark age, resilience, adaptation, regeneration, revitalization, reorganization, rearrangement, rebirth, transition, transformation, experimentation."

171

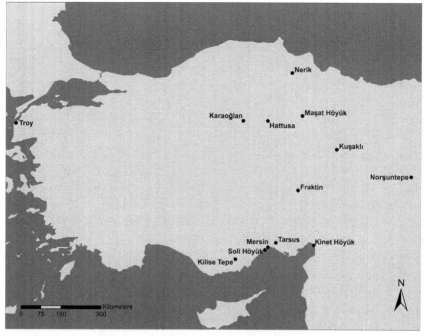

Figure 5.1. Map of sites with a destruction event ca. 1200 BCE in Anatolia.

destruction affecting Anatolia ca. 1200 BCE. He noted that destruction appears to have occurred essentially east or south of the Halys River in central Anatolia stating that, "Indications from archaeological excavations are that only a small number of sites of the Hittite world were actually destroyed" (2005, 247).[4] This, in combination with the fact that 46 percent of all cited destruction in Anatolia are false destructions, and given the large geographic area that Anatolia represents, there was indeed little destruction ca. 1200 BCE. Only thirteen sites have evidence of destruction at the end of the Late Bronze Age. However, some of the sites that did suffer a destruction event are the most famous in all of Anatolia, including Troy of ancient fame and Hattusa, capital of the Hittite Empire. With these major and eminent sites experiencing a destruction ca. 1200 BCE this has helped fuel the hype surrounding the little destruction that actually took place in Anatolia at the end of the Late Bronze Age. Therefore, to better understand how destruction affected Anatolia and the Hittite Empire, we must examine those sites that did suffer destruction ca. 1200 BCE (fig. 5.1), beginning with perhaps the most notorious: Troy.

---

4. This assertion was based on Bittel 1983 and his discussion of destruction.

DESTRUCTION IN ANATOLIA AND THE FALL OF THE HITTITE EMPIRE 173

Hisarlık-Troy — Scale: Site-Wide — Cause: Warfare

Situated on the Küçük Menderes River on the northwestern Anatolian coast is the mound of Hisarlık, which has for nearly two centuries been identify with Priam's Troy of legend.[5] The site has been excavated off and on for nearly 150 years, beginning with Heinrich Schliemann in the 1870s, whose excavations were continued by Wilhelm Dörpfeld (1902) in the 1890s, with Carl Blegen (Blegen et al. 1950) later returning to the site in the 1930s, and most recently by Manfred Korfmann (2001, 2004a) during the late twentieth century.[6] There has been much controversy surrounding Troy's physical size, particularly the extent of the lower city, and by proxy the population and prominence of Troy during the thirteenth century BCE, whether it was indeed the rich city described by Homer or if was more of a provincial backwater town.[7] Regardless of the exact size and importance of Troy ca. 1200 BCE, the city suffered a site-wide destruction event at some time between 1230–1190/1180 at the end of Troy VIIa.[8]

For our purposes here, the majority of the useful information for this destruction derives from the excavations led by Blegen. Much as with Mycenae and Tiryns, the Schliemann and Dörpfeld excavations do not provide much useful data, though some of the ten houses that Dörpfeld partially unearthed were completely exposed during Blegen's excavations at Troy and were included in his summary of finds (Blegen et al. 1950, 3–5). Evidence of destruction including burnt rubble, fallen debris, crushed pottery, and evidence of burning were revealed in every house Blegen excavated. House 700, which was situated inside of the former South Gate, was destroyed by fire and was filled with stone rubble, some of which had been cracked and calcined by the heat, while carbonized wheat was uncovered on the floor and in a basin, along with a great deal of crushed pottery. Some fragments of a human skull were found in the doorway of the vestibule and other scanty human remains were uncovered just outside of House 700. Blegen (Blegen et al. 1950, 62–66) interpreted these as the remains of at least one victim of this destruction. Similar signs of destruction were uncovered in Houses 701, 705, 722, which abutted the fortification wall, and Houses 721, 725, 730, 731, 732, and 741 along with Houses VIIζ and VIIγ (Blegen et al. 1950, 69–116, 120–22). House 741 lay outside of the eastern wall

---

5. It is also possible that Troy was Wilusa known from thirteenth century BCE Hittite texts. For discussions of this possible association, see Easton et al. 2002, 94–101; Latacz 2004, 75–100; Bryce 2006, 107–21; Pantazis 2009. This was the favored identification of Korfmann (2004b, 2007).

6. For a historical overview of the excavations, see Cline 2013; Easton 2014.

7. For some of the back and forth on the topic, see Korfmann 2001; Easton et al. 2002; Heimlich 2002; Hertel and Kolb 2003.

8. Mountjoy 1999a, 297–301; 2017, 91. See also Korfmann (2004a, 37; 2004b, 15; 2007, 25), who agrees with Mountjoy's suggested date for the end of the Phase VIIa.

174   CHAPTER FIVE

of the citadel and underneath in the burnt debris from Troy VIIa was a broken mandible, likely from an adult male (11). Burning was also evident on the pavement in Square J7, as well as on Street 710 and 711 East, which were also covered with burnt debris. The lower jaw bone of a human was uncovered on Street 711 East among fallen stones, while on Street 710 a bronze arrowhead was discovered in the middle of the street, which Blegen took as a key piece of evidence suggesting that Troy VIIa was destroyed in an act of warfare (Blegen et al. 1950, 11–12, 50–51, 56–57, 106). Down on the western slope of the citadel Blegen uncovered another possible victim of this destruction. The skeleton was uncovered, "in an awkward position, as if the body had not been properly buried, but had been struck down and left to lie as it fell" (12).

In the more recent excavation conducted by Korfmann, further evidence of this destruction was uncovered in the lower city. Of the several excavated houses, only one was completely unearthed. The Terrace House was located in the western suburb of the lower town, and it too was destroyed by fire. In the debris were cooking implements and other markers of domestic activity, but along with these mundane everyday household objects were several arrowheads and numerous sling bullets that were discovered in multiple rooms of the building. Outside on the street next to the Terrace House were three piles of sling stones seemingly prepared for active combat (Korfmann 2004a, 37; Becks 2006, 159; Aslan 2019, 50). Korfmann also uncovered an undefined number of skeletons, one of which he (2004c) described as, "a girl, I think sixteen, seventeen years old, half buried, the feet were burned by fire. Half of the corpse was underground." Korfmann (1996, 11; 2004a, 37; 2004b, 15; 2007, 25), much like Blegen, believed that the weaponry, the massive destruction, and the loss of human life indicated that Troy VIIa ended in an act of war.

From all of the above evidence, it is clear that Troy suffered a site-wide destruction at the end of the Late Bronze Age, even if the date for this destruction could have fallen at nearly any time in the defined period between 1225–1175 BCE. What is also evident is that there is no reason to disagree with either Blegen or Korfmann that Troy VIIa ended in an act of warfare. However, the rationale for this identification is not the widespread nature of the destruction or even the human victims. Rather, it is the dispersed weaponry found on a street as well as scattered in the Terrace House that suggest warfare as the likely causal factor for the destruction and the death of at least several individuals. Who brought about this destruction and if the battle that raged in Troy VIIa had anything to do with the mythical war recorded by Homer will remain an area of contentious historical debate.[9] However, no matter exactly

---

9. See Latacz 2004, 278–287; Bryce 2005, 357–71; 2006, 180–94; Dickinson 2008; Rose 2014, 40–43. See Hiller (1991) who suggests that both the VIh and VIIa destruction events were combined in historical memory into one mythic event.

DESTRUCTION IN ANATOLIA AND THE FALL OF THE HITTITE EMPIRE   175

who it was that put the city to the torch, what is evident is that Troy suffered a massive destruction at the hands of man at the end of the Late Bronze Age.

Karaoğlan — Scale: Partial — Cause: Unknown

Karaoğlan, situated south of Ankara near the upper reaches of the Sangarios River, is like so many sites where there is a general lack of published information on the end of the Late Bronze Age. There exist only a handful of sentences that describe the end of the Hittite period, dubbed Level 3, as virtually the same preliminary report was published in German, French, and Turkish in 1939.[10] From the little information available, Remzi Oğuz Arık (1939a, 221; 1939b; 54–55) describes the end of the Hittite level as a massive destruction, the excavated structures were severely burned and blackened, stones were cracked from the heat, metals were at least partially melted, while walls had been toppled over. He states (1939b, 55) that the "Hittite layer ... must have been destroyed, entirely and at once, as a result of a terrible invasion or a formidable earthquake." Unfortunately, there is little information to go on both for the extent of this destruction and also the exact date. There are no published descriptions of any of the buildings that were uncovered, and it is impossible to say how much of the site was destroyed. Moreover, Arık never gave a specific date for the destruction. He (1939a, 1939b, 1939c) only states that this destruction represented the end of the Hittite period prior to the onset of the Phrygian level. The ca. 1200 BCE date was first assigned by Kurt Bittel (1983) in his seminal article on Anatolian destruction, a date that was repeated by Robert Drews (1993, 9), Amos Nur and Eric Cline (2000, 60), Nur and Dawn Burgess (2008, 225 fig. 8.1), and Cline (2014, 126; 2021, 121). However, the requisite study of the materials from Karaoğlan that could help to pinpoint the date of this destruction was never conducted, and it is only an assumption that the Hittite layer ended ca. 1200 BCE. Suffice it to say that there is also no information that indicates the possible cause for the partial destruction of Karaoğlan. Arık never mentions any weapons of war, and while he (1939b, 44, 54–55) notes that throughout the millennia there is possible evidence of earthquake damage at the site, there is no clear evidence that this particular destruction was caused by an earthquake.

While Karaoğlan did indeed suffer a destruction, perhaps ca. 1200 BCE, this is not to say that false information about this destruction has not crept into the scholarly zeitgeist. In Drews 1993 (9), Nur and Cline 2000 (60), as well as Cline 2014 (126) and 2021 (121), each of the authors report that several human skeletons or victims were uncovered in the destruction. The root citation for

---

10. Arık 1939a, 1939b, 1939c. There are some minor differences, particularly in the German report.

176 CHAPTER FIVE

this claim is Bittel 1983 (31), who does indeed state that several individuals lost their lives in this event.[11] However, this was an error by Bittel. While several bodies were uncovered in the destruction, only one of them was human, a male some 20–25 years old who was "crushed by the landslide of large stones near a hearth."[12] The other bodies that were excavated and that had been burnt in the destruction were unspecified animals (Arık 1939a, 221). Yet, when Bittel cited Arık 1939a, he only reported that bodies were uncovered and not that only one of these bodies belonged to a human.

Oymaağaç Höyük-Nerik — Scale: Single-Building — Cause: Unknown

Oymaağaç Höyük, ancient Nerik, lies seven kilometers from the Kızılırmak River and some 150 kilometers northeast of Hattusa. A single-building destruction event has been uncovered at the site as a temple, dubbed the "Jüngerer Tempel" or New Temple, was destroyed at some point during the reign of Suppiluliuma II ca. 1200 BCE. The date for the destruction is based on texts uncovered in the remains, as well as C14 dates derived from the destruction debris, though a more exact date cannot be given at this time (Czichon et al. 2011, 213–18; 2016, 16–25, 60, 101; 2019, 66; Pavol Hnila pers. comm. 02/12/21). Much of the temple was removed during later building activities, leaving no floors with in situ finds (Czichon et al. 2012, 213–18; 2016, 16–25). However, it is apparent that the building was burned as Hnila (pers. comm. 02/12/21) has informed me that,

> Most of the wooden beams in the walls completely disappeared, only very few of them were carbonized. Some of those carbonized beams were found still inside the walls (in various rooms), while a couple of collapsed beams were found on the walking surfaces along the outside face of the temple (the highest concentration in square 7384). Many of the walls were baked into a hard mass, which we designate as a "conglomerate." This consists of limestones turned into lime, with admixtures of baked mud bricks. The fire that destroyed the building must have continued as a smoldering fire underground, since the walls were burnt down to the foundation stones, which were often more than 2 meters deep below the floor. The rooms fill from the construction time of the temple (under the floor level) was also burnt to various degrees—with clearest traces of heat and smoke close to the walls.

Unfortunately, due to the state of preservation, there are no clues as to what caused this destruction event, and it remains a single-building destruction of unknown cause.

---

11. Drews cites Bittel 1983, while Nur and Cline cite both Drews 1993 and Bittel 1983, while Cline only cites Drews 1993.

12. Arık 1939b, 58. See also Arık 1939a, 212 fig. 4 for a photograph of the skeleton in situ. For a complete description of the remains, see Kansu and Tunakan 1948, 760–62.

Boğazköy-Hattusa — Scale: Multibuilding — Cause: Arson

Hattusa, the once great former capital of the Hittite kingdom sits within the great loop of the Kızılırmak River near modern day Boğazkale. Jürgen Seeher (2001), one of the former directors of the excavations at Hattusa has already laid out an excellent review of the "destruction" of Hattusa that took place within the first decades of the twelfth century BCE. Seeher has gone to great lengths demonstrating that the city was not burnt down in a catastrophic conflagration brought on by the hands of some invading force. Rather, as he summarizes the situation (2010, 221):

> (1) There is no burnt "horizon," only a certain number of burnt ruins the date of whose destruction is not established; (2) for the most part these burnt ruins contained no finds, which suggests that they burnt down only after they had lost their function and had been emptied of artefacts; (3) the emptying was presumably carried out by inhabitants of the city—after all, an enemy that is attacking a city does not go to the trouble of emptying buildings virtually down to the last pot before torching them; (4) the only buildings to have burnt are official ones—temples, palace buildings—while the residential districts remained unscathed; this too argues against an assault from outside.

To enumerate a little further on Seeher's statement, while there was evidence of destruction at Hattusa, there is no uniform pattern in terms of its intensity or exactly what was destroyed. The royal palace with its heavy wooden timber framing was at points burnt so thoroughly that the meter-thick walls had been completely blackened, while limestone cracked in the heat and turned to chalk (Seeher 2001, 627). A similar situation was true for the great temple in the lower town, which too was burnt; however, of the twenty-five temples uncovered in the central temple district, only nine have any signs of action by fire (fig. 5.2). The remainder appear to have been simply abandoned without having been destroyed, which is also true for the residential buildings and workshops from the last phase of the central temple district's use (Seeher 2001, 626, 628). Seeher (2001, 625–26) notes that one of the crucial pieces of information in interpreting this destruction event is the finds that were left behind. Generally speaking, these fall within three categories, clay tablets, stationary pithoi that could hold up to 1750 L, and thus, too difficult to remove, and clay seals. Seeher reasonably reasons that no attacking enemy in the middle of a ferocious battle while fires raged all around would take the time or have the time to remove nearly every last scrap and fragment of pottery and the means to transport it. Rather, it is more likely that the inhabitants removed the majority of all objects from these buildings.[13] Because of the systemic emptying of the buildings at

---

13. Seeher 2001, 631. Seeher quotes Neve (1969, 13) who, when describing the situation in the northeast magazine, states, "On the floors preserved in all rooms, deeply sunk under the load of

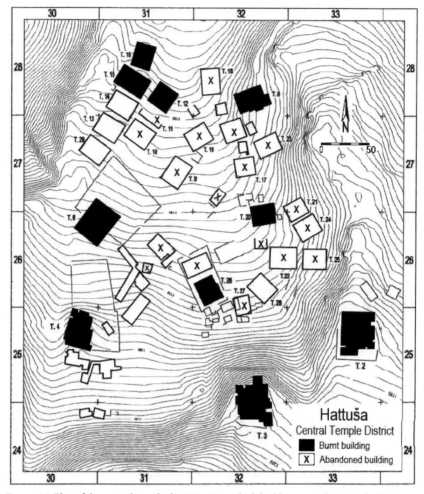

Figure 5.2. Plan of the central temple district noting which buildings were burnt and which were abandoned. For unmarked buildings, the situation is not clear. From Seeher 2001, 629 Abb 1. Courtesy of Jürgen Seeher.

Hattusa, which has left few chronological markers, there is no clear destruction horizon, and it is quite possible that there were months or even years between the burning and destruction of the individual buildings.[14] While Bittel (1977, 41) assumed that the targeted destruction of the monumental buildings or those

---

the destruction debris and clay-hard fired by fire, there was not a single object in situ, with the exception of two bronze hooks."

14. Seeher 2001, 634. As Seeher (626) also points out, there are also sizable distances between these buildings such as the five hundred meters between Temple 2 and Temple 7, meaning that trying to stratigraphically tie these structures together is a task in and of itself.

with an official function indicated that the destruction must have occurred at one time, Seeher (2001, 632) has remarked that while there might have been a uniform intention to destroy these buildings, "In this case, the uniformity of intention does not necessarily lead to a uniformity in the time of destruction."

As Seeher rightly concludes, due to the targeted nature of the destruction and the near complete emptying of many of Hattusa's buildings, the destruction was caused by humans rather than by some natural or accidental cause. Moreover, he (2001, 634) points out that there is little evidence for warfare in the ruins of the once great city. More than likely as he (633) and Hermann Genz (2013, 471–72) have argued, Suppiluliuma II and his entourage abandoned the city prior to any buildings being burned, seeking a new capital further south. Seeher suggests that rather than some kind of outside force attacking and burning parts of the city, it was the disgruntled inhabitants who had been left behind, abandoned by Suppiluliuma II, who emptied the buildings and eventually burned some of them.[15] Thus, in the end according to Seeher (2001, 633), "Hattuša was not fought and besieged as a thriving capital, but its end was brought about by 'other difficulties.' It was not conquered, but gradually given up; it was not destroyed, it decayed."

It is quite clear that the destruction, no matter over what period of time it took place, was caused by humans. However, there is no clear indication exactly who caused the destruction. It is possible that the inhabits left behind decided to torch some buildings, but it is also as likely that after the city was largely abandoned and emptied by Suppiluliuma II that it was attacked and partially burnt by the Kaska or some other group while there was essentially no one there to defend the city.[16] It could also be argued, though admittedly without any historical precedent from the period, that Suppiluliuma II himself torched some these buildings when he left Hattusa, leaving the once mighty city largely useless, lest any other group should come and easily take over the former capital.[17] Without any new information being brought to light that could help illuminate the existing evidence in a more profound way, there is no clear group(s) responsible for the destruction(s) of some of the buildings at Hattusa ca. 1200 BCE. Indeed, it is quite possible that various buildings fell prey

---

15. Seeher 2001, 633–34. Though importantly Seeher notes that hostile actions should not be completely ruled out, as there are burn marks on some of the city's fortifications and gates.

16. Müller-Karpe (2017, 151–54) prefers a scenario where the Kaska attacked the city prior to any abandonment and simply plundered everything in sight. However, while he makes several objections to Seeher's interpretation, he does not attempt to explain the totality of the missing materials from these buildings. In other instances of destruction by warfare, as discussed in this book, while there will be some degree of plundering, it is unlikely that the Kaska would have removed every piece of pottery from dozens of buildings. It remains the most likely explanation that the city was abandoned prior to any burning events.

17. Which I have suggested as a possible scenario for the fall of Gla in Greece in ch. 4.

180   CHAPTER FIVE

to different actors at different times and were destroyed for diverse reasons
even beyond those suggested here.

Maşat Höyük — Scale: Single-Building — Cause: Unknown

Maşat Höyük is located some 150 km east of Hattusa and 20 km south of Zile.
Once again, while evidence of a likely end of the Late Bronze Age destruction
was uncovered at the site, there is barely any published information describing
it. What is clear is that Maşat Höyük Level II suffered extensive destruction in the
late fourteenth century BCE, and while there was another phase characterized
by Hittite material culture that was built atop the burnt debris of the former
Hittite palace, Level I had lost its palatial attributes (Özgüç 1980, 1982). Even
though Tahsin Özgüç reported that several houses were uncovered that dated
to Level I, there is only a basic description of a single house excavated on the
citadel. This three-room house had been built on the ruins of the Level II palace,
and it was destroyed by fire at some time between 1275–1200 BCE. The house
was filled with pottery, most of which was cooking related (Özgüç 1978, 65–66;
1982, 77, 100). This; however, is the extent of the information on the destruction.
Özgüç (1982, 77) vaguely mentions that another house had been excavated to
the west and that its floor was covered with broken pottery, though he makes
no mention of any burning. Another foundation dated to Level I was uncovered
on the western slope, and its floor too was strewn with pottery, jar covers,
rhyta, stamp seals, stone molds; yet, once again there is no mentioned evidence
of destruction (Özgüç 1982, 100). From the limited information, while it appears
that much of the material culture was left in the structures, there is only enough
published evidence to confirm that one of these houses was destroyed, which
may or may not have been ca. 1200 BCE.

For the cause of this destruction, again, the limited information is a great
hinderance to defining a probable cause. Özgüç (1982, 100) assumed that the
houses had been sacked by the Kaska, and there is some possible evidence that
Maşat Höyük was attacked, as an arrowhead was uncovered in Level I along with
a three-pronged bronze weapon excavated on the East terrace that may belong
to Level I (Özgüç 1982, 112–13). However, there is no contextual information
where these weapons were uncovered, and they cannot conclusively be
associated with warfare. Likewise, there is also no clear evidence that Maşat
Höyük was actually destroyed ca. 1200 BCE. An LH IIIB stirrup jar(s) was
excavated in Level I, which Özgüç (1978, 66; 1980, 309) dated to the first half
of the thirteenth century BCE if not a little latter.[18] A tablet was also uncovered
from Level I dating to the mid-thirteenth century BCE (Özgüç 1982, 152), which

---

18. See also Mee 1978 (132–33) who reports that from what Elizabeth French had seen of the
pottery, the sherds possibly made up six stirrup jars dating to the LH IIIA2–B.

DESTRUCTION IN ANATOLIA AND THE FALL OF THE HITTITE EMPIRE   181

when combined with the imported Mycenean ceramics could give a date for this single-building destruction in the mid-thirteenth century BCE or at least act as a *terminus post quem*. However, until the material from Maşat Höyük is reexamined, there will be no concrete date for this destruction, as an analysis of the wooden remains from the site cannot provide any further information for the absolute date of this destruction event (Mielke 2006a, 84–87).

Fraktin — Scale: Single-Building — Cause: Unknown

Situated fifty kilometers south of Kayseri near the Gümüşören village of Develi was a small Hittite settlement at Fraktin (also spelled Firaktin or Firakdin Höyük), which is better known for the rock relief of Hattusili III and his queen Puduhepa situated two kilometers away from the site (see Bittel 1939; Laroche 1989). Excavations were carried out at Fraktin, but as with many sites, it has been insufficiently published, unlike its more famous relief (Özgüç 1948, 1955a, 1955b). At least one house was uncovered that was burnt in the early twelfth century BCE, as a LH IIIC stirrup jar was uncovered in the destruction debris (Özgüç 1948, 265–67; 1955a; 1955b, 301–2; Mee 1978, 128). Several metal objects were discovered on the floor of one room of the house, while there was also an abundance of pottery that was uncovered in the destruction. Several arrowheads were also discovered on the floor of the burnt house that could be evidence of warfare, but the published information is not clear enough to make this distinction (Özgüç 1948, 267; 1955a; 1955b, 301–4). Suffice it to say, there is not nearly enough information to conclude how extensive this destruction was or what caused it.

Kuşaklı-Sarissa — Scale: Multibuilding — Cause: Warfare

Kuşaklı, which was the ancient Hittite city of Sarissa, is situated some four kilometers from the village of Altınyayla in the Sivas Province.[19] While a destruction event was uncovered at the end of Period III ending the Hittite settlement, the exact date of the destruction is not entirely clear based on the currently available material. According to Andreas Müller-Karpe (2017, 148), based on the style of the Hittite script uncovered on the tablets found in the destruction, this would place the destruction toward the end of the thirteenth century, as a cuneiform sign form on one tablet fragment from the site does not occur prior to the reign of Tudhaliya IV (1240–1220 BCE). It is also possibile that the destruction was later, during the first decades of the twelfth century

---

19. The reports on the excavations at Sarissa have been fragmented over a number of articles that contain the requisite information on this destruction as well as pertinent information on the previous destruction events that rocked the city. See Müller-Karpe 1995, 1996, 1997, 1998, 1999, 2000a, 2000b, 2001, 2002, 2004a, 2004b, 2006, 2009, 2017.

182 CHAPTER FIVE

BCE. One tablet might bear the name of Kuzi-Teshub, the future Great King of Carchemish, and Müller-Karpe (2017, 149–50) has suggested that there may not have been a large gap between the destructions of Sarissa and Hattusa. However this is all speculative and the date of the destruction could have occurred anywhere between ca. 1240–1180 and may or may not be connected to the end of the Late Bronze Age.[20]

No matter when the final destruction of the Hittite settlement at Sarissa occurred, the apparent focus was on Temple 1 situated on the northeast of the mound (see Müller-Karpe 1995, 9–20; 1996, 84; 2017, 108–20, 146–47). Temple 1 was clearly destroyed by fire, as masses of burnt mud brick were uncovered throughout the structure, along with ash and charcoal. In some areas the heat was so intense that it partially deformed or fused pottery as well as burned and charred grain, mostly barley (Müller-Karpe 1995, 16–20; 2017, 146). While an exact inventory of the temple has not been published, Müller-Karpe has stated that it appears as if the building was at least partially plundered before it was burnt, as the majority of the valuable objects seem to have been removed prior to burning. Interestingly, a likely quiver of twelve arrows was discovered in the corner of Room 4.[21] At least one person died in the fire, as a half-preserved human skeleton was uncovered in the rubble of the west wing of the temple (Müller-Karpe 2017, 146). Müller-Karpe (2017, 146–47) reports that the fire likely started in the basement of the northeast wing where a jug was uncovered that had burnt with such intensity that it was fused, and this may have been an incendiary device employed to start the fire that eventually burned the entirety of Temple 1.

Other evidence of destruction by fire was uncovered in Buildings A, B, and D on the opposite side of the mound from Temple 1 (Müller-Karpe 1995, 27; 1997, 105–6; 2002, 334; 2017, 147). However, there are no clear descriptions of exactly how damaged these buildings were. Müller-Karpe (2017, 147) only states that unlike Temple 1, few of the air-dried mud bricks used in the construction of the superstructures for Buildings A, B, and D were completely fired until they were hardened and red in color. Thus, while it is possible that these buildings suffered damage by fire, the exact extent of it is currently unclear.[22] Another

---

20. The wood samples taken from the site have not been a help in dating the material; see discussion in Mielke 2006a, 89.

21. Müller-Karpe 1995, 15–17. However, there remained a large quantity of ceramics as over 36,000 fragments were recorded from Temple 1 (Müller-Karpe 1996, 84). Müller-Karpe (1995, 15–16) has also suggested that there is some evidence that at some point after the building had burnt people came back and dug into the temple in search of valuables.

22. Müller-Karpe suggests that more of the site was destroyed based on the geomagnetic survey conducted at Sarissa, which indicates there are additional structures with signs of burning yet to be excavated. He assumes that these buildings date to the end of the Hittite period and were destroyed at the same time as Temple 1 and Buildings A, B, and D (Müller-Karpe 2017, 147). He bases this presumption on the assumption that the debris from previous destruction events would have

point of interest is that a dagger, a lance tip, and arrowheads were uncovered in several locations within this destruction, though Müller-Karpe (2017, 147) is not clear on the exact find spots. Müller-Karpe (2017, 147) has also asserted that evidence of destruction was uncovered in some of the houses of the *Westhang*; however, due to the severe erosion that affected the slope on this side of the mound, there is no clear indication of what happened to these houses at the end of Period III (Mielke 2006b, 178). From the general information provided thus far by Müller-Karpe (2017, 147, 154), Sarissa did suffer a multibuilding destruction event in an act of war. There is nevertheless an important caveat that needs to be taken into consideration when examining the impact that this destruction might have had on Sarissa.

Much like Hattusa, the background to this destruction event must be taken into consideration, as Sarissa was hardly a thriving metropolis whenever Temple 1 was burnt. Large swaths of the site were already in ruins prior to this final destruction event. The grand temple of the storm god, dubbed Building C, was burnt to the ground along with the northwest gate, and part of Building D, sometime near the end of the fourteenth century BCE. Yet, none of these structures were rebuilt and their ruins were left rotting in some of the most prominent positions on the mound (Müller-Karpe 2017, 141–43). Building E, which is situated to the northeast of Building C, was abandoned without any evidence of destruction, likely before the destruction of Building C (Arnhold 2009, 135–36, 2014, 9; Müller-Karpe 2002, 337; 2017, 144). The caravanserai, the royal stable, was also destroyed in a separate but slightly later destruction, most likely by the earthquake that struck Sarissa in the early to mid-thirteenth century BCE, burying at least one horse alive (Müller-Karpe 2017, 144–45). Thus, Sarissa at the time of Temple 1's destruction was hardly a thriving city, as the majority of the excavated structures were already burnt ruins and the city's defenses were at least partially defunct, which would have left the city essentially open to attack.[23] We cannot view this destruction event as a prosperous city taken by surprise; rather, it was a city already in decline that was finally snuffed out with the burning of Temple 1.

---

been cleared away. This is, however, a strange claim to make as much of the site lay in literal piles of burnt and collapsed mud bricks at the time when Temple 1 was burnt. Thus, while it is possible there are more buildings which were burnt at the same time as Temple 1, it is just as likely that these buildings were burnt when Building C was burnt ca. 1300 BCE or during the early to mid-thirteenth century earthquake that struck Sarissa.

23. The southwest gate that was also excavated may have been out of use as well, but there are no definitive dates for the end of this structure (Müller-Karpe 1998, 129–137; 1999, 69–79).

184 CHAPTER FIVE

Kilise Tepe — Scale: Site-Wide — Cause: Unknown

Just west of the Göksu River is the mound of Kilise Tepe. The main structure excavated that dates to the end of the Late Bronze Age is the Stele Building, which was named after a sandstone stele uncovered in Room 3, indicating that at least part of the building had a cultic function.[24] The Stele Building was destroyed by fire at the end of its Phase IIc, which the excavators date to ca. 1190 BCE.[25] But it is not clear exactly how much of the building was burnt, as the floor levels differed throughout the structure and the higher floors were completely obliterated by later construction activity leaving few traces of destruction (Hansen and Postgate 1998, 112). In Room 3, the sandstone altar, cracked by the fire, was discovered in more than seventy pieces, while the floor was covered by mud bricks containing pieces of carbonized wooden beams. Room 4 too was filled with destruction debris, a burnt beam, and there was a large storage jar filled with burnt einkorn (Postgate and Thomas 2007, 123–28).

Another important find in Room 4 was a single arrowhead, which was the only weapon of war uncovered in this destruction event.[26] Room 5 was likewise burnt and contained burnt lentils and barley, while the eastern wall had been heated to such a degree that it had been transformed into a jumble of vitrified mud bricks.[27] Room 6 had its floor burnt orange while in Room 7 the fire burned so intensely it created a sixty-centimeter-deep layer of highly vitrified destruction debris that lay on the floor and against the walls. The floor of Room 8 had also been burnt orange and jars filled with burnt seeds and cleaned barley were discovered in the room (Postgate and Thomas 2007, 131–36). Outside of the Stele Building, destruction by fire was also uncovered in the East Building, which was most striking in its Room 20, which contained one meter of calcined and distorted mud bricks, as well as a silver figurine and jewelry (Postgate and Thomas 2007, 138–42). The Northeast Annex, a triangular space with a variety of fire installations that may have acted as the kitchen for the Stele Building, was covered with heavily burnt destruction debris (142–43). Thus, it appears that Kilise Tepe suffered a site-wide destruction at some point in the early twelfth century BCE. However, there are questions as to what might have caused this massive fire that touched every structure at the site.

---

24. A possible altar was also found in Room 3, while a cache of astragali was uncovered in Room 7. This further suggests that there was some kind of cultic function for at least part of the structure, though not necessarily the whole building, which likely had some administrative or storage purpose (Postgate and Thomas 2007, 123–26, 137).

25. Hansen and Postgate 1998, 112; Postgate and Thomas 2007, 35; Bouthillier et al. 2014; Postgate 2017, 5.

26. Postgate and Thomas 2007, 36, 129. Find number 1572 K19/150.

27. Postgate and Thomas 2007, 130. The excavators assume that oil may have been stored in the room, which could explain the high heat witnessed in Room 5.

One issue is that while a single arrowhead was uncovered in the destruction debris, an arrowhead is not positive proof for warfare. More revealing is that the buildings may have been partially abandoned prior to the destruction. As Postgate and Thomas (2007, 147) note, "It seems possible that the users of the building had warning [before the destruction]: few artefacts were found in situ on the floors, but perhaps more tellingly several of the pot emplacements in Rooms 4, 5, 7 and 8 no longer held vessels." Moreover, a thick layer of loose aggregates across several of the floors may be an indication that the building was abandoned prior to the destruction, allowing time for this natural buildup of material to accumulate. There is also some indication that some of the timbers were removed from the walls, all of which would indicate that the inhabitants might have fled prior to this burning episode (Postgate and Thomas 2007, 147). However, there is no clear indication what might have caused this destruction or why, if the people had fled, they left their foodstuffs behind to be burnt.

Soli Höyük — Scale: Partial — Cause: Unknown

Eleven kilometers west of the city of Mersin lies Soli Höyük, and unfortunately there is limited information as to exactly what transpired at the site ca. 1200 BCE at the end of its Period VI.1. Evidence of destruction dating to the beginning of the twelfth century BCE is sparse. An ashy layer was excavated in Squares E9 and F9 that contained burnt and broken kitchen wares; however, both of these squares are situated on the slope of the mound and there was no secure architecture associated with these finds. In Square G8, which is adjacent to Square F9, some remains of a building with a fallen roof that covered burnt and broken pottery was also uncovered (Yağcı 2007a, 800; 2007b, 367, 384; 2008, 238; Novák et al. 2017, 155; Remzi Yağcı pers. comm. 03/04/20). Remzi Yağcı (2007b, 384, 384; 2008, 239) associated this burning with the arrival of the Sea Peoples; however, from the severely limited information, it is entirely unclear what caused the burning or how extensive this partial destruction event was.

Mersin-Yumuktepe — Scale: Multibuilding — Cause: Unknown

Yumuktepe is located on the northwestern periphery of the city of Mersin. The site was originally excavated by John Garstang (1953) in the early twentieth century and a renewed excavation at the site has been ongoing since the late twentieth century.[28] Unfortunately, there is limited information on the destruction event originally excavated by Garstang. He uncovered evidence of destruction at the end of his Level V, which he dated to ca. 1200 BCE and

---

28. Köroğlu 1998; Caneva and Sevin 2004; Jean 2006; Caneva and Köroğlu 2010; Caneva and Jean 2016; Novák et al. 2017.

186   CHAPTER FIVE

correlated with the actions of the Sea Peoples.[29] However, his description of the destruction is regrettably lacking in many details that could have provided a fuller understanding of the extent and possible cause behind this destruction event. In his description of the destruction, Garstang (1953, 239–40) notes that, "the street..., the stone foundations of the fortress wall, and the whole area to the northwest, were found buried beneath half a metre of ashes and brick refuse." He goes on to say that in many places along the fortification wall the heat appears to have been so intense that many of the stones had turned into a white powder when they were heated to the point that they were calcined and had disintegrated (240). However, in the houses Garstang (240) noted that, "Comparatively little burnt debris was found inside the houses, the floors of which at this period occur somewhat above the level of the street outside. But here and there (notably in Rooms 42 and 52) scattered bricks lay actually upon the pavements." Unfortunately, this is the extent of the information on the destruction from Garstang's excavations. While from his description, the fire appears to have been intense, particularly against the fortification wall, it is not clear to what degree, if any, the destruction affected the houses.[30] In Garstang's original excavation, he focused his attention on the western side of the mound, while the renewed excavation uncovered evidence of Level V in their Southern Trench. Here too possible evidence of Garstang's destruction, dubbed Level "Vb," may have been uncovered, though what was uncovered was fragmentary as only scorched or calcined earth with traces of fire were found (Caneva and Sevin 2004, 75). Thus, it is possible that the destruction was more widespread, affecting more of the mound, but this is unclear based on the currently available evidence.

Finally, there is the issue of the date of this multibuilding destruction of unknown cause. While Garstang dated the destruction to before 1200 BCE prior to the destruction event at nearby Tarsus (Barnett 1940, 100; Garstang 1953, 243), the renewed excavation has cast some doubt on this date. The possible destruction uncovered in the southern trench at the end of Level "Vb" at Yumuktepe was not the last Hittite settlement, as another one followed, dubbed Level "Va" by the current excavators. This was the last Late Bronze Age level, one that apparently was not found or noticed by Garstang. Thus, at the moment, all that can be said for the date of the destruction uncovered in Level V and perhaps "Vb" is that it occurred in the second half of the thirteenth century BCE while Level "Va" too belongs to the late thirteenth century (Caneva and

---

29. Barnett 1940, 100; Garstang 1953, 243. Mee notes that based on the Mycenean pottery uncovered by Garstang the date of the destruction is before 1200 BCE without being able to clarify a more precise end of Level V (Mee 1978, 133).

30. Because of this ambiguity and if the houses were destroyed or not, the scale of the destruction is only a multibuilding, as there is insufficient evidence that it was site-wide.

Sevin 2004, 82; Jean 2006, 328; Novák et al. 2017, 160). It remains a distinct possibility that the Level V destruction took place before the end of the Late Bronze Age. Hopefully, further excavations at Yumuktepe will be able to clarify this chronological quandary.

Tarsus-Gözlükule — Scale: Site-Wide — Cause: Unknown

Located on the southern periphery of modern Tarsus, the double-peaked mound of Gözlükule hosted a Hittite settlement that was largely exposed by Hetty Goldman in the early twentieth century dubbed the LB IIa phase.[31] As with many of the older excavations, the vague nature of the published evidence makes coming to any conclusion for the destruction event a difficult task.

The Hittite settlement was uncovered in both Goldman's Sections A and B. A monumental structure was excavated in Section A that Goldman (Goldman et al. 1956, 49–50) originally assumed was a temple, as at the time it was the only monumental Hittite building excavated outside of Hattusa and Alaca Höyük. However, after further analysis, it is unclear exactly what specific function the building had. It could have been a temple, palace, or an administrative structure, though as Aslı Özyar (2015, 283) has made clear, it was used both as a metal workshop and for administrative purposes. Unfortunately, Goldman did not publish any record of the destruction, as she simply states that Section A had been burnt.[32] Steven Karacic, who had access to the original field notes, states that the unpublished dairies yielded some clues to the fate of the monumental structure as its "mud-brick superstructure, wood beams, and stone foundation all preserved evidence of destruction by fire."[33] Yet, this limited description is the extent of our knowledge about the fate of this building.

For Section B, there is at least a slightly more detailed account. Two large houses, the East House and West House, were uncovered, and at least the East House may have been the residence of an official, given the presence of several seal-impressed bullae (Goldman et al. 1956, 51–57; Özyar 2015, 283). Both houses were destroyed by fire. The East House was filled with burnt debris and the fire had burned especially hot in the so-called Manger Room, where the superstructure had been baked to a cement-like hardness, while the stone foundation had been calcined and there were the remains of burnt beams. Goldman (Goldman et al. 1956, 51–55) assumed that the room stored

---

31. Goldman et al. 1956; Özyar et al. 2012; Yalçin 2013; Karacic 2014; Özyar 2015; Ünlü 2016; Novák et al. 2017, 161–63.

32. Goldman et al. 1956, 51. And this too was only in the context of comparing it to Section B where she states, "As in section A, all buildings [in Section B] ended in a great conflagration" (51).

33. Karacic 2014, 119. Slane (1987) also addressed the architecture of the Hittite settlement, however, her analysis does not provide any additional information outside of what can be found in Goldman et al. 1956.

188   CHAPTER FIVE

fodder, which would have provided the fuel to create such an intense fire. In
Room 9, a bronze lancehead was uncovered at the stub of a wall, while two
arrowheads were also uncovered in the East House, though no specific find
context was listed.[34] The West House too was destroyed by fire and was filled
with burnt debris and remains of burnt wood. Goldman (Goldman et al. 1956,
56–57) notes that it appears that most objects, other than a bin of charred
wheat, had been taken out of the building prior to the destruction. Another
briefly mentioned building, the South House, was also described as destroyed
by fire (58). Goldman assumed that both Sections A and B were destroyed at
the same time by the Sea Peoples in the last quarter of the thirteenth century
BCE. She supposed that the Sea Peoples had largely emptied the site of most if
its precious goods before ransacking it (63, 350–51). The renewed excavations
at Gözlükule did not reach any substantial remains dating to the end of the
Late Bronze Age. What was uncovered was characterized by debris, sometimes
with traces of burning, though nothing else can be said at this time (Özyar et
al. 2012; Yalçin 2013; Ünlü 2016).

From the at times very limited information, it is again a difficult task to
pin down a possible cause for this site-wide destruction event; however, it is
likely that warfare was involved. Several weapons of war were uncovered in
the LB IIa Hittite destruction; seven derived from Section A and at least the tip
of a spear along with the tang of a sword were uncovered in the monumental
building from Section A.[35] Two arrowheads were uncovered in the East House
from Section B along with a spearhead, while another arrowhead was found
in an unspecified location in Section B.[36] Unfortunately, the majority of these
finds are without a clear context, and while a street was uncovered in both
Sections A and B, we do not know if any of these weapons were discovered
on either of these streets. No gold was uncovered in either Section A or B
dating to the time of the destruction.[37] Given that the West Building was largely
emptied prior to its destruction, and in combination with the weapons of war,
of which at least four were uncovered in a residential building, the hand of man
was likely involved in this destruction, but this cannot be confirmed beyond a
reasonable doubt.

One recent discovery, which may alter our interpretation of this destruction,
is connected to the question of when it occurred. Radiocarbon measurements
from charcoal uncovered during the renewed excavation tentatively places the

---

34. Goldman et al. 1956, 55, 291–92. The lancehead is Bronze #97 while the two arrowheads are
Bronze #83 and #88.

35. Goldman et al. 1956, 291–93. From Section A: Bronze #78, #79, #80, #84, #89, #90, #92; from
the monumental building: spearhead: Bronze #96, sword: Bronze #109.

36. Goldman et al. 1956, 291–292. Bronze #82, #83, #88, #97.

37. Goldman et al. 1956, 301. Two pieces of gold dating to some nebulous time in LB II as a
whole were recovered.

destruction between 1522–1258 BCE with a 2-sigma probability (Özyar, Ünlü, and Pilvaci 2019, 55). Thus, further investigation may place this destruction before the end of the Late Bronze Age, which could also push back the date for the destruction witnessed at Yumuktepe.

Kinet Höyük — Scale: Partial — Cause: Unknown

Kinet Höyük is located in southeastern Cilicia thirty-five kilometers north of Iskenderun, and as with many another Anatolian sites, there is little information about what occurred at the site ca. 1200 BCE. Part of a single house from Period 13.1 was burnt ca. 1200 BCE. Burnt mud bricks from the collapsed superstructure were uncovered on the floor, which unfortunately was highly affected by later pitting activities. Two ovens and several objects used in food preparation were uncovered in the attached courtyard (Gates 1998, 265; 2000, 194–95; 2006, 301–2; Novák et al. 2017, 178–79). Due to the limited information there is no way to assign a possible cause, or even to know the extent of this partial destruction.

Norşuntepe — Scale: Multibuilding — Cause: Warfare

Norşuntepe is now an island in the Keban Dam Lake and was excavated by Harald Hauptmann during the 1970s prior to the dam's completion. While an end of the Late Bronze Age destruction was found at Norşuntepe, the lack of a meaningful final publication leaves little information to draw from to help interpret this destruction event, as what information there is remains fragmentary. Level III at Norşuntepe was the final Hittite phase for the site and the destruction event that burnt at least a significant portion of the excavated remains took place within the early twelfth century BCE (von Gladiß and Hauptmann 1974, 17; Hauptmann 2001, 602; Müller 2005, 112–13). While Hauptmann and Günther Korbel (von Gladiß and Hauptmann 1974, 17; Korbel 1985, 45, 53; Hauptmann 2001, 602) report that evidence of destruction by fire was uncovered in every area where Level III was excavated, the reports describing the Level III buildings and their associated finds are sparse and lacking crucial information or descriptions.

The remains of a highly disturbed house, which Hauptmann described as destroyed by fire, was uncovered on the southern terrace and importantly, an arrowhead was discovered in the rubble (Hauptmann 1972, 111; Korbel 1985, 28). On the acropolis, two building complexes separated by a street were also excavated and both are reported as having been burnt. Within the destruction debris were carnelian beads, several bronze tools, and three bronze arrowheads, one of which was lodged in a wall according to Korbel (Hauptmann 1974, 89; Korbel 1985, 22–23, 53). Unfortunately, while other Level III structures were

190   CHAPTER FIVE

excavated, there are no adequate descriptions to shed light on what their fate
was, and because of this it is completely unclear exactly how much of the site
was actually destroyed by fire.[38] Given that several arrowheads were uncovered
in disparate structures, one of which was likely lodged in a wall when it was
excavated, warfare seems to be a reasonable conclusion for this destruction.
However, it needs to be said that this is based on the highly preliminary, often
fragmented, and at times conflicting reports on the end of Level III.[39] Because of
this the classification itself should be considered preliminary until the material
from Level III is properly published.

Did Destruction Fell the Hittite Empire?

At the beginning of this chapter, I noted that nearly twenty years ago Bryce
had pointed out that Anatolia in general suffered little destruction at the end of
the Late Bronze Age. Indeed, this sentiment has been borne out by this study,
as demonstrated in chapter 3: eleven of the twenty-four cited destruction
events are false destructions. Sites such as Kaman-Kalehöyük and Beycesultan
endured destruction well before ca. 1200 BCE, while Tille Höyük and Lidar
Höyük suffered a destruction event well after 1200 BCE. While thirteen sites in
this vast geographic area did indeed undergo some kind of destruction event ca.
1200 BCE, the pattern of evidence indicates that these destruction events were
unlikely to have brought about or sped along the end of the Hittite Empire in
one dramatic flair. This is evident when observing the patterns of destruction,
particularly around the former Hittite capital of Hattusa, where one might
expect to find the most damning evidence of destruction-induced collapse.

Four sites—Hattusa, Alishar Höyük, Maşat Höyük, and Alaca Höyük—have
all been cited as destroyed ca. 1200 BCE. However, this thorough examination
of the archaeological evidence reveals a pattern that indicates that destruction
was not the prime mover behind the fall of the Hittite Empire, but rather that the
region suffered a gradual degradation that finally ended with the abandonment
of Hattusa. This all began with the destruction event in Maşat Höyük's Level
II, where the Hittite palace was burnt, ending the monumental phase of the
site's Late Bronze Age history ca. 1300 BCE. What was left behind were only
some houses built on the ruins of a once thriving Hittite town. It was during
the final phase of habitation, Level I, that this no-longer-thiving settlement
experienced a single-building destruction—and even this was most likely not
at the end of the Late Bronze Age, as two key chronological markers, a tablet

---

38. Thus, the scale is classified as a multibuilding destruction though it very well may have
been site-wide.

39. E.g., Hauptmann only says that the arrowheads were uncovered in the structures on the
acropolis and that they were buried in the rubble, while Korbel, who provides a more detailed
overview of Level III, specifically states that one was lodged in a wall.

and Mycenean pottery, both dating to the mid-thirteenth century BCE were found, likely placing this relatively finite destruction well before 1200 BCE. At Alishar Höyük, the site did not even make it to the end of the Hittite Empire, as it was abandoned without destruction ca. 1250 BCE (Gorny 1990, 378, 434–35). Alaca Höyük too, while commonly cited as having been destroyed ca. 1200 BCE, experienced no destruction at the end of the Late Bronze Age (see ch. 3). Given the lack of destruction, it is most likely that the religiously significant site was simply abandoned.

Alaca Höyük's abandonment without destruction can be correlated with the circumstances surrounding the end of Hattusa. It too was largely abandoned without destruction, leaving the city and its beleaguered inhabitants open either to attack or self-desecration by those same disenchanted residents. Hattusa was not in a state of supreme condition when some of its buildings were destroyed, as Genz has keenly noted. Several of the city's gates were hastily blocked while several of the temples in the central temple district were utilized as quarries for the building of small houses and workshops (Genz 2013, 471–72). This is clear evidence of crisis architecture and that not all was well even before any destruction took place. Even though there is no indication from the textual material uncovered at Hattusa suggesting that the city and the empire were in decline or on the verge of collapse (see discussion in Miller 2020), the archaeological evidence speaks of decline, crisis, and abandonment. Consequently, by the time Hattusa suffered the burning of some of its buildings, it was in a period of crisis; it had been abandoned by its ruler, and had lost its function as the capital of the Hittite Empire. The eventual destruction of some of the major structures at the site did not create this situation or cause the city to lose its royal and political function. Rather, the final multibuilding destruction simply served as the capstone to an already ongoing process of degradation and abandonment. The fact that Hattusa was left to lie in ruins with only meager remains dating to the early Iron Age was not the result of the destruction event(s).[40] Rather, it was the multitude of events preceding the burning of some buildings that ultimately led to the fall of the city. Therefore, taking all of this together, no destruction ca. 1200 BCE forced the Hittites from any of these sites, and destruction was not a causal factor in the end of the empire in the Hittite heartland.

The same could be said for two other geographically disparate sites, Troy and Kuşaklı-Sarissa, who share a commonality. Both sites did undergo destructions at the end of the Late Bronze Age, but the lead-up to those destructions is as important as the destruction themselves. For Troy, while Troy VIIa was destroyed in an act of war, the site appears to have been in an impoverished state with temporary housing, crowded living spaces, and an

---

40. For a discussion of the early Iron Age material see Genz 2013, 472 and the references therein.

192 CHAPTER FIVE

emphasis on storage, which appears to have been the aftershock of the major destruction event at the end of Troy VIh ca. 1300 BCE.[41] Whether or not the crisis architecture witnessed in Troy VIIa was the result of hasty preparation in the face of an advancing army as Blegen saw it or the attempts of the populace to rebuild after the devastating earthquake of Troy VIh as Penelope Mountjoy proposes, the fact of the matter is that the city was hardly thriving when it was attacked.[42] Moreover, what we must recall is that Troy VIIa should have had nearly a century to recover after the VIh destruction event. A relatively brief period of impoverishment would be the commonsense result of the VIh destruction, as Mountjoy suggests. However, this crisis should not have endured for one hundred years. Under normal circumstances a city could, given this amount of time, regain its standing after a shock, as was the case for many other cities throughout the Late Bronze Age Eastern Mediterranean. Therefore, after the VIh destruction there must have been other systemic cultural and economic changes at Troy, leaving it in a position where it could not rebuild or be revitalized to the degree that it once enjoyed. Thus, of the two destructions, VIh and VIIa, the critical one, the one that truly hampered and devalued the city was the destruction at the end of Troy VIh. The circumstances surrounding this particular destruction must have created a situation in which the inhabitants would not or could not recover from, even with nearly a century of time on their side.

In a like manner, the same can be said of Kuşaklı-Sarissa. As detailed above, much of Sarissa was laid waste prior to the destruction of Temple 1, which may or may not have been at the end of the Late Bronze Age. At least one of the city's gates, the stable, and, most significantly, the once magnificent temple to the storm god were all piles of rubble well before 1200 BCE. In

---

41. Blegen et al. 1950; Blegen, Caskey, and Rawson 1953; Blegen 1975, 161; Mountjoy 1999b, 296–97; 2017, 88; Nur and Cline 2000, 56–57; Cline 2013, 93–94. The VIh destruction was likely brought on by earthquake. Blegen (1975, 161) describes Troy VIIa as, "The houses themselves, for the most part small, were numerous; they were crowded closely together, often with party walls, and they seem to have filled the whole area inside the fortification, where they were superposed over the earlier buildings, as well as the considerable spaces that had previously been left open. Another distinctive feature is the presence in almost every house of large pithoi or storage jars: ranging in number from one or two to eight or ten or even twenty, they were sunk deeply beneath the floors so that the mouth, covered by a stone slab, projected only an inch or two above the ground."

42. Blegen et al. 1950; Blegen 1975, 162. As Blegen (1975, 162) describes it, "The crowding together of a great number of small houses within the fortress and the installation of innumerable huge storage jars to lay up a supply of provisions are factors that suggest preparations for a siege, and the final holocaust was the usual accompaniment of the capture, sacking and burning of an ancient town. The general agreement of this evidence with the accounts preserved in Greek tradition cannot safely be disregarded: if a Troy of Priam, besieged and taken by an Agamemnon, ever actually existed in fact, it must be identified with the settlement called VIIa." Mountjoy 1999b, 296–97; 2017, 88.

both cases, while Troy and Sarissa suffered destruction at the end of the Late Bronze Age, the more impactful destruction had already occurred one hundred or more years prior, leaving these once great cities in a more or less ruined state much like Maşat Höyük. From an archaeological perspective, they no longer held the prominence that they once enjoyed, a standing that was forever marred by their respective destructions during the fourteenth century BCE.[43] Consequently, while the final destructions at both sites would have been devastating to their respective communities, the timing of these events at ca. 1200 BCE is unlikely to have been a factor in the subsequent abandonment of Late Bronze Age characteristics at both sites. Rather, this outcome would have obtained regardless of when the destructions had occurred, even if it had been earlier in the thirteenth century BCE.

Further afield, this was indeed the case for the once mighty Hazor in the southern Levant, which faced a period of crisis prior to its final multibuilding destruction in the mid-thirteenth century BCE. After this event the site lost its Late Bronze Age Canaanite characteristics and was abandoned, even though this was long before the "end of the Late Bronze Age" (Zuckerman 2007; Ben-Tor and Zuckerman 2008). The same could also be said of Qatna in Syria, which experienced a destruction event ca. 1340 BCE, and what developed from this event was only a scanty and impoverished settlement (Pfälzner 2007, 42–43; 2012, 774, 778–79; Bonacossi 2013, 119–21). The chronological date did not matter for either of these sites, and it is unlikely that just because Troy and Sarissa suffered destruction ca. 1200 BCE that the timing itself was the crucial factor in the changes witnessed at both sites.

Turning away from Troy and Sarissa, the region of Cilicia too does not offer a portrait of sudden violent destruction at the end of the Late Bronze Age. As laid out in chapter 3, both Porsuk and Domuztepe have no evidence of an end of the Late Bronze Age destruction. From here, there is a clear attenuated process of destruction that likely took place over the course of several decades, perhaps beginning well into the thirteenth century BCE. At Tarsus, the recent C14 dates preliminarily suggest that Goldman's destruction was in the first half of the thirteenth century BCE. Given that the destruction of Yumuktepe may have occurred before the destruction uncovered at Tarsus, and that a subsequent Hittite phase was uncovered dating after Garstang's Level V, it is at least likely that both destructions occurred sometime in the thirteenth century BCE prior to the end of the Late Bronze Age or ca. 1200 BCE. As a

---

43. An interesting possibility for the reason why Maşat Höyük and Sarissa may not have built back after their end of the fourteenth-century BCE destruction events is that these could be linked to the plague of Mursili II (for a discussion of the plague prayers, see Beckman 1997; Singer 2002). It is at least reasonable to entertain the idea that if the area was gripped by a plague, that after the destruction events there simply was not the manpower needed to rebuild.

194   CHAPTER FIVE

result, there were likely several decades between these two destruction events
and the site-wide destruction at Kilise Tepe ca. 1190 BCE. The destructions
at both Soli Höyük and Kinet Höyük may have also occurred during the
first decades of twelfth century BCE. However, there is as yet no evidence of
how extensive these destructions were nor what might have caused them, as
both could simply have been accidental or natural destructions—or perhaps
not even destructions at all. Given the probable chronological dispersion of
these destruction events in Cilicia, it is unlikely that they are temporally or
causally correlated with one another. To this point, even though Soli Höyük
and Yumuktepe are only a handful of kilometers away from each other, the
time separating their respective destruction events negates any correlation
between the two events.

A tangential point to go along with this discussion is that traditionally
Qode has been presumed to be the region of Cilicia, and given that it was
one of the regions listed as "cutoff" by the Sea Peoples, this has led many to
assume that the destruction in Cilicia was brought on by the Sea Peoples.[44]
However, as Zsolt Simon (2011, 263) has recently pointed out, there is currently
no reasonable linguistic evidence to pinpoint where exactly Qode was located
other than that it was in, "North Syria, and, more precisely, the territory of
Naharina/Mittani." Since there is no linguistic and thus no historical evidence
placing the Sea Peoples in Cilicia at the time, it stands to reason that they had
no dealings in any of these destructions.[45] Moreover, it is more than likely that
the destructions uncovered at Yumuktepe and Tarsus occurred well before the
Sea Peoples' supposed destructive march through Anatolia and Syria, and these
destruction events should be separated from the now mythical figures of Late
Bronze Age destruction.

Moving further afield to the final four destructions in Anatolia ca. 1200
BCE, while a multibuilding destruction was uncovered at Norşuntepe dating
to the beginning of the twelfth century BCE, other sites in the region such as
Tille Höyük and Lidar Höyük appear to have survived ca. 1200 BCE intact and
their Late Bronze Age characteristics were only extinguished nearly a century
or more later. Thus, while Norşuntepe might have succumbed to an attack, the
region surrounding the site was not washed over by a tide of destruction. At
both Fraktin and Karaoğlan, the limited published evidence of destruction does
not bespeak a national tragedy; rather, no matter what the cause was for either

---

44. See Simon 2011 for an overview of all of the traditional and modern theories for the location of Qode, and why all of these suggestions fail to offer a realistic solution for its. For a more
complete analysis of the texts related to the Sea Peoples and the inherent problems in associating
the Sea Peoples with any destruction in the Eastern Mediterranean, see ch. 7 and the references
therein.

45. Nor is there any evidence that they were in the region of Ugarit, as will be discussed in
detail in ch. 7.

event, these were local disasters whose effects would not reach far beyond the borders of the site. Moreover, given that LH IIIC pottery was uncovered at Fraktin, it is likely that its single-building destruction occurred after the Hittite Empire had already collapsed, and thus could not have been a causal factor in said collapse. Likewise, the temple that was burned at Oymaağaç Höyük-Nerik reveals nothing other than that it burnt, but not the cause or affect of that event, as the settlement continued after the destruction event (Czichon et al. 2011, 2016).

The question that must be asked in light of this evidence is, What role, if any, did destruction play in the fall of the Hittite Empire? There are of a course a legion of theories attempting to explain exactly how the Hittite Empire might have fallen, which have been discussed and documented at length elsewhere.[46] These include political instabilities; dynastic changes; grain shortages resulting from drought or overstressing a fragile ecosystem; war in both the east and west of the empire; earthquakes; destruction by the Kaska; disloyal vassal states bucking their duties while withholding their obligatory support; the activities of the Sea Peoples on the Cilician coast bringing destruction while hampering trade; as well as deaths in the royal family, among other factors mingled together that could have brought about the end of the empire.

While this study of destruction cannot answer the question, it can remove from the predominate theories some of the extraneous hypothetical suggestions that are not borne out by the archaeological record. The first of these is of course the proposed effect that earthquakes might have had on Anatolia. There is currently no evidence that earthquakes caused any of the recorded damage in the thirteen sites in Anatolia that suffered a destruction ca. 1200 BCE. It remains a possibility that Karaoğlan was struck by a seismic event at some unspecified time in the thirteenth century BCE; however, even if the site was harmed by an earthquake, the damage done to one site by one earthquake would not have been enough to bring down the Hittite Empire.[47]

The Sea Peoples can also be written off as harmful agents moving against the Hittite Empire during its final years. While they have not been utilized as a causal explanation for the damage at Hattusa for decades (see discussion in Genz 2013, 477); nevertheless, they are still factored in as a disruptive force on

---

46. Bittel 1983; Yakar 1993, 2006; Singer 2000; Nur and Cline 2001; Seeher 2001; Bryce 2005, 327–56; Collins 2007, 65–80; Beal 2011; Genz 2013; Middleton 2017, 155–81; Müller-Karpe 2017, 151–54; de Martino 2018; Schachner 2020. See Alaura 2020 for further references.

47. As mentioned above, Sarissa likely suffered damage from an earthquake during the mid-thirteenth century BCE, well before the end of the Late Bronze Age. The excavators from Oymaağaç Höyük-Nerik have also suggested that the site experienced an earthquake during the mid-thirteenth century BCE (Czichon et al. 2011, 215; 2016, 37). If both sites did suffer an earthquake in the mid-thirteenth century BCE it would not have been the same event, as the sites are separated by more than three hundred kilometers.

196 CHAPTER FIVE

the Cilician coast. However, as mentioned above, there is no historical evidence placing the Sea Peoples in Cilicia ca. 1200 BCE, and Yumuktepe and Tarsus suffered destruction before their supposed warpath even began. Moreover, while Ugarit's loyalty to the crown in Hattusa was fraught during the final years of the Late Bronze Age (Singer 1999, 709–29), it remained an active port of trade for the empire up until the final destruction of the city. Since it appears that the Hittite Empire fell prior to the destruction of Ugarit (de Martino 2018, 23–24), trade would have been able to continue and move overland where the Hittites maintained control. In addition, if Suppiluliuma II had gained some sort of sovereignty over Alashiya as he claims (Bryce 2005, 332–33), then in the closing years of the empire, the Hittites would have had sovereignty over the coastal lands in the entire northeastern Mediterranean basin. This would have allowed for trade to go to any number of ports before heading to the heartland.[48] Of course, piratical activity or coastal warfare in the region would have had a negative impact (see Emanuel 2016; 2018; 2020, 90–124). Nevertheless, there is not enough historical or archaeological evidence that trade was greatly disturbed prior to the fall of the empire and certainly not resulting from any destruction.[49]

This brings us back to the question, What effect, if any at all, did destruction ca. 1200 BCE have on the fall of the Hittite Empire? The straightforward answer is likely little to none, based on the plain fact that most Hittite sites simply were not destroyed ca. 1200 BCE, and of the few that did suffer a destruction event, several, such as Maşat Höyük, Sarissa, or Hattusa, were already shells of their former selves. The destruction of Troy, while dramatic, should not be causally connected with the fall of the Hittite Empire, particularly if we separate its destruction and the supposed swath of destruction caused by the Sea Peoples. Moreover, the distance between Troy and Hattusa is more than eight hundred kilometers as the crow flies, and the two destruction events, while chronologically close, are causally discounted. Of the other destructions that took place, they were likely spread out over the course of fifty or more years, as several of these events have insubstantial rational for being end of the Late Bronze Age destructions. Moreover, given that seven of the false destruction events in Anatolia are misdated destruction events, since further research revealed that they did not occur ca. 1200 BCE, it is more than likely in my opinion that several of the destruction events, such as those from Maşat Höyük, Karaoğlan, and perhaps even Yumuktepe, Tarsus, and Sarissa will also

---

48. An example of this trade might be encapsulated by the Cape Gelidonya shipwreck that sank off the southern coast of Turkey ca. 1200 BCE; see Bass 1961, 2010, 2013.

49. There is also the issue that there is little evidence that the Hittites participated or even needed to participate in interregional trade; see discussion in Genz 2011.

prove to fall outside of the end of the Late Bronze Age.[50] Most likely these destructions occurred earlier in the thirteenth century BCE, but this suggestion will only be confirmed or negated after further investigation.

We must recall that violence, forced abandonment, open field warfare, and other hostile actions that can be carried out against an empire need not result in destruction. The two phenomena must be separated. For example, it is unlikely that Suppiluliuma II joyfully packed up his capital city to move to a trendier location simply because it was the thing to do at the time. Rather, Hattusa must have been vulnerable from some expected force or threat that required Suppiluliuma to leave for his own safety in an attempt at maintaining power, a move that ultimately failed. Importantly for this discussion is that whatever the stressor(s) was, it was not a vast swath of destruction surrounding Hattusa crippling the hinterland and sites further afield ca. 1200 BCE. The reasons for the fall of the Hittite Empire should not be connected with destruction. Moreover, as Stefano de Martino (2018, 38) has recently pointed out, this situation did not even begin ca. 1200 BCE. Rather, as he describes it, "The Hittite kingdom was a wounded body in the second half of the 13th century BCE." Given the struggles, warfare, coups, plague, a shifting capital, one of the greatest military battles in ancient history, and more that afflicted the Hittite Empire from the end of the fourteenth through the thirteenth century BCE, it is a wonder that the empire did not collapse prior and the last kings of the empire should be credited for holding it together rather than being blamed for letting it fall apart.[51] What can be confirmed is that there is no substantial evidence that destruction itself was a factor in the collapse of the Hittite Empire ca. 1200 BCE.

---

50. Anatolia being second only to the southern Levant's fifteen misdated destructions while every other region combined had only five.

51. See the discussions in Bryce 2005; Beal 2011; Miller 2020.

CHAPTER SIX

Cyprus and the Absence of Destruction at the End of the Late Bronze Age

Cyprus: Destroyed or Not Destroyed ca. 1200 BCE?

For Cyprus, no substantive debate has taken place regarding the causes of the supposed destruction events on the island ca. 1200 BCE, as the explanations fall into one of two general camps: The destruction was caused by the Sea Peoples; or while the destructions are mentioned, no causal explanation for who or what caused them is given.[1] Even Amos Nur (Nur and Cline 2001; Nur and Burgess 2008), who championed the theory that an earthquake storm struck the entire Eastern Mediterranean, never suggested that any site on Cyprus was destroyed by an earthquake. What has already been discussed extensively in the literature is exactly how much destruction took place on the island at the end of the LC IIC. Depending upon which recent book or article one chooses to reference, one will find that Alassa, Kalavasos-*Ayios Dhimitrios*, Kition, Kouklia *Palaepaphos*, Kourion (*Episkopi*)-*Bamboula*, and Maroni-*Vournes* were either destroyed or not destroyed.[2] Bernard Knapp and to some degree Peter Fischer have tended to cite more destruction at the end of the LC IIC, while Maria Iacovou and Artemis Georgiou have downplayed the amount of destruction. This is not to say that there is not some agreement between the two camps, as both state that Enkomi, Maa *Paleokastro*, and Sinda were destroyed ca. 1200 BCE. Nevertheless, as I have already demonstrated in chapter 3, 61 percent of all cited destruction ca. 1200 BCE on Cyprus never happened, including Sinda. Moreover, as we will see in the following pages, of the remaining five sites that did suffer a destruction event at the end of the LC IIC (fig. 6.1), most were scarcely affected. It is obvious, based on the archaeological record, that no major site on Cyprus experienced a truly devastating destruction event, and indeed, as has been reported for nearly two decades, parts of Cyprus experienced a period of growth rather than decline after 1200 BCE (Iacovou 2008, 2013a, 2013b, 2014; Georgiou 2011, 2012a, 2012b, 2015, 2017; Georgiou and Iacovou 2020).

---

1. For the Sea Peoples, see Dikaios 1969, 1971; Maier 1969; Fischer 2017, 2019, 2020; Fischer and Bürge 2018. For no causal explanation, see Knapp 1997, 2009, 2013; Iacovou 2008, 2013a, 2013b, 2014; Georgiou 2011, 2012a, 2012b, 2015, 2017; Knapp and Manning 2016; Georgiou and Iacovou 2020.

2. For destroyed, see Knapp 1997, 54–55 table 2; Steel 2004, 188; Knapp 2009; Knapp and Manning 2016; 132; Fischer 2017, 195, 198 table 1. For not destroyed, see Georgiou 2011, 2015; Iacovou 2013a, 2014; Georgiou and Iacovou 2020.

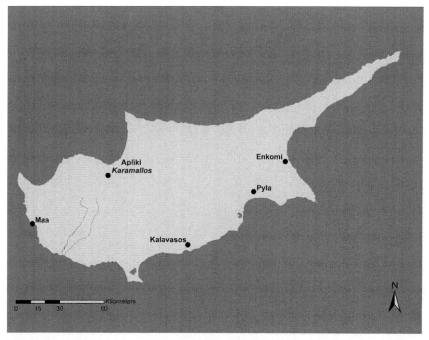

Figure 6.1. Map of sites with a destruction event ca. 1200 BCE on Cyprus.

Enkomi — Scale: Partial — Cause: Unknown

Situated three kilometers southwest of Salamis on the east coast of Cyprus, Enkomi is one of the supposed major destruction events ca. 1200 BCE, as it appears on nearly all maps and lists of destruction for the end of the Late Bronze Age.[3] It has been explored by several archaeological expeditions, though the material presented here pertains to the finds uncovered during the Cypriot excavations. The discoveries by the French expedition remain largely unpublished; moreover, what has been published from Claude Schaeffer's excavations unfortunately does not offer many clues to what happened at the end of the LC IIC at Enkomi.[4] Of the two buildings where there is sufficient published information, Building 18 and the Ingot God Sanctuary, there are no relevant finds that might help illuminate what transpired ca. 1200 BCE. In Building 18, an ashy layer with charcoal was uncovered on the floor of Sol VI that dates to Porphyrios Dikaios's Level II. However, it is unclear when exactly

---

3. Drews 1993, 9 fig. 1; Nur and Cline 2000, 56; Nur and Burgess 2008, 225 fig 8.1; Kaniewski et al. 2011, fig. 1; Cline 2014, 110–11, 128 fig. 10; Kaniewski, Guiot, and Van Campo 2015, 370 fig. 1; Knapp and Manning 2016, 130.

4. See Schaeffer 1952, 239–369; 1971; Courtois 1972, 151–362; Ionas 1984; Courtois, Lagarce, and Lagarce 1986.

during Level II Sol VI dates and there is no clear stratigraphical connection between Sol VI and Dikaios's Level IIB. Nor is there a clear origin or context for the ash based on the limited finds from Building 18 (Ionas 1984, 52). Consequently, no clear evidence exists that Building 18 suffered any kind of destruction ca. 1200 BCE, either from the material remains or the chronological end date for Sol VI. For the Ingot God Sanctuary, the earliest dated deposits derived from several soundings under the floor of the sanctuary from a preexisting building. These finds, from Sols VI and V, are likely associated with Dikaios's Level IIIA (Ionas 1984, 60; see also Mountjoy 2005) or after the supposed destruction of Level IIB. In sum, from the published remains from the French excavations at Enkomi, currently no evidence of a ca. 1200 BCE destruction event exists.

The typical evidence for the destruction of Enkomi is derived from Dikaios's excavations. However, what is most interesting about the supposed ca. 1200 BCE destruction event at Enkomi is that it became more drastic over the course of the excavation reports, though the evidence remained the same. Thus, in Dikaios's (1971, 513) "Summary and Historical Conclusions" from volume 2, he describes the destruction at the end of Level IIB Floor IV in Areas III and I as a, "terrific disaster that must have affected the whole town." Yet, going through the descriptions of the individual rooms and the tables summarizing the evidence for destruction published two years prior, a different image emerges of this possible destruction event, one that is far less severe than is commonly reported.

From the excavation reports, it is clear that the Area III Level IIB Floor IV Structure was not destroyed in a cataclysmic event (fig. 6.2). Twenty-four rooms, nearly half the rooms in the building, showed no signs of destruction.[5] No walls had collapsed nor were there any traces of fire that can be attributed to a destruction.[6] In some cases, Dikaios assumed that part of the building was destroyed, even though there was a lack of physical destruction debris. This was the case with the North Gate in Area III, as Dikaios neither mentions nor describes any evidence of destruction. Despite this, he (1969, 70) still assumed that it had been destroyed, even though there was a lack of visible damage. He stated that, "The damage to the gate must have been severe but is not now seen since it was repaired by those who repaired not only the building but also the fortifications" (1969, 89). Given that Dikaios presumed the site was destroyed by attacking Mycenaeans, in this view it would make sense that he supposed the gate was attacked and destroyed, even though no physical evidence of this

---

5. Rooms 1, 4, 5, 6, 7, 8, 9, 12, 17, 19, 40, 41, 42, 43, 45, 47, 60, 70, 77, 78, 79, 79a, 87 and 88 (Dikaios 1969, 46–73). Room 19 had bits of charcoal on the floor.

6. E.g., Dikaios mentions that in Room 47 there was some evidence of a fire, but this is likely due to the hearth found in the room. Likewise, Rooms 78 and 87 from the West Sector both have traces of burning on their floors, but both rooms were active copper smelting areas and the burning is more than likely due to this industrial activity (Dikaios 1969, 56–57, 62–63, 87, 90–91).

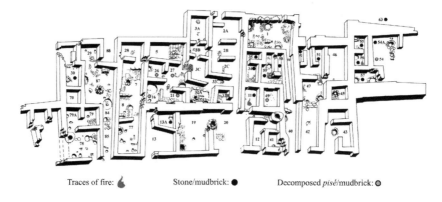

Figure 6.2. Modified plan of Enkomi Area III Level IIB detailing where possible traces of destruction were uncovered. Dikaios 1969, pl. 252.

destruction was discovered (Dikaios 1971, 513–14). This is a case where the assumption surpassed the archeological evidence.

There were some rooms from the Area III structure that had moderate to more pronounced signs of destruction. On the mild side of the spectrum, seven rooms had only a hard layer of either decomposed *pisé* or mud brick while four rooms had some stone collapse on the floors and another twelve rooms yielded partial or complete fallen mud bricks.[7] Only two rooms, Rooms 11 and 56, had significant marks of destruction, as both were found with fallen walls and traces of fire (Dikaios 1969, 52, 64). Two other rooms, the so-called East and West Megara, were believed to be destroyed by Dikaios (1969, 85, 89) based on some stones found on the floor and their general condition. Nevertheless, as the floors were seemingly cleared of any debris, if this part of the structure suffered any damage is unclear.

A similar situation is also true for Area I Level IIB Floor IV's structure (fig. 6.3). Comparable to Area III, there is a spectrum of damage, most of it mild. Four rooms had only a decomposed layer of mud brick or *pisé* (Rooms 113, 114, 116, and 117), while Rooms 135 and 140 had both a layer of mud brick or *pisé* in conjunction with ashes and traces of fire on their floors (Dikaios 1969, 164–68). Rooms 128 and 129 had traces of fire or carbonization on their floors; yet, there was no evidence of structural collapse. Only five rooms showed significant signs of damage. Carbonized material, ashes, fallen stones, and mud

---

7. Mild destruction: Rooms 16, 21, 26, 27, 28, 49 and 54 (Dikaios 1969, 46–73). Stone collapse: Rooms 13, 29, 30 and 55 (Dikaios 1969, 46–73); though in the description of the rooms, Dikaios originally says that the pebble layer found in Room 29 was too thin to be considered part of the destruction (1969, 61); yet, he includes it in the table of destruction as evidence of destruction (1969, 90). Fallen mud bricks: Rooms 11, 34, 35, 46, 51, 52, 54a, 56, 57, 58, 59 and 63 (Dikaios 1969, 46–73).

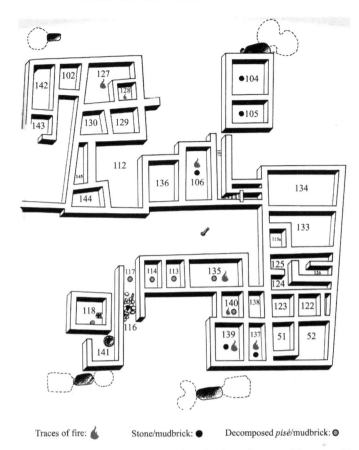

Figure 6.3. Modified plan of Enkomi Area I Level IIB detailing where possible traces of destruction were uncovered. Dikaios 1969, pl. 272.

bricks were found in Rooms 106, 137, and 139, while fallen boulders and debris were uncovered in Rooms 104 and 105 (164–68). The only weapons from Level IIB were discovered in Area I underneath the floor of Level IIIA's Room 12 in the south eastern section of the structure, where the hilt of a dagger, one arrowhead, and one sling bullet were recovered and were believed to belong to the Level IIB building (256–57). However, given their context, these weapons are not an indication for warfare.

Again, Dikaios (1971, 513) described this destruction as a "terrific disaster that must have affected the whole town." He believed the destructive agents to have been at least in part Mycenaeans fleeing destruction on Greece, and after leaving the city in ruins, came back some ten to twenty years later bringing about the architectural changes and improvements witnessed in Level IIIA (Dikaios 1971, 513–14). However, the physical evidence recorded in Areas III and I reveals a more moderate interpretation for this "destruction" at the end of the LC IIC.

As discussed above, the physical presence of destruction debris from Area III and I is varied, with most of it being moderate or mild evidence of damage. Multiple rooms yielded no traces of destruction, while others had only a layer of decomposed mud brick, *pisé*, some fallen stones, or mud bricks. It is unclear if this is even related to a destruction event or if these materials simply fell from the walls after a period of neglect, for example, during the ten-to-twenty-year hiatus Dikaios proposed took place after this supposed "destruction." Thus, it is quite possible that the buildings were not destroyed at all, as only two rooms from the Area III structure and five rooms from the Area I structure had significant traces of physical destruction with fallen mud bricks, stones, and in a few cases evidence of burning not related to industrial activities. It is because of this ambiguity that the destruction is listed as a partial destruction, but it is well within the realm of possibility that Enkomi did not suffer a destruction event at the end of the LC IIC. It then goes without saying that there is no clear cause for this possible partial destruction.[8]

Part of the overemphasis on the amount of "destruction" that took place at Enkomi originates from the way in which Dikaios published the information. For each level he included a chart that noted which rooms had what type of damage from destruction. Yet, what is particularly problematic about these charts is that while they are seemingly helpful tools describing what evidence of destruction was uncovered in what room, the charts are in fact misleading. Dikaios only lists the rooms where "evidence of destruction" was uncovered, while leaving out those rooms where there was no evidence of destruction. For example, the chart for the Level IIB Area III building only lists thirty-three of the more than fifty rooms in the structure (Dikaios 1969, 90–92). Likewise, for the Area I structure, of the thirty-five rooms, Dikaios only included nine in his chart of the "destruction."[9] This leads the reader to assume the destruction was worse than it was or that it affected the entire structure, as Dikaios simply left out any areas or rooms that had no debris, while also including rooms that had evidence of fire that derived from industrial activities. Consequently, the possible Level IIB Floor IV destruction was magnified in the final publication beyond what was archaeologically attestable.

---

8. A single wall from Room 63, one of the casemates, was found dislodged and inclined toward the center of the room (Dikaios 1969, 82 pl. 13:3). While this could be taken as evidence of earthquake, there is no other convincing evidence that would indicate that the wall did not lean due to lack of maintenance or faulty construction.

9. Dikaios 1969, 170–71. This is a problem for every chart of destruction throughout the entire final publication of the Cypriot excavations at Enkomi.

Cyprus and the Absence of Destruction

Pyla-Kokkinokremos — *Scale: Partial* — *Cause: Earthquake*

Pyla-*Kokkinokremos* was founded at the end of the LC IIC and is situated some ten kilometers east of Kition.[10] It is believed to have been built as a short-term defensive settlement (Karageorghis 2001; Karageorghis and Kanta 2014, 155–62) or as a planned gateway settlement by Kition (Stanley-Price 1979; Georgiou 2012a, 2012b; Georgiou and Iacovou 2020, 1143). The site had a short life span of only some fifty years, and generally in the scholarly literature Pyla-*Kokkinokremos* is listed as abandoned without destruction sometime in the beginning of the LC IIIA shortly after it was constructed.[11] However, Louise Steel listed it as destroyed with other sites such as Enkomi, Kition, and Maa *Paleokastro*, which she states were destroyed in a wave of destruction overtaking the island at the end of the LC IIC.[12] Athanasia Kanta also maintained the possibility that Pyla was destroyed stating, "the *destruction* or abandonment date of the site of Pyla is set by imported early LH IIIC pottery, at ca. 1175–1170 BC."[13] More recently, Joachim Bretschneider, Jan Driessen, and Athanasia Kanta (2021, 6) have listed the site as destroyed along with other sites such as Enkomi, Maa *Paleokastro*, Tell Tweini, and Tell Kazel. The picture presented by the archaeological remains indicates that Pyla did suffer a destruction event, but the exact extent of this destruction and what resulted from it are more elusive.

In Area II Complex B, much of the east wall was leaning toward the east along with the east walls in Rooms 11 and 12. The east wall in Room 5, the west wall in Room 27, and the east wall of the casemate south of Complex C were all leaning east while in Room 25 large slabs were dislodged and leaning west (Karageorghis and Demas 1984, 15, 23–24, 116). It is unlikely that these walls all leaned east due to settling, as the buildings were built on bedrock (6). Rubble and stones filled Rooms 11, 12, 20, 32 and the room associated with the eastern wall of the casemate, while Room 27 had a light scatter of rubble, which was noted as being the case for most rooms in Area II. The entrance to Room 24 was filled with rubble and the entrance to Room 11 too was blocked by rubble. A layer of mud brick was also uncovered underneath the rubble in Room 11 suggesting that the superstructure had collapsed first. Mud-brick debris was also uncovered in Rooms 5 and 10 (Karageorghis and Demas 1984, 14–15, 17,

---

10. See Caraher, Moore, and Pettegrew 2014, 43–46, and their discussion of the discovery of a prehistoric harbor that existed at Pyla-Kokkinokremos.

11. Karageorghis and Demas 1984, 67–68; Karageorghis 1992, 80; Georgiou 2012a, 2012b; Karageorghis and Kanta 2014, 159–60; Georgiou and Iacovou 2020, 1143.

12. Steel 2004, 188. Steel on the same page in the next sentence also states that the site was abandoned.

13. Karageorghis and Kanta 2014, 111 (emphasis added). In a recent publication Kanta (2021, 70, 72) has again noted that the site possibly suffered destruction prior to the abandonment.

206 CHAPTER SIX

23–24). Burning was only seen in two rooms. In Room 24 of Complex D, patches of ashes were discovered against the east wall. Vassos Karageorghis and Martha Demas (1984, 17–19) state that a considerable amount of ash was mixed in the rubble filling the entrance of the room. Likewise, in Complex E Room 31, in the northern half of the room, ash covered the floor, likely indicating a localized burning event.

The recent excavations by Karageorghis and Kanta (2014, 7, 17, 20, 26, 47, 74, 88, 106) have uncovered additional evidence of a destruction event. In Complex F, Room 2A part of its floor was covered with small stones and pebbles. Likewise, in Complex G, Room 3 had a layer of loose stones that they associate with wall collapse. The corridor dubbed Room 4 had one of its in situ vases crushed by falling debris, and in Room 8 stones fell over the entrance. In Complex H, fallen stones were found in Room 6 and in Complex I many fallen stones covered smashed pottery in Room 19, while fallen stones were also found in Room 45. In the brief excavation and survey carried out by Michael Brown (2017, 283, 292) between 2007 and 2009, in sounding EU11 a layer of collapsed and burnt mud-brick superstructure overlaid an occupational deposit that he suggests might be an indication of a violent end for the site. Likewise, in the subsequent excavations by Bretschneider, Kanta, and Driessen (2015, 8–10, 17; see also 2017), in their Trench 3.3 they uncovered a rubble layer over top of crushed pottery that they associate with a collapsed wall, while ash and burnt matter were found in Trench 3.2. In the South Complex, Room 10 had some indications that its roof collapsed over the top of several smashed vessels containing burnt material. Recently, Kanta (Bretschneider, Driessen, and Kanta 2018) uncovered evidence of a possible natural disaster in Sector 4.2 stating that, "Specific stratigraphic details point to a natural disaster, possibly a seismic event, which led to the collapse of part of the plateau and the partial sealing of rooms built against it." She assumes this might indicate a seismic event that struck the site before it was abandoned.

In their original report, Karageorghis and Demas interpreted the leaning walls and rubble as evidence of a partial destruction of Complexes B and C by an earthquake. They state that, "The layer of mudbrick below the rubble in room 11 would suggest a collapse of the superstructure. The west wall of Room 27 as well as much of the east wall of Complex B was leaning considerably to the east. It would seem that the affect of some natural disaster, probably an earthquake, is the only plausible explanation for the partial destruction of Complexes B and C."[14] Karageorghis and Demas (1984, 15) did not, however, believe that the

---

14. Karageorghis and Demas 1984, 15. Likewise for Room 25 they (23) state, "Much of the east wall of Complex B can be seen leaning distinctly eastward. The east wall of Rooms 11 and 12 are buttressed by rubble filling inside and outside. Clearly the leveling for the wall was never properly achieved when, as we suspect, an earthquake shook the foundations and caused collapse."

CYPRUS AND THE ABSENCE OF DESTRUCTION

site was destroyed nor that this was the cause of the abandonment, as they conclude that the residents attempted to buttress the exterior of Room 25 of Complex D, as the wall appeared disturbed and possibly unstable because of the shaking.

Given the information presented above, it does seem likely that an earthquake struck Pyla-*Kokkinokremos* at some point in its brief history. This would explain the slanting walls, as settling of the foundation cannot account for the leaning since the buildings were built on bedrock. Moreover, several walls from different complexes were all leaning in the same direction. Given the pattern of differentiated destruction, leaning walls, the partial collapse of the plateau covering over several rooms, Pyla-*Kokkinokremos* suffered a partial destruction, likely by an earthquake. The reason this is attributed a partial destruction is that no complex was completely destroyed, that is, not all rooms had evidence of destruction. Moreover, it is not clear if all of the damage listed above was contemporaneous. While it may be that the damage done to Complexes B and C as well as the collapse of the plateau in Sector 4.2 were all part of the same seismic event, much of the remaining evidence could have resulted from postabandonment structural collapse. In this case, much as Karageorghis and Demas suggested in 1984, the site suffered some minor damage by earthquake, but this did not inhibit habitation at the site, and it was only abandoned later on.

Recently, Driessen, Bretschneider, and Kanta (forthcoming) have stressed the sudden nature of the abandonment of Pyla-*Kokkinokremos*. As they state,

> The sudden abandonment of the settlement at Pyla-*Kokkinokremos* is worth stressing: most rooms were left with their pottery in place as well as other objects, including quite a few in metal, which is usually rather rare in contexts of abandonment. The rich floor deposits present throughout the settlement— including undoubtedly very valuable ceramic vessels and calcite vases—seem to indicate that the abandonment process was precipitous.

Whether or not the seismic event suggested by Karageorghis and Demas, Kanta, and myself was the cause of this sudden abandonment is at the moment unclear. It is possible that there was some human force behind the abandonment, as arrowheads, armor plates, spear points, and sling bullets have been uncovered in the excavation by Driessen, Bretschneider, and Kanta. Unfortunately, the exact find locations for these weapons has not yet been published, and Driessen, Bretschneider, and Kanta have stated that weapons are rare finds.[15] Driessen, Bretschneider, and Kanta (forthcoming) have suggested that the abandonment could have been preceded by some violent action or alternatively that, "The

---

15. Driessen, Bretschneider, and Kanta forthcoming. An arrowhead was also uncovered in Gate Area Complex 1 Room 1 that was recovered among broken pottery (Karageorghis and Kanta 2014, 106).

208   CHAPTER SIX

abandonment could have been because of fear of enemy attack, exposure to sickness, death, bad luck or evil spirits, or caused by famine. It could also have taken the character of a migration. A potential scenario could be, for example, that the inhabitants had launched a (military?) expedition (e.g., to Egypt), which may have been so unsuccessful that the boats were ruined, preventing return." For the moment, however, there remains neither a clear cause behind the abandonment nor information on exactly how much of the site was damaged by destruction. Nevertheless, the scenario that Pyla-*Kokkinokremos* was damaged by an earthquake at some point in its relatively short life cycle remains likely.

Kalavasos-Ayios Dhimitrios — *Scale: Single-Building* — *Cause: Accidental*

Kalavasos-*Ayios Dhimitrios* is situated in the Vasilikos River Valley some three kilometers from the Mediterranean coast. The original excavator, Alisson South (1980; 1982; 1983; 1984a, 24; 1984b; 1988; 1991; 1992; 1996; 1997), found that the majority of the site was peacefully abandoned at the end of the LC IIC, a conclusion that was further supported by the recent excavations at the site that too uncovered no evidence of destruction (Fisher et al. 2019). Only a single structure, Building X, had any signs of damage ca. 1200 BCE (South 1983, 96–98, 101; 1984a, 23; 1984b, 15). Traces of burning were witnessed in many but not all rooms of Building X. Large pieces of carbonized beams, charcoal chunks, and some burnt mud-brick fragments were uncovered in nine rooms, while smaller amounts of ash were on the floors of four additional rooms.[16] Many of the floors in the eastern section of the structure did not survive; however, where floors were uncovered in Rooms A. 155 and 173 no ash or burning was detected (South pers. comm. 09/04/2018). This suggests that much of the western and central sections of the building were burnt while the eastern half likely remained untouched. The question then is, as always, what might have caused this single-building destruction, as there are neither signs of warfare nor destruction in any of the other buildings at the site, which would exclude a natural disaster such as an earthquake?[17]

---

16. More severe damage: Rooms A. 151, 152, 153, 154, 157, 161, 165, 175, 176; smaller amounts of ash: Rooms A.163, 164, 167, 168 (Alisson South pers. comm. 09/04/2018).

17. Ash was also found on the floor of Building XII to the south of Building X (South pers. comm. 09/04/2018); however, there is no clear evidence to say this ash came from a destruction event. Rather the ash likely originated from the burning of Building X. The direction of the prevailing winds in the Kalavasos region during the day blows in a southern to southwesterly direction (Pashardes and Christofides 1995, 413). As South noted, the ash in Room A. 152 was thickest in the southern half of the room (South 1983, 98). With Building XII lying to the south of Building X, and since ash but no further evidence of burning was uncovered, this likely represents windblown ash from the burning of Building X rather than any further signs of destruction.

South (1984a, 25; 1984b, 14–15) has pointed out that this fire likely occurred after the building and the rest of the site was abandoned. All moveable objects in Building X were removed and the structure had very few finds in it, even in comparison to the other abandoned buildings at Kalavasos-*Ayios Dhimitrios*. South also pointed out that a layer of naturally built-up dust was discovered at the bases and inside of the pithoi in Room A. 152, the pithos hall, implying that the room had been out of use for some time when the structure was partially burnt. This is further indicated by the lack of any vitrification in either of the two pithos halls, which likely would have been the case if the pithoi were still filled with olive oil. This suggests that any remaining olive oil was removed or used before the building's abandonment and partial destruction. While this evidence could be taken as a targeted anthropogenic destruction, as the emptying and burning of the most monumental structure Kalavasos-*Ayios Dhimitrios* calls to mind the similar destructions at Dimini, and Gla. However, there is another more likely cause for this fire since the initial abandonment was not the last time Building X was occupied before it burnt.

From Building X, there is little evidence to suggest that it functioned as a residence or had a domestic component (Russell 1986, 315). It appears that this building and the other monumental structures in the Northeast Area seem to have played an administrative role in the production and storage of olive oil, while the remainder of the site was residential. Only Building XIII may have been a residential structure in the Northeast Area (South 1996). Thus, from the initial phase of use, it is unlikely that there would be traces of humans living in the structure. Yet, several finds suggest that Building X was inhabited briefly after its initial abandonment.

In Room A. 151, the entrance to the corridor was obstructed by a "late blocking wall." Inside the room, sheep and goat bones were discovered on the floor in association with high quantities of course wares, the most common shape being the shallow pan and monochrome wares (Russell 1986, 318). Also discovered in Room A. 151 was the upper part of a Canaanite storage jar placed upside down against the southern wall of the room. Inside the jar, and the room, there were pieces of copper slag and scraps of metal that too were unusual finds, as there is generally no evidence of major metallurgical activity at the site other than a possible "copper smith's" workshop in Building IX (South 1983, 97–98; 1996, 41). Pamela Russell has already suggested that, "the late blocking wall may have served to define a working area, and conceivably the vessels were used by squatters, or at least by people living in makeshift quarters after the building had ceased to function in its original manner." The suggestion that Building X was used by "squatters" is further supported by other evidence, such as one kilogram of animal bones, mainly sheep and goat with some duck

210   CHAPTER SIX

bones, that were found against the western wall of the courtyard Room A. 157.[18] Here, the percentage of course and monochrome wares was the highest in the building (Russell 1986, 316; South 1983, 97–98; 1996, 41). Likewise, grinding equipment was discovered on the floor of Room A. 157 (South 2008, 312).

Another unusual find was uncovered at the southern end of Room A. 152, the pithos hall. Here, a pithos base with its edges shaped to a circular platter was uncovered resting on a thin gypsum slab, which South (1983, 98 pl. XV:4), at the time concluded was a makeshift hearth. In a room used to store processed, valuable, and flammable olive oil why would there be a hearth, which surely would have put soot and ashes into the oil or caught the room ablaze? Likely, the answer is that after the building went out of use it was reused temporarily by "squatters." The hearth in Room A. 152, the domestic wares and animal bones in Room A. 151, along with the late blocking wall, and the animal bones and domestic wares in the courtyard Room A. 157 all suggest a "squatter's" phase after the initial abandonment of Building X. Likewise, similar evidence was discovered outside of Building XI, the second olive oil production structure that is nearby Building X. A large quantity of animal bones, occupation debris, and ash were in association with a Canaanite jar without a neck and base built into a wall-like construction that was likely used as an oven (South 1997, 158). This further suggests a brief reuse of the area by squatters.

This type of "squatter's" phase has been detected at several sites in the southern Levant at the end of the Late Bronze Age. At Tell el-Fukhar in Jordan, a monumental structure was apparently abandoned before it was reused as a temporary residence. Crude walls were built partially blocking the entrance that was associated with a fireplace added to the final floor before the building was destroyed (Strange 2015a, 35–38). A similar situation was seen at another site in Jordan, Tall al-'Umayri. Here too, a once monumental structure, Building C, which apparently had a cultic function, was seemingly abandoned and reused

---

18. South (2008) has argued that feasting may have taken place in the central courtyard of Building X, as a number of artifacts and faunal remains were uncovered in Area 173, which is close to Building X, and it appears to indicate that feasting took place somewhere in the area. This feasting, in her view, may account for the faunal remains uncovered in Room A. 157. However, given the variety of evidence that Russell (1986) and I have presented, more likely the remains found in the courtyard resulted from a brief reuse of Building X. As South herself suggests, the courtyard in Building X has no "hearth, benches, or further protectoral elaboration," which would indicate feasting took place in the courtyard. Rather, as she also notes, the partially excavated Building XII to the south of Building X would have been more suitably equipped to handle feasting than the courtyard in Building X (South 2008, 312–13). Papasavvas (2014) has argued that the remains found in Area 173 may be evidence of a closure ceremony based on South's assessment. However, if this feasting deposit is evidence of a closure ceremony, of which there is no substantial evidence, as we cannot even say in which building it might have taken place; it would only indicate that this ceremony took place before the abandonment of the site and the subsequent reuse of Building X. It is not akin to a termination ritual that results in the sacred destruction of a building, and thus does not account for the burning that was discovered in the structure, as the building was reused by squatters.

before it was destroyed, likely by an earthquake. Again, several doors were blocked with crude walls and two hearths were added in the final phase. One hearth was found in Room C5 along with everyday household ceramics, though in the previous phase Room C5 had a cultic function, suggested by a niche with five standing stones that was built into the wall of the room (Bramlett 2008, 113–21). Thus, the finds from Kalavasos-*Ayios Dhimitrios* fit in well with other monumental buildings in the wider Levantine region that were abandoned and reused by "squatters" at the end of the Late Bronze Age.[19]

What this indicates for the possible cause of the fire is as follows. Since it appears the site as a whole was abandoned before most of Building X was burned, and because there no evidence of warfare at the site, it is unlikely that this fire was caused by humans burning the building as an act of war or arson. If, as Russell and I suggest, Building X was briefly reused after its abandonment, this would be further evidence against an attack on the site, as the building survived the abandonment process long enough for perhaps a few meals to be eaten in the courtyard and in Room A. 151. This likely indicates an accidental fire occurred postabandonment of the site in general. With only a few people in the building, an uncontrolled fire could have quickly gotten out of hand, partially burning the structure before it was abandoned for a second time.[20]

Apliki Karamallos — *Scale: Single-Building — Cause: Unknown*

Apliki *Karamallos* is located in the valley of the Marathasa, one of the rivers running down the northern slopes of the Troodos. The site was excavated by Joan Du Plat Taylor (1952; Du Plat Taylor and Kling 2007; Kling et al. 2007) where she uncovered a Late Bronze Age mining village. Only a single structure from Area A dubbed the "Storehouse" had evidence of destruction, as the other domestic structures excavated in Area B were abandoned without signs of destruction.[21] The "Storehouse" was a small L-shaped house and evidence of destruction by fire was uncovered in every room except for Room A1, possibly because it was separated from the remainder of the structure by a wall. Rooms A2–A8 were discovered with varying amounts of burnt timbers, ashes, broken pottery, fallen mud bricks, burnt grain, and fallen walls (Du Plat Taylor and Kling 2007, 8–36). Based on the pottery, the date of the destruction was after 1200 BCE (38) though radiocarbon measurements derived partially from the burnt grain uncovered in Room A3 suggests a date for the destruction between

---

19. See ch. 7 for a discussion of the destruction events from both sites.

20. Todd 2013, 97, has suggested that there was a small, short-lived and sporadic occupation during the LC IIIA. South (pers. comm. 09/04/2018) clarified that this was found only in Building XIV, as a late floor level just below the topsoil. Around eight sherds were identified as LC IIIA.

21. Du Plat Taylor and Kling 2007, 8, 41. Other architectural remains were also uncovered in Area C; however, no documentation of these remains exists (64).

212   CHAPTER SIX

1180–1130 BCE, which could put this destruction event outside of the end of the Late Bronze Age as defined here (Manning and Kuniholm 2007, 326–28).

The cause of the single-building destruction is unclear, as there is no apparent evidence for any natural, accidental, or manmade cause for the fire. No weapons of war were found in the building or the remainder of the site.[22] While slag was uncovered in Rooms A2, A5, and A7 and tuyères in Rooms A2, A3, A5, and A6, they were all in storage at the time of the destruction; moreover, there is no indication that metallurgical activity was taking place in the building nor is there any indication that the tuyères were ever used (Kassianidou 2018, 349). Since there was no active industrial activity in the building, an out-of-control industrial fire is not an option. It is my opinion that the single-building destruction was likely accidental, given the lack of evidence for arson, warfare, or a natural disaster, but as there is no burden of proof to fully support this claim the cause remains unknown.

Maa Paleokastro — *Scale: Site-Wide — Cause: Warfare*

Situated some twenty-five kilometers north of Kouklia, the short-lived settlement at Maa *Paleokastro*, like Pyla, was possibly a defensive settlement (Karageorghis 2001) or a planned settlement of Paphos (Georgiou 2012a; 2012b; Georgiou and Iacovou 2020, 1143) that persisted for a short fifty years. The site was excavated first by Dikaios followed by a more extensive excavation led by Karageorghis and Demas. Signs of destruction were uncovered in every area at the end of Floor II dating to the beginning of the LC IIIA1. At the northern end of the site, in Area II, the traces of destruction were not as direct as those witnessed in the other areas. Building I Rooms 19 and 42 had their plaster floors burnt, while Room 20 only had an area of burning at the center of the room. Room 43's floor was burnt and covered in ashes, though the ash could have been derived from the hearth in the room. For Rooms 20B, 23, and 25, there is no mentioned evidence of burning or wall collapse (Karageorghis and Demas 1988, 12–14, 64). More clear evidence of burning along with some whole and fragmentary mud bricks were uncovered in Area 44, the space between Building I and the "Tower" to the north of it. In the "Tower" Rooms 45 and 46, both floors were covered with a layer of fine ash. To the south of Area II, another structure was uncovered with a burnt plaster floor covered with a layer of debris (14–17).

The most severe evidence for destruction was uncovered in Area III between Areas I and II. Destruction debris was witnessed throughout Buildings

---

22. Originally Du Plat Taylor (1952, 163) interpreted several objects found in a number of rooms from the "Storehouse" as maceheads. However, the objects upon further analysis were perforated stone hammers and not weapons at all (Swiny 1986, 15; Kassianidou 2007, 280).

CYPRUS AND THE ABSENCE OF DESTRUCTION   213

II, III, and IV, where burnt floors, mud-brick debris, including whole mud-bricks, burnt clay, and plaster was uncovered. Ash, debris, and burning were also exposed outside of the buildings (Karageorghis and Demas 1988, 20–29). At the southern end of the site, in Area I, Dikaios discovered whole mud bricks, lumps of mortar burnt hard with the impressions of thin reeds and branches in his Rooms 1 and 2, while Karageorghis and Demas (1988, 3–9) noted traces of burning and a layer of ash in their Rooms 6 and 18 along with some burnt plaster. Karageorghis and Demas (1988, 266) assumed this destruction came at the hands of some attacking force, which they presumed to be pirates, though they were not certain this was the case. As they (1988, 266) describe it, "We might suggest that they were 'pirates,' 'adventurers' or remnants of the 'Sea Peoples,' but this is simply another way of saying that we do not know."

The presences of weapons within this destruction indicates that Maa *Paleokastro* was destroyed in an act of war. Four bronze arrowheads, four bronze sling bullets, two bronze daggers, and part of a bronze knife were discovered scattered throughout the site, not stored together.[23] Several of these objects particularly point to warfare, as an arrowhead was discovered on Street A north of the "Tower" in Area II. For Area III, in the space between Buildings II and III called Area 88, two arrowheads and one sling bullet were uncovered along with a dagger that was outside of Room 77 (Karageorghis and Demas 1988, 16, 39). These certainly would not have been places to store weapons of war and likely remained there after the attack. Moreover, there is no evidence that would suggest that the site was struck by an earthquake. The fact that weapons of war were found in the structures, in open spaces, and on a street, combined with the lack of evidence for a seismic event, leads to the conclusion that the destruction was likely caused by an act of war. According to Karageorghis and Demas (1988, 51, 65, 265–66), it seems as if people were able to get away with their belongs before Maa *Paleokastro* was destroyed. The local populace came back and rebuilt the site a short time after it was burnt, perhaps better fortifying the dog-leg gate in the north of town before Maa *Paleokastro* was abandoned without evidence of destruction at the end of Floor I.[24] Thus, even though the site suffered a site-wide destruction by warfare, this was not the end of the settlement.

---

23. Karageorghis and Demas 1988, 16, 22, 24, 27, 29, 32, 39, 103, 108, 109, 111, 114, 118, 119, 128. One arrowhead was found in Area II Street A. Another was uncovered in Area III Building III Room 79, while two more were found in the open-air Area 88 between Buildings II and III. A bronze sling bullet was unearthed north of Area II in Room 55, while another was found in Room 60. Another sling bullet was discovered in Area III Building III Room 84, while another was found in Area 88. The point of a bronze dagger was found in Area III Building II Room 65, while another was uncovered in Building III Room 84. An additional bronze dagger was found south of Room 77. One other bronze dagger was discovered in Pit a from Building II. However, as it was found in a pit it is not certain it was from this likely attack.

24. Georgiou (2012b, 72) describes Floor I at Maa as "Characterized by hasty constructions. The

214   CHAPTER SIX

The Lack of Destruction on Cyprus ca. 1200 BCE

The accounts of the amount and severity of destruction that the island of Cyprus witnessed ca. 1200 BCE have been grievously misrepresented, as well as any effect destruction could have had on the island. As demonstrated in chapter 3, of the thirteen destruction events, eight are false, equating to a 61 percent error rate, including sites such as Sinda, Kition, Hala Sultan Tekke, Maroni-*Vournes*, Alassa, Kouklia *Palaepaphos*, Myrtou-*Pigadhes*, and Kourion. This as an error rate is already an astounding figure by itself and demonstrates the general lack of destruction ca. 1200 BCE on the island. Moreover, this general lack of destruction is further highlighted by the sites on Cyprus that have physical evidence of destruction, as much of this "destruction" was not nearly as severe as one might be led to believe.

This is most palpable in Enkomi's Level IIB Floor IV partial destruction that is a staple of end of the Late Bronze Age destruction maps.[25] Yet, the structures excavated in Areas I and III yielded minimal evidence that they were burnt, and much of the "destruction debris" may have resulted from the buildings simply being abandoned for a short period, rather than from a destruction event. Consequently, Enkomi may not have suffered a destruction event at all ca. 1200 BCE. For Pyla-*Kokkinokremos*, the site was likely struck by an earthquake, causing damage to some structures and facilitating the collapse of part of the plateau that may or may not have preceded the site's abandonment. Nevertheless, what should be noted is that Pyla-*Kokkinokremos* was not a major settlement and was likely only an offshoot of another local polity. Therefore, even though it suffered a partial destruction, this destruction event likely did not affect the island as a whole—or even the local region. This was a limited event that did not affect much more than those living at the site, as nearby Kition flourished during the same period.

The situation for Maa *Paleokastro*, which suffered the only site-wide destruction on Cyprus, is similar. While the site was destroyed in an act of war, this destruction event was likely a local disaster, one that did not affect the region or island, as the destruction did not even bring an end to the site. It was rebuilt and reoccupied until it was abandoned without a destruction in the LC IIIA. The destruction by warfare was not part of any wave of savagery overtaking the island and likely represents a single instance of regional violence, and much like Pyla-*Kokkinokremos*, nearby Paphos flourished at the same time. Both sites were likely failed experiments, and neither were

---

structures assigned to Floor I occupation are much more numerous compared to these of Floor II, presumably indicating a population increase."

25. See, Drews 1993, 9 fig. 1; Nur and Cline 2000, 44 fig. 1; Kaniewski et al. 2011, 2 fig. 1; Cline 2014, 110–11 fig. 10; Kaniewski, Guiot, and Van Campo 2015, 2 fig. 1.

major settlements. The destruction events at both sites would not have been a significant disruption to life on the island, or even in their local regions.

At Kalavasos-*Ayios Dhimitrios*, the destruction that did take place was extremely limited, as the majority of the site was abandoned without any traces of destruction, and only Building X was partially burnt. Based on several finds in Building X, from a layer of naturally built-up dust in the pithos hall indicating a period of abandonment before the fire, to signs of a "squatter" occupation in the building, all the evidence points away from a violent destruction by locals or the Sea Peoples. If it were an attacking force, one might expect that the other monumental structures would have also been burnt; yet, this is not the case. One might also expect that Building X would have been destroyed during its initial phase of occupation when it was still the seat of local power, not while "squatters" were living in an already abandoned building. It is more likely that an accidental fire got out of control, and once it began to burn the building there were too few people to manage and put it out. Lastly, for Apliki *Karamallos* only a single storehouse was burnt, while the remainder of the mining site was abandoned without destruction. In sum, there is no evidence that any major site on Cyprus suffered a destruction ca. 1200 BCE and the destruction that did occur was minimal or affected minor sites.

The general lack of destruction on Cyprus in and around 1200 BCE further illuminates the distinctive nature of the transition from the thirteenth to the twelfth century BCE on the island in comparison to many of its Eastern Mediterranean counterparts. The shift from the LC IIC to the LC IIIA was not a period of traumatic upheavals shaking the island to its core. Rather, a nucleation of power occurred, where several sites such as Enkomi and Hala Sultan Tekke maintained a seat of prominence during the LC IIIA while others such as Kition and Paphos entered into a period of prosperity. This was coupled with a cultural continuity seen in architecture, tomb use, pottery styles, religious practices, and town planning across the LC IIC/LC IIIA divide.[26] As Georgiou (2015, 138) has neatly summarized the situation:

> Cyprus constitutes a particular case on a Mediterranean-wide level, since the island did not suffer a collapse of socio-political structures, such as that which fell upon the Mycenaean palaces and the Hittite rule. The Mediterranean "crisis" caused upheavals to the island's settlement pattern, but it was by no means devastating. It affected only regional systems, and this is why we see the purposeful abandonment of some settlements. The Cypriot polities that made it through the 12th century exercised the same political and economic functions as in the previous centuries.

---

26. Coldstream 1989; Rupp 1989; Karageorghis 1992; Sherratt 1994, 1998; Steel 2004, 185; Iacovou 2008, 2013a, 2013b, 2014; Georgiou 2011, 2015, 2017; Knapp 2013, 451; Georgiou and Iacovou 2020, 1142–44. For a more recent thorough study of the transition from the Late Bronze Age to the early Iron Age on Cyprus see, Meyer and Knapp 2021.

216   CHAPTER SIX

Indeed, the Late Bronze Age on Cyprus did not even end with the LC IIC. Rather the Bronze Age persisted until the end of the LC IIIA, as old sites of power gradually waned until up-and-coming cities such as Kourion and Salamis began their ascent to power in the true onset of the Iron Age at the beginning of the LC IIIB (Iacovou 2008, 635–37; 2014, 662–63, 667). In this way, Cyprus stands out from many of its counterparts in the Eastern Mediterranean. None of the major urban centers on Cyprus, such as Enkomi, Kition, Hala Sultan Tekke, Kalavasos-*Ayios Dhimitrios*, Maroni-*Vournes*, Alassa, and Kouklia *Palaepaphos*, suffered a devastating destruction, nor did any destruction event precede the abandonment of a major settlement. This lack of destruction combined with the continuation of the Late Bronze Age culture and the continued dominance of many of the major Cypriot sites into the twelfth century BCE indicates Cyprus does not fit neatly into many of the typical crisis scenarios for the Eastern Mediterranean at the end of the thirteenth century BCE. It fits in with the trends already seen on Crete and in the central Levant that experienced little or no destruction ca. 1200 BCE.

The question remains, did destruction actually have any sort of effect on the polities of Cyprus ca. 1200 BCE? The answer to this question is a definitive "no." For example, while the major sites in the valleys of the Vasilikos and the Kouris were abandoned over the course of some fifty years beginning at the end of the LC IIC and stretching into the LC IIIA, this was in no way precipitated by destruction, as none of the sites were destroyed.[27] Moreover, as Georgiou and Iacovou (2020, 1144) significantly point out, "Paphos and Kition profited from the economic demise of their neighbors" as both sites constructed the first ever central urban sanctuaries waxing in power and influence after Alassa, Kalavasos-*Ayios Dhimitrios*, and Maroni-*Vournes* waned and were abandoned (Webb 1999, 58–84, 292; Georgiou and Iacovou 2020, 1144). Likewise, the only site to suffer a major destruction event— Maa *Paleokastro*—was not a major site, as it was only a short-lived, recently built, planned village that could in no way be called vital to the overall health and well-being of Cyprus.

The supposed disruption of trade was also not affected by any sort of destruction. The only major port that might have suffered some damage was Enkomi; however, Level III was reconstructed on a grander scale than before (Dikaios 1969, 96–133, 188–215). As Georgiou and Iacovou (2020, 1144) describe it, "The LC IIIA material evidence [from Enkomi] provides a rich and detailed testimony to a merchant society's determination to meet the economic realities of a new era. It is not unlikely that Enkomi, like Phoenicia and the Carmel coast, received at this time an influx of merchants from the destroyed commer-

---

27. Being Alassa, Kalavasos-*Ayios Dhimitrios*, and Maroni-*Vournes*. Hadjisavvas 1994; 1996; 2000; 2007; 2009; 2017, 129–214, 256–73; Hadjisavvas and Hadjisavva 1997; South 1996; Cadogan 2011, 401.

cial hub of Ugarit." That is, destruction could not have played a role in affecting Cyprus ca. 1200 BCE outside, perhaps, of the destruction of Ras Shamra, which might have been a boon for the local Cypriot economies.

Meanwhile, the supposed loss of trade between Cyprus ca. 1200 BCE and the remainder of the Eastern Mediterranean is largely witnessed by the cessation of imported Cypriot vessels.[28] However, at least for Egypt and the southern Levant, trade in Cypriot pottery appears to have drastically decreased well before the traditional 1200 BCE date. Robert Merrillees (1968, 201–2) and Celia Bergoffen (1989, 211–12) have both noted that Cypriot exchange with Egypt appears to have stopped or decelerated already after the Amarna period ca. 1300 BCE. The same can be said for the southern Levant. Barry Gittlen (1977, 1981), Bergoffen (1989, 1991), and I (Millek 2019c, forthcoming a) have found that exchange in Cypriot pottery either stopped or greatly decreased at the end of the LB IIA ca. 1300 BCE not the LB IIB. Even without a vast amount of destruction on Cyprus, trade in Cypriot pottery had already suffered a major decrease in consumption some one hundred years before the end of the Late Bronze Age. This situation calls to mind the trade in imported Mycenaean pottery to the Levant discussed in chapter 4, which too was not affected by destruction ca. 1200 BCE, as trade in Argolid-made Mycenean pottery had already ended ca. 1250 BCE.

On the other hand, Cypriot oxhide ingots, or fragments thereof, have been found throughout Sicily and Sardinia dating to the twelfth and eleventh centuries BCE, and all oxhide ingots from Sardinia have been shown to be consistant with a Cypriot origin (Hauptmann 2009; Lo Schiavo 2009; Lo Schiavo, Procelli, and Mair 2009; Kassianidou 2012). As Vasiliki Kassianidou (2013, 145) describes the situation, "In the 11th century [BCE] the Late Bronze Age [on Cyprus] comes to an end but not the production and trade of Cypriot copper which continues to thrive in the Iron Age." Thus, one of the vital industries for Cyprus, the production and trade in copper, did not end ca. 1200 BCE even if the market appears to have shifted to the west as the east moved toward sourcing copper from the Faynan during the twelfth and eleventh centuries BCE (see Yahalom-Mack et al. 2014 and references therein).

What this all points to is that, as Iacovou (2008, 2013a, 2013b, 2014) and Georgiou (2011, 2015, 2017; Georgiou and Iacovou 2020) propose, there is more evidence of abandonment and continuity without destruction during the transition from the LC IIC to the LC IIIA than there is for widespread destruction. There is no physical evidence suggesting that violence initiated the changes witnessed on the island during the twelfth century BCE, much of which could even be described as a flourishing rather than a decline. Cyprus was in no way

---

28. See Gittlen 1977, 1981; Bergoffen 1989, 1991; Bell 2006; Papadimitriou 2013, 2015; Greener 2015, 2016; Vilian 2015; Millek 2019c, forthcoming a.

greatly affected by destruction ca. 1200 BCE despite the traditional claims to the contrary. As for the role of the Sea Peoples in all of this, at least in terms of destruction, there is no evidence that the Sea Peoples caused any damage on the island ca. 1200 BCE, nor is there even a historical connection suggesting that they destroyed anything on the island. This is a topic that I will discuss in greater detail in the following chapter.

CHAPTER SEVEN

The Levant: A Mixed Bag of Destruction

Levantine Destruction: Sea Peoples, Egyptians, and Peasant Uprisings

The Levant as a geographic area was not affected equally by destruction ca. 1200 BCE; however, in general the amount of destruction is far less than typically claimed. As detailed in chapter 3, the central Levant experienced no destruction ca. 1200 BCE, while there is a 70 percent error rate with regard to the twenty cited destruction events in the northern Levant, and the same is true for the southern Levant's sixty-three cited destruction events, as 67 percent are false destructions. As there was not nearly as much destruction as has been previously proposed, destruction consequently played less of a role in the "collapse" ca. 1200 BCE. There remain, however, twenty-eight destruction events that did occur ca. 1200 BCE in the northern and southern Levant.

A range of possible causes for these destructions, encompassing many of the common explanations, are often cited for the end of the Late Bronze Age. The Sea Peoples loom large over the destruction in the northern Levant, be they the traditional nineteenth century-style Sea Peoples or famine-driven peasants later known as the Sea Peoples, while the Arameans have also been accused of bring destruction to the region.[1] Earthquakes have been an assumed factor for the entire Levant, as Claude Schaeffer (1948, 2; 1968, 763) claimed that Ugarit was destroyed by an earthquake, an assertion that was extended to the whole of the Levant by Amos Nur and Eric Cline.[2] For the southern Levant, the Sea Peoples are also cited as a culprit, with the Egyptians, rival city-states, or Canaanites rising up against their Egyptian overlords also being named as the assailants of various sites throughout the region ca. 1200 BCE.[3]

---

1. For the Sea Peoples, see Katzenstein 1973, 59; Barnett 1975, 370; Lund 1986, 186; Courbin 1990, 504; Lagarce and Lagarce 1995, 149; Badre 2006, 94; Yon 2006, 21; Bretschneider, Van Vyve, and Jans 2011, 77–78; Kaniewski et al. 2011; 2015, 369–82; Langgut, Finkelstein, and Litt 2013, 166. See also discussion in Millek 2019a. For the Arameans, see Singer 1987, 2000.

2. Nur and Cline 2000; Nur and Burgess 2008. Callot (1994, 204–11) believes that an earthquake did strike Ugarit but that this event took place in mid-thirteenth century BCE, not at the end of the Late Bronze Age, and that the city was rebuilt subsequent to the seismic event, only to be destroyed ca. 1185 BCE.

3. For the Sea Peoples, see Dever 1992; Weinstein 1992, 2012; Bietak 1993; Stager 1995; Stern 2013; see also discussion in Millek 2017. For other assailants, see Morris 2005, 709; Barako 2007a; Gadot 2009; Kreimermann 2017, 193; Oritz and Wolff 2019.

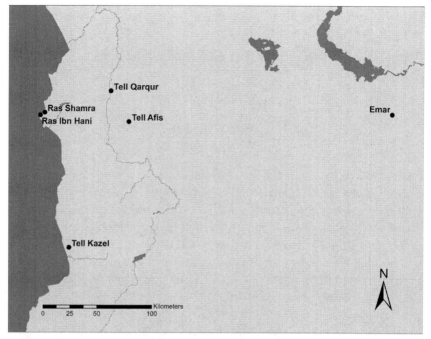

Figure 7.1. Map of sites with a destruction event ca. 1200 BCE in the northern Levant.

While a host of possible explanations have been offered for these destructions, the same issues that have plagued the other regions in question have infected the Levant as well, as many of the destruction events that did occur were not as severe as previously proposed. We begin our examination of the Levantine destructions in the north at Ras Shamra, the former capital city and trading emporium of Ugarit.

Northern Levant (fig. 7.1)

Ras Shamra-Ugarit — Scale: Site-Wide — Cause: Warfare

Located on the coast of northern Syria, Ras Shamra, the capital city of Ugarit, was destroyed ca. 1190–1185 BCE (see Millek 2020, 105–8). This destruction has been well documented over the many decades that the settlement has been excavated. Throughout the city there were signs of destruction from burnt plaster, fallen roofs, burnt brick hardened by fire, heaps of ash, and collapsed walls found in both administrative and domestic contexts (Schaeffer 1979, 51–52; Yon 1992, 117–18; Callot 1994, 212–13). Nevertheless, the entire city was not set ablaze, as both Claude Schaeffer (1963, 206; 1966, 132) and Olivier Callot (1994, 212–13) note that in the *Ville sud*, there were houses that did not have any signs of fire. Despite the fact that the *Ville sud* was not burnt, this destruction is still classified as site-wide, given that the majority of all excavated areas have evidence of destruction throughout widespread sections of the city.

As for the cause of this destruction, finds in the debris point to an act of armed conflict (fig. 7.2). Marguerite Yon (1992, 117) notes that twenty-five arrowheads were scattered about in the *Centre de la ville*. The arrowheads were not found in stockpiles, and thus appear to have been randomly distributed as the result of a military engagement, though no further information about their specific find spots has been given. Callot, in his presentation of the material from the *Ville sud*, notes that thirty-two arrowheads were discovered scattered about the area and twelve of these arrowheads were discovered on the streets and in the open spaces of the area. Along with the arrowheads, two bronze lance heads, four bronze javelin heads, five bronze daggers, one bronze sword, and three bronze pieces of armor were scattered throughout the houses and streets.[4] An undefined number of arrowheads were uncovered in the *Maison aux albâtres*, which were discovered, "inside the building, along the western and southern facades, with a greater frequency toward the southern corner of the structure. We would therefore be tempted to attribute the outbreak of the fire to disturbances during which the residence was attacked mainly from the west" (Contenson et al. 1974, 10). An additional two arrowheads and one bronze armor plate were recently uncovered in the *chantier du Rempart* in the 2007–2008 excavations (Al-Maqdissi et al. 2010, 28). Moreover, two hundred arrowheads were discovered in the *Palais royal*, where at least some were concentrated at the main entrance, which Schaeffer assumed to be evidence of a guardpost where quivers full of arrows were stored. Unfortunately, there is no further detailed information on how these arrowheads were dispersed throughout the *Palais royal*, nor is there any additional information on the pieces of armor and sling bullets that Schaeffer also uncovered in the structure (Vita and Matoïan, 2008, 258–59). No human remains were ever discovered in the destruction debris, leading many to conclude that the inhabitants fled the city, hiding some of their belongings, before the city was sacked and burnt, with the attacking force looting many of the valuable objects (Callot 1994, 212; Singer 1999, 730; Yon 2006, 22).

The lack of human remains, and the supposed "low" number of arrowheads have led both Issam Halayqa (2010, 325–26) and Klaus Sommer (2016, 209–11) to argue that there could not have been a fierce fight in the city. Yet, as Jordi Vidal (2014, 71–74) has pointed out, the general narrative that the populace of Ras Shamra escaped before a battle or that there was no battle at all does not

---

4. Callot 1994, 219–25; see as well fig. 309 "Les armes" on p. 383. Yon (1992, 117) notes that thirty arrowheads were found in the area but does not mention the additional weaponry.

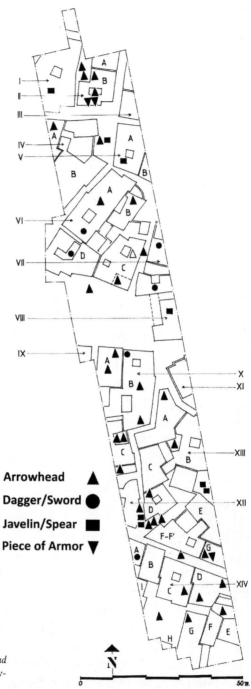

Figure 7.2. Plan of the *Ville Sud* noting where weapons were uncovered. Courtesy of Olivier Callot.

match the archaeological record. As he argues, while there may be a lack of skeletons, the mere presence of weapons of war scattered throughout the city indicates that a conflict occurred, and for a conflict to happen there must be combatants on both sides suggesting that at least some people had remained in the city fighting the attackers. He (72) also argues that the number of arrowheads is not low, and while he does not cite much corroborating evidence, he is correct. The 259 plus arrowheads and the 12 daggers, lances, javelins, and sword from the *Villa sud* are the most weapons of war found in any destruction event likely caused by an act of war from the end of the Late Bronze Age in the entirety of the Levant, if not the Eastern Mediterranean as a whole. The only destruction level ca. 1200 BCE that yielded more weapons of war was the destruction of the "Palace of Nestor" at Pylos and only because more than 500 bronze arrowheads were in storage at the time of the destruction.

Nonetheless, given that there is a relatively even distribution of weapons in the *Ville Sud*, as they were discovered on the streets, in the open spaces, and in the houses of the area, this indicates that they were not stockpiled and were likely deposited as a result of a conflict. If one argues that those weapons from domestic structures, open spaces, and streets are not evidence of warfare, as their contexts seems to suggest, then a compelling explanation must be given for why they were found in these contexts and especially on streets. It is highly doubtful to me that the citizens of Ras Shamra would leave a lance, sword, dagger, or arrowhead simply lying on the street for a child to pick up. While these weapons of war were likely deposited during the battle that was waged in the city, other depositions are likely indicators of weapon storage. Of the two hundred arrowheads discovered in the *Palais royal*, at least some were found concentrated at the main entrance, which Schaeffer assumed to be evidence of a guardpost where quivers full of arrows were stored (Vita and Matoïan, 2008, 258–59). Unfortunately, much like the arrowheads in the *Centre de la ville*, the find contexts for this wealth of weaponry are not provided. Nevertheless, it appears that at least some may have been in storage at the time of the destruction.

Regardless, the destruction of Ugarit is one of the best examples of a destruction by warfare from the end of the Late Bronze Age. While some of the inhabitants might have escaped, others did not, as indicated by the battle that scattered arrowheads and other weapons throughout the city. Thus, it is reasonable to agree with Yon (2006, 21) that the site was destroyed in an act of war, though whether or not it was the Sea Peoples as she claims is another matter, one to which I will return at the end of this chapter, as both the textual and archeological narrative for the destructive incursion of the Sea Peoples must be questioned at length.

224   CHAPTER SEVEN

Ras Ibn Hani — Scale: Single-Building — Cause: Arson

At a short distance to the southwest of Ras Shamra lies Ras Ibn Hani. Of the several Late Bronze Age structures uncovered at the site, evidence of destruction was found only in the *Palais Nord* (see Millek 2020, 109–11). Élisabeth and Jacques Lagarce (2006) have already presented this destruction in great detail. From their research, they discovered that while the building as a whole was set on fire, there was a differentiation in the intensity of burning throughout the structure. The fire reached its highest temperatures south of the courtyard and along its east side, as well as in the southeast wing of the building. The northwest of the building was also burned, but the temperature of the fire was much lower than in the southeast wing (225). Their conclusion, based on the pattern and intensity of the fire found throughout the *Palais Nord*, is that it was arson. They point out that the areas with the most intense fire were close to the front of the building and the easiest to reach. Moreover, the materials used to construct the building do not appear to have been sufficient enough to feed the fire to such a degree that it would create the intense heat witnessed in these areas. This indicates that fuel would have had to have been brought into the building and then set on fire (258).

Yet, it appears that before any burning took place, the building was largely emptied of most of the movable objects, as almost all ceramics were taken out, and those that remained were not complete vessels. It appears that the objects that were left, such as tablets and lead ingots, were not important enough at the time for the inhabitants to take with them upon the evacuation of the site.[5] The evidence thus suggests that the *Palais Nord* was burned in a targeted destruction by human hands. There is no evidence of earthquake damage, and an accidental fire is unlikely, as much of the material from the building was removed prior to the burning event. Much as with the destruction of Megaron B at Dimini, one cannot plan an accidental fire. Moreover, what is clear is that this destruction was targeted, as the remainder of the site has not yielded any evidence for destruction at all, even in the structures adjacent to the *Palais Nord*.

To the east of the *Palais Nord*, a set of rooms assumed to be a service building yielded no evidence of a destruction event. Likewise, *Bâtiment B*, to the southwest of the *Palais Nord*, was also found without any evidence of destruction. Neither of these buildings appear to have been emptied of their contents and were simply abandoned without destruction.[6] In the *Palais Sud*,

---

5. Two objects of note that were left in the building: an arrowhead was found in Room XVII, which was used for metalworking and is thus not likely an indicator of a direct assault, and a javelin head was found in Room XXIV, though whether or not it was being stored there cannot be determined (Bounni, Lagarce, and Lagarce 1998, 69).

6. Bounni et al. 1981, 284–86; Bordreuil et al. 1984, 399; Lagarce and Lagarce 1995, 146; Bounni, Lagarce, and Lagarce 1998, 14, 87–88; Curtis 1999, 26.

traces of fire were detected in the courtyard, while the remainder of the building had deteriorated without evidence of burning. This minor evidence of burning is not sufficient enough reason to conclude that the building was destroyed, and likely represents other activities going on in the courtyard. Much like in the *Palais Nord*, the *Palais Sud* was devoid of most finds, as they were seemingly cleared out even more systematically than the *Palais Nord*. If someone had tried to set the building ablaze as was done to the *Palais Nord*, it appears that their efforts were unsuccessful.[7]

The date of this single-building destruction is not clear from the archaeological remains. Adnan Bounni, É. Lagarce, and J. Lagarce (1998, 86–88), put the destruction of the *Palais Nord* at some time shortly before the destruction of Ras Shamra, giving a date of ca. 1185 BCE. They claim that the inhabitants left Ras Ibn Hani to seek shelter in Ras Shamra with the arrival of the Sea Peoples before the entire region of Ugarit was destroyed. This is based on the assumption that the Sea Peoples destroyed the land in one fell swoop. However, the documentary evidence uncovered at Ras Ibn Hani dates at the latest to 1230 BCE, which led the excavators to assume that the tablets from the *Palais Nord* represented a "dead archive," one that was stored and forgotten and does not represent the life cycle of the building (Lagarce et al. 1987, 287–88; Bounni, Lagarce, and Lagarce 1998, 86). Yet, if the archive is used to date the destruction, much like the archives at Ras Shamra have been used to date its destruction, then that places the destruction well before that of Ras Shamra and the incursions supposedly caused by the Sea Peoples. So, while the destruction *may* be contemporaneous, or at least within several years of the destruction found at Ras Shamra, this conclusion is not certain.

Tell Kazel — Scale: Multi-Building — Cause: Warfare

Tell Kazel, located on the 'Akkar plain of southern Syria, suffered a destruction event shortly after 1200 BCE (Jung 2018a, 47–51) at the end of the Late Bronze Age in its Area II North-Eastern sector Level 6 final, Area II Southern sector Level 5b, and Area IV Level 5 upper (see also Millek 2020, 114–16). Much like Ras Ibn Hani, the destruction was targeted, and much like Ras Shamra, there is sufficient evidence that this was an act of war or conflict. In Area II the North-Eastern sector, its Building I only had traces of fire in areas with a cooking or industrial function and it does not appear that the building was destroyed (Badre et al. 1994, 310–32). Likewise, in Building II from Area II the North-Eastern sector, traces of fire were not pronounced, and it does not appear as

---

7. Two arrowheads were discovered in the *Palais Sud*, though whether or not these are indicative of conflict is not clear from the preliminary reports, as no clear find contexts were given (Bounni et al. 1976, 241; 1979, 231–32; Bounni 1979, 286; Bounni, Lagarce, and Lagarce 1998, 86).

226 CHAPTER SEVEN

if the building was destroyed (Badre et al. 1994, 345; Capet and Gubel 2000, 434–36; Capet 2003, 66–96). In the southern sector of Area II, based on the preliminary reports from Buildings A and B, burning was only uncovered in one room; however, a full assessment of these buildings must await further publication.[8] Nevertheless, the picture presented by the archaeological evidence uncovered in Area II demonstrates that these domestic and industrial structures were unaffected by destruction. The situation was vastly different for the Temple Complex uncovered in Area IV. Traces of fire were found in the Cella and the Eastern Back Room of the temple though there is no mention of fire in the entrance to the temple (Badre and Gubel 1999–2000, 170–74). The fire appears to have been particularly intense in the Eastern Back Room, where a meter of severely burnt material with few ashes covered a large number of vessels stored therein. Leila Badre and Eric Gubel (1999–2000, 172) assume that the vessels likely stored olive oil, which could account for the severe burning witnessed in the room.

On either side of the temple were the Southern and Northern Complexes. These two structures had several domestic features such as tannurs, grinders, and storage jars, indicating that while they may be related to the temple, they could also have been independent domestic residences (Badre and Gubel 1999–2000, 197–98). In the Southern Complex, Room A was destroyed by fire along with Room B, though there is no mention of burning in Room C (170). In the Northern Complex, a thick layer of burnt material was uncovered in Rooms A and B that caused some of the material in the rooms to calcinate. Again, the likely cause for this was olive oil produced by the olive press in Room B. Once again, there is no mention of burning in the Northern Complex's Room C (180–85).

From the evidence for this destruction, there is no apparent evidence of damage by a natural disaster in the destruction of Tell Kazel. Moreover, given that only the most monumental structure was targeted, along with the buildings on either side, an earthquake is an unlikely culprit, as it would not be so selective as to destroy the sole prominent building at the site while leaving no traces of destruction behind in Buildings I and II. An accidental fire could be a reasonable explanation for the cause of this destruction given the wealth of olive oil stored and produced in the buildings. However, an accidental fire cannot account for the weapons of war scattered among the buildings in Area IV and II.

Throughout Area IV several weapons were uncovered; a bronze arrowhead was recovered in the cella while a bronze spearhead was found in Room A

---

8. Capet 2003, 96–99. Chiti and Pedrazzi (2014, 69) have stated that there is evidence of fire in this area, but the statement is too general to know if there is actually evidence of fire and if this was in conjunction with industrial activity as it was in much of Area II.

from the Southern Complex. In Room B from the Northern Complex, two bronze lance heads were recovered along with a bronze spearhead and two bronze armor plates (Badre and Gubel 1999–2000, 172, 177, 185). In general, the temple area does not appear as if it was looted or emptied before it was destroyed, which would suggest that the destruction was sudden (Badre 2008, 261–62). Additional weapons of war were uncovered in Building II from Area II the North-Eastern sector. A small arrowhead was recovered from Street L, and three arrowheads were uncovered in Rooms A, K, and S, with each room yielding one arrowhead. No weapons were retrieved from contexts that might suggest storage or as part of the bronze industry, and this is especially true for the arrowhead found on Street L, as this is not a likely place to store a weapon (Capet 2003, 68, 72, 74, 92).

At the same time, several weapons were uncovered that cannot be cited as evidence of conflict. In Building I and in the Southern sector of Area II, several weapons were discovered within the structures; however, these were uncovered in association with the bronze workshops (Badre et al. 1994, 327, 332; Capet 2003, 96–99; Jung, 2009, 42). Therefore, these weapons cannot be conclusively assigned to an act of war, as they may have been part of the industry situated in Building I and in the Southern sector of Area II. Given that the destruction uncovered at Tell Kazel was directed at the site's sacred building, that weapons were found in domestic structures, and that one arrowhead was discovered on a street, armed conflict was likely the cause for this destruction. As with Ras Shamra and Ras Ibn Hani, the supposed destroyers of Tell Kazel were the Sea Peoples, and Tell Kazel may be the singular site in the whole of the Eastern Mediterranean where the textual evidence might indicate that the Sea Peoples caused this multibuilding destruction.[9] This discussion will be taken up below.

Tell Afis — Scale: Multibuilding — Cause: Unknown

Some sixty kilometers south of Aleppo, a destruction event was uncovered at Tell Afis in its Area E4 Level Vb (fig. 7.3), where three buildings were uncovered, Buildings A, B, and E (see Millek 2019a, 164). Buildings A and E to the north are separated from Building B by Street C to the south, and based on the size and quality of the architecture, Building A appears to have been the most important structure uncovered in the area (Venturi 2012, 6). Meanwhile Building B's walls were much thinner, and it appears that this structure served as a domestic unit (Venturi 2010, 2). Both Building A and E were destroyed by fire in the first half of the twelfth century BCE.[10] The exterior mud bricks

---

9. Badre and Gubel 1999–2000, 197–98; Capet 2003, 118; Badre 2006, 94; Jung 2009, 42.

10. Venturi 2008, 368; 2010, 4; 2012; 2013, 238. Knapp and Manning (2016, 130) mistakenly place the destruction of Tell Afis in the mid-fourteenth or thirteenth century BCE along with the ca. 1340 BCE destruction found at Qatna and the ca. 1370 BCE destruction of Hama Level G3.

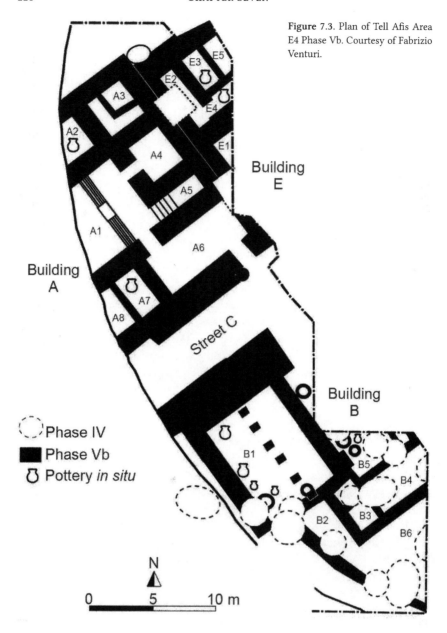

Figure 7.3. Plan of Tell Afis Area E4 Phase Vb. Courtesy of Fabrizio Venturi.

of Building A were vitrified by the heat of the fire, while inside burnt debris measured up to two meters thick. Remains of burnt wood were uncovered in Rooms A1 and A5, while the ceiling in Room A6 was burnt and had collapsed onto the floor. Similar evidence of destruction was also uncovered in Building E adjacent to Building A. To the north of Building A and E was Area D, which was a plastered space or courtyard that had no evidence of action by fire or debris on its surface. To the south of Building A, E, and Street C, lay Building B, which does not appear to have suffered the same fate as both Building A and E. No burning was found in Room B1, the Pillared Room. Burnt wood was recovered from the floors of Rooms B3 and B5, but as Fabrizio Venturi (2007, 129–34; 2010, 2; 2012, 6; 2020, 10–15; pers. comm. 09/08/2018) notes, this may be from everyday human activity, as two tannurs were situated in Room B5. Only Room B2 had clear signs of action by fire, but here the thickness of the ash and charcoal was only between five to ten centimeters and the mud bricks show no signs of vitrification indicating that the fire had not burned at any great intensity.

The cause of this multibuilding destruction is not evident from the excavated materials. No weapons of war nor any clear signs of a natural disaster were seen in the destruction of Building A and E. This destruction event also does not appear to have affected the site as a whole and may have been targeted. Not only was little evidence of a destruction seen in Building B, but in Area N on the other side of the acropolis, one room so far uncovered of a building belonging to the same phase also had no traces of a destruction (Venturi pers. comm. 09/08/2018). Thus, it may be that this was an act of arson targeting the, as of yet, most monumental structure, while the domestic Building B was left alone. However, the evidence is not strong enough to make this judgment at this time and the cause remains unknown.

Tell Qarqur — Scale: Multibuilding — Cause: Unknown

Tell Qarqur is situated in the Orontes River Valley of western Syria. Jesse Casana has reported that the site suffered a massive destruction dated to the early twelfth century BCE. The destruction was witnessed both in excavation and was possibly seen in a geophysical survey of the high mound.[11] However, as Eric Jensen (2018, 112; see also 2020, 6) has made clear, the physical evidence for destruction is limited, as Late Bronze Age material was only uncovered in a portion of Area B. In the Step Trench and square B13, part of what appears to have been a storage facility was uncovered. The floor was obscured by a meter of burnt debris, and under this debris were the remains of numerous storage jar fragments (Jensen 2018, 112). In square B2 another building, likely used for food preparation or consumption, was uncovered and it too was destroyed. Jensen (2018, 115, 117) describes the building's condition as, "The great intensity of the conflagration that destroyed this building left burnt and tumbled mudbrick

---

11. Casana, Herrmann, and Fogel 2008; Casana 2017, 166. The date for the destruction is not clear, as the best radiocarbon samples were lost during the Syrian Civil War (Jesse Casana pers. comm. 07/22/2020).

230 CHAPTER SEVEN

destruction debris at over a meter in depth ... the stones themselves exhibited scorch and burn marks with many stones deeply cracked, and although they still retained their original shape upon excavation, the stones could be taken apart and reassembled, piece by jagged piece."

While it is clear that several buildings were affected by destruction, Jensen (2018, 123) cautions that given the current state of excavations at the site, "Whether the entire Late Bronze Age II settlement at Tell Qarqur met with the same fiery destruction as the areas currently excavated is uncertain." In sum, there is no clear evidence for how extensive this burning event was nor is there any indication of what might have caused it.[12] For the time being the destruction is classified as a multibuilding destruction of unknown cause; however, this classification should be considered preliminary, as it could have been more extensive if the geophysical survey detected the same destruction event, or it could be less extensive if only certain rooms related to storage or cooking burnt in an accidental, but eventually controlled, fire.

Meskene-Emar — Scale: Multibuilding — Cause: Arson

Located on the middle Euphrates in northwestern Syria, Emar experienced a multibuilding destruction event between 1187 and 1175 BCE (Arnaud 1975, 92; Cohen and d'Alfonso 2008, 24; see Millek 2019a, 167–69). Unfortunately, while both the French and the German expeditions excavated large portions of the site, the description of the site's final destruction is minimal, as the scholarly focus has been on the rich archival materials uncovered at Emar.[13] The best description of Emar's destruction event was published in 1975. In this report, Jean-Claude Margueron (1975a) noted that evidence of fire was uncovered in Areas A, C, E, J, L, and a part of Areas M, O, and T. However, in the houses from Areas D, H, M, P, and Q, no evidence of action by fire was seen. Moreover, virtually no objects, and in most cases not even ceramics, were recovered in these areas, which suggested to Margueron (1975a, 68–69) a possible partial abandonment of the city before the remainder of the site was burned. Within the destruction, seven arrowheads, three daggers, two armor plates, and one sword were uncovered; however, the context for these finds has not been published (Beyer 1982, 119–21). Thus, while these weapons might be direct evidence of

---

12. Jensen (2018, 59–60; 2020, 6) claims that the destruction was caused by some invading force and he equates changes in the subsistance patterns in the following Iron Age as evidence of a disruptive event where attackers must have destroyed the perennial crops as well as taking, killing, or scattering the site's sheep and goats. However, based on the currently available evidence, there is no indication of the cause or if the destruction event itself was the causal factor in the change in subsistance patterns.

13. Margueron 1975a, 1975b, 1982a, 1982b, 1982c, 1983; Margueron and Boutte 1995; Finkbeiner 2001, 2002; Finkbeiner and Sakal 2003, 2015.

warfare, without the contextual information this can only be assumed based on the apparent pattern of evidence, which indicates arson.

What caused this destruction, or more generally speaking, who caused this destruction has been a matter of some scholarly debate.[14] The perpetrators have been assumed to be the Sea Peoples (Caubet 1992, 129), the Aramaeans (Singer 1987, 413–21), or ,based on the textual sources from Emar, a mysterious group known only as *ṭár-wu*, which Daniel Arnaud (1986) translated as "hordes." This group of people is known from several texts, such as AOSI 2.2–3, which states, "in the year when hordes (?) of troops besieged the city" (Adamthwaite 2001, 270), or as AOSI 44.32–3, which reads, "in the year of distress when hordes (?) of troops besieged the city of Emar" (270). It is unknown if the term *ṭár-wu* is referencing an as of yet unknown ethnic group by that name, or if it is a place holder for a group whose name was not known to the scribes of Emar (271).

From an archaeological perspective there is no clear answer as to who did the destroying. Leaving aside the texts for a moment, it is likely, based on the archaeological evidence, that this destruction was committed by human hands. Areas of importance, such as the palace in Area A, the temples of Ba'al and Astarte in Area E, as well as the temple in Area M, were destroyed, while the houses in Area M were left alone. This, along with the fact that other domestic structures were spared the torch in Areas D, H, P, and Q, suggests a guiding hand rather than a random fire or natural disaster. Moreover, since at least part of the city was abandoned prior to the destruction event, it was not a sudden accidental or natural disaster. Rather, whoever destroyed the monumental structures at Emar were expected and planned for. Accordingly, the destruction was most likely by arson and possibly an act of war, as the eleven weapons and two armor plates may suggest. Who it was that destroyed the monumental buildings is unknown, but as neither the Sea Peoples nor the Arameans were ever mentioned as actively destroying anything in the region of Emar, there is no textual or archaeological bases to assume it was either of these two groups.

Southern Levant (fig. 7.4)

Tel Yin'am — Scale: Multibuilding — Cause: Unknown

Tel Yin'am is situated in Yavne'el Valley of the eastern Galilee. While there is evidence of destruction at the end of the last Late Bronze Age phase at the site, the exact date of this destruction may be well before ca. 1200 BCE at some time during the LB IIB (Liebowitz 2003, 18, 100; see also Millek 2019c, 174–75). However, since there is still the possibility that the destruction dates to the end

---

14. For an overview, see Adamthwaite 2001, 270–80.

232　　　　　　　　　　　　　Chapter Seven

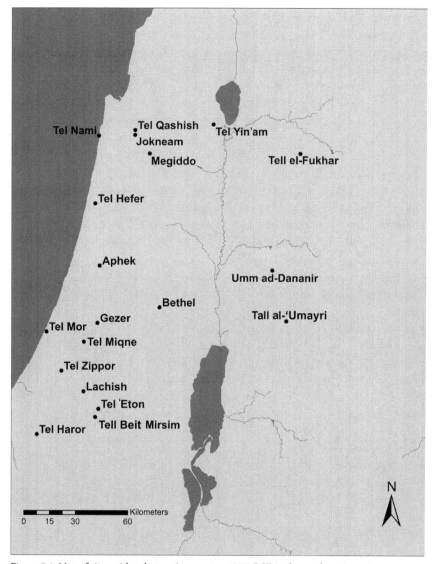

Figure 7.4. Map of sites with a destruction event ca. 1200 BCE in the southern Levant.

of the thirteenth century, which is Harold Liebowitz's preferred date, it will be included here.

Stratum XIIA represents the last Late Bronze Age phase at Tel Yin'am. Buildings 1, 2, 5, 6, and 7 were destroyed at the end of Stratum XIIA, as they were filled with mud-brick collapse, burnt debris, and ash, but no evidence of destruction was seen in Building 3 upper and Building 8 (Liebowitz 2003, 60–100). Building 6 appears to have been the most affected by the fire, as the heat

THE LEVANT: A MIXED BAG OF DESTRUCTION   233

was so intense that it created a layer of vitrified mud brick that lay atop the floor of the structure (87–97). After the destruction, there was a brief squatter settlement in Buildings 1, 3 Upper, 5, and 7 prior to the Iron Age resettlement of the site (83–98). While it is clear the Tel Yin'am suffered a multibuilding destruction, as most but not all structures from Stratum XIIA were burnt, there is no clear cause. The site was already in a period of crisis prior to the destruction as Building 1, which was possibly the residence of the local ruler (Leibowitz 1993, 1516). It had been transformed from the most well-built structure to one filled with flimsy and poorly built walls and was partially converted into an industrial smelting area (Millek 2019c, 174–75). Nevertheless, there is no clear evidence as to what caused this destruction.

Tel Qashish — Scale: Partial — Cause: Unknown

Located in the northwestern section of the Jezreel Valley, little is known about the end of the Late Bronze Age at Tel Qashish. Material dating to the end of the Late Bronze Age was only excavated in a single square in Area A (Square S/18), which was highly disturbed by events during Israel's War of Independence in 1948, as several trenches were dug and a cement bunker was constructed in the area. This was only compounded by the fact that the Late Bronze Age materials lay close to the surface and were severely damaged by erosion and plowing (Ben-Tor and Bonfil 2003b, 331; 2003c, 369). Stratum V represents the last Late Bronze Age occupation at the site.[15] The only description of the possible destruction event was provided by Amnon Ben-Tor (1993a, 1203) who stated that, "Traces of the fierce destruction by fire of the Late Bronze Age settlement (layers of ash, brick rubble, and an abundance of pottery) are evident wherever remains of the period have been uncovered." Unfortunately, there is no further information concerning this possible destruction event (Ben-Tor and Bonfil 1988, 108; 2003a 245, 276). Given the fragmentary nature of the remains and the limited area that was uncovered, it is unknown if there was a destruction at the end of the Late Bronze Age; however, much as with Teichos Dymaion in Greece, to err on the side of caution, a partial destruction is still attributed to Tel Qashish, even though it may not have been destroyed ca. 1200 BCE.

Jokneam — Scale: Multibuilding — Cause: Unknown

The archeological site of Jokneam is located near the modern city Yokneam Illit in the western Jezreel Valley. Little is known of the Late Bronze Age, as much of

---

15. Though due to the disturbed nature of the finds it was not always clear what walls and ceramics belonged to Stratum V or to the following Iron Age Stratum IV (Ben-Tor and Bonfil 2003b, 331, 337).

234 CHAPTER SEVEN

the settlement either remains under the Iron Age buildings or was completely removed by the Iron Age construction activity (Millek 2019c, 182–83). What we know of the Late Bronze Age site is based on two areas, A4 and A1, uncovered outside of the Iron II walls (Ben-Tor 1993b, 808). In Area A4, what has been excavated of Stratum XIXa, which dates to the end of the Late Bronze Age, was destroyed in a fire. A meter of debris was uncovered in the structure, while collapsed mud bricks were found uncovered in an alleyway next to it. In Area A1, another burn layer was excavated, though it was not as substantial as what had been uncovered in Area A4 (Ben-Ami 2005a, 154, 164). Doron Ben-Ami (2005b, 183) suggests that the destruction may have been abrupt, given the numerous intact and nearly intact vessels discovered in the debris; however, there is no clear cause for this multibuilding destruction, nor is there clear evidence that it was sudden, and the cause remains unknown.

Tel Nami — Scale: Partial — Cause: Natural

Located on the southern Carmel coast about fifteen kilometers south of Haifa, little information has been published about the LB IIB settlement at Tel Nami, which suffered a destruction event at the beginning of the twelfth century BCE (Artzy 1990a, 23; 1990b, 75; 1993, 1096–97; 1995, 22; 2013, 10). In Area D1, the area was sealed by a thick layer of mud and fallen mud bricks that might have been from a collapsed roof (Artzy 1990a, 34; 1990b, 76; 1992, 24). Area G was found to contain a large amount of crushed pottery, while a basalt basin had been knocked off its base, crushing pottery underneath it; however, other than this, there is no other published information on the destruction (Artzy 1991, 197; 1995, 23). Unfortunately, based on the preliminary reports, it is unclear exactly how much of each area was affected by this destruction.

Weapons of war were found in both areas D1 and G; however, these were likely part of the metal recycling industry at Tel Nami, and thus there is no clear evidence of warfare (Artzy 1990a, 34; 1991, 197; 1992, 25; 1993, 1096; 1995, 22–23). Moreover, the lack of any evidence of action by fire indicates that humans were not involved in the destruction, and it of course could not have been destroyed in an accidental fire. Area G contained numerous precious objects of bronze and pieces of gold and silver (Artzy 1993, 1096), perhaps indicating that the destruction took place before these objects could be removed.

The most likely explanation for this destruction is that Tel Nami experienced a severe storm that resulted in the collapse of some of the superstructure, which would explain the layer of mud in Area D1. If this was not the case, at the least, the partial destruction was likely brought on by some kind of natural cause, as there is no evidence suggesting the hand of man.

THE LEVANT: A MIXED BAG OF DESTRUCTION

Megiddo Stratum VIIB — Scale: Single-Building — Cause: Unknown

Megiddo, situated on the western end of the Jezreel Valley, was one of the most preeminent sites in the southern Levant during the Late Bronze Age, and given its importance, it too is a common example of destruction ca. 1200 BCE.[16] Two destruction events have been ascribed to Megiddo Stratum VII (Finkelstein et al. 2017a; Martin 2017). David Ussishkin (1995, 1998, 2000, 2008) has argued that the palace only suffered one destruction at the end of Stratum VIIA, but this has been convincingly refuted by Amihai Mazar (2002), Inbal Samet (2009), Israel Finkelstein et al. (2017a), and Mario Martin (2017), leaving two destruction events, one at the end of VIIB and one in VIIA. However, as Finkelstein et al. (2017a, 274–75) and Martin (2017, 279–84) have argued and as mentioned in chapter 3, the date for the destruction of Stratum VIIA appears to fall in the eleventh century BCE based on radiocarbon dates and correlations with recent finds in Area H, though as also mentioned in chapter 3, the date could also be in the mid-twelfth century BCE. Nevertheless, no matter which of these two dates is correct for Stratum VIIA, this destruction occurred outside of the transition from the Late Bronze Age to the Iron Age and was not part of the events that brought about the transformations witnessed in the southern Levant.

This would leave the supposed destruction of the palace during Stratum VIIB dating to ca. 1185 BCE (Martin 2017, 283); however, there is little physical evidence that Megiddo suffered a destruction at the beginning of the twelfth century BCE (Millek 2018b, 249–50). In Area K, Unit 04/K/57, which was attached to Building 04/K/44, was filled with a half meter of destruction debris on an earthen floor and was covered by an ash layer. However, no evidence of a destruction was witnessed in Building 04/K/44, though complete vessels remained on the floor, which seems to indicate that it was "hastily" abandoned.[17] No destruction was uncovered in Areas H or F (Finkelstein and Ussishkin 2000, 593–94; Martin 2017, 279), and the burning uncovered in Unit 04/K/57 is not even enough evidence to assume that any building in Area K was destroyed.

Traditionally, the focus of destruction at the end of the Late Bronze Age at Megiddo was assumed to be the palace in Area AA. However, the actual evidence of destruction is meagre at best. Gordon Loud (1948, 29) described the destruction as, "The Stratum VIIB palace obviously suffered violent destruction so extensive that the Stratum VIIA builders deemed it more expedient to level off the resulting debris and build over it than to remove all of it." He (29) goes

---

16. Dever 1992, 100 fig. 13.1; Drews 1993, 9 fig. 1; Nur and Cline 2000, 44 fig. 1; Bell 2006, 137 map 1; Nur and Burgess 2008, 225 fig 8.1; Kaniewski et al. 2011 fig. 1; Kaniewski, Guiot, and Van Campo 2015, 370 fig. 1; Knapp and Manning 2016, 130. For a previous discussion of the destruction at Megiddo, see Millek 2018b, 249–50; 2019c, 171–74.

17. Finkelstein, Ussishkin, and Halpern 2006, 847–48; Gadot, Martin, and Blockman 2006, 90–92; Arie and Nativ 2013, 171–74; Martin, Blockman, and Bidmead 2013, 153, 160

236 CHAPTER SEVEN

on to describe the meter and a half of fallen stones over which the Stratum VIIA pavement was constructed, and some charred horizontal lines found, "Here and there on the walls of the rooms to the north of the court." What Loud's account of this destruction is generally lacking is evidence of a destruction. He only notes a large quantity of fallen stones and assumed that the palace was so badly destroyed that the following builders did not remove the resulting rubble. However, much like the North Gate at Enkomi that Dikaios assumed was destroyed, there is no clear evidence that suggests that the Stratum VIIB palace was in fact destroyed ca. 1200 BCE. The palace could have been torn down and remodeled during Stratum VIIA rather than destroyed, much like the temples from Kition.

To err on the side of caution, Megiddo is still assigned a single-building destruction, as the destruction may not have been properly catalogued during the attempted total excavation of Megiddo. However, given that there is no other evidence of destruction even in the adjacent Area H, it is highly likely that Megiddo experienced no destruction ca. 1200 BCE. At most, if there was a destruction, this damage was minimal and was followed by rebuilding activities and a Late Bronze Age cultural affinity that lasted for half a century or more.

Tel Hefer — Scale: Partial — Cause: Unknown

Situated about five kilometers inland from the Mediterranean Sea in the central Sharon Plain, little is known about the end of the Late Bronze Age at Tel Hefer (also known as Tell Ifshar). In fact, little is actually known about the Late Bronze Age as a whole, as the majority of the Late Bronze Age finds came from a single storage room that was reused throughout the LB II. The last LB level Phase A/7 dated to ca. 1200 BCE was another iteration of the storage room and it was destroyed by fire, as burnt mud bricks covered the floor along with debris from the collapsing building. Eight storage jars were discovered in the debris, while some Cypriot milk bowl sherds were on the floor (Porath and Paley 1982a, 66; 1982b, 42; 1993, 612). However, there is no other information about this destruction, and there is no way to know what caused this partial destruction, or if it was even a destruction event at all.

Aphek — Scale: Site-Wide — Cause: Warfare

Situated near the headwaters of the Yarqon River, Aphek at the time of its final Egyptian phase was dominated by a single building at the top of the site.[18] This building, Palace VI, was a continuation of the two previous Egyptian buildings,

---

18. For a discussion of this destruction regarding the Sea Peoples invasion and the fall of Egyptian hegemony, see Millek 2017, 2018a.

THE LEVANT: A MIXED BAG OF DESTRUCTION   237

Palaces V and IV. Palace VI was built on the southwest corner of Palace V, and it was destroyed at the end of the Late Bronze Age in an apparent military battle. Throughout the destroyed building, remains of carbonized wood and burnt plaster were uncovered. Items from the second floor crashed down to the floor below, and the charred remains of a wooden door were found at the entrance of a stairway connecting to the building's piazza. Remains of destruction were not limited to Palace VI alone, as burnt material, detritus burnt bricks, and ash were scattered over the top of the tell. Much of this material was against the stumps of the palace's walls, but it was also spread for several meters due to the years of erosion following the building's destruction and abandonment (Gadot 2009, 55–63).

Palace VI seems to have been destroyed with all its goods intact, indicating that the inhabitants did not have time to take their belongings out before the destruction. In the destruction debris from Stratum X12, six or possibly seven arrowheads were found in the wreckage.[19] One arrowhead was inside of the structure, and the remainder were scattered outside of the building, both south and east of the palace, while an armor scale was also discovered in the destruction debris (Gadot 2009, 66; Yahalom-Mack and Shalev 2009, 417). Moshe Kochavi (1978, 15; 1990, xii) reported that the arrowheads were embedded in the floors and the walls of the palace. He states that, "No less dramatic were the bronze arrowheads found with their tips penetrating the southern façade of the building or stuck into the surface of the alley."[20] However, this was not mentioned in the final report and it is unclear if these arrowheads were simply not recorded or if they were the arrowheads described in the final report, but the contexts do not match Kochavi's initial statements. Nevertheless, since the arrowheads that were recorded in the final report were not gathered together as if being stored in the building, but were scattered outside it, this would suggest an attack against the building from the outside. With this evidence, including the complete destruction of the sole building on the site, and the intact assemblage inside of the building, it is reasonable to conclude that Aphek Stratum X12 was destroyed by an enemy force. However, who that force was cannot be said from the archaeological remains. The destruction of Stratum X12 at Aphek could be classified as either a single-building or a site-wide destruction. Since Palace VI was the only structure known for this period at the site, it is classified as a site-wide destruction rather than as a single-building, even though there was only a sole structure to destroyed, yet the site as a whole was indeed destroyed (Millek 2018b, 249).

---

19. Gadot 2009, 67–68; Yahalom-Mack and Shalev 2009, 416–17. One of the arrowheads possibly came from Stratum X13.

20. Kochavi 1978, 15. See fig. 7, "Arrowheads found stuck in the walls and floors." Five arrowheads are shown.

238   CHAPTER SEVEN

Bethel — Scale: Partial — Cause: Unknown

Bethel, situated in the central hill country, suffered a destruction event that has
been dated by Finkelstein and Lily Singer-Avitz (2009, 37) to the late thirteenth
or early twelfth century BCE. The site was excavated both by William Foxwell
Albright (1934) in the 1930s and James Kelso (1968) in the 1950s; however,
the published evidence for the end of Phase 2, the last Late Bronze phase, is
minimal. Albright (1934, 9) described the destruction in Area I simply as a
"tremendous conflagration," while in Area II he noted that there was a mass
of fallen burnt mud bricks filled with ash that extended for twenty meters
(9). Albright described this destruction by saying that, "We have never seen
indications of a more destructive conflagration in any Palestinian excavations"
(9) Albright (1934, 11) assumed that Bethel had been destroyed by the Israelites
in the mid-thirteenth century BCE.

The excavation carried out by Kelso also uncovered evidence of this
destruction, and much like Albright's excavations, there is little information
to go off in assessing the scale or cause of the destruction. Kelso (1968, 31)
describes the situation as, "The last LB town was utterly destroyed by a great
conflagration and the succeeding Israelite town was strikingly different";
however, this is about the extent of the description of the destruction. In Area II,
a wall was excavated that had been burnt in an intense fire, cracking the rocks,
while traces of action by fire was uncovered throughout the area. A pavement
was seen to have heavy burning on top of it, and a stone foundation had ash
atop it. Additionally, Kelso states that the expedition found two breaches in
the city's defenses. On the south side of the city an Iron I house had been built
partially on the stub of the city wall and partially on 1.75 m of ash and brick
debris. A similar find was found in the western portion of the site, as Iron I
houses were built over at times 1 to 1.5 m of ashes charcoal, brick, and earth
(Kelso 1968, 30, 49). Some cracking was seen in a wall of Area II, which could be
taken as evidence for an earthquake, though structural failure is just as likely
an explanation (29). However, of great importance is that the excavators noted
that, at Bethel, all the expeditions found much smaller amounts of pottery
from the LB II than normal. A number of rooms yielded no pottery or any
other objects, and according to the Kelso (1968, 48), the city seems to have been
thoroughly plundered before it was given to the torch.

From the descriptions given by both Albright and Kelso, Phase 2 did suffer a
destruction; however, the exact extent of the damage is unclear. While Albright
states that Area I was destroyed by a conflagration, there is no published
evidence from either excavation to support this. Likewise, while it is clear that
the site's wall suffered damage, it is entirely unclear how many buildings were
actually burnt. Because of this, the end of Phase 2 is currently assigned a partial

THE LEVANT: A MIXED BAG OF DESTRUCTION   239

destruction, even though it may have been more extensive, as the published material is not clear enough to make an estimation of how much of the site was actually destroyed ca. 1200 BCE.[21] There is also no clear burden of proof for what caused the destruction. Much as at Ras Ibn Hani and Emar, it appears that Bethel might have been partially abandoned prior to this burning event, as some rooms had no finds in them whatsoever. And as with Gla, it is unlikely that invaders would take everything out of the rooms, including seemingly worthless pottery. This may point to an organized partial abandonment of the site prior to destruction; nevertheless, this is only a suggestion, as the published material is not sufficient enough to make a reasonable judgment.

Gezer — Scale: Single-Building — Cause: Unknown

Gezer sits at the foothills of the Judaean Mountains roughly midway between Jerusalem and Tel Aviv. A destruction event ca. 1200 BCE at the end of General Stratum XIV has been attributed to Merenptah by Steven Ortiz and Samuel Wolff (2012, 75; 2019, 82). However, the only convincing evidence of a destruction event ca. 1200 BCE comes from the recent excavation conducted by Ortiz and Wolff, who date their single-building destruction to the end of William Dever's General Stratum XIV (Ortiz and Wolff 2019, 74). However, the evidence for destruction from the Dever excavations is equivocal at best. In Field I Stratum 5A, there was a large amount of rockfall in the eastern portion of surface 3012 over wall 3011A, inside the wall above Surface 3009A and over the north corner of Wall 2011. Additionally, in the whole area in and around this rockfall there was orange-buff brick detritus up to twenty centimeters deep, along with forty-five to fifty-five centimeters of debris, mostly made of dark-brown rubble, patches of ash, some plaster fragments, and bones (Dever et al. 1970, 23–24). In Field II, much of Stratum 12 had been disturbed by building activities in Stratum 11, and it is unclear if there was any destruction. Some collapsed stones, rubbly mud-brick detritus, plastery debris, charred wood, ashes, and sherds, were uncovered; however, not all of this material was in situ (Dever et al. 1974, 51). In Field VI Stratum 7 the only evidence for human activity was the extensive digging of trenches (Dever et al. 1986, 50–59).

From the Dever excavations at Gezer, there are only ephemeral remains of a settlement during General Stratum XIV and any possible evidence of destruction was disturbed by the following construction activities in Stratum XIII. Dever was not convinced that there was a destruction at the end of

---

21. Kreimerman (2017, 186) has opted to maximally interpret the evidence and lists the destruction of Bethel as his most devastating type of destruction.

240   CHAPTER SEVEN

Stratum XIV saying that, "This stratum ends with no apparent destruction, but the following Str. XIII shows major changes."[22]

However, evidence of a single-building destruction has been uncovered in the recent expedition to Gezer led by Ortiz and Wolff.[23] A large building complex made up of several rooms as well as a courtyard and auxiliary room had been burned, and the fire took the lives of two adults and one child. The remains of one adult and a child were discovered in Unit A near an industrial installation. Both skeletons had been badly burnt and the adult's hands were positioned over their head at the time of death (Ortiz and Wolff 2019, 75–79). Skeletal remains of a female were uncovered in the southwest corner of Unit D, who was possibly shielding herself from the stone and mud bricks that crushed and covered over her body (79).

The building dates to the LB IIB, but Ortiz and Wolff assume that this destruction dates to the time of Merenptah, as he claims to have subdued Gezer in the so-called Israel Stele, and given that the following occupation was Iron I, they assume that this places the destruction to ca. 1200 BCE (74–75). However, much as Michael Hasel has already pointed out, there is no record of Merenptah actually destroying Gezer, or Ashkelon, which is also mentioned on the stele. Merenptah's scribes described his action as Ashkelon being "brought in" and Gezer as "captured" (Hasel 1998, 241–54; 2016, 221). Thus, the text does not mention actual destruction but rather forced subjugation. Moreover, as Donald Redford (1986, 199) has noted about the Israel Stele in general, "The sort of triumphal sweep of arms which the above snippet of poetry conjures up is quite unhistorical, and the passage must be rejected as a reliable source." Hence, there is no textual basis to assume that Merenptah destroyed Gezer, as Ashkelon has no evidence of a destruction from this period (see ch. 3) and the language that Merenptah invoked does not connote a destruction (Hasel 1988, 29–64). Moreover, as no weapons have been uncovered and there is no clear evidence of destruction elsewhere in the site, there is no evidence that this destruction was even caused by humans and the souls who died could have been caught unaware in an accidental fire.

Tel Mor — Scale: Single-Building — Cause: (VII: Unknown) (VI: Natural)

North of Ashdod and one kilometer from the Mediterranean Sea lies the small mound of Tel Mor, which was home to an Egyptian garrison at the end of the Late Bronze Age (see Barako 2007a, 2007b, 2013; Martin and Barako 2007). Both Building B of Stratum VII and the subsequently constructed Building F of

---

22. Dever and Seger 2014, 14. Dever (1993, 504) also mentioned in 1993 that there is no evidence of a destruction at the end of General Stratum XIV.

23. For an overview of this expedition to Gezer, see Oritz and Wolff 2012, 2017, 2019.

THE LEVANT: A MIXED BAG OF DESTRUCTION   241

Stratum VI were destroyed in two separate destruction events (fig. 7.5), the first at the end of the thirteenth century BCE and the second at the beginning of the twelfth century BCE (Dothan 1993c, 1073; Barako 2007b, 242). Tristan Barako (2007a, 26) describes the destruction of Building B as:

> A heavy destruction layer, in places as thick as 1.5 meters, covered the buildings of Stratum VII. Although thickest in the north of Building B, this layer was exposed in every room excavated. Unlike the collapse that separated Strata VIII and VII, it contained a large amount of ash and burnt mudbrick. Apparently, the site was abandoned for a time after this fiery destruction, as evidenced by a thin, superimposed layer of windblown sand.

Moshe Dothan (1993c, 1073) attributed this destruction either to the Egyptians in the punitive campaign by Merenptah or to the Israelites. However, Barako believes that given the continued presence of Egyptian pottery at the site, the Egyptian answer is unlikely. He (2007b, 242) states that "It is more reasonable to suppose, instead, that attacks on Egyptian garrisons (such as Tel Mor) by rebellious Canaanites (e.g., Gezer) prompted Merneptah's campaign ... If any group, then, is to claim responsibility for the destruction of Stratum VII, it should probably be the Canaanites." Nevertheless, there is no clear answer for what caused this destruction, as there is no positive evidence that points especially to arson, warfare, an accident, or a natural disaster. Further, while Building B was destroyed and subsequently abandoned, there was nevertheless strong cultural continuity at the site, both in the local Canaanite pottery and in the Egyptian and Egyptian-style pottery leading to the construction of Building F (Barako 2007c; Martin and Barako 2007).

Occupation was renewed at Tel Mor with the construction of Building F in Stratum VI (LB IIB/IA I transitional). Building F was constructed to the east of Building B with the western edge of the structure resting on the destroyed remains of Building B's eastern side. Dothan (1993c, 1073) described the square building with massive four-meter-thick walls as a *migdol.* Building F was also destroyed, which Barako (2007a, 30) describes as, "Stratum VI also ended in destruction. Numerous whole or almost whole vessels lay smashed on the floors of building F, particularly in room 71. On top of these vessels were fallen mudbricks and ten more broken pots." No reason or cause for this destruction was given by either Dothan or Barako. The key to understanding the likely cause for this destruction comes from understanding the potential hazards of the construction techniques utilized in Building F. Building F was constructed in a traditional Egyptian style, that is, without a stone foundation, and in addition, under the mud-brick foundation was a layer of sand (Barako 2007a, 26). This faulty foundation would have been more prone to damage by earthquakes or other natural causes, such as storms or settling. As Baruch Brandl (2010, 254) notes, the use of sand as a foundation may have allowed for water to seep

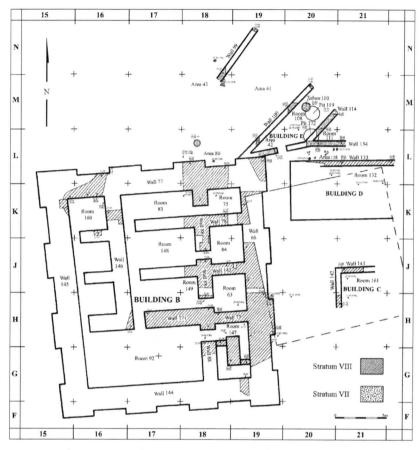

Figure 7.5. Tel Mor, Strata VIII–VII. Courtesy of Tristen Barako.

below the foundation, causing structural weakness. He (254–55) goes on to point out that this was likely part of a foundation ritual, referencing James Weinstein's (1973, 5–6) sixth act of an Egyptian foundation ceremony ritual. Therefore, it is likely that the collapse of Building F was caused either by some natural cause, be it settling or a storm.[24] While there is no clear answer for what caused the burning and collapse of the Stratum VII Building B, for Building F, it likely collapsed due an engineering oversight, as sand as a foundation may have been appropriate for the climate in Egypt, but was not suited for the rainier climate of the southern Levantine coast.

---

24. This is also likely the reason behind the similar destruction of the Stratum VIII Building B; see Millek 2018a.

Tel Miqne-Ekron — Scale: Single-Building — Cause: Unknown

One of the five cities of the Philistine pentapolis, Tel Miqne-Ekron is about thirty-seven kilometers southwest of Jerusalem at the point where the Judaean hills meet the coastal plain. It is the only city of the Philistine pentapolis that suffered a destruction event at the end of the Late Bronze Age.[25] Stratum VIIIB (formerly Stratum IX) represents the LB IIB period of Tel Miqne-Ekron. From the little amount of LB IIB material that has been excavated, it appears Ekron was a small town or village, mainly consisting of domestic structures and/or possibly an industrial area.[26] Stratum VIIIB Field I Upper ended in a fire that burnt a single mud-brick storage unit containing a layer of burnt debris and fallen mud bricks covering over complete vessels resting on the floor. One storage jar was filled with carbonized figs and another contained carbonized lentils (Killebrew 1998, 381; 2013, 81, 83; Dothan 1998, 151). There is no further evidence at this time that any more of the site was destroyed.[27] And similar to many other sites in the southern Levant, there is no clear cause for this single-building destruction.

Tel Zippor — Scale: Single-Building — Cause: Unknown

Tel Zippor (also spelled Sippor), located near the main road from Qiryat Gat to Ashkelon suffered a single-building destruction ca. 1200 BCE at the end of its Stratum III.[28] A possible "Canaanite" cultic building was uncovered in Stratum III featuring a raised mud-brick platform, while a bronze statue of a god and a stone statue that most likely depicted a "Canaanite" king were discovered inside the structure. However, there was no evidence that this cultic building was destroyed (Biran and Negbi 1964, 285; 1965, 256; 1966, 163; Biran 1993, 1527). Another structure from Stratum III, likely a storage unit, was destroyed by fire, as the rooms were filled with ash and burnt material up to half a meter. The bricks in the lower course were burnt until they were black and brittle and in the debris were the burnt remains of plants.[29] While this single storage unit was burned ca. 1200 BCE, the excavators made it clear that the site as a

---

25. As noted in ch. 3, Tell eṣ-Ṣafi/Gath, Ashkelon, and Ashdod were not destroyed ca. 1200 BCE. There is currently no information on the fate of Gaza, owing to a lack of excavations of the Late Bronze Age and Iron Age settlement, if it even still exists; see Millek 2017 for a more extensive discussion of this destruction and its aftermath.

26. Killebrew 2013, 80–81. The possible industrial activities are indicated by large amounts of flint debitage, flint tools, slag, copper, and olive pits.

27. Contrary to Stager 1995, 342 who states, "[At Ekron] the Philistines encountered a small Canaanite city ... of four ha and destroyed it in an intense conflagration. Over its ruins and beyond, the Philistines built a city five times larger than the old Canaanite one."

28. See Millek 2017 for further discussion of the impact of the destruction at Tel Zippor.

29. Biran and Negbi 1965, 256. The type of plants was never specified.

244 CHAPTER SEVEN

whole was not destroyed. Avraham Biran and Ora Negbi (1965, 256) stated that, "The result of this season's excavation confirmed the conclusion that the Philistine settlement on Tel Sippor did not bring in its wake the destruction of the Canaanite settlement which preceded it ... the Canaanite remains were discovered immediately beneath the Philistine floors, with no trace of fire or destruction intervening between the two," and (1966, 163), "Here again, no evidence of fire could be detected below the plastered floor of Stratum II, which sealed the remains of Stratum III." Thus, this single-building destruction did not in any way represent the destruction of the site as a whole. While there is no evidence regarding the cause of the fire, it was most likely an accidental or natural one. If this was an act of arson the question arises, Why did the arsonists burn a storage unit rather than the cultic structure, which is the case in so many other destructions by warfare or arson? Thus, while we cannot confirm what the cause was, at the least there is no evidence that it was brought on by warfare, arson, or a natural disaster such as an earthquake.

Lachish Level VII — Scale: Single-Building — Cause: Accidental and Arson

Lachish is situated in the Judaean hill country some thirty-eight kilometers southeast of Jerusalem. While the major site-wide destruction witnessed at the end of the Level VI occurred well after the end of the Late Bronze Age, as discussed in chapter 3, a destruction or destructions affected Lachish at the end of its Level VIIA ca. 1200 BCE.[30] In Area S, a domestic structure was uncovered that had been destroyed in a fire (Barkay and Ussishkin 2004, 344, 347). A possible indication of the cause of this destruction is the location where the fire and destruction appear to have made the most damage: both Units 3766 and 3782 Upper, which suffered the most damage by fire, seem to have been part of a kitchen or food preparation area. Destruction was also found in Unit 3783, which is directly behind unit 3782. Unit 3783 also had a tabun at its south wall W1017, which is the same wall shared by the tabun in Unit 3782. The destruction in Unit 3783 also covered several complete storage jars (350–51). It is quite possible that this fire was caused by an accidental kitchen fire, as both rooms that suffered the most damage shared a single wall that had a tabun on either side (Millek 2017, 127).

An objection to the suggestion that the domestic structure from Area S Level VIIA was destroyed in a kitchen/house fire would of course be the destruction of Fosse Temple III, which was also burned in a fire at the end of the Level VII. The Fosse Temple is situated in the former Middle Bronze Age fosse, and is some distance from the settlement proper. Inside the destroyed

---

30. For the Level VI destruction, see discussion in Barkay and Ussishkin 2004; Ussishkin 2004b, 2004d; Millek 2017; Weissbein et al. 2020.

Fosse Temple III were large amounts of pottery, and surrounding the shrine the excavators uncovered vessels and ornaments of ivory, glass, faience, alabaster, scarabs, cylinder seals, and beads, all of which lay burnt and broken in a confused mass (Tufnell, Inge, and Harding 1940, 42), while in the Southern Niche C, thirty-five complete bowls were discovered (42). An ivory hand and eye were excavated in a rubbish pit outside of the temple that were possibly part of a composite statue; however, no more of this statue was recovered. No metal objects were recovered from the temple nor were any other parts of a god or goddess. It appears that many of the valuable objects and materials were removed prior to the destruction of the temple (27–28, 42).

The fire appears to have been the fiercest at the back of the temple where the altar was situated. The back walls of the shrine had been turned red like a kiln, glass had begun to melt, and ivory was blackened, and in some cases calcined (Tufnell, Inge, and Harding 1940, 42). This suggested to Olga Tufnell (42) that there was a deliberate effort to destroy the temple, and this suggestion is most likely correct. However, the question remains why it was destroyed. It is of key importance that after Fosse Temple III was burnt, the building was left alone. The inhabitants of Level VI did not dig into the temple hoping to uncover treasures, no other building was built on top of it, and it was gradually covered over with wash from the tell (Tufnell, Inge, and Harding 1940, 28; Ussishkin 2004b, 62). This leads to another possible explanation for this fire; namely, that it was destroyed in a termination ritual signifying the end of its function. This would explain why the deity or deities were removed before destruction, and also why the temple seemed to remain sacred after the fire (Millek 2017, 128). It is also possibly no coincidence that directly after this fire, a grand new temple was built in Area P Level VI, which David Ussishkin (1993, 900) has suggested was, "Either instead of the Fosse Temple or as a part of the royal palace."

At the moment, it appears that Lachish suffered two separate destruction events at the end of Level VII ca. 1200 BCE: one resulting from an accidental fire, and the other from a termination ritual. However, recent excavations at Lachish call into question whether this was the case or not. In several initial reports based on the 2013–2017 excavations, it has been reported that underneath the newly uncovered North-East Temple dating to Level VI as well as in several other excavation squares in Area BB, black ash, collapsed mud bricks, and complete pottery vessels shattered on the floors were uncovered (Weissbein et al. 2016, 48; 2020, 21; Garfinkel et al. 2019, 7; Itamar Weissbein pers. comm. 02/18/2020). If it is indeed the case that evidence of destruction is present, this would indicate that the destruction of Fosse Temple III, the domestic structure in Area S, and the burnt material from Area BB were likely the result of one and the same event. To assume that these three separated structures were caught up in three separate destructions would stretch coincidence. Thus, if there is

246 CHAPTER SEVEN

evidence of destruction from Area BB at the end of Level VII it would likely indicate that the site was mostly destroyed by human hands as the destruction of the Fosse Temple III suggests.

However, in a recently published report from the excavation team delineating the results from 2013–2017 excavations, there is no reported mention, description, or photographic evidence of this supposed destruction event (Garfinkel et al. 2021, 435–38). What is described in the report is that on the eastern slope of the tell were the remains of three thick stone walls, which the excavators suggest was a fortress similar to the recently uncovered Middle Bronze Age fortress (435–36). Yet, there is no mentioned evidence of destruction debris or burning associated with this fortress. One would expect this to be the case if indeed the site had been assaulted resulting in a general destruction level, as a fortress would be a likely target of an attack. In the western section of Area BB, "segments of rooms and part of a pillar building" were uncovered (436). Two plaque figurines were found in this building, and it shares certain similarities with the Level VI Pillared Building, but, yet again, there is no mentioned or photographic evidence of a destruction event. Several other buildings without a coherent plan were found west of this structure, and again there is no mentioned destruction (436). Finally, in the Late Bronze Age strata below the Level VI temple from Area BB, while imported pottery and typical Canaanite pottery were recovered, no evidence is mentioned for the previously stated destruction (436–38). In the article, the authors (438) state that, "Radiometric dating from the western segment of Area BB indicates that Level VII was destroyed during the last quarter of the 13th century rather than around 1200"; however, this is the extent of any mention of a Level VII destruction in Area BB. Therefore, while it is still possible that there is evidence of a destruction that was not featured in the most up-to-date site report, for the moment there is no significant published evidence to substantiate a destruction event was uncovered at the end of the Level VII in area BB.

There are several caveats that must be addressed regardless of the possible evidence of destruction in Area BB at the end of Level VII, since Lachish Level VII was not destroyed wholesale. While Ussishkin (2004c, 198) assumed that the possible cultic structure from Area P Level P-1 was destroyed along with the Area S domestic structure and the Fosse Temple III (Area P is also situated next to Area S), there is no evidence of any fire or destruction. In fact, the following temple in Level VI lay immediately on top of the Level P-1 structure, following the same orientationn and was roughly the same size, though there were different internal divisions. Moreover, the Level VI temple may have even reused the floor from the Level P-1 structure, which shows no signs of burning (Ussishkin 2004c, 191, 193; 2004d, 224). What seems more likely is that the building from Level VII Level P-1 was removed, making way for the Stratum

VI temple, otherwise known as the Acropolis Temple (Ussishkin 2004d, 261). It appears that the building was dismantled, as there are no signs of fire (Ussishkin 2004c, 193), and it cannot and should not be assumed that the Level P-1 structure was destroyed.

The construction activities that were witnessed throughout Level VI demonstrate as well that, while several sections of Lachish were destroyed at the end of the Level VII in one or more events, this was in no way a interruption to the site. Indeed, the structures of Level VI were more magnificent than their Level VII predecessors. The domestic structure in Area S was replaced by a monumental public structure dubbed the Pillared Building (Barkay and Ussishkin 2004). The Area P Level P-1 structure was replaced by the richly built and luxuriously furnished Acropolis Temple (Ussishkin 2004d), and in Area BB as well a second impressive temple was constructed during Level VI (Weissbein et al. 2020). Much like Enkomi and other sites on Cyprus, the beginning of the twelfth century BCE was not a period of deficiency at Lachish, despite it enduring one or more destruction events ca. 1200 BCE. Rather, it was a time of architectural flourishing that only ended closer to the end of the twelfth century BCE, when the site experienced a time of crisis and ultimately a site-wide destruction (see Ussishkin 2004b; Zuckerman 2007; Millek 2017; Weissbein et al. 2020).

Tel 'Eton — Scale: Partial — Cause: Unknown

Tel 'Eton is located in the trough valley of the southeastern Judean Shephelah. The Late Bronze Age settlement has only been found in a very limited section of the excavation. From the limited material uncovered to date, a possible destruction has been discovered dating to the first half of the twelfth century BCE. Evidence of the Late Bronze Age have been uncovered in both Areas B and C, though the Late Bronze Age site likely covered the mound (Faust 2014, 588; Faust and Katz 2015, 90–91). In situ vessels have been uncovered in Area B and in square V46, a massive layer of burnt mud bricks was excavated (Faust 2011, 213; 2014, 588). With the current state of excavation, it is impossible to know if a destruction occurred at the site, and if so, what might have been the possible cause, or even if it occurred at the end of the Late Bronze Age.[31]

Tell Beit Mirsim — Scale: Partial — Cause: Unknown

Tell Beit Mirsim is situated at the border between the Shephelah and Mount Hebron. It was excavated by Albright during the late 1920s and early 1930s

---

31. Faust (2014, 588) is also hesitant in assessing this possible destruction stating that, "We must wait for more data before any definite conclusion can be reached." See also Faust et al. 2014, 56, which states that there is only a hint of destruction at the end of the Late Bronze Age settlement.

248 CHAPTER SEVEN

and became a model for future excavations in the southern Levant. As with any older excavation from the infancy of archaeology, the recording methods leave much to be desired by modern standards. Thus, while Albright (1930, 6; 1932, 52; 1938, 63–66; 1974, 100; 1993, 178–79) claims that the LB II city of Level C2 was destroyed in an intense conflagration brought on by the invading Israelites, the recorded evidence for said destruction is lacking. Albright mentions that several houses, including a possible palace, were uncovered from the C2 city; however, he (1938, 63) does not say if these houses were burnt or not. The only physical evidence of burning was from a portion of a fallen roof that contained four horizontal carbonized beams (Albright 1938, 64; see also Albright 1938, 114 pl. 18b). Nevertheless, the structure that this portion of roof belonged to was not excavated, as Albright (1938, 64) states that the roofing fell down the hill with the collapse of the unexcavated structure. Outside of this portion of burnt roof, no other evidence of a destruction is recorded.[32] Albright mentions that ashes were uncovered; yet, ash can be derived from any number of sources, and need not reflect a destruction event. The find context for a scarab of Amenophis III was described as both, "below a great mass of ash-filled earth from the destruction of phase C2" (Albright 1938, 71) and as, "below the bed of ashes mingled with earth which marks the destruction of the second phase of C" (Albright 1930, 6). These two descriptions are not congruent with one another, and without any section drawings or photographs, it is unclear exactly how much ash was present; and, as the find spot of Queen Twosert's scarab from Acco teaches us, scarabs discovered in ashes do not always derive from destruction events. Thus, unless further excavations can provide a better understanding of the end of the Late Bronze Age at Tell Beit Mirsim, there is only evidence that it suffered a partial destruction of an unknown cause.

Tel Haror — Scale: Partial — Cause: Unknown

Tel Haror is situated in the western Negev desert, twenty-five kilometers northwest of Beersheba. Unfortunately, while excavations were conducted at Tel Haror for several years, as with so many sites there exists only a handful of brief excavation reports on the findings. From these reports it is evident that Tel Haror did not suffer a tremendous destruction at the end of the Late

---

32. Albright also claims that a temple that he had not found or excavated was destroyed by the Israelites with the rest of C2. He makes this assertion because a libation tray, lion statue, several Astarte plaques, and ox bones were uncovered in "debris" (Albright 1938, 66). He (66) reasons that, "The invaders who destroyed city C evidently sacked the temple, breaking the sacred objects which it contained or throwing them into the rubbish outside." However, as it is not even clear if there was a temple, let alone if it was destroyed, there is no evidence that a temple was sacked and looted, particularly since these objects were not ritually terminated, as the faces and hands were not mutilated (Albright 1938, 119–24, pls. 23, 24, 25, 26, 27, 38).

Bronze Age (see Millek 2017, 126). In area K, Stratum K3 appears to have been a domestic area attested to by the sizable refuse pits, poorly preserved mud-brick walls, and pits filled with ash and organic remains. This stratum is dated to the LB IIB, and there is no apparent evidence that this area was destroyed ca. 1200 BCE (Oren 1995, 113; 1997b, 475). In Area B, Stratum B7 a fiery destruction of a mud-brick building that is dated to the end of the Late Bronze Age was uncovered under the Stratum B6 structure (Oren 1993b, 100; 1993c, 582; 1995, 116). However, there is so little information that all that can be said is that Tel Haror experienced a partial destruction some time close to the end of the Late Bronze Age. While there is some evidence of destruction in Area B, it appears to have been so unimportant to the excavators that it was not even mentioned in a later summary of the history of Tel Haror (Oren 1997b, 475).

Tell el-Fukhar — Scale: Single-Building — Cause: Unknown

Tell el-Fukhar is located some ten kilometers north of Irbid. While remains of an LB IIB settlement were excavated in four areas, the material uncovered in both Areas B and F were too fragmented to come to any conclusion as to what happened at the end of the Late Bronze Age (see Millek 2019b, 122–24). The LB IIB remains from Stratum V found in Area B were mostly robbed out to the floor levels by the following Iron I occupation (Ottosson 2015, 15–16), while in Area F, a number of houses were excavated from Stratum V but were too fragmented to allow for a determination of what occurred at the end of the Late Bronze Age. As Jonathan Strange (2015b, 71) describes it, "Whether the houses were destroyed by violent action or whether it was an earthquake, as it is evidenced in the palace in CIII, or the lower settlement was simply abandoned, cannot be said."

The only clear evidence for destruction derives from Area C and possibly Area D. A partially uncovered public building, possibly a palace, was discovered in Area CIII Stratum V. Two rooms of this building were exposed along with a monumental entrance, though the exact dimensions of the building are unknown, leaving it currently at fifteen by twenty meters. It is possible that it stretched into Area D, which would make the building considerably larger (Strange 2015a, 35–37). Charred pieces of wood, burnt beams of oak, pottery mixed with ashes, massive mud-brick collapse, and burnt mud bricks were uncovered in the destruction at the end of Stratum V Phase 3. One of the large stones in a wall of the building was broken in half, which the excavators suggest is a sign of possible earthquake damage, though they also postulate that it could have been cracked due to the heat of the fire. The only other signs of an earthquake were seen in the bedrock further down the tell. The excavators claim that no evidence of arson or warfare was uncovered, and they

250 CHAPTER SEVEN

believe the cause of the destruction was an earthquake ca. 1200 BCE (Strange 2015a, 38–39; 2015c, 420).

From the little evidence uncovered it is not clear what exactly caused the destruction of the so-called palace found in Area C, as little else is known about the final Late Bronze Age phase at the site. If only this former public building was destroyed while domestic structures were left alone, this might indicate a guiding hand in the destruction, as a natural disaster would have likely affected more than a single building. Whether or not this is the case is unknown from the currently available evidence. Likewise, there is insufficient evidence to conclude that an earthquake caused the destruction. Given that the building was also being utilized as a "squatter's" house prior to the destruction as described in chapter 6 (Strange 2015a, 38–39; Millek 2019b, 123; and see p. 210 above), it might have caught on fire accidentally and, without the resources to contain it, the public building burnt down, as was likely the case for Kalavasos-*Ayios Dhimitrios*. However, without any other information on the remainder of the site ca. 1200 BCE, the cause must be left as unknown.

Khirbet Umm ad-Dananir — Scale: Partial — Cause: Unknown

Located in the Baqʻah Valley, a quarter of an LB I–II structure was excavated at Khirbet Umm ad-Dananir (see Millek 2019b, 129). Evidence of a fire and several carbonized roof beams were uncovered in the structure; yet, little else has been published describing this event. This partial destruction occurred at some time in the thirteenth century BCE, though a more precise date is unknowable given the limited amount of the building that was excavated (McGovern 1989, 128, 130, 134). There is currently not enough information to determine the cause of this fire, the date of the fire, or to what extent the building was affected by this fire. Patrick McGovern (1989, 128) does note that while a wealth of finds in the form of a dedicatory fill was found underneath the floor of the structure, few artifacts were found on the floor itself. This might indicate that the building was in the process of being abandoned or was already abandoned when part of the building suffered from a fire, though this is far from certain.

Tall al-ʻUmayri — Scale: Single-Building — Cause: Earthquake

Tall al-ʻUmayri is situated between the Queen Alia Airport highway and Amman National Park.[33] Remains from Late Bronze Age have only been uncovered to a limited extent, as the Late Bronze Age material from Field F consisted of only some debris layers, a few walls, and some earthen layers dating to the LB IIB. The main structure dating to the end of the Late Bronze Age was a large five-

---

33. For a more extended discussion, see Millek 2019b, 131–32.

THE LEVANT: A MIXED BAG OF DESTRUCTION   251

room, possible temple complex, called Building C uncovered in Field B Phase 14.[34] Evidence of destruction was in all the rooms of Building C, as burnt bricks, burnt remains of roofing beams, collapsed mud brick, and roofing detritus filled every room. In Room 4, an ascending staircase was split down the middle, a doorjamb was also split down the middle, and the eastern exterior wall was partially separated, all of which the excavators believe point to a destruction by earthquake (Bramlett 2008, 123; Clark 2011, 48–49). An earthquake would appear to be the likely candidate for the single-building destruction of Building C, though, as mentioned in chapter 6, this was only after the structure had been transformed into squatter's abode.[35]

What Did the Sea Peoples and Others Destroy ca. 1200 BCE?

Despite the fact that there are eighty-seven cited destruction events for the entire Levant, the actual amount of damage ca. 1200 BCE was exceedingly minor when compared to what is typically reported. In this vast geographic area consisting of hundreds of sites, there were only twenty-eight destructions ca. 1200 BCE. As I demonstrated in chapter 3, in total 70 percent of all cited destructions in the Levant were misdated, assumed, or simply false citations. The central Levant experienced no destruction ca. 1200 BCE, while Transjordan had only three destructions, one of which was only some burning uncovered in one corner of a partially excavated building.[36] For the other two Transjordan destruction events at Tell el-Fukhar and Tall al-'Umayri, while the two public buildings were burned, this was only after they had been turned into homes for squatters and no longer reflected their former Late Bronze Age glory.

Moreover, as discussed in chapter 3, several major destruction events in Transjordan fall well outside of the end of the Late Bronze Age, for example, the major site-wide destruction by earthquake at Tell Deir Alla, which occurred

---

34. Herr 1998, 253–54; 2000, 170; 2008, 1849; Bramlett 2008, 107; Herr, Clark, and Bramlett 2009, 76; Clark 2011, 43.

35. See pp. 210–11 above. Cline (2021, 110) has recently claimed that the earthquake that struck Tall al-'Umayri was possibly the same that destroyed Tell Deir Alla. However, as mentioned in ch. 3, the Tell Deir Alla earthquake occurred decades after the Tall al-'Umayri Phase 14 destruction event and can not be the same earthquake.

36. It is true that for the moment there are no destructions at all in the central Levant dating to the end of the Late Bronze Age; however, it would be no surprise to me if an excavation at some site in the central Levant discovered a destruction ca. 1200 BCE, as it is highly unlikely that during a fifty year or more period of time no one ever caught the house on fire because they weren't watching the tabun, no storm knocked down a house, no uncontrolled forest fire lit a village aflame, no army from another warring city torched a public building, and no flying spark caused an unfortunate explosion when too much flour was in the air. It is likely that in the future a ca. 1200 BCE destruction will be excavated; however, this should not be viewed as proof of the supposed cataclysmic times surrounding the end of the Late Bronze Age. Rather we must remember that destruction happens and was not uncommon in the ancient world, just as house fires, industrial explosions, and arson are not uncommon in our modern world.

252 CHAPTER SEVEN

ca. 1150 BCE. The destruction event uncovered at Pella could have taken place at the same time or later, at the end of the twelfth or beginning of the eleventh century BCE, and Tell es-Sa'idiyeh's site-wide destruction possibly took place toward the end of the twelfth century BCE or well into the Iron IIA. Consequently, for both the central Levant and Transjordan, destruction was not a factor in the transition to the Iron Age owing to the fact that there was essentially no destruction ca. 1200 BCE, and the destruction that did occur only took place after the Late Bronze Age administrative system had been abandoned at Tell el-Fukhar and Tall al-'Umayri.

Of those sites that actually suffered a destruction event ca. 1200 BCE in the northern and southern Levant, particularly Cisjordan, the amount of damage is again less than the typical narrative for the end of the Late Bronze Age claims. Five were partial destructions, while another eleven were single-building destructions, meaning that nearly 60 percent of the destructions that did occur ca. 1200 BCE in the Levant were minor events that affected a small part of each individual site. While it is true that a site such as Bethel might have experienced more widespread destruction than the partial destruction designation suggests, it is also true that sites such as Megiddo VIIB, Tel 'Eton, Tel Hefer, Tel Qashish, and Khirbet Umm ad-Dananir, among others, might not even have suffered any destructions ca. 1200 BCE.

Of course, several sites did indeed experience more severe destruction at the end of the Late Bronze Age as six sites underwent a multibuilding destruction, while only two experienced a site-wide destruction. One of these site-wide destructions, Aphek, was only a single structure at the time of its destruction, though by the criteria here it stands as a site-wide destruction. Ras Shamra too suffered a site-wide destruction, but again the *Ville Sud* was spared the torch, and as discussed in chapter 2, it could be considered a multibuilding destruction. Indeed, many of the "major" end of the Late Bronze Age destruction events in the Levant did not occur at the end of the Late Bronze Age. Hama, Qatna, Hazor, Megiddo VIIA, Tel Azekah, Lachish Level VI, Tell Deir Alla, Tell es-Sa'idiyeh, and Beth-Shean S-3, all suffered multibuilding or site-wide destructions, and yet, these events occurred decades before or after 1225–1175 BCE. The number of major destructions that rocked the region in the supposed time of trouble was in actuality far less than typically assumed, that is, unless one chooses to extend the "end of the Late Bronze Age" beyond a reasonable span of time.

This leaves twenty-eight destruction events that must be dealt with, and the overriding question of course is, What caused the destructions that did occur and what effect did they have on the Levant? To begin, the destructions were not caused by earthquakes. While Schaeffer (1948, 2; 1968, 763) assumed that Ras Shamra's final destruction was caused by an earthquake, Nur and Cline (2000) extend this to the whole of the Levant), there is abundant evidence that the destruction was caused by an act of war, and no site in Syria has any evidence that could lead to the conclusion that an earthquake was at fault.[37] Likewise, in the southern Levant, only Building C from Tall al-'Umayri was likely destroyed by an earthquake ca. 1200 BCE, and this was only after the building had been turned into temporary housing for squatters. It is unlikely that the earthquake played any major role in ending the Late Bronze Age cultural affinities or political system at the site as, for all intents and purposes, this had ended once the initial cultic or administrative function of Building C had ended. A major earthquake destroyed Tell Deir Alla, at least part of Beth-Shean, and possibly parts of Pella; however, this occurred well after the end of the Late Bronze Age ca. 1150 BCE (Millek 2019b; see also discussion in ch. 3). Thus, nowhere in the Levant is there any substantial evidence that: (1) earthquakes disproportionately destroyed settlements ca. 1200 BCE, and (2) that they helped to bring about the end of the Bronze Age.

Perhaps the most notorious group associated with the end of the Late Bronze Age and destruction throughout the Levant are the Sea Peoples.[38] There have been countless books and articles discussing the historical and archeological validity of the Sea Peoples, their possible origin, and their material culture.[39] But there are two glaring issues with the assertion that the Sea Peoples caused a vast swath of destruction in the Levant on their way to Egypt: (1) there is no textual evidence that suggests that the Sea Peoples as we know them from the Egyptian sources destroyed multiple cities and towns in the Levant and elsewhere, and (2) there is no archeological evidence of this destruction either.

To begin, there are basic problems with the textual evidence for Sea Peoples–induced destruction. The genesis for much of the assumed destruction caused by the Sea Peoples comes from the texts uncovered in Egypt and Ugarit

---

37. Geology pun is intended.

38. Though it should be noted that the term "Sea Peoples" is a modern invention, as it is translated from the French *peuples de la mer* coined by French Egyptologist Maspero (1886; Killebrew and Lehmann 2013a, 2). The groups making up the "Sea Peoples" consisted of the Lukka, Sherden, Shekelesh, Teresh, Eqwesh, Denyen, Sikil/Tjekker, Weshesh, and Peleset (Philistines). However, as previously noted by Killebrew and Lehmann (2013a, 2 n. 1), the designation "of the sea" appears only in relation to the Sherden, Shekelesh, and Eqwesh.

39. The following is only a brief sampling of the research on the Sea Peoples from the textual and material culture points of view. The volumes and articles provide a rich bibliographic source to follow the complex, varied, and often contentious history of scholarship on the Sea Peoples: Edgerton and Wilson 1936; Dothan 1982; Sanders 1985; Cifola 1988, 1994; Dothan and Dothan 1992; Lesko 1992; Bietak 1993; Sherratt 1998; Silberman 1998; Drews 2000; O'Connor 2000; Oren 2000; Redford 2000, 2018; Cline and O'Connor 2003; Jung and Mehofer 2009; Boileau et al. 2010; Kahn 2010, 2011; Yasur-Landau 2010; Charaf 2011; Adams and Cohen 2013; Bargueño et al. 2013; Killebrew and Lehmann 2013b; Ben-Dor Evian 2015, 2016, 2017, 2019; Middleton 2015, 2018; Popko 2016; Fischer and Burge 2017b; James 2017; Janeway 2017; Millek 2017, 2020, 2021b; Jung 2018b; Feldman et al. 2019; Baumann 2020.

254   CHAPTER SEVEN

that supposedly describe these people groups. Ramesses III's Year 8 inscriptions and their related reliefs from Medinet Habu are the most infamous of this group. These texts have been debated at length in terms of their historical value; however, the question that I take up here is not whether the texts are historically accurate or verbose propaganda; rather, the question is where the texts ever mention destruction (see Millek 2020, 2021b). The opening lines of Ramesses III's Year 8 inscription are normally called upon to describe the path of destruction wrought by the Sea Peoples. It reads:

> Year 8 under the majesty of (Ramesses III).... The foreign countries made a conspiracy in their islands. All at once the lands were removed and scattered in the fray. No land could stand before their arms, from Khatte, Qode,[40] Carchemish, Arzawa,[41] and Alashiya[42] on, being cut off at [one time]. A camp [was set up] in one place in Amor. They desolated its people, and its land was like that which has never come into being. They were coming forward toward Egypt, while the flame was prepared before them. Their confederation was the Philistines, Tjekru, Shekelesh, Denye(n), and Washosh, lands united. They laid their hands upon the lands as far as the circuit of the earth, their hearts confident and trusting: "Our plans will succeed!" (Edgerton and Wilson 1936)

One of the first problems with employing this text to pin any destruction in the Levant on the Sea Peoples is the omission of almost the entirety of the Levantine coast. Of the key areas of the Levantine coast only Amurru is actually named in the text and the nebulous region of Djahy, which may or may not be in the Levant.[43] However, Canaan, all of the Lebanese coastal sites that were well known to the Egyptians, and Ugarit are conspicuously missing from the text. For at least Ugarit, Mario Liverani (1995a, 49) has argued that while the site itself was not mentioned in the Medinet Habu texts, this is only because the text describes states not regions. Thus, Ugarit would be subsumed under Carchemish in the list of lands "cutoff." However, the conflation of Carchemish and Ugarit in the Egyptian texts glosses over the Egyptian precedent already set in Ramesses II's texts of the Battle of Kadesh where Ugarit and Carchemish are clearly separate entities (Millek 2020; Wilson 1927). As Hasel (2011, 72–75)

---

40. The location of Qode has traditionally been assumed to be Kizzuwatna or more recently Tarḫuntašša in Cilica. However, as Simon (2011, 263) has pointed out, there is currently no reasonable linguistic evidence to pinpoint where exactly Qode was located other than that it was in "North Syria, and, more precisely, the territory of Naharina/Mittani." See Simon 2011 for an overview of all of the traditional and modern theories for the location of Qode and why all of these suggestions fail to offer a realistic solution for Qode's location.

41. Arzawa as a political entity no longer existed at the time of Ramesses III, as the Hittites had rearranged the region at the end of the fourteenth century and divided it into several vassal states (Müller 2001, 301).

42. Alashiya is ancient Cyprus, which as seen in the previous chapter did not suffer destructions from the Sea Peoples, as there were essentially no destruction on the island ca. 1200 BCE.

43. See Bietak 1993; Kahn 2011; Ben-Dor Evian 2017; Hoffmeier 2018.

has noted, Ramesses II's text describes city-states (e.g., Aleppo, Carchemish, Kadesh, Ugarit, and Tunip), regions (e.g., Amurru, Arzawa, Dijahy, Kizzuwatna, and Retenu), and a foreign country (Hatti). The absence of Ugarit in the Medinet Habu text is not because it was linguistically subsumed under Hittite Carchemish; rather, Ugarit, like the southern and central Levant, simply was not considered as "cutoff" by the Sea Peoples in the Egyptian view of events. Therefore, for nearly the entirety of the Levant, there is no Egyptian historical source that suggests that the sites were destroyed by the confederation of the Sea Peoples, as no other Egyptian text—including Merenptah's Year 5 inscriptions, Ramesses III's Year 5 inscriptions, and Papyrus Harris—mentions any kind of "destruction" in the southern or central Levant, or in Ugarit brought on by the Sea Peoples.[44]

One of the most striking issues with Ramesses III's inscriptions from Medinet Habu is that, while it is often cited as referring to the destruction of the six northern lands, it does not actually say that they were destroyed. As Uwe Müller has pointed out, the Medinet Habu text describes these regions and cities as being "*fdq*"; however, as he notes, this word does not denote destruction. Normally a city or country that is destroyed is "*fḫ*" (Hasel 1998, 33–34), or "*sksk*" also "to destroy" (Faulkner 1962, 262), while "*fdq*" as a noun means "part/section/portion" and as a verb means "taking apart/split/chop" (Faulkner 1962, 99). Thus, the countries in the list were not "destroyed," but were separated or split apart from each other.[45] According to Müller, only Amurru can be said to have actually suffered a destruction in the Medinet Habu texts.

As Dan'el Kahn (2010, 15–16) has pointed out, in Ramesses III's fifth regnal year, he describes an Egyptian invasion of Amurru where he boasts that as a result of this campaign, "Amurru is (but) ashes." This presents the possibility that Amurru was first invaded by Ramesses and was thus not destroyed by the Sea Peoples. At minimum, from a historical point of view, one cannot say with any certainty which group—the Egyptians or the Sea Peoples—was responsible for the destruction. The Medinet Habu texts, in sum, do not describe any destruction in Anatolia, Cyprus, or the Levant other than perhaps in the isolated locale of Amurru, as the words themselves do not suggest destruction by armed conflict or by fire. Yet, in the scholarly literature there has been blatant fudging

---

44. See the texts in Breasted 1906a, 241, 243, 249; 1906b, 201. An interesting point made by Lesko (1992, 154) is that in Ramesses III's temple at Karnak, which was likely completed in his thirtieth year, no mention is made of the Sea Peoples whatsoever, a curious omission for such a supposedly important historical event.

45. Müller 2001, 301. Müller's (303) view is that this list represents the Hittite Empire as it was at the time, as texts from Hatti describe Cyprus as being under Hittite control toward the end of the Late Bronze Age. Thus, the fact that these were split or cut off indicates the fragmentation of the Hittite Empire, which he presumes was engulfed in a civil war, and that this helped bring about the fall of the Hittite Empire and led to the turmoil in the Egyptian border regions.

of what the text actually says. This is clear, for example, from David Kaniewski et al. 2011, which rewrote the quote to say, "No land could stand before their arms: from Hatti, Qode, Carchemish, Arzawa, and Alashiya on, *being cut off (destroyed) at one time*."[46] The article cites James Pritchard 1969 (262) for the quotation, who, however, in his translation of the text does not include the word "destroyed." This addition, not in brackets but parentheses, therefore implying the word "destroyed" was in Pritchard's translation, completely alters what the text actually says and is a fallacious modification of the historical narrative.

Much as for the southern and central Levant and Ugarit, the Egyptian textual records also do not mention destruction for any other region. Merenptah's Year 5 Great Karnak Inscription, Ramesses III's Year 5 inscription, the remainder of the Year 8 inscription, and Papyrus Harris are all silent as far as the Sea Peoples causing any kind of destruction anywhere. All that is said in these texts is that Merenptah or Ramesses destroyed and killed the various groups of the Sea Peoples, not that the Sea Peoples themselves caused any destruction (Edgerton and Wilson 1936; Breasted 1906a, 241, 243, 249; 1906b, 201; Redford 2018, 21–41). The Egyptian textual records that mention the Sea Peoples are employed to demonstrate the destruction caused by the Sea Peoples, but only through an overinterpretion of the texts and the addition of destructions and regions destroyed that no Egyptian text relating to the Sea Peoples ever describes as destroyed. This is a historical reconstruction of events that does not accurately reflect the historical records that those events are purportedly based on.[47]

The only region of the Levant that may have its own textual references to the Sea Peoples is Ugarit. However, even here there are issues with the assertion that these groups or enemies mentioned in the Ugaritic texts are the Sea Peoples as we know them from the Egyptian sources. The first issue at hand is that no known "tribes" of the Sea Peoples are ever named as destroyers in any of the letters from Ugarit. While the assailants are referred to at times as "ships of the enemy" (RS 20.238), Bernard Knapp and Sturt Manning (2016, 120) have rightly pointed out that the texts from Ugarit only make it clear that in the last fifty years of the site's history it was, "harassed periodically by enemy ships from the sea and by land-based troops on their own border." Moreover, while it is typically assumed that the enemies on ships are referencing the Sea Peoples known in the Egyptian textual record, three of the "tribes" of the Sea Peoples were known to the people of Ugarit and yet are not named as attackers

---

46. Kaniewski et al. 2011, 1 (emphasis added). This edited quote from Medinet Habu with the addition of "destroyed" where there is no linguistic rational for this addition has recently been published in Bretschneider, Driessen, and Kanta 2021, 7.

47. See also Silberman 1998 and Müller 2001 for the modern historical background and the role that the Sea Peoples played in early twentieth century social Darwinism and European expansion.

in the Ugaritic texts. Lukka of course was known to Ugarit, as Ammurapi II claims all of his ships were stationed in Lukka at the time when the enemy ships were distressing him (RS 20.238). The Shardana, were well known in Egypt and Ugarit and had served both countries as mercenaries.[48] As Oswald Loretz has pointed out, if they too were part of the attack on Ugarit, they are never mentioned, and given Ugarit's historical relations with the group, it seems doubtful that they would not be named. Loretz (1995, 125–34) posits that it might even be that they were killed along with the people from Ugarit to whom they were in service.

Finally, there is the text RS 34.129, in which an unnamed Hittite king, likely Suppiluliuma II, asks to interview one Ibnadušu, "whom the people from Šikila-who live on ships had abducted" (Dietrich and Loretz 1978, 53–56; Hoftijzer and Van Soldt 1998, 343). These Šikila have been equated with the Egyptian Shekelesh, one of the five "tribes" who attacked Egypt during the eighth year of Ramesses III and are described as "of the sea" in the Egyptian historical records (Killebrew and Lehmann 2013a, 2 n. 1). Because of this single reference the text was assumed to provide evidence that the unnamed enemies on boats present in the other texts from Ugarit were in fact the Sea Peoples of Egyptian notoriety (Singer 1999, 722). However, there are several issues with this assertion. The first and most glaring is that the text itself never describes the Šikila as causing any destruction or harm to any city or town. The only crime the Šikila have committed is that they abducted Ibnadušu and are not well known to the Hittite king. Moreover, much like the Lukka and the Shardana, if we are to assume the Šikila/Shekelesh attacked Ugarit, even though they were known to the people of Ugarit, they are never mentioned as being among the enemies on ships, despite the fact that they were mentioned in RS 34.129 by name. What can be taken from the literary evidence from Ugarit is that while three groups of the Sea Peoples were known by name, none of these groups is ever mentioned as being the enemies on ships. To argue that the naval forces mentioned in the Ugaritic texts are in some way related to the Sea Peoples mentioned in the Egyptian texts is to argue from silence, taking a logical leap where there is no textual bridge between these two accounts.

Taken all together, there is in fact no reliable historical source that claims the Sea Peoples caused any kind of destruction toward the end of the Late Bronze Age other than perhaps in Amurru. The Egyptian sources never mention that any destruction took place, nor do they mention the majority of the Levant. And the Medinet Habu text has been read in a way where one line that linguistically does not even say that the northern regions and cities were destroyed has been transmuted into evidence that the Sea Peoples caused

---

48. For an overview concerning the historical sources relating to the Shardana, see Emanuel 2013.

a vast amount of destruction. Likewise, in the texts from Ugarit, despite the fact that several of the "tribes" of the Sea Peoples were known, they are never mentioned in any of the attacks on the city or its environs. All that can be said is that people on boats attacked the city, which could indicate any coastal group in the Eastern Mediterranean. Therefore, from a textual perspective, there is no strong link between the Sea Peoples and destruction in the Levant.

On the archaeological side, there is also a dearth of evidence indicating that the Sea Peoples caused any destruction in the Levant. The majority of sites that have a supposed Sea Peoples destruction were never destroyed in the first place.[49] Other sites, such as Tel Mor, Aphek, and Tel Miqne-Ekron, while they did suffer destruction events ca. 1200 BCE, it does not appear that these were at the hands of the Sea Peoples. After the Stratum VI single-building destruction, Tel Mor was rebuilt in an Egyptian style and it was only after the site was peacefully abandoned that there was any introduction of Philistine material culture (Millek 2018). Aphek was destroyed and the Egyptian presence ceased; however, following the destruction was a local Canaanite phase, and only after this phase was there a peaceful intrusion of Philistine material culture, as there was no intervening destruction event between the Canaanite and Philistine layers. The same can be said for Tel Miqne/Ekron, as after the single-building destruction there was a small Canaanite phase that was followed by the Philistine city with no intervening destruction (Millek 2017). Thus, the cultures at the sites were not supplanted after the destruction, rather they continued and there is no archeological or historical evidence that the Sea Peoples violently intruded into them, which would be in agreement with the texts, which never state that the Sea Peoples caused any harm in the southern Levant.[50]

For the northern Levant, while Ras Shamra and Ras Ibn Hani suffered destructions from warfare and arson, there is no archaeological evidence that specifies who carried out the destructions, and for Ras Ibn Hani it is not even clear exactly when the destruction took place. Moreover, in the same period where the "enemies on boats" were harassing Ugarit, a land invasion also came from the region of Mukish.[51] Thus, while there is textual and archaeological evidence of warfare and arson in the region of Ugarit, there are any number of possible groups that could have brought on the destruction, and there is no

---

49. These are from north to south: Ras el-Bassit, Tell Tweini, Tell Sukas, Arwad, Byblos, Sidon, Tyre, Achzib, Tell Keisan, Acco, Shiqmona, Tell Abu Hawam, Tel Dor, Tel Mevorakh, Tel Zeror, Tel Michal, Tel Gerisa, Ashdod, Ashkelon, Tell eṣ-Ṣafi/Gath, Beth-Shemesh, and Tell Jemmeh; see the discussion in ch. 3 as well as Millek 2017, 2019a, 2019c, 2020, 2021b.

50. This peaceful intrusion of Sea Peoples or Philistine material culture is also apparent at sites such as Tell eṣ-Ṣafi/Gath, Ashkelon, Ashdod, Tel Zeror, and many others; see discussion in Millek 2017.

51. RS 16.402; RS 34.143; Singer 1999, 723–25. For a historical overview on the theory that the Mushki are to be associated with the mythical Phrygians, see Kopanias 2015.

THE LEVANT: A MIXED BAG OF DESTRUCTION

actual evidence that it was the Sea Peoples, nor is there concrete evidence of the time frame within which these destructions fall. They could have been days to decades apart.

The only site that may have suffered destruction at the hands of the Sea Peoples based on the historical and archaeological evidence is Tell Kazel, which was possibly the ancient capital of the kingdom of Amurru, Sumur/Simyra (Badre 2006). Tell Kazel did indeed suffer a destruction by warfare in a time frame that could be associated with the influx of the Sea Peoples. However, there are two issues with definitively placing the blame on the Sea Peoples. The first, as mentioned above, is that Ramesses III is also a possible contender for this destruction. Thus, from the same pharaoh's records, there are two possible historical candidates for the destruction, neither of which is more likely than the other. The second issue is that Handmade Burnished ware, one of the supposed material cultural signals of the Sea Peoples, appeared at Tell Kazel *prior* to the destruction event, representing a peaceful intrusion of Sea Peoples material culture. This has led the excavators at Tell Kazel to assume that some members of the Sea Peoples arrived at the site and integrated with the local populace before the site was destroyed by another wave of the Sea Peoples (Badre and Gubel, 1999–2000, 197–98; Capet 2003, 118; Badre 2006, 94). However, there is no certain evidence that this destruction event was brought on by the Sea Peoples over another local group—or even Ramesses III himself. Thus, it remains a possibility that Tell Kazel was attacked by the Sea Peoples, but a possibility is all it is. Consequently, despite the rich scholarly history that has attributed all, much, or at least some of the destruction in the Levant ca. 1200 BCE to the Sea Peoples, realistically only one site may have experienced some destruction at their hands, and even this is questionable.

One point that must also be mentioned, albeit briefly, regards the textual and material cultural evidence recovered from Tell Tayinat pointing to a link between the kingdom of Palistin/Walistin with the Peleset tribe of the Sea Peoples and the Philistines of the southern Levant.[52] Over the past two decades, while the case has been made for a Sea Peoples presence at Tell Tayinat, recent research, both on the textual record and the material culture uncovered from the site, has cast doubt on the Sea Peoples connection during the early and mid-twelfth century BCE. For the written material, K. Lawson Younger has recently laid out several difficulties in trying to tie the name Palisitn/Walistin to the Peleset and the Philistines. The chief of these issues is the final "n" of Palistin/Walistin, which has never been found in any of the spellings of the southern

---

52. Hawkins 2011, 51; 2013, 499. For a general discussion of Tell Tayinat as well as a discussion of the epigraphic evidence for the kingdom of Palistin/Walistin arguing both sides of this discussion, see Harrison 2009a, 2009b, 2010, 2013; Hawkins 2009, 2011, 2013; Kahn 2011; Weeden 2013, 2015; Younger 2016, 127–35; Janeway 2017; Welton 2019; Welton et al. 2019; Emanuel 2020, 256–60.

Levant's "Philistines" during the Iron Age (Younger 2016, 129–31). Moreover, as Younger (134) states, "it may be more likely that the gentilic *Palistiniza-/Walistiniza* has an Anatolian derivation that is separate from the *plšt* of the southern Levant." As he (127–35) goes on to point out, there are also no personal names from the existing written record uncovered in the Amuq that have an Aegean link. All of the above has created several hurdles to circumvent should on wish to associate Palistin/Walistin with the Philistines from a textual and linguistic perspective. As Younger (133–34) so aptly summarizes the situation,

> There seems to be an assumption that the Neo-Hittite state's name was based on the people connected with the Aegean pottery. But there is actually no textual evidence of the identity of these people; nor is there any evidence that they provided the name Palistin/Walistin to the Luwian entity. Why would the Neo-Hittite state that built the monumental structures in Phase I, a polity in which Luwian was the language of its inscriptions want to assume the name of an intrusive earlier settlement? There seems to be nothing "Philistine" or its equivalent (i.e., Aegean) in the Luwian inscriptions or the later material culture of Palistin/Walistin.

Lynn Welton has also recently called into question the relation to the Aegean witnessed in the material culture uncovered at Tell Tayinat. She notes that the oft-cited statistic that 95 percent of the Phase N, or Iron I, ceramics were Aegean-style pottery is inaccurate.[53] Indeed, as Welton goes on to demonstrate, in the earliest phase of the reoccupation, dubbed FP 6c, less than 1 percent of the painted diagnostic sherds belong to LH IIIC style deep bowls. This number increase in the next phase FP 6b to about 5 percent. Based on radiocarbon measurements taken from Field 1, phase FP 6b likely dates to the late twelfth century BCE while FP 6c likely dates to the mid-twelfth century BCE.[54] As she (2019, 82–83) sums up the results of this renewed investigation,

> Aegeanizing influences that are often associated with the arrival of the so-called "Sea Peoples" do not appear immediately upon Tayinat's reoccupation, but take hold rather later, during FP 6b, likely dating to the late 12th century BCE, and appear alongside these continuing Late Bronze Age material traditions. The late appearance of these features is problematic for reconstructions that would like to see Tayinat and the kingdom of Palastin as a waypoint created *en route* by migrating Sea Peoples on their way south.... What is emerging as a fairly clear pattern is that it is the late 12th century that represents the time period of the most rapid change in the Amuq, rather than the early 12th century.

---

53. Welton 2019, 71. As she states, "This figure drastically overestimates the Aegeanizing component of the material culture at Tell Tayinat, and is likely a reflection of the fact that other contemporaneous ceramic material was not recognized at the time of its excavation in the 1930s, and that the LH IIIC material was preferentially collected because of its distinctive and easily recognizable characteristics."

54. Welton 2019, 79–81; Welton et al. 2019, 322–25; see also discussion in Janeway 2017, 116–17.

It is clear from the recent reviews of the data is that there is considerable reasonable doubt that Tell Tayinat was related to the Peleset tribe of the Sea Peoples or the Philistines. Moreover, if there were to be such a connection it would be long after the end of the Late Bronze Age, not until close to the end of the twelfth century BCE. This same conclusion was reached by Jeffrey Emanuel (2020, 260) who, after reviewing the current state of the evidence, stated, "It appears, therefore, that the Early Iron Age settlement at Tell Tayinat cannot be directly connected to the events depicted by Ramesses III or to the initial establishment of the Philistines' foothold in the southern coastal plain of Canaan."

Finally, the question remains, what effect did these destructions have on the Levant ca. 1200 BCE. To begin in the southern Levant, it is evident that destruction did not bring about the end of Egyptian hegemony, influence, and their physical presence in the region.[55] The two general explanations for the exit of Egypt from the southern Levant are either that they were forced out by the Sea Peoples or that local Canaanite anti-Egyptian forces destroyed their bases and forced them out (see Weinstein 1992, 2012; Bietak 1993; Morris 2005, 709). However, Egypt's withdrawal from the southern Levant was neither sudden nor violent, as it was protracted over a nearly one-hundred-year period. Sites such as Ashkelon, Deir el-Balah, and Tell el-Far'ah (South) were abandoned by the Egyptians without destruction. For the Egyptian garrison at Tel Mor, while it suffered three separate destruction events, two of which were likely from the faulty foundation of sand, it was rebuilt each time, and was finally abandoned without any evidence of destruction. Beth-Shean suffered a multibuilding destruction by earthquake, which only served as an archaeological marker for the already ongoing process of Egypt's exit from the site. While both Aphek and Jaffa's Gate complex were destroyed in acts of war and are geographically close to each other (Burke et al. 2017; Millek 2018), these destruction events were separated by nearly a century and were not part of any string of events bringing about the end of Egyptian hegemony. Rather, internal pressures and woes in Egypt likely caused them to look closer to home as they gradually abandoned their garrisons in the southern Levant over the course of decades if not a century (Millek 2018).

What then about the supposed disruption of trade networks ca. 1200 BCE? While it is the case that certain forms of exchange for all intents and purposes ended, such as the importation of Cypriot and Mycenaean pottery to the southern Levant, the date for the cessation of trade was fifty to one hundred years prior to the end of the Late Bronze Age.[56] Thus, destruction ca. 1200 BCE had nothing to do with the cessation of this trade. In other instances,

---

55. See full discussion in Millek 2018.
56. See Gittlen 1977; 1981; Bergoffen 1989, 1991; Stockhammer 2017, 2019; Millek 2019c.

262 CHAPTER SEVEN

trade continued after 1200 BCE; this is very apparent in the continued use and utilization of tin in the production of tin bronze. Tin has no nearby local sources in the entire Levant. Bronze and Iron Age tin was possibly mined in Afghanistan, Kazakhstan, the Bolkardag region of the south-central Taurus Mountains, or as far away as Cornwall, England.[57] Regardless of where the metal came from, whether the distant northwest or the east, it had to be imported to make bronze. Originally, it was assumed that a shortage of tin at the end of the Late Bronze Age caused the transition away from tin bronze to the development and use of iron objects.[58] Moreover, it has also been postulated that Ugarit acted as the main distributor of tin and with its destruction the tin trade was destabilized (Bell 2009, 2012). However, archeometallurgical studies from the past thirty years have demonstrated that there was never a drop in the amount of available tin in the Levant and Cyprus during the Iron I.[59] Moreover, arsenic, antimony, and zinc were not employed to a greater degree as a replacement alloying agent during the Iron I, indicating that tin was still available in sufficient quantities that these other elements were not needed as substitutes (Pickles and Peltenburg 1998, 68). As Naama Yahalom-Mack and Adi Eliyahu-Behar (2015, 298) have recently summarized the situation:

> With respect to the question of tin availability for the production of bronze, analysis of 95 copper-based artifacts from LB II–Iron II contexts showed that tin-bronze was continuously used and that the average tin (Sn) content (5–6 wt percent) was maintained throughout the periods. This supports earlier studies that showed there was no shortage of tin during the transition period.

As there is no evidence that access to tin substantially decreased during the Iron I, and because tin is a nonlocal metal that had to have originated from far-flung sources, trade in tin continued after 1200 BCE even without Ugarit.[60] If

---

57. Stöllner et al. 2011; Galili et al. 2013; Erb-Satullo, Gilmour, and Khakhutaishvili 2015; Garner 2015; Berger et al. 2019. Powell et al. 2021.

58. For an overview on the history of this theory, see Yahalom-Mack and Eliyahu-Behar 2015; Palermo 2018, 27–29.

59. See Waldbaum 1989, 1999; Pickles and Peltenburg 1998; Yahalom-Mack et al. 2014; Yahalom-Mack and Eliyahu-Behar 2015; Ashkenazi, Bunimovitz, and Stern 2016.

60. For a counter argument, see Meyer and Knapp 2021, 12–15. One argument that Meyer and Knapp make is that comparing the amount of tin on board the Uluburun shipwreck to that on the Cape Gelidonya shipwreck gives a reflection of the differences in availability. They note that the Uluburun ship had one ton of tin compared to the sixteen kilograms of tin on the Cape Gelidonya, stating (15) that, "The contrasting availability of tin as represented in these two shipwrecks separated by about a hundred years suggests that, by the end of the Late Bronze Age, metallic tin was less readily or less reliably available." However, a major difficulty when making this comparison is that, as Bass (Bass et al. 1967, 82–83) noted in the 1967 report on the Cape Gelidonya wreck, "The tin oxide, however, was found only where it had been covered and preserved by masses of copper and sea concretion, and it would be impossible to estimate the amount that might have been washed away from more exposed areas." Thus, it is impossible to determine how much tin was originally on board the Cape Gelidonya wreck and the two shipwrecks and the amount of tin

The Levant: A Mixed Bag of Destruction · 263

Ugarit had played a primary role in tin distribution, an assumption that has not been verified, some other actors would have taken over this trade. It is apparent that destruction did not hinder the tin trade, as it never ceased. Indeed, several other forms of exchange continued, at least in the southern Levant, as various materials and objects from Egypt were imported during the Iron I, perhaps in greater quantities than during the Late Bronze Age, or at least they were more diffused in their availability (Millek 2019c, 217–38). The likely reason why trade was not disrupted by destruction is that at large, virtually no coastal sites were destroyed ca. 1200 BCE. In the over six hundred kilometers of Levantine coastline, only five sites suffered some kind of destruction ca. 1200 BCE.[61] Thus, even though Ugarit was destroyed and abandoned ca. 1185 BCE, other agents of exchange, be they Cyprus, the central Levant, or the Carmel in the southern Levant, took over this trade and likely benefited from Ugarit's downfall (Gilboa, Waiman-Barak, and Sharon 2015, 101; Georgiou and Iacovou 2020, 1144).

A common objection that might be brought up against the above evidence for the continuation of the tin trade, is that bronze was being recycled to some higher degree after the end of the Late Bronze Age due to a shortage of fresh tin. Broken bronze objects, which are believed to be evidence of scrap metal intended for reuse, were found in the Cape Gelidonya shipwreck and at Tel Nami.[62] However, while these finds imply that bronze was being recycled ca. 1200 BCE, the notion that this was in a response to a lack of tin faces several difficulties. The first is of course that bronze was likely being recycled at all points during the Bronze Age, and there is no substantial evidence that more was being recycled post-1200 BCE.[63] Second, when the Cape Gelidonya ship

---

cannot be compared. Moreover, it should be remembered that there were ten tons of copper aboard the Uluburun ship compared to the nine hundred kilograms of copper aboard the Cape Gelidonya ship, which had been well preserved (Bass 2010; Pulak 2010). Since there was about a 1 to 10 ratio of tin to copper aboard the Uluburun shipwreck, if we used this same measure, then there would have only needed to be ninety kilograms of tin aboard the Cape Gelidonya to be equal to the Uluburun in terms of ratios. Moreover, it must be remembered that the lading of the Uluburun and the Cape Gelidonya were vastly different, with that of the Uluburun representing a wide variety of costly goods, while that of the Cape Gelidonya was generally more modest. Thus, in general, comparing the two ships will lead to faulty results. Based on this type of comparison, one could also argue that there was less copper available at the end of the Late Bronze Age—for which there is no evidence—since the Cape Gelidonya ship carried less than ten percent of the copper that was aboard the Uluburun.

61. Tel Mor, Tel Nami, Tell Kazel, Ras Ibn Hani, and Ras Shamra.

62. For Cape Gelidonya this included "plowshares, axes, adzes, an ax-adze, chisels, pruning hooks, a spade, knives, and casting waste" (Bass 2010, 800). For Tel Nami, see Bass 2010, 800; Artzy 1997, 9; 2013, 338.

63. This was recently demonstrated in a pXRF analysis of some 206 copper-based objects from Enkomi. There was an even distribution of bronze objects with lower levels of tin (below 5 percent) throughout all of Enkomi's chronological phases both before and after 1200 BCE, with no clear clustering in one particular phase (Charalambous, Papasavvas, and Kassianidou 2021, 5). As Charalambous, Papasavvas, and Kassianidou argue, this likely resulted from old bronze

264 CHAPTER SEVEN

sank between 1250–1150 BCE, there was over nine hundred kilograms of copper, and an unknown amount of tin, on board the ship in addition to the bronze tools possibly meant for recycling.[64] Thus, while some of the bronze cargo was likely destined to be recycled, the main cargo of the Cape Gelidonya shipwreck was still copper and tin ready to be made into new bronze. The third issue is the evidence already discussed, that there never was an absence of tin hampering trade and compelling bronze recycling as the only means of attaining bronze.[65] In sum, there is no substantial evidence that supports the hypothesis that more bronze was being recycled after ca. 1200 BCE than before, while there is a large body of evidence indicating the continued trade in tin. The Cape Gelidonya shipwreck may date well into the twelfth century BCE and could itself be a testament to this continued tin trade.

In the northern Levant, there is also evidence of ongoing trade, as Welton has recently elucidated for Tell Tayinat during the twelfth century BCE. As she (2019, 83) states,

> The results of ceramic petrographic analysis ... suggest that, contrary to the view that communities in the Iron Age I were fairly isolated and that trade relationships had largely disappeared after the collapse of the Late Bronze Age, there was in fact quite a healthy system of interregional exchange continuing into the 12th century. This view is confirmed by the small finds, which display wide-ranging parallels throughout the Mediterranean and the presence of luxury raw materials, such as gold, ivory, and carnelian.

For the southern Levant it is difficult to pinpoint any impact caused by destruction ca. 1200 BCE on the various polities and people groups. Egyptian hegemony persisted for some seventy years after 1200 BCE. The arrival of the "Philistines" was not predicated on the vast destruction of the settlements of the southern coastal plain, as Canaanite culture did not even end at these so-called Philistine sites.[66] Likewise, prominent Late Bronze Age sites such as Megiddo, Beth-Shean, Tel Azekah, Tell Deir Alla, and Lachish continued on in their Late Bronze Age cultural traditions unimpeded by the year 1200 BCE until later in the twelfth century BCE. This is despite the fact that Lachish suffered one or more destructions ca. 1200 BCE; yet, the following period was initially defined as a period of growth, even if it ended some seventy years later in a time of crisis. In general, there is a lack of evidence for warfare or arson in the

---

being mixed with fresh copper, which produced the lower levels of tin, a process that took place throughout the site's history.

64. Bass 2010, 800. The tin had converted into tin oxide, which had the consistency of toothpaste, meaning there was no way to assess the original amount of tin that was aboard the ship.

65. Interestingly, a small number of bronze objects from Enkomi have higher levels of tin—more than 13 percent. Of these nineteen high-tin objects, eleven derive from Levels IIIA, IIIB, and IIIC and postdate 1200 BCE (Charalambous, Papasavvas, and Kassianidou 2021, 5–6).

66. Stager 1995, 334; Mazar 2008, 94; Hitchcock and Maeir 2013; Maeir and Hitchcock 2017.

southern Levant ca. 1200 BCE, as only Lachish and Aphek experienced some destruction by human hands. This absence of destruction by warfare or arson in fact matches with the historical view, as there are no textual references from the period that would indicate that the years surrounding 1200 BCE were filled with violent destruction brought on by murderous hordes (see discussion in Millek 2018b, 288–92). In all, destruction could not have been a causal factor in the transformation and transitions at the end of the Late Bronze Age in the southern Levant, as there was barely any destruction ca. 1200 BCE; the major destruction events we commonly think of occurred before or after the end of the Late Bronze Age, while the changes that did occur took place gradually over more than a century.

In the northern Levant, the situation was markedly different. While destruction was still less rampant than oftentimes claimed, the northern Levant experienced far more destruction by warfare and arson. However, much as Joseph Maran asked for Tiryns in Greece, we must ask why these destructions would have had a more devastating impact on sites such as Ras Shamra or Emar than those prior to ca. 1200 BCE? Ras Shamra was struck by an earthquake at some time in the mid-13th century BCE (Callot 1994, 204–11); yet, this destruction did not bring about the abandonment of Ugarit. Emar suffered several attacks by the Hurrians, an attempted coup d'état, as well as the attacks by the *ṭár-wu*, but again this did not cause the abandonment of the city (Adamthwaite 2001, 233–80). Rather, a set of underly preexisting factors is likely to have brought on the abandonment of these cities, and the destruction was only the capstone to a range of difficulties faced by these sites. Indeed, looking at the archeological record, there appears to be a pattern of abandonment at many northern Levantine sites. Ras Ibn Hani was abandoned before the destruction of the *Palais Nord*. This might also be the case for Ras el-Bassit, as the *grand bâtiment* was emptied of its contents, which might indicate an end of the Late Bronze Age abandonment, even though the site itself was not destroyed. The same could be said of Tell Tweini, as Michel Al-Maqdissi reports that many of the structures appear to have been abandoned. At Tell Kazel, in both Area IV and Area II of the North-Eastern sector, it appears as if they were abandoned and reoccupied before the site was attacked, while at Emar, five residential areas were abandoned prior to the destruction of the site's ritual and monumental structures (Millek 2019a, 174). Thus, rather than a sudden unexpected invasion, preexisting conditions caused several sites to abandon house and home prior to any destruction.

From here, we can postulate to some degree what those preexisting conditions were for Ugarit and why it was abandoned, but this can only be done by stepping into the realm of more extreme speculation, what one might call "informed imagination" (Sherratt 2010, 91). By piecing together the patterns of

266   CHAPTER SEVEN

events mentioned in the texts and the archaeological recorded, we can envision a scenario that explains the downfall of Ugarit and the near permanent abandonment of Ras Shamra. To begin, we must take into consideration the background to these events. Based on the surviving documentation, there are several instances where certain texts mention a famine in the land of Ugarit, Hatti, or Emar and the need for grain shipments (see Singer 1999, 714–19; Knapp and Manning 2016, 120–23). This has regularly been cited as evidence for climate change causing unfavorable growing conditions.[67] While it is unclear exactly how bad this famine was, let us assume that there was at least some food stress on Ugarit and its environs ca. 1200 BCE.

The second aspect that needs to be taken into consideration are the texts that do speak of the approaching enemy (see Astour 1965; Singer 1999, 719–31; Knapp and Manning 2016, 118–20). Within this body of texts, for many of which it is not certain when they were written, there is the clear indication that Ugarit was being attacked by land and by sea.[68] Perhaps the most famous of these is RS 20.238, which was sent by an unnamed king of Ugarit to the king of Alashiya saying:

> My father behold, the enemy's ships came (here); my cities(?) were burned, and they did evil things in my country. Does not my father know that all my troops and chariots(?) are in the Land of Hatti, and all my ships are in the Land of Lukka?... Thus, the country is abandoned to itself. May my father know it: the seven ships of the enemy that came here inflicted much damage upon us. (Singer 1999, 720)

While the unnamed Ugaritic king, perhaps Ammurapi II, mentions that his cities were burned, the archaeological evidence from the surrounding sites does not suggest that this was the case. This can be seen in the recently translated letter RS 94.2475 from the "House of Urenu" that provides some clarifying information. It states:

> To the king, my lord say, thus Ammurapi, your servant ... I wrote you twice, thrice, [new]s regarding the enemy!... May my lord know that now the enemy forces are stationed at Ra'šu [Ras Ibn Hani] and their avant-guard forces were sent to Ugarit. Now may my lord send me forces and chariots and may my lord save me from the forces of this enemy![69]

---

67. Kaniewski et al. 2010, 2011, 2013, 2019; Kaniewski, Guiot, and Van Campo 2015; Kaniewski and Van Campo 2017a, 2017b; Cohen 2020.

68. As Knapp and Manning (2016, 119 table 1) have noted, RS 20.18; 88.2009; 19.11; 20.162; 94.2523; 94.2530; 18.113A 34.147; and RSL 1 all do not have a clear date for when they were written. RS 20.033 was likely written in the fourteenth to thirteenth centuries BCE; RS 34.129 was likely written sometime during the thirteenth century BCE; while RS 20.238 was written during thirteenth to twelfth centuries BCE.

69. Lackenbacher and Malbran-Labat 2016, 40–41, no. 16. English translation in Cohen 2020. See Na'aman 2004 for the identification of Ras Ibn Hani with Ra'šu.

Even in this letter noting that the enemy was stationing itself at nearby Ras Ibn Hani, it does not say that the site was destroyed, which corresponds with the archaeological evidence. Rather, another text, RS 19.11, sent from Drdn to his lord in Ugarit, gives perhaps a more realistic measure of the situation. It states:

> When your messenger arrived, the army was humiliated and the city was sacked. *Our food in the threshing floors was burnt and the vineyards were also destroyed.* Our city is sacked. May you know it! May you know it!" (RS 19.11; Singer 1999, 726, emphasis added)

What should be noted here is that while the city was sacked and the army humiliated, the burning mentioned in the text is highly specific. It was the foodstuffs and vineyards that were destroyed. What can be taken from this is that: (1) RS 19.11 indicates that if there was famine in the land it was not total and there was still food that the people had been able to grow themselves, and (2) the attack was perhaps at harvest time, since the food was on the threshing floor. The importance of this is clear. The attacking force was not necessarily concerned with destroying buildings; rather, they were attempting to limit the food supply reaching Ugarit, exaggerating the famine through the willful destruction of the vineyards and the grain. What this also tells us is that the attacking forces were themselves not starving, as many of the climate proponents might suggest; a starving population does not burn the food they are seeking out.

From here it becomes clear what transpired at least in this hypothetical reconstruction of events. Ugarit was already under pressure from a famine, which at least placed some food stress on the region, while an army came with the intention of destroying Ugarit itself. They managed this feat through a combination of seaborne raids, which would have helped to elicit fear as well as helping to cut off aid, be that military or food, from arriving at Ras Shamra. This was coupled with the willful destruction of the recently grown food in the surrounding region, which would have placed an even greater stress on the inhabitants of the city. The enemy also clearly waited to attack Ras Shamra until the end. Ras Ibn Hani was already abandoned prior to its single-building destruction, and whether or not the enemies burned the *Palais Nord* is not the point, as the importance is that they forced the abandonment or evacuation of the sites surrounding Ras Shamra and stationed themselves in a position to attack their main target, which is alluded to in the recently translated RS 94.2475. Moreover, Ugarit's army had already lost several battles by the time the enemy came to the gates of Ras Shamra. This is clear from RS 19.11 as well as in RS 4.425, which states that at least a portion of the Ugaritic army had already been defeated (Singer 1999, 726). Thus, the enemy gained the upper hand by taking control of the sea, as well as gradually closing in on Ras Shamra until finally the city itself was attacked and burned.

The question then naturally arises, Why was this destruction any different than those that preceded it? Why was Ugarit abandoned if even after the mid-thirteenth century BCE earthquake it was rebuilt? Again, the answer is clear, given what we can piece together and if we reframe the question asking, Who could or would rebuild Ugarit after its destruction? Herein lies the key: there was no one to rebuild the city. As mentioned in the chapter 5, the Hittite Empire had likely already fallen by the time Ras Shamra was destroyed (see de Martino 2018). Thus, even if the Hittites had wished to rebuild its vassal state, which was already bucking its duties (see Singer 1999, 693–708), the Hittite Empire was not even able to rebuild itself, let alone Ugarit.

While Ammurapi II wrote to the king of Alashiya, no one on Alashiya had any reason to help reestablish the city. This is clear from RS 20.18, which was sent by Eshuwara a high-ranking Alashiyan official, who suggested that Ammurapi defend himself; yet, he offered no actual help while Ugarit was actively being harassed (Cline and O'Connor 2003, 138). Moreover, Ugarit was likely a commercial rival to the ports of Alashiya. Sites such as Enkomi, Kition, and Hala Sultan Tekke, among others might have been better off without Ugarit, as they could position themselves as the key trading hubs in the northeastern Mediterranean basin.

Carchemish too would not have been any help, as Kuzi-Teshub was consolidating his power as a newly minted Great King of his own Neo-Hittite kingdom. While the Carchemish official Urhi-Teshub promised help to the elders of Ugarit as they defended the city, this aid likely never arrived or did so only after the city had been burned (Singer 1999, 729; RS 88.2009).

Then there is Ammurapi II himself; however, he would have been in no position to rebuild. After the possible mid-thirteenth century BCE earthquake, there was the ability to rebuild, as the political structure was still in place and Ugarit would have had the aid of Hatti or Carchemish, as the times were relatively peaceful. However, the opposite was true ca. 1185 BCE. Ugarit's army had been defeated, they were forced to go on the defensive, and since Ammurapi and the elites were likely trapped in the city when it was attacked, many if not most of the ruling class were possibly killed or imprisoned for the remainder of their lives. Consequently, there would have been no one to rebuild Ugarit after it had fallen, which meant the final destruction of Ras Shamra ca. 1185 BCE.

With no one from the outside or inside to rebuild the kingdom of Ugarit it collapsed, leaving Ras Shamra, the once great city, open to be used as a pen for animals.[70] As mentioned above, there is no clear answer to who the enemies

---

70. See discussion in Callot 2008, who notes the evidence of postdestruction reuse of parts of the site, likely by nomads.

were nor is there any textual evidence that would convict the Sea Peoples, but one possibility is that this was a coordinated attack on Ugarit to destroy it over some period of time.

It bears repeating that the above scenario is an excursion into informed imagination, and it relies heavily upon many assumptions that cannot be proven and thus is only an extremely hypothetical set of events. To this point, as Knapp and Manning (2016, 118–20) have already noted, many of the texts that speak of warfare are undated or do not have a precise date. Thus, there is no clear sequence of events, as we do not know in what order these letters were written or what the time frame was in which they were written. Likewise, while climate change coming in the form a three-hundred-year long period of more arid conditions might have caused a famine, several recent studies have placed doubt on the effect of climate change on the northern Levant ca. 1200 BCE. As Knapp and Manning (2016, 137) have summarized, "Based on a series of proxy indicators, there is clearly some sort of shift to cooler and more arid and unstable conditions generally between the 13th and 10th centuries B.C.E., but not necessarily any one key 'episode.'" Moreover, from the study of stable isotopes and the plant varieties grown during and after 1200 BCE in the Levant, Doğa Karakaya and Simone Riehl (2019, 155) have convincingly demonstrated that, "there is no clear evidence that the Late Bronze Age and the Iron Age were periods of dearth and widespread famine, as some climate models have presupposed. On the contrary, the cultivation of drought-susceptible crop plants becomes progressively more widespread during the Iron Age." Likewise, they have demonstrated that there is minimal evidence of stress on the plants during the supposed "Megadrought" (a term coined in Kaniewski and Van Campo 2017a, 2017b) related to water availability (Karakaya and Riehl 2019). Thus, we do not know if there actually was a severe famine that could have been exacerbated in the region of Ugarit ca. 1200 BCE by the willful destruction of foodstuffs.

We must keep in mind that not all cities, kingdoms, or empires could be rebuilt regardless of the timing of those events. While we speculate on the fall of Ugarit or the Hittite Empire, not nearly as much attention has been given to the fall of the kingdom of Mitanni, which was subdivided by the Hittites and Assyrians during the fourteenth century BCE, despite its similarities to the events at Ugarit (see Klengel 2013). This is likely due to the fact that we know many of the actors in the fall of Mitanni and need not speculate, nor are there any mythic connotations to its fall as there are with the end of the kingdoms and empires at the end of Late Bronze Age. Moreover, what needs to be taken into further consideration are the regional and subregional differences at the end of the Late Bronze Age. Take, for example, Carchemish and Emar. Both were important sites during the Late Bronze Age, both are located in the northern Levant, and both are situated on the Euphrates River. However, despite this, their trajectories were vastly different at the end of the Late Bronze Age. Carchemish was not destroyed or abandoned, and it became the seat of a Neo-Hittite kingdom. Emar was partially abandoned, had its public and monumental structures burned, and then was completely abandoned. To come closer to understanding what those factors might have been, we must take a subregional and site by site approach. Thus, while there is no definite answer why once-vital sites such as Ras Shamra and Emar were abandoned, even if we can speculate on those causes, it is likely that the destructions that preceded these events were only the capstone on a long period of political turmoil, and the destruction was not the de facto cause for the abandonments.

CHAPTER EIGHT

Overview and Impact on Mediterranean Societies

Destruction by the Numbers

Destruction and the end of the Late Bronze Age have been inextricably linked since the nineteenth century, even before the modern periodization existed that would create a Bronze Age to end. Many of these early destructions were caught up in myth, taking Homer, other Greek poets, and historians at their word, while at the same time archaeology lent credence to the lore of yesteryear. After nearly 150 years of excavations, deciphering tablets and monuments, adding in environmental data, and the continuous building up and tearing down of old and new theories for the collapse(s), crisis, or transition, through all of this destruction became and has maintained its role as an integral cog in the mechanisms that brought about the end of the Late Bronze Age. As mentioned in chapter 1, this sentiment was epitomized by Robert Drews (1993, 4) who stated that, "Within a period of forty to fifty years at the end of the thirteenth and the beginning of the twelfth century almost every significant city in the eastern Mediterranean world was destroyed, many of them never to be occupied again," and more recently (2020, 230) that "there is little controversy about which cities were destroyed [ca. 1200 BCE]." Indeed, the list of sites destroyed has grown with every passing year, and while at times scholars will correct certain false destructions, most have remained in the literature.[1] Beyond this, of those destructions that did occur ca. 1200 BCE, the majority are listed or simply described as destroyed and the severity of most destructions has been misrepresented by the phrase, "X sites were destroyed ca.1200 BCE." Nevertheless, over the course of the last five chapters, this common view of the end of the Late Bronze Age and the amount of destruction ca. 1200 BCE has been taken to task. To put the amount and severity of destruction into its proper place, it is appropriate to give a brief overview here of just how much destruction actually took place ca. 1200 BCE based on the information provided in chapters 3 through 7.

To begin, I have uncovered 153 destruction events from 148 sites in the scholarly literature that have been cited as occurring ca. 1200 BCE. There are

---

1. E.g., Cline removed Alalakh from his map of destruction and noted that recent examinations of the site's stratigraphy showed no destruction ca. 1200 BCE, while Knapp and Manning removed Hama and Qatna as end of the Late Bronze Age destructions, noting that both had suffered destruction during the fourteenth century BCE.

likely to be more than this in the literature from smaller site reports or in one of the thousands of articles, book chapters, dissertations, and books on the end of the Late Bronze Age or the beginning of the Iron Age. That said, given that the number of destructions examined in this book represents nearly three times as many destructions as have been discussed in other major works on the end of the Late Bronze Age (e.g., Drews 1993; Cline 2014, 2021; Knapp and Manning 2016), these 153 destruction events should be taken as fairly representative of the situation in the scholarly debate. However, astoundingly, 94, or 61 percent, of these destructions have either been misdated, are based on loose evidence for destruction, or are simply false citations, and generally there is a fairly even spread among the three categories. There are 33 misdated destructions, including major sites such as Lefkandi, Knossos, Koukounaries of Paros, Miletus, Arslantepe, Hazor, Beth-Shean, Tell Deir Alla, Tell es-Sa'idiyeh, and Tel Azekah.

For the assumed destructions there are 35 sites that did not yield the requisite evidence of a destruction, including major placeholders on end of the Late Bronze Age lists and charts of destruction, such as Orchomenos, Krisa, Khania, Alishar Höyük, Sinda, Ras el-Bassit, Tell Tweini, Tell Sukas, Acco, Ashdod, and Tell eṣ-Ṣafi/Gath. It is possible for certain of these assumed destructions, such as Tell Tweini or Sinda, that further excavations may reveal a destruction event, but based on the currently available evidence, there is no justification to assume that these sites were destroyed. This is particularly true given that oftentimes these assumed destructions at sites, such as Sinda and Tell Tweini, are compared to other major destruction events, such as the site-wide destructions uncovered at Maa *Paleokastro* and Ras Shamra. However, there is no comparison between these destructions by warfare and the evidence uncovered at Sinda and Tell Tweini, comprising some ash found on some floors or on a wall, is in no way analogous to the cumulative evidence of site-wide burning and destruction at Maa *Paleokastro* and Ras Shamra.

The most pernicious of the group of false destructions are the twenty-six false citations that include several of the supposed major destructions ca. 1200 BCE. Many of these have been featured destructions in the majority of the foremost publications on the end of the Late Bronze Age from the past several decades. Sites such as Korakou, Hama, Qatna, and Ashkelon have been repeatedly cited as destroyed, even though neither the excavators nor those working on the material from the sites ever claimed that they were destroyed. Perhaps one of the most egregious false destructions is the "destruction by fire" of Alaca Höyük, the genesis of which lay with Kurt Bittel selecting from, at the time, fifty years of excavations, picking the one place from the first season of excavation prior to the establishment of the site's stratigraphy where a "destruction" was mentioned though not in association with ca. 1200 BCE.

Yet, despite being one of the standard end-of-the-Late Bronze Age destruction events for Anatolia, in the nearly one hundred years of off and on excavations at Alaca Höyük, no evidence of this supposed destruction was ever uncovered, and this fact has been washed over by a sea of citations claiming the opposite, while deferring to Bittel rather than referring to the actual excavation reports.

Then there are the other instances of false citations where it is entirely unclear how certain sites came to be cited as destroyed ca. 1200 BCE. For example, Drews, while claiming that Kition was destroyed ca. 1200 BCE, cites an article by Vassos Karageorghis, who specifically states that Kition was not destroyed. Or for the repeated citations over the past thirty years that Tel Batash was destroyed ca. 1200 BCE; this has gone on despite the numerous quotations from the excavators, who clearly state that the site was not destroyed. In other instances, it is confounding how certain sites were credited with a destruction. For instance, Drews's claim that Khirbet Rabud was destroyed ca. 1200 BCE relied on a citation that never mentioned Khirbet Rabud, but only that the biblical city of Debir was destroyed. Yet, both William Foxwell Albright and Paul Lapp, who were Drews's source of information, did not identify Debir with Khirbet Rabud, as they believed Debir was Tell Beit Mirsim, and Albright specifically argued against Khirbet Rabud being Debir. Yet, this was the reference Drews chose to use to argue that Khirbet Rabud was destroyed. There is also the addition of Phaistos to David Kaniewski et al. 2011 and Kaniewski, Jöel Guiot, and Elise Van Campo 2015 maps of destruction by the Sea Peoples, and yet there is not even a reference to the site in either article outside of its placement on the map of destruction. There is no a question if the site was destroyed or not as the answer is a resounding no.

It should come as a surprise that the quantity of false destructions ca. 1200 BCE is so high. If it were the case that more than 50 percent of all imported Mycenean pottery in the Levant simply didn't exist or that one out of every two excavated temples reported in the scholarly literature was nonexistent, this would rightly cause some controversy. However, the issues plaguing destruction at the end of the Late Bronze Age do not end with the ninety-four false destructions, as the destruction events that did occur were in general far less drastic than commonly believed. Of the fifty-nine destruction events that did take place ca. 1200 BCE, seventeen were partial destructions, while another nineteen were single-building destructions. Thus, 61 percent of the destructions ca. 1200 BCE in the Eastern Mediterranean caused marginal physical damage. Many of the partial destructions may not even be destructions at all, as the currently published evidence from sites such as Tel 'Eton, Tel Qashish, Umm ad-Dananir, Enkomi, Soli Höyük, Gouves, Kannia, Teichos Dymaion, and Prophetis Elias is so minimal that further excavation or examination of the unpublished excavated materials may well reveal that these sites did not suffer

274   CHAPTER EIGHT

a destruction ca. 1200 BCE.[2] This ambiguity extends even to the single-building destructions, as it is not clear if there was a destruction at Megiddo at the end of Stratum VIIB. Consequently, destruction ca. 1200 BCE was far less rampant than has been assumed for over a century, and the majority of the destruction events that did occur were minor in their scale. However, there remain the twenty-three multibuilding and site-wide destructions and the question of what effect, if any, these events had on hastening or bringing about the end of sites, empires, and the Late Bronze Age in general.

Cause and Effect: Destruction's Impact on Societies ca. 1200 BCE

Herein lies the crucial question: Did destruction actually bring about or speed along many of the supposed negative consequences oftentimes associated with the end of the Late Bronze Age and the years surrounding 1200 BCE? What impact, if any, did destruction have on a local, regional, and superregional level? The answer is that, in general, ca. 1200 BCE destruction is unlikely to have had much of an effect on the societies of Late Bronze Age Eastern Mediterranean. There are several reasons, though one of the most significant is simply the lack of destruction in many of the regions under discussion. For the two partial destructions at Gouves and Kannia on Crete there is no evidence that these events would have had wide-reaching effects. Kannia, at the time, was only the reuse of three rooms from a LM I building that collapsed, likely by some natural phenomenon, and would not have had a major impact on society at large other than perhaps those visiting the shrine. For Gouves, there is no clear indication how much of the site was even affected by the destruction event. On the Cycladic Islands there was no destruction ca. 1200 BCE, which too was the case for the entirety of the central Levant. Therefore, destruction could not have caused a great deal of harm or change in either of these regions owing to the fact that there simply was no destruction.

On Cyprus, the only site that has significant evidence of destruction is Maa *Paleokastro*; however, this site was not a major center whose destruction would have imploded the commercial activities of the island. Moreover, Maa *Paleokastro* was not even abandoned after its destruction. No major Cypriot site has evidence of destruction, as the evidence from Enkomi is equivocal whether there even was a destruction or not, and if there was it was minor. The single-building destruction of Building X from Kalavasos-*Ayios Dhimitrios* only took place after the site had been abandoned and the structure was turned into a squatters' abode. Indeed, while Kalavasos-*Ayios Dhimitrios*, Maroni-

---

2. The only partial destructions that may have been more widespread were those uncovered at Bethel and Karaoğlan. However, even here the Karaoğlan destruction event provides no definitive evidence it was an end of the Late Bronze Age destruction event.

Vournes, and Alassa (*Pano Mandilaris* and *Paliotaverna*) were all abandoned, this was not as a result of destruction. Thus, there is no evidence suggesting that destruction could have had any impact on Cypriot society or it polities, as the one area where major sites were abandoned ca. 1200 BCE was not the result of destruction, while other regions on the island flourished after the end of the Late Bronze Age.

In the southern Levant too there is little evidence suggesting that destruction would have had a great effect on the region ca. 1200 BCE. There is no evidence suggesting that the Sea Peoples or Philistines violently destroyed the local villages and cities, supplanting them or even intermingling with the population through force. Rather, the arrival of the Sea Peoples or Philistine material culture is archaeologically and historically absent of violence, as there are no texts suggesting that the Sea Peoples caused any destruction in Canaan, nor is there any physical evidence of a violent intrusion.

Likewise, destruction and particularly destruction ca. 1200 BCE did not force out the Egyptians or their ability to exert influence over the southern Levant, as this did not end for another seventy or more years after 1200 BCE. The more logical solution for the disappearance of Egypt's ability to maintain hegemony over the southern Levant was the political turmoil in Egypt proper rather than violent uprisings or the influx of the Sea Peoples in Canaan. Outside of this, there too was very little actual destruction ca. 1200 BCE in the southern Levant. Of the twenty-one destruction events that did occur, eight were partial destructions and ten were single-building destructions. There is little evidence that Megiddo Level VIIB suffered a single-building destruction event, and consequently there is no evidence that any major site suffered destruction ca. 1200 BCE in the southern Levant.[3]

Only one site suffered a site-wide destruction ca. 1200 BCE, Aphek, and even here it was the sole building on the mound at the time of its destruction by warfare, which would not have had a drastic effect on the region or on Egypt's hold on power. Likewise, for Transjordan, there is no evidence of a massive string of destruction. The major earthquake that likely affected several sites occurred ca. 1150 BCE. For both Tell el-Fukhar and Tall al-ʿUmayri Phase 14, while both sites' monumental buildings were destroyed in single-building destructions, this was only after they had lost their function as shrines or seats of local power. Much like Building X from Kalavasos-*Ayios Dhimitrios*, both buildings had been transformed into squatters' abodes, indicating that the Late

---

3. Again it is possible that Lachish Level VII, rather than being two single-building destructions was one multibuilding destruction, and, if so, the above statement would need to be amended. However, as mentioned in ch. 7, following Level VII was initially a period of flourishing not impoverishment. Thus, even if the Level VII destruction was more widespread, it did not "kill" the site or even cause a decline.

276 CHAPTER EIGHT

Bronze Age administrative system at the sites ended prior to the destructions rather than after. Therefore, for the southern Levant in general there is no evidence that destruction had a major effect on the region ca. 1200 BCE, as many of the major destructions appear to have hit the region seventy or more years later.[4]

In Anatolia, there is again no evidence suggesting that destruction itself was the main factor in bring about the end of the Late Bronze Age Hittite Empire. For the Hittite heartland, Alaca Höyük was not destroyed and Alishar Höyük had been abandoned, likely without destruction, in the mid-thirteenth century BCE. Maşat Höyük was a shadow of its former fourteenth-century BCE self when it suffered a single-building destruction, likely during the mid-thirteenth century BCE, while Hattusa had already been abandoned during a period of crisis prior to the destruction of some of its monumental structures.

Again, this does not discount the real possibility of nondestructive violence in the Hittite heartland ca. 1200 BCE, but there is no indication that this supposed violence brought about any destruction. While there was a multibuilding destruction at Kuşaklı-Sarissa, the site was not in prime condition at the time of the destruction event, as the major temple of the storm god had lain in ruins for a century, along with at least one gate and several other buildings.

There is virtually no evidence of destruction in western Anatolia and, while Troy VIIA suffered a site-wide destruction by warfare, the site itself was not in an optimal condition, at least not when compared to the remains from Troy VIh. The destruction of Troy certainly would have had an impact on the local region, but this was an isolated event and cannot be associated with any of the other destructions in Anatolia ca. 1200 BCE.

For the region of Cilicia, there is a great deal of ambiguity surrounding the timing of the multibuilding destruction at Mersin-Yumuktepe and the site-wide destruction of Tarsus-Gözlükule along with the site-wide destruction of Kilise Tepe. It is quite possible that both Mersin and Tarsus suffered their destruction events before the end of the Late Bronze Age, and at the very least, there were likely several decades between their destruction events and the site-wide destruction of Kilise Tepe. From the current information, it appears that many of the destructions in Anatolia were spaced out over the course of a half century or more; therefore, destruction ca. 1200 BCE could not have been a major factor in the downfall of the Hittite Empire.

In sum, for Crete, the Cycladic Islands, Anatolia, Cyprus, and the central and southern Levant, there is no evidence suggesting that destruction had a major impact on the societies ca. 1200 BCE or that destruction, no matter the

---

4. This would include the site-wide destructions of Tel Azekah, Lachish Level VI, Tell Deir Alla, as well as the multibuilding destruction at Beth-Shean. One could also include the multibuilding destruction of Hazor, though this of course was before the events of the end of the Late Bronze Age.

cause, helped to bring about the collapse, transition, or transformation during the twelfth century BCE. However, the situation is dissimilar for parts of Mycenean Greece and portions of the northern Levant.

For Greece, there is more pronounced evidence of arson and warfare, as Pylos and Midea were likely destroyed in acts of war, while Tiryns, Gla, and Dimini suffered destruction events by arson, as was possibly also the case at Kastro-Palaia. Nevertheless, we should not assume that this was some kind of massive string of destruction sweeping over the Greek mainland, as not only is there a clear differentiation in the timing of these events, but there are also separate patterns in the destructions. In the north, at Kastanas, while there was a multibuilding destruction, this did not end the life of the site, and it appears that the settlement had a proclivity for destruction, given that nearly every phase had some kind of destruction event. Thus, this destruction is unlikely to have caused any major long-lasting damage to the site or the region.

For the three sites near Volos, there is no clear evidence of warfare in either of the single-building destructions at Dimini and Kastro-Palaia, while Pefkakia was abandoned without destruction. Moreover, only a single monumental structure from both Dimini and Kastro-Palaia were selected for burning, and at least in the case of Megaron B, this was preceded by the emptying of part of the building, which may have been the case for the "palace" at Kastro-Palaia. Thus, in neither of these cases was the destruction rampant, nor does it appear to have been sudden, and life at both sites did not end with these destruction events. For Gla, the abandonment of the site was premeditated and systematic, and it certainly did not come as a surprise to the residents, nor were nearby Orchomenos and Krisa destroyed ca. 1200 BCE. While Thebes suffered some kind of destruction event, it does not appear to be part of some kind of wider regional pattern in Boeotia and Phocis.

In the Argolid, the situation varies from its northern counterparts. At both Midea and Tiryns, the destruction was more widespread, with a site-wide and multibuilding destruction respectively, which affected monumental and domestic structures alike, and both were likely caused by the hand of man. An earthquake cannot explain the evidence of warfare, nor is there any significant proof suggesting that the physical damage was caused by a seismic event. While it is unclear exactly what caused the destruction at Mycenae ca. 1200 BCE, an earthquake is an unlikely solution given its proximity to Tiryns and Midea.

On the other hand, there is more evidence of rampant violence in the Argolid ca. 1200 BCE, though again we cannot say in what time frame these destructions took place. Again, it should be mentioned that not all sites in the area suffered a destruction event, as Iria's LH IIIC early supposed "destruction" comprised only some burnt material in a pit with no evidence of damage to the site's architecture. Once again, in Messenia there is no clear pattern of

278 CHAPTER EIGHT

destruction, as Nichoria was abandoned without destruction, as was the former palatial site of Iklaina (Cosmopoulos 2019, 365). However, Pylos was destroyed in a site-wide destruction by warfare, marking the end of the settlement; nevertheless, this was a singular event not in concert with other destruction in the region.

In light of the above, it is unlikely, given the differences in these destructions, that they were brought on by a connected cause, a conclusion supported by the decades that separated certain of the destruction events, such as those at Gla and Pylos. Moreover, while destruction certainly was not a "good thing," it is not entirely clear how much of a role it played in the changes witnessed during the LH IIIC. This is clear given the lack of destruction at many sites and the preconditions prior to destruction at others. For example, it is unlikely that the single-building destruction at Dimini caused the eventual abandonment of the settlement after the brief period of rebuilding during the LH IIIC Early. Rather, some structural change in the social fabric likely caused this, which could have been induced by violence, but not by the physical destruction of the site's architecture.

Likewise, for Messenia, destruction likely acted in a similar manner as I proposed for the abandonment of Ras Shamra. There is no indication of rampant violence and destruction in the region, but with the complete destruction of the palace by warfare in conjunction with the probable death of many of the rulers and elites, there would have been no one to rebuild. It should be remembered that nearby Iklaina could have capitalized on Pylos's misfortune if it had not already suffered a site-wide destruction during the mid-thirteenth century BCE that was only followed by a period of impoverishment at the site.[5] Thus, much like for Ras Shamra, there was no one to rebuild, and whoever destroyed Pylos had no interest in its reconstruction.

It is again within the realm of "informed imagination" that a similar situation occurred in the Argolid if we assume—which is a big assumption— that the destruction events were more or less contemporaneous. Given that at least two of the three major settlements suffered a destruction event at the hand of man, it is perhaps probable that there was simply no one to rebuild. If the prior major destruction events during the thirteenth century BCE were precipitated by an earthquake, then again there would have been a social order in place to reerect the great cities. However, if many of the elites or rulers were killed ca. 1200 BCE, this would have made it a more difficult task, leaving those who remained to focus on their own settlement, such as the reconstruction activities at Tiryns. Unfortunately, we lack any historical evidence from the Argolid that might help to elucidate the situation ca. 1200 BCE, and the above

---

5. I am currently working with Michael Cosmopoulos on the investigation and review of the material from this destruction event.

scenario is only a very assumption-laden reconstruction, as it does not explain the other outside causes that would have affected the palatial system's ability to reconstruct itself. Thus, to reiterate Maran's point, there is no clear reason why these destruction events were so impactful on the sites in the Argolid ca. 1200 BCE.[6]

Much as there is more pronounced evidence of warfare and arson in parts of Greece, the same is true for Syria, though much as with every other region, this did not affect the whole of the region. Alakah, Hama, Qatna, and Tell Nebi Mend/Kadesh all were without destruction ca. 1200 BCE. There is no evidence of destruction from the Temple of the Storm God at Aleppo nor is there any reason to assume that Carchemish was destroyed. Ras el-Bassit, Tell Sukas, Tell Tweini, and Arwad all were without destruction ca. 1200 BCE, though it is possible that both Ras el-Bassit and Tell Tweini were abandoned briefly at the end of the Late Bronze Age. Indeed, Syria has the highest rate of false destructions in the entire Eastern Mediterranean with a 70 percent error rate.[7] Thus, for much of the Syrian coast, and the Orontes River Valley, the physical destruction of sites had little impact on the societies of these regions ca. 1200 BCE, given the lack of destruction.

While there is evidence of destruction by the hand of man at several sites, such as Ras Shamra, Ras Ibn Hani, Emar, Tell Kazel, and possibly Tell Afis, I would doubt that this represents a string of contemporaneous disasters by the same causal agent. The destruction event from Tell Afis can only be dated to the first half of the twelfth century BCE, leaving a wiggle room of fifty years for its multibuilding destruction. While it is possible that the single-building destruction at Ras Ibn Hani occurred close in time to the destruction of Ras Shamra, it is also possible that the site had been abandoned and the *Palais Nord* was destroyed several decades prior to Ras Shamra. As mentioned in the previous chapter, it is my speculative opinion that the site-wide destruction at Ras Shamra, and the multibuilding destruction at Emar were only the capstones on a set of preexisting conditions.

For Emar, while the previous attacks by the Hurrians, the attempted coup d'état, as well as the attacks by the *ṭár-wu*, did not bring about the end of the site, it is unlikely that they brought health and prosperity. Since it appears that

---

6. Maran's (2015, 280) statement is, "Why this particular [destruction] should have had much more devastating and enduring consequences than all the others which had occurred earlier in the Palatial period."

7. It is possible that sites such as Tell Faq'ous, Tell Rifa'at, and Tell Abu Danné suffered a destruction ca. 1200 BCE. However, for the moment, the meager remains of a possible destruction event at each site cannot be reliably dated to any time close to ca. 1200 BCE. Obviously, if after a review of the ceramics or if any other materials arise that can help to date the possible destructions to ca. 1200 BCE, the sites would be removed as being false destructions and would be listed as partial destructions.

280 CHAPTER EIGHT

Emar was at least partially abandoned prior to the multibuilding destruction, and that the monumental and ceremonial structures were targeted for destruction, it raises the question of who could have rebuilt the site. Once again, there are no clear contenders, as the overarching Hittite Empire had been taken out of the picture, while Carchemish was busy helping itself. One could step deeply into the realm of informed imagination and make the wild suggestion that it was Carchemish who attacked the site in an attempt at consolidating power. After the fall of the Hittite Empire, there would have been no reason for Emar to stay under the control of Carchemish, and Emar could have tried to take the title of Great King for itself, which would not have boded well with Kuzi-Teshub, resulting in a retaliatory measure from the newly minted Great King. However, to reiterate, this is purely speculation of the highest degree.

Again, as mentioned in the previous chapter, Ugarit may have fallen to a deliberate military campaign, not necessarily focused on the destruction of buildings, but on the burning and constriction of the region's food supply while slowly cornering Ras Shamra. While the scenario I laid out is purely informed imagination, I believe that the reason for the site's abandonment and the collapse of the kingdom of Ugarit likely follows from my proposed solution. That is, there simply was no one who would or could rebuild the site and its political and economic framework. In this way, destruction likely had a long-term impact on Emar and Ugarit; however, this was only because these destruction events occurred in concert with other preexisting conditions in conjunction with the lack of any one to restore these petty kingdoms.

In all, on the superregional scale of the Eastern Mediterranean, destruction did not play a significant role in ending the Late Bronze Age, bringing down empires, or causing the death of untold number of peoples. While it is likely that certain destruction events in Greece and the northern Levant had a greater toll on the regional societies, it is not entirely clear exactly how it affected these sites without reaching into the realm of less empirical speculation. Nevertheless, the most significant point that warrants repeating is that based on the available evidence, there was no string of destructions between 1225 and 1175 BCE and the majority of the regions in the Eastern Mediterranean did not overtly suffer from massive destruction events. Moreover, in many cases when there was a destruction, it was only after the site in question had been partially abandoned.

Furthermore, in general, we should exclude the notion of prosperous cities and towns being runover by ransacking marauders or crushed by an unexpected earthquake in the night. Many of these sites were on their last leg to begin with, and the destruction only left a visible mark for archaeologists to find, while many other sites in the same predicament were simply abandoned without destruction ca. 1200 BCE. Consequently, based on all of

OVERVIEW AND IMPACT ON MEDITERRANEAN SOCIETIES 281

this and generally speaking, destruction did not have an overt impact on the majority of societies in the Eastern Mediterranean ca. 1200 BCE, as indicated by the lack of destruction.

Destruction and Theorizing the End of the Late Bronze Age in the Eastern Mediterranean

With all of the above information in hand, we can see what effect this study has on many of the theories for the end of the Late Bronze Age as briefly laid out in chapter 1. First and foremost, despite the claims of Claude Schaeffer, Klaus Kilian, Amos Nur, Dawn Burgess, and Eric Cline, there is no evidence of an earthquake storm ca. 1200 BCE. Many of the major earthquakes that supposedly took place ca. 1200 BCE either did not take place at all—such as those affecting Tiryns and Midea—or they pre- and postdate 1200 BCE, as at Troy VIh, Ras Shamra, Beth-Shean, Tell Deir Alla, and the possible earthquake-related damage uncovered at Kynos. Only two sites, Pyla-*Kokkinokremos* on Cyprus and Tall al-'Umayri in Transjordan suffered earthquake-induced damage ca. 1200 BCE. For Pyla, the damage appears to have been minimal, and it is unclear if the harm caused by this earthquake impeded life at the site or not. For Tall al-'Umayri, Building C was already a squatter's house and the earthquake would not have had a major effect on the site, as whatever caused the initial abandonment was the true prime factor in the site's downfall, not the earthquake.

Recently, Cline (2021, 136) has claimed that numerous sites suffered a destruction by earthquake between 1225–1175 BCE, including Mycenae, Thebes, Pylos, Kynos, Lefkandi, the Menelaion, Kastanas in Thessaly, Korakou, Prophetis Elias, Gla, Tiryns, Midea, Troy, Karaoğlan, Hattusa, Ugarit, Beth-Shean, Tell Deir Alla, Tell es-Sa'idiyeh, Tall al-'Umayri, Ashdod, and Acco. However, as discussed in chapters 3 through 7, there is no evidence of any earthquake damage ca. 1200 BCE at Pylos, Kynos, Lefkandi, the Menelaion, Kastanas, Korakou, Prophetis Elias, Gla, Tiryns, Midea, Troy, Hattusa, Ugarit, Beth-Shean, Tell Deir Alla, Tell es-Sa'idiyeh, Ashdod, and Acco, and there is no conclusive evidence of earthquake-related damage at Mycenae, Thebes, and Karaoğlan. The supposed destruction by earthquake at Enkomi is not the Level IIB Floor IV possible destruction event discussed in chapter 6. Rather this refers to a separate destruction event at the end of Dikaios's Level IIIB, which took place at the end of the twelfth century BCE.[8] This list of sites

---

8. Dikaios 1971, 530–31. See as well discussion in Mountjoy 2005, 154. This is largely based on several key finds in the Ashlar Building from Area I, which Dikaios himself originally noted as evidence of an earthquake, such as an inclined wall in Room 9 from the Ashlar Building found in association with a fallen doorjamb; the crushed child in Room 8 as well as the two other children who died and had been seemingly dumped in Room 2 attesting that the building collapsed before they could escape; a ritual may have been going on at the time in Rooms 10 and 9, where the horned god

was based on the faulty assessment presented in Nur and Cline 2000, which included a number of false destructions, as well as destructions that clearly were not caused by an earthquake, while also forcing together destructions likely by earthquake that took place over nearly two centuries. Consequently, there is simply no physical evidence supporting the theory that earthquakes at one time or over time greatly affected the Eastern Mediterranean ca. 1200 BCE, or that earthquakes were in any way an exacerbator or causal factor in the collapse or transition.

Likewise, no evidence exists that supports any theory relying on a massive string of destructions, such as Drews's marauders with advanced weaponry, or those incorporating the Sea Peoples in any of their many forms, as there simply was not a massive string of destructions, let alone one caused by warfare and arson. Moreover, for the Sea Peoples theories at large, neither is there archaeological evidence to suggest that the Sea Peoples caused a massive amount of destruction, nor is there any clear historical document pinning any destruction on them. No text from Egypt or Ugarit ever mentions any group of the Sea Peoples causing any kind of destruction. Their role as destructive agents was written into history by more recent scholars who have at times deliberately changed the words of the texts to fit a paradigm, thereby altering the eyewitness accounts of the events to fit a modern theory rather than the ancient reality.

Regions such as Cilicia, Ugarit, and the southern Levant were written into the ancient texts by modern historians and archaeologists, even though these well-known geographic locations were excluded from the Egyptian lists of regions, sites, and countries "cutoff" by the Sea Peoples. While it remains possible that Tell Kazel could have suffered a multibuilding destruction at the hands of the Sea Peoples, no evidence suggests that this was the case for any other site in the Eastern Mediterranean. No site on Cyprus has a destruction that can be attributed to them. The destruction events at Tarsus and Mersin occurred well before the Sea Peoples supposedly started their violent trek across the Eastern Mediterranean. Moreover, for the majority of sites where locally made Sea Peoples or Philistine pottery appeared during the early decades of the twelfth century BCE, this material arrived without an intervening destruction. In sum, there is simply no evidence that the Sea Peoples were a major threat at the end of the Late Bronze Age or that they caused any kind of major perceivable damage to the coastal or inland sites of the Eastern Mediterranean.[9]

---

was uncovered, which was stopped by the sudden collapse of the structure, as the legs of animals were found still articulated as if they had been freshly offered (Dikaios 1969, 197, 211–12).

9. See also the recent discussion in Emanuel 2020, 251–63, where he notes that there is no reasonable polity or polities that could have mustered a naval force to cause the kind of damage typically attributed to the Sea Peoples.

For the climate theories, particularly that suggested by Kaniewski et al. (2010, 2011, 2013, 2019) the problem is that even if a prolonged drought preceded a population movement, there is no evidence that this resulted in destruction. Moreover, if we assume groups of people were moving about in search of food, why was food so often left behind to be burnt? Foodstuffs were burnt at Dimini, Gla, Midea, Mycenae, Troy, Kuşaklı, Tarsus, Kilise Tepe, Apliki *Karamallos*, Tel Miqne-Ekron, and Tel Zippor. In many cases, for example, at Gla, Dimini, Midea, and Kilise Tepe, while other objects appear to have been removed prior to the destruction, the foodstuffs were left behind, indicating that those leaving the site were not in desperate need of the food, nor were those who caused the burning at Gla, Dimini, and Midea. If starvation was a real threat, the inhabitants of Gla would have left the pottery in the Melathron and taken the grain. Moreover, as RS 19.11 indicates, while there might have been some food stress on Ugarit, it appears that there still was the ability to grow crops that were the specific target of destruction rather than the prized possession of a starving horde seeking food. Thus, while climate change certainly should not be discounted as a stressor, it does not appear to have been as severe as previously claimed, as noted by Bernard Knapp and Sturt Manning (2016) and Doğa Karakaya and Simone Riehl (2019), nor did it produce catastrophic ruin resulting in climate-driven destruction.

Similar issues plague the notion of a system collapse, as the majority of the ports of trade were not destroyed ca. 1200 BCE. The tin trade continued after 1200 BCE; trade continued between Egypt and Canaan; and at least for the southern Levant, the majority of the trade in Mycenaean or Cypriot pottery ended prior to 1250 BCE, well before the end of the Late Bronze Age. Moreover, regions that should have suffered from the theoretical collapsing system did not. Cyprus and the central Levant, who supposedly relied on trade for their livelihood, flourished or at least continued seemingly unimpeded by events ca. 1200 BCE.

It can also be argued that much of the assumed interconnected system is also a product of modern scholarship looking to globalization as a means of understanding the past. Yet, the physical evidence for connection during the Late Bronze Age between many of these regions is flimsy. As Hermann Genz (2013) has pointed out, there is no clear indication that the Hittite Empire was part of any great trading network. The quantity of nonlocal materials imported to the Aegean over the course of four hundred years is a paltry amount, and the little that was imported was highly concentrated in a few select sites, mainly in the Argolid (see Manning and Hulen 2005; Murray 2013, 312–17). Moreover, there is little indication that Mycenaean Greece was highly connected to any polity or empire in the rest of the Eastern Mediterranean, as Linear B tablets are silent on the supposed interregional trade, while the quantity of exported

284   CHAPTER EIGHT

Mycenean pottery is for the most part negligible and chronologically dispersed across two centuries.[10] While there certainly was contact between these regions, there is not sufficient evidence to say that they had a tightly connected political and economic system, one in which the failure of one would cause a breakdown in the others. Nevertheless, even if one assumes there was a system to collapse, it is clear that destruction could not have been a causal factor in that collapse.

Destruction, the End of the Late Bronze Age, and Where We Go from Here

This study has sought to challenge the more than a century of research and excavations that have erroneously embedded destruction into the core of the end of the Late Bronze Age narrative. But it also brings to the fore several other important points that need to be taken into further consideration. The first is, as stressed in chapter 2, there is the need for a strict definition of what constitutes a destruction, as well as a systematic method to define and describe destruction events. None of the following suggestions will bear any fruit if there is no accepted concept for what is or is not a destruction. Until such a time when a definition and system for demarcating destruction is broadly accepted, such as the one presented here, there can be no hope of having an informed conversation on the subject, as everyone will continue to talk past each other, much as they would if there was no standard typology of Late Helladic pottery. If a system such as this one can be widely adopted then we can address the following issues to help bring more clarity not only to the end of the Late Bronze Age, but to the ancient world in general.

One of the issues that needs to be addressed in the future is the subconscious assumption that periods of transition are fraught with more destruction than the periods before the transition or collapse. This is obvious, as most periods of transition are oftentimes assumed to be accompanied by a string of destructions or "destruction horizon."[11] However, it is my opinion that it is unlikely that only the end of the Late Bronze Age suffers from false destructions in any of their three forms. Indeed, this has already been demonstrated for another period in the southern Levant, as Jodi Magness (1993, 43, 53, 66–71, 86–88, 90–91, 118) has uncovered that many of the destruction events associated with the Muslim conquest of Palestine were misdated by more than a century and had only been artificially constricted into a single chronological horizon. Like-

---

10. For further details, see the discussion in Millek 2019c, 122–40, 200–204.

11. This is indeed the case for the southern Levant, which has a "destruction horizon" at the end of the Early Bronze Age, Middle Bronze Age, and, as discussed in this book, Late Bronze Age. For the Early Bronze Age, see Butzer 1997, 271–72; Richard 2014, 343; Prag 2014, 388; Gallo 2014. For the Middle Bronze Age, see Burke 2014, 411.

wise, Ryan Boehm (2013, 319–25) has demonstrated that, despite the traditional view that the *synoikismos* in the late fourth and third centuries BCE in northern Greece and western Asia Minor was a period of widespread destruction, in fact there is an overwhelming lack of evidence for destruction at this time. It is more than likely that many of the supposed "destruction horizons" are either generally false, as is the case for the end of the Late Bronze Age, or that at the least there is less destruction than has oftentimes been presumed to be the case.

Much of the reason for this theoretical supposition that destruction was rampant in periods of transition likely stems from the assumption that the end of a period or age must be preceded by violent destruction. Thus, as was the case with many of the assumed or false citations discussed in chapter 3, sites were presumed destroyed not based on any evidence, but rather because the site had a layer dated to ca. 1200 BCE. Since the underlying assumption dictated that all or almost all sites were destroyed ca. 1200 BCE many sites were presumed destroyed, even if there was a general lack of evidence, or what was found likely represented burning in only a single room or the day-to-day use of a hearth.[12] Consequently, in many cases of false destruction ca. 1200 BCE, the theory superseded the physical archaeological evidence. It is more than likely that this is also the case in other periods and regions that have lists of sites destroyed ca. any given date.

Moreover, in many instances where destruction was uncovered, it was simply assumed that the destruction was caused by violent warfare or by an earthquake, depending on the theoretical leaning of the excavator interpreting the material. Because of this, other possible causes were overlooked or ignored, as the evidence had to fit into a preconceived theoretical mold that did not allow for accidental fires, structural engineering failures, or even evidence of warfare in sites that were supposedly destroyed by an earthquake. Thus, there needs to be a reappraisal of all so-called destruction horizons, to see what sites actually have evidence of destruction, when the evidence dates to, whether there is evidence of abandonment or crisis prior to the destruction event, and what the scale and possible causes for the destructions are. Until this work is undertaken, any discussion of a "destruction horizon" should be taken with a measure of caution, as it is more than likely that these other "horizons of destruction" too are rife with errors that need to be expunged.

This leads to two other vital points. The first of these is that typically during these periods of crisis, collapse, transition, or change, depending on how one chooses to view it, there is the undercurrent in the literature that these were more violent points in history than in the times preceding them. Thus, not only is there supposedly more evidence for widespread destruction, but violence and

---

12. I have provided several quotations in the previous chapters where many have stated just this, that all sites in a given region were destroyed.

unrest is typically assumed to be at greater levels than in the preceding decades. The end of the Late Bronze Age is an excellent example of this assumption, yet, there is nothing to suggest that the years surrounding 1200 BCE were any more violent than the previous centuries. If we were to ask the people of the Levant if the LB I or LB II were without violence, the inhabitants of Megiddo would likely answer no, as they were utterly defeated by Thutmoses III and put under Egyptian subjugation along with the majority of the Levant. The Amarna Letters do not provide a picture of peace and tranquility during the fourteenth century BCE in Canaan and the central Levant, but rather portray fighting between petty polities who were also harassed by groups of Habiru (Ahlström, Rollefson, and Edelman 1993, 239–71). The situation at Qatna certainly challenges the notion that the period during the Late Bronze Age was less violent than its end, as the site suffered a massive destruction, likely at the hands of Suppiluliuma I, and it never regained its former glory. Ugarit was caught in a tug of war between Egypt, Mitanni, and the Hittites, while Mitanni itself was completely obliterated as an entity by the Hittites and Assyrians.

Other sites that could challenge the prevailing view of the intra Late Bronze Age periods are Troy VIh, Beycesultan, Maşat Höyük, and Kuşaklı, which all suffered greater damage during the course of the Late Bronze Age than at its end ca. 1200 BCE. While historians bemoan the loss of Linear B and writing in Greece at the end of the Late Bronze Age, what is oftentimes lost in the discussion is the complete annihilation of Linear A, which resulted in the disappearance of an entire language group at the end of the fifteenth century BCE (Tomas 2010; Wiener 2015). The loss of Linear A was in many ways worse than the disappearance of Linear B, as at least Greek survived, while whatever language Linear A represented appears to have gone out of existence. From here, the list could go on, as Egypt, Hatti, Mitanni, Babylonia, Assyria, and others were constantly at war with someone, extending their reach through violent and at times destructive conquest, while they too faced threats from uprisings, other kingdoms and empires, as well as from population groups they could not control, such as the Kaska, Habiru, Sashu, Libyans, pirates, and bandits, to name only a few.

Thus, while the end of the Late Bronze Age is typically described as a period of more overt violence and destruction, the historical record does not indicate that it was any more tumultuous than the Late Bronze Age as a whole—that is, unless one reaches into the realm of Greek myth and the bombastic narration provided by one pharaoh on one of his monuments that largely reflects violence done against the Sea Peoples by the Egyptians rather than the other way around.

This then leads into the second point, which is that the assumption that transitional periods such as the end of the Late Bronze Age were fraught with more destruction, and not only that, but also more-devastating destruction than in the preceding centuries, is not based on any factual evidence or systematic study. It is merely an assumption. If one were to ask how many destruction events occurred during the LB I in the Levant, what was their scale, what were the probable causes, and what resulted after the destruction, no lists or maps exist to answer this question. Destruction during a period or age has gone largely unstudied as a phenomenon. While the amount of destruction at the end of the Late Bronze Age is outwardly compared to destruction during the Late Bronze Age, we simply do not know how much destruction actually took place in any given period for any given region. Consequently, we cannot say that there was more destruction and more devastating destruction at the end of the Late Bronze Age, as we do not know how much destruction occurred before it or after it. Thus, much as all periods of collapse, crisis, transition, and their "destruction horizons" need to be reevaluated, the entire archaeological record requires reexamination, as we cannot compare one data set to another data set that does not currently exist in any tangible form. If there is to be any comparison, we must first understand how destruction affected sites during a period to see if there are drastic differences between interperiod destructions and destructions at the end of a period or age. Until that time, it is fruitless to say there was more destruction at the end of a period such as the Late Bronze Age, as we simply do not know what the rate of destruction was, the average scale, distribution of cause, and the effect of these destructions during any fifty-to-one-hundred-year span of time.

From here it is clear where the study of destruction needs to go. Essentially, every destruction event from every period needs to be critically reexamined, while interperiod destruction events need to be sought out. If Late Helladic pottery had been accumulating over the course of the past one-hundred-plus years from hundreds of excavations without ever being examined under a common rubric or typology, while it would be a monumental task to study this body of material, the effort would be worthwhile. It would reveal troves of information that have gone undetected, challenging theories and upending assumptions.

Likewise, attempting to reinvestigate all destruction events would be a mammoth task; however, it too will be worth the while. Over the course of such an endeavor, theories and reconstructions of the past will be challenged, upended, or shown to be fallacious, while also reaffirming others when the evidence warrants it. We can examine how populations reacted to destructive crises both during and outside periods of transition. The method of analyzing destruction would be refined, improved, and expanded, just as what has been presented here was not meant to be the end of the discussion on examining and interpreting destruction, but merely the beginning. This endeavor of course will not happen all at once, and it will need to be done site by site and destruction horizon by destruction horizon, but if it is completed, the benefits to our understanding of the ancient world will far outweigh the cost in time.

Only by thoroughly studying destruction over the millennia can we come to a better understanding of how destruction in its myriad of forms affected ancient societies and discover what new knowledge lies lurking in the darkness of the unstudied destruction event.

Appendix

Overview of Destructions ca. 1200 BCE

Misdated Destructions	
Site	**Description**
Lefkandi	No destruction at the end of the LH IIIB. Phase 1b destruction event occurred after the end of the Late Bronze Age.
Kynos	Destruction of the storerooms occurred in the LH IIIC Middle.
Knossos	Final Palace was destroyed in the fourteenth century BCE.
Palaikastro Kastri	Floor 2 ended during the mid-thirteenth century BCE.
Koukounaries of Paros	Mycenean citadel was destroyed ca. 1150 BCE.
Çine-Tepecik	Level II la destruction dates to the mid-twelfth century BCE.
Miletus	Third Building Period or Miletus VI dates to 1130–1060 BCE. No evidence of destruction ca. 1200 BCE.
Beycesultan	Level II destruction dates to ca. 1530–1410 BCE.
Zeyve Höyük-Porsuk	Level V destruction event occurred between 1514–1430 BCE.
Arslantepe	Imperial Gate destruction dates to the first half of the thirteenth century BCE.
Tille Höyük	Burning of the gate complex took place after 1090 BCE.
Lidar Höyük	Layer <7> and the possible destruction dates to late in the twelfth century BCE.
Tell Rifa'at	Level III material and possible destruction can only be dated to the Late Bronze Age.
Alalakh (Tell Atchana)	Level I dates to ca. 1300 BCE. No clear evidence of destruction was uncovered at the end of Level I.
Tel Dan	Ceramics and C14 dates from Level VIIA1 place the possible destruction between 1150–1130 BCE.
Hazor	Stratum XIII and 1A multibuilding destruction took place ca. 1250 BCE.

290 APPENDIX

Misdated Destructions	
Tell Keisan	Based on recent analysis of the ceramics the Stratum 13 destruction took place ca. 1150 BCE.
Shiqmona	The possibly destroyed public building dates to the fourteenth century BCE. No end of the Late Branze Age destruction was uncovered.
Megiddo Stratum VIIA	Stratum VIIA dates to the mid-twelfth or beginning of the eleventh century BCE.
Beth-Shean	The Stratum S-3a earthquake took place in the mid-twelfth century BCE, likely ca. 1150 BCE.
Jaffa	Based on the renewed excavations the Stratum RG-3a destruction took place between 1134–1115 BCE.
Tel Harasim	The destruction event occurred in the mid-thirteenth century BCE.
Tel Azekah	The Late Bronze Age site was destroyed in a site-wide destruction ca. 1130 BCE.
Tel Zayit	The destruction event took place at some point during the early to mid-LB IIB.
Lachish Level VI	The Level VI site-wide destruction took place ca. 1130 BCE.
Tell el-Hesi, Pilaster Building	The Pilaster building was destroyed between 1150–1130 BCE.
Tel Sera'	The Egyptian garrison was destroyed in the middle or third quarter of the twelfth century BCE.
Tell Jemmeh	The Phase G–H destruction dates to the Iron II. No evidence of destruction ca. 1200 BCE.
Tell el-Far'ah (South)	The destruction took place at the end of the twelfth century BCE. Egyptian presence disappeared prior to this destruction.
Tell Irbid	C14 dates derived from short-lived samples places the destruction event between 1395–1260 BCE.
Pella	The destruction occurred at the end of the twelfth century BCE, possibly in association with Tell Deir Alla.
Tell Deir Alla	The earthquake induced destruction of Phase E occurred ca. 1150 BCE.
Tell es-Sa'idiyeh	The destruction of Stratum XII occurred either between 1150 and 1120 BCE or during the Iron IIA.

APPENDIX

Assumed Destructions	
Site	Description
Orchomenos	Only broken pottery, fallen plaster, and pieces of melted lead were recovered from the floor of the courtyard.
Krisa	There is only a statement that the site was destroyed with no published evidence of destruction in any structure.
Iria	Some burnt material in a pit was assumed to be a destruction. There was no damage visible to the buildings.
Athens	The Houses on the North slope were not houses at all. It was refuse that was dumped on the stairs.
Ayios Stephanos	Burning was uncovered in one room from Trench Beta 11. No other damage was recorded.
Khania (Kydonia)	Burning was only uncovered in part of Room A of Building 1. This was likely a contained accidental fire.
Alishar Höyük	Drews misquoted von der Osten saying the site was destroyed by fire. The site was abandoned ca. 1250 BCE.
Kouklia *Palaepaphos*	Some burnt sherds from the wells at Evreti were cited as destruction. The settlement itself has not been found.
Myrtou-*Pigadhes*	No burning or wall collapse was uncovered, though the altar may have been destroyed by humans.
Alassa (Pano Mandilaris and Paliotaverna)	No evidence of LC IIC destruction. Building II suffered two separate fires that did not destroy the structure.
Hala Sultan Tekke	Melted silver was uncovered in City Quarter 2, the Northwestern Structure, Room 44. No further evidence of destruction was recorded.
Sinda	Only ash with no other evidence of destruction was uncovered.
Aleppo: Temple of the Storm God	There is no published evidence of a destruction. This supposed destruction only exists on two tables with no clear date.
Tell Abu Danné	There is little published evidence of a destruction nor a clear date for the end of Level V.
Tell Faq'ous	The pottery from a possible destruction can only be dated to the Late Bronze Age. It was assumed it took place with the destruction of Emar.
Ras el-Bassit	Traces of fire and carbonized wood were discovered near a wall of a house. No other evidence of destruction was recorded.

Assumed Destructions	
Tell Tweini	Some floors yielded layers of ash. Most buildings were abandoned without any evidence of burning.
Tell Sukas	Patches of burnt floor and ash were highly localized. No destruction debris was uncovered.
Tyre	Stratum XV had a black ashy layer on its floor, likely from domestic cooking activity.
Kamid el-Loz	Evidence of burning was only uncovered in three rooms of Temple T1. No other structures have destruction debris.
Achzib	No end of the Late Bronze Age site has been uncovered and there is no evidence the Middle Bronze Age defenses were destroyed ca. 1200 BCE.
Acco	Ash from an industrial context was assumed to be evidence of a destruction event.
Tell Abu Hawam	There is no evidence of destruction from the settlement. The defenses deteriorated naturally and were not destroyed.
Tel Dor	Stern assumed the site was destroyed by the Sea Peoples. He noted that no destruction had been found.
Tel Mevorakh	There is no evidence of a destruction. It appears to have been abandoned.
Tel Zeror	Some burnt beams were uncovered on a floor. No other evidence of destruction was seen on either mound.
Tel Gerisa	An unspecified burning event from a 1929 letter was taken as a 1200 BCE destruction. No further evidence of a destruction was uncovered.
Beth-Shemesh	No evidence of destruction was uncovered in the renewed excavations, while the original account is questionable.
Tell Zira'a	The occasional fallen wall and ash were assumed to be destruction. Likely the site was abandoned resulting in some collapse.
Tell Abu al-Kharaz	There were scanty remains from Phase VIII, which lacked clear evidence of a destruction event.
Amman Airport Structure	Evidence of burning in Room VII can be attributed to the hearth in that room.
Ashdod	Some ash from Area A does not indicate a destruction, as all other areas lack destruction debris.

APPENDIX 293

Assumed Destructions	
Tell eṣ-Ṣafi/Gath	Pottery on a floor from Area E was assumed to be a destruction. No other debris has been uncovered.
Qubur el-Walaydah	No burning or wall collapse was uncovered. It was simply assumed that the site was destroyed.
Tell el-Ḥesi, City Sub-IV Egyptian Governor's Residence	City Sub-IV Egyptian governor's residence has no clear published evidence of a destruction.

False Citations	
Site	**Description**
Pefkakia	Adrimi-Sismani repeatedly cited a destruction, even though the excavators clearly stated the site was abandoned.
Korakou	Drews created a destruction assuming that the lack of evidence was not the lack of a destruction.
Nichoria	An initial trial trench from 1959 led the excavators to assume the site was destroyed. Full-scale excavations proved this to be a false assumption, as the site was abandoned without destruction.
Phaistos	Kaniewski et al. simply placed it on a map as destroyed by the Sea Peoples with no citations. No evidence of an end of the Late Bronze Age destruction has been found.
Alaca Höyük	Bittel chose a sentence from the first season excavation as evidence for destruction even though all excavations have shown no evidence of destruction.
Kaman-Kalehöyük	Drews claimed a mid-eighteenth-century BCE destruction was ca. 1200 BCE.
Domuztepe near Karatepe-Aslantaş	The date of a possible destruction was changed to ca. 1200 BCE over several citations. No ca. 1200 destruction was uncovered.
Kourion (Episkopi)-Bamboula	Neither Benson nor Weinberg claimed the site was destroyed. No destruction was uncovered ca. 1200 BCE.
Maroni-*Vournes*	Olive pressing debris was assumed to be a fire in a room. No evidence of destruction was uncovered and the site was abandoned.
Kition	Karageorghis and Demas both state the site was not destroyed. Older references have been cited over newer works.

False Citations	
Carchemish	No evidence of a destruction was uncovered in the old or renewed excavations.
Aleppo	Drews misquoted Woolley, creating a destruction when Woolley never claimed there was one.
Hama	Drews misquoted Barret who never claimed it was destroyed. Fugmann too noted there was no destruction.
Qatna	Astour listed Qatna as destroyed without evidence, which Drews recited and popularized.
Tell Nebi Mend (Kadesh)	Astour listed Kadesh as destroyed without evidence, which Drews recited and popularized.
Arwad	Nothing is known about the Late Bronze Age site as all remains except for those from the Roman period have been removed.
Byblos	Kaniewski et al. simply placed it on a map as destroyed by the Sea Peoples with no citations. No evidence of an end of the Late Bronze Age destruction has been found.
Sidon: College Site	No evidence of an end of the Late Bronze Age destruction was uncovered.
ʿAfula	Dever claimed it was destroyed by the Sea Peoples. No end of the Late Bronze Age settlement has been uncovered.
Tel Michal	Stern claimed it was destroyed by the Sea Peoples. The site was abandoned ca. 1300 BCE.
Tel Batash (Timnah)	Kelm and Mazar have stated the site was not destroyed, but it has been repeatedly cited as destroyed ca. 1200 BCE.
Tell ej-Judeideh	There was a settlement gap at the site between the EB III and the Iron II.
Tel Burna	No evidence of an end of the Late Bronze Age destruction has been excavated. The end of the Late Bronze Age at the site remains unclear.
Khirbet Rabud	Drews claimed Debir was destroyed citing Lapp, who assumed Debir was Tell Beit Mirsim not Khirbet Rabud.
Ashkelon	Phythian-Adams uncovered a layer of ash that was not a destruction. No destruction was seen in the renewed excavations.
Tell el-ʿAjjul	Bell simply placed it on a map as destroyed with no citations. There was no settlement ca. 1200 BCE.

Destruction ca. 1200 BCE by region

Region/Site	Scale	Cause	Description
Greece			
Kastanas	Multibuilding	Unknown	Trapezhaus and the Antenbau were burnt. No clear cause. Site was prone to burning events.
Dimini	Single-Building	Arson/Termination Ritual	Only Megaron B was burnt after being emptied and the building was left undisturbed during the LH IIIC. Possible termination ritual.
Kastro-Palaia in Volos	Single-Building	Unknown	Only the Palace was burnt, as houses were left alone. No clear cause, though arson is possible. The building may have been emptied prior to destruction.
Gla	Multibuilding	Arson	The site was largely emptied prior to the burning of the gates and Melathron. Destruction appears premeditated and planned.
Thebes	Multibuilding	Unknown	Several buildings were burnt, though there is no clear chronological connection between them. No clear cause, as there is no evidence for warfare or earthquake.
Teichos Dymaion	Partial	Unknown	Burning and debris were uncovered, but the extent is unclear based on the current state of publication.
Mycenae	Multibuilding	Unknown	Much of the destruction was excavated without record. No clear cause, though an earthquake seems untenable based on finds at Midea and Tiryns.
Midea	Site-Wide	Warfare	Fifty weapons, mainly arrowheads, were scattered throughout the destruction suggesting warfare. No clear evidence of earthquake.

Region/Site	Scale	Cause	Description
Tiryns	Multibuilding	Arson/Warfare	Monumental structures were targeted and no evidence of earthquake. Weapons were uncovered in domestic structures.
Prophetis Elias/ Katsingri	Partial	Unknown	Burning was uncovered but it is not clear if this is a destruction or not based on the state of publication.
Pylos	Site-Wide	Warfare	Weapons were scattered throughout the Palace of Nestor suggesting it was destroyed completely in an act of war.
Menelaion	Single-Building	Unknown	Much of the Menelaion was excavated without record, leaving little clues for the possible cause. No other structures were destroyed ca. 1200 BCE.
Crete			
Kannia	Partial	Natural	Three refurbished rooms from a LM I villa collapsed without burning. This was likely from a natural cause, though not necessarily an earthquake.
Kato Gouves	Partial	Unknown	Some structural collapse with no evidence of burning was uncovered. The state of publication is too sparse to conclude the extent or cause.
Anatolia			
Hisarlık-Troy	Site-Wide	Warfare	Weapons were uncovered in nonstorage locations. Destruction was rampant and several individuals were killed.
Karaoğlan	Partial	Unknown	At least one individual died in the destruction. However, the published information is unclear on the cause or scale. Destruction may predate the end of the Late Bronze Age.

Region/Site	Scale	Cause	Description
Oymaağaç Höyük-Nerik	Single-Building	Unknown	The Jüngerer Tempel was burnt, but it had been cleared to the floor level by later activities at the site. There is no indication of cause.
Boğazköy-Hattusa	Multibuilding	Arson	The site was abandoned prior to the burning of some but not all of the monumental structures.
Maşat Höyük	Single-Building	Unknown	A single house was burnt, which possibly took place in the mid-thirteenth century BCE, not ca. 1200 BCE. No indication of cause.
Fraktin	Single-Building	Unknown	A single house was burnt, likely after the Hittite Empire had already collapsed, based on a LH IIIC stirrup jar uncovered in the debris.
Kuşaklı-Sarissa	Multibuilding	Warfare	Much of the site lay in ruins when Temple 1 and other structures were burnt. Weapons were found in the destruction debris. It was possibly prior to ca. 1200 BCE.
Kilise Tepe	Site-Wide	Unknown	The site was burnt, likely after it had been partially abandoned. There is no clear cause. It likely took place well after the destructions at Mersin and Tarsus.
Soli Höyük	Partial	Unknown	The remains are so fragmentary it is unclear if there was a destruction, and if so, what was the cause or extent.
Mersin-Yumuktepe	Multibuilding	Unknown	Burning was found in several structures, though the houses may have been avoided. This event possibly took place earlier in the thirteenth century BCE.

Region/Site	Scale	Cause	Description
Tarsus-Gözlükule	Site-Wide	Unknown	All buildings were burnt, possibly by warfare. C14 dating might indicate this took place earlier in the thirteenth century BCE.
Kinet Höyük	Partial	Unknown	Evidence of burning is minor based on the paucity of finds from the end of the Late Bronze Age. It is unclear if there was a destruction, and if so, what was the cause or extent.
Norşuntepe	Multibuilding	Warfare	An arrowhead was lodged in a wall, likely indicating warfare. This is provisional as the publications are sparse in details.
Cyprus			
Enkomi	Partial	Unknown	It is unclear if this was a destruction, as burning was rare. Much of the debris could have resulted from a brief hiatus, causing the partial deterioration of some walls.
Pyla-*Kokkinokremos*	Partial	Earthquake	Several walls were tilted east, and part of the plateau collapsed on several rooms. Unclear if this preceded the site's abandonment or if abandonment occurred later.
Kalavasos-*Ayios Dhimitrios*	Single-Building	Accidental	Building X was reused by squatters after the site had been abandoned. It partially burned, likely in an accidental fire.
Apliki *Karamallos*	Single-Building	Unknown	A single storage building burned, possibly accidentally. No other buildings were damaged. There is no clear cause.
Maa *Paleokastro*	Site-Wide	Warfare	Weapons were uncovered strewn throughout the site indicating warfare. The site was rebuilt after destruction and was later abandoned without destruction.

Region/Site	Scale	Cause	Description
Northern Levant			
Ras Shamra	Site-Wide	Warfare	Dozens of weapons were scattered throughout open spaces and streets in a domestic area. All areas of the site were burnt except for the *Ville Sud*.
Ras Ibn Hani	Single-Building	Arson	Only the *Palais Nord* was burnt, as all other buildings were untouched. It appears that the site was abandoned prior to this destruction event.
Tell Kazel	Multibuilding	Warfare	Only the buildings in Area IV show evidence of destruction. Scattered weapons throughout domestic structures and on a street indicate warfare.
Tell Afis	Multibuilding	Unknown	Possibly arson, as the monumental structure may have been targeted, though this is unclear. The date is possibly after end of the Late Bronze Age.
Tell Qarqur	Multibuilding	Unknown	Evidence of destruction has been uncovered in two structures, but there is no clear extent or cause based on the current information.
Meskene-Emar	Multibuilding	Arson	Site was partially abandoned and only the monumental structures were burnt. Houses were left untouched, even those adjoining a temple that was burnt.
Southern Levant			
Tel Yin'am	Multibuilding	Unknown	Several buildings were burnt while others were untouched. The destruction was possibly earlier in the thirteenth century BCE.
Tel Qashish	Partial	Unknown	The end of the Late Bronze Age remains were highly disturbed. It is unclear if there was a destruction, and if so, what was the cause or extent.

Region/Site	Scale	Cause	Description
Jokneam	Multibuilding	Unknown	Two buildings show evidence of burning. No clear cause, as much of the Late Bronze Age site was removed or is covered by Iron II remains.
Tel Nami	Partial	Natural	No burning was uncovered. A natural event appears to have caused the superstructure to collapse, perhaps during a storm, given the layer of mud on the floor.
Megiddo VIIB	Single-Building	Unknown	There is no evidence of destruction outside of some possible material from Area AA, which is equivocal. It is possible Megiddo had no destruction ca. 1200 BCE.
Tel Hefer	Partial	Unknown	A storage room burnt. However, it is unclear if there was a destruction, and if so, what was the cause or extent.
Aphek	Site-Wide	Warfare	Palace VI was the sole structure when it was destroyed by fire. Arrowheads were scattered in the debris. This was followed by a local Canaanite phase.
Bethel	Partial	Unknown	The destruction was possibly more extensive, but the publications are unclear and lacking crucial details.
Gezer	Single-Building	Unknown	No evidence of destruction from the Dever excavations. In the renewed excavations, a single building was burnt. Merenptah does not claim he destroyed Gezer.
Tel Mor VII	Single-Building	Unknown	The Egyptian garrison was burnt with no clear cause. A new building was constructed that maintained the Egyptian characteristics in Stratum VI.

Region/Site	Scale	Cause	Description
Tel Mor VI	Single-Building	Natural	Structural collapse without fire, likely as a result of mud bricks on a foundation of sand. The building was rebuilt and then abandoned without destruction.
Tel Miqne-Ekron	Single-Building	Unknown	Single storage unit was burnt. This was followed by a local Canaanite phase that was then replaced by the Philistine city without an intervening destruction.
Tel Zippor	Single-Building	Unknown	A single storage unit was burnt, while the nearby temple was left untouched. It is possible this was accidental, but this is unclear.
Lachish: Area S	Single-Building	Accidental	A domestic structure was burnt in a likely accidental fire, as the most intense damage was in the kitchen. New excavations may change this interpretation.
Lachish: Fosse Temple	Single-Building	Arson/Termination Ritual	Building appears to have been ritually terminated. It may have been replaced by the temple in Area P Level VI. Area P was not abandoned without destruction ca. 1200 BCE.
Tel 'Eton	Partial	Unknown	It is unclear from the limited finds if there was a destruction, and if so, what was its cause or extent.
Tell Beit Mirsim	Partial	Unknown	Albright published no clear evidence of a destruction. It might be that the site did not suffer a destruction ca. 1200 BCE.
Tel Haror	Partial	Unknown	A mud-brick building was burnt with no other evidence of destruction. No clear cause based on the limited published information.

Region/Site	Scale	Cause	Description
Tell el-Fukhar	Single-Building	Unknown	The palace was burnt only after it had been transformed into a squatter's abode. There is no clear cause, as there is no overt evidence of an earthquake.
Umm ad-Dananir	Partial	Unknown	One corner of a building had evidence of burning. It is unclear if there was a destruction, and if so, what was the cause or extent.
Tall al-'Umayri	Single-Building	Earthquake	Building C was burnt after an apparent earthquake. The building had already been transformed into a squatter's abode prior to destruction.

References

Adams, Matthew J. and Margaret Cohen 2013. "The 'Sea Peoples' in Primary Sources." Pages 645–64 in *The Philistines and Other "Sea Peoples" in Text and Archaeology*. Edited by Ann E. Killebrew and Gunnar Lehmann. ABS 15. Atlanta: Society of Biblical Literature.

Adamthwaite, Murray R. 2001. *Late Hittite Emar: The Chronology, Synchronisms, and Socio-Political Aspects of a Late Bronze Age Fortress Town*. ANESSup 8. Louvain: Peeters.

Adler, Wolfgang, and Silvia Penner 2001. *Die spätbronzezeitlichen Palastanlagen*. Kāmid el-Lōz 18. Saarbrücker Beiträge zur Altertumskunde 62. Bonn: Habelt.

Adrimi-Sismani, Vassiliki 1994a. "Η Μυκηναϊκή πόλη στο Διμήνι: Νεότερα δεδομένα για την αρχαία Ιωλκό." Pages 17–43 in *Νεότερα δεδομένα των ερευνών για την Αρχαία Ιωλκό: Πρακτικά Επιστημονικής Συνάντησης, 12 Μαΐου 1993*. Volos: Graphe A.E.

———. 1994b. "Ο Μυκηναϊκός οικισμός του Διμηνίου." Pages 225–32 in volume 1 of *ΘΕΣΣΑΛΙΑ: Δεκαπέντε χρόνια αρχαιολογι κης έρευνας, 1975–1990; Αποτελέσματα και Προοπτικές: Πρακτικά διεθνούς ευνεδρίου, Λυών, 17–22 απριλίου 1990*. 2 vols. Athens: Kapon.

———. 2003. "Μυκηναϊκή Ιωλκός." *Αρχαιολογικά Ανάλεκτα εξ Αθηνών* 32–34:71–100.

———. 2004. "Le Palais de Iolkos et sa Destruction." *BCH* 128–129:1–54. DOI:10.3406/bch.2004.7349.

———. 2006. "The Palace of Iolkos and Its End." Pages 465–81 in *Ancient Greece: From the Mycenaean Palaces to the Age of Homer*. Edited by Sigrid Deger-Jalkotzy and Irene S. Lemos. Edinburgh Leventis Studies 3. Edinburgh: Edinburgh University Press.

———. 2007a. "Mycenaean Northern Borders Revisited: New Evidence from Thessaly." Pages 159–77 in *Rethinking Mycenaean Palaces II*. Edited by Michael L. Galaty and William A. Parkinson. 2nd ed. Monograph 60. Los Angeles: Cotsen Institute of Archaeology, University of California.

———. 2007b. "Iolkos: Myth, Archaeology and History" Pages 20–32 in vol. 1 of *The Argonautica and World Culture*. Edited by Rismag Gordeziani. 2 vols. Phasis 10. Tbilisi: Ivane Javakhishvili State University.

———. 2011. "Habitation Changes in the Eastern Coastal Thessaly Following the Destruction of the Palaces at the End of LH IIIB2." Pages 313–30 in *The "Dark Ages" Revisited: Acta of an International Symposium in Memory of William D. E. Coulson, University of Thessaly, Volos, 14–17 June 2007*. Edited by Alexander Mazarakis Ainian. 2 vols. Volos: University of Thessaly Press.

———. 2013. *Ο μυκηναϊκός οικισμός Διμηνίου, 1977–1997: 20 χρόνια ανασκαφών*. Volos: Hellenic Ministry of Culture, Archaeological Institute of Thessalian Studies.

———. 2016. "Dimini: An Urban Settlement of the Late Bronze Age in the Pagasitic Gulf." Pages 39–61 in *RA-PI-NE-U: Studies on the Mycenaean World Offered to Robert Laffineur for His 70th Birthday*. Edited by Jan M. Driessen. Aegis 10. Louvain: Presses Universitaires de Louvain.

304 REFERENCES

———. 2020. "The Destruction of Mycaenean Centres in Eastern Thessaly." Pages 23–34 in *Collapse and Transformation: The Late Bronze Age to Early Iron Age in the Aegean.* Edited by Guy D. Middleton. Oxford: Oxbow. DOI: 10.2307/j.ctv13pk6k9.10.

Ahlström, Gösta W., Gary Orin Rollefson, and Diana Vikander Edelman. 1993. *The History of Ancient Palestine from the Palaeolithic Period to Alexander's Conquest.* JSOTSup 146. Sheffield: JSOT Press.

Alaura, Silvia. 2020. "The Much-Fabled End of the Hittite Empire: Tracing the History of a Crucial Topic." Pages 9–30 in *Anatolia between the 13th and 12th Century BCE.* Edited by Stefano de Martino and Elena Devecchi. Eothen 23. Firenze: LoGisma.

Albright, William Foxwell. 1926. "The Excavations at Tell Beit Mirsim." *BASOR* 23:2–14. DOI: 10.2307/1354957.

———. 1930. "The Third Campaign at Tell Beit Mirsim." *BASOR* 39:1–10. DOI: 10.2307/1354839.

———. 1932. *The Pottery of the First Three Campaigns.* Vol. 1 of *The Excavation of Tell Beit Mirsim in Palestine.* AASOR 12. New Haven: Yale University Press.

———. 1934. "The Kyle Memorial Excavation at Bethel." *BASOR* 56:2–15. DOI: 10.2307/1355123.

———. 1935. "A Summary of Archaeological Research during 1934 in Palestine, Transjordan, and Syria." *AJA* 39:137–48. DOI: 10.2307/498771.

———. 1938. *The Excavation of Tell Beit Mirsim.* Vol. 2: *The Bronze Age.* AASOR 17. New Haven, Conn.: Yale University Press.

———. 1939. "The Israelite Conquest of Canaan in the Light of Archaeology." *BASOR* 74:11–23. DOI: 10.2307/3218878.

———. 1963. *The Biblical Period from Abraham to Ezra.* Harper Torchbooks. New York: Harper & Row.

———. 1967. "Debir." Pages 207–20 in *Archaeology and Old Testament Study: Jubilee Volume of the Society for Old Testament Study 1917–1967.* Edited by David Winston Thomas. Oxford: Clarendon.

———. 1974. *The Archaeology of Palestine and the Bible.* Richards Lectures 1931. Cambridge: American Schools of Oriental Research.

———. 1993. "Beit Mirsim, Tell." *NEAEHL* 1:177–80.

Alkim, U. Bahadir. 1952a. "Summary of Archaeological Work in Turkey during 1951: Karatepe." *AnSt* 2:19–20. DOI: 10.2307/3642364.

———. 1952b. "Sixth Season's Work at Karatepe." *Belleten* 16:134–36.

———. 1952c. "The Results of the Recent Excavations at Domuztepe." *Belleten* 16:238–50.

Al-Maqdissi, Michel, Massaoud Badawy, Joachim Bretschneider, Greta Jans, Klaas Vansteenhuyse, Gabriella Voet, and Karel Van Lerberghe. 2008. "The Occupation Levels of Tell Tweini and Their Historical Implications." Pages 341–350 in *Proceedings of the 51st Rencontre Assyriologique Internationale, Held at the Oriental Institute of the University of Chicago, July 18–22, 2005.* Edited by Robert D. Biggs, Jennie Myers, and Martha T. Roth. SAOC 62. Chicago: Oriental Institute of the University of Chicago.

Al-Maqdissi, Michel, Yves Calvet, Valérie Matoïan, Khozama Al-Bahloul, Christophe Benech, Jean-Claude Bessac, Éric Coqueugniot, et al. 2010. "Rapport préliminaire sur les activités de la mission syro-française de Ras Shamra-Ougarit en 2007 et 2008 (67e et 68e campagnes)." *Syria* 87:21–51.

Ålin, Per. 1962. *Das Ende der mykenischen Fundstätten auf dem griechischen Festland.* Studies in Mediterranean Archaeology 1. Lund: Boktryckeri.

REFERENCES 305

Amador, María Correas. 2013. "Ethnoarchaeology as a Tool for a Holistic Understanding of Mudbrick Domestic Architecture in Ancient Egypt." *Cuadernos de Prehistoria y Arqueología* 39:65–80.

Ambers, Janet, Keith Matthews, and Sheridan Bowman. 1989. "British Museum Natural Radiocarbon Measurements XXI." *Radiocarbon* 31:15–32. DOI: 10.1017/S0033822200013205.

Ambraseys, N. N. 2006. "Earthquakes and Archaeology." *JArS* 33:1008–16. DOI: 10.1016/j.jas.2005.11.006.

Anati, Emmanuel. 1963. "Soundings at Tell Abu Hawam." *IEJ* 13:142–43.

———. 1975. "Tell Abu Hawam." *EAEHL* 1:9–12.

Anderson, John J. 1881. *New Manual of General History: With Particular Attention to Ancient and Modern Civilization.* New York: Maynard, Merrill & Co.

Anderson William P. 1988. *Sarepta I, the Late Bronze and Iron Age Strata of Area II,Y: The University Museum of the University of Pennsylvania Excavations at Sarafand, Lebanon.* Beirut: Département des publications de l'Université libanaise.

Andreadaki-Vlazaki, Maria. 2010. "Khania (Kydonia)." Pages 518–28 in *The Oxford Handbook of the Bronze Age Aegean (ca. 3000–1000 BC).* Edited by Eric H. Cline. Oxford Handbooks. Oxford: Oxford University Press.

Andrikou, Eleni. 1999. "The Pottery from the Destruction Layer of the Linear B Archive in Pelopidou Street, Thebes." Pages 79–102 in *Floreant Studia Mycenaea: Akten des X Internationalen Mykenologischen Colloquiums in Salzburg (vom 1–5 Mai 1995).* Edited by Sigrid Deger-Jalkotzy. Veröffentlichungen der Mykenischen Kommission 18. Vienna: Österreichischen Akademie der Wissenschaften.

Andrikou, Eleni, Vassilis L Aravantinos, Louis Godart, Anna Sacconi, and Joanita Vroom. 2006. *Thèbes fouilles de la Cadmée II.2: Les tablettes en Linéaire B de la Odos Pelopidou; Le contexte archéologique; La céramique de la Odos Pelopidou et la chronologie du Linéaire B.* Biblioteca di "Pasiphae" 2. Pisa: Istituti Editoriali e Poligrafici Internazionali.

Aravantinos, Vassilis, Louis Godar, and Anna Sacconi. 2001. *Thèbes fouilles de la Cadmée.* Biblioteca di "Pasiphae" 1. Pisa: Istituti Editoriali e Poligrafici Internazionali.

Arie, Eran, and Assaf Nativ. 2013. "Part II: Level K-6." Pages 165–77 in vol. 1 of *Megiddo V: The 2004–2008 Seasons.* Edited by Israel Finkelstein, David Ussishkin, and Eric H Cline. 3 vols. SMNIA 31. Winona Lake, IN: Eisenbrauns. DOI: 10.5325/j.ctv2321hmw.10.

Arık, Remzi Oğuz. 1937a. *Les fouilles d'Alaca Höyük entreprises par la Société d'histoire turque: Rapport préliminaire sur les travaux en 1935.* Publications de la Sociéré d'histoire turque 1. Ankara: Société d'histoire turque.

———. 1937b. "Les premiers résultat des fouilles d'Alaca hüyük." *Belleten* 1:222–34.

———. 1939a. "Ein neuer hethitischer Fundort im Süden von Ankara." *AA* 54:207–23.

———. 1939b. "Le Höyük de Karaöğlan." *Belleten* 3:43–60.

———. 1939c. "Anadolu'nun En Garp Eti İstasyonu Karaoğlan Höyüğü." *Belleten* 3:27–42.

Arnaud, Daniel. 1975. "Les textes d'Emar et la chronologie de la fin du bronze recent." *Syria* 52:87–92.

———. 1986. *Recherches au pays d'Aštata. Emar, VI/3: Textes sumeriens et accadiens.* Synthèse 18. Paris: Editions Recherche sur les civilisations.

Arnhold Simone. 2009. *Das hethitische Gebäude E auf der Akropolis von Kuşaklı.* Kuşaklı-Sarissa 4. Rahden: Leidorf.

———. 2014. "Die Altınyayla Ovası Das Umland von Kuşaklı-Sarissa. Entwicklung und

Ressourcennutzung der Kulturlandschaft in einer Zentralanatolischen Siedlungskammer." PhD diss., Philipps-Universität Marburg.

Artzy, Michel. 1985. "Merchandise and Merchantmen: On Ships and Shipping in the Late Bronze Age Levant." Pages 135–140 in *Acts of the Second International Cyprological Congress*. Edited by Theodoros Papadopoullos and Stelios Chatzestylli. Nicosia: Society of Cypriot Studies.

———. 1990a. "Tel Nami 1985/1988." *ESI* 9:22–24.

———. 1990b. "Nami Land and Sea Project, 1985–1988." *IEJ* 40:73–76.

———. 1991. "Nami Land and Sea Project, 1989." *IEJ* 41:194–97.

———. 1992. "Tel Nami: 1989/1991." *Excavations and Surveys in Israel* 12:24–27.

———. 1993. "Nami, Tel." *NEAEHL* 3:1095–98.

———. 1995. "Nami: A Second Millennium International Maritime Trading Center in the Mediterranean." Pages 17–40 in *Recent Excavations in Israel: A View to the West; Reports on Kabri, Nami, Miqne-Ekron, Dor, and Ashkelon*. Edited by Seymour Gitin. Dubuque: Kendall/Hunt Publishing Co.

———. 1997. "Nomads of the Sea." Pages 1–16 in *Res Maritimae: Cyprus and the Eastern Mediterranean from Prehistory to Late Antiquity*. Edited by Stuart Swiny, Robert L. Hohlfelder, and Helena Wylde Swiny. ASORAR 4. Atlanta: Scholars Press.

———. 1998. "Routes, Trade, Boats and 'Nomads of the Sea.'" Pages 439–48 in *Mediterranean Peoples in Transition: Thirteenth to Early Tenth Centuries B.C.E.; In Honor of Professor Trude Dothan*. Edited by Seymour Gitin, Amihai Mazar, and Ephraim Stern. Jerusalem: Israel Exploration Society.

———. 2006. "The Carmel Coast during the Second Part of the Late Bronze Age: A Center for Eastern Mediterranean Transshipping." *BASOR* 343:45–64. DOI: 10.1086/BASOR25066964.

———. 2007. "Tell Abu Hawam: News from the Late Bronze Age." Pages 357–66 in *The Synchronization of Civilizations in the Eastern Mediterranean in the Second Millennium B.C. III: Proceedings of the SCIEM 2000–2nd EuroConference, Vienna, 28th of May–1st of June 2003*. Edited by Manfred Bietak. Denkschriften der Gesamtakademie 37. Vienna: Austrian Akademie of Sciences.

———. 2013. "The Importance of the Anchorages of the Carmel Coast in the Trade Networks during the Late Bronze Period." *Michmanim* 24:7–24.

Artzy, Michel, and R. Beeri. 2010. "Tel Akko." Pages 15–23 in *One Thousand Nights and Days: Akko through the Ages*. Edited by Ann E. Killebrew and Vered Raz-Romeo. Hecht Museum Catalogue 31. Haifa: Hecht Museum.

Artzy, Michel, and Svetlana Zagorski. 2012. "Cypriot 'Mycenaean' IIIB Imported to the Levant." Pages 1–12 in *All the Wisdom of the East: Studies in Near Eastern Archaeology and History in Honor of Eliezer D. Oren*. Edited by Mayer Gruber, Shmuel Aḥituv, Gunnar Lehmann, and Zipora Talshir. OBO 255. Fribourg: Academic Press; Göttingen: Vandenhoeck & Ruprecht.

Ashkenazi, Dana, Shlomo Bunimovitz, and Adin Stern 2016. "Archaeometallurgical Investigation of Thirteenth–twelfth Centuries BCE Bronze Objects from Tel Beth-Shemesh, Israel." *JArS: Reports* 6:170–81. DOI: 10.1016/j.jasrep.2016.02.006.

Aslan, Carolyn. 2019. "The West Sanctuary at Troy in the Protogeometric, Geometric, and Archaic Periods: Late Bronze Age; Troy VI, VIIA, and VIIB Phases." Pages 42–62 in *Troy Excavation Project Final Reports: The West Sanctuary I; Iron Age–Classical*. Edited by Charles Brian Rose, Kathleen M. Lynch, and Getzel M. Cohen. Bonn: Habelt.

REFERENCES 307

Asscher, Yotam, Dan Cabanes, Louise A Hitchcock, Aren M. Maeir, Steve Weiner, and Elisabetta Boaretto. 2015a. "Radiocarbon Dating Shows an Early Appearance of Philistine Material Culture in Tell Es-Safi/Gath, Philistia." *Radiocarbon* 57:825–50. DOI: 10.2458/azu_rc.57.18391.

Asscher, Yotam, Gunnar Lehmann, Steven A. Rosen, Steve Weiner, and Elisabetta Boaretto. 2015b. "Absolute Dating of the Late Bronze to Iron Age Transition and the Appearance of Philistine Culture in Qubur el-Walaydah, Southern Levant." *Radiocarbon* 57:77–97. DOI: 10.2458/azu_rc.57.16961.

Åström, Paul. 1985. "The Sea Peoples in the Light of New Excavations." *Cahiers du Centre d'Etudes Chypriotes* 3:3–18.

———. 1986. "Hala Sultan Tekke: An International Harbour Town of the Late Cypriot Bronze Age." *OpAth* 16:7–17.

———. 1998. "Continuity or Discontinuity: Indigenous and Foreign Elements in Cyprus around 1200 BCE." Pages 80–86 in *Mediterranean Peoples in Transition: Thirteenth to Early Tenth Centuries B.C.E.; In Honor of Professor Trude Dothan.* Edited by Seymour Gitin, Amihai Mazar, and Ephraim Stern. Jerusalem: Israel Exploration Society.

———. 2001. "The Travels of Opheltas: Catastrophes in Greece and Cyprus c. 1190 BC." *Archaeologia Cypria* 4:115–22.

Åström, Paul, and Katie Demakopoulou. 1986. "New Excavations in the Citadel of Midea, 1983–1984." *OpAth* 16:19–25.

———. 1996. "Signs of an Earthquake at Midea?" Pages 37–40 in *Archaeoseismology.* Edited by Stathis C. Stiros and R. E. Jones. Fitch Laboratory Occasional Papers 7. Athens: Institute of Geology & Mineral Exploration; British School at Athens.

Åström, Paul, Katie Demakopoulou, Nicoletta Divari-Valakou, and Peter. M. Fischer. 1992. "Excavations in Midea, 1989–1990." *OpAth* 19:11–22.

Åström, Paul, Katie Demakopoulou, Nicoletta Divari-Valakou, and Gisela Walberg. 1990. "Excavations in Midea 1987." *OpAth* 18:9–22.

Åström, Paul, Katie Demakopoulou, and Gisela Walberg. 1988. "Excavations in Midea, 1985." *OpAth* 17:7–11.

Astour, Michael. 1959. "Les étrangers a Ugarit et le statut juridique des Ḫabiru." *RA* 53:70–76.

———. 1965. "New Evidence on the Last Days of Ugarit." *AJA* 69:253–58. DOI: 10.2307/502290.

Avigad, Nahman. 1976. "Jerishe, Tell." *EAEHL* 2:575–78.

Avi-Yonah, Michael, and Israel Eph'al. 1975. "Ashkelon." *EAEHL* 1:121–30.

Bachhuber, Christoph, and R. Gareth Roberts, eds. 2009 *Forces of Transformation: The End of the Bronze Age in the Mediterranean; Proceedings of an International Symposium Held at St. John's College, University of Oxford, 25–6th March 2006.* Oxford: Oxbow.

Badre, Leila. 1997. "Arwad." *OEANE* 1:218–19.

———. 2006. "Tell Kazel–Simyra: A Contribution to a Relative Chronological History in the Eastern Mediterranean during the Late Bronze Age." *BASOR* 343:65–95. DOI: 10.1086/BASOR25066965.

———. 2008. "The Religious Architecture in the Bronze Age: Middle Bronze Beirut and Late Bronze Tell Kazel." Pages 253–70 in *Interconnections in the Eastern Mediterranean Lebanon in the Bronze and Iron Ages: Proceedings of the International*

308 REFERENCES

Symposium Beirut 2008. Edited by Anne-Marie Maïla-Afeiche. BAAL 6. Beirut: Minstère de la culture, Direction Générale des Antiquités.

Badre, Leila, and Eric Gubel. 1999–2000. "Tell Kazel, Syria: Excavations of the AUB Museum, 1993–1998; Third Preliminary Report." *Berytus* 44:123–203.

Badre, Leila, Eric Gubel, Emmanuelle Capet, Nadine Panayot, Dominique Collon, and Françoise Briquel-Chatonnet. 1994. "Tell Kazel (Syrie), Rapport préliminaire sur les 4e–8e campagnes de fouilles (1988–1992)." *Syria* 71:259–351+353–59.

Balensi Jacqueline. 2004. "Relativité du phénomène mycénien à Tell Abou Hawam: un 'proto-marketing'?" Pages 141–81 in *La Céramique mycénienne de l'Égée au Levant: Hommage à Vronwy Hankey; Table ronde internationale, Maison de l'Orient et de la Méditerranée, 20 mars 1999.* Edited by Jacqueline Balensi, Jean-Yves Monchambert, and Sylvie Muller Celka. Travaux de la Maison de l'Orient et de la Méditerranée 41. Lyon: Maison de l'Orient et de la Méditerranée.

Baltacıoğlu, Hatçe. 2008. "Alaca Höyük Geç Tunç Çağı Yapı Kompleksinin (Tapınak/ Tapınak-Saray/Saray) Tanımı." Pages 23–39 in *Batı Anadolu ve Doğu Akdeniz Geç Tunç Çağı Kültürleri Üzerine Yeni Araştırmalar.* Edited by Armağan Erkanal-Öktü, Sevinç Günel, and Ulaş Deniz. Ankara: Hacettepe Üniversitesi.

Barako, Tristan. J. 2007a. "Stratigraphy and Building Remains." Pages 11–42 in *Tel Mor: The Moshe Dothan Excavations, 1959–1960.* Edited by Tristan J. Barako. IAAR 32. Jerusalem: Israel Antiquities Authority.

———. 2007b. "Summary and Historical Conclusions." Pages 239–48 in *Tel Mor: The Moshe Dothan Excavations, 1959–1960.* Edited by Tristan J. Barako. IAAR 32. Jerusalem: Israel Antiquities Authority.

———. 2007c. "Canaanite and Philistine Pottery." Pages 43–128 in *Tel Mor: The Moshe Dothan Excavations, 1959–1960.* Edited by Tristan J. Barako. IAAR 32. Jerusalem: Israel Antiquities Authority.

———. 2013. "Philistines and Egyptians in the Southern Coastal Canaan during the Early Iron Age." Pages 37–51 in *The Philistines and Other "Sea Peoples" in Text and Archaeology.* Edited by Ann E. Killebrew and Gunner Lehman. ABS 15. Atlanta: Society of Biblical Literature.

Barber, Robin L. 1981. "The Late Cycladic Period: A Review." *ABSA* 76:1–21.

Bargueño, Javier García, Jesús García García, José María Martín García, and Paz Ramírez Valiente. 2013. "Los Pueblos del Mar a través de las tendencias historiográficas." *Ab Initio: Revista digital para estudiantes de Historia* 4.8:3–43.

Barkay, Gabriel, and David Ussishkin 2004. "Area S: The Late Bronze Age Strata." Pages 316–410 in vol. 1 of *The Renewed Archaeological Excavations at Lachish (1973–1994).* Edited by David Ussishkin. 5 vols. SMNIA 22. Tel Aviv: Emery and Claire Yass Publications in Archaeology.

Barnett, Richard David. 1940. "Explorations in Cilicia, The Nielsen Expedition: Fifth Interim Report; Excavation at Mersin, 1938–39; The Greek Pottery." *AAA* 26:98–130.

———. 1975. "The Sea Peoples." Pages 359–78 in *The Middle East and the Aegean Region c. 1380–1000 BC.* Edited by I. E. S. Edwards, C. J. Gadd, N. G. L. Hammond, and E. Sollberger. 3rd ed. CAH 2.2. Cambridge: Cambridge University Press.

Bass, George. F. 1961. "The Cape Gelidonya Wreck: Preliminary Report." *AJA* 65:267–76. DOI: http://doi.org/10.2307/501687

———. 2010. "Cape Gelidonya Shipwreck." Pages 797–803 in *The Oxford Handbook of the*

REFERENCES 309

Bronze Age Aegean (ca. 3000–1000 BC). Edited by Eric H. Cline. Oxford Handbooks. Oxford: Oxford University Press.

——. 2013. "Cape Gelidonya Redux." Pages 62–71 in *Cultures in Contact: From Mesopotamia to the Mediterranean in the Second Millennium B.C.* Edited by Joan Aruz, Sarah B. Graff, and Yelena Rakic. New Haven: Yale University Press.

Bass, George F., Peter Throckmorton, Joan Du Plat Taylor, J. B. Hennessy, Alan R. Shulman, and Hans-Günter Buchholz. 1967. "Cape Gelidonya: A Bronze Age Shipwreck." *TAPA* 57:1–177. DOI: 10.2307/1005978.

Batziou-Efstathiou, Anthi. 2012. "Ανασκαφή μυκηναϊκού οικισμού στα Πευκάκια 2006–2008." Pages 177–92 in Αρχαιολογικο εργο Θεσσαλιας και Στερεας Ελλαδας 3: Πρακτικα επιστημονικης συναντησης, Βολος 27.2–2.3.2003. 2 vols. Volos: Hypourgeio.

——. 2016. "Η τελική φάση κατοίκησης του Μυκηναϊκού οικισμού στα Πευκάκια." Pages 135–44 in vol. 1 of Αρχαιολογικο εργο Θεσσαλιας και Στερεας Ελλαδας 4: Πρακτικα επιστημονικης συναντησης, Βολος 15.3–18.3.2012. Volos: Ekdosē tou Tameiou Archaiologikōn Porōn & Apallotriōseōn.

Baumann, Stefan W. E. 2020. "Historicity and Visual Language in the War Scenes of Ramses III and the Sea People." Pages 339–70 in *From Past to Present: Studies in Memory of Manfred O. Korfmann*. Edited by Stefan W. E. Baumann, Turan Efe, Tobias L. Kienlin, and Ernst Pernicka. Studia Troica Monographien 11. Bonn: Habelt.

Baumbach, Lydia. 1983. "An Examination of the Evidence for a State of Emergency at Pylos c. 1200 B.C. from the Linear B Tablets." Pages 28–40 in *Res Mycenaeae: Akten des VII. Internationalen mykenologischen Colloquiums in Nürnberg 1981 vom 6.–10. April 1981*. Edited by A. Heubeck and Günter Neumann. Göttingen: Vandenhoeck & Ruprecht.

Beal, Richard H. 2011. "Hittite Anatolia: A Political History." Pages 579–603 in *The Oxford Handbook of Ancient Anatolia 10,000–323 B.C.E.* Edited by Sharon R. Steadman and Gregory McMahon. Oxford Handbooks. Oxford: Oxford University Press.

Bechar, Shlomit, Amnon Ben-Tor, Ido Wachtel, Daphna Ben-Tor, Elisabetta Boaretto, and Philipp Stockhammer. 2021. "The Destruction of Late Bronze Age Hazor." *AeL* 31:45–74. https://doi.org/10.1553/AEundL31s45

Beckman, Gary. 1997. "Plague Prayers of Muršili II." *COS* 1.60:156–60.

Becks, Ralf. 2006. "Troia in der späten Bronzezeit: Troia VI und Troia VIIa." Pages 155–66 in *Troia: Archäologie eines Siedlungshügels und seiner Landschaft*. Edited by Manfred Korfmann. Mainz: von Zabern.

Bell, John, Joseph Jopling, John Laird, D. K. Clark, Duglad Cambell, and Henry W. Reveley. 1859. *The Journal of the Society of Arts* 7:475–90.

Bell, Carol. 2006 *The Evolution of Long Distance Trading Relationships across the LBA/ Iron Age Transition on the Northern Levantine Coast*. BARIS 1574. Oxford: Archaeopress.

——. 2009. "Continuity and Change: The Divergent Destinies of Late Bronze Age Ports in Syria and Lebanon across the LBA/Iron Age Transition." Pages 30–38 in *Forces of Transformation: End of the Bronze Age in the Mediterranean; Proceedings of an International Symposium Held at St. John's College, University of Oxford, 25–26th March 2006*. Edited by Cristopher Bachhuber and R. Gareth Roberts. Oxford: Oxbow.

——. 2012. "The Merchants of Ugarit: Oligarchs of the Late Bronze Age Trade in Metals?" Pages 180–87 in *Eastern Mediterranean Metallurgy and Metalwork in the Second Millennium BC: A Conference in Honour of James D. Muhly; Nicosia 10–11 October 2009.* Edited by Vasiliki Kassianidou and George Papasavvas. Oxford: Oxbow.

Ben-Ami, Doron. 2005a. "The Architecture and Stratigraphy of the Late Bronze Age." Pages 141–64 in *Yoqne'am III the Middle and Late Bronze Ages Final Report of the Archaeological Excavations (1977–1988).* Edited by Amnon Ben-Tor, Doron Ben Ami, and Ariella Livneh. Qedem Reports 7. Jerusalem: Institute of Archaeology.

———. 2005b. "The Pottery of the Late Bronze Age." Pages 165–240 in *Yoqne'am III the Middle and Late Bronze Ages Final Report of the Archaeological Excavations (1977–1988).* Edited by Amnon Ben-Tor, Doron Ben Ami, and Ariella Livneh. Qedem Reports 7. Jerusalem: Institute of Archaeology.

Bendall, Lisa M. 2003. "A Reconsideration of the Northeastern Building at Pylos: Evidence for a Mycenaean Redistributive Center." *AJA* 107:181–231.

———. 2013. "Pylos." Pages 5677–78 in vol. 10 of *The Encyclopedia of Ancient History.* Edited by Roger S. Bagnall, Kai Brodersen, Craige Brian Champion, Andrew Erskine, and Sabine R. Huebner. 13 vols. Chichester: Wiley-Blackwell.

Ben-Dor Evian, Shirly. 2015. "'They Were *thr* on Land, Others at Sea': The Etymology of the Egyptian Term for 'Sea–Peoples.'" *Sem* 57:57–75. DOI: 10.2143/SE.57.0.3115456.

———. 2016. "The Battles between Ramesses III and the 'Sea-Peoples.'" *ZÄS* 143:151–68. DOI: 10.1515/zaes-2016-0010.

———. 2017. "Ramesses III and the 'Sea–Peoples': Towards a New Philistine Paradigm; Ramesses III and the 'Sea Peoples.'" *OJA* 36:267–85. DOI: 10.1111/ojoa.12115

———. 2019. "Représentations des 'peuples de la mer' dans l'iconographie du Proche-Orient ancien: Vers la formulation d'un nouveau paradigme philistin." Pages 127–41 in *Représenter dieux et hommes dans le Proche-Orient ancien et dans la Bible: Actes du colloque organisé par le Collège de France,Paris, les 5 et 6 mai 2015.* Edited by Thomas Römer, Hervé Gonzalez, and Lionel Marti. OBO 287. Leuven: Peeters.

Ben-Dov, Rachel. 2009. *Dan III: Avraham Biran Excavations 1966–1999: The Late Bronze Age.* Jerusalem: Nelson Glueck School of Biblical Archaeology/Hebrew Union College.

Ben-Shlomo, David. 2011. "Early Iron Age Domestic Material Culture in Philistia and an Eastern Mediterranean Koiné." Pages 183–206 in *Household Archaeology in Ancient Israel and Beyond.* Assaf Yasur-Landau, Jennie R. Ebeling, and Laura B. Mazow. CHANE 50. Leiden: Brill. DOI: 10.1163/ej.9789004206250.i-452.64.

———. 2012. "Tell Ğemme during the Bronze Age and Canaanite Household Archaeology." *ZDPV* 128:133–57.

———. 2014a. "Field I: The Late Bronze Age." Pages 209–336 in *The Smithsonian Institution Excavation at Tell Jemmeh, Israel, 1970–1990.* Edited by David Ben-Shlomo and Gus W. Van Beek. SCAn 50. Washington, DC: Smithsonian Institution Scholarly Press.

———. 2014b. "Synthesis and Conclusions: The Significance of Tell Jemmeh." Pages 1054–65 in *The Smithsonian Institution Excavation at Tell Jemmeh, Israel, 1970–1990.* Edited by David Ben-Shlomo and Gus W. Van Beek. SCAn 50. Washington, DC: Smithsonian Institution Scholarly Press.

Benson, Jack Leonard. 1969. "Bamboula at Kourion." *RDAC* 1969:1–28.

———. 1970. "Bamboula at Kourion." *RDAC* 1970:25–74.

REFERENCES   311

Ben-Tor, Amnon. 1993a. "Qashish, Tel." *NEAEHL* 4:1200–1203.

———. 1993b. "Jokneam." *NEAEHL* 3:805–11.

———. 1998. "The Fall of Canaanite Hazor: The 'Who' and 'When' Questions." Pages 456–67 in *Mediterranean Peoples in Transition: Thirteenth to Early Tenth Centuries B.C.E.; In Honor of Professor Trude Dothan*. Edited by Seymour Gitin, Amihai Mazar, and Ephraim Stern. Jerusalem: Israel Exploration Society.

———. 2002. "Hazor: A City State between the Major Powers; A Rejoinder." *SJOT* 16:303–8.

———. 2006. "The Sad Fate of Statues and the Mutilated Statues of Hazor." Pages 3–16 in *Confronting the Past: Archaeological and Historical Essays on Ancient Israel in Honor of William G. Dever*. Edited by Seymour Gitin, J. Edward Wright, and J. P. Dessel. Winona Lake, IN: Eisenbrauns.

———. 2013. "Who Destroyed Canaanite Hazor?" *BAR* 39.4:26–36, 58–60.

Ben-Tor, Amnon, and Ruhama Bonfil. 1988. "Tel Qashish, 1984/1985 Seasons." *ESI* 6:106–8.

———. 2003a. "The Stratigraphy and Pottery Assemblages of the Middle and Late Bronze Ages in Area A." Pages 185–276 in *Tel Qashish: A Village in the Jezreel Valley; Final Report of Archaeological Excavations (1978–1987)*. Edited by Amnon Ben-Tor, Ruhama Bonfil, and Sharon Zuckerman. Qedem Reports 5. Jerusalem: Institute of Archaeology.

———. 2003b. "The Translational Late Bronze/Iron Age Phase to the Persian Period in Area A." Pages 331–63 in *Tel Qashish: A Village in the Jezreel Valley; Final Report of Archaeological Excavations (1978–1987)*. Edited by Amnon Ben-Tor, Ruhama Bonfil, and Sharon Zuckerman. Qedem Reports 5. Jerusalem: Institute of Archaeology.

———. 2003c. "The Middle Bronze Age to the Ottoman Period in Area B." Pages 364–86 in *Tel Qashish: A Village in the Jezreel Valley; Final Report of Archaeological Excavations (1978–1987)*. Edited by Amnon Ben-Tor, Ruhama Bonfil, and Sharon Zuckerman. Qedem Reports 5. Jerusalem: Institute of Archaeology.

Ben-Tor, Amnon, and Maria Teresa Rubiato 1999. "Excavating Hazor, Part 2: Did the Israelites Destroy the Canaanite City?" *BAR* 25.3:22–39.

Ben-Tor, Amnon, and Sharon Zuckerman. 2008. "Hazor at the End of the Late Bronze Age: Back to Basics." *BASOR* 350:1–6. DOI: 10.1086/BASOR25609263.

Ben-Tor, Amnon, Sharon Zuckerman, Shlomit Bechar, and Débora Sandhaus. 2017. *Hazor VII: The 1990–2012 Excavations. The Bronze Age*. Jerusalem: Hebrew University of Jerusalem.

Berger, Daniel, Jeffrey S. Soles, Alessandra R. Giumlia-Mair, Gerhard Brügmann, Ehud Galili, Nicole Lockhoff, and Ernst Pernicka. 2019. "Isotope Systematics and Chemical Composition of Tin Ingots from Mochlos (Crete) and Other Late Bronze Age Sites in the Eastern Mediterranean Sea: An Ultimate Key to Tin Provenance?" *PLoS ONE* 14.6:e0218326. DOI: 10.1371/journal.pone.0218326.

Bergoffen, Celia J. 1989. "A Comparative Study of the Regional Distribution of Cypriot Pottery in Canaan and Egypt in the Late Bronze Age." PhD diss., New York University.

———. 1991. "Overland Trade in Northern Sinai: The Evidence of the Late Cypriot Pottery." *BASOR* 284:59–76. DOI: 10.2307/1357194.

Betancourt, Philip P. 1976. "The End of the Greek Bronze Age." *Antiquity* 50:40–47. DOI: 10.1017/S0003598X00070617.

———. 2000. "The Aegean and the Origin of the Sea Peoples." Pages 297–304 in *The Sea

312   References

Peoples and Their World: A Reassessment. Edited by Eliezer Oren. Museum Monograph 108. Philadelphia: University Museum, University of Pennsylvania. DOI: 10.9783/9781934536438.297.

Beyer, Dominique. 1982. "Bronzes." Pages 119–21 in *Meskéné–Emar: Dix ans de travaux 1972–1982.* Edited by Dominique Beyer. Paris: Éditions recherche sur les civilisations.

———. 2005. "Porsuk (Zeyve Höyük): Rapport sommaire sur la campagne de fouilles de 2004." *AnAnt* 13:295–318.

———. 2008. "Zeyve Höyük (Porsuk): Rapport sommaire sur la campagne de fouilles de 2007." *AnAnt* 16:314–44.

———. 2010. "From the Bronze Age to the Iron Age at Zeyve Höyük/Porsuk: A Temporary Review." Pages 97–109 in *Geo-Archaeological Activities in Southern Cappadocia, Turkey.* Edited by Lorenzo D'Alfonso. StMed 22. Pavia: Italian University Press.

———. 2015. "Quelques nouvelles données sur la chronologie des phases anciennes de Porsuk, du Bronze Moyen à la réoccupation du Fer." Pages 101–10 in *La Cappadoce méridionale de la préhistoire à la période byzantine: 3èmes rencontres d'archéologie de l'IFEA, Istanbul 8–9 Novembre, 2012.* Edited by Dominique Beyer, Olivier Henry, and Aksel Tibet. Istanbul: Institut Français d'Etudes Anatoliennes Georges-Dumézil. DOI: 10.4000/books.ifeagd.3283.

Beyer Dominique, Chalier Isabelle, Françoise Laroche-Traunecker, Stéphane Lebreton, Julie Patrier, and Aksel Tibet. 2006. "Zeyve Höyük (Porsuk): Rapport sommaire sur la campagne de fouilles de 2005." *AnAnt* 14:205–44.

Beyer, Dominique, and Françoise Laroche-Traunecker. 2017. "Le site de zeyve-höyük-porsuk aux époques hittite et néo-hittite: Remarques sur la succession des systèmes défensifs." Pages 229–44 in *Hittitology Today: Studies on Hittite and Neo-Hittite Anatolia in Honor of Emmanuel Laroche's 100th Birthday/L'hittitologie aujourd'hui: études sur l'Anatolie hittite et néo-hittite à l'occasion du centenaire de la naissance d'Emmanuel Laroche.* Edited by Alice Mouton. Istanbul: Institut Français d'Études Anatoliennes Georges Dumézil. DOI: 10.4000/books.ifeagd.3567.

Bietak, Manfred. 1993. "The Sea Peoples and the End of the Egyptian Administration in Canaan." Pages 292–306 in *Biblical Archaeology Today: Proceedings of the Second International Congress on Biblical Archaeology, Jerusalem 1990.* Edited by Avraham Biran, Joseph Aviram, and Alan Paris-Shadur. 2 vols. Jerusalem: Israel Exploration Society.

Bikai, Patricia Maynor. 1978. *The Pottery of Tyre.* Warminster: Aris & Phillips.

———. 1992. "The Phoenicians." Pages 132–41 in *The Crisis Years: The 12th Century B.C.; From Beyond the Danube to the Tigris.* Edited by William A. Ward and Martha Sharp Joukowsky. Dubuque, IA: Kendall/Hunt Publishing.

Biran, Avraham. 1993. "Zippor, Tel." *NEAEHL* 4:1526–27.

Biran, Avraham, and Ora Negbi. 1964. "Tel Ṣippor." *IEJ* 14:284–85.

———. 1965. "Tel Ṣippor." *IEJ* 15:255–56.

———. 1966. "The Stratigraphical Sequence at Tel Ṣippor." *IEJ* 16:160–73.

Bittel, Kurt. 1939. "Untersuchungen in Fraktin." *AA* 54:566–68.

———. 1970. *Hattusha: The Capital of the Hittites.* New York: Oxford University Press.

———. 1977. "Das Ende des Hethiterreiches aufgrund archäologischer Zeugnisse." Pages 36–56 in *Jahresbericht des Instituts für Vorgeschichte der Universität Frankfurt am Main 1976.* Edited by Hermann Müller-Karpe. Munich: Beck.

REFERENCES   313

———. 1983. "Die archäologische Situation in Kleinasien um 1200 v.Chr. und während der nachfolgenden vier Jahrhunderte." Pages 25–47 in *Griechenland, die Agais und die Levante wahrend der Dark Ages vom 12. bis zum 9. Jahrhundert v. Chr.* Edited by Sigrid Deger-Jalkotzy. Mykenische Studien 10. Vienna: Österreichische Akademie der Wissenschaften.

Blakely, Jeffrey A. 2000. "Petrie's Pilaster Building at Tell el-Hesi." Pages 66–80 in *The Archaeology of Jordan and Beyond: Essays in Honor of James A. Sauer.* Edited by Lawrence E. Stager, Joseph A. Greene, and Michael D. Coogan. SAHL 1. Winona Lake, IN: Eisenbrauns. DOI: 10.1163/9789004369801_011.

———. 2018. "Tell el-Hesi: A Type Site for Reevaluating So-Called 'Egyptian Governors' Residencies' of the South." *PEQ* 150:271–95. DOI: 10.1080/00310328.2018.1531537.

Blaylock, S. R., D. H. French, G. D. Summers, C. S. Lightfoot, J. J. Coulton, P. Catling, P. Roberts, and Stephen J. Hill. 1991. "The Year's Work." *AnSt* 41:3–22. DOI: 10.2307/3642928.

Blegen, Carl William. 1921. *Korakou: A Prehistoric Settlement near Corinth.* Boston: American School of Classical Studies at Athens.

———. 1962. *The Mycenaean Age: The Trojan War, the Dorian Invasion, and Other Problems.* Lectures in Memory of Louise Taft Semple 1. Cincinnati: University of Cincinnati.

———. 1975. "Troy VII." Pages 161–64 in *The Middle East and the Aegean Region c. 1380–1000 BC.* Edited by I. E. S. Edwards, C. J. Gadd, N. G. L. Hammond, and E. Sollberger. 3rd ed. CAH 2.2. Cambridge: Cambridge University Press.

Blegen, Carl William, Alfred R. Bellinger, Dorothy Burr Thompson, George Robert Rapp, and John A. Gifford. 1950. *Troy: Excavations Conducted by the University of Cincinnati, 1932–1938.* Princeton: Princeton University Press.

Blegen, Carl William, John L Caskey, and Marion Rawson. 1953. *Troy III: The Sixth Settlement.* 2 vols. Princeton: Princeton University Press.

Blegen, Carl William, and Marion Rawson. 1966. *The Palace of Nestor at Pylos in Western Messenia.* Vol. 1: *The Buildings and Their Contents.* Princeton: Princeton University Press.

———. 1973. *The Palace of Nestor at Pylos in Western Messenia.* Vol. 3: *Acropolis and Lower Town, Tholoi, Grave Circle, and Chamber Tombs, Discoveries Outside the Citadel.* Princeton: Princeton University Press.

Bliss, Frederick Jones. 1894. *A Mound of Many Cities: Or Tell El Hesy Excavated.* London: Watt & Son.

Boehm, Ryan. 2013. "Catastrophe or Resilience? Destruction and Synoikismos in the Hellenistic World." Pages 319–27 in *Destruction: Archaeological, Historical and Philological Perspectives.* Edited by Jan Driessen. Louvain-La-Neuve: Presses Universitaires de Louvain.

Boileau, Marie-Claude, Leila Badre, Emmanuelle Capet, Reinhard Jung, and Hans Mommsen. 2010. "Foreign Ceramic Tradition, Local Clays: The Handmade Burnished Ware of Tell Kazel (Syria)." *JArS* 37:1678–89. DOI: 10.1016/j.jas.2010.01.028.

Bonacossi, D. Morandi. 2013. "The Crisis of Qatna at the Beginning of the Late Bronze Age II and the Iron Age II Settlement Revival: A Regional Trajectory towards the Collapse of the Late Bronze Age Palace System in the Northern Levant." Pages 113–46 in *Across the Border: Late Bronze–Iron Age Relations between Syria and Anatolia; Proceedings of a Symposium Held at the Research Center of Anatolian*

314 REFERENCES

Studies, Koç University, Istanbul, May 31–June 1, 2010. Edited by K Aslihan Yener. ANESSup 42. Leuven: Peeters.

Bordreuil, Pierre, Jacques Lagarce, Élisabeth Lagarce, Adnan Bounni, and Nassib Saliby. 1984. "Les découvertes archéologiques et épigraphiques de Ras Ibn Hani (Syrie) en 1983: Un lot d'archives administratives." *CRAI* 128:398–438.

Borgna, Elisabetta. 1997. "Some Observations on Deep Bowls and Kraters from the "Acropoli Mediana" at Phaistos, in Late Minoan III Pottery." Pages 273–98 in *Chronology and Terminology: Acts of a Meeting Held at the Danish Institute at Athens, August 12–14, 1994.* Edited by Erik Hallager and Birgitta P Hallager. Monographs of the Danish Institute at Athens 1. Athens: Danish Institute at Athens.

———. 2003. "Regional Settlement Patterns, Exchange Systems and Sources of Power in Crete at the End of the Late Bronze Age: Establishing a Connection." *SMEA* 45:153–83.

———. 2007. "LM IIIC Pottery at Phaistos: An Attempt to Integrate Typological Analysis with Stratigraphic Investigation." Pages 55–72 in *LH III C Chronology and Synchronisms II: LH III C Middle; Proceedings of the International Workshop Held at the Austrian Academy of Sciences at Vienna, October 29th and 30th, 2004.* Edited by Sigrid Deger-Jalkotzy and Michaela Zavadil. Veröffentlichungen der Mykenischen Kommission 28. Vienna Österreichische Akademie der Wissenschaften.

———. 2011. "To Return to Late Palatial Phaistos: Preliminary Notes on the LM III Occupation of Chalara." Pages 477–91 in *Proceedings of the 10th International Cretological Congress, Khania, 2006.* Edited by E.G. Kapsomenos, M. Andreadaki-Vlazaki, M. Andrianakis, and E. Papadopoulou. Khania: Literary Society "Chryssostomos."

———. 2017. "10. LM IIIB Pottery at Phaistos." Pages 313–29 in *How Long Is a Century? Late Minoan IIIB Pottery: Relative Chronology and Regional Differences.* Edited by Charlotte Langohr. Aegis 12. Louvain-La-Neuve: Presses Universitaires de Louvain.

Boulotis, Christos. 2000. "Η τέχνη των τοιχογραφιών στην μυκηναϊκή Βοιωτία." Pages 1095–1149 in vol. 3.1 of *Διεθνές Συνέδριο Βοιωτικών Μελετών (Θήβα, 4–8 Σεπτεμβρίου 1996).* Edited by Vassilis Aravantinos. Athens: Society of Boeotian Studies.

Bounni Adnan. 1979. "La quatrième campagne de fouilles (1978) à Ras Ibn Hani: Lumières nouvelles sur le royaume d'Ugarit, les Peuples de la Mer et la ville hellénistique." *CRAI* 123: 277–94.

Bounni, Adnan, Elisabeth Lagarce, and Jacques Lagarce 1998. *Ras Ibn Hani I: Le palais nord du bronze récent; Fouilles 1979–1995, synthèse préliminaire.* Bibliothèque archéologique et historique 151. Beirut: Beyrouth Institut Français d'Archéologie du Proche-Orient.

Bounni, Adnan, Elisabeth Lagarce, Jacques Lagarce, and Nassib Saliby. 1976. "Rapport préliminaire sur la première campagne de fouilles (1975) à Ibn Hani (Syrie)." *Syria* 53:233–79.

Bounni, Adnan, Elisabeth Lagarce, Jacques Lagarce, Nassib Saliby, Leila Badre, P. Leriche, and M. Touma. 1981. "Rapport préliminaire sur la quatrième campagne de fouilles (1978) à Ibn Hani (Syrie)." *Syria* 58:215–97.

Bounni, Adnan, Elisabeth Lagarce, Nassib Saliby, Leila Badre, and Jacques Lagarce. 1979.

REFERENCES 315

"Rapport préliminaire sur la troisieme campagne de fouilles (1977) à Ibn Hani (Syrie)." *Syria* 56:217–291+293–315+317–24.

Bourke, Stephen J. 1993. "The Transition from the Middle to the Late Bronze Age in Syria: The Evidence from Tell Nebi Mend." *Levant* 25:155–95. DOI: 10.1179/lev.1993.25.1.155.

———. 2012a. "The Six Canaanite Temples of *Ṭabaqāt Faḥil*: Excavating Pella's 'Fortress' Temple (1994–2009)." Pages 159–201 in *Temple Building and Temple Cult: Architecture and Cultic Paraphernalia of Temples in the Levant (2.–1. Mill. B.C.E.); Proceedings of a Conference on the Occasion of the 50th Anniversary of the Institute of Biblical Archaeology at the University of Tübingen (28–30 May 2010)*. Edited by Jens Kamlah. ADPV 41. Weisbaden: Harrassowitz.

———. 2012b. "Tell Nebi Mend in the 3rd/2nd Millennia BC." *Bulletin for the Council for British Research in the Levant* 7:50–52. DOI: 10.1179/1752726012Z.0000000006.

———. 2020. "Tell Nebi Mend and the Iron Age I in the Upper Orontes Valley." *AHL* 52–53:19–45.

Bouthillier, Christina, Carlo Colantoni, Sofie Debruyne, Claudia Glatz, Mette Marie Hald, David Heslop, Ekin Kozal. Bob Miller, Peter Popkin, Nicholas Postgate, Caroline S. Steele, and Adam Stone. 2014 "Further Work at Kilise Tepe, 2007–2011: Refining the Bronze to Iron Age Transition." *AnSt* 64:95–161. DOI: 10.1017/S0066154614000076.

Boz, Başak 2016. "Considering The Re-Use of Late Bronze Age Buildings in Light of Contextual Information and Human Remains at Beycesultan." *Mediterranean Archaeology & Archaeometry* 16.2:75–86. DOI:10.5281/zenodo.48531.

Bramlett, Kent. 2008. "Eastern Front: The Transjordan Highlands in Late Bronze Age Hegemonic Conquest." PhD diss., University of Toronto.

Brandl, Baruch 2010. "The Egyptian Origin of the Architecture at Deir el-Balaḥ." Pages 251–65 in *Deir el-Balaḥ: Excavations in 1977–1982 in the Cemetery and Settlement. Vol. 1: Stratigraphy and Architecture*. Edited by Trude Krakauer Dothan and Baruch Brandl. Qedem 49. Jerusalem: Institute of Archaeology, Hebrew University of Jerusalem.

Breasted, James. Henry. 1906a. *Ancient Records of Egypt Vol. 3*. Chicago: University of Chicago Press.

———. 1906b. *Ancient Records of Egypt Vol. 4*. Chicago: University of Chicago Press.

Breasted, James H., and Robert M. Engberg. 1935. "The Oriental Institute Archaeological Report on the Near East: First Quarter, 1935." *AJSL* 51:252–77. DOI: 10.1086/370463.

Bretschneider, Joachim, Jan Driessen, and Athanasia Kanta. 2018. "Pyla-Kokkinokremos: Short Report of the 2018 Campaign." https://www.academia.edu/37281038/PYLA-KOKKINOKREMOS_Short_report_of_the_2018_Campaign.

———. 2021. "Cyprus and Ugarit at the End of the Late Bronze Age: Insights from Pyla-Kokkinokremos." Pages 607–38 in *Ougarit, un anniversaire: Bilans et recherches en cours*. Edited by Valérie Matoïan. RSO 28. Leuven: Peeters.

Bretschneider, Joachim, Greta Jans, and Anne-Sophiee Van Vyve. 2014. "Once Upon a Tell in the East: Tell Tweini through the Ages." *UF* 45:347–72.

Bretschneider, Joachim, Greta Jans, Anne-Sophie Van Vyve, Hendrik Hameeuw, and Klaas Vansteenhuyse. 2019. "Tell Tweini: A Long Story Short." Pages 1–30 in *About Tell Tweini (Syria): Artefacts, Ecofacts and Landscape; Research Results of*

316 Indexes

the Belgian Mission. Edited by Joachim Bretschneider and Greta Jans. Leuven: Peeters. DOI: 10.2307/j.ctv1q26pt4.5.

Bretschneider, Joachim, Athanasia Kanta, and Jan Driessen. 2017. "Pyla-Kokkinokremos (Cyprus): Preliminary Report on the 2015–2016 Campaigns." *UF* 48:39–120.

Bretschneider, Joachim, and Karel Van Lerberghe. 2008. "Tell Tweini, Ancient Gibala, between 2600 BCE and 333 BCE." Pages 11–68 in *Search of Gibala: An Archaeological and Historical Study Based on Eight Seasons of Excavations at Tell Tweini (Syria) in the A and C Fields (1999–2007)*. Edited by Joachim Bretschneider and Karel van Lerberghe. AuOrSup 24. Barcelona: AUSA.

———. 2010. "Rapport Préliminaire sur les Activités de la Mission Syro-Belge de Tell Tweini entre 2007 et 2008 sur Le Chantier A." *Chronique Archéologique en Syrie: Special Issue Documenting the Annual Excavation Reports concerning the Archaeological Activities in Syria Excavation Reports of 2008* 4:133–45.

———. 2014. "Das Reich von Ugarit vor und nach dem Seevölkersturm: Neue Forschungen im antiken Gibala." Pages 149–70 in *Krieg und Frieden im Alten Vorderasien: 52e Rencontre Assyriologique Internationale, International Congress of Assyriology and Near Eastern Archaeology, Münster, 17.–21. Juli 2006*. Edited by Hans Neumann, Reinhard Dittmann, Susanne Paulus, Georg Neumann, and Anais Schuster-Brandis. AOAT 401. Münster: Ugarit-Verlag.

Bretschneider, Joachim, Anne-Sophie Van Vyve, and Greta Jans. 2011. "Tell Tweini: A Multi-Period Harbour Town at the Syrian Coast." Pages 73–87 in *Egypt and the Near East – the Crossroads: Proceedings of an International Conference on the Relations of Egypt and the Near East in the Bronze Age, Prague, September 1–3, 2010*. Edited by Jana Mynářová. Prague: Charles University Czech Institute of Egyptology.

Broneer, Oscar. 1933. "Excavations on the North Slope of the Acropolis in Athens, 1931–1932." *Hesperia* 2:329–417. DOI: 10.2307/146642.

———. 1939. "A Mycenaean Fountain on the Athenian Acropolis." *Hesperia* 8:317–433. DOI: 10.2307/146495.

Brown, Brian. 2013. "The Structure and Decline of the Middle Assyrian State." *JCS* 65:97–126. DOI: 10.5615/jcunestud.65.2013.0097.

Brown, Michael. 2017. "Landscape and Settlement in Late Bronze Age Cyprus: Investigations at Pyla-Kokkinokremos, 2007–2009." *PEQ* 149:274–94. DOI: 10.1080/00310328.2017.1320909.

Bruins, Hendrik J., Johannes van der Plicht, and J. Alexander MacGillivray. 2009. "The Minoan Santorini Eruption and Tsunami Deposits in Palaikastro (Crete): Dating by Geology, Archaeology, 14C, and Egyptian Chronology." *Radiocarbon* 51:397–411. DOI: 10.1017/S003382220005579X.

Bryce, Trevor. 2005. *The Kingdom of the Hittites*. Oxford: Oxford University Press.

———. 2006. *The Trojans and Their Neighbours*. London: Routledge.

———. 2012. *The World of the Neo-Hittite Kingdoms: A Political and Military History*. Oxford: Oxford University Press.

Budka, Julia, C. Geiger, P. Heindl, V. Hinterhuber, and H. Reschreiter. 2019. "The Question of Fuel for Cooking in Ancient Egypt and Sudan." *EXARC.net* 2019.1. https://exarc.net/ark:/88735/10398.

Bunch, Ted E., Malcolm A. LeCompte, A. Victor Adedeji, James H. Wittke, T. David Burleigh, Robert E. Hermes, Charles Mooney, Dale Batchelor, Wendy S. Wolbach, Joel Kathan, Gunther Kletetschka, Mark C. L. Patterson, Edward C. Swindel,

Timothy Witwer, George A. Howard, Siddhartha Mitra, Christopher R. Moore, Kurt Langworthy, James P. Kennett, Allen West, and Phillip J. Silvia. 2021. "A Tunguska Sized Airburst Destroyed Tall el-Hammam a Middle Bronze Age City in the Jordan Valley near the Dead Sea." *Scientific Reports* 11.1:18632. DOI: 10.1038/s41598-021-97778-3.

Bundgaard, Jens Andreas. 1976. *Parthenon and the Mycenaean City on the Heights*. Copenhagen: National Museum of Denmark.

Burke, Aaron A. 2011. "Early Jaffa: from the Bronze Age to the Persian Period." Pages 63–78 in *The History and Archaeology of Jaffa I*. Edited by Martin Peilstöcker and Aaron A. Burke. Monumenta Archaeologica 25. Los Angeles: Cotsen Institute of Archaeology Press.

———. 2014. "Introduction to the Levant during the Middle Bronze Age." Pages 403–13 in *The Oxford Handbook of the Archaeology of the Levant c. 8000–332 BCE*. Edited by Margreet Steiner and Ann E Killebrew. Oxford Handbooks. Oxford: Oxford University Press.

Burke, Aaron A., and Krystal V. Lord. 2010. "Egyptians in Jaffa: A Portrait of Egyptian Presence in Jaffa during the Late Bronze Age." *NEA* 73:2–30. DOI: 10.1086/NEA20697244.

Burke, Aaron A., and Martin Peilstöcker. 2017. "Chapter 2. Excavations of the Jaffa Cultural Heritage Project, 2008–2014." Pages 27–61 in *The History and Archaeology of Jaffa II*. Edited by Aaron A. Burke, Katherine Strange Burke, and Martin Peilstöcker. Monumenta Archaeologica 41. Los Angeles: Cotsen Institute of Archaeology Press.

Burke, Aaron A., Martin Peilstöcker, Amy Karoll, George A. Pierce, Krister Kowalski, Nadia Ben-Marzouk, Jacob C. Damm, Andrew J. Danielson, Heidi D. Fessler, Brett Kaufman, Krystal V. L. Pierce, Felix Höflmayer, Brian N. Damiata, and Michael Dee. 2017. "Excavations of the New Kingdom Fortress in Jaffa, 2011–2014: Traces of Resistance to Egyptian Rule in Canaan." *AJA* 121:85–133. DOI: 10.3764/aja.121.1.0085.

Bury, John Bagnell, Stanley Arthur Cook, Frank E. Adcock, Martin Percival Charlesworth, and Norman Hepburn Baynes. 1924. *The Egyptian and Hittite Empires to c. 1000 BC*. CAH 2. Cambridge: Cambridge University Press.

Bushnell, Lesley. 2013. "The Socio-Economic Implications of the Distribution of Juglets in the Eastern Mediterranean during the Middle and Late Bronze Age." PhD diss., University College London.

Butzer, Karl W. 1997. "Sociopolitical Discontinuity in the Near East C. 2200 B.C.E.: Scenarios from Palestine and Egypt." Pages 245–96 in *Third Millennium BC Climate Change and Old World Collapse*. Edited by H Nüzhet Dalfes, George Kukla, and Harvey Weiss. Berlin: Springer.

Cadogan, Gerald. 1985. "Maroni." Pages 195–97 in *Archaeology in Cyprus 1960–1985*. Edited by Vassos Karageorghis. Nicosia: Zavallis.

———. 1986. "Maroni II." *RDAC* 1986:40–44.

———. 1996. "Maroni: Change in Late Bronze Age Cyprus." *Studies in Mediterranean Archaeology and Literature Pocket-book* 126:15–23.

———. 2011. "Bronze Age Maroni-Vournes: A Review." Pages 397–404 in vol. 1.2 of *Proceedings of the IV International Cyprological Congress Lefkosia 29 April–3 May 2008*. Edited by Andreas Demetriou. Lefkosia: Society of Cypriot Studies.

Cadogan, Gerald, and M. Domurad. 1989. "Maroni V." *Report of the Department of Antiquities, Cyprus* 1989:77–81.

Cadogan, Gerald, Ellen Herscher, Pamela Russell, and Sturt Manning. 2001. "Maroni-Vournes: A Long White Slip Sequence and Its Chronology." Pages 75–88 in *The White Slip Ware of Late Bronze Age Cyprus: Proceedings of an International Conference Organized by the Anastasios G. Leventis Foundation, Nicosia in Honour of Malcolm Wiener, Nicosia 29th–30th October.* Edited by Vasso Karageorghis. CCEM 2. Vienna: Österreichischen Akademie der Wissenschaften.

Callot, Olivier. 1994. *La tranchée "Ville Sud," Études d 'architecture domestique.* RSO 10. Paris: Éditions Recherche sur les civilisations.

———. 2008. "Réflexions sur Ougarit après ca 1180 av. J.-C." Pages 119–25 in *Ougarit au Bronze moyen et au Bronze recent: Actes du colloque international tenu à Lyon en novembre 2001.* Edited by Yves Calvet and Marguerite Yon. TMO 47. Lyon: Maison de l'Orient et de la Méditerranée-Jean Pouilloux.

Çambel, Halet. 1984. "Karatepe Kazıları." *Kazı Sonuçları Toplantısı* 5:153–61.

———. 1986. "Karatepeaslantaş ve Domuztepe 1984 yılı Çalışmaları." *Kazı Sonuçları Toplantısı* 7:271–85.

Çambel, Halet, Mehmet Akif Ism, and James E. Knudstad. 1996. "Karatepeaslantaş ve Domuztepe 1993–1994 yılı Çalışmaları." *Kazı Sonuçları Toplantısı* 17:229–47.

Çambel, Halet, Mehmet Akif Ism, and Serge Sadler. 1987. "Karatepe-aslantaş ve Domuztepe: 1985 yılı Çalışmaları." *Kazı Sonuçları Toplantısı* 8:329–43.

Çambel, Halet, and Mehmet Özdoğan. 1985. "1983 yılı Domuztepe Çalışmaları." *Kazı Sonuçları Toplantısı* 6:259–72.

Caneva, Isabella, and Éric Jean. 2016. "Mersin-Yumuktepe: Une mise au point sur les derniers travaux." *AnAnt* 24:13–34. DOI: 10.4000/anatoliaantiqua.368.

Caneva, Isabella, and Gülgün Köroğlu. 2010. *Yumuktepe: A Journey through Nine Thousand Years.* Istanbul: Ege Yayınları.

Caneva, Isabella, and Veli Sevin. 2004. *Mersin-Yumuktepe: A Reappraisal.* Galatina: Congedo.

Capet, Emmanuelle. 2003. "Tell Kazel (Syrie), rapport préliminaire sur les 9e–17e campagnes de fouilles (1993–2001) du musée de l'université américaine de Beyrouth: Chantier II." *Berytus* 47:63–122.

Capet, Emmanuelle, and Éric Gubel. 2000. "Tell Kazel: Six Centuries of Iron Age Occupation (c. 1200–612 BC)." Pages 425–57 in *Essays on Syria in the Iron Age.* Edited by Guy Bunnens. ANESSup 7. Leuven: Peeters.

Cappers, René T. J., and Reinder Neef. 2012. *Handbook of Plant Palaeoecology.* Groningen: Barkhuis.

Caraher, William R., R. Scott Moore, and David K. Pettegrew. 2014. *Pyla-Koutsopetria I: Archaeological Survey of an Ancient Coastal Town.* ASORAR 21. Boston: American Schools of Oriental Research.

Carpenter, Rhys. 1966. *Discontinuity in Greek Civilization.* J. H. Gray Lectures 1965. New York: Norton.

Casana, Jesse. 2017. "The Northern Levant: Archaeology." Pages 159–76 in *Hittite Landscape and Geography.* Edited by Mark Weeden, Lee Z. Ullmann, and Zenobia Homan. HdO 121. Leiden: Brill.

Casana, Jesse, Jason, T. Herrmann, and Aaron Fogel. 2008. "Deep Subsurface Geophysical Prospection at Tell Qarqur, Syria." *Archaeological Prospection* 15:207–25. DOI: 10.1002/arp.335.

Casson, Stanley. 1921. "The Dorian Invasion Reviewed in the Light of Some New Evidence." *Antiquaries Journal* 1:199–221. DOI: 10.1017/S0003581500002249.

———. 1922. *Ancient Greece: A Study.* Oxford: Oxford University Press.

Catling, Hector W. 1975. "Cyprus in the Late Bronze Age." Pages 188–216 in *The Middle East and the Aegean Region c. 1380–1000 BC.* Edited by I. E. S. Edwards, C. J. Gadd, N. G. L. Hammond, and E. Sollberger. 3rd ed. CAH 2.2. Cambridge: Cambridge University Press.

———. 1976–1977. "Excavations at the Menelaion, Sparta, 1973–1976." *ArRep* 23:24–42. DOI: 10.2307/581107.

———. 2009. *Sparta: Menelaion I the Bronze Age.* Vol. 1: *The Text.* British School at Athens Supplementary Volume 45.1. London: British School at Athens.

Caubet, Anne. 1992. "Reoccupation of the Syrian Coast after the Destruction of the 'Crisis Years.'" Pages 123–31 in *The Crisis Years: The 12th Century B.C.; From Beyond the Danube to the Tigris.* Edited by William A. Ward and Martha Sharp Joukowsky. Dubuque, IA: Kendall/Hunt Publishing.

Çelik, Duygu. 2008. "Alacahöyük Hitit Barajı." *Aykut Çınaroğlu'na Armağan* 2008:87–104.

Chapman, Rupert L. 1989. "The Three Ages Revisited: A Critical Study of Levantine Usage, Part I; The Critique." *PEQ* 121:89–111. DOI: 10.1179/peq.1989.121.2.89.

Charaf, Hanan 2008. "New Light on the End of the Late Bronze Age at Tell Arqa." *AHL* 26–27:70–98.

———. 2011. "Over the Hills and Far Away: Handmade Burnished Ware and Mycenaean Cooking Pots at Tell Arqa, Lebanon." Pages 203–18 in *On Cooking Pots, Drinking Cups, Loomweights and Ethnicity in Bronze Age Cyprus and Neighbouring Regions: An International Archaeological Symposium Held in Nicosia, November 6th –7th 2010.* Edited by Vassos Karageorghis and Ourania Kouka. Nicosia: Leventis Foundation.

Charaf, Hanan, and Lynn Welton. eds. 2019. *The Iron Age I in the Levant: A View from the North; Part 1.* AHL 50–51. London: Lebanese British Friends of the National Museum.

———, eds. 2020. *The Iron Age I in the Levant: A View from the North; Part 2.* AHL 52–53. London: Lebanese British Friends of the National Museum.

Charalambous, Andreas, George Papasavvas, and Vasiliki Kassianidou. 2021. "Enkomi (Cyprus): Using pXRF Spectroscopy to Identify LBA Copper Alloys." *JArS: Reports* 35:102726. DOI: 10.1016/j.jasrep.2020.102726.

Chatzi-Vallianou, Despina. 2017. "5. The Late Minoan IIIB Pottery of Gouves Potters Quarter and Workshop." Pages 103–52 in *How Long Is a Century? Late Minoan IIIB Pottery: Relative Chronology and Regional Differences.* Edited by Charlotte Langohr. Aegis 12. Louvain-La-Neuve: Presses Universitaires de Louvain.

Chiti, Barbara, and Tatiana Pedrazzi. 2014. "Tell Kazel (Syria), Area II: New Evidence from a Late Bronze/Iron Age Quarter." Pages 205–22 in *Proceedings of the 8th International Congress on the Archaeology of the Ancient Near East. 30 April–4 May 2012, University of Warsaw.* Vol. 2: *Excavation and Progress Reports, Posters.* Edited by Piotr Bieliński and Michał Gawlikowski Wiesbaden: Harrassowitz.

Cifola, Barbara. 1988. "Ramses III and the Sea Peoples: A Structural Analysis of the Medinet Habu Inscriptions." *Or* 5:275–306.

———. 1994. "The Role of the Sea Peoples and the End of the Late Bronze Age: A Reassessment of Textual and Archaeological Evidence." *Orientis Antiqui Miscellanea* 1:1–23.

Çinaroğlu, Aykut, and Duygu Çelik. 2010. *Atatürk & Alaca Höyük.* Ankara: Ekici Form Ofset.

Clark, Douglas. R. 2011. "The Late Bronze and Early Iron Ages at Tall al-'Umayri." Pages 43–57 in *The Madaba Plains Project: Forty Years of Archaeological Research into Jordan's Past.* Edited by Douglas R. Clark, Larry G. Herr, Øystein Sakala LaBianca, and Randall W. Younker. London: Routledge.

Cline, Eric H. 2013. *The Trojan War: A Very Short Introduction.* New York: Oxford University Press.

———. 2014. *1177 B.C.: The Year Civilization Collapsed.* Princeton: Princeton University Press.

———. 2021. *1177 B.C.: The Year Civilization Collapsed.* Rev. and expanded. Princeton: Princeton University Press.

Cline, Eric. H., and David O'Connor. 2003. "The Mystery of the 'Sea Peoples." Pages 107–38 in *Mysterious Lands: Encounters with Ancient Egypt.* Edited by David O'Connor and Stephen Quirke. London: UCL Press.

Cohen, Yoram. 2020. "The 'Hunger Years' and the 'Sea Peoples': Preliminary Observations on the Recently Published Letters from the 'House of Urtenu' Archive at Ugarit." Pages 47–61 in vol. 1 of *Ve-'Ed Ya'aleh (Gen 2:6): Essays in Biblical and Ancient Near Studies Presented to Edward L. Greenstein.* Edited by Peter Machinist, Robert A. Harris, Joshua A. Berman, Nili Samet, and Noga Ayali-Darshan. 2 vols. WAWSup 5. Atlanta: Society of Biblical Literature.

Cohen, Yoram, and Lorenzo d'Alfonso. 2008. "The Duration of the Emar Archives and the Relative and Absolute Chronology of the City." Pages 3–25 in *The City of Emar among the Late Bronze Age Empires: History, Landscape, and Society; Proceedings of the Konstanz Emar Conference (2006).* Edited by Lorenzo D'Alfonso, Yoram Cohen, and Dietrich Sürenhagen. AOAT 349. Münster: Ugarit-Verlag.

Coldstream, Jonathan N. 1989. "Status Symbols in Cyprus in the Eleventh Century BC." Pages 325–35 in *Early Society in Cyprus.* Edited by Edgar Peltenburg. Edinburgh: Edinburgh University Press.

Collins, Billie Jean. 1996. "The End of the Bronze Age: Changes in Warfare and the Catastrophe ca. 1200 B.C." *Classical Bulletin* 72.2:129–31.

———. 2007. *The Hittites and Their World.* ABS 7. Atlanta: Society of Biblical Literature.

Contenson, Henri de, Jacques-Claude Courtois, Élisabeth Lagarce, Jacques Lagarce, and Rolf A. Stucky. 1974. "XXXIVe campagne de fouilles à Ras Shamra en 1973: Rapport préliminaire." *Syria* 51:1–30. DOI: 10.3406/syria.1974.6432.

Cook, Arthur. 1929. "Notes on Recent Excavations." *PEQ* 61:111–18. DOI: 10.1179/peq.1929.61.2.111.

Courbin, Paul. 1975. "Rapport sur la 4eme Campagne de Fouille (1974) à Ras el Bassit." *AAAS* 25:59–71.

———. 1976. "Rapport sur la 5ème campagne de fouille à Ras el Bassit." *AAAS* 26:63–69.

———. 1983. "Bassit, campagnes 1980–1982." *Syria* 60:290–92.

———. 1986. "Bassit." *Syria* 63:175–220. DOI: 10.3406/syria.1986.8665.

———. 1990. "Bassit–Posidaion in the Early Iron Age." Pages 503–10 in *Greek Colonists and Native Populations: Proceedings of the First Australian Congress of Classical Archaeology Held in Honour of Emeritus Professor A. D. Trendall, Sydney 9–14 July 1985.* Edited by Jean-Paul Descœudres. Oxford: Humanities Research Centre.

REFERENCES   321

Courtois, Jacques-Claude. 1971. "Le Sanctuaire du dieu au Lingot d'Enkomi Alasia."
Pages 151–362 in *Alasia 1: À l'occasion de la XXe Campagne de Fouilles à Enkomi-Alasia (1969)*. Edited by Claude F.-A. Schaeffer. Mission archéologique d'Alasia 4.
Paris: Mission archéologique d'Alasia.

Courtois, Jacques-Claude, Jacques Lagarce, and Elisabeth Lagarce. 1986. *Enkomi et le bronze récent à Chypre*. Nicosie: Leventis Foundation.

Cosmopoulos, Michael B. 2018. *Iklaina: The Monumental Buildings*. Archaeological Society at Athens Library 316. Athens: Library of the Archaeological Society at Athens.

———. 2019. "State Formation in Greece: Iklaina and the Unification of Mycenaean Pylos." *AJA* 123:349–80. DOI: 10.3764/aja.123.3.0349.

Cosmopoulos, Michael B., Susan E. Allen, Danielle J. Riebe, Deborah Ruscillo, Maria Liston, and China Shelton. 2019. "New Accelerator Mass Spectrometry 14C Dates from the Mycenaean Site of Iklaina." *JArS: Reports* 24:888–99. DOI: 10.1016/j.jasrep.2019.02.034.

Cucuzza, Nicola. 2009. "Progetto Kannià: resoconto preliminare sullo studio della villa minoica." *Annuario della Scuola Archeologica di Atene* 87:927–33.

———. 2015a. "La coroplastica di Kannià: Osservazioni preliminari." *Creta antica* 16:45–57.

———. 2015b. "Il complesso della villa di Kannià (Messarà) fra Tardo Minoico I e Tardo Minoico III." Pages 183–96 in *Géosciences, archéologie et histoire en Crète de l'Âge du Bronze récent à l'époque archaïque: Actes du colloque international pluridisciplinaire de Strasbourg, 16–18 octobre 2013*. Edited by Daniela Lefèvre-Novaro, Laetitia Martzolff, Matthieu Ghilardi, Jasper Donelan, and Claire Camberlein. Padova: Bottega d'Erasmo.

———. 2017. "11. Preliminary Observations on LM IIIB Pottery from Kannia." Pages 331–40 in *How Long Is a Century? Late Minoan IIIB Pottery: Relative Chronology and Regional Differences*. Edited by Charlotte Langohr. Aegis 12. Louvain-La-Neuve: Presses Universitaires de Louvain.

———. 2018. "The Minoan Villa at Kannia: Preliminary Report on a New Project." Pages 309–18 in Πεπραγμένα του ΙΑ' Διεθνούς Κρητολογικού Συνεδρίου, (Ρέθυμνο, 21–27 Οκτωβρίου 2011): Ρέθυμνο: Ιστορική και Λαογραφική Εταιρεία Ρεθύμνου.

Cunningham, Timothy. 2017. "13. Postpalatial Palaikastro: The Settlement and Its Ceramics in LM IIIB." Pages 355–95 in *How Long Is a Century? Late Minoan IIIB Pottery: Relative Chronology and Regional Differences*. Edited by Charlotte Langohr. Aegis 12. Louvain-La-Neuve: Presses Universitaires de Louvain.

Cunningham, Timothy, and Jan Driessen. 2017. *Crisis to Collapse: The Archaeology of Social Breakdown*. Aegis 11. Louvain-la-Neuve: Presses Universitaires de Louvain.

Curtis, Adrian H. W. 1999. "Ras Shamra, Minet el-Beida, and Ras Ibn Hani: The Material Sources." Pages 5–27 in *Handbook of Ugaritic Studies*. Edited by Wilfred G. E. Watson and Nicholas Wyatt. HdO 39. Leiden: Brill. DOI: 10.1163/9789004294103_003.

Czichon, Rainer Maria, Jörg Klinger, Peter Breuer, Jacob Eerbeek, Sherry C. Fox, Elena Marinova-Wolff, Henning Marquardt, Harald Von der Osten-Woldenburg, Silvio Reichmuth, Simone Riehl, and Theodor Johannsen. 2011. "Archäologische Forschungen am Oymaagac Höyük/Nerik(?) in den Jahren 2007–2010." *MDOG* 143:169–250.

Czichon, Rainer Maria, Jörg Klinger, Pavol Hnila, Dirk Paul Mielke, Sonja Behrendt, Herbert Böhm, Michael Breuer, Christoph Forster, Carol Griggs, Marie Klein, Marko Koch, Günther Karl Kunst, Monika Lehmann, Brita Lorentzen, Sturt W.

Manning, Kathryn Marklein, Christoph Purschwitz, Corinna Rössner, Claudia Tappert, and Margherita Andrea Valsecchi Gillmeister. 2019. "Archäologische Forschungen am Oymaağaç Höyük/Nerik 2016–2018." *MDOG* 151:37–200.

Czichon, Rainer Maria, Jörg Klinger, Pavol Hnila, Dirk Paul Mielke, Herbert Böhm, Christoph Forster, Carol Griggs, Martin Kähler, Günther Karl Kunst, Monika Lehmann, Brita Lorentzen, Sturt Manning, Kathryn Marklein, Henning Marquard, Silvio Reichmuth, Jana Richter, Corinna Rössner, Burhan Sadıklar, Katherine Seufer, Robert Sobott, Irene Traub-Sobott, Harald von der Osten-Woldenburg, Melanie Weber, Horst Wolter, and Mehmet Ali Yılmaz. 2016. "Archäologische Forschungen am Oymaağaç Höyük/Nerik 2011–2015." *MDOG* 148:1–141.

Dagan, Yehuda. 2004. "Results of the Survey: Settlement Patterns in the Lachish Region." Pages 2672–90 in vol. 5 of *The Renewed Archaeological Excavations at Lachish (1973–1994)*. Edited by David Ussishkin. 5 vols. SMNIA 22. Tel Aviv: Emery and Claire Yass Publications in Archaeology.

D'Agostino, Anacleto. 2020. "Tracing Fire Events and Destructions of Late Bronze Age Date: The End of the Hittite Building on the Citadel of Uşaklı Höyük." Pages 69–93 in *Anatolia between the 13th and 12th Century BCE*. Edited by Stefano de Martino and Elena Devecchi. Eothen 23. Firenze: LoGisma.

Dakoronia, Fanouria. 1993. "Homeric Towns in East Lokris: Problems of Identification." *Hesperia* 62:115–27. DOI: 10.2307/148252.

———. 1996. "Earthquakes of the Late Helladic III Period (12th Century BC) at Kynos (Livanates, Central Greece)." Pages 41–44 in *Archaeoseismology*. Edited by Stathis C. Stiros and R. E. Jones. Fitch Laboratory Occasional Papers 7. Athens: Institute of Geology & Mineral Exploration; British School at Athens.

Dakouri-Hild, Anastasia. 2001. "The House of Kadmos in Mycenaean Thebes Reconsidered: Architecture, Chronology and Context." *ABSA* 96:81–122.

———. 2010. "Thebes." Pages 690–711 in *The Oxford Handbook of the Bronze Age Aegean (ca. 3000–1000 BC)*. Edited by Eric H. Cline. Oxford Handbooks. Oxford: Oxford University Press.

Damm-Meinhardt, Ursula. 2015. *Baubefunde und Stratigraphie der Unterburg (Kampagnen 1976 bis 1983): Die mykenische Palastzeit (SH III B2) und beginnende Nachpalastzeit (Beginn SH III C)*. Tiryns 17. Wiesbaden: Reichert.

Daniel, John Franklin, Oscar Broneer, and H. T. Wade-Gery. 1948. "The Dorian Invasion: The Setting." *AJA* 52:107–10. DOI: 10.2307/500556.

Daux Georges. 1960. "Chronique des fouilles et découvertes archéologiques en Grèce en 1960." *BCH* 85:601–953.

———. 1962. "Chronique des fouilles et découvertes archéologiques en Grèce en 1961." *BCH* 86:629–974.

Davis, Jack L. 2010. "Pylos." Pages 680–89 in *The Oxford Handbook of the Bronze Age Aegean (ca. 3000–1000 BC)*. Edited by Eric H. Cline. Oxford Handbooks. Oxford: Oxford University Press.

Dawkins, Boyd. 1897. "The Present Phase of Prehistoric Archaeology, Being the Opening Address of the Antiquarian Section at the Dorchester Meeting." *Archaeological Journal* 54:377–94. DOI: 10.1080/00665983.1897.10852746.

Dawkins, Richard M., and Arthur M. Woodward. 1910. "Laconia: I. Excavations at Sparta." *ABSA* 16:1–61.

Dedeoğlu, Fulya, 2014. "Beycesultan Höyük Excavation Project: New Archaeological Evidence from Late Bronze Age Layers." *Arkeoloji Dergisi* 17:1–39.

REFERENCES 323

Dedeoğlu, Fulya, and Erim Konakçı. 2015. "Local Painted Pottery Tradition from Inland Southwest Anatolia and Its Contribution to Second Millennium BC Chronology." *Mediterranean Archaeology and Archaeometry* 15:191–214.

Deger-Jalkotzy, Sigrid. 2008. "Decline, Destruction, Aftermath." Pages 387–416 in *The Cambridge Companion to the Aegean Bronze Age*. Edited by Cynthia W Shelmerdine. Cambridge: Cambridge University Press.

Demakopoulou, Katie. 1995. "Mycenaean Citadels: Recent Excavations on the Acropolis of Midea in the Argolid," *BICS* 40:151–76.

———. 2003. "The Pottery from the Destruction Layers in Midea: Late Helladic III B2 Late or Transitional Late Helladic III B2/Late Helladic III C Early?" Pages 77–92 in *LH III C Chronology and Synchronisms II: LH III C Middle; Proceedings of the International Workshop Held at the Austrian Academy of Sciences at Vienna, October 29th and 30th, 2004*. Edited by Sigrid Deger-Jalkotzy and Michaela Zavadil. Veröffentlichungen der Mykenischen Kommission 28. Vienna Österreichische Akademie der Wissenschaften.

———. 2007. "The Role of Midea in the Network of Mycenaean Citadels in the Argolid." Pages 65–80 in *Keimelion: Elitenbildung und elitärer Konsum von der mykenischen Palastzeit bis zur Homerischen Epoche; Akten des internationalen Kongresses vom 3. bis 5. Februar 2005 in Salzburg* = *The Formation of Elites and Elitist Lifestyles from Mycenaen Palatial Times to the Homeric Period*. Edited by Eva Alram-Stern, Georg Nightingale, Anna Elisabeth Bächle, and Sigrid Deger-Jalkotzy. Vienna: Österreichischen Akademie der Wissenschaften.

———. 2015. "The Mycenaean Acropolis of Midea: New Discoveries and New Interpretations." Pages 185–97 in *Mycenaeans Up to Date: The Archaeology of the Northeastern Peloponnese; Current Concepts and New Directions*. Edited by Iphiyenia Tournavitou and Ann-Louise Schallin. Skrifter utgivna av Svenska institutet i Athen 56. Stockholm: Svenska Instituten vid Rom och Athen.

Demakopoulou, Katie, Nicoletta Divari-Valakou, Paul Åström, and Gisela Walberg. 1996. "Excavations in Midea 1994." *OpAth* 21:13–32.

———. 1998. "Excavations in Midea 1995–1996." *OpAth* 22–23:57–90.

———. 2001. "Work in Midea 1997–1999: Excavation, Conservation, Restoration." *OpAth* 25–26:35–52.

Demakopoulou, Katie, Nicoletta Divari-Valakou, Maria Lowe Fri, Madeleine Miller, Monica Nilsson, and Ann-Louise Schallin. 2010. "Excavations in Midea 2008–2009." *OpRomAth* 3:7–32.

Demakopoulou, Katie, Nicoletta Divari-Valakou, Monica Nilsson, and Ann-Louise Schallin. 2006–2007. "Excavations in Midea 2005." *OpAth* 31–32:7–29.

———. 2008. "Excavations in Midea 2006." *OpAthRom* 1:7–30.

———. 2009. "Excavations in Midea 2007." *OpAthRom* 2:7–30.

Demakopoulou, Katie, Nicoletta Divari-Valakou, Ann-Louise Schallin, Gunnel Ekroth, A. Lindblom, Monica Nilsson, and Lena Sjögren. 2002. "Excavations in Midea 2000 and 2001." *OpAth* 27:27–58.

Demakopoulou, Katie, Nicoletta Divari-Valakou, Ann-Louise Schallin, Lena Sjögren, and Monica Nilsson. 2003. "Excavations in Midea 2002." *OpAth* 28:7–28.

———. 2004. "Excavations in Midea 2003." *OpAth* 29:9–27.

———. 2005. "Excavations in Midea 2004." *OpAth* 30:7–34.

Demakopoulou, Katie, Nicoletta Divari-Valakou, and Gisela Walberg. 1994. "Excavations and Restoration Work in Midea 1990–1992." *OpAth* 20:19–41.

324 REFERENCES

Desborough, Vincent Robin d'Arba. 1964. *The Last Mycenaeans and Their Successors: An Archaeological Survey c. 1200–c. 1000 B.C.* Oxford: Clarendon.

———. 1975. "The End of Mycenaean Civilization and the Dark Age: (a) The Archaeological Background." Pages 658–77 in *The Middle East and the Aegean Region c. 1380–1000 BC.* Edited by I. E. S. Edwards, C. J. Gadd, N. G. L. Hammond, and E. Sollberger. 3rd ed. CAH 2.2. Cambridge: Cambridge University Press.

Dever, William G. 1992. "The Late Bronze–Early Iron I Horizon in Syria-Palestine: Egyptians, Canaanites, 'Sea Peoples,' and Proto-Israelites." Pages 99–110 in *The Crisis Years: The 12th Century B.C.; From Beyond the Danube to the Tigris.* Edited by William A. Ward and Martha Sharp Joukowsky. Dubuque, IA: Kendall/Hunt Publishing.

———. 1993. "Gezer." *NEAEHL* 2:496–506.

———. 2017. *Beyond the Texts: An Archaeological Portrait of Ancient Israel and Judah.* Atlanta: SBL Press.

Dever, William G., H. Darrell Lance, Reuben G. Bullard, Dan P. Cole, and Joe D. Seger. 1974. *Gezer II: Report of the 1967–70 Seasons in Fields I and II.* Jerusalem: Hebrew Union College/Nelson Glueck School of Biblical Archaeology.

Dever, William G., H Darrell Lance, and Reuben G Bullard. 1986. *Gezer IV: The 1969–71 Seasons in the Field VI, the "Acropolis."* Jerusalem: Hebrew Union College/Nelson Glueck School of Biblical Archaeology.

Dever, William G., H. Darrell Lance, and G. Ernest Wright. 1970. *Gezer I: Preliminary Report of the 1964–66 Seasons.* Jerusalem: Hebrew Union College/Nelson Glueck School of Biblical Archaeology.

Dever, William G., and Joe D. Seger. 2014. "A Brief Summary of the Stratigraphy and Cultural History of Gezer." Pages 8–17 in *Gezer VI: The Objects from Phases I and II (1964–1974).* Edited by Garth Gilmour. Winona Lake, IN: Eisenbrauns. DOI: 10.1515/9781575068909-006.

Dickinson, Oliver T. P. K. 2008. "Was There Really a Trojan War?" Pages 189–97 in *Dioskouroi: Studies Presented to W. G. Cavanagh and C. B. Mee on the Anniversary of Their 30-Year Joint Contribution to Archaeology.* Edited by Chrysanthi Gallou, M. Georgiadis, and G. M. Muskett. BARIS 1889. Oxford: Archaeopress.

———. 2010. "The Collapse at the End of the Bronze Age." Pages 483–90 in *The Oxford Handbook of the Bronze Age Aegean (ca. 3000–1000 BC).* Edited by Eric H. Cline. Oxford Handbooks. Oxford: Oxford University Press.

Dietrich, Manfried, and Oswald Loretz. 1978. "Das 'seefahrende Volk' von Sikila (RS 34.129)." *UF* 10:53–56.

Dikaios, Porphyrios. 1969. *Enkomi Excavations 1948–1958.* Vol. 1: *The Architectural Remains the Tombs.* Mainz: von Zabern.

———. 1971. *Enkomi Excavations 1948–1958.* Vol. 2: *Chronology, Summary and Conclusions, Catalogue, Appendices.* Mainz: von Zabern.

Döhl, Hartmut. 1973. "Iria: Die Ergebnisse der Ausgrabungen 1939." Pages 127–94 in *Frühhelladische Keramik auf der Unterburg von Tiryns.* Edited by Wolf Rudolph, Hartmut Döhl, Ulrich Willerding, and Walter Voigtländer. Tiryns 6. Mainz: von Zabern.

Dörpfeld, Wilhelm. 1902. *Troja Und Ilion.* Greece: Beck & Barth.

Dothan, Moshe. 1955. *The Excavations at 'Afula.* Jerusalem: Israel Department of Antiquities and Museums.

REFERENCES 325

———. 1971. *Ashdod II–III: The Second and Third Seasons of Excavations 1963, 1965 Soundings in 1967*. Jerusalem: Israel Department of Antiquities and Museums.

———. 1981. "Akko, 1980." *IEJ* 31:110–12.

———. 1988. "The Significance of Some Artisans' Workshops along the Canaanite Coast." Pages 295–303 in *Society and Economy in the Eastern Mediterranean (c. 1500–1000 BC): Proceedings of the International Symposium Held at the University of Haifa from the 28th of April to the 2nd of May 1985*. Edited by Michael Heltzer and Edward Lipiński. OLA 23. Leuven: Peeters.

———. 1993a. "Acco." *NEAEHL* 1:16–31.

———. 1993b. "'Afula." *NEAEHL* 1:37–39.

———. 1993c. "Mor, Tel." *NEAEHL* 3:1073–74.

Dothan, Moshe, and David Ben-Shlomo. 2005. *Ashdod VI: The Excavations of Areas H and K The Fourth-Sixth Seasons of Excavations (1968–1969)*. IAAR 24. Jerusalem: Israel Antiquity Authority.

Dothan, Moshe, and David Noel Freedman. 1967. *Ashdod I: First Season of Excavations 1962*. 'Atiqot 7. Jerusalem: Israel Department of Antiquities and Museums.

Dothan, Moshe, and Yehoshua Porath. 1993. *Ashdod V: Excavation of Area G The Fourth-Sixth Seasons of Excavation 1968–1970*. 'Atiqot 23. Jerusalem: Israel Antiquities Authority.

Dothan, Trude. 1982. *The Philistines and Their Material Culture*. New Haven: Yale University Press.

———. 1983. "Some Aspects of the Appearance of the Sea Peoples and Philistines in Canaan." Pages 99–117 in *Griechenland, die Agais und die Levante wahrend der Dark Ages vom 12. bis zum 9. Jahrhundert v. Chr*. Edited by Sigrid Deger-Jalkotzy. Mykenische Studien 10. Vienna: Österreichische Akademie der Wissenschaften.

———. 1998. "Initial Philistine Settlement: From Migration to Coexistence." Pages 148–61 in *Mediterranean Peoples in Transition: Thirteenth to Early Tenth Centuries B.C.E.; In Honor of Professor Trude Dothan*. Edited by Seymour Gitin, Amihai Mazar, and Ephraim Stern. Jerusalem: Israel Exploration Society.

Dothan, Trude, and Moshe Dothan. 1992. *People of the Sea: The Search for the Philistines*. New York: Macmillan.

Doumet-Serhal, Claude 2021–2022. "Sidon from the End of the 13th to the 10th Century BC: The Temple." *AHL* 54–55:1–442.

Drake, Brandon L. 2012. "The Influence of Climatic Change on the Late Bronze Age Collapse and the Greek Dark Ages." *JArS* 39:1862–70. DOI: 10.1016/j.jas.2012.01.029.

Drews, Robert. 1993. *The End of the Bronze Age: Changes in Warfare and the Catastrophe ca. 1200 BC*. Princeton: Princeton University Press.

———. 2000. "Medinet Habu: Oxcarts, Ships, and Migration Theories." *JNES* 59:161–90. DOI: 10.1086/468830.

———. 2020. "Catastrophe Revisited." Pages 229–35 in *Collapse and Transformation: The Late Bronze Age to Early Iron Age in the Aegean*. Edited by Guy D. Middleton. Oxford: Oxbow. DOI: 10.2307/j.ctv13pk6k9.29.

Driessen, Jan. 1995. "'Crisis Architecture'? Some Observations on Architectural Adaptations as Immediate Responses to Changing Socio-Cultural Conditions." *Topoi* 5:63–88.

———, ed. 2013. *Destruction: Archaeological, Historical and Philological Perspectives*. Louvain-La-Neuve: Presses Universitaires de Louvain.

———, ed. 2018. *An Archaeology of Forced Migration: Crisis-Induced Mobility and the Col-*

lapse of the 13th c. BCE Eastern Mediterranean. Aegis 15. Louvain-La-Neuve: Presses Universitaires de Louvain.

———. 2019. "The Santorini Eruption: An Archaeological Investigation of Its Distal Impacts on Minoan Crete." *Quaternary International* 499:195–204. DOI: 10.1016/j.quaint.2018.04.019.

Driessen, Jan, Joachim Bretschneider, and Anastasia Kanta. Forthcoming. "Prelude to Crisis? A Closer Look at Pyla-Kokkinokremos." In *The Decline of Bronze Age Civilisations in the Mediterranean: Cyprus and Beyond; Studies in Mediterranean Archaeology.* Edited by Peter. M. Fischer and Teresa Bürge. Uppsala: Åström.

Drower, Margaret. 1985. *Flinders Petrie: A Life in Archaeology.* London: Gollanz.

Du Plat Taylor, Joan. 1952. "A Late Bronze Age Settlement at Apliki, Cyprus." *Antiquaries Journal* 32:133–67. DOI: 10.1017/S0003581500076800.

———. 1957. *Myrtou-Pigadhes: A Late Bronze Age Sanctuary.* Oxford: Ashmolean Museum.

Du Plat Taylor, Joan, and Barbara Kling. 2007. "Overview of the Excavated Areas." Pages 7–91 in *Joan du Plat Taylor's Excavations at the Late Bronze Age Mining Settlement at Apliki Karamallos, Cyprus.* Edited by Barbara Kling, James David Muhly, Vasiliki Kassianidou, and Joan du Plat Taylor. Studies in Mediterranean Archaeology 134. Sävedalen: Åström.

Dupré, Sylvestre. 1983. *Porsuk I: La céramique de l'âge du bronze et de l'âge du fer.* Mémoire 20. Paris: Éditions Recherche sur les civilisations.

Easton, Donald F. 2014. "The First Excavations at Troy: Brunton, Calvert and Schliemann." Pages 32–103 in *Troia 1987–2012: Grabungen und Forschungen 1.* Edited by Ernst Pernicka, Charles Brian Rose, and Peter Jablonka. Studia Troica Monographien 5. Bonn: Habelt.

Easton, Donald F., J. David Hawkins, Andrew G. Sherratt, and E. Susan Sherratt. "Troy in Recent Perspective." *AnSt* 52 (2002):75–109. DOI: 10.2307/3643078.

Edgerton, William. F., and John A. Wilson. 1936. *Historical Records of Ramses III: The Texts in Medinet Habu Vols. I and II.* SAOC 12. Chicago: University of Chicago Press.

van Effenterre, Henri, and Jean Jannoray. 1937. "Fouilles de Krisa (Phocide)." *BCH* 61:299–326. DOI: 10.3406/bch.1937.2732.

———. 1938. "Fouilles de Krisa (Phocide)." *BCH* 62:110–48. DOI: 10.3406/bch.1938.2698.

Elayi, Josette. 2018. *The History of Phoenicia.* Atlanta: Lockwood Press.

Elgavish, Joseph. 1993. "Shiqmona." *NEAEHL* 4:1373–78.

Emanuel, Jeffrey P. 2013. "'Šrdn from the Sea': The Arrival, Integration, and Acculturation of a 'Sea People.'" *Journal of Ancient Egyptian Interconnections* 5:14–27. DOI: 10.2458/azu_jaei_v05i1_emanuel.

———. 2015. "King Taita and His 'Palistin': Philistine State or Neo-Hittite Kingdom?" *Antiguo Oriente* 13:11–40.

———. 2016. "Maritime Worlds Collide: Agents of Transference and the Metastasis of Seaborne Threats at the End of the Bronze Age." *PEQ* 148:265–80. DOI: 10.1080/00310328.2016.1250359.

———. 2018. "Differentiating Naval Warfare and Piracy in the Late Bronze–Early Iron Age Mediterranean: Possibility or Pipe Dream?" Pages 68–80 in *Change, Continuity, and Connectivity: North-Eastern Mediterranean at the Turn of the Bronze Age and in the Early Iron Age.* Edited by Lukasz Niesiołowski-Spanò; Marek Wecowski. Philippika 118. Wiesbaden: Harrassowitz.

REFERENCES 327

———. 2020. *Naval Warfare and Maritime Conflict in the Late Bronze and Early Iron Age Mediterranean.* CHANE 117. Leiden: Brill.

Erb-Satullo, Nathaniel L., Brian J. J. Gilmour, and Nana Khakhutaishvili. 2015. "Crucible Technologies in the Late Bronze–Early Iron Age South Caucasus: Copper Processing, Tin Bronze Production, and the Possibility of Local Tin Ores." *JArS* 61:260–76. DOI: 10.1016/j.jas.2015.05.010.

Evely, Don, ed. 2006. *Lefkandi IV: The Bronze Age; The Late Helladic IIIC Settlement at Xeropolis.* Supplementary Volume 39. London: British School of Archaeology at Athens.

Faulkner, Raymond O. 1962. *Concise Dictionary of Middle Egyptian.* Oxford: Griffith Institute.

Faust, Avraham. 2011. "Tel 'Eton Excavations (2006–2009): A Preliminary Report." *PEQ* 143:198–224. DOI: 10.1179/003103211X13092562976171.

———. 2014. "The History of Tel 'Eton Following the Results of the First Seven Seasons of Excavations (2006–2012)." Pages 585–604 in *Proceedings of the 8th International Conference on the Archaeology of the Ancient Near East (ICAANE).* Vol. 2: *Excavation and Progress Reports; Posters.* Edited by Piotr Bieliński, Michał Gawlikowski, Rafał Koliński, Dorota Ławecka, Arkadiusz Sołtysiak, and Zuzanna Wygnańska. Weisbaden: Harrassowitz Verlag.

———. 2017. "Tel 'Eton and the History of the Shephelah during the Iron Age." Pages 21–43 in *Le-ma'an Ziony: Essays in Honor of Ziony Zevit.* Edited by Frederick E. Greenspahn and Gary Rendsburg. Eugene, OR: Cascade.

Faust, Avraham, and Hayah Katz. 2015. "A Canaanite Town, a Judahite Center, and a Persian Period Fort: Excavating Over Two Thousand Years of History at Tel 'Eton." *NEA* 78.2:88–102. DOI: 10.5615/neareastarch.78.2.0088.

Faust, Avraham, Hayah Katz, David Ben-Shlomo, Yair Sapir, and Pirchiya Eyall. 2014. "Tēl 'Ēṭōn/Tell 'Ēṭūn and Its Interregional Contacts from the Late Bronze Age to the Persian-Hellenistic Period: Between Highlands and Lowlands." *ZDPV* 130:43–76.

Feldman, Michal, Daniel M. Master, Raffaela A. Bianco, Marta Burri, Philipp W. Stockhammer, Alissa Mittnik, Adam J. Aja, Choongwon Jeong, and Johannes Krause. 2019. "Ancient DNA Sheds Light on the Genetic Origins of Early Iron Age Philistines." *Science Advances* 5.7. DOI: 10.1126/sciadv.aax0061.

Ferry, Matthieu, Mustapha Meghraoui, Najib Abou Karaki, Masdouq Al-Taj, and Lutfi Khalil. 2011. "Episodic Behavior of the Jordan Valley Section of the Dead Sea Fault Inferred from a 14-ka-Long Integrated Catalog of Large Earthquakes Episodic Behavior of the Jordan Valley Section of the Dead Sea Fault." *Bulletin of the Seismological Society of America* 101:39–67. DOI: 10.1785/0120100097.

Finkbeiner, Uwe. 2001. "Emar 1999: Bericht über die 3. Kampagne der syrisch-deutschen Ausgrabungen." *BaM* 32:41–120.

———. 2002. "Emar 2001: Bericht über die 4. Kampagne der syrisch-deutschen Ausgrabungen." *BaM* 33:109–46.

Finkbeiner, Uwe, and Ferhan Sakal. 2003. "Emar 2002: Bericht über die 5. Kampagne der syrisch-deutschen Ausgrabungen." *BaM* 34:9–118.

———. 2015. *Emar after the Closure of the Tabqa Dam: The Syrian-German Excavations 1996–2002.* Vol. 2: *Excavation Method, Architecture and Stratigraphy.* Subartu 35. Turnhout: Brepols.

Finkelstein, Israel. 2009. "Destructions: Megiddo as a Case Study." Pages 113–26 in *Ex-*

ploring the Long Durée: Essays in Honor of Lawrence E. Stager. Edited by J. David Schloen. Winona Lake, IN: Eisenbrauns.

———. 2016. "The Levant and the Eastern Mediterranean in the Early Phases of the Iron Age: The View from Micro-Archaeology." Pages 112–22 in *Assyria to Iberia: Art and Culture in the Iron Age.* Edited by Joan Aruz and Michael Seymour. Metropolitan Museum of Art Symposia. New York: Metropolitan Museum of Art.

Finkelstein, Israel, Eran Arie, Mario A. S. Martin, and Eli Piasetzky. 2017a. "New Evidence on the Late Bronze/Iron I Transition at Megiddo: Implications for the End of the Egyptian Rule and the Appearance of Philistine Pottery." *AeL* 27:261–80.

Finkelstein, Israel, Dafna Langgut, Meirav Meiri, and Lidar Sapir-Hen. 2017b. "Egyptian Imperial Economy in Canaan: Reaction to the Climate Crisis at the End of the Late Bronze Age." *AeL* 27:249–60.

Finkelstein, Israel, and Lily Singer-Avitz. 2009. "Reevaluating Bethel." *ZDPV* 125:33–48.

Finkelstein, Israel, and David Ussishkin. 2000. "Archaeological and Historical Conclusions." Pages 576–605 in *Megiddo III: The 1992–1996 Seasons.* Edited by Israel Finkelstein, David Ussishkin, and Baruch Halpern. SMNIA 18. Tel Aviv: Emery and Claire Yass Publications in Archaeology.

Finkelstein, Israel, David Ussishkin, and Baruch Halpern. 2006. "Archaeological and Historical Conclusions." Pages 843–59 in *Megiddo IV: The 1998–2002 Seasons.* Edited by Israel Finkelstein, David Ussishkin, and Baruch Halpern. 2 vols. SMNIA 24. Tel Aviv: Emery and Claire Yass Publications in Archaeology.

Finné, Martin, Karin Holmgren, Chuan-Chou Shen, Hsun-Ming Hu, Meighan Boyd, and Sharon Stocker. 2017. "Late Bronze Age Climate Change and the Destruction of the Mycenaean Palace of Nestor at Pylos." *PLoS ONE* 12: e0189447. DOI: 10.1371/journal.pone.0189447.

Fischer, Bettina, ed. 2003. *Identifying Changes: The Transition from Bronze to Iron Ages in Anatolia and Its Neighbouring Regions; Proceedings of the International Workshop, Istanbul, November 8–9, 2002.* Istanbul: Turk Eskicagi Bilimleri enstitusu.

Fischer, Peter M. 2006. *Tell Abu al-Kharaz in the Jordan Valley.* Vol. 2: *The Middle and Late Bronze Ages.* CCEM 11. Vienna: Österreichischen Akademie der Wissenschaften.

———. 2011. "The New Swedish Cyprus Expedition 2010: Excavations at Dromolaxia Vizatzia/Hala Sultan Tekke; Preliminary Results." *OpAthRom* 4:69–98.

———. 2013. "The New Swedish Cyprus Expedition 2012 Excavations at Hala Sultan Tekke." *OpAthRom* 6:45–79.

———. 2014. "The Southern Levant (Transjordan) during the Late Bronze Age." Pages 561–76 *The Oxford Handbook of the Archaeology of the Levant c. 8000–332 BCE.* Edited by Margreet Steiner and Ann E. Killebrew. Oxford Handbooks. Oxford: Oxford University Press.

———. 2017. "The 13th/12th Century BCE Destructions and the Abandonment of Hala Sultan Tekke, Cyprus." Pages 177–206 in *"Sea Peoples" Up-to-Date: New Research on the Transformations in the Eastern Mediterranean in the 13th–11th Centuries BCE.* Edited by Peter M. Fischer and Teresa Bürge. CCEM 35. Vienna: Österreichische Academie der Wissenschaften. DOI: 10.2307/j.ctt1v2xvsn.15.

———. 2019. "Hala Sultan Tekke, Cyprus: A Late Bronze Age Trade Metropolis." *NEA* 82:236–47. DOI: 10.1086/705491.

———. 2020. "The Occupational History of the Bronze Age Harbour City of Hala Sultan Tekke, Cyprus." *AeL* 29:188–229. DOI: 10.1553/AEundL29s189.

REFERENCES 329

Fischer, Peter M., and Teresa Bürge. 2014. "The New Swedish Cyprus Expedition 2013 Excavations at Hala Sultan Tekke." *OpAthRom* 7:61–106. DOI: 10.30549/opath-rom-07-04.

———. 2015. "The New Swedish Cyprus Expedition 2014 Excavations at Hala Sultan Tekke." *OpAthRom* 8:27–79. DOI: 10.30549/opathrom-08-03.

———. 2017a. "The New Swedish Cyprus Expedition 2016 Excavations at Hala Sultan Tekke (The Söderberg Expedition)." *OpAthRom* 10:50–93. DOI: 10.30549/opath-rom-10-03.

———. eds. 2017b. *Sea Peoples Up-to-Date: New Research on Transformation in the Eastern Mediterranean in 13th–11th Centuries BCE*. CCEM 35. Vienna: Österreichischen Akademie der Wissenschaften. DOI: 10.2307/j.ctt1v2xvsn.

———. 2018. *Two Late Cypriot City Quarters at Hala Sultan Tekke: The Söderberg Expedition 2010–2017*. Studies in Mediterranean Archaeology 147. Uppsala: Åström.

Fisher, Kevin D., Sturt W. Manning, and Thomas M. Urban. 2019. "New Approaches to Late Bronze Age Urban Landscapes on Cyprus: Investigations at Kalavasos-Ayios Dhimitrios, 2012–2016." *AJA* 123:473–507. DOI: 10.3764/aja.123.3.0473.

Fischer, Peter M., and Moain Sadeq. 2000. "Tell el-'Ajjul 1999: A Joint Palestinian-Swedish Field Project: First Season Preliminary Report." *AeL* 10:211–26.

———. 2008. "'Ajjul, Tell el-." *NEAEHL* 5:1565–66.

Fischer, Peter M., Moain Sadeq, Anne Lykke, Rainer Feldbacher, Michael Weigl, and Christa Mlina. 2002. "Tell el-'Ajjul 2000 Second Season Preliminary Report." *AeL* 12:109–53. DOI: 10.1553/AEundL12s109.

Forrer, Emil O. 1936. "The Hittites in Palestine. I." *PEQ* 68:190–203. DOI: 10.1179/peq.1936.68.4.190.

Forsdyke, Edgar John. 1957. *Greece before Homer: Ancient Chronology and Mythology*. New York: Norton.

Frangipane, Marcella. 2011. "Arslantepe-malatya: A Prehistoric and Early Historic Center in Eastern Anatolia." Pages 968–92 in *The Oxford Handbook of Ancient Anatolia 10,000–323 B.C.E*. Edited by Sharon R. Steadman and Gregory McMahon. Oxford Handbooks. Oxford: Oxford University Press.

Frank, Andre Gunder. 1993. "Bronze Age World System Cycles." *CA* 34:383–429.

Franken, Hendricus Jacobus. 1975. "Palestine in the Time of the Nineteenth Dynasty: (b) Archaeological Evidence." Pages 331–37 in *The Middle East and the Aegean Region c. 1380–1000 BC*. Edited by I. E. S. Edwards, C. J. Gadd, N. G. L. Hammond, and E. Sollberger. 3rd ed. CAH 2.2. Cambridge: Cambridge University Press.

———. 1992. *Excavations at Tell Deir ʿAllā: the Late Bronze Age Sanctuary*. DMOA 16. Leuven: Peeters.

French, Elizabeth B. 2002. *Mycenae, Agamemnon's Capital: The Site in Its Setting*. Stroud: History Press.

———. 2010. "Mycenae." Pages 671–79 in *The Oxford Handbook of the Bronze Age Aegean (ca. 3000–1000 BC)*. Edited by Eric H. Cline. Oxford Handbooks. Oxford: Oxford University Press.

French, Elizabeth B., and Spyros E. Iakovidis. 2003. *Archaeological Atlas of Mycenae*. Athens: Archaeological Society of Athens.

French, Elizbeth B., Philipp W. Stockhammer, Ursula Damm-Meinhardt. 2009. "Mycenae and Tiryns: The Pottery of the Second Half of the Thirteenth Century BC-Contexts and Definitions." *ABSA* 104:175–232. DOI: 10.1017/S006824540000023X.

French, Elizabeth B., and William Taylour. 2007. *Well Built Mycenae: The Helleno-British*

330 REFERENCES

Excavations within the Citadel at Mycenae 1959–1969. Fascicule 13: *The Service Areas of the Cult Centre.* Oxford: Oxbow.

Fugmann, Ejnar. 1958. *Hama: Fouilles et recherches de la Fondation Carlsberg 1931–1938, II.1; L'architecture des périodes pré–hellénistiques.* Copenhagen: Fondation Carlsberg.

Furumark, Arne, and Charles Martin Adelman. 2003. *Swedish Excavations at Sinda, Cyprus: Excavations Conducted by Arne Furumark 1947–1948.* Skrifter utgivna av Svenska institutet i Athen 50. Stockholm: Åström.

Gadot, Yuval. 2009. "The Late Bronze Age (Strata X14–X12)." Pages 41–72 in *Aphek-Antipatris II: The Remains on the Acropolis; The Moshe Kochavi and Pirhyia Beck Excavations.* Edited by Yuval Gadot, Esther Yadin, and Gabriella Bachi. SMNIA 27. Tel Aviv: Emery and Claire Yass Publications in Archaeology.

———. 2010. "The Late Bronze Egyptian Estate at Aphek." *TA* 37:48–66. DOI: 10.1179/033 443510x12632070179388.

Gadot, Yuval, Mario Martin, and Noga Blockman. 2006. "Area K (Levels K-5 and K-4, the 1998–2002 Seasons)." Pages 87–103 in *Megiddo IV: The 1998–2002 Seasons.* Edited by Israel Finkelstein, David Ussishkin, and Baruch Halpern. 2 vols. SMNIA 24. Tel Aviv: Emery and Claire Yass Publications in Archaeology.

Galanakis, Yannis. 2013a. "Korakou in Korinthia." Pages 3810–11 in vol. 7 of *The Encyclopedia of Ancient History.* Edited by Roger S. Bagnall, Kai Brodersen, Craige Brian Champion, Andrew Erskine, and Sabine R. Huebner. 13 vols. Chichester: Wiley-Blackwell.

———. 2013b. "Dhimini in Thessaly." Pages 2062 in vol. 4 of *The Encyclopedia of Ancient History.* Edited by Roger S. Bagnall, Kai Brodersen, Craige Brian Champion, Andrew Erskine, and Sabine R. Huebner. 13 vols. Chichester: Wiley-Blackwell.

———. 2013c. "Iolkos in Thessaly." Pages 3485 vol. 7 of in *The Encyclopedia of Ancient History.* Edited by Roger S. Bagnall, Kai Brodersen, Craige Brian Champion, Andrew Erskine, and Sabine R. Huebner. 13 vols. Chichester: Wiley-Blackwell.

Galili, Ehud, Noel Gale, and Baruch Rosen. 2013. "A Late Bronze Age Shipwreck with a Metal Cargo from Hishuley Carmel, Israel." *International Journal of Nautical Archaeology* 42:2–23. DOI: 10.1111/j.1095-9270.2012.00344.x.

Galil, Gershon, Ayelet Levinzon-Gilboa, Aren M. Maeir, Dan'el Kahn, and Ayelet Gilboa, eds. 2012. *The Ancient Near East in the 12th–10th Centuries BCE: Culture and History; Proceedings of the International Conference Held at the University of Haifa, 2–5 May, 2010.* AOAT 392. Münster: Ugarit-Verlag.

Gallet, Yves, Agnès Genevey, Maxime Le Goff, Frédéric Fluteau, and Safar Ali Eshraghi. 2006. "Possible Impact of the Earth's Magnetic Field on the History of Ancient Civilizations." *Earth and Planetary Science Letters* 246:17–26. DOI: 10.1016/j. epsl.2006.04.001.

Galling, Kurt. 1954. "Studien aus dem Deutschen evangelischen Institut für Altertumswissenschaft in Jerusalem. 50. Zur Lokalisierung von Debir." *ZDPV* 70:135–41.

Gallo, Elisabetta. 2014. "Destructions in Early Bronze Age Southern Levant." Pages 141–69 in *Overcoming Catastrophes: Essays on Disastrous Agents Characterization and Resilience Strategies in Pre-Classical Southern Levant.* Edited by Lorenzo Nigro. ROSAPAT 11. Rome: La Sapienza.

Garbati, Giuseppe, and Tatiana Pedrazzi. 2015. *Transformations and Crisis in the Mediterranean: Identity and Interculturality in the Levant and Phoenician West during the*

REFERENCES   331

12th–8th centuries BCE: Proceedings of the International Conference Held in Rome, CNR, May 8–9 2013. RSFSup 42. Rome: Istituto di Studi sul Mediterraneo Antico.

Garfinkel, Yosef. 2017. "The Ethnic Identification of Khirbet Qeiyafa: Why It Matters." Pages 149–67 in *The Wide Lens in Archaeology: Honoring Brian Hesse's Contributions to Anthropological Archaeology*. Edited by Allan Gilbert, Justin Lev-Tov, and Paula Wapnish. Archaeobiology 2. Atlanta: Lockwood Press.

Garfinkel, Yosef, Michael G. Hasel, Martin G. Klingbeil, Hoo-Goo Kang, Gwanghyun Choi, Sang-Yeup Chang, Soonhwa Hong, Saar Ganor, Igor Kreimerman, and Christopher Bronk Ramsey. 2019 "Lachish Fortifications and State Formation in the Biblical Kingdom of Judah in Light of Radiometric Datings." *Radiocarbon* 61.3:1–18 DOI:10.1017/RDC.2019.5

Garfinkel, Yosef, Michael G. Hasel, Martin G. Klingbeil, Igor Kreimerman, Michael Pytlik, Jon W. Carroll, Jonathan W. B. Waybright, Hoo-Goo Kang, Gwanghyun Choi, SangYeup Chang, Soonhwa Hong, Arlette David, Itamar Weissbein, and Noam Silverberg. 2021. "The Canaanite and Judean Cities of Lachish, Israel: Preliminary Report of the Fourth Expedition, 2013–2017." *AJA* 125:419–59. DOI: 10.3764/aja.125.3.0419.

Garner, Jennifer. 2015. "Bronze Age Tin Mines in Central Asia." Pages 135–44 in *Archaeometallurgy in Europe III: Proceedings of the 3rd International Conference Deutsches Bergbau-Museum Bochum June 29–July 1, 2011*. Edited by Andreas Hauptmann and Diana Modarressi-Tehrani. Bochum: Deutsches Bergbau-Museum.

Garstang, John. 1910. *The Land of the Hittites: An Account of Recent Explorations and Discoveries in Asia Minor, with Descriptions of the Hittite Monuments*. London: Constable.

———. 1953. *Prehistoric Mersin, Yümük Tepe in Southern Turkey: The Neilson Expedition in Cilicia*. Oxford: Clarendon.

Gates, Marie-Henriette. 1996. "Archaeology in Turkey." *AJA* 100:277–335. DOI: 10.2307/506905.

———. 1998. "1997 Archaeological Excavations at Kinet Höyük (Yesil-Dörtyol, Hatay)." *Kazı Sonuçları Toplantısı* 20:259–82.

———. 2000. "1998 Excavations at Kinet Höyük (Yeşil-Dörtyol, Hatay)." *Kazı Sonuçları Toplantısı*, 21:193–208.

———. 2006. "Dating the Hittite Levels at Kinet Höyük: A Revised Chronology." Pages 293–309 in *Strukturierung und Datierung der hethitischen Archäologie: Voraussetzungen, Probleme, Neue Ansätze; Internationaler Workshop Istanbul, 26–27. November 2004*. Edited by Dirk Paul Mielke, Ulf-Dietrich Schoop, and Jürgen Seeher. Byzas 4. Istanbul: Ege Yayınları.

———. 2013. "From Late Bronze to Iron Age on Syria's Northwest Frontier: Cilicia and the Amuq." Pages 95–116 in *Syrian Archaeology in Perspective: Celebrating 20 Years of Excavations at Tell Afis; Proceedings of the International Meeting; Percorsi di Archeologia Siriana; Giornate di studio Pisa 27–28 Novembre 2006*. Edited by Stefania Mazzoni and Sebastiano Soldi. Pisa: ETS.

Gauss, Walter. 2000. "Neue Forschungen zur prähistorischen Akropolis von Athen." Pages 167–89 in *Österreichische Forschungen zur ägäischen Bronzezeit 1998: Akten der Tagung am Institut für Klassische Archäologie der Universität Wien, 2.–3. Mai 1998*. Edited by Fritz Blakolmer. Wiener Forschungen zur Archäologie 3. Vienna: Phoibos.

———. 2003. "Late Mycenaean Pottery from the Northslope of the Athenian Acropolis

of Athens." Pages 93–104 in *LH III C Chronology and Synchronisms II. LH III C Middle: Proceedings of the International Workshop Held at the Austrian Academy of Sciences at Vienna, October 29th and 30th, 2004.* Edited by Sigrid Deger-Jalkotzy and Michaela Zavadil. Veröffentlichungen der Mykenischen Kommission 28. Vienna: Österreichische Akademie der Wissenschaften.

Gazis, Michael. 2010. "Η προϊστορική ακρόπολη του Τείχους Δυμαίων: Σε αναζήτηση ταυτότητας." Pages 237–55 in *Ίρις: Μελέτες στη μνήμη της καθηγήτριας Αγγελικής Πιλάλη-Παπαστερίου.* Edited by Nikos Merousis, Evaggelia Stefani, and Marianna Nikolaidou. Thessalonike: Kornilia-Sfakianaki.

Genz, Hermann. 2011. "Foreign Contacts of the Hittites." Pages 301–31 in *Insights into Hittite History and Archaeology.* Edited by Hermann Genz and Dirk Paul Mielke. Colloquia Antiqua 2. Leuven: Peeters.

———. 2013. "'No Land Could Stand before Their Arms, from Hatti ... on ...'? New Light on the End of the Hittite Empire and the Early Iron Age in Central Anatolia." Pages 469–78 in *The Philistines and Other "Sea Peoples" in Text and Archaeology.* Edited by Ann E. Killebrew and Gunner Lehman. ABS 15. Atlanta: Society of Biblical Literature.

Georgiou, Artemis. 2011. "The Settlement Histories of Cyprus at the Opening of the Twelfth Century BC." *Cahier du Centre d'Études Chypriotes* 41:109–31.

———. 2012a. "Pyla-Kokkinokremos, Maa-Palaeokastro and the Settlement Histories of Cyprus in the Twelfth Century B.C." PhD diss., University of Oxford.

———. 2012b. "Pyla-Kokkinokremos and Maa-Palaeokastro: A Comparison of Two Naturally Fortified Late Cypriot Settlements." Pages 65–83 in *Cyprus: An Island Culture; Society and Social Relations from the Bronze Age to the Venetian Period.* Edited by Artemis Georgiou. Oxford: Oxbow.

———. 2015. "Cyprus during the 'Crisis Years' Revisited." Pages 129–45 in *The Mediterranean Mirror: Cultural Contacts in the Mediterranean Sea between 1200 and 750 B.C.* Edited by Andrea Babbi, Friederike Bubenheimer-Erhart, Beatriz Marín-Aguilera, and Simone Mühl. RGZM-Tagungen 20. Mainz: Verlag des Römisch-Germanischen Zentralmuseums.

———. 2017. "Flourishing amidst a 'Crisis': The Regional History of the Paphos Polity at the Transition from the 13th to the 12th Centuries BCE." Pages 207–28 in *"Sea Peoples" Up-to-Date: New Research on the Transformations in the Eastern Mediterranean in the 13th–11th Centuries BCE.* Edited by Peter M. Fischer and Teresa Bürge. CCEM 35. Vienna: Österreichische Academie der Wissenschaften. DOI: 10.2307/j.ctt1v2xvsn.16.

Georgiou, Artemis. and Maria Iacovou 2020. "Cyprus." Pages 1133–62 in vol. 2 of *A Companion to the Archaeology of Early Greece and the Mediterranean.* Edited by Irene M. Lemos and Antonios Kotsonas. 2 vols. BCAW. Hoboken, NJ: Wiley-Blackwell.

Gershuny, Lilly. 1981. "Stratum V at Tell Abū Hawām." *ZDPV*:36–44.

Gibson, Shimon. 1994. "The Tell ej-Judeideh (Tel Goded) Excavations: A Reappraisal Based on Archival Records in the Palestine Exploration Fund." *TA* 21:194–234. DOI: 10.1179/tav.1994.1994.2.194.

Gilboa, Ayelet, and Ilan Sharon. 2003. "An Archaeological Contribution to the Early Iron Age Chronological Debate: Alternative Chronologies for Phoenicia and Their Effects on the Levant, Cyprus, and Greece." *BASOR* 332:7–80. DOI: 10.2307/1357808.

———. 2017. "Fluctuations in Levantine Maritime Foci across the Late Bronze/Iron Age Transition: Charting the Role of the Sharon-Carmel (Tjeker) Coast in the Rise

REFERENCES 333

of Iron Age Phoenician Polities." Pages 285–98 in *"Sea Peoples" Up-to-Date: New Research on the Transformations in the Eastern Mediterranean in the 13th–11th Centuries BCE*. Edited by Peter M. Fischer and Teresa Bürge. CCEM 35. Vienna: Österreichische Academie der Wissenschaften. DOI: 10.2307/j.ctt1v2xvsn.20.

Gilboa, Ayelet, Ilan Sharon, Jeffrey R. Zorn, and Sveta Matskevich 2018. *Excavations at Dor: Final Report*. Vol. IIA: *Area G, the Late Bronze and Iron Ages: Synthesis, Architecture and Stratigraphy*. Qedem Reports 10. Jerusalem: Hebrew University of Jerusalem.

Gilboa, Ayelet, Paula Waiman-Barak, and Ilan Sharon. 2015. "Dor, the Carmel Coast and Early Iron Age Mediterranean Exchanges." Pages 85–109 in *The Mediterranean Mirror: Cultural Contacts in the Mediterranean Sea between 1200 and 750 B.C.* Edited by Andrea Babbi, Friederike Bubenheimer-Erhart, Beatriz Marín-Aguilera, and Simone Mühl. RGZM-Tagungen 20. Mainz: Verlag des Römisch-Germanischen Zentralmuseums.

Gitin, Seymour, Amihay Mazar, and Ephraim Stern, eds. 1998. *Mediterranean Peoples in Transition: Thirteenth to Early Tenth Centuries BCE; In Honor of Professor Trude Dothan*. Jerusalem: Israel Exploration Society.

Gittlen Barry M. 1977. "Studies in the Late Cypriote Pottery Found in Palestine." PhD diss., University of Pennsylvania.

——. 1981. "The Cultural and Chronological Implications of the Cypro-Palestine Trade during the Late Bronze Age." *BASOR* 241:49–59. DOI: 10.2307/1356710.

Givon, Shmuel. 2008. "Harasim (Tel)." *NEAEHL* 5:1766–77.

von Gladiß, Almut, and Harald Hauptmann. 1974. "Norşuntepe." *AW* 5.2: 9–19.

Goetze, Albrecht. 1975. "The Hittites and Syria (1300–1200 BC)." Pages 252–73 in *The Middle East and the Aegean Region c. 1380–1000 BC*. Edited by I. E. S. Edwards, C. J. Gadd, N. G. L. Hammond, and E. Sollberger. 3rd ed. CAH 2.2. Cambridge: Cambridge University Press.

Goldman, Hetty, Frederick R. Matson, Machteld Johanna Mellink, and Ignace J. Gelb. 1956. *Excavations at Gözlü Kule, Tarsus*. Vol. 2: *From the Neolithic through the Bronze Age*. Princeton: Princeton University Press.

Gonnella, Julia, Wahid Khayyata, and Kay Kohlmeyer. 2005. *Die Zitadelle von Aleppo und der Tempel des Wettergottes: Neue Forschungen und Entdeckungen*. Münster: Rhema.

Gordon, Douglas H. 1953. "Fire and the Sword: The Technique of Destruction." *Antiquity* 27.105:149–52. DOI: 10.1017/S0003598X00024790.

Gorman, Vanessa B. 2001. *Miletos, the Ornament of Ionia: A History of the City to 400 B.C.E.* Ann Arbor: University of Michigan Press.

Gorny, Ronald. 1990. "Alişar Höyük in the Second Millennium B.C." PhD diss., University of Chicago.

——. 1994. "The 1993 Season at Alişar Höyük in Central Turkey." *Anatolica* 20:191–202.

——. 1995a. "Alişar Höyük in the Late Second Millennium BC." Pages 159–71 in *Atti del II Congresso internazionale di hittitologia*. Edited by Onofrio Carruba, Mauro Giorgieri, and Clelia Mora. Pavia: Iuculano.

——. 1995b. "Hittite Imperialism and Anti-Imperial Resistance as Viewed from Alişar Höyük." *BASOR* 299/300:65–89. DOI: 10.2307/1357346.

Görsdorf, Jochen, Harald Hauptmann, and Gundela Kaschau. 2002. "14C-Datierungen zur Schichtabfolge des Lidar Höyük, Südost-Türkei." *Berliner Beiträge zur Archäometrie* 19:63–70.

334 REFERENCES

Gottlieb, Yulia. 2016. "Beer-Sheba under Attack: A Study of Arrowheads and the Story of the Destruction of the Iron Age Settlement." Pages 1192–1228 in *Beer-Sheba III: The Early Iron IIA Enclosed Settlement and the Late Iron IIA-Iron IIB Cities.* Edited by Ze'ev Herzog, Lily Singer-Avitz, and Itzhaq Beit-Arieh. SMNIA 33. Winona Lake, IN: Eisenbrauns.

Grant, Elihu. 1929. *Beth Shemesh (Palestine).* Biblical and Kindred Studies 2. Haverford: Haverford College.

———. 1939. *Ain Shems Excavations (Palestine).* Biblical and Kindred Studies. Haverford: Haverford College.

Greaves, Alan M. 2002. *Miletos: A History.* London: Routledge.

Green, John D. M. 2006. "Ritual and Social Structure in the Late Bronze and Early Iron Age Southern Levant: The Cemetery at Tell es-Sa'idiyeh, Jordan." PhD diss., University of London, University College London.

Greener, A. 2015. "Late Bronze Age Imported Pottery in the Land of Israel: Between Economy, Society and Symbolism." PhD diss., Bar-Ilan University.

———. 2016. "Analyzing the Late Bronze Age Imported Pottery Distribution in the Southern Levant: Overcoming Methodological Challenges." Pages 463–43 in *Proceedings of the 9th International Congress on the Archaeology of the Ancient Near East, June 9–13, 2014, University of Basel.* Volume 3: *Reports.* Edited by Rolf A. Stucky, Oskar Kaelin, and Hans-Peter Mathys. ICAANE 9. Wiesbaden: Harrassowitz.

Greenberg, Raphael. 2019. *The Archaeology of the Bronze Age Levant: From Urban Origins to the Demise of City-States, 3700–1000 BCE.* Cambridge World Archaeology. Cambridge: Cambridge University Press.

Greenfield, Tina, Chris McKinny, and Itzhaq Shai. 2017. "'I Can Count All My Bones:' A Preliminary Report of the Late Bronze Faunal Remains from Area B1 at Tel Burna, Israel." Pages 419–41 in *The Wide Lens in Archaeology: Honoring Brian Hesse's Contributions to Anthropological Archaeology.* Edited by Justin Lev-Tov, Paula Wapnish, and Allan Gilbert. Archaeobiology 2. Atlanta: Lockwood Press.

Griggs, Carol B., and Sturt W. Manning. 2009. "A Reappraisal of the Dendrochronology and Dating of Tille Höyük (1993)." *Radiocarbon* 51:711–20. DOI: 10.1017/S0033822200056046.

Grigson, Caroline. 2015. "The Fauna of Tell Nebi Mend (Syria) in the Bronze and Iron Age—A Diachronic Overview, Part 1: Stability and Change—Animal Husbandry." *Levant* 47:5–29. DOI: 10.1179/0075891415Z.00000000055.

Günel, Sevinç. 2010. "Mycenaean Cultural Impact on the Çine (Marsyas) Plain, Southwest Anatolia: The Evidence from Çine-Tepecik." *AnSt* 60:25–49.

———. 2015a. "Ein Zentrum mit interregionalen Beziehungen in Westanatolien in der Bronzezeit: Çine-Tepecik/Bronz Çağında Batı Anadolu'da Bölgelerarası Bağlantıları Gösteren Bir Merkez: Çine-Tepecik." Pages 205–16 in *Anatolien-Brücke der Kulturen: Aktuelle Forschungen und Perspektiven in den deutsch-türkischen Altertumswissenschaften; Tagungsband des Internationalen Symposiums "Anatolien – Brücke der Kulturen" in Bonn vom 7. bis 9. Juli 2014.* Edited by Ünsal Yalçin and Hans-Dieter Bienert. Bonn: Deutsches Bergbau-Museum.

———. 2015b. "Çine-Tepecik: New Contributions on Late Bronze Age Cultures in Western Anatolia." Pages 627–46 in *NOSTOI: Indigenous Culture, Migration, Integration in the Aegean Islands, Western Anatolia during the Late Bronze Age-Early Iron Age, Koç University, Istanbul.* Edited by Nikolaos Chr Stampolidis, Çiğdem Maner, and Konstantinos Kopanias. Istanbul: Koç University Press.

REFERENCES

335

———. 2016. "A New Centre of Intercultural Relations in Western Anatolia during the Late Bronze Age: Çine-Tepecik." Pages 347–59 in vol. 3 of *Proceedings of the 9th International Congress on the Archaeology of the Ancient Near East (ICAANE)*. Edited by Oskar Kaelin and Hans-Peter Mathys. Wiesbaden: Harrassowitz.

Gur-Arieh, Shira, Ruth Shahack-Gross, Aren M. Maeir, Gunnar Lehmann, Louise A. Hitchcock, and Elisabetta Boaretto. 2014. "The Taphonomy and Preservation of Wood and Dung Ashes Found in Archaeological Cooking Installations: Case Studies from Iron Age Israel." *JArS* 46:50–67. DOI: 10.1016/j.jas.2014.03.011.

Gursan-Salzmann, Ayse. 1992. "Alaca Hoyuk: A Reassessment of the Excavation and Sequence of the Early Bronze Age Settlement." PhD diss., University of Pennsylvania.

Hadjisavvas, Sophocles. 1986. "Alassa: A Late Cypriot Site." *RDAC* 1986:62–67.

———. 1989. "A Late Cypriot Community at Alassa." Pages 32–42 in *Early Society in Cyprus*. Edited by Edgar Peltenburg. Edinburgh: Edinburgh University Press.

———. 1991. "LC IIC to LC IIIA without Intruders: The Case of Alassa-Pano Mandilaris." Pages 173–80 in *Cypriot Ceramics: Reading the Prehistoric Record*. Edited by Jane A. Barlow. Museum Monograph 74. Philadelphia: University Museum of Archaeology and Anthropology.

———. 1994. "Alassa Archaeological Project 1991–1993." *RDAC* 1994:107–14.

———. 1996. "Alassa: A Regional Centre of Alassa?" Pages 23–38 in *Late Bronze Age Settlement in Cyprus: Function and Relationship*. Edited by Paul Åström and Ellen Herscher. Studies in Mediterranean Archaeology and Literature 126. Jonsered: Åström.

———. 2000. "Dating Alassa." Pages 431–36 in *The Synchronisation of Civilisations in the Eastern Mediterranean in the Second Millennium B.C. II: Proceedings of the SCIEM 2000 – Euro Conference Haindorf, 2nd of May–7th of May 2001*. Edited by Manfred Bietak. CCEM 29. Vienna: Österreichischen Akademie der Wissenschaften.

———. 2007. "Who Were the Residents of the Ashlar Buildings in Cyprus?" Pages 1–7 in *Patrimoines culturels en Méditerranée orientale: Recherche scientifique et enjeux identitaires. 1er atelier (29 novembre 2007); Chypre, une stratigraphie de l'identité*. Edited by Jean-Claude David and Sylvie Müller-Celka. Lyon: Rencontres scientifiques en ligne de la Maison de l'Orient et de la Méditerranée.

———. 2009. "Aspects of Regionalism in Late Cypriot Architecture and the Case of Alassa." Pages 127–34 in *The Formation of Cyprus in the 2nd Millennium B.C.: Proceedings of a Workshop Held at the 4th Cyprological Congress May 2nd, 2008, Lefkosia, Cyprus*. Edited by Irmgard Hein. CCEM 20. Vienna: Österreichischen Akademie der Wissenschaften.

———. 2017. *Alassa: Excavations at the Late Bronze Age Sites of Pano Mantilaris and Paliotaverna 1984–2000*. Lefkosia: Department of Antiquities, Cyprus.

Hadjisavvas, Sophocles, and I. Hadjisavva. 1997. "Aegean Influence at Alassa." Pages 143–48 in *Praktika tu diethnus archaiologiku synedriou Hē Kypros kai to Aigaio stēn archaiotēta: apo tēn proïstorikē periodo ōs ton 7o aiōna m. Ch.: Leukōsia 8–10 dekembriu 1995 = Proceedings of the International Conference Cyprus and the Aegean in Antiquity*. Edited by Maroni Tsaroukkas. Nicosia: Department of Antiquities, Cyprus.

Halayqa, Issam K. H. 2010. "The Demise of Ugarit in the Light of Its Connections with Hatti." *UF* 42:297–330.

336 REFERENCES

Hall, Harry Reginald. 1901. *The Oldest Civilization of Greece: Studies of the Mycenaean Age.* London: Nutt.

———. 1902. "Keftiu and the Peoples of the Sea." *ABSA* 8:157–89.

Hallager, Birgitta. 2017. "2. The LM IIIB Settlements at Khania West Crete." Pages 37–52 in *How Long Is a Century? Late Minoan IIIB Pottery: Relative Chronology and Regional Differences.* Edited by Charlotte Langohr. Aegis 12. Louvain-La-Neuve: Presses Universitaires de Louvain.

Hallager, Erik, and Birgitta Hallager. 2003. *The Greek-Swedish Excavations at the Agia Aikaterini Square, Kastelli, Khania 1970–1987 and 2001.* Vol. 3: *The Late Minoan IIIB; 2 Settlement.* Skrifter utgivna av Svenska institutet i Athen 47. Stockholm: Åström.

Hamilton, Robert William. 1935. "Excavations at Tell Abu Hawam." *QDAP* 4:1–69.

Hänsel, Bernhard. 1979. "Die Ausgrabungen von Kastanas in Zentralmakedonien 1975–1978." *Jahrbuch des Romisch-Germanischen Zentral-Museums Mainz* 26:167–202. DOI: 10.11588/jrgzm.1979.0.51332.

———. 1989. *Kastanas: Ausgrabungen in einem Siedlungshügel der Bronze- und Eisenzeit Makedoniens 1975–1979.* Vol. 6: *Die Grabungen und der Baubefund.* Berlin: Spiess.

Hansen, Cavidan K., and J. Nicholas Postgate. 1999. "The Bronze to Iron Age Transition at Kilise Tepe." *AnSt* 49:111–21. DOI: 10.2307/3643066.

Harrison, Karl. 2004. "Fire and Burning in a Neolithic Settlement: Çatalhöyük." *Çatalhöyük Archive Reports.* www.catalhoyuk.com/archive_reports/2004/ar04_38.html.

———. 2008. "Fire and Burning at Çatalhöyük, 2008." *Çatalhöyük Archive Report 2008*: 273–80.

———. 2013. "The Application of Forensic Fire Investigation Techniques in the Archaeological Record." *JArS* 40:955–59. DOI: 10.1016/j.jas.2012.08.030.

Harrison, Timothy. P. 2008. *Cyprus, the Sea Peoples, and the Eastern Mediterranean: Regional Perspectives on Continuity and Change.* Toronto: Canadian Institute for Mediterranean Studies.

———. 2009a. "Neo-Hittites in the 'Land of Palistin': Renewed Investigations at Tell Ta'yinat on the Plain of Antioch." *NEA* 72:174–89. DOI: 10.1086/NEA25754026.

———. 2009b. "Lifting the Veil on a 'Dark Age': Ta'yinat and the North Orontes Valley during the Early Iron Age." Pages 171–84 in *Exploring the Long Durée: Essays in Honor of Lawrence Stager.* Edited by David Schloen. Winona Lake, IN: Eisenbrauns.

———. 2010. "The Late Bronze/Early Iron Age Transition in the North Orontes Valley." Pages 83–102 in *Societies in Transition: Evolutionary Processes in the Northern Levant between Late Bronze II and Early Iron Age.* Edited by Fabrizio Venturi. Studi e testi orientali 9. Bologna: CLUEB.

———. 2013. "Tayinat in the Early Iron Age." Pages 61–87 in *Across the Border: Late Bronze–Iron Age Relations between Syria and Anatolia; Proceedings of a Symposium Held at the Research Center of Anatolian Studies, Koç University, Istanbul, May 31–June 1, 2010.* Edited by Aslihan K. Yener. ANESSup 42. Leuven: Peeters.

Hasel, Michael G. 1998. *Domination and Resistance: Egyptian Military Activity in the Southern Levant, ca. 1300–1185 B.C.* PAe 11. Leiden: Brill.

———. 2011. "The Battle of Kadesh: Identifying New Kingdom Polities, Places, and Peoples in Canaan and Syria." Pages 65–86 in *Egypt, Canaan and Israel: History, Imperialism, Ideology and Literature Proceedings of a Conference at the University of*

REFERENCES 337

Haifa, 3–7 May 2009. Edited by Shay Bar, Dan'el Kahn, and J. J. Shirley. CHANE 52. Leiden: Brill. DOI: 10.1163/ej.9789004194939.i-370.27.

———. 2016. "The Archaeology of Destruction: Methodological Desiderata." Pages 205–28 in *From Sha'ar Hagolan to Shaarayim: Essays in Honor of Prof. Yosef Garfinkel.* Edited by Sa'ar Ganor, Igor Kreimerman, Katharina Streit, and Madeleine Mumcuoglu. Jerusalem: Israel Exploration Society.

Häser, Jutta, Katja A. P. Soennecken, and Dieter Vieweger. 2016. "Tall Zira'a in North-West Jordan between Aram and Israel." Pages 121–37 in *In Search for Aram and Israel: Politics, Culture, and Identity.* Edited by Omer Sergi, Manfred Oeming, and Izaak J. Hulster. ORA 20. Tübingen: Mohr Siebeck.

Hatzaki, Eleni 2004. "From Final Palatial to Postpalatial Knossos: A View from the Late Minoan II to Late Minoan IIIB Town." *British School at Athens Studies* 12:121–26.

———. 2005. "Postpalatial Knossos: Town and Cemeteries from LM IIIA2 to LM IIIC." Pages 65–95 in *Ariadne's Threads: Connections between Crete and the Greek Mainland in Late Minoan III (LM IIIA2 to LM IIIC); Proceedings of the International Workshop Held at Athens, Scuola archeologica italiana, 5–6 April 2003.* Edited by Anna Lucia D'Agata, Jennifer Moody, and Erin Williams. Tripodes 3. Atene: Scuola archeologica italiana di Atene.

———. 2017. "3. To Be or Not to Be in LM IIIB Knossos." Pages 53–77 in *How Long Is a Century? Late Minoan IIIB Pottery: Relative Chronology and Regional Differences.* Edited by Charlotte Langohr. Aegis 12. Louvain-La-Neuve: Presses Universitaires de Louvain.

Hatzaki, Eleni and Antonis Kotsonas 2020. "Knossos and North Central Crete." Pages 1029–53 in vol. 2 of *A Companion to the Archaeology of Early Greece and the Mediterranean.* Edited by Irene M. Lemos and Antonios Kotsonas. 2 vols. BCAW. Hoboken, NJ: Wiley-Blackwell.

Hauptmann, Andreas. 2009. "Lead Isotope Analysis and the Origin of Sardinian Metal Objects." Pages 494–509 in *Oxhide Ingots in the Central Mediterranean.* Edited by Fulvia Lo Schiavo. Nicosia: A.G. Leventis Foundation; Rome: CNR-Istituto di studi sulle civilta dell'Egeo e del vicino oriente.

Hauptmann, Harald. 1972. "Norşuntepe Kazıları, 1970." Pages 87–119 in *Keban Projesi 1970 Çalışmaları.* Keban Projesi yayınları 1.3. Ankara: Türk Tarih Kurumu Basımevi.

———. 1974. "Norşuntepe KazıHın, 1971." Pages 71–83 in *Keban Projesi 1971 Çalışmalan.* Keban Projesi yayınları 1.4. Ankara: Türk Tarih Kurumu Basımevi.

———. 1981. "Lidar Höyük, 1980." *AnSt* 31:197–98. DOI: 10.2307/3642767.

———. 1987. "Lidar Höyük and Nevali Cori, 1986." *AnSt* 37:203–7. DOI: 10.2307/3642895.

———. 2001. "Norşuntepe." Pages 596–604 in *Reallexikon der Assyriologie* Vol. 9. Edited by Erich Ebeling et al. Berlin: de Gruyter.

Hawkins, John David. 1988. "Kuzi–Tešub and the 'Great Kings' of Karkamiš." *AnSt* 38:99–108. DOI: 10.2307/3642845.

———. 2009. "Cilicia, the Amuq, and Aleppo: New Light in a Dark Age." *NEA* 72:164–73. DOI: 10.1086/NEA25754025.

———. 2011. "The Inscriptions of the Aleppo Temple." *AnSt* 61:35–54.

———. 2013. "The Luwian Inscriptions from the Temple of the Storm-God of Aleppo." Pages 493–500 in *Across the Border: Late Bronze–Iron Age Relations between Syria and Anatolia; Proceedings of a Symposium Held at the Research Center of Anato-*

lian Studies, Koç University, Istanbul, May 31–June 1, 2010. Edited by Aslihan K. Yener. ANESSup 42. Leuven: Peeters.

Heeren, Arnold H. L. 1817. *Handbuch der Geschichte der Staaten des Alterthums mit besonderer Rücksicht auf ihre Verfassungen, ihren Handel und ihre Colonien; Nach der neuesten Ausgabe.* Wien: Härter.

———. 1826. *Ideen über die Politik, den Verkehr und den Handel, der vornehmsten Völker der alten Welt. Theil 2: Afrikanische Völker.* Abt. 2: *Aegypter.* Göttingen: Vandenhoeck & Ruprecht.

———. 1838. *Historical Researches into the Politics, Intercourse, and Trade of the Carthaginians, Ethiopians, and Egyptians.* 2nd ed. 2 vols. Oxford: Talboys.

Heimlich, Rüdiger. 2002. "The New Trojan Wars." *Archaeology Odyssey* 5 (July–August):16–23.

Heinz, Marlies. 2016. *Kamid el-Loz: 4000 Years and More of Rural and Urban Life in the Lebanese Beqa'a Plain.* Beirut: Lebanese British Friends of the National Museum.

Heinz, Marlies, Sabina Kulemann-Ossen, Julia Linke, and Elisabeth Wagner. 2010a. *Kamid el-Loz: Intermediary between Cultures; More than 10 Years of Archaeological Research in Kamid el-Loz (1997 to 2007).* BAAL 7. Beirut: Directorate General of Antiquities, Ministry of Culture.

Heinz, Marlies, Elisabeth Wagner-Durand, Julia Linke, Alexandra Walther, Antonietta Catanzariti, Jan-Matthias Müller, and Martin Weber. 2010b. "Kamid el-Loz: Report on the Excavations in 2008 and 2009." *BAAL* 14:9–134.

Hennessy, John Basil. 1966. "Excavation of a Late Bronze Age Temple at Amman." *PEQ* 98:155–62. DOI: 10.1179/peq.1966.98.2.155.

———. 1985. "Thirteenth Century B.C. Temple of Human Sacrifice at Amman." Pages 85–104 in *Phoenicia and Its Neighbours: Proceedings of the Colloquium Held on the 9th and 10th of December 1983 at the "Vrije Univ. Brussel," in Cooperation with the "Centrum voor Myceense en Archaisch-Griekse Cultuur."* Edited by Eric Gubel. StPhoe 3. Leuven: Peeters.

Herr, Larry G. 1983. "The Amman Airport Structure and the Geopolitics of Ancient Transjordan." *BA* 46:223–29.

———. 1998. "Tell el-'Umayri and the Madaba Plains Region during the Late Bronze-Iron Age I Transition." Pages 251–64 in *Mediterranean Peoples in Transition: Thirteenth to Early Tenth Centuries B.C.E.; In Honor of Professor Trude Dothan.* Edited by Seymour Gitin, Amihai Mazar, and Ephraim Stern. Jerusalem: Israel Exploration Society.

———. 2000. "The Settlement and Fortification of Tell al-'Umayri in Jordan during the LB/ Iron I Transition." Pages 167–79 in *The Archaeology of Jordan and Beyond: Essays in Honor of James A. Sauer.* Edited by Lawrence E. Stager, Joseph A. Greene, Michael D. Coogan, and James A Sauer. Winona Lake, IN: Eisenbrauns.

———. 2008. "'Umeiri, Tell el-." *NEAEHL* 5:1848–51.

Herr, Larry G., Douglas R. Clark, and Kent Bramlett. 2009. "From the Stone Age to the Middle Ages in Jordan: Digging up Tall al-'Umayri." *NEA* 72:68–97. DOI: 10.1086/NEA20697220.

Hertel, Dieter, and Frank Kolb. 2003. "Troy in Clearer Perspective." *AnSt* 53:71–88. DOI: 10.2307/3643087.

Herzog, Ze'ev. 1982. "Tel Gerisa—1981/1982." *ESI* 1:28–31.

———. 1983. "Tel Gerisa, 1982." *IEJ* 33:121–23.

———. 1988. "Tel Gerisa, 1986." *ESI* 7:60–62.

———. 1989. "Middle and Late Bronze Age Settlements (Strata XVII–XV)." Pages 29–43

Excavations at Tel Michal, Israel. Edited by Ze'ev Herzog, George Rapp, and Ora Negbi. Minneapolis: University of Minnesota Press.

———. 1990. "Tel Gerisa, 1988." *ESI* 9:51–52.

———. 1991. "Tel Gerisa, 1989/90." *ESI* 10:121–22.

———. 1993a. "Gersia, Tel." *NEAEHL* 2:480–84.

———. 1993b. "Michal, Tel." *NEAEHL* 3:1036–41.

———. 1997. *Archaeology of the City: Urban Planning in Ancient Israel and Its Social Implications.* SMNIA 13. Tel Aviv: Emery and Claire Yass Archaeology Press.

———. 2001. "Archaeology and History at Tel Michal." Pages 21–30 in *Maritime Tel Michal and Apollonia.* Edited by Eva Grossmann. BARIS 915. Oxford: Archaeopress.

Herzog, Ze'ev, and Tsvika Tsuk 1996. "Tel Gerisa, 1991/92." *ESI* 15:60–62.

Hiller, Stefan. 1991. "Two Trojan Wars? On the Destructions of Troy VIh and VIIa." *Studia Troica* 1:145–54.

Hinzen, Klaus-G., Joseph Maran, Hector Hinojosa-Prieto, Ursula Damm-Meinhardt, Sharon K. Reamer, Jana Tzislakis, Kilian Kemna, Gregor Schweppe, Claus Fleischer, and Katie Demakopoulou. 2018. "Reassessing the Mycenaean Earthquake Hypothesis: Results of the HERACLES Project from Tiryns and Midea, Greece." *Bulletin of the Seismological Society of America* 108:1046–70. DOI: 10.1785/0120170348.

Hitchcock, Louise A., and Aren M. Maeir. 2013. "Beyond Creolization and Hybridity: Entangled and Transcultural Identities in Philistia." *Archaeological Review from Cambridge* 28:51–74.

Hoffmeier, James K. 2018. "A Possible Location in Northwest Sinai for the Sea and Land Battles between the Sea Peoples and Ramesses III." *BASOR* 380:1–25. DOI: 10.5615/bullamerschoorie.380.0001.

Hofstra, Susanne Ursula. 2000. "Small Things Considered: The Finds from LH IIIB Pylos in Context." PhD diss., University of Texas at Austin.

Hoftijzer, J., and W. H. van Soldt 1998. "Texts from Ugarit Pertaining to Seafaring." Pages 333–44 in *Seagoing Ships and Seamanship in the Bronze Age Levant.* Edited by Shelley Wachsmann. College Station: Texas A & M University Press.

Hooker, John T. 1976. *Mycenaean Greece.* States and Cities of Ancient Greece. London: Routledge.

Hruby, Julie. 2006. "Feasting and Ceramics: A View from the Palace of Nestor at Pylos." PhD diss., University of Cincinnati.

Humbert, Jean-Baptiste. 1981. "Récents travaux à Tell Keisan (1979–1980)." *RB* 88:373–98.

———. 1993. "Keisan, Tell." *NEAEHL* 3:862–67.

Hurwit, Jeffrey M. 1999. *The Athenian Acropolis: History, Mythology, and Archaeology from the Neolithic Era to the Present.* Cambridge: Cambridge University Press.

Iacovou, Maria. 2008. "Cultural and Political Configurations in Iron Age Cyprus: The Sequel to a Protohistoric Episode." *AJA* 112:625–57. DOI: 10.3764/aja.112.4.625.

———. 2013a. "Aegean-Style Material Culture in Late Cypriot III: Minimal Evidence, Maximal Interpretation." Pages 585–618 in *The Philistines and Other "Sea Peoples" in Text and Archaeology.* Edited by Ann E. Killebrew and Gunner Lehman. ABS 15. Atlanta: Society of Biblical Literature.

———. 2013b. "Historically Elusive and Internally Fragile Island Polities: The Intricacies of Cyprus's Political Geography in the Iron Age." *BASOR* 370:15–47. DOI: 10.5615/bullamerschoorie.370.0015.

———. 2014. "Cyprus during the Iron Age I Period (Late Cypriot IIC– IIIA): Settlement

Pattern Crisis (LC IIC–IIIA) to the Restructuring (LC IIIB) of Its Settlement Pattern." Pages 660–74 in *The Oxford Handbook of the Archaeology of the Levant c. 8000–332 BCE.* Edited by Margreet Steiner and Ann E Killebrew. Oxford Handbooks. Oxford: Oxford University Press.

Iakovidis, Spyros E. 1983. *Late Helladic Citadels on Mainland Greece.* Momumenta graeca et romana 4. Leiden: Brill.

———. 1986. "Destruction Horizons at Late Bronze Age Mycenae." Pages 233–60 in vol. 1 of *Φίλια Έπη εις Γεώργιον Μυλωνάν διά τα 60 έτη του ανασκαφικού του έργου.* 2 vols. Library of the Athens Archaeological Society 103. Athens: Athens Archaeological Society.

———. 1989. *Γλας I: Η Ανασκαφή 1955–1961.* Library of the Athens Archaeological Society 107. Athens: Athens Archaeological Society.

———. 1992. "The Mycenaean Fortress of Gla." Pages 607–15 in *Mykenaïka: Actes du IXe Colloque international sur les textes mycéniens et égéens organisé par le Centre de l'antiquité grecque et romaine de la Fondation hellénique des recherches scientifiques et l'Ecole française d'Athénes (Athénes, 2–6 octobre 1990).* Edited by Jean Pierre Olivier. Athens: Ecole française d'Athènes.

———. 1993. "The Impact of Trade Disruption on the Mycenaean Economy in the 13th–12th Centuries B.C.E." Pages 314–20 in *Biblical Archaeology Today, 1990: Proceedings of the Second International Congress on Biblical Archaeology, Jerusalem, June–July 1990.* Edited by Avraham Biran, Joseph Aviram, and Alan Paris-Shadur. Jerusalem: Israel Exploration Society.

———. 1995. "Γλας και Ορχομενός." Pages 69–81 in *Β' Διεθνές Συνέδριο Βοιωτικών Μελετών: Λειβαδιά, 6–10 Σεπτεμβρίου 1992.* Edited by Alexandra Christopoulou. Athens: Society of Boeotian Studies.

———. 1998. *Γλας II: Η Ανασκαφή 1981–1991.* Library of the Athens Archaeological Society 173. Athens: Athens Archaeological Society.

———. 2001. *Gla and the Kopais in the 13th Century B.C.* Library of the Athens Archaeological Society 221. Athens: Archaeological Society at Athens.

———. 2013. *Ανασκαφές Μυκηνών. IV. Η Οικία στις Πλάκες.* Library of the Athens Archaeological Society 288. Athens: Athens Archaeological Society.

Ilan, David. 2019. *Dan IV: The Iron Age I Settlement; The Avraham Biran Excavations (1966–1999).* Jerusalem: Nelson Glueck School of Biblical Archaeology/Hebrew Union College.

Ionas, I. 1984. "Stratigraphies of Enkomi." *RDAC* 1984:50–66.

Issar, Arie S., and Mattanyah Zohar. 2007. *Climate Change: Environment and History of the Near East.* 2nd ed. Berlin: Springer.

James, Peter. 2017. "The Levantine War-Records of Ramesses III: Changing Attitudes, Past, Present and Future." *Antiguo Oriente* 15:57–147.

James, Simon. 2013. "The Archaeology of War." Pages 91–127 in *The Oxford Handbook of Warfare in the Classical World.* Edited by Brian Campbell and Lawrence A. Tritle. Oxford Handbooks. Oxford: Oxford University Press. DOI: 10.1093/oxfordhb/9780195304657.013.0005.

Janeway, Brian. 2017. *Sea Peoples of the Northern Levant? Aegean-Style Pottery from Early Iron Age Tell Tayinat.* SAHL 7. Winona Lake, IN: Eisenbrauns.

Jantzen, Detlef, Ute Brinker, Jörg Orschiedt, Jan Heinemeier, Jürgen Piek, Karlheinz Hauenstein, Joachim Krüger, Gundula Lidke, Harald Lübke, Reinhard Lampe, Sebastian Lorenz, Manuela Schult, and Thomas Terberger. 2011. "A Bronze Age

REFERENCES 341

Battlefield? Weapons and Trauma in the Tollense Valley, North-Eastern Germany." *Antiquity* 85:417–33. DOI: 10.1017/S0003598X00067843.

Jean, Éric. 2006. "The Hittites at Mersin-Yumuktepe: Old Problems and New Directions." Pages 311–32 in *Strukturierung und Datierung der hethitischen Archäologie: Voraussetzungen, Probleme, Neue Ansätze; Internationaler Workshop Istanbul, 26–27. November 2004*. Edited by Dirk Paul Mielke, Ulf-Dietrich Schoop, and Jürgen Seeher. Byzas 4. Istanbul: Ege Yayınları.

Jensen, Eric. 2018. "The Endurance of Tell Qarqur: Settlement Resilience in Northwestern Syria during the Late Bronze and Iron Ages (ca. 1200–700 BC)." PhD diss., University of Arkansas.

———. 2020. "Iron I Settlement Resilience and Recovered at Tell Qarqur, Syria." Pages 2–18 in *The Iron Age I in the Levant: A View from the North; Part 2*. Edited by Hanan Charaf and Lynn Welton. AHL 52–53. London: Lebanese British Friends of the National Museum.

Jung, Reinhard. 2002. *Kastanas: Die Drehscheibenkeramik der Schichten 19 bis 11*. 2 vols. Prähistorische Archäologie in Südosteuropa 18. Berlin: Spiess.

———. 2003. "Late Helladic IIIC at the Toumbes of Kastanás and Ólynthos – and the Problems of Macedonian Mycenaean Pottery." Pages 131–44 in *LH III C Chronology and Synchronisms Proceedings of the International Workshop Held at the Austrian Academy of Sciences at Vienna, May 7th and 8th, 2001*. Edited by Sigrid Deger-Jalkotzy and Michaela Zavadil. Veröffentlichungen der Mykenischen Kommission 20. Vienna: Österreichischen Akademie der Wissenschaften.

———. 2009. "Sie vernichteten sie, als ob sie niemals existiert hätten"—Was blieb von den Zerstörungen der Seevölker?" Pages 31–48 in *Schlachtfeldarchäologie/Battlefield Archaeology: 1. Mitteldeutscher Archäologentag vom 09. Bis 11. Oktober 2008 in Halle (Saale)*. Edited by Harald Meller. Tagungen des Landesmuseums für Vorgeschichte Halle 2. Halle: Landesamt für Denkmalpflege und Archäologie Sachsen-Anhalt, Landesmuseum für Vorgeschichte.

———. 2010. "End of the Bronze Age." Pages 171–84 in *The Oxford Handbook of the Bronze Age Aegean (ca. 3000–1000 BC)*. Edited by Eric H. Cline. Oxford Handbooks. Oxford: Oxford University Press.

———. 2012a. "Kastanas in Macedonia." Pages 3704–5 in vol. 7 of *The Encyclopedia of Ancient History*. Edited by Roger S. Bagnall, Kai Brodersen, Craige Brian Champion, Andrew Erskine, and Sabine R. Huebner. 13 vols. Chichester: Wiley-Blackwell.

———. 2012b. "Can We Say, What's Behind All Those Sherds? Ceramic Innovations in the Eastern Mediterranean at the End of the Second Millennium." Pages 104–20 in *Materiality and Social Practice: Transformative Capacities of Intercultural Encounters*. Edited by in Joseph Maran and Philipp W. Stockhammer. Oxford: Oxbow.

———. 2016. "Friede den Hütten, Krieg den Palästen! In the Bronze Age Aegean." Pages 553–578 in vol. 2 of *Arm und Reich: Zur Ressourcenverteilung in prähistorischen Gesellschaften; Rich and Poor; Competing for Resources in Prehistoric Societies; 8 Mitteldeutscher Archäologentag vom 22. bis 24. Oktober 2015 in Halle (Saale)*. Edited by Harald Meller, Hans Peter Hahn, Reinhard Jung, and Roberto Risch. 2 vols. Tagungen des Landesmuseums für Vorgeschichte Halle 14. Halle: Landesamt für Denkmalpflege und Archäologie Sachsen-Anhalt.

———. 2018a. "Mycenaean Pottery in Coastal Syria." Pages 47–155 in *Tell Kazel au Bronze recent: Études céramiques*. Edited by Leila Badre, Barbara Vitale, and Emmanuelle Capet. Bibliothèque archéologique et historique 211. Beirut: Presses de l'Ifpo.

342   REFERENCES

——. 2018b. "Push and Pull Factors of the Sea Peoples between Italy and the Levant." Pages 273–306 in *An Archaeology of Forced Migration: Crisis-Induced Mobility and the Collapse of the 13th c. BCE Eastern Mediterranean*. Edited by Jan Driessen. Aegis 15. Louvain-La-Neuve: Presses Universitaires de Louvain.

Jung, Reinhard, and Mathias Mehofer. 2009. "A Sword of Naue II Type from Ugarit and the Historical Significance of Italian-Type Weaponry in the Eastern Mediterranean." *Aegean Archaeology* 8:111–35.

Jusseret, Simon. 2017. "Archaeoseismological Research on Minoan Crete: Past and Present." Pages 223–47 In *Minoan Earthquakes: Breaking the Myth through Interdisciplinarity*. Edited by Simon Jusseret and Manuel Sintubin. Studies in Archaeological Sciences 5. Leuven: Leuven University Press.

Jusseret, Simon, Charlotte Langohr, and Manuel Sintubin. 2013. "Tracking Earthquake Archaeological Evidence in Late Minoan IIIB (~1300–1200 B.C.) Crete (Greece): A Proof of Concept." *Bulletin of the Seismological Society of America* 103:3026–43. DOI: 10.1785/0120130070.

Kafafi, Zeidan A., and Gerrit van der Kooij. 2013. "Tell Dēr ʿAllā during the Transition from Late Bronze Age to Iron Age." *ZDPV* 129:121–31.

Kahn, Dan'el. 2010. "Who Is Meddling in Egypt's Affairs? The Identity of the Asiatics in the Elephantine Stele of Sethnakhte and the Historicity of the Medinet Habu Asiatic War Reliefs." *Journal of Ancient Egyptian Interconnections* 2:14–23. DOI: 10.2458/azu_jaei_v02i1_kahn.

——. 2011. "The Campaign of Ramesses III against Philistia." *Journal of Ancient Egyptian Interconnections* 3:1–11. DOI: 10.2458/azu_jaei_v03i4_kahn.

Kaniewski, David, Joël Guiot, and Elise Van Campo. 2015. "Drought and Societal Collapse 3200 Years Ago in the Eastern Mediterranean: A Review." *Wiley Interdisciplinary Reviews: Climate Change* 6:369–82. DOI: 10.1002/wcc.345.

Kaniewski, David, Nick Marriner, Joachim Bretschneider, Greta Jans, Christophe Morhange, Rachid Cheddadi, Thierry Otto, Frédéric Luce, and Elise Van Campo. 2019. "300-Year Drought Frames Late Bronze Age to Early Iron Age Transition in the Near East: New Palaeoecological Data from Cyprus and Syria." *Regional Environmental Change* 19:2287–97. DOI: 10.1007/s10113-018-01460-w.

Kaniewski, David, Etienne Paulissen, Elise Van Campo, Harvey Weiss, Thierry Otto, Joachim Bretschneider, and Karel Van Lerberghe. 2010. "Late Second–Early First Millennium BC Abrupt Climate Changes in Coastal Syria and Their Possible Significance for the History of the Eastern Mediterranean." *Quaternary Research* 74:207–15. DOI: 10.1016/j.yqres.2010.07.010.

Kaniewski, David, and Elise Van Campo. 2017a. "3.2 Ka BP Megadrought and the Late Bronze Age Collapse." Pages 161–82 in *Megadrought and Collapse: From Early Agriculture to Angkor*. Edited by Harvey Weiss. Oxford: Oxford University Press.

——. 2017b. "The Climatic Context of the 3.2 kyr calBP Event." Pages 85–93 in *"Sea Peoples" Up-to-Date: New Research on the Transformations in the Eastern Mediterranean in the 13th–11th Centuries BCE*. Edited by Peter M. Fischer and Teresa Bürge. CCEM 35. Vienna: Österreichische Academie der Wissenschaften. DOI: 10.2307/j.ctt1v2xvsn.9.

Kaniewski, David, Elise Van Campo, Joël Guiot, Sabine Le Burel, Thierry Otto, and Cecile Baeteman. 2013. "Environmental Roots of the Late Bronze Age Crisis." *PLoS ONE* 8:e71004. DOI: 10.1371/journal.pone.0071004.

Kaniewski, David., Elise Van Campo, Karel Van Lerberghe, Tom Boiy, Klaas Vansteen-

REFERENCES 343

huyse, Greta Jans, Karin Nys, Harvey Weiss, Christophe Morhange, Thierry Otto, and Joachim Bretschneider. 2011. "The Sea Peoples, from Cuneiform Tablets to Carbon Dating." *PLoS ONE* 6:e20232. DOI: 10.1371/journal.pone.0020232.

Kansu, Ş. A., and S. Tunakan. 1948. "Karaoğlan Höyüğünden Çıkarılan Eti, Erik ve Klasik Devir İskeletlerinin Antropolojik İncelenmesi (Etüde Anthropologigue des sguelettes datant des epoques Hittite et Phrygienne et de l'Âge classigue, provenant des fouilles du Höyük de Karaoğlan, 1937–1938)." *Belleten* 12:759–74.

Kanta, Athanasia. 2021. "Sardinians at Pyla- Kokkinokremos in Cyprus." Pages 67–75 in *Cultural Contacts and Trade in Nuragic Sardinia: The Southern Route (Sardinia, Sicily, Crete, Cyprus) Proceedings of the Fourth Festival of the Nuragic Civilization (Orroli, Cagliari)*. Edited by Mauro Perra and Fulvia Lo Schiavo. Cagliari: Arkadia.

Kaplan, Jacob. 1967. "Jaffa's History Revealed by the Spade." Pages 113–18 in *Archaeological Discoveries in the Holy Land*. New York: Bonanza Books.

———. 1972. "The Archaeology and History of Tel Aviv-Jaffa." *BA* 35:65–95. DOI: 10.2307/3211001.

Karacic, Steven. 2014. "The Archaeology of Hittite Imperialism and Ceramic Production in Late Bronze Age IIA Tarsus-Gözlükule, Turkey." PhD diss., Bryn Mawr College.

Karageorghis, Vassos. 1962. "Recent Archaeological Investigations at Kition." *Kypriakai spoudai* 26:167–71.

———. 1963a. "Chronique des fouilles à Chypre en 1962." *BCH* 87:325–87.

———. 1963b. "Excavations at Kition, 1963." *RDAC* 1963:3–15.

———. 1982. *Cyprus: From the Stone Age to the Romans*. Ancient Peoples and Places. London: Thames & Hudson.

———. 1990. *The End of the Late Bronze Age in Cyprus*. Nicosia: Pierides Foundation.

———. 1992. "The Crisis Years: Cyprus." Pages 79–86 in *The Crisis Years: The 12th Century B.C.; From Beyond the Danube to the Tigris*. Edited by William A. Ward and Martha Sharp Joukowsky. Dubuque, IA: Kendall/Hunt Publishing.

———. 2000. "Cultural Innovations in Cyprus Relating to the Sea Peoples." Pages 255–79 in *The Sea Peoples and Their World: A Reassessment*. Edited by Eliezer D. Oren. Museum Monograph 108. Philadelphia: University Museum, University of Pennsylvania, 2013. DOI: 10.9783/9781934536438.255.

———. 2001. "Patterns of Fortified Settlements in the Aegean and Cyprus c. 1200 B.C." Pages 1–10 in *Defensive Settlements of the Aegean and the Eastern Mediterranean after c. 1200 B.C.: Proceedings of an International Workshop Held at Trinity College Dublin, 7th–9th May, 1999*. Edited by Vassos Karageorghis and Christine Morris. Nicosia: Leventis Foundation.

Karageorghis, Vassos, and Martha Demas. 1984, *Pyla-Kokkinokremos, A Late 13th Century B. C. Fortified Settlement in Cyprus*. Nicosia: Department of Antiquities.

———. 1985. *Excavations at Kition. V: The Pre-Phoenician Levels*. Nicosia: Department of Antiquities.

———. 1988. *Excavations at Maa-Palaeokastro 1979–1986*. Nicosia: Department of Antiquities.

Karageorghis, Vassos, and Athanasia Kanta. 2014. *Pyla-Kokkinokremos: A Late 13th Century BC Fortified Settlement in Cyprus; Excavations 2010–2011*. Studies in Mediterranean Archaeology 141. Uppsala: Åström.

Karakaya, Doğa, and Simone Riehl. 2019. "Subsistence in Post-Collapse Societies: Pat-

344 REFERENCES

terns of Agroproduction from the Late Bronze Age to the Iron Age in the Northern Levant and Beyond." Pages 136–63 in *The Iron Age I in the Levant: A View from the North; Part 1*. Edited by Hanan Charaf and Lynn Welton. AHL 50–51. London: Lebanese British Friends of the National Museum.

Karouzou, Eleni. 2018. "Thessaly, from the Late Bronze Age to the Early Iron Age (c. 1600–700 BC)." PhD diss., University of Oxford, 2018.

Kase, Edward W. 1970. "A Study of the Role of Krisa in the Mycenaean Era." MA thesis, Loyola University.

Kassianidou, Vasiliki. 2007. "Ground Stone Tools from Apliki Karamallos." Pages 277–306 in *Joan du Plat Taylor´s Excavations at the Late Bronze Age Mining Settlement at Apliki Karamallos, Cyprus*. Edited by Barbara Kling, James David Muhly, Vasiliki Kassianidou, and Joan du Plat Taylor. Studies in Mediterranean Archaeology 134. Sävedalen: Åström.

———. 2012. "The Origin and Use of Metals in Iron Age Cyprus." Pages 229–60 in *Cyprus and the Aegean in the Early Iron Age: The Legacy of Nicolas Coldstream*. Edited by Maria Iacovou. Nicosia: Bank of Cyprus Cultural Foundation.

———. 2013. "The Production and Trade of Cypriot Copper in the Late Bronze Age: An Analysis of the Evidence." *Pasiphae* 7:133–46.

———. 2018. "Apliki Karamallos on Cyprus: The 13th Century BCE Miners' Settlement in Context." Pages 345–56 in *Mining for Ancient Copper: Essays in Memory of Beno Rothenberg*. Edited by Erez Ben-Yosef. SMNIA 37. Tel Aviv: Emery and Claire Yass Archaeology Press.

Katzenstein, H. Jacob. 1973. *The History of Tyre from the Beginning of the Second Millennium B.C.E. until the Fall of the Neo-Babylonian Empire in 538 B.C.E*. Jerusalem: Schocken Institute.

Kelm, George L., and Amihai Mazar. 1982. "Three Seasons of Excavations at Tel Batash: Biblical Timnah." *BASOR* 248:1–36. DOI: 10.2307/1356672.

———. 1995. *Timnah: A Biblical Town in the Sorek Valley*. Winona Lake, IN: Eisenbrauns.

Kelso, James Leon. 1968. *The Excavation of Bethel (1934–1960)*. AASOR 39. Cambridge: American Schools of Oriental Research.

———. 1993. "Bethel." *NEAEHL* 1:192–94.

Keswani, Priscilla. 2016. "Fragmentary Pithoi." Pages 217–34 in *Feasting, Crafting and Depositional Practice in Late Bronze Age Palaepaphos: The Well Fillings of Evreti*. Edited by Constance von Rüden, Artemis Georgiou, Ariane Jacobs, and Paul Halstead. Bochumer Forschungen Zur Ur- und Frühgeschichtlichen Archäologie 8. Rahden: Leidorf.

Kilani, Marwan. 2016. "Byblos in the Late Bronze Age: Interactions between the Levantine and Egyptian Worlds." PhD diss., Queen's College University of Oxford.

———. 2020. *Byblos in the Late Bronze Age: Interactions between the Levantine and Egyptian Worlds*. SAHL 9. Leiden Brill.

Kilian, Klaus. 1983. "Civiltà micenea in Grecia: Nuovi aspetti storici ed interculturali." Pages 53–96 in *Magna Grecia E Mondo Miceneo: Atti del ventiduesimo Convegno di Studi sulla Magna Grecia (Taranto, Ottobre 7–11, 1982)*. Edited by Lucia Vagnetti. Taranto: Istituto per la Storia e l'Archeologia della Magna Grecia.

———. 1988. "Mycenaeans Up to Date, Trends and Changes in Recent Research." Pages 115–52 in *Problems in Greek Prehistory: Papers Presented at the Centenary Conference of the British School of Archaeology at Athens, Manchester April 1986*. Edited by Elizabeth B. French and K. A. Wardle. Bristol: Bristol Classical Press.

REFERENCES 345

————. 1996. "Earthquakes and Archaeological Context at 13th Century BC Tiryns." Pages 63–68 in *Archaeoseismology*. Edited by Stathis C. Stiros and R. E. Jones. Fitch Laboratory Occasional Papers 7. Athens: Institute of Geology & Mineral Exploration; British School at Athens.

Killebrew, Ann E. 1998. "Ceramic Typology and Technology of the Late Bronze II and Iron I Assemblages from Tel Miqne-Ekron: The Transition from Canaanite to Philistine Culture." Pages 379–405 in *Mediterranean Peoples in Transition: Thirteenth to Early Tenth Centuries B.C.E.; In Honor of Professor Trude Dothan*. Edited by Seymour Gitin, Amihai Mazar, and Ephraim Stern. Jerusalem: Israel Exploration Society.

————. 2005. *Biblical Peoples and Ethnicity: An Archaeological Study of Egyptians, Canaanites, Philistines, and Early Israel, 1300–1100 B.C.E.* ABS 9. Atlanta: Society of Biblical Literature.

————. 2013. "Early Philistine Pottery Technology at Tel Minqe-Ekron: Implications for the Late Bronze–Early Iron Age Transition in the Eastern Mediterranean." Pages 77–129 in *The Philistines and Other "Sea Peoples" in Text and Archaeology*. Edited by Ann E. Killebrew and Gunner Lehman. ABS 15. Atlanta: Society of Biblical Literature.

Killebrew, Ann E., and Gunner Lehmann. 2013a. "The World of the Philistines and Other 'Sea Peoples.'" Pages 1–18 in *The Philistines and Other "Sea Peoples" in Text and Archaeology*. Edited by Ann E. Killebrew and Gunner Lehman. ABS 15. Atlanta: Society of Biblical Literature.

————, eds. 2013b. *The Philistines and Other "Sea Peoples" in Text and Archaeology*. ABS 15. Atlanta: Society of Biblical Literature.

Kitchen, Kenneth. 2009. "Egyptian New-Kingdom Topographical Lists: An Historical Resource with 'Literary' Histories." Pages 129–35 in *Causing His Name to Live: Studies in Egyptian Epigraphy and History in Memory of William J. Murnane*. Edited by Peter J. Brand and Louise Cooper. CHANE 37. Leiden: Brill. DOI: 10.1163/ej.9789004176447.i-240.47.

Kleiman, Sabine, Yuval Gadot, and Oded Lipschits. 2016. "A Snapshot of the Destruction Layer of Tell Zakarīye/Azekah Seen against the Backdrop of the Final Days of the Late Bronze Age." *ZDPV* 132:105–33.

Klengel, Horst. 2013. "Syria 1350–1200 BC." Pages 339–44 in *Archéologie et Histoire de la Syrie*. 1: *La Syrie de l'époque néolithique à l'âge du fer*. Edited by Winfried Orthmann, Paolo Matthiae, and Michel Al-Maqdissi. Schriften zur vorderasiatischen Archäologie 1. Wiesbaden: Harrassowitz.

Kling, Barbara, James D. Muhly, Vasiliki Kassianidou, and Joan du Plat Taylor. 2007. *Joan du Plat Taylor's Excavations at the Late Bronze Age Mining Settlement at Apliki Karamallos, Cyprus*. Studies in Mediterranean Archaeology 134. Sävedalen: Åström.

Knapp, A. Bernard. 1997. *The Archaeology of Late Bronze Age Cypriot Society: The Study of Settlement, Survey and Landscape*. Occasional Papers 4. Glasgow: University of Glasgow Department of Archaeology.

————. 2008. *Prehistoric and Protohistoric Cyprus: Identity, Insularity, and Connectivity*. Oxford: Oxford University Press.

————. 2009. "Monumental Architecture, Identity and Memory." Pages 47–59 in *Proceedings of the Symposium: Bronze Age Architectural Traditions in the East Mediterranean: Diffusion and Diversity (Gasteig, Munich, 7–8 May, 2008)*. Edited by A.

346   REFERENCES

Bernard Knapp. Weilheim: Verein zur Förderung der Aufarbeitung der Hellenischen Geschichte e.V.

———. 2013. *The Archaeology of Cyprus: From Earliest Prehistory through the Bronze Age.* Cambridge World Archaeology. Cambridge: Cambridge University Press.

Knapp, A. Bernard, and Sturt Manning. 2016. "Crisis in Context: The End of the Late Bronze Age in the Eastern Mediterranean." *AJA* 120:99–149. DOI: 10.3764/aja.120.1.0099.

Knauf, Ernst Axel. 2008. "From Archeology to History, Bronze and Iron Ages with Special Regard to the Year 1200 B.C.E, and the Tenth Century." Pages 72–85 in *Israel in Transition: From the Late Bronze II to the Iron IIa (c. 1250–850 BCE).* Vol. 1: *The Archaeology.* Edited by Lester L. Grabbe. LHBOTS 491. New York: T&T Clark.

Kochavi, Moshe. 1974. "Khirbet Rabud = Debir." *TA* 1:2–33. DOI: 10.1179/033443574788593494.

———. 1978. "Canaanite Aphek." *Expedition* 20:12–17.

———. 1990. *Aphek in Canaan: The Egyptian Governor's Residence and Its Finds.* Jerusalem: Israel Museum.

———. 1993. "Zeror, Tel." *NEAEHL* 4:1524–26.

Kochavi, Moshe, Raphael Greenberg, and Adi Keinan. "Rabud, Khirbet." 1975. *EAEHL* 4:995.

Kohlmeyer, Kay. 2000. *Der Tempel des Wettergottes von Aleppo.* Münster: Rhema.

———. 2009. "The Temple of the Storm God in Aleppo during the Late Bronze and Early Iron Ages." *NEA* 72:190–202. DOI: 10.1086/NEA25754027.

———. 2012. "Der Tempel des Wettergottes von Aleppo: Baugeschichte und Bautyp, räumliche Bezüge, Inventar und bildliche Ausstattung." Pages 55–78 in *Temple Building and Temple Cult: Architecture and Cultic Paraphernalia of Temples in the Levant (2.–1. Mill. B.C.E.); Proceedings of a Conference on the Occasion of the 50th Anniversary of the Institute of Biblical Archaeology at the University of Tübingen (28–30 May 2010).* Edited by Jens Kamlah. ADPV 41. Weisbaden: Harrassowitz.

———. 2013. "The Temple of the Storm-God of Aleppo." Pages 511–24 in *Archéologie et Histoire de la Syrie.* 1: *La Syrie de l'époque néolithique à l'âge du fer.* Edited by Winfried Orthmann, Paolo Matthiae, and Michel Al-Maqdissi. Schriften zur vorderasiatischen Archäologie 1. Wiesbaden: Harrassowitz.

———. 2016. "The Temple of Hadad at Aleppo: The Greatest Urban Sanctuary of Northern Syria in Historical Perspective." Pages 295–336 in *Giornate di studio L'archeologia del sacro e l'archeologia del culto: Sabratha, Ebla, Ardea, Lanuvio (Roma, 8–11 ottobre 2013); Ebla e la Siria dall'Età del bronzo all'Età del ferro.* Edited by Paolo Matthiae. Rome: Bardi.

Kohlmeyer, Kay, and Arie Kai-Browne. 2020. *The Temple of the Weather God of Aleppo.* Münster: Rhema.

Kolonas, Lazaros. 2009. *Teichos Dymaion.* Athens: Kapon.

van der Kooij, Gerrit. 2006. "Tell Deir 'Alla: The Middle and Late Bronze Age Chronology." Pages 199–226 in *The Chronology of the Jordan Valley during the Middle and Late Bronze Ages: Pella, Tell Abu Al-Kharaz, and Tell Deir 'Alla.* Edited by Peter M. Fischer and Stephen Bourke. CCEM 12. Vienna: Österreichischen Akademie der Wissenschaften.

Kopanias, Konstantinos. 2015. "The Mushki/Phrygian Problem from the Near Eastern Point of View." Pages 211–26 in *NOSTOI: Indigenous Culture, Migration, Integration in the Aegean Islands, Western Anatolia during the Late Bronze Age-Early Iron*

REFERENCES 347

Age, Koç University, Istanbul. Edited by Konstantinos Kopanias, Çiğdem Maner, and Nikolaos Chr Stampolidis. Istanbul: Koç University Press.

Kopanias, Konstantinos, Çiğdem Maner, and Nikolaos Chr Stampolidis. eds. 2015. *NOSTOI: Indigenous Culture, Migration, Integration in the Aegean Islands, Western Anatolia during the Late Bronze Age-Early Iron Age, Koç University, Istanbul.* Istanbul: Koç University Press.

Korbel, Günther. 1985. *Die Spätbronzezeitliche keramik von Norsuntepe.* Hanover: Insitut für Bauen und Planen.

Korfmann, Manfred. 1996. "Troia-Ausgrabungen 1995." *Studia Troica* 6:1–63.

———. 2001. *Troia: Traum und Wirklichkeit: Begleitband zur Ausstellung "Troia - Traum und Wirklichkeit."* Stuttgart: Theiss.

———. 2004a. "Was There a Trojan War?" *Archaeology* 57:36–41.

———. 2004b. "Die Arbeiten in Troia/Wilusa 2003; Work at Troia/Wilusa in 2003." *Studia Troica* 14:3–31.

———. 2004c. Transcript of the BBC documentary "The Truth of Troy." http://www.bbc.co.uk.proxy.lib.umich.edu/science/horizon/2004/troytrans.shtml.

———. 2007. "Was There a Trojan War? Troy between Fiction and Archaeological Evidence." Pages 20–26 in *Troy: From Homer's Iliad to Hollywood Epic.* Edited by Martin M. Winkler. Malden, MA: Blackwell.

Köroğlu, Kemalettin. 1998. *5 yılında Yumuktepe = The V. Anniversary of the Excavations at Yumuktepe (1993–1997).* Eskičag Bilimleri Enstitüsü yayınları 12. Istanbul: Ege Yayınları.

Koşay, Hâmit Zübeyr. 1939–1940. "Results of the Excavations Alacahöyük." *La Turquie Kemaliste* 32–40:20–26.

———. 1940. "Les Fouilles D'Alacahöyük, Entreprises par la Société D'Histoire Turque Travaux Exécutés en 1940 et leurs Résultats." *Belleten* 5:9–16.

———. 1944. *Ausgrabungen von Alaca Höyük: Ein Vorbericht über die im Auftrage der Türkischen Geschichts kommission im Sommer 1936 durchgeführten Forschungen und Entdeckungen.* Veröffentlichungen der Türkischen Geschichtskommission 5/2. Ankara: Türk Tarih Kurumu Basımevi.

———. 1951. *Türk Tarih Kurumu tarafından yapılan Alaca Höyük kazısı; Türk Tarih Kurumu yayınlarından 1937–1939.* Türk tarih kurumu yayinlarindan 5/5. Ankara: Türk Tarih Kurumu Basımevi.

———. 1954. *Alacahöyük.* Ankara: Turkish Press, Broadcasting and Tourist Dept.

———. 1973. *Türk Tarih Kurumu tarafindan yapilan Alaca Höyük kazisi; 1963–1967 çalişmalari ve keşiflere ait ilk rapor.* Ankara: Türk Tarih Kurumu Basimevi.

Koşay, Hâmit Zübeyr, and Mahmut Akok. 1966. *Türk Tarih Kurumu tarafindan yapilan Alaca Höyük kazisi, 1940–1948 deki çalişmalara ve keşiflere ait ilk rapor; Ausgrabungen von Alaca Höyük: Vorbericht über die Forschungen und Entdeckungen von 1940–1948.* Türk tarih kurumu yayinlarindan 5/6. Ankara: Türk Tarih Kurumu Basimevi.

Kounouklas, Petros. 2011. "The Late Helladic IIIC Middle-Early Protogeometric Settlement at Kynos, East Lokris, Greece: Architecture, Spatial Organisation, Pottery, and Function." PhD diss., University of Bristol.

Kreimerman, Igor. 2017. "A Typology for Destruction Layers: The Late Bronze Age Southern Levant as a Case Study." Pages 173–203 in *Crisis to Collapse: The Archaeology of Social Breakdown.* Edited by Timothy Cunningham and Jan Driessen. Aegis 11. Louvain-la-Neuve: Presses Universitaires de Louvain.

Kreimerman, Igor, and Ruth Shahack-Gross. 2019. "Understanding Conflagration of One-Story Mud-Brick Structures: An Experimental Approach." *Archaeological and Anthropological Sciences* 11:2911–28. DOI: 10.1007/s12520-018-0714-7.

Kristiansen, Kristian, and Paulina Suchowska-Ducke. 2015. "Connected Histories: The Dynamics of Bronze Age Interaction and Trade 1500–1100 BC." *Proceedings of the Prehistoric Society* 81:361–92. DOI: 10.1017/ppr.2015.17.

Kuniholm, Peter I., Maryanne W. Newton, Carol B. Griggs, and Pamela J. Sullivan. 2005. "Dendrochronological Dating in Anatolia: The Second Millennium BC." *Der Anschnitt* 18:41–47.

Lackenbacher, Sylvie, and Florence Malbran-Labat. 2016. *Lettres en Akkadien de la "Maison d'Urtenu": Fouilles de 1994.* RSO 23. Leuven: Peeters.

LaFayette-Hogue, Shannon. 2011. "The Destruction and Afterlife of the Palace of Nestor at Pylos: The Making of a Forgotten Landmark." PhD diss., University of Cincinnati.

———. 2016. "New Evidence of Post-Destruction Reuse in the Main Building of the Palace of Nestor at Pylos." *AJA* 120:151–57. DOI: 10.3764/aja.120.1.0151.

Lagarce, Élisabeth, and Jacques Lagarce. 2006. "L'incendie du Palais Nord de Ras Ibn Hani: Traces et modalités d'une catastrophe." *Syria* 83:247–58. DOI: 10.4000/syria.239.

Lagarce, Jacques, and Élisabeth Lagarce. 1995. "Ras Ibn Hani au Bronze Recent." Pages 141–54 in *Le pays d'Ougarit autour de 1200 av. J.-C.: Histoire et archéologie; Actes du colloque international, Paris, 28 juin–1er juillet 1993.* Edited by Marguerite Yon, Maurice Sznycer, and Pierre Bordreuil. RSO 11. Paris: Éditions Recherche sur les civilisations.

Lagarce, Jacques, Élisabeth Lagarce, Adnan Bounni, and Nassib Saliby. 1987. "Les dixième et onzième campagnes de fouilles (1984 et 1986) à Ras Ibn Hani (Syrie)." *CRAI* 131:274–88.

Langgut, Dafna, Israel Finkelstein, and Thomas Litt. 2013. "Climate and the Late Bronze Collapse: New Evidence from the Southern Levant." *TA* 40:149–75. DOI: 10.1179/033443513X13753505864205.

Lapp, Paul W. 1967. *The Conquest of Palestine in the Light of Archaeology.* St. Louis: Concordia.

Laroche, Emmanuel. 1989. "Les reliefs de Fraktin." Pages 301–2 in *Anatolia and the Ancient Near East: Studies in Honor of Tahsin Özgüç.* Edited by Kutlu Emre. Ankara: Türk Tarih Kurumu.

Latacz, Joachim. 2004. *Troy and Homer: Towards a Solution of an Old Mystery.* Oxford: Oxford University Press.

Lazar, Michael, Eric H. Cline, Roey Nickelsberg, Ruth Shahack-Gross, and Assaf Yasur-Landau. 2020. "Earthquake Damage as a Catalyst to Abandonment of a Middle Bronze Age Settlement: Tel Kabri, Israel." *PLoS ONE* 15:e0239079. DOI: 10.1371/journal.pone.0239079.

Lehmann, Gustav Adolf. 1985. *Die mykenisch-frühgriechische Welt und der östliche Mittelmeerraum in der Zeit der "Seevölker"-Invasionen um 1200 v. Chr.* Opladen: Westdeutscher.

Lehmann, Gunner. 2017. "The Late Bronze-Iron Age Transition and the Problem of the Sea Peoples Phenomenon in Cilicia." Pages 229–55 in *"Sea Peoples" Up-to-Date: New Research on the Transformations in the Eastern Mediterranean in the 13th–11th Centuries BCE.* Edited by Peter M. Fischer and Teresa Bürge. CCEM 35.

REFERENCES 349

Vienna: Österreichische Academie der Wissenschaften. DOI: 10.2307/j.ctt1v2x-vsn.17.

Lemos, Irene S. 2006. "Athens and Lefkandi: A Tale of Two Sites." Pages 505–30 in *Ancient Greece: From the Mycenaean Palaces to the Age of Homer*. Edited by Sigrid Deger-Jalkotzy and Irene S. Lemos. Edinburgh Leventis Studies 3. Edinburgh: Edinburgh University Press.

Lenzen, Cherie J. 1997. "Irbid." *OEANE* 3:181.

Lenzen, Cherie J., Richard L. Gordon, and Alison M. McQuitty. 1985. "Excavations at Tell Irbid and Beit Ras, 1985." *ADAJ* 29:151–59.

Lenzen, Cherie J., and Alison M. McQuitty. 1988. "The 1984 Survey of the Irbid/Bet Ras Region." *ADAJ* 32:265–74.

Lerat, Lucien, and Jean Jannoray. 1936. "Premieres recherches sur l'Acropole de Krisa (Phocide)." *RAr* 8:129–45.

Lesko, Leonard. H. 1992. "Egypt in the 12th Century B.C." Pages 151–56 in *The Crisis Years: The 12th Century B.C.; From Beyond the Danube to the Tigris*. Edited by William A. Ward and Martha Sharp Joukowsky. Dubuque, IA: Kendall/Hunt Publishing.

Levi, Doro. 1959. "La Villa rurale minoica di Gortina." *BArte* 44:237–65.

Liebowtiz, Harold A. 1993. "Yin'am, Tel." *NEAEHL* 4:1515–16.

———. 2003. *Tel Yin'am I: The Late Bronze Age*. Studies in Archaeology 42. Austin: Texas Archeological Research Laboratory, the University of Texas at Austin.

Lipschits, Oded, Yuval Gadot, and Manfred Oeming. 2017. "Four Seasons of Excavations at Tel Azekah: The Expected and (Especially) Unexpected Results." Pages 1–25 in *The Shephelah during the Iron Age: Recent Archaeological Studies*. Edited by Oded Lipschitz and Aren M. Maeir. Winona Lake, IN: Eisenbrauns. DOI: 10.5325/j.ctv1bxh4cw.4.

Littaver, M. A, J. H. Crouwel, and Harald Hauptmann. 1991. "Ein Spätbronzezeitliches Speichenrad vom Lidar Höyük in der Südost-Türkei." *AA* 3:349–58.

Liverani, Mario. 1987. "The Collapse of the Near Eastern Regional System at the End of the Bronze Age: The Case of Syria." Pages 66–73 in *Centre and Periphery in the Ancient World*. Edited by Michael Rowlands, Mogens Larsen, and Kristian Kristiansen. Cambridge: Cambridge University Press.

———. 1995a. "Le royaume d'Ougarit." Pages 47–54 in *Le pays d'Ougarit autour de 1200 av. J.–C.: Histoire et archéologie; Actes du colloque international, Paris, 28 juin–1er juillet 1993*. Edited by Marguerite Yon, Maurice Sznycer, and Pierre Bordreuil. RSO 11. Paris: Éditions Recherche sur les civilisations.

———. 1995b. "La fin d'Ougarit: Quand? pourquoi? comment?" Pages 113–17 in *Le pays d'Ougarit autour de 1200 av. J.–C.: Histoire et archéologie; Actes du colloque international, Paris, 28 juin–1er juillet 1993*. Edited by Marguerite Yon, Maurice Sznycer, and Pierre Bordreuil. RSO 11. Paris: Éditions Recherche sur les civilisations.

———. 2003. *Israel's History and the History of Israel*. Bible World. London: Equinox.

———. 2012. "Melid in the Early and Middle Iron Age: Archaeology and History." Pages 327–44 in *The Ancient Near East in the 12th–10th Centuries BCE: Culture and History; Proceedings of the International Conference Held at the University of Haifa, 2–5 May, 2010*. Edited by Gershon Galil, Ayelet Levinzon-Gilboa, Aren M. Maeir, Dan'el Kahn, and Ayelet Gilboa AOAT 392. Münster: Ugarit-Verlag.

———. 2020. "A History of the Ancient Near East." Pages 11–26 in *A Companion to the*

350 REFERENCES

Ancient Near East. Edited by Daniel C. Snell. 2nd ed. BCAW Hoboken, NJ: Wiley Blackwell.

Livieratou, Antonia. 2012. "Kynos." Pages 3842 in vol. 7 of *The Encyclopedia of Ancient History.* Edited by Roger S. Bagnall, Kai Brodersen, Craige Brian Champion, Andrew Erskine, and Sabine R. Huebner. 13 vols. Chichester: Wiley-Blackwell.

———. 2020. "East Locris and Phocis." Pages 815–35 in vol. 2 of *A Companion to the Archaeology of Early Greece and the Mediterranean.* Edited by Irene M. Lemos and Antonios Kotsonas. 2 vols. BCAW. Hoboken, NJ: Wiley-Blackwell.

Lloyd, Seton. 1972. *Late Bronze Age Architecture.* Beycesultan 3.1. London: British Institute of Archaeology at Ankara.

Lloyd, Seton, and James Mellaart. 1955. "Beycesultan Excavations: First Preliminary Report." *AnSt* 5:39–92. DOI: 10.2307/3642324.

———. 1956. "Beycesultan Excavations: Second Preliminary Report, 1955." *AnSt* 6:101–35. DOI: 10.2307/3642405.

Loretz, Oswald. 1995. "Les Serdanu et la fin d'Ougarit: À propos des documents d'Égypte, de Byblos et d'Ougarit relatifs aux Shardana." Pages 125–36 in *Le pays d'Ougarit autour de 1200 av. J.-C.: Histoire et archéologie; Actes du colloque international, Paris, 28 juin–1er juillet 1993.* Edited by Marguerite Yon, Maurice Sznycer, and Pierre Bordreuil. RSO 11. Paris: Éditions Recherche sur les civilisations.

Lo Schiavo, Fulvia. 2009. "Oxhide Ingots in Nuragic Sardinia." Pages 225–390 in *Oxhide Ingots in the Central Mediterranean.* Edited by Fulvia Lo Schiavo. Nicosia: A.G. Leventis Foundation; Rome: CNR-Istituto di studi sulle civilta dell'Egeo e del vicino oriente.

Lo Schiavo, Fulvia. R. M. Albanese Procelli, and Alessandra Giumlia Mair. 2009. "Oxhide Ingots from Sicily." Pages 135–221 in *Oxhide Ingots in the Central Mediterranean.* Edited by Fulvia Lo Schiavo. Nicosia: A. G. Leventis Foundation; Rome: CNR-Istituto di studi sulle civilta dell'Egeo e del vicino oriente.

Loud, Gordon. 1948. *Megiddo II: Seasons of 1935–39.* 2 vols. OIP 42. Chicago: University of Chicago Press.

Luckenbill, Daniel David. 1914. "The Hittites." *AmJT* 18:24–58.

Lund, John. 1986. *Sūkās VIII: The Habitation Quarters.* Publications of the Carlsberg Expedition to Phoenicia 10. Copenhagen: Royal Danish Academy.

MacDonald, Colin. 2010. "Knossos." Pages 529–542 in *The Oxford Handbook of the Bronze Age Aegean (ca. 3000–1000 BC).* Edited by Eric H. Cline. Oxford Handbooks. Oxford: Oxford University Press.

Maggidis, Christofilis. 2020. "Glas and Boeotia." Pages 107–20 in *Collapse and Transformation: The Late Bronze Age to Early Iron Age in the Aegean.* Edited by Guy D. Middleton. Oxford: Oxbow. DOI: 10.2307/j.ctv13pk6k9.19.

Maeir, Aren M. 2012. "The Tell es-Safi/Gath Archaeological Project 1996–2010: Introduction, Overview and Synopsis of Results." Pages 1–88 in *Tell es-Safi/Gath I: The 1996–2005 Seasons.* Part 1: *Text.* Edited by Aren M. Maeir. ÄAT 69. Wiesbaden: Harrassowitz.

———. 2013. "Philistia Transforming: Fresh Evidence from Tell eṣ-Ṣafi/Gath on the Transformational Trajectory of Philistine Culture." Pages 191–242 in *The Philistines and Other "Sea Peoples" in Text and Archaeology.* Edited by Ann E. Killebrew and Gunner Lehman. ABS 15. Atlanta: Society of Biblical Literature.

———. 2020. "Introduction and Overview." Pages 3–52 in *Tell es-Safi/Gath II: Excavations and Studies.* Edited by Aren M. Maeir and Joe Uziel. ÄAT 105. Münster: Zaphon.

REFERENCES

Maeir, Aren M., Jeffrey R. Chadwick, Amit Dagan, Louise A. Hitchcock, Jill Katz, Itzhaq Shai, and Joe Uziel. 2019. "The Late Bronze Age at Tell es-Safi/Gath and the Site's Role in Southwestern Canaan." Pages 1–18 in *The Late Bronze and Early Iron Ages of Southern Canaan.* Edited by Aren M. Maeir, Chris McKinny, and Itzhaq Shai. Archaeology of the Biblical Worlds 2. Berlin: de Gruyter. DOI: 10.1515/9783110628371-001.

Maeir, Aren M., and Louise A. Hitchcock. 2017. "The Appearance, Formation and Transformation of Philistine Culture: New Perspectives and New Finds." Pages 149–62 *"Sea Peoples" Up-to-Date: New Research on the Transformations in the Eastern Mediterranean in the 13th–11th Centuries BCE.* Edited by Peter M. Fischer and Teresa Bürge. CCEM 35. Vienna: Österreichische Academie der Wissenschaften. DOI: 10.2307/j.ctt1v2xvsn.13.

Maier, Franz Georg. 1969. "Excavations at Kouklia (Palaepaphos): Third Preliminary Report; Season 1968." *RDAC* 1968:33–42.

Maier, Franz Georg, and Vassos Karageorghis. 1984. *Paphos: History and Archaeology.* Nicosia: Leventis Foundation.

Maier, Franz Georg, and Marie-Louise von Wartburg. 1985. "Reconstructing History from the Earth, c. 2800 BC–1600 AD: Excavating at Palaepaphos, 1966–1984." Pages 142–72 in *Archaeology in Cyprus 1960–1985.* Edited by Vassos Karageorghis. Nicosia: Zavallis.

Magness, Jodi. 1993. *Jerusalem Ceramic Chronology: Circa 200–800 CE.* JSOT-ASOR Monographs 9. Sheffield: JSOT Press.

Maisler, Benjamin. 1951. "The Stratification of Tell Abū Huwâm on the Bay of Acre." *BASOR* 124:21–25. DOI: 10.2307/1355697.

Manning, Sturt W. 2007. "Why Radiocarbon Dating 1200 BC Is Difficult: A Sidelight on Dating the End of the Late Bronze Age and the Contrarian Contribution." *Scripta Mediterranea* 27/28:53–80.

Manning, Sturt W., Georgia-Marina Andreou, Kevin D. Fisher, Peregrine Gerard-Little, Catherine Kearns, Jeffrey F. Leon, David A. Sewell, and Thomas M. Urban. 2014. "Becoming Urban: Investigating the Anatomy of the Late Bronze Age Complex, Maroni, Cyprus." *Journal of Mediterranean Archaeology* 27:3–32. DOI: 10.1558/jmea.v27i1.3.

Manning, Sturt W., and Linda Hulin. 2005. "Maritime Commerce and Geographies of Mobility in the Late Bronze Age of the Eastern Mediterranean." Pages 270–302 in *The Archaeology of Mediterranean Prehistory.* Edited by Emma Blake and A. Bernard Knapp. Blackwell Studies in Global Archaeology. Hoboken, NJ: Wiley-Blackwell. DOI: 10.1002/9780470773536.ch11.

Manning, Sturt W., and Peter Ian Kuniholm. 2007. "Absolute Dating at Apliki Karamallos." Pages 325–35 in *Joan du Plat Taylor's Excavations at the Late Bronze Age Mining Settlement at Apliki Karamallos, Cyprus.* Edited by Barbara Kling, James David Muhly, Vasiliki Kassianidou, and Joan du Plat Taylor. Studies in Mediterranean Archaeology 134. Sävedalen: Åström.

Manolova, Tzveta. 2020. "The Levant." Pages 1185–1214 in vol. 2 of *A Companion to the Archaeology of Early Greece and the Mediterranean.* Edited by Irene M. Lemos and Antonios Kotsonas. 2 vols. BCAW. Hoboken, NJ: Wiley-Blackwell.

Manuelli, Federico. 2013. *Arslantepe, Late Bronze Age: Hittite Influence and Local Traditions in an Eastern Anatolian Community.* Arslantepe 9. Rome: Sapienza Università di Roma.

352 REFERENCES

Manuelli, Federico, and Lucia Mori. 2016. "The King at the Gate: Monumental Fortifications and the Rise of Local Elites at Arslantepe at the End of the 2nd Millennium BCE." *Origini* 39:209–42.

Manuelli, Federico, Cristiano Vignola, Fabio Marzaioli, Isabella Passariello, and Filippo Terrasi. 2021. "The Beginning of the Iron Age at Arslantepe: A 14C Perspective." *Radiocarbon* 63:885–903. DOI: 10.1017/RDC.2021.19.

Maran, Joseph. 2008. "Nach dem Ende: Tiryns – Phönix aus der Asche." Pages 63–73 in *Zeit der Helden: Die, "dunklen Jahrhunderte Griechenlands" 1200–700 v. Chr. Katalog zur Ausstellung im Badischen Landesmuseum Karlsruhe (2008).* Edited by Claus Hattler. Karlsruhe: Badisches Landesmuseum.

———. 2009. "The Crisis Years? Reflections on Signs of Instability in the Last Decades of the Mycenaean Palaces." *Scienze dell'antichità Storia Archeologia Antropologia* 15:241–62.

———. 2010. "Tiryns." Pages 722–34 in *The Oxford Handbook of the Bronze Age Aegean (ca. 3000–1000 BC).* Edited by Eric H. Cline. Oxford Handbooks. Oxford: Oxford University Press.

———. 2015. "Tiryns and the Argolid in Mycenaean Times: New Clues and Interpretations." Pages 277–293 in *Mycenaeans up to Date: The Archaeology of the North-Eastern Peloponnese; Current Concepts and New Directions.* Edited by Ann-Louise Schallin and Iphigeneia Turnabitu. Skrifter utgivna av Svenska institutet i Athen 56. Stockholm: Svenska Instituten vid Rom och Athen.

Marchetti, Nicolò. 2012. "Karkemish on the Euphrates: Excavating a City's History." *NEA* 75:132–47. DOI: 10.5615/neareastarch.75.3.0132.

———. 2013. "The 2011 Joint Turco–Italian Excavations at Karkemish." *Kazı Sonuçları Toplantısı* 34:349–63.

———. 2014. "The 2012 Joint Turco–Italian Excavations at Karkemish." *Kazı Sonuçları Toplantısı* 35:233–48.

———. 2015a. "The 2014 Joint Turco–Italian Excavations at Karkemish." *Kazı Sonuçları Toplantısı* 37:363–80.

———. 2015b. "Karkamış – Türk-İtalyanHeyeti'nin 2011–2014 yıllararasındaki kazı çalışmaları." *Arkeolji ve Sanat* 148:39–52.

Marco, Shmuel. 2008. "Recognition of Earthquake-Related Damage in Archaeological Sites: Examples from the Dead Sea Fault Zone." *Tectonophysics* 453:148–56. DOI: 10.1016/j.tecto.2007.04.011.

Marco, Shmuel, Amotz Agnon, Israel Finkelstein, and David Ussishkin. 2006. "Megiddo Earthquakes." Pages 568–75 in *Megiddo IV: The 1998–2002 Seasons.* Edited by Israel Finkelstein, David Ussishkin, and Baruch Halpern. 2 vols. SMNIA 24. Tel Aviv: Emery and Claire Yass Publications in Archaeology.

Margueron, Jean-Claude. 1975a. "Quatre campagnes de fouilles à Emar (1972–1974): Un bilan proviso ire." *Syria* 52:53–85.

———. 1975b. "Rapport préliminaire sur les deux premières campagnes de fouilles à Meskéné/Emar 1972–1973." *AAAS* 25:73–86.

———. 1980. "Emar: Un exemple d'implantation hittite en terre syrienne." Pages 285–312 in *Le Moyen Euphrate: Zone de contacts et d'échanges; Actes du Colloque de Strasbourg 10–12 mars 1977.* Edited by Jean-Claude Margueron. Travaux du Centre de recherche sur le Proche-Orient et la Grèce antiques 5. Leiden: Brill.

———. 1982a. "Architecture et Urbanisme." Pages 23–39 in *Meskéné–Emar: Dix ans de*

REFERENCES 353

travaux 1972–1982. Edited by Dominique Beyer. Paris: Éditions recherche sur les civilisations.

———. 1982b. "Aux marches de l'Empire Hittite: Une campagne de fouilles à Tell Faq'ous (Syrie), citadelle du pays d'Astata." Pages 47–66 in *La Syrie au bronze récent: Recueil publié à l'occasion du cinquantenaire de la découverte d'Ougarit–Ras Shamra*. Edited by Marguerite Yon. Paris: Editions Recherche sur les civilisations.

———. 1982c. "Rapport Préliminaire sur les 3°, 4°, 5° et 6° campagne de fouilles à Meskene/Emar." *AAAS* 32:233–49.

———. 1983. "Emar." *AAAS* 33:175–85.

Margueron, Jean-Claude, and Veronica Boutte. 1995. "Emar, Capital of Aštata in the Fourteenth Century BCE." *BA* 58:126–38. DOI: 10.2307/3210445.

Martin, Mario A. S. 2017. "The Fate of Megiddo at the End of the Late Bronze IIB." Pages 267–86 in *Rethinking Israel: Studies in the History and Archaeology of Ancient Israel in Honor of Israel Finkelstein*. Edited by Oded Lipschits, Yuval Gadot, and Matthew J Adams. Winona Lake, IN: Eisenbrauns.

Martin, Mario A. S., and Tristan J. Barako. 2007. "Egyptian and Egyptianized Pottery." Pages 129–65 in *Tel Mor: The Moshe Dothan Excavations, 1959–1960*. Edited by Tristan J. Barako. IAAR 32. Jerusalem: Israel Antiquities Authority.

Martin, Mario A. S., Noga Blockman, and Julye Bidmead. 2013. "Part I: Levels K-8 and K-7." Pages 153–64 in Megiddo V: The 2004–2008 Seasons, vol. 1. Edited by Israel Finkelstein, David Ussishkin, and Eric H. Cline. Monograph Series of the Sonia and Marco Nadler Institute of Archaeology 31. Winona Lake, IN: Eisenbrauns.

de Martino, Stefano. 2018. "The Fall of the Hittite Kingdom." *Mesopotamia* 53:23–48.

de Martino, Stefano, and Elena Devecchi. eds. 2020. *Anatolia between the 13th and the 12th Century BCE*. Eothen 23. Firenze: LoGisma.

Marzolff, P. 2008. "Ein Neu Entdeckter Gang an der Nordspitze der Unterburgmauer von Tiryns." *AA* 25:97–109.

Maspero, Gaston. 1873. Review of *Etudes sur l'antiquité d'après les sources égyptiennes et Les Monuments réputés préhistoriques*, by François Joseph Chabas. *Review Critique d'Histoire et de Litterature* 2:84–85.

———. 1886. *Histoire ancienne des peuples de l'Orient: Ouvrage contenant 3 ct. et quelques spécimens des écritures hiéroglyphiques et cunéiformes*. Paris: Hachette.

———. 1896. *The Struggle of the Nations: Egypt, Syria and Assyria*. New York: Appleton.

Mastrokostas, Efthymios. 1962. "Ἀνασκαφαί τοῦ Τείχους Δυμαίων." *ΠΑΕ* 1962:127–33.

———. 1963. "Ἀνασκαφαί τοῦ Τείχους Δυμαίων." *ΠΑΕ* 1963:93–98.

———. 1964. "Ἀνασκαφή τοῦ Τείχους Δυμαίων." *ΠΑΕ* 1964:60–67.

———. 1965. "Ἀνασκαφή τοῦ Τείχους Δυμαίων." *ΠΑΕ* 1966:121–36.

———. 1966. "Ἀχαΐα: Τεῖχος Δυμαίων." Ἔργον: 156–65.

Matthiae, Paolo. 2018. *Dalla terra alla storia: Scoperte leggendarie di archeologia orientale*. Torino: Scoperte leggendarie di archeologia orientale.

Maunder, Samuel. 1850. *The Treasury of History: Comprising a General Introductory Outline of Universal History, Ancient and Modern, and a Series of Separate Histories of Every Principal Nation That Exists, Their Rise, Progress, Present Condition*. London: Longman, Brown, Green, Longmans, & Roberts.

Mazar, Amihai. 1990. *Archaeology of the Land of the Bible 10,000–586 B.C.E*. ABRL. New York: Doubleday.

———. 1997. *Timnah (Tel Batash) I: Stratigraphy and Architecture*. Qedem 37. Jerusalem: Institute of Archaeology, Hebrew University of Jerusalem.

354 REFERENCES

——. 2002. "Megiddo in the Thirteenth–Eleventh Centuries BCE: A Review of Some Recent Studies." Pages 264–82 in *Aharon Kempinski Memorial Volume: Studies in Archaeology and Related Disciplines*. Edited by Shmuel Ahituv and Eliezer D. Oren. Beer-Sheva 15. Beer-Sheva: Ben-Gurion University of the Negev Press.

——. 2008. "From 1200 to 850 B.C.E.: Remarks on Some Selected Archaeological Issues." Pages 86–120 in *Israel in Transition: From the Late Bronze II to the Iron IIa (c. 1250–850 BCE)*. Vol. 1: *The Archaeology*. Edited by Lester L. Grabbe. LHBOTS 491. New York: T&T Clark.

——. 2009a. "Introduction and Overview." Pages 1–32 in *Excavations at Tel Beth-Shean 1989–1996*, vol. 3: *The 13th–11th Centuries BCE (Areas S and N)*. Edited by Nava Panitz-Cohen and Amihai Mazar. Jerusalem: Institute of Archaeology, Hebrew University of Jerusalem; Israel Exploration Society.

——. 2009b. "Area N North South: Stratigraphy and Architecture." Pages 72–93 in *Excavations at Tel Beth-Shean 1989–1996*, vol. 3: *The 13th–11th Centuries BCE (Areas S and N)*. Edited by Nava Panitz-Cohen and Amihai Mazar. Jerusalem: Institute of Archaeology, Hebrew University of Jerusalem; Israel Exploration Society.

——. 2010. "Tel Beth-Shean: History and Archaeology." Pages 237–72 in *One God – One Cult – One Nation: Archaeological and Biblical Perspectives*. Edited by Reinhard Gregor Kratz and Hermann Spieckermann. BZAW 405. Berlin: de Gruyter.

Mazar, Amihai, and George L. Kelm. 1993. "Batash, Tel (Timnah)." *NEAEHL* 1:152–57.

Mazar, Amihai, and Nava Panitz-Cohen. 2019. "Tel Batash in the Late Bronze Age: A Retrospect." Pages 86–121 in *The Late Bronze and Early Iron Ages of Southern Canaan*. Edited by Aren M. Maeir, Chris McKinny, and Itzhaq Shai. Archaeology of the Biblical Worlds 2. Berlin: de Gruyter. DOI: 10.1515/9783110628371-005.

McClellan, Thomas L. 1992. "12th Century BC Syria: Comments on Sader's Paper." Pages 164–73 in *The Crisis Years: The 12th Century B.C.; From Beyond the Danube to the Tigris*. Edited by William A. Ward and Martha Sharp Joukowsky. Dubuque, IA: Kendall/Hunt Publishing.

McDonald, William Andrew. 1972. "Excavations at Nichoria in Messenia: 1969–71." *Hesperia* 41:218–73. DOI: 10.2307/147682.

McDonald, William Andrew, C. T. Shay, Nancy Wilkie, R. Hope Simpson, William P. Donovan, Harriet Blitzer, and J. Rosser. 1975. "Excavations at Nichoria in Messenia: 1972–1973." *Hesperia* 44:69–141. DOI: 10.2307/147426.

McDonald, William Andrew, and R. Hope Simpson. 1960. "Where a Whole Mycenaean World Awaits the Spade." *Illustrated London News* April 30, 1960:740–41.

McDonald, William Andrew, and Nancy C. Wilkie, eds. 1992. *Excavations at Nichoria in Southwest Greece*. Vol. 2: *The Bronze Age Occupation*. Minneapolis: University of Minnesota Press.

McGovern, Patrick E. 1989. "The Baq'ah Valley Project 1987: Khirbet Umm ad-Dananir and al-Qesir." *ADAJ* 33:123–36.

McKinny, Chris, Deborah Cassuto, and Itzhaq Shai. 2015. "Tel Burna: The Late Bronze and Iron Age Remains after Five Seasons." *The Bible and Interpretation*. https://bibleinterp.arizona.edu/articles/2015/04/mck398002.

McKinny, Chris, Aharon Tavger, Deborah Cassuto, Casey Sharp, Matthew J. Suriano, Steven M. Ortiz, and Itzhaq Shai. 2020. "Tel Burna after a Decade of Work: The Late Bronze and Iron Ages." *NEA* 83:4–15. DOI: 10.1086/705490.

McKinney, Chris, Aharon Tavger, and Itzhaq Shai. 2019. "Tel Burna in the Late Bronze Age: Assessing the 13th Century BCE Landscape of the Shephelah." Pages 148–

References

70 in *The Late Bronze and Early Iron Ages of Southern Canaan*. Edited by Aren M. Maeir, Chris McKinny, and Itzhaq Shai. Archaeology of the Biblical Worlds 2. Berlin: de Gruyter. DOI: 10.1515/9783110628371-008.

Mee, Christopher. 1978. "Aegean Trade and Settlement in Anatolia in the Second Millennium BC." *AnSt* 28:121–56. DOI: 10.2307/3642747.

Mellaart, James. 1970. "The Second Millennium Chronology of Beycesultan." *AnSt* 20:55–67. DOI: 10.2307/3642588.

Mellaart, James, and Ann Murray. 1995. *Late Bronze Age and Phrygian Pottery and Middle and Late Bronze Age Small Objects*. Beycesultan 3.2. London: British Institute of Archaeology at Ankara.

Merrillees, Robert S. 1968. *The Cypriot Bronze Age Pottery Found in Egypt*. Studies in Mediterranean Archaeology 18. Lund: Blom.

Du Mesnil du Buisson, Robert. 1935. *Le site archéologique de Mishrifé-Qatna*. Collection de textes et documents d'Orient 1. Paris: de Boccard.

Metzger, Martin. 1991. *Die spätbronzezeitlichen Tempelanlagen: Stratigraphie, Architektur und installationen*. Kamid el-Loz 7. Bonn: Habelt.

———. 1993. *Die spätbronzezeitlichen Tempelanlagen: Die Kleinfunde*. Kämid el-Loz 8. Bonn: Habelt

Meyer, Nathan, and A. Bernard Knapp. 2021. "Resilient Social Actors in the Transition from the Late Bronze to the Early Iron Age on Cyprus." *Journal of World Prehistory* 34:433–87. DOI: 10.1007/s10963-021-09163-7.

Middleton, Guy D. 2010. *The Collapse of Palatial Society in LBA Greece and the Postpalatial Period*. BARIS 2110. Oxford: Archaeopress.

———. 2012. "Nothing Lasts Forever: Environmental Discourses on the Collapse of Past Societies." *Journal of Archaeological Research* 20:257–307.

———. 2015. "Telling Stories: The Mycenaean Origins of the Philistines." *OJA* 34:45–65. DOI: 10.1111/ojoa.12048.

———. 2017. *Understanding Collapse: Ancient History and Modern Myths*. Cambridge: Cambridge University Press.

———. 2018. "'I Would Walk 500 Miles and I Would Walk 500 More': The Sea Peoples and Aegean Migration at the End of the Late Bronze Age." Pages 95–115 in *Change, Continuity, and Connectivity: North-Eastern Mediterranean at the Turn of the Bronze Age and in the Early Iron Age*. Edited by Lukasz Niesiołowski-Spanò and Marek Wecowski. Philippika 118. Wiesbaden: Harrassowitz.

———. 2020a. "Mycenaean Collapse(s) c. 1200 B.C." Pages 9–22 in *Collapse and Transformation: The Late Bronze Age to Early Iron Age in the Aegean*. Edited by Guy D. Middleton. Oxford: Oxbow. DOI: 10.2307/j.ctv13pk6k9.9.

———, ed. 2020b. *Collapse and Transformation: The Late Bronze Age to Early Iron Age in the Aegean*. Oxford: Oxbow.

Mielke, Dirk Paul. 2006a. "Dendrochronologie und hethitische Archäologie—Einige kritische Anmerkungen." Pages 77–94 in *Strukturierung und Datierung der hethitischen Archäologie: Voraussetzungen, Probleme, Neue Ansätze; Internationaler Workshop Istanbul, 26–27. November 2004*. Edited by Dirk Paul Mielke, Ulf-Dietrich Schoop, and Jürgen Seeher. Byzas 4. Istanbul: Ege Yayınları.

———. 2006b. *Die Keramik vom Westhang*. Kuşaklı Sarissa 2. Rahden: Leidorf.

Millek, Jesse Michael. 2017. "Sea Peoples, Philistines, and the Destruction of Cities: A Critical Examination of Destruction Layers 'Caused' by the 'Sea Peoples.'" Pages 113–40 in *"Sea Peoples" Up-to-Date: New Research on the Transformations in the*

356 REFERENCES

Eastern Mediterranean in the 13th–11th Centuries BCE. Edited by Peter M. Fischer and Teresa Bürge. CCEM 35. Vienna: Österreichische Academie der Wissenschaften. DOI: 10.2307/j.ctt1v2xvsn.11.

———. 2018a. "Destruction and the Fall of Egyptian Hegemony over the Southern Levant." *Journal of Ancient Egyptian Interconnections* 19:1–21.

———. 2018b. "Just How Much Was Destroyed? The End of the Late Bronze Age in the Southern Levant." *UF* 49:239–74.

———. 2019a. "Destruction at the End of the Late Bronze Age in Syria: A Reassessment." *Studia Eblaitica* 5:157–90.

———. 2019b. "Crisis, Destruction, and the End of the Late Bronze Age in Jordan: A Preliminary Survey." *ZDPV* 135:119–42.

———. 2019c. *Exchange, Destruction, and a Transitioning Society: Interregional Exchange in the Southern Levant from the Late Bronze Age to the Iron I.* Tübingen: Tübingen University Press.

———. 2020. "'Our City Is Sacked. May You Know It!' The Destruction of Ugarit and Its Environs by the 'Sea Peoples.'" Pages 102–32 in *The Iron Age I in the Levant: A View from the North; Part 2.* Edited by Hanan Charaf and Lynn Welton. AHL 52–53. London: Lebanese British Friends of the National Museum.

———. 2021a. "Why Did the World End in 1200 BCE?" *Ancient Near East Today* 9.8. https://www.asor.org/anetoday/2021/08/world-end-1200-bce.

———. 2021b. "Just What Did They Destroy? The Sea Peoples and the End of the Late Bronze Age." Pages 59–98 in *The Mediterranean Sea and the Southern Levant: Archaeological and Historical Perspectives from the Bronze Age to Medieval Times.* Edited by Jens Kamlah and Achim Lichtenberger. ADPV 48. Wiesbaden: Harrassowitz.

———. Forthcoming a. "The Impact of Destruction on Trade at the End of the Late Bronze Age in the Southern Levant." *Jerusalem and the West: Perspectives from Archaeology.* Edited by Felix Hagemeyer. Tübingen: Mohr Siebeck.

———. Forthcoming b. "Troy, the Sea Peoples, and 1200 BC: The Origins and Future of an Iconic Date." *UF* 52.

Miller, Jared L. 2020. "Are There Signs of the Decline of the Late Hittite State in the Textual Documentation from Hattuša?" Pages 237–55 in *Anatolia between the 13th and 12th Century BCE.* Edited by Stefano de Martino and Elena Devecchi. Eothen 23. Firenze: LoGisma.

Milojcic, Vladimir. 1972. "Neue deutsche Ausgrabungen in Demetrias/Thessalien, 1967–1972." *Jahrbuch der Heidelberger Akademie der Wissenschaften* 1972:61–74.

Mock, Shirley Boteler. 1998. "Prelude." Pages 3–18 in *The Sowing and the Dawning: Termination, Dedication, and Transformation in the Archaeological and Ethnographic Record of Mesoamerica.* Edited by Shirley Boteler Mock. Albuquerque: University of New Mexico Press.

Monroe, Christopher. M. 2009. *Scales of Fate: Trade, Tradition, and Transformation in the Eastern Mediterranean ca. 1350–1175 BCE.* AOAT 357. Münster: Ugarit-Verlag.

Montesanto, Mariacarmela. 2020. "Lost in Transition: The Late Bronze–Iron Age Pottery Assemblage in Tell Atchana/Alalakh." *Studia Eblaitica* 6:57–88.

Montesanto, Mariacarmela, and Marina Pucci. 2019. "The Iron Age at Alalakh." Pages 93–135 in *The Iron Age I in the Levant: A View from the North; Part 1.* Edited by Hanan Charaf and Lynn Welton. AHL 50–51. London: Lebanese British Friends of the National Museum.

REFERENCES 357

Moore, Andrew M. T., James P. Kennett, William M. Napier, Ted E. Bunch, James C. Weaver, Malcolm LeCompte, A. Victor Adedeji, Paul Hackley, Gunther Kletetschka, Robert E. Hermes, James H. Wittke, Joshua J. Razink, Michael W. Gaultois, and Allen West. 2020. "Evidence of Cosmic Impact at Abu Hureyra, Syria at the Younger Dryas Onset (~12.8 ka): High-Temperature Melting at >2200 °C." *Scientific Reports* 10:4185. DOI: 10.1038/s41598-020-60867-w.

Morhange, Christophe, Amos Salamon, Guéna Bony, Clément Flaux, Ehud Galili, Jean-Philippe Goiran, and Dov Zviely. 2014. "Geoarchaeology of Tsunamis and the Revival of Neo-catastrophism in the Eastern Mediterranean." Pages 31–51 in *Overcoming Catastrophes: Essays on Disastrous Agents Characterization and Resilience Strategies in Pre-Classical Southern Levant*. Edited by Lorenzo Nigro. RO-SAPAT 11. Rome: La Sapienza.

Morris, Ellen. 2005. *The Architecture of Imperialism: Military Bases and the Evolution of Foreign Policy in Egypt's New Kingdom*. PAe 22. Leiden: Brill.

Morris, Joseph. 1925. *The German Air Raids on Great Britain, 1914–1918*. London: Low, Marston & Co.

Mountjoy, Penelope A. 1993. *Mycenaean Pottery: An Introduction*. Oxford University School of Archaeology Monograph 36. Oxford: Oxford University School of Archaeology.

——. 1997. "The Destruction of the Palace at Pylos Reconsidered." *ABSA* 92:109–37. DOI: 10.1017/S0068245400016658.

——. 1999a. "The Destruction of Troia VIh." *Studia Troica* 9:253–93.

——. 1999b. "Troia VII Reconsidered." *Studia Troica* 9:295–346.

——. 2004. "Miletos: A Note." *ABSA* 99:189–200. DOI: 10.1017/S006824540002116X.

——. 2005. "The End of the Bronze Age at Enkomi, Cyprus: The Problem of Level III B." *ABSA* 100:125–214.

——. 2008. "The Cyclades during the Mycenaean period." Pages 467–78 in *Horizon: A Colloquium on the Prehistory of the Cyclades*. Edited by Neil Brodie, Jenny Doole, Gioros Galvalas, and Colin Renfrew. Cambridge: McDonald Institute for Archaeological Research.

——. 2017. *Troy VI Middle, VI Late and VII: The Mycenaean Pottery*. Bonn: Habelt.

Müller, K. 1930. *Tiryns III: Die Architektur der Burg und des Palastes*. Augsburg: Filser.

Müller, Uwe, 1999 "Die eisenzeitliche Stratigraphie von Lidar Höyük." *AnSt* 49:123–31. DOI: 10.2307/3643067.

——. 2001. "Invasionen oder Bürgerkrieg? Zur Neuinterpretation von Textquellen anhand archäologischer Ergebnisse." Pages 299–303 in *Lux Orientis: Archäologie zwischen Asien und Europa; Festschrift für Harald Hauptmann, 2001*. Edited by Rainer M. Boehmer and Joseph Maran. Rahden: Leidorf.

——. 2003. "A Change to Continuity: Bronze Age Traditions in Early Iron Age." Pages 137–49 in *Identifying Changes: The Transition from Bronze to Iron Ages in Anatolia and Its Neighbouring Regions; Proceedings of the International Workshop, Istanbul, November 8–9, 2002*. Edited by Bettina Fischer. Istanbul: Türk Eskiçag Bilimleri Enstitüsü.

——. 2005 "Norsuntepe and Lidar Höyük: Two Examples for Cultural Change in Early Iron Age." Pages 107–14 in *Proceedings of the 5th Anatolian Iron Ages Colloquium Held at Van in 2001*. Edited by Altan Cilingiroglu and Gareth Darbyshire. British Institute of Archaeology at Ankara Monograph 31. London: British Institute of Archaeology at Ankara.

358 References

Müller-Karpe, Andreas. 1995. "Untersuchungen in Kusakli 1992–94." *MDOG* 127:5–36.

———. 1996. "Untersuchungen in Kusakli 1995." *MDOG* 128:69–94.

———. 1997. "Untersuchungen in Kusakli 1996." *MDOG* 129:103–42.

———. 1998. "Untersuchungen in Kusakli 1997." *MDOG* 130:93–174.

———. 1999. "Untersuchungen in Kusakli 1998." *MDOG* 131:57–113.

———. 2000a. "Untersuchungen in Kusakli 1999." *MDOG* 132:311–53.

———. 2000b. "Die Akropolis der hethitischen Stadt Kuşaklı-Sarissa." *Nürnberger Blätter zur Archäologie* 16:91–110.

———. 2001. "Untersuchungen in Kusakli 2000." *MDOG* 133:225–50.

———. 2002. "Untersuchungen in Kusakli 2001." *MDOG* 134:331–51.

———. 2004a. "Untersuchungen in Kusakli 2002." *MDOG* 136:103–35.

———. 2004b. "Untersuchungen in Kusakli 2003." *MDOG* 136:137–72.

———. 2006. "Untersuchungen in Kusakli 2004 und 2005." *MDOG* 138:15–42.

———. 2009. "The Rise and Fall of the Hittite Empire in the Light of Dendroarchaeological Research." Pages 253–62 in *Tree-Rings, Kings and Old World Archaeology and Environment: Papers Presented in Honor of Peter Ian Kuniholm*. Edited by Sturt W. Manning and Mary Jaye Bruce. Oxford: Oxbow.

———. 2017. *Sarissa: Die Wiederentdeckung einer hethitischen Königsstadt*. Darmstadt: von Zabern.

Mumford, Gregory. 2015. "The Amman Airport Structure: A Re-Assessment of Its Date-Range, Function and Overall Role in the Levant." Pages 89–198 in *Walls of the Prince: Egyptian Interactions with Southwest Asia in Antiquity; Essays in Honour of John S. Holladay, Jr*. Edited by Timothy P. Harrison, Edward B. Banning, and Stanley Klassen. CHANE 77. Leiden: Brill. DOI: 10.1163/9789004302563_007.

Murray, Sarah C. 2013. "Trade, Imports, and Society in Early Greece." PhD diss., Stanford University.

———. 2018. "Imported Exotica and Mortuary Ritual at Perati in Late Helladic IIIC East Attica." *AJA* 122:33–64. DOI: 10.3764/aja.122.1.0033.

Mylonas, George E. 1964. "Priam's Troy and the Date of Its Fall." *Hesperia* 33:352–80. DOI: 10.2307/147283.

———. 1966. "The East Wing of the Palace of Mycenae." *Hesperia* 35:419–26. DOI: 10.2307/147570.

Na'aman, Nadav. 2004. "Ra'shu, Re'si-ṣuri, and the Ancient Names of Ras Ibn Hani." *BASOR* 334:33–39. DOI: 10.2307/4150105.

Nahshoni, Pirhiya. 2013. "A Thirteenth-Century BCE Site on the Southern Beach of Ashdod." *'Atiqot* 74:59–122.

Negbi, Oron. 1989. "Bronze Age Pottery (Strata XVII – XV)." Pages 43–63 in *Excavations at Tel Michal, Israel*. Edited by Ze'ev Herzog, George Rapp, and Ora Negbi. Minneapolis: University of Minnesota Press.

Nelson, Michael. 2001. "The Architecture of Epano Englianos, Greece." PhD diss., University of Toronto.

Neve, Peter. 1969. "Der große Tempel und die Magazine." Pages 9–19 in *Funde aus den Grabungen 1967 und 1968*. Edited by Kurt Bittel. Boğazköy 4. ADOG 14. Berlin: Mann.

Niemeier, Wolf-Dietrich. 2007. "Milet von den Anfängen menschlicher Besiedlung bis zur Ionischen Wanderung." Pages 3–20 in *Frühes Ionien: Eine Bestandsaufnahme; Panionion-Symposion Güzelçamlı, 26. September–1. Oktober 1999*. Edited by Justus Cobet. Milesische Forschungen 5. Mainz: von Zabern.

REFERENCES   359

Niemeier, Wolf-Dietrich, and Barbara Niemeier. 1997. "Milet 1994–1995: Projekt 'Minoisch-mykenisches bis protogeometrisches Milet'; Zielsetzung und Grabungen auf dem Stadionhügel und am Athenatempel." *AA* 1997:189–248.

Niesiołowski-Spanò, Lukasz, and Marek Węcowski, eds. 2018. *Change, Continuity, and Connectivity: North-Eastern Mediterranean at the Turn of the Bronze Age and in the Early Iron Age*. Philippika 118. Wiesbaden: Harrassowitz Verlag.

Nougayrol, Jean, Emmanuel Laroche, Charles Virolleaud, and Claude F.-A. Schaeffer. 1968. *Ugaritica V: Nouveaux textes accadiens, hourrites et ugaritiques des archives et bibliothèques privées d'Ugarit*. MRS 16. Paris: Geuthner.

Novák, Mirko, Anna Lucia D'Agata, Isabella Caneva, Christine Eslick, Charles Gates, Marie-Henriette Gates, K. Serdar Girginer, Özlem Oyman-Girginer, Éric Jean, Gülgün Köroğlu, Ekin Kozal, Sabina Kulemann-Ossen, Gunnar Lehmann, Aslı Özyar, Tülay Ozaydın, J. Nicholas Postgate, Fatma Şahin, Elif Ünlü, Remzi Yağcı, and Deniz Yaşin Meier. 2017. "Cilician Chronology Group: A Comparative Stratigraphy of Cilicia." *AoF* 44: 150–86. DOI: 10.1515/aofo-2017-0013.

Nowicki, Krzystof. 2018. "The Late 13th c. BCE Crisis in the East Mediterranean: Why the Case of Crete Matters." Pages 117–48 in *An Archaeology of Forced Migration: Crisis-Induced Mobility and the Collapse of the 13th c. BCE Eastern Mediterranean*. Edited by Jan Driessen. Aegis 15. Louvain-La-Neuve: Presses Universitaires de Louvain.

Núñez, Francisco J. 2018. "The Impact of the Sea Peoples in Central Levant: A Revision." Pages 116–40 in *Change, Continuity, and Connectivity: North-Eastern Mediterranean at the Turn of the Bronze Age and in the Early Iron Age*. Edited by Lukasz Niesiołowski-Spanò and Marek Węcowski. Philippika 118. Wiesbaden: Harrassowitz.

Nur, Amos, and Dawn Burgess. 2008. *Apocalypse: Earthquakes, Archaeology, and the Wrath of God*. Princeton: Princeton University Press.

Nur, Amos, and Eric H. Cline. 2000. "Poseidon's Horses: Plate Tectonics and Earthquake Storms in the Late Bronze Age Aegean and Eastern Mediterranean." *JArS* 27:43–63. DOI: 10.1006/jasc.1999.0431.

Nur, Amos, and Hagai Ron. 1997. "Armageddon's Earthquakes." *International Geology Review* 39:532–41. DOI: 10.1080/00206819709465287.

O'Connor, David. 2000. "The Sea Peoples and the Egyptian Sources." Pages 85–102 in *The Sea Peoples and Their World: A Reassessment*. Edited by Eliezer D. Oren. Museum Monograph 108. Philadelphia: University Museum, University of Pennsylvania, 2013. DOI: 10.9783/9781934536438.85.

Ohata, Kiyoshi. 1966. *Tel Zeror I: Preliminary Report of the Excavation, First Season, 1964*. Tokyo: Society for Near Eastern Studies in Japan.

Ohata, Kiyoshi, and Moshe Kochavi. 1964. "Tel Zeror." *IEJ* 14:283–84.

Omura, Sachihiro. 2011. "Kaman-Kalehöyük Excavations in Central Anatolia." Pages 1095–1111 in *The Oxford Handbook of Ancient Anatolia 10,000–323 B.C.E.* Edited by Sharon R. Steadman and Gregory McMahon. Oxford Handbooks. Oxford: Oxford University Press.

Oren, Eliezer D. 1982. "Ziglag: A Biblical City on the Edge of the Negev." *BA* 45:155–66. DOI: 10.2307/3209810.

———. 1984. "Governor's Residencies in Canaan under the New Kingdom: A Case Study of Egyptian Administration." *Journal of the Society for the Study of Egyptian Antiquities* 14.2:37–56.

360 References

———. 1992. "Palaces and Patrician Houses in the Middle and Late Bronze Ages." Pages 105–20 in *The Architecture of Ancient Israel: From the Prehistoric to the Persian Period; In Memory of Immanuel (Munya) Dunayevsky*. Edited by Aharon Kempinski, Ronny Reich, and Hannah Katzenstein. Jerusalem: Israel Exploration Society.

———. 1993a. "Sera', Tel." *NEAEHL* 4:1329–35.

———. 1993b. "Tel Haror – 1990/1990 – תל הרור." *Hadashot Arkheologiyot* 1993:97–100.

———. 1993c. "Haror, Tel." *NEAEHL* 2:580–84.

———. 1995. "Tel Haror—1990." *ESI* 13:113–16.

———. 1997a. "Sera', Tel." *OEANE* 5:1–2.

———. 1997b. "Haror, Tel." *OEANE* 2:474–76.

———. ed. 2000. *The Sea Peoples and Their World: A Reassessment*. University Museum Monograph 108. Philadelphia: University Museum, University of Pennsylvania.

Oren, Eliezer D., and E. Netzer 1974. "Tel Sera' (Tell esh-Shari'a)." *IEJ* 24:264–66.

Ortiz, Steven, and Samuel Wolff. 2012. "Guarding the Border to Jerusalem: The Iron Age City of Gezer." *NEA* 75:4–19. DOI: 10.5615/neareastarch.75.1.0004

———. 2017. "Tel Gezer Excavations 2006–2015: The Transformation of a Border City." Pages 61–102 in *The Shephelah during the Iron Age: Recent Archaeological Studies*. Edited by Oded Lipschitz and Aren M. Maeir. Winona Lake, IN: Eisenbrauns.

———. 2019. "A Reevaluation of Gezer in the Late Bronze Age in Light of Renewed Excavations and Recent Scholarship." Pages 62–85 in *The Late Bronze and Early Iron Ages of Southern Canaan*. Edited by Aren M. Maeir, Chris McKinny, and Itzhaq Shai. Archaeology of the Biblical Worlds 2. Berlin: de Gruyter. DOI: 10.1515/9783110628371-004.

von der Osten, Hans Henning. 1937. *The Alishar Huyuk: Seasons of 1930–32, Part 2*. OIP 29. Chicago: University of Chicago.

Ottosson, M. 2015. "1990–93 – Area B." Pages 15–28 in *Tall al-Fukhār: Results from Excavations in 1990–93 and 2002*, vol. 1: *Text*. Edited by John Strange. Proceedings of the Danish Institute in Damascus 9. Aarhus: Aarhus University Press.

Özgüç, Tahsin. 1948. "Excavations at Fraktin near Develi and Researches in Anti-Taurus Region." *Belleten* 12:266–67.

———. 1955a. "Fraktin." *AnSt* 5:20. DOI: 10.2307/3642322.

———. 1955b. "Firakdin eserleri/Finds at Firakdin." *Belleten* 19:301–7.

———. 1978. *Maşat Höyük Kazıları ve Çevresindeki Araştırmalar = Excavations at Maşat Höyük and Investigations in Its Vicinity*. Türk Tarik Kurumu Yayınları 5/38. Ankara: Türk Tarih Kurumu Basımevi.

———. 1980. "Excavations at the Hittite Site, Maşat Höyük: Palace, Archives, Mycenaean Pottery." *AJA* 84:305–9. DOI: 10.2307/504705.

———. 1982. *Maşat Höyük II: A Hittite Center Northeast of Boghazköy*. Ankara: Türk Tarih Kurumu Basımevi.

———. 2002. "Alacahöyük: Ein Kultort im Kerngebiet des Reiches." Pages 172–75 in *Die Hethiter und ihr Reich: Das Volk der 1000 Götter/Hititler ve Hitit İmparatorluğu; 1000 Tanrılı Halk, Bonn Hitit Sergi Kataloğu*. Edited by Tahsin Özgüç and Ayşe Baykal-Seeher. Bonn: Kunst-und Ausstellungshalle der Bundesrepublik Deutschland.

Özyar, Aslı. 2015. "Contributions of Tarsus-Gözlükule to Hittite Studies." Pages 279–86 in *The Discovery of an Anatolian Empire = Bir Anadolu İmparatorluğunun Keşfi: A Colloquium to Commemorate the 100th Anniversary of the Decipherment of the Hittite Language (November 14th and 15th, 2015; Istanbul Archaeological Museum-*

REFERENCES 361

Library). Edited by Meltem Doğan-Alparslan, Andreas Schachner, and Metin Alparslan. Istanbul: Türk Eskiçağ Bilimleri Enstitüsü.

Özyar, Aslı, Elif Ünlü, Steve Karacic, Çiğdem Külekçioğlu, and Türkan Pilavcı. 2012. "Tarsus-Gözlükule 2010 Yılı Kazısı." *Kazı Sonuçları Toplantısı* 33:413–31.

Özyar, Aslı, Elif Ünlü, and Türkan Pilavcı. 2019. "Recent Fieldwork at Tarsus-Gözlükule: The Late Bronze Age Levels." Pages 53–71 in *The Archaeology of Anatolia*, vol. 3: *Recent Discoveries (2017–2018)*. Edited by Sharon R. Steadman and Gregory McMahon. Newcastle-upon-Tyne: Cambridge Scholars.

Palermo, Joanna. 2018. "The Impact of Iron Technology on the Economy of the Aegean and Cyprus from 1200–850 BCE." PhD diss., University of Oxford.

Panitz-Cohen, Nava, and Amihai Mazar. 2009. "Area S: Stratigraphy and Architecture." Pages 94–193 in *Excavations at Tel Beth-Shean 1989–1996*, vol. 3: *The 13th–11th Centuries BCE (Areas S and N)*. Edited by Nava Panitz-Cohen and Amihai Mazar. Jerusalem: Institute of Archaeology, Hebrew University of Jerusalem; Israel Exploration Society.

Pantazis, Vangelis D. 2009. "Wilusa: Reconsidering the Evidence." *Klio* 91:291–310. DOI: 10.1524/klio.2009.0014.

Papadimitriou, Nikolas. 2013. "Regional or 'International' Networks? A Comparative Examination of Aegean and Cypriot Imported Pottery in the Eastern Mediterranean." *Talanta* 44:92–136.

———. 2015. "Aegean and Cypriot Ceramic Trade Overseas during the 2nd Millennium BCE." Pages 423–45 in *There and Back Again – the Crossroads II: Proceedings of an International Conference Held in Prague, September 15–18, 2014.* Edited by Jana Mynářová, Pavel Onderka, and Peter Pavúk. Prague: Charles University, Faculty of Arts.

Papadopoulos, Thanasis J. 1979. *Mycenaean Achaea.* 2 vols. Studies in Mediterranean Archaeology 55. Göteborg: Åström.

Papasavvas, George. 2014. "Feasting, Deposition and Abandonment in the Sanctuary of the Horned God at Enkomi." Pages 245–60 in *Structure, Measurement and Meaning: Insights into the Prehistory of Cyprus; Studies on Prehistoric Cyprus in Honour of David Frankel.* Edited by Jennifer M. Webb. Studies in Mediterranean Archaeology 143. Uppsala: Åström.

Parr, Peter J. 1983. "The Tell Nebi Mend Project." *AAAS* 33:99–117.

———. 1991. "The Tell Nebi Mend Project." *Journal of the Ancient Chronology Forum* 4:78–85.

———. 1997. "Tell Nebi Mend." *OEANE* 4:114–15.

Pashardes, Stelios, and Constantinos Christofides. 1995. "Statistical Analysis of Wind Speed and Direction in Cyprus." *Solar Energy* 55:405–14. DOI: 10.1016/0038-092X(95)00064-X.

Paz, Yitzhak. 2011. "'Raiders on the Storm': The Violent Destruction of Leviah, an Early Bronze Age Urban Centre in the Southern Levant." *Journal of Conflict Archaeology* 6:3–21. DOI: 10.1179/157407811X12958693492891.

Pecorella, Paolo Emilio. 1975. *Malatya III: Rapporto preliminare delle campagne 1963–1968; Il livello eteo imperiale e quelli neoetei.* Orientis antiqui collectio 12. Rome: Centro per le Antichità e la Storia dell'Arte del Vicino Oriente.

Peker, Hasan. 2017. "Some Remarks on the Imperial Hittite Sealings from the 2017 Excavations at Karkemish." *NABU* 2017.4:178–79, no. 101.

———. 2020. "New Evidence for the Late 13th Century BCE Administrative Structure

362 REFERENCES

at Karkemiš." Pages 317–23 in *Anatolia between the 13th and 12th Century BCE*. Edited by Stefano de Martino and Elena Devecchi. Eothen 23. Firenze: LoGisma.

Pelon, Olivier. 1992. "Quatre campagnes à Porsuk (Cappadoce Méridionale) de 1986 à 1989." *Syria* 69:305–47. DOI: 10.3406/syria.1992.7292.

———. 1993. "La fouille de Porsuk-Ulukışla." Pages 14–19 in *Anatolie antique: Fouilles françaises en Turquie; Catalogue de l'exposition; Gypsothèque de l'Université Lumière Lyon II, 23 octobre–23 décembre 1990*. Edited by Jean-Louis Bacqué-Grammont, Michel Amandry, and Alain Davesne. Varia Anatolica 4/2. Istanbul: Institut Français d'Études Anatoliennes-Georges Dumézil.

Petrie, W. M. Flinders. 1890. "The Egyptian Bases of Greek History." *JHS* 11:271–77. DOI: 10.2307/623432.

———. 1891. *Tell el Hesy (Lachish)*. Cambridge: Cambridge University Press.

———. 1896. "Egypt and Israel." *The Contemporary Review* May 1896:617–27.

———. 1928. *Gerar*. British School of Archaeology in Egypt Publications 43. London: British School of Archaeology in Egypt.

———. 1930. *Beth-Pelet I (Tell Fara)*. London: British School of Archaeology in Egypt.

Pezard, Maurice. 1931. *Qadesh: Mission archeologique a Tell Nebi Mend, 1921–1922*. Bibliothèque archéologique et historique 15. Paris: Geuthner.

Pfälzner, Peter. 2007. "Archaeological Investigations in the Royal Palace of Qatna." Pages 29–64 in *Urban and Natural Landscapes of an Ancient Syrian Capital: Settlement and Environment at Tell Mishrifeh/Qatna and in Central-Western Syria; Proceedings of the International Conference Held in Udine, 9–11 December 2004*. Edited by Daniele Morandi Bonacossi. Studi archeologici su Qatna 1. Udine: Forum.

———. 2012. "Levantine Kingdoms of the Late Bronze Age." Pages 770–96 in vol. 2 of *A Companion to the Archaeology of the Ancient Near East*. Edited by Daniel T. Potts. 2 vols. BCAW. Hoboken, NJ: Wiley-Blackwell.

Phythian-Adams, W. J. 1923. "Report on the Stratification of Askalon." *PEQ* 55:60–84. DOI: 10.1179/peq.1923.55.2.60.

Pickles, Sydney, and Peltenburg, Edgar. 1998. "Metallurgy, Society and the Bronze/Iron Transition in the East Mediterranean and the Near East." *RDAC* 1998:67–100.

Platon, N., and E. Touploupa. 1965. "Καδμεῖον: Οἰκόπεδον Δημ. Παυλογιαννοπούλου (Πελοπίδου 28)" *ArchDelt* 20:233–35.

Popko, Lutz. 2016. "Die hieratische Stele MAA 1939.552 aus Amara West: Ein neuer Feldzug gegen die Philister." *ZÄS* 143:214–33.

Porath, Yosef, and Samuel M. Paley. 1982a. "The Regional Project in 'Emeq Hefer, 1981." *IEJ* 32:66–67.

———. 1982b. "Tel Ifshar – 1981." *ESI* 1:42–43.

———. 1993. "Hefer, Tel." *NEAEHL* 2:609–14.

Postgate, J. Nicholas. ed. 2017. *Excavations at Kilise Tepe 2007–2011: The Late Bronze and Iron Ages*. https://tinyurl.com/kilisetepe.

Postgate, J. Nicholas, and David Thomas, eds. 2007. *Excavations at Kilise Tepe, 1994–98: From Bronze Age to Byzantine in Western Cilicia; Text*. British Institute of Archaeology at Ankara Monograph 30.1. Cambridge: McDonald Institute for Archaeological Research.

Powell, Wayne, Michael Johnson, Cemal Pulak, K. Aslihan Yener, Ryan Mathur, H. Arthur Bankoff, Linda Godfrey, Michael Price, and Ehud Galili. 2021. "From Peaks to Ports: Insights into Tin Provenance, Production, and Distribution from

REFERENCES 363

Adapted Applications of Lead Isotopic Analysis of the Uluburun Tin Ingots." *JArS* 134:105455. DOI: 10.1016/j.jas.2021.105455.

Prag, Kay. 2014. "The Southern Levant during the Intermediate Bronze Age." Pages 388–400 in *The Oxford Handbook of the Archaeology of the Levant c. 8000–332 BCE*. Edited by Margreet Steiner and Ann E Killebrew. Oxford Handbooks. Oxford: Oxford University Press.

Prausnitz, Moshe W. 1963. "Achzib." *IEJ* 13:337–38.

———. 1965. "Tel Achzib." *IEJ* 15:256–58.

———. 1993. "Achzib." *NEAEHL* 1:32–35.

Prince, Philip Alexander. 1838. *Parallel Universal History: Being an Outline of the History and Biography of the World Divided into Periods*. London: Whittaker.

Pritchard James B. 1969. *Ancient Near Eastern Texts Related to the Old Testament*. 3rd ed. with supplement. Princeton: Princeton University Press.

Puglisi, Dario. 2013. "The View from the Day After: Some Observations on the Late Bronze Age I Final Destructions in Crete." Pages 171–82 in *Destruction: Archaeological, Historical and Philological Perspectives*. Edited by Jan Driessen. Louvain-La-Neuve: Presses Universitaires de Louvain.

Pulak, Camel. 2010. "Uluburun Shipwreck." Pages 862–76 in *The Oxford Handbook of the Bronze Age Aegean (ca. 3000–1000 BC)*. Edited by Eric H. Cline. Oxford Handbooks. Oxford: Oxford University Press.

Rakoczy, Lila, ed. 2008. *The Archaeology of Destruction*. Newcastle: Cambridge Scholars.

Ramsay, W. M. 1882. "Some Phrygian Monuments." *JHS* 3:256–63. DOI: 10.2307/623540.

Rapp, George Jr. 1986. "Assessing Archaeological Evidence for Seismic Catastrophies." *Geoarchaeology* 1:365–79. DOI: 10.1002/gea.3340010403.

Reade, Wendy J., Dan Barag, and Eliezer D. Oren. 2017. "Glass Vessels and Beads from the Late Bronze Age Temple at Tel Sera', Israel." *Journal of Glass Studies* 59:11–21.

Redford, Donald B. 1986. "The Ashkelon Relief at Karnak and the Israel Stela." *IEJ* 36:188–200.

———. 2000. "Egypt and Western Asia in the Late New Kingdom: An Overview." Pages 1–20 in *The Sea Peoples and Their World: A Reassessment*. Edited by Eliezer D. Oren. Museum Monograph 108. Philadelphia: University Museum, University of Pennsylvania, 2013. DOI: 10.9783/9781934536438.1.

———. 2018. *The Medinet Habu Records of the Foreign Wars of Ramesses III*. CHANE 91. Leiden: Brill.

Redsicker, David R., and John J. O'Connor. 1997. *Practical Fire and Arson Investigation*. 2nd ed. New York: CRC Press.

Reinisch, Leo. 1864. *Die Stele des Basilicogrammaten Schay im ägyptischen Cabinete in Wien: Mit Interlinear-Version und Commentar*. Philosophisch-Historische Klasse: Sitzungsberichte 10. Vienna: Hof.

Richard, Suzanne. 2014. "The Southern Levant (Transjordan) during the Early Bronze Age." Pages 330–52 in *The Oxford Handbook of the Archaeology of the Levant c. 8000–332 BCE*. Edited by Margreet Steiner and Ann E Killebrew. Oxford Handbooks. Oxford: Oxford University Press.

Ridder, André de. 1894. "Fouilles de Gha (pl. X–XI)." *BCH* 18:271–310. DOI: 10.3406/bch.1894.3696.

Riis, Poul Jørgen. 1970. *Sūkās I: The North–East Sanctuary and the First Settling of Greeks in Syria and Palestine*. Copenhagen: Munksgaard.

de Roos, Johan. 2007. *Hittite Votive Texts*. Uitgaven van het Nederlands Instituut voor het Nabije Oosten te Leiden 109. Leiden: Nederlands Instituut voor het Nabije Oosten.

Rose, Charles Brian. 2014. *The Archaeology of Greek and Roman Troy*. New York: Cambridge University Press.

Rothbaum, H. P. 1963. "Spontaneous Combustion of Hay." *Journal of Applied Chemistry* 13:291–302. DOI: 10.1002/jctb.5010130704.

de Rouge, Emmanuel. 1855. *Notice de quelques textes hiéroglyphiques récemment publiés par M. Greene: Mit 1 Tafel (Extrait de l'Athenaeum français)*. Paris: Thunot.

———. 1867. *Extraits d'un memoire sur les attaques dirigées contre l'Egypte par les peuples de la Mediterranee vers le quatorzième siécle avant notre ére*. Paris: Didier.

Routledge, Bruce, and Kevin McGeough 2009. "Just What Collapsed? A Network Perspective on 'Palatial' and 'Private' Trade at Ugarit." Pages 20–27 in *Forces of Transformation: End of the Bronze Age in the Mediterranean; Proceedings of an International Symposium Held at St. John's College, University of Oxford, 25–26th March 2006*. Edited by Cristopher Bachhuber and R. Gareth Roberts. Oxford: Oxbow.

Rova, Elena. 2014. "Tannurs, Tannur Concentrations and Centralised Bread Production at Tell Beydar and Elsewhere: An Overview." Pages 121–70 in *Paleonutrition and Food Practices in the Ancient Near East: Towards a Multidisciplinary Approach*. Edited by Lucio Milano. HANEM 14. Padova: SARGON.

von Rüden, Constance, Artemis Georgiou, Ariane Jacobs, and Paul Halstead, eds. 2016. *Feasting, Crafting and Depositional Practice in Late Bronze Age Palaepaphos: The Well Fillings of Evreti*. Bochumer Forschungen zur Ur- und Frühgeschichtlichen Archäologie 8. Rahden: Leidorf.

Rupp, David W. 1989. "Puttin' on the Ritz: Manifestations of High Status in Iron Age Cyprus." Pages 336–62 in *Early Society in Cyprus*. Edited by Edgar Peltenburg. Edinburgh: Edinburgh University Press.

Russell, Pamela Jaye. 1986. "The Pottery from the Late Cypriot IIC Settlement at Kalavasos-Ayios Dhimitrios, Cyprus: The 1979–1984 Excavation Seasons." PhD diss., University of Pennsylvania.

Rutter, Jeremy. B. 1974. "The Late Helladic IIIB and IIIC periods at Korakou and Gonia in the Corinthia." PhD diss., University of Pennsylvania.

———. 2015. "The Floor Deposits of LH IIIC Early at Korakou: Some Unconventional Approaches to Ceramic Analysis Made Possible by More Fully Preserved Pots." Presentation at the Οξυδερκειν at Korakou: A Centennial Celebration of C. W. Blegen's 1915–1916 Excavations; A Conference Sponsored by the Institute of Aegean Prehistory and by the American School of Classical Studies at Athens, September 4–6, 2015.

Sackett, L. Hugh, Mervyn R. Popham, Peter M. Warren, and Lars Engstrand. 1965. "Excavations at Palaikastro VI." *ABSA* 60:248–315.

Sader, Hélène. 1992. "The Twelfth Century BC in Syria: The Problem of the Rise of the Aramaeans." Pages 157–63 in *The Crisis Years: The 12th Century B.C.; From Beyond the Danube to the Tigris*. Edited by William A. Ward and Martha Sharp Joukowsky. Dubuque, IA: Kendall/Hunt Publishing.

———. 2014. "The Northern Levant during the Iron Age I Period." Pages 607–23 in *The Oxford Handbook of the Archaeology of the Levant c. 8000–332 BCE*. Edited by Margreet Steiner and Ann E Killebrew. Oxford Handbooks. Oxford: Oxford University Press.

REFERENCES 365

———. 2019. *The History and Archaeology of Phoenicia*. ABS 25. Atlanta: SBL Press

Salamon, Amos, Thomas Rockwell, Steven N. Ward, Emanuela Guidoboni, and Alberto Comastri. 2007. "Tsunami Hazard Evaluation of the Eastern Mediterranean: Historical Analysis and Selected Modeling." *Bulletin of the Seismological Society of America* 97:704–25. DOI: 10.1785/0120060147.

———. 2011. "A Critical Evaluation of Tsunami Records Reported for the Levant Coast from the Second Millennium BC to the Present." *Israel Journal of Earth Sciences* 58:327–54. DOI: 10.1785/0120060147.

Samet, Inbal. 2009. "Canaanite Rulership in Late Bronze Age Megiddo." MA thesis, Tel Aviv University.

Sampson, Adamiantos. 1980. "Ὁδός Πελοπίδου (οικόπεδο Μ. Λούκου)." *ArchDelt* 35:217–20.

———. 1985. "La Destruction d'un Atelier Palatial Mycénien à Thèbes," *BCH* 109:21–29. DOI: 10.3406/bch.1985.1816.

Sandars, Nancy K. 1985. *The Sea Peoples: Warriors of the Ancient Mediterranean, 1250–1150 BC*. Rev. ed. London: Thames & Hudson.

Sayce, Archibald Henry. 1888. *The Hittites: The Story of a Forgotten Empire*. London: Religious Tract Society.

———. 1909. "The Latest Hittite Discoveries." *Biblical World* 33:367–81.

Schaeffer, Claude F.-A. 1948. *Stratigraphie Comparée et Chronologie de l'Asie Occidentale*. London: Oxford University Press.

———. 1952. *Enkomi-Alasia: Nouvelles missions en Chypre 1946–1950*. Paris: Klincksieck.

———. 1963. "Neue Entdeckungen in Ugarit. (23. und 24. Kampagne, 1960–1961)." *AfO* 20:206–15.

———. 1966. "Neue Entdeckungen und Funde in Ugarit (1962–1964)." *AfO* 21:131–37.

———. 1968. "Commentaires sur les lettres et documents trouvés dans les bibliothèques privés d'Ugarit." Pages 607–768 in *Ugaritica V: Nouveaux textes accadiens, hourrites et ugaritiques des archives et bibliothèques privées d'Ugarit*. Edited by Jean Nougayrol, Emmanuel Laroche, Charles Virolleaud, and Claude F.-A. Schaeffer. MRS 16. Paris: Geuthner.

———. 1971. *Alasia I: À l'occasion de la XXe Campagne de Fouilles à Enkomi-Alasia (1969)*. Paris: Mission archéologique d'Alasia.

———. 1979. *Ras Shamra 1929–1979, par la Mission Archéologique de Ras Shamra*. Paris: Guichard.

Schachner, Andreas. 2020. "The 14th and 13th Centuries BC in the Hittite Capital City Hattuša: A (Re-)Assessment." Pages 381–410 in *Anatolia between the 13th and 12th Century BCE*. Edited by Stefano de Martino and Elena Devecchi. Eothen 23. Firenze: LoGisma.

Schilardi, Demetrius. 1980. "The Destruction of the LH IIIB Citadel of Koukounaries on Paros." Pages 158–79 in *Papers in Cycladic Prehistory*. Edited by Jack L. Davis and John F. Cherry. Institute of Archaeology Monograph 14. Los Angeles: Institute of Archeology, University of California.

———. 2012. "Koukounaries of Paros and Zagora of Andros: Observations on the History of Two Contemporary Communities." *Mediterranean Archaeology* 25:89–105.

———. 2016. *Koukounaries, Paros: The Excavations and History of a Most Ancient Aegean Acropolis*. Athens: Paros Excavations, Center of Historical and Archaeological Studies.

Schliemann, Heinrich. 1880. *Mycenae: A Narrative of Researches and Discoveries at Mycenæ and Tiryns.* New York: Scribners.

———. 1886. *Tiryns: The Prehistoric Palace of the Kings of Tiryns; The Results of the Latest Excavations.* London: Murray.

Schloen, David. 2008. "British and Israeli Excavations." Pages 153–64 in *Ashkelon 1: Introduction and Overview.* Edited by Lawrence E. Stager, David Schloen, Daniel M. Master. Winona Lake, IN: Eisenbrauns.

Schuler, Einar Von. 1957. *Hethitische Dienstanweisungen für höhere Hof-und Staatsbeamte: Ein Beitrag zum antiken Recht Kleinasiens.* AfOB 10. Graz: Selbstverl.

Seeher, Jürgen. 2001. "Die Zerstorung der Stadt Hattuša." Pages 623–34 in *Akten des IV. Internationalen Kongresses für Hethitologie, Würzburg, 4.–8. Oktober 1999.* Edited by Gernot Wilhelm. StBoT 45. Wiesbaden: Harrassowitz.

———. 2010. "After the Empire: Observations on the Early Iron Age in Central Anatolia." Pages 220–29 in *Ipamati kistamati pari tumatimis: Luwian and Hittite Studies Presented to J. David Hawkins on the Occasion of His 70th Birthday.* Edited by Itamar Singer. SMNIA 28. Tel Aviv: Tel Aviv University.

Selover, Stephanie LeSan. 2015. "Excavating War: The Archaeology of Conflict in Early Chalcolithic to Early Bronze III Central and Southeastern Anatolia." PhD diss., University of Chicago.

Seton-Williams, Marjory Veronica. 1961. "Preliminary Report on the Excavations at Tell Rifa'at." *Iraq* 23:68–87. DOI: 10.2307/4199696.

Shahack-Gross, Ruth, Ron Shaar, Erez Hassul, Yael Ebert, Mathilde Forget, Norbert Nowaczyk, Shmuel Marco, Israel Finkelstein, and Amotz Agnon. 2018. "Fire and Collapse: Untangling the Formation of Destruction Layers Using Archaeomagnetism." *Geoarchaeology* 33:513–28. DOI: 10.1002/gea.21668.

Shai, Itzhaq, Chris McKinny, and Joe Uziel. 2015. "Late Bronze Age Cultic Activity in Ancient Canaan: A View from Tel Burna." *BASOR* 374:115–33. DOI: 10.5615/bullamerschoorie.374.0115.

Shai, Itzhaq, Joe Uziel, Jeffrey R. Chadwick, and Aren M. Maeir. 2017. "The Late Bronze Age at Tell eṣ-Ṣâfi/Gath." *NEA* 80:292–95. DOI: 10.5615/neareastarch.80.4.0292.

Shai, Itzhaq, Joe Uziel, and Aren M. Maeir. 2012. "The Stratigraphy and Architecture of Area E: Strata E1–E5." Pages 221–34 in *Tell es-Safi/Gath I: The 1996–2005 Seasons.* Part 1: *Text.* Edited by Aren M. Maeir. ÄAT 69. Wiesbaden: Harrassowitz.

———. 2020a. "The Late Bronze Age Stratigraphy and Architecture." Pages 381–98 in *Tell es-Safi/Gath II: Excavations and Studies.* Edited by Aren M. Maeir and Joe Uziel. ÄAT 105. Münster: Zaphon.

———. 2020b. "Overview of the Late Bronze Age Remains from Area E." Pages 499–520 in *Tell es-Safi/Gath II: Excavations and Studies.* Edited by Aren M. Maeir and Joe Uziel. ÄAT 105. Münster: Zaphon.

Sharon, Ilan, and Ayelet Gilboa 2013. "The *SKL* Town: Dor in the Early Iron Age." Pages 393–468 in *The Philistines and Other "Sea Peoples" in Text and Archaeology.* Edited by Ann E. Killebrew and Gunner Lehman. ABS 15. Atlanta: Society of Biblical Literature.

Shear, Ione Mylonas. 1987. *The Panagia Houses at Mycenae.* University Museum Monograph 68. Philadelphia: University Museum, University of Pennsylvania.

Shelmerdine, Cynthia W. 1997. "Review of Aegean Prehistory VI: The Palatial Bronze Age of the Southern and Central Greek Mainland." *AJA* 101:537–85. DOI: 10.2307/507109.

———. 1999. "'Pylian Polemics: The Latest Evidence on Military Matters.'" Pages 403–10 in *Polemos: Le Contexte Guerrier en Égée à l'âge du Bronze; Actes de la 7e Rencontre Égéenne Internationale, Université de Liège, 14–17 Avril 1998*. Edited by Robert Laffineur. Aegaeum 19. Liège: Université de Liège

———. 2001. "The Palatial Bronze Age of the Southern and Central Greek Mainland." Pages 329–82 in *Aegean Prehistory: A Review*. Edited by Tracey Cullen. AJASup 1. Boston: Archaeological Institute of America.

Sherratt, Andrew, and Susan Sherratt. 1991. "From Luxuries to Commodities: The Nature of Mediterranean Bronze Age Trade Systems." Pages 351–86 in *Bronze Age Trade in the Mediterranean: Papers Presented at the Conference Held at Rewley House, Oxford, in December 1989*. Edited by Noël H. Gale. Studies in Mediterranean Archaeology 90. Jonsered: Aströms.

———. 1993. "The Growth of the Mediterranean Economy in the Early First Millennium BC." *World Archaeology* 24:361–78.

———. 1998. "Small Worlds: Interaction and Identity in the Ancient Mediterranean." Pages 329–43 in *The Aegean and the Orient in the Second Millennium: Proceedings of the 50th Anniversary Symposium, Cincinatti, 18–20 April 1997*. Edited by Eric H. Cline. Aegaeum 18. Liège: Liège Université de Liège, Histoire de l'Art et Archéologie de la Grèce Antique.

Sherratt, Susan. 1994. "Commerce, Iron and Ideology: Metallurgical Innovation in 12th–11th Century Cyprus." Pages 59–106 in *Proceedings of the International Symposium: Cyprus in the 11th Century BC*. Edited by Vassos Karageorghis. Nicosia: Leventis Foundation.

———. 1998. "'Sea Peoples' and the Economic Structure of the Late Second Millennium in the Eastern Mediterranean." Pages 292–313 in *Mediterranean Peoples in Transition: Thirteenth to Early Tenth Centuries B.C.E.; In Honor of Professor Trude Dothan*. Edited by Seymour Gitin, Amihai Mazar, and Ephraim Stern. Jerusalem: Israel Exploration Society.

———. 1999. "E Pur si muove: Pots, Markets, and Values in the Second Millennium Mediterranean." Pages 163–211 in *The Complex Past of Pottery: Production, Circulation and Consumption of Mycenaean and Greek Pottery (Sixteenth to Early Fifth Centuries BC)*. Edited by Jan Paul Crielaard, Vladimir Stissi, and Gert Jan van Wijngaarden. Amsterdam: Gieben.

———. 2000. "Circulation of Metals and the End of the Bronze Age in the Eastern Mediterranean." Pages 82–98 in *Metals Make the World Go Round: The Supply and Circulation of Metals in Bronze Age Europe; Proceedings of a Conference Held at the University of Birmingham in June 1997*. Edited by Christopher F. E. Pare. Oxford: Oxbow.

———. 2003. "The Mediterranean Economy: 'Globalization' at the End of the Second Millennium B.C.E." Pages 37–62 in *Symbiosis, Symbolism, and the Power of the Past: Canaan, Ancient Israel, and Their Neighbors from the Late Bronze Age through Roman Palaestina; Proceedings of the Centennial Symposium W. F. Albright Institute of Archaeological Research and American Schools of Oriental Research, Jerusalem, May 29–May 31, 2000*. Edited by William G. Dever and Seymour Gitin. Winona Lake, IN: Eisenbrauns. DOI: 10.5325/j.ctv1bxh1vp.8.

———. 2010. "The Aegean and the Wider World: Some Thoughts on a World-Systems Perspective." Pages 81–106 in *Archaic State Interaction: The Eastern Mediterranean in the Bronze Age.* Edited by William A Parkinson and Michael L Galaty. Santa Fe: School for Advanced Research Press.

Shtienberg, Gilad, Assaf Yasur-Landau, Richard D. Norris, Michael Lazar, Tammy M. Rittenour, Anthony Tamberino, and Omri Gadol. 2020. "A Neolithic Mega-Tsunami Event in the Eastern Mediterranean: Prehistoric Settlement Vulnerability along the Carmel Coast, Israel." *PLoS ONE* 15:e0243619. DOI: 10.1371/journal. pone.0243619.

Silberman, Neil Asher. 1998. "The Sea Peoples, the Victorians, and Us: Modern Social Ideology and Changing Archaeological Interpretations of the Late Bronze Age Collapse." Pages 268–75 in *Mediterranean Peoples in Transition: Thirteenth to Early Tenth Centuries B.C.E.; In Honor of Professor Trude Dothan.* Edited by Seymour Gitin, Amihai Mazar, and Ephraim Stern. Jerusalem: Israel Exploration Society.

Simon, Zsolt. 2011. "The Identification of Qode: Reconsidering the Evidence." Pages 249–69 in *Egypt and the Near East: The Crossroads; Proceedings of an International Conference on the Relations of Egypt and the Near East in the Bronze Age, Prague, September 1–3, 2010.* Edited by Jana Mynářová. Prague: Czech Institute of Egyptology.

Simpson, R. Hope. 1965. *A Gazetteer and Atlas of Mycenaean Sites.* Bulletin Supplement 16. London: Institute of Classical Studies.

Simpson, R. Hope, and Oliver T. P. K. Dickinson. 1979. *A Gazetteer of Aegean Civilization in the Bronze Age: The Mainland and Islands.* Studies in Mediterranean Archaeology 52. Göteborg: Åström.

Singer, Itamar. 1987. "Dating the End of the Hittite Empire." *Hethitica* 8:413–21.

———. 1999. "A Political History of Ugarit." Pages 603–733 in *Handbook of Ugaritic Studies.* Edited by Wilfred G. E. Watson and Nicholas Wyatt. HdO 39. Leiden: Brill. DOI: 10.1163/9789004294103_016.

———. 2000. "New Evidence on the End of the Hittite Empire." Pages 21–33 in *The Sea Peoples and Their World: A Reassessment.* Edited by Eliezer D. Oren. Museum Monograph 108. Philadelphia: University Museum, University of Pennsylvania, 2013. DOI: 10.9783/9781934536438.21.

———. 2002. *Hittite Prayers.* Edited by Harry A. Hoffner Jr. WAW 11. Atlanta: Society of Biblical Literature.

———. 2007. "Who Were the Kaška?" *Phasis* 10:166–81.

Slane, Dorothy Anne. 1987. "Middle and Late Bronze Age Architecture and Pottery in Gözlu Kule, Tarsus: A New Analysis." PhD diss., Bryn Mawr College.

Skafida, Evangelia, Artemis Karnava, and Jean-Pierre Olivier. 2012. "Two New Linear B Tablets from the Site of Kastro-Palaia in Volos." Pages 55–73 in *Études mycéniennes 2010: Actes du XIIIe colloque international sur les textes égéens, Sèvres, Paris, Nanterre, 20–23 septembre 2010.* Edited by Pierre Carlier. Pisa: Fabrizio Serra.

Skafida, Evangelia, Artemis Karnava, Iakovos Georgiou, Dimitris Agnousiotis, Topa Karouzou, Kalogianni Eleni, Asderaki Emilia, Eleni Vaxevanopoulos, Georgiou Markos, Chara Rea, Manos Dionysiou, Elisabeth Tzoumousli, and M. Margaritov. 2020. "Ο οικισμός της Ύστερης Εποχής Χαλκού στο 'Κάστρο-Παλαιά' του Βόλου: Αποτελέσματα του ερευνητικού διεπιστημονικού προγραμμάτος και των πρόσφατων ερευνών, 2012–2014." Pages 57–68 in *Archaeological Work of Thessaly and Central Greece* 5. Edited by Alexandros Mazarakis Ainian. Volos: Ministry of Culture and Sports, Fund for Archaeological Resources and Expropriations and Laboratory of Archeology, University of Thessaly.

REFERENCES 369

Skafida, Evagelia, Artemis Karnava, Jean-Pierre Olivier, Thilo Rehren, Eleni Asderaki-Tzoumerkioti, Markos Vaxevanopoulos, Ioannis Maniatis, Georgia Tsartsidou, Iakovos Georgiou, Maria Tsigara, 2015. "Ο οικισμός της Ύστερης Εποχής Χαλκού στο 'Κάστρο-Παλαιά' Βόλου: Από τις ανασκαφικές έρευνες του Δ. Θεοχάρη στα νέα ευρήματα της πρόσφατης διεπιστημονικής έρευνας." Pages 135–57 in *Archaeological Work of Thessaly and Central Greece* 4. Edited by Alexandros Mazarakis Ainian. Volos: Ministry of Culture and Sports, Fund for Archaeological Resources and Expropriations and Laboratory of Archeology, University of Thessaly.

Smith, Cecil. 1892. "Egypt and Mycenaean Antiquities." *Classical Review* 6.10:462–66.

Smith, P. 2004. "Skeletal Remains from Level VI." Pages 2504–7 in vol. 5 of *The Renewed Archaeological Excavations at Lachish (1973–1994)*. Edited by David Ussishkin. 5 vols. SMNIA 22. Tel Aviv: Emery and Claire Yass Publications in Archaeology.

Smith, Robert H., and Timothy Potts. 1992. "The Middle and Late Bronze Ages." Pages 35–82 in *Pella in Jordan, 2: 1982–1985*. Edited by Anthony McNicoll, John Basil Hennessy, and Robert H Smith. Sydney: Meditarch.

Soennecken, Katia. 2017. "Kulturelle Umbrüche in der südlichen Levante der Übergang von der Bronze- zur Eisenzeit unter besonderer Berücksichtigung des Tall Zirāʿa." PhD diss., University of Wuppertal.

Sommer, Klaus. 2016. *Der 21. Januar 1192 v. Chr.: Der Untergang Ugarits?* Münchner Studien zur Welt 14. Munich: Utz.

Snodgrass, Anthony. 1987. *An Archaeology of Greece: The Present State and Future Scope of a Discipline*. Sather Classical Lectures 53. Berkeley: University of California Press.

South, Alisson K. 1980. "Kalavasos-Ayios Dhimitrios 1979: A Summary Report." *RDAC* 1980:22–53.

———. 1982. "Kalavasos-Ayios Dhimitrios 1980–1981." *RDAC* 1982:60–68.

———. 1983. "Kalavasos-Ayios Dhimitrios 1982." *RDAC* 1983:92–116.

———. 1984a. "Kalavasos-Ayios Dhimitrios 1983." *RDAC* 1984:14–41.

———. 1984b. "Kalavasos-Ayios Dhimitrios and the Late Bronze Age Cyprus." Pages 11–18 in *Cyprus at the Close of the Late Bronze Age*. Edited by Vassos Karageorghis. Nicosia: Leventis Foundation.

———. 1988. "Kalavasos-Ayios Dhimitrios 1987: An Important Ceramic Group from Building X." *RDAC* 1988:223–28.

———. 1991. "Kalavasos-Ayios Dhimitrios 1990." *RDAC* 1991:131–39.

———. 1992. "Kalavasos-Ayios Dhimitrios 1991." *RDAC* 1992:134–46.

———. 1996. "Kalavasos-Ayios Dhimitrios and the Organization of Late Bronze Age Cyprus." Pages 39–49 in *Late Bronze Age Settlement in Cyprus: Function and Relationship*. Edited by Paul Åström and Ellen Herscher. Studies in Mediterranean Archaeology and Literature 126. Jonsered: Åström.

———. 1997. "Kalavasos-Ayios Dhimitrios 1992–1996." *RDAC* 1997:151–75.

———. 2008. "Feasting in Cyprus: A View from Kalavasos." Pages 309–16 in *DAIS: The Aegean Feast; Proceedings of the 12th International Aegean Conference, 12e Rencontre égéenne internationale, University of Melbourne, Centre for Classics and Archaeology, 25–29 March 2008*. Edited by Louise Hitchcock, Robert Laffineur, and Janice L Crowley. Aegaeum 29. Liège: Université de Liège, Histoire de l'art et archéologie de la Grèce antique.

370   References

Spyropoulos, Theodoros. 1971. "Οἰκόπεδον Δημ. Παυλογιαννοπούλου (ὁδός Πελοπίδου)." *ArchDelt* 26:209.

———. 1973. "Ὀρχομενός." *ArchDelt* 28:258–63.

———. 1974. "To Anakritoro tou Minyou eis to Boiotikon Orchomenon." *Athens Annals of Archaeology* 7:313–25.

———. 2015. "Wall Paintings from the Mycenaean Palace of Boiotian Orchomenos." Pages 355–70 in *Mycenaean Wall Painting in Context: New Discoveries, Old Finds Reconsidered*. Edited by Hariclia Brecoulaki, Jack L. Davis, and Sharon R. Stocker. Μελετηματα 72. Athens: National Hellenic Research Foundation.

Spyropoulos, Theodoros, and John Chadwick. 1975. *Thebes Tablets II*. Minos Supplement 4. Salamanca: Universidad de Salamanca.

Stager, Lawrence E. 1993. "Ashkelon." *NEAEHL* 1:103–12.

———. 1995. "The Impact of the Sea Peoples in Canaan (1185–1050 BCE)." Pages 332–48 in *The Archaeology of Society in the Holy Land*. Edited by Thomas E. Levy. London: Leicester University Press.

Stager, Lawrence E., J. David Schloen, Daniel M. Master, Michael D. Press, and Adam Aja. 2008. "Stratigraphic Overview." Pages 215–326 in *Ashkelon 1: Introduction and Overview*. Edited by Lawrence E. Stager, David Schloen, and Daniel M. Master. Winona Lake, IN: Eisenbrauns.

Stanley-Price, N. 1979. *Early Prehistoric Settlement in Cyprus: A Review and Gazetteer of Sites, c. 6500–3000 BC*. BARIS 65. Oxford: British Archaeological Reports.

Steel, Louise. 2004. *Cyprus before History: From the Earliest Settlers to the End of the Bronze Age*. London: Duckworth.

van der Steen, Eveline J. 1996. "The Central East Jordan Valley in the Late Bronze and Early Iron Ages." *BASOR* 302:51–74. DOI: 10.2307/1357128.

Stern, Ephraim. 1978. *Excavations at Tel Mevorakh I (1973–1976). From the Iron Age to the Roman Period*. Qedem 9. Jerusalem: Hebrew University of Jerusalem.

———. 1984. *Excavations at Tel Mevorakh II (1973–1976): The Bronze Age*. Qedem 18. Jerusalem: Hebrew University of Jerusalem.

———. 1992. "The Many Masters of Dor." *BAR* 19:22–31, 76–78.

———. 2000. *Dor, Ruler of the Seas: Nineteen Years of Excavations at the Israelite-Phoenician Harbor Town on the Carmel Coast*. Jerusalem: Israel Exploration Society.

———. 2012. "Archaeological Remains of the Northern Sea People along the Sharon and Carmel Coasts and the Acco and Jezreel Valleys." Pages 473–507 in *The Ancient Near East in the 12th–10th Centuries BCE: Culture and History; Proceedings of the International Conference Held at the University of Haifa, 2–5 May, 2010*. Edited by Gershon Galil, Ayelet Levinzon-Gilboa, Aren M. Maeir, Dan'el Kahn, and Ayelet Gilboa AOAT 392. Münster: Ugarit-Verlag.

———. 2013. *The Material Culture of the Northern Sea Peoples in Israel*. SAHL 5. Winona Lake, IN: Eisenbrauns.

Stevanović, Mirjana. 1997. "The Age of Clay: The Social Dynamics of House Destruction." *Journal of Anthropological Archaeology* 16:334–95. DOI: 10.1006/jaar.1997.0310.

Stiros, Stathis C. 1996. "Identification of Earthquakes from Archaeological Data: Methodology, Criteria and Limitations." Pages 129–52 in *Archaeoseismology*. Edited by Stathis C. Stiros and R. E. Jones. Fitch Laboratory Occasional Papers 7. Athens: Institute of Geology & Mineral Exploration; British School at Athens.

Stockhammer, Philipp, W. 2017. "How Aegean Is Philistine Pottery? The Use of Aegean-Type Pottery in the Early 12th Century BCE Southern Levant." Pages 379–88

REFERENCES 371

in *"Sea Peoples" Up-to-Date: New Research on the Transformations in the Eastern Mediterranean in the 13th–11th Centuries BCE*. Edited by Peter M. Fischer and Teresa Bürge. CCEM 35. Vienna: Österreichische Academie der Wissenschaften. DOI: 10.2307/j.ctt1v2xvsn.24.

———. 2019. "Shifting Meanings and Values of Aegean-Type Pottery in the Late Bronze Age Southern Levant." Pages 233–46 in *The Late Bronze and Early Iron Ages of Southern Canaan*. Edited by Aren M. Maeir, Chris McKinny, and Itzhaq Shai. Archaeology of the Biblical Worlds 2. Berlin: de Gruyter. DOI: 10.1515/9783110628371-012.

Stöllner, Thomas, Zeinolla Samaschev, Sergej Berdenov, Jan Cierny, Monika Doll, Jennifer Garner, Anton Gontscharov, Alexander Gorelik, Andreas Hauptmann, Rainer Herd, Galina A. Kusch, Viktor Merz, Torsten Riese, Beate Sikorski, and Benno Zickgraf. 2011. "Tin from Kazakhstan–Steppe Tin for the West?" Pages 231–51 in *Anatolian Metal V*. Edited by Ünsal Yalçin. Veröffentlichungen aus dem Deutschen Bergau-Museum 180. Bochum: Deutsches Bergbau-Museum.

Strange, Jonathan. 2008. "The Late Bronze Age." Pages 281–310 in *Jordan: An Archaeological Reader*. Edited by Russell B. Adams. London: Equinox Publishing.

———. 2015a. "1990–93 Area C and D." Pages 29–62 in *Tall al-Fukhār: Results from Excavations in 1990–93 and 2002*, vol. 1: *Text*. Edited by John Strange. Proceedings of the Danish Institute in Damascus 9. Aarhus: Aarhus University Press.

———. 2015b. "2002 – Area F." Pages 63–72 in *Tall al-Fukhār: Results from Excavations in 1990–93 and 2002*, vol. 1: *Text*. Edited by John Strange. Proceedings of the Danish Institute in Damascus 9. Aarhus: Aarhus University Press.

———. 2015c. "The History and Significance of Tall al-Fukhār." Pages 419–22 in *Tall al-Fukhār: Results from Excavations in 1990–93 and 2002*, vol. 1: *Text*. Edited by John Strange. Proceedings of the Danish Institute in Damascus 9. Aarhus: Aarhus University Press.

Stubbings, Frank H. 1975. "The Recession of Mycenaean Civilization." Pages 338–58 in *The Middle East and the Aegean Region c. 1380–1000 BC*. Edited by I. E. S. Edwards, C. J. Gadd, N. G. L. Hammond, and E. Sollberger. 3rd ed. CAH 2.2. Cambridge: Cambridge University Press.

Sukenik, E. L. 1935. "Tell el Jerishe." *QDAP* 4:208–9.

———. 1938. "Tell el Jerishe." *QDAP* 6:225.

———. 1944. "Tell el Jerishe." *QDAP* 10:198–99.

Summers, Geoffrey D. 1993. *Tille Höyük 4: The Late Bronze Age and the Iron Age Transition*. British Institute of Archaeology at Ankara Monograph 15. London: British Institute of Archaeology at Ankara.

———. 2010. "Revisiting the End of the Late Bronze Age and the Transition to the Early Iron Age at Tille Höyük." *Iraq* 72:193–200. DOI: 10.1017/S0021088900000656.

———. 2013. "Some Implications of Revised C14 and Dendrochronological Dating for the 'Late Bronze Levels' at Tille Höyük on the Euphrates." Pages 311–28 in *Across the Border: Late Bronze–Iron Age Relations between Syria and Anatolia; Proceedings of a Symposium Held at the Research Center of Anatolian Studies, Koç University, Istanbul, May 31–June 1, 2010*. Edited by Aslihan K. Yener. ANESSup 42. Leuven: Peeters.

Summers, Geoffrey. D., D. H. French, C. S. Lightfoot, Stuart Blaylock, J. J. Coulton, Stephen J. Hill, and H. F. Russell. 1989. "The Year's Work." *AnSt* 39:3–16. DOI: 10.2307/3642807.

Swenson, Loyd S., Jr. 2013. *The Ethereal Aether: A History of the Michelson-Morley-Miller Aether-Drift Experiments, 1880–1930*. Austin: University of Texas Press.

Swiny, Stuart. 1986. *The Kent State University Expedition to Episkopi Phaneromeni*. Studies in Mediterranean Archaeology 74. Göteborg: Åström.

Symeonoglou, Sarantis. 1985. *The Topography of Thebes from the Bronze Age to Modern Times*. Princeton: Princeton University Press.

Tappy, Ron E. 2008. "Zayit, Tel." *NEAEHL* 5:2082–83.

Taylor, James, Amy Bogaard, Tristan Carter, Michael Charles, Scott Haddow, Christopher J. Knüsel, Camilla Mazzucato. 2015. "'Up in Flames': A Visual Exploration of a Burnt Building at Çatalhöyük in GIS." Pages 127–49 in *Assembling Çatalhöyük I*. Edited by Ian Hodder and Arkadiusz Marciniak. Themes in Contemporary Archaeology 1. Leeds: Maney.

Taylour, William, and Richard Janko. 2008. *Ayios Stephanos: Excavations at a Bronze Age and Medieval Settlement in Southern Laconia*. Supplementary Volume 44. London: British School at Athens.

Taylour, William, Elizabeth French, and K. A. Wardle. 1999. *Well Built Mycenae: The Helleno-British Excavations within the Citadel at Mycenae*. Fascicule 10: *The Temple Complex*. Oxford: Oxbow.

Thareani, Yifat, Michael Jasmin, and Philippe Abrahami. 2016. "Tel Achziv–Israel Preliminary Report, 2016: The Third Season of Excavations." https://telachziv.files.wordpress.com/2016/04/2016-achziv-preliminary-report.pdf.

———. 2017. "Tel Achziv–Israel Preliminary Report, 2017: The Fourth Season of Excavations." https://telachziv.files.wordpress.com/2016/04/2017-achziv-preliminary-report.pdf.

Theochares, Demetrios R. 1956. "Ἰωλκός (Βόλος)." *Ἔργον* 1956:43–50.

———. 1957. "Thessalie." *BCH* 81:590–97. DOI: 10.3406/bch.1957.2393.

———. 1958. "Iolkos: Whence Sailed the Argonauts." *Archaeology* 11:13–18.

———. 1960. "Ἀνασκαφαί εν Ἰωλκῷ." *ΠΑΕ* 1960:49–59.

———. 1961. "Ἀνασκαφαί Ἰωλκού." *ΠΑΕ* 1961:45–54.

Tefnin, Roland. 1978/1979. "Tell Abou Danné." *AfO* 26:145–47.

———. 1979. "Une ville fortifiée de l'Age du Bronze en Syrie du Nord: Tell Abou Danné." *Archéologia* 129:42–49.

———. 1980. "Deux campagnes de fouilles au Tell Abou Danné (1975–1976)." Pages 179–99 in *Le Moyen Euphrate: Zone de contacts et d'échanges; Actes du Colloque de Strasbourg 10–12 mars 1977*. Edited by Jean-Claude Margueron. Travaux du Centre de recherche sur le Proche-Orient et la Grèce antiques 5. Leiden: Brill.

Todd, Ian. A. 2013. *Vasilikos Valley Project 12: The Field Survey of the Vasilikos Valley*. Vol. 3: *Human Settlement in the Vasilikos Valley*. Studies in Mediterranean Archaeology 71.12. Göteborg: Åström.

Tomas, Helena. 2010. "Cretan Hieroglyphic and Linear A." Pages 340–55 in *The Oxford Handbook of the Bronze Age Aegean (ca. 3000–1000 BC)*. Edited by Eric H. Cline. Oxford Handbooks. Oxford: Oxford University Press.

Tsountas, Chrestos, and J. Irving Manatt. 1897. *The Mycenaean Age: A Study of the Monuments and Culture of Pre-Homeric Greece*. London: Houghton, Mifflin.

Tubb, Jonathan N. 1986. "Tell es-Sa'idiyeh 1986: Interim Report of the Second Season of Excavations." *ADAJ* 30:115–29.

———. 1988a. "Tell es-Sa'idiyeh 1987: Third Season Interim Report." *ADAJ* 32:41–58.

References

———. 1988b. "Tell es-Saʿidiyeh: Preliminary Report on the First Three Season of Renewed Excavation." *Levant* 20:23–88. DOI: 10.1179/lev.1988.20.1.23.

———. 1990. "Preliminary Report on the Fourth Season of Excavations at Tell es-Saʿidiyeh in the Jordan Valley." *Levant* 22:21–42. DOI: 10.1179/lev.1990.22.1.21.

———. 1993. "Saʾdiyeh, Tell-es." *NEAEHL* 4:1295–1300.

———. 1998. *Canaanites*. Peoples of the Past. London: British Museum.

Tubb, Jonathan N., and Peter G. Dorrell. 1991. "Preliminary Report of the Fifth (1990) Season of Excavations at Tell es-Saʿidiyeh." *ADAJ* 35:181–94.

———. 1993. "Tell es-Saʿidiyeh: Interim Report on the Sixth Season of Excavations." *PEQ* 125:50–74.

Tubb, Jonathan N., Peter G. Dorrell, and Felicity J. Cobbing. 1996. "Interim Report on the Eighth (1995) Season of Excavations at Tell es-Saʿidiyeh." *PEQ* 128:16–40.

———. 1997. "Interim Report on the Ninth Season (1996) of Excavations at Tell es-Saʿidiyeh, Jordan." *PEQ* 129:54–77.

Tufnell, Olga, Charles H. Inge, and Lankester Harding. 1940. *Lachish II (Tell ed Duweir) The Fosse Temple*. Oxford: Oxford University Press.

Tufnell, Olga, and Aharon Kempinski. 1993. "ʾAjjul, Tell el-." *NEAEHL* 1:49–53.

Uhlig, Tobias, Joachim Krüger, Gundula Lidke, Detlef Jantzen, Sebastian Lorenz, Nicola Ialongo, and Thomas Terberger. 2019. "Lost in Combat? A Scrap Metal Find from the Bronze Age Battlefield Site at Tollense." *Antiquity* 93:1211–30. DOI: 10.15184/aqy.2019.137.

Ünlü, Elif. 2016. "Tarsus-Gözlükule Höyüğü Geç Tunç IIb Katmanında Rastlanan Seramik Devamlılıkları = Tarsus-Gözlükule Höyük: The Continuity of Late Bronze Age IIb Ceramic Finds." *Cedrus: The Journal of Mediterranean Civilisations Studies* 4:1–9. DOI: 10.13113/CEDRUS.201601.

Ussishkin, David. 1985. "Levels VII and VI Lachish and the End of the Late Bronze Age in Canaan." Pages 213–30 in *Palestine in the Bronze and Iron Ages: Papers in Honour of Olga Tufnell*. Edited by Jonathan N. Tubb. Publications of the Institute of Archaeology 16. London: Institute of Archaeology.

———. 1993. "Lachish." *NEAEHL* 3:897–911.

———. 1995. "The Destruction of Megiddo at the End of the Late Bronze Age and Its Historical Significance." *TA* 22:240–67. DOI: 10.1179/tav.1995.1995.2.240.

———. 1998. "The Destruction of Megiddo at the End of the Late Bronze Age and Its Historical Significance." Pages 197–219 in *Mediterranean Peoples in Transition: Thirteenth to Early Tenth Centuries B.C.E.; In Honor of Professor Trude Dothan*. Edited by Seymour Gitin, Amihai Mazar, and Ephraim Stern. Jerusalem: Israel Exploration Society.

———. 2000. "Area G: Soundings in the Late Bronze Gate." Pages 25–74 in *Megiddo III: The 1992–1996 Seasons*. Edited by Israel Finkelstein, David Ussishkin, and Baruch Halpern. SMNIA 18. Tel Aviv: Emery and Claire Yass Publications in Archaeology.

———. 2004a. "The Expedition and Its Work." Pages 3–22 in vol. 1 of *The Renewed Archaeological Excavations at Lachish (1973–1994)*. Edited by David Ussishkin. 5 vols. SMNIA 22. Tel Aviv: Emery and Claire Yass Publications in Archaeology.

———. 2004b. "A Synopsis of the Stratagraphical, Chronological and Historical Issues." Pages 50–119 vol. 1 of *The Renewed Archaeological Excavations at Lachish (1973–1994)*. Edited by David Ussishkin. 5 vols. SMNIA 22. Tel Aviv: Emery and Claire Yass Publications in Archaeology.

374   REFERENCES

———. 2004c. "Area P: The Late Bronze Age Strata." Pages 188–214 in vol. 1 of *The Renewed Archaeological Excavations at Lachish (1973–1994)*. Edited by David Ussishkin. 5 vols. SMNIA 22. Tel Aviv: Emery and Claire Yass Publications in Archaeology.

———. 2004d. "Area P: The Level VI Temple." Pages 215–81 in vol. 1 of *The Renewed Archaeological Excavations at Lachish (1973–1994)*. Edited by David Ussishkin. 5 vols. SMNIA 22. Tel Aviv: Emery and Claire Yass Publications in Archaeology.

———. 2004e. "Area D: The Bronze Age Strata." Pages 282–315 in vol. 1 of *The Renewed Archaeological Excavations at Lachish (1973–1994)*. Edited by David Ussishkin. 5 vols. SMNIA 22. Tel Aviv: Emery and Claire Yass Publications in Archaeology.

———. 2007. "Lachish and the Date of the Philistine Settlement in Canaan." Pages 601–8 in *The Synchronisation of Civilisations in the Eastern Mediterranean in the Second Millennium B.C. III: Proceedings of the SCIEM 2000 – 2nd EuroConference Vienna, 28th of May–1st of June 2003*. Edited by Manfred Bietak and Ernst Czerny. CCEM 9. Vienna: Österreichischen Akademie der Wissenschaften.

———. 2008. "The Date of the Philistine Settlement in the Coastal Plain: The View from Megiddo and Lachish." Pages 203–18 in *Israel in Transition: From the Late Bronze II to the Iron IIa (c. 1250–850 BCE)*, Vol. 1: *The Archaeology*. Edited by Lester L. Grabbe. LHBOTS 491. New York: T&T Clark.

———. 2021. "The Late Bronze III–II Royal Palaces at Megiddo: A Rejoinder." *AeL* 31:473–86.

Vacek, Alexander. 2020. "Ugarit, Al Mina, and Coastal North Syria." Pages 1163–84 in vol. 2 of *A Companion to the Archaeology of Early Greece and the Mediterranean*. Edited by Irene M. Lemos and Antonios Kotsonas. 2 vols. BCAW. Hoboken, NJ: Wiley-Blackwell.

Vallianou, Despina. 1995. "Μινωικά κεραμικά εργαστήρια: Μια εθνογραφική προσέγγιση με νέα δεδομένα." Pages 1035–58 in *Pepragmena tu 7. Diethnus Krētologiku Synedriu. 1,1, Tmēma archaiologiko*. Edited by Nikolaos E. Papadogiannakēs. Rethymno: Dēmos Rethymnēs, Istorikē. kai Laographikē Etaireia Rethymnēs.

———. 1996. "New Evidence of Earthquake Destructions in Late Minoan Crete." Pages 153–68 in *Archaeoseismology*. Edited by Stathis C. Stiros and R. E. Jones. Fitch Laboratory Occasional Papers 7. Athens: Institute of Geology & Mineral Exploration; British School at Athens.

———. 1997. "The Potters' Quarter in LM III Gouves." *Aegaeum* 16:333–44.

Van Beek, Gus W. 1993. "Jemmeh, Tell." *NEAEHL* 2:667–74.

Van De Mieroop Marc. 2008. *The Eastern Mediterranean in the Age of Ramesses II*. New York NY: John Wiley & Sons.

Van Leuven, J. V. 1979. "Prehistoric Grain Explosions." *Antiquity* 53:138–40. DOI: 10.1017/S0003598X00109123.

Vanschoonwinkel, Jacques. 2002. "Earthquakes and the End of the Mycenaean Palaces." *Les Études Classiques* 70:123–37.

Venturi, Fabrizio. 2007. *L'Siria nell'età delle trasformazioni (XIII–X sec. a.C.): Nuovi contributi dallo scavo di Tell Afis*. Studi e testi orientali 8. Bologna: CLUEB.

———. 2008. "The Sea People in the Levant: A North–Syrian Perspective." Pages 365–82 in vol. 3 of *Proceedings of the 5th International Congress of the Archaeology of the Ancient Near East*. Edited by Joaquín Maria Córdoba Zoilo, Miquel Molist, Maria Carmen Pérez, Isabel Rubio, and Sergio Martínez. Madrid: Universidad Autónoma de Madrid.

———. 2010. "Cultural Breakdown or Evolution? The Impact of Changes in 12th B.C. Tell

REFERENCES 375

Afis." Pages 1–27 in *Societies in Transition: Evolutionary Processes in the Northern Levant between Late Bronze Age II and Early Iron Age; Papers Presented on the Occasion of the 20th Anniversary of the New Excavation in Tell Afis, Bologna, 15th November 2007.* Edited by Fabrizio Venturi. Studi e testi orientali 9. Bologna: CLUEB.

———. 2012. "Hittites at Tell Afis, I: New Evidence of Cultural Links between Syria and Anatolia through Analysis of Late Bronze Age II Tell Afis Material Culture." *Or* 81:1–31.

———. 2013. "The Transition from the Late Bronze Age to the Early Iron Age at Tell Afis, Syria (Phases VII–III)." Pages 227–59 in *Across the Border: Late Bronze–Iron Age Relations between Syria and Anatolia; Proceedings of a Symposium Held at the Research Center of Anatolian Studies, Koç University, Istanbul, May 31–June 1, 2010.* Edited by Aslihan K. Yener. ANESSup 42. Leuven: Peeters.

———. 2020. *Tell Afis: The Excavations of Areas E2–E4; Phases V–I; The End of the Late Bronze/Iron Age I Sequence; Stratigraphy, Pottery and Small Finds.* 2 vols. Studi di Archeologia Siriana 4. Firenze: Le lettere.

Vermeule, Emily Townsend. 1960. "The Fall of the Mycenaean Empire." *Archaeology* 13:66–76.

Vidal, Jordi. 2014. "Violence against Non-Combatant Population in the Levant in the Late Bronze Age." Pages 65–78 in *The Other Face of the Battle: The Impact of War on Civilians in the Ancient Near East.* Edited by Davide Nadali and Jordi Vidal. AOAT 413. Münster: Ugarit-Verlag

Vieweger, Dieter. 2011. "The Transition from the Bronze to the Iron Age in Northern Palestine: Archaeological and Archaeometric Investigations on Tall Zirā ʿa." *AeL* 21:305–17.

———. 2013. "The Transition from Bronze to Iron Ages in Northern Palestine: Archaeological and Archaeometric Investigations at Tall Zarʿā." *SHAJ* 11:231–42.

Vincent, L. H. 1929. "L'Annee archeologique 1927–8 en Palestine." *RB* 38:92–114.

Vita, Juan-Pablo, and Valérie Matoïan, 2008. "Le roi et l'armée." Pages 258–64 in *"L'Orient des palais": Le Palais royal d'Ougarit au Bronze recent.* Edited by Michel Al-Maqdissi and Valérie Matoïan. Documents d'archéologie syrienne 15. Damascus: Ministère de la culture, Direction générale des antiquités et des musées.

Voskos, Ioannis, and A. Bernard Knapp. 2008. "Cyprus at the End of the Late Bronze Age: Crisis and Colonization or Continuity and Hybridization?" *AJA* 112:659–84.

Wace, Alan John Bayard. 1964. *Mycenae: An Archaeological History and Guide.* 2nd ed. Princeton: Princeton University Press.

———. 1980. *Excavations at Mycenae, 1939–1955.* British School at Athens Supplementary Volume 12. Athens: British School of Archaeology at Athens.

Wace, Alan John Bayard, W. A. Heurtley, Winifred Lamb, Leicester B. Holland, and C. A. Boethius. 1923. "The Report of the School Excavations at Mycenae, 1920–1923." *ABSA* 25:1–434.

Wagner-Durand, Elisabeth. 2020. "Kamid el-Loz during the Early Centuries of the Iron Age." Pages 73–101 in *The Iron Age I in the Levant: A View from the North; Part 2.* Edited by Hanan Charaf and Lynn Welton. AHL 52–53. London: Lebanese British Friends of the National Museum.

Walberg, Gisela. 1998. *Excavations on the Acropolis of Midea: Results of the Greek-Swedish Excavations under the Direction of Katie Demakopoulou and Paul Åström.* Skrifter utgivna av Svenska institutet i Athen 49. Stockholm: Åström.

376 REFERENCES

———. 2007. *Midea: The Megaron Complex and Shrine Area; Excavations on the Lower Terraces, 1994–1997.* Prehistory Monographs 20. Phildelphia: INSTAP Academic Press.

Waldbaum, Jane C. 1989. "Copper, Iron, Tin, Wood: The Start of the Iron Age in the Eastern Mediterranean." *Archeomaterials* 3:111–122.

———. 1999. "The Coming of Iron in the Eastern Mediterranean: Thirty Years of Archaeological and Technological Research." Pages 27–58 in *The Archaeometallurgy of the Asian Old World.* Edited by Vincent C Pigott. University Museum Monographs 89. Philadelphia: University Museum, University of Pennsylvania.

Ward, William A., and Martha Sharp Joukowsky. 1992. *The Crisis Years: The 12th Century B.C.: From Beyond the Danube to the Tigris.* Dubuque, IA: Kendall/Hunt Publishing

Ward, William Hayes. 1896. "Early Palestine." *Biblical World* 7:401–10.

Webb, Jennifer M. 1999. *Ritual Architecture, Iconography and Practice in the Late Cypriot Bronze Age.* Studies in Mediterranean Archaeology and Literature 75. Jonsered: Åström.

Webster, Lyndelle C., Omer Sergi, Sabine Kleiman, Oded Lipschits, Quan Hua, Geraldine E. Jacobsen, Yann Tristant, and Yuval Gadot. 2017. "Preliminary Radiocarbon Results for Late Bronze Age Strata at Tel Azekah and Their Implications." *Radiocarbon* 60:309–31. DOI: 10.1017/RDC.2017.85.

Weeden, Mark. 2013. "After the Hittites: The Kingdoms of Karkamish and Palistin in Northern Syria." *BICS* 56.2:1–20. DOI: 10.1111/j.2041-5370.2013.00055.x.

———. 2015. "The Land of Walastin at Tell Tayınat." *NABU* 2015.2:65–66, no. 44.

Weiberg, Erika, and Martin Finné. 2018. "Resilience and Persistence of Ancient Societies in the Face of Climate Change: A Case Study from Late Bronze Age Peloponnese." *World Archaeology* 50:584–602. DOI: 10.1080/00438243.2018.1515035.

Weinberg, Saul. 1983. *Bamboula at Kourion: The Architecture.* University Museum Monograph 42. Philadelphia: University Museum, University of Pennsylvania.

Welton, Lynn. 2019. "A New Start or Business as Usual? Evidence from the Earliest Iron Age I Levels at Tell Tayinat." Pages 70–92 in *The Iron Age I in the Levant: A View from the North; Part 1.* Edited by Hanan Charaf and Lynn Welton. AHL 50–51. London: Lebanese British Friends of the National Museum.

Welton, Lynn, Timothy Harrison, Stephen Batiuk, Elif Ünlü, Brian Janeway, Doğa Karakaya, David Lipovitch, David Lumb, and James Roames. 2019. "Shifting Networks and Community Identity at Tell Tayinat in the Iron I (ca. 12th to Mid–10th Century B.C.E.)." *AJA* 123:291–333. DOI: 10.3764/aja.123.2.0291.

Wiener, Malcolm H. 2015. "The Mycenaean Conquest of Minoan Crete." Pages 131–42 in *The Great Islands: Studies of Crete and Cyprus Presented to Gerald Cadogan.* Edited by Stylianos Andreu, Eleni Hatzaki, and Colin F. MacDonald. Athens: Kapon.

Weinstein, James Morris. 1973. "Foundation Deposits in Ancient Egypt." PhD diss., University of Pennsylvania.

———. 1992. "The Collapse of the Egyptian Empire in the Southern Levant." Pages 142–50 in *The Crisis Years: The 12th Century B.C.; From Beyond the Danube to the Tigris.* Edited by William A. Ward and Martha Sharp Joukowsky. Dubuque, IA: Kendall/Hunt Publishing.

———. 2012. "Egypt and the Levant in the Reign of Ramesses III." Pages 160–80 in *Ramesses III: The Life and Times of Egypt's Last Hero.* Edited by Eric H. Cline and David Bourke O'Connor. Ann Arbor: University of Michigan Press.

REFERENCES 377

Weiss, Barry. 1982. "The Decline of Late Bronze Age Civilization as a Possible Response to Climatic Change." *Climatic Change* 4:173–98. DOI: 10.1007/BF02423389.

Weissbein, Itamar, Yosef Garfinkel, Michael G. Hasel and Martin G. Klingbeil. 2016. "Goddesses from Canaanite Lachish." *Strata: Bulletin of the Anglo-Israel Archaeological Society* 34:41–55.

Weissbein, Itamar, Yosef Garfinkel, Michael G. Hasel, Martin G. Klingbeil, Baruch Brandl, and Hadas Misgav. 2020. "The Level VI North-East Temple at Tel Lachish." *Levant* 51:76–104. DOI: 10.1080/00758914.2019.1695093.

van Wijngaarden, Gert. J. 2002. *Use and Appreciation of Mycenaean Pottery in the Levant, Cyprus and Italy (ca. 1600–1200 BC).* Amsterdam Archaeological Studies 8. Amsterdam: Amsterdam University Press.

Wilson, John A. 1927. "The Texts of the Battle of Kadesh." *AJSL* 43:266–87. DOI: 10.1086/370157.

Wood, Bryant. G. 1991. "The Philistines Enter Canaan: Were They Egyptian Lackeys or Invading Conquerors?" *BAR* 17.6:44–52, 89–90, 92.

Woodhouse, Robert. 2009. "An Overview of Research on Phrygian from the Nineteenth Century to the Present Day." *Studia Linguistica Universitatis Iagellonicae Cracoviensis* 126:167–88. DOI: 10.2478/v10148-010-0013-x.

Woolley, Leonard C. 1921. *Carchemish: Report on the Excavations at Djerabis.* Part 2: *The Town Defences.* London: The Trustees of the British Museum.

———. 1955. *Alalakh: An Account of the Excavations at Tell Atchana in the Hatay, 1937–1949.* Oxford: Oxford University Press.

———. 1959. *A Forgotten Kingdom: Being a Record of the Results Obtained from the Excavations of Two Mounds, Atchana and Al Mina, in the Turkish Hatay.* London: Parrish.

Wright, G. Ernest. 1939. "Iron: The Date of Its Introduction into Common Use in Palestine." *AJA* 43:458–63.

Yağcı, Remzi. 2007a. "Hittites at Soli (Cilicia)." Pages 797–814 in vol. 2 of *VI Congresso Internazionale di Ittitologia, Roma, 5–9 settembre 2005.* Edited by Alfonso Archi and Rita Francia. 2 vols. Studi micenei ed egeo-anatolici 50. Rome: CNR, Istituto di studi sulle civilta dell'Egeo e del Vicino Orienre.

———. 2007b. "Soli (Kilikia) Miken IIIC Kapları." Pages 367–76 in *Patronvs: Coşkun Özgünel'e 65. Yaş Armağanı = Festschrift für Coşkun Özgünel zum 65. Geburtstag.* Edited by Erhan Öztepe and Musa Kadıoğlu. Istanbul: Homer Kitebavi.

———. 2008. "The Invisible Presence of the Sea Peoples in Cilicia - Kilikya'da Deniz Kavimleri Sorunu." Pages 233–40 in *Bati Anadolu ve Dogu Akdeniz Gec Tunc Cagi Kulturleri Uzerine Yeni Arastirmalar.* Edited by Armağan Erkanal-Öktü, Sevinç Günel, Ulaş Deniz, Sevinç Günel, and Armağan Erkanal-Öktü. Arkeoloji-Sanat Tarihi Bölümü. Ankara: Hacettepe Üniversitesi.

Yahalom-Mack, Naama, and Adi Eliyahu-Behar. 2015. "The Transition from Bronze to Iron in Canaan: Chronology, Technology, and Context." *Radiocarbon* 57:285–305. DOI: 10.2458/azu_rc.57.18563.

Yahalom-Mack, Naama, Ehud Galili, Irina Segal, Adi Eliyahu-Behar, Elisabetta Boaretto, Sana Shilstein, and Israel Finkelstein. 2014. "New Insights into Levantine Copper Trade: Analysis of Ingots from the Bronze and Iron Ages in Israel." *JArS* 45:159–77. DOI: 10.1016/j.jas.2014.02.004.

Yahalom-Mack, Naama, and Sariel Shalev. 2009. "Metal Objects." Pages 419–43 in *Aphek-Antipatris II: The Remains on the Acropolis; The Moshe Kochavi and Pirhyia Beck*

378 REFERENCES

Excavations. Edited by Yuval Gadot, Esther Yadin, and Gabriella Bachi. SMNIA 27. Tel Aviv: Emery and Claire Yass Publications in Archaeology.

Yalçin, Serdar. 2013. "A Re-Evaluation of the Late Bronze to Early Iron Age Transitional Period: Stratigraphic Sequence and Plain Ware of Tarsus-Gözlükule." Pages 195–212 in *Across the Border: Late Bronze–Iron Age Relations between Syria and Anatolia; Proceedings of a Symposium Held at the Research Center of Anatolian Studies, Koç University, Istanbul, May 31–June 1, 2010.* Edited by Aslihan K. Yener. ANESSup 42. Leuven: Peeters.

Yakar, Jak. 1993. "Anatolian Civilization Following the Disintegration of the Hittite Empire: An Archaeological Appraisal." *TA* 20:3–28. DOI: 10.1179/tav.1993.1993.1.3.

———. 2006. "Dating the Sequence of the Final Destruction/Abandonment of LBA Settlements: Towards a Better Understanding of Events That Led to the Collapse of the Hittite Kingdom." Pages 33–51 in *Strukturierung und Datierung der hethitischen Archäologie: Voraussetzungen, Probleme, Neue Ansätze; Internationaler Workshop Istanbul, 26–27. November 2004.* Edited by Dirk Paul Mielke, Ulf-Dietrich Schoop, and Jürgen Seeher. Byzas 4. Istanbul: Ege Yayınları.

———. 2007. "The Archaeology of the Kaška." Pages 817–27 in *VI Congresso Internazionale di Ittitologia, 5–9 settembre 2005.* Edited by Alfonso Archi. Studi Micenei ed Egeo-Anatolici 50. Rome: CNR, Istituto di studi sulle civilta dell'Egeo e del Vicino Orienre.

Yannai, Eli. 2002. "A Stratigraphic and Chronological Reappraisal of the 'Governor's Residence' at Tell el-Far'ah (South)." Pages 368–76 in *Aharon Kempinski Memorial Volume: Studies in Archaeology and Related Disciplines.* Edited by Eliazer Oren and Shmuel Ahituv. Beer-Sheva 15. Beer-Sheva: Ben-Gurion University of the Negev Press.

Yasur-Landau, Assaf. 2010. *The Philistines and Aegean Migration at the End of the Late Bronze Age.* Cambridge: Cambridge University Press, 2010.

Yisraeli, Yael. 1993. "Far'ah, Tell El - (South)." *NEAEHL* 2:441–44.

Yener, K. Aslihan. 2013a. "New Excavations at Alalakh: The 14th–12th Centuries B.C.E." Pages 11–35 in *Across the Border: Late Bronze–Iron Age Relations between Syria and Anatolia; Proceedings of a Symposium Held at the Research Center of Anatolian Studies, Koç University, Istanbul, May 31–June 1, 2010.* Edited by Aslihan K. Yener. ANESSup 42. Leuven: Peeters.

———, ed. 2013b. *Across the Border: Late Bronze–Iron Age Relations between Syria and Anatolia; Proceedings of a Symposium Held at the Research Center of Anatolian Studies, Koç University, Istanbul, May 31–June 1, 2010.* ANESSup 42. Leuven: Peeters.

———. 2017. "Cult and Ritual at Late Bronze Age II Alalakh: Hybridity and Power under Hittite Administration." Pages 215–24 in *Hittitology Today: Studies on Hittite and Neo-Hittite Anatolia in Honor of Emmanuel Laroche's 100th Birthday/L'hittitologie aujourd'hui: études sur l'Anatolie hittite et néo-hittite à l'occasion du centenaire de la naissance d'Emmanuel Laroche.* Edited by Alice Mouton. Istanbul: Institut Français d'Études Anatoliennes Georges Dumézil. DOI: 10.4000/books.ifeagd.3548.

Yener, K. Aslihan, and Murat Akar. 2013. "Alalakh-Tell Atchana." Pages 264–71 in *Hittites: An Anatolian Empire.* Edited by Meltem Doğan-Alparslan and Metin Alparslan. Anadolu uygarlıkları serisi 3. Istanbul: Tüpraş.

Yon, Marguerite. 1992. "The End of the Kingdom of Ugarit." Pages 111–22 in *The Crisis Years: The 12th Century B.C.; From Beyond the Danube to the Tigris.* Edited

REFERENCES 379

by William A. Ward and Martha Sharp Joukowsky. Dubuque, IA: Kendall/Hunt Publishing.

———. 2006. *The City of Ugarit at Tell Ras Shamra*. Winona Lake, IN: Eisenbrauns.

Younger, K. Lawson, Jr. 2016. *A Political History of the Arameans: From Their Origins to the End of Their Polities*. ABS 13. Atlanta: SBL Press.

Zuckerman, Alexander. 2010. "On Aegean Involvement in Trade with the Near East during the Late Bronze Age." *UF* 42: 887–901.

Zuckerman, Sharon. 2007. "Anatomy of a Destruction: Crisis Architecture, Termination Rituals and the Fall of Canaanite Hazor." *Journal of Mediterranean Archaeology* 20:3–32. DOI: 10.1558//jmea.2007.v20i1.3.

———. 2009. "The Last Days of a Canaanite Kingdom: A View from Hazor." Pages 100–107 in *Forces of Transformation: End of the Bronze Age in the Mediterranean; Proceedings of an International Symposium Held at St. John's College, University of Oxford, 25–26th March 2006*. Edited by Cristopher Bachhuber and R. Gareth Roberts. Oxford: Oxbow.

———. 2013. "Area S: Renewed Excavations in the Lower City of Hazor." *NEA* 76:94–97. DOI: 10.5615/neareastarch.76.2.0094.

Zuckerman, Sharon, David Ben-Shlomo, Penelope A. Mountjoy, and Hans Mommsen. 2010. "A Provenance Study of Mycenaean Pottery from Northern Israel." *Journal of Archaeological Science* 37:409–16.

Zwickel, Wolfgang. 2011. "Jaffa in Its Regional Context during the Late Bronze and Iron Ages." Pages 79–93 in *The History and Archaeology of Jaffa I*. Edited by Martin Peilstöcker and Aaron A. Burke. Monumenta Archaeologica 25. Los Angeles: Cotsen Institute of Archaeology Press.

INDEX

SITE NAMES

A

Abu al-Kharaz, Tell 100–101, 292
Abu Danné, Tell 88, 279, 291
Abu Hawam, Tell 9, 96, 120, 167, 258, 292
Abu Hureyra, Tell 40
Acco 93, 95–96, 120, 126, 129, 248, 258,
    272, 281, 292
Achzib 93–95, 120, 258, 292
Afis, Tell 227–29, 279, 299
'Afula 9, 119–20, 122, 294
'Ajjul, Tell el- 124, 129, 294
Alaca Höyük 9, 11, 55, 108–11, 187,
    190–91, 272–73, 276, 293
Alalakh 9, 64, 65, 271, 289
Alassa *Paliotaverna* and *Pano Mandilaris*
    14, 27, 42–43, 80, 83–86, 199, 214, 216,
    275, 291
Aleppo 64, 87–88, 115–16, 227, 255, 279,
    291, 294
Alishar Höyük 81–82, 190–91, 272, 276,
    291
Amman Airport Structure 101, 292
Ankuwa 82
Aphek 9, 16, 33–34, 45, 47, 236–37, 252,
    258, 261, 265, 275, 300
Apliki *Karamallos* 211–12, 215, 283, 298
Arslantepe 14, 62–63, 272, 289
Arwad 118, 258, 279, 294
Ashdod 9, 27, 102, 123, 240, 243, 258, 272,
    281, 292
Ashkelon 9, 15, 69, 123–24, 126, 240, 243,
    258, 261, 272, 294
Atchana, Tell 64–65
Athens 9, 77–79, 133, 291
Ayios Stephanos 79, 291
Azekah, Tel 14, 17, 69, 121, 252, 264, 272,
    276, 290

B

Batash, Tel 9, 120, 273, 294
Beer-Sheba 71
Beit Mirsim, Tell 8–9, 123, 247, 248, 273,
    301, 304
Bethel 8, 9, 238–39, 274, 300
Beth-Shean 17, 40, 65, 68, 72, 252–53,
    261, 264, 272, 276, 281, 290
Beth-Shemesh 8, 99–100, 258, 292
Beycesultan 30, 61, 127, 190, 286, 289
Boğazköy-Hattusa 6, 8, 9, 32, 34, 43–44,
    49, 165, 171–72, 176–80, 182–83, 187,
    190–91, 195–97, 276, 281, 297
Burna, Tel 122, 294
Byblos 118–19, 129, 258, 294

C

Carchemish 8–10, 115–17, 182, 254–56,
    268–70, 279–80, 294
Çine-Tepecik 59, 289

D

Dan, Tel 65, 128, 289
Debir 122–23, 273, 304, 330, 346
Deir Alla, Tell 9, 17, 39, 72–74, 251–53,
    264, 272, 276, 281, 290
Deir el-Balah 261
Dimini 105, 134–37, 142, 154, 163–65,
    167–68, 209, 224, 277–78, 283, 295
Domuztepe 111–12, 193, 293
Dor, Tel 9, 96–97, 120, 258, 292

E

Ekron. *See* Miqne-Ekron, Tel
Enkomi 9, 18, 27, 86, 114–15, 167, 199,
    200–202, 204–5, 214–17, 236, 247,
    263–64, 268, 273–74, 281, 298
'Eton, Tel 247, 252, 273, 301

382 INDEX

F

Faq'ous, Tell 88–89, 279, 291
Far'ah (South), Tell el- 71–72, 104, 261, 290
Fraktin 9, 181, 194–95, 297, 312, 348, 360
Fukhar, Tell el- 210, 249, 251–52, 275, 302

G

Gerisa, Tel 8, 98–99, 258, 292
Gezer 8, 9, 239–40, 300
Gla 8, 16, 49, 138–42, 154, 163–65, 167–68, 179, 209, 239, 277–78, 281, 283, 295
Gouves. *See* Kato Gouves

H

Hala Sultan Tekke 6, 9, 48–49, 86, 127, 214–16, 268, 291
Hama 9, 10, 116–17, 227, 252, 271–72, 279, 294
Hammam, Tall al- 40
Harasim, Tel 69, 121, 290
Haror, Tel 9, 248–49, 301
Hazor 6, 9, 10, 14–15, 35, 43, 65–67, 74, 117, 122–23, 128, 165, 193, 252, 272, 276, 289
Hefer, Tel 236, 252, 300
Hesi, Tell el- 53, 70, 104, 290, 293
Hisarlık-Troy 4, 7–8, 12–15, 32, 34, 53, 172–75, 191–93, 196, 276, 281, 283, 286, 296

I

Ifshar, Tell. *See* Hefer, Tel
Iklaina 14, 169, 278
Irbid, Tell 72, 290
Iria 11, 26, 76–77, 127, 277, 291

J

Jaffa 68–69, 261, 290
Jemmeh, Tell 10, 71, 104, 258, 290
Jokneam 233, 300, 311
Judeideh, Tell ej- 121–22, 294

K

Kadesh. *See* Nebi Mend, Tell

Kalavasos-*Ayios Dhimitrios* 14, 41, 50, 199, 208–9, 211, 215–16, 250, 274–75, 298
Kaman-Kalehöyük 30, 111, 190, 293
Kamid el-Loz 49, 92–93, 292
Kannia 160, 162, 273–74, 291, 296
Karaoğlan 8–9, 175–76, 194–96, 274, 281, 296
Kastanas 9, 132–34, 163, 277, 281, 295
Kastro-Palaia 8, 32, 105, 137–38, 163–64, 165, 277, 295
Kato Gouves 160–62, 273–74, 296
Katsingri. *See* Prophetis Elias
Kazel, Tell 45, 47, 205, 225–27, 259, 263, 265, 279, 282, 299, 307–8, 313, 318–19, 341
Keisan, Tell 9, 67, 120, 128, 258, 290
Khania (Kydonia) 80–81, 127, 272
Khirbet Rabud 11, 122–23, 273, 294
Kilise Tepe 184, 193–94, 276, 283, 297
Kinet Höyük 189, 194, 298
Kition 9, 10, 113–15, 199, 205, 214–16, 236, 268, 273, 293
Knossos 57–58, 115, 160, 272, 289
Korakou 106–7, 272, 281, 293
Kouklia *Palaepaphos* 82, 199, 214, 216, 291
Koukounaries of Paros 11, 59, 162, 272, 289
Kourion 112, 199, 214, 216, 293
Krisa 8, 11, 76–77, 272, 277, 291
Kuşaklı-Sarissa 6, 38, 181–83, 191–93, 195–96, 276, 283, 286, 297, 305, 356, 358
Kydonia. *See* Khania
Kynos 56–57, 281, 289

L

Lachish 6, 9, 14–17, 34–35, 41, 44, 70, 117, 123, 244–47, 252, 264–65, 275–76, 290, 301
Level VII 244–47
Lefkandi 9, 15, 56, 128, 272, 281, 289
Lidar Höyük 10, 63–64, 128, 190, 194, 289

M

Maa *Paleokastro* 9, 32, 47, 166, 199, 205, 212–14, 216, 272, 274, 298
Maroni-*Vournes* 14, 112, 199, 214, 216,

INDEX   383

274, 293
Maşat Höyük 9, 180–81, 190, 193, 196,
   276, 286, 297, 360
Megiddo 8, 9, 14–15, 236, 264
   Stratum VIIA 15, 68, 252, 290
   Stratum VIIB 235–36, 252, 300
Menelaion 8, 11, 144, 159–60, 163, 281,
   296
Mersin-Yumuktepe 16, 185, 276, 282, 297
Meskene-Emar 6, 9, 32, 35, 88–89, 165,
   230–31, 239, 265–66, 269–70, 279–80,
   291, 299
Mevorakh, Tel 97, 120, 258, 292
Michal, Tel 120, 122, 129, 258, 294
Midea 9, 11, 39, 47, 144, 147–54, 163–65,
   168, 277, 281, 283, 295
Miletus 8, 59, 60, 272, 289
Miqne-Ekron, Tel 32, 123, 243, 258, 283,
   301
Mor, Tel 39, 240–42, 258, 261, 263,
   300–301
Mycenae 4, 8, 11, 42, 44, 53, 74, 76, 132,
   144, 146–47, 154, 163–65, 168–69, 173,
   277, 281, 283, 295
Myrtou-*Pigadhes* 83, 214, 291

N

Nami, Tel 234, 263, 300
Nebi Mend, Tell 10, 116–18, 279, 294
Nichoria 8, 107–8, 126, 278, 293
Norşuntepe 9, 189–90, 194, 298, 333, 337

O

Orchomenos 8, 11, 74–77, 127, 133, 272,
   277, 291
Oymaağaç Höyük-Nerik 176, 195, 297

P

Palaikastro Kastri 58–59, 289
Paphos 212, 215–16
Pefkakia 105, 135, 277, 293
Pella 72, 100, 252, 253, 290
Phaistos 108, 124, 129, 273, 293
Porsuk. *See* Zeyve Höyük-Porsuk
Prophetis Elias/Katsingri 9, 156–57, 273,
   281, 296
Pyla-*Kokkinokremos* 205, 205–8, 214, 281,
   298, 315–16, 332, 343

Pylos 6, 8, 11, 14, 26, 32, 45, 107, 142, 144,
   153, 157–59, 163–64, 166, 168–69, 223,
   277–78, 281, 296

Q

Qarqur, Tell 229–30, 299
Qashish, Tel 233, 252, 273, 299
Qatna 10, 16, 116–18, 193, 227, 252,
   271–72, 279, 286, 294
Qubur el-Walaydah 104, 127, 293

R

Ras el-Bassit 9, 89–90, 258, 265, 272, 279,
   291
Ras Ibn Hani 9, 31, 224–25, 227, 239, 258,
   263, 265–67, 279, 299
Ras Shamra-Ugarit 1–2, 6, 8–9, 16,
   33–34, 45–47, 60, 89, 117, 165, 167, 194,
   196, 217, 219–25, 227, 252–58, 262–63,
   265–70, 272, 278–83, 286, 299
Rifaʿat, Tell 64, 279, 289

S

Şafi/Gath, Tell eş- 102–3, 121–23, 127,
   243, 258, 272, 293
Saʿidiyeh, Tell es- 73, 252, 272, 281, 290
Sarepta 14, 167
Seraʾ, Tel 9, 71, 290
Shariah, Tell esh-. *See* Seraʾ, Tel
Shiqmona 67, 120, 258, 290
Sidon 119, 167, 258, 294
Sinda 9, 86–87, 114, 199, 214, 272, 291
Sippor. *See* Zippor, Tel
Soli Höyük 31, 185, 194, 273, 297
Sukas, Tell 9, 91, 258, 272, 279, 292

T

Tarsus-Gözlükule 8–9, 16, 111, 117, 186–
   89, 193–94, 196, 276, 282–83, 297–98
Tayinat, Tell 259–61, 264
Teichos Dymaion 11, 31, 145, 156, 163,
   233, 273, 295
Thebes 3, 9, 11, 143–45, 163, 168, 277,
   281, 295
Tille Höyük 10, 14, 63, 128, 190, 194, 289
Tiryns 4, 8, 11, 32, 34, 53, 131, 144, 147,
   150, 154–57, 163–70, 173, 265, 277–78,
   281, 295–96

384 INDEX

Troy. *See* Hisarlık-Troy
Tweini, Tell 90–91, 127, 205, 258, 265, 272, 279, 292
Tyre 92, 167, 258, 292

U

'Umayri, Tall al- 210, 250–53, 275, 281, 302
Umm ad-Dananir 250, 252, 273, 302

Y

Yin'am, Tel 231–33, 299
Yumuktepe 8, 9, 185–87, 189, 193–94, 196, 276, 297

Z

Zayit, Tel 69, 121, 290
Zeror, Tel 9, 97–98, 258, 292
Zeyve Höyük-Porsuk 14, 61–62, 193, 289
Zippor, Tel 9, 42, 243, 283, 301
Zira'a, Tell 100, 292

MODERN AUTHORS

A

Abrahami, Philippe 95, 372
Adrimi-Sismani, Vassiliki 105, 134–36
Albright, William Foxwell 71, 122, 238, 247–48, 273
Ålin, Per 8, 42, 107
Alkim, U. Bahadir 111
Al-Maqdissi, Michel 91, 265, 345–46, 375
Anderson, John J. 13–14
Andreadaki-Vlazaki, Maria 81
Astour, Michael 117–18
Aravantinos, Vassilis 143, 145
Arık, Remzi Oğuz 109–10, 175
Arnaud, Daniel 231
Artzy, Michel 96
Åström, Paul 9, 48, 131, 323, 335, 369, 376

B

Badre, Leila 226, 313–14, 342
Balensi, Jacqueline 96, 308
Barako, Tristan 241
Barnett, Richard David 116
Bar, Shay 67–68

Batziou-Efstathiou, Anthi 105
Bell, Carol 10, 96, 124
Ben-Ami, Doron 234
Ben-Shlomo, David 71, 102
Benson, Jack Leonard 112
Ben-Tor, Amnon 165, 233, 309–11
Bergoffen, Celia 217
Beyer, Dominique 62–63
Bikai, Patricia M. 92
Biran, Avraham 244
Bittel, Kurt 11, 110, 176, 178
Blakely, Jeffrey 104
Blegen, Carl 8, 26, 106, 157, 173–74, 192
Bliss, Frederick Jones 104
Boehm, Ryan 285
Bourke, Stephen 117–18
Brandl, Baruch 241
Bretschneider, Joachim 90–91, 205, 304, 316, 326, 342–43
Broneer, Oscar 78
Bunimovitz, Shlomo 100
Burgess, Dawn 56, 107, 115–16, 175, 281
Bürge, Teresa 86

C

Cadogan, Gerald 112
Çambel, Halet 112
Catling, Hector W. 9, 159–60
Caubet, Anne 9
Chadwick, John 143
Chatzi-Vallianou, Despina 160–61
Cline, Eric 5, 10, 15, 56, 58, 60–61, 91, 107, 114–16, 123, 126–28, 133, 175, 219, 252, 271, 281–82
Cook, Arthur 98
Cosmopoulos, Michael 278
Courbin, Paul 89–90
Cucuzza, Nicola 160
Cunningham, Timothy 59–60

D

Dakoronia, Fanouria 56–57
Dakouri-Hild, Anastasia 143
Damm-Meinhardt, Ursula 155–56
Dawkins, Boyd 159
Demakopoulou, Katie 131
Demas, Martha 113–15, 206, 212–13
Desborough, Vincent Robin d'Arba 60,

107
Dever, William 7, 9, 119, 239
Dickenson, Oliver T. P. K. 169
Dikaios, Porphyrios 200–204, 212, 236, 281
Döhl, Hartmut 11, 26, 77
Dörpfeld, Wilhelm 173
Dothan, Moshe 95, 95–96, 241, 308, 325, 353
Dothan, Trude 95, 306–7, 311, 325, 333, 338, 345, 367–68, 373
Doumet-Serhal, Claude 119
Drews, Robert 4, 6, 10–11, 15, 56, 58–61, 63–64, 71, 79, 95–96, 106–7, 111, 114–18, 122–23, 125–28, 175, 271, 282
Driessen, Jan 205, 313, 315–16, 321, 342, 348, 359, 363
Du Mesnil du Buisson, Robert 117
Dunand, Maurice 118
Du Plat Taylor, Joan 83, 211–12, 309

E

Effenterre, Henri van 76
Elayi, Josette 118
Elgavish, Joseph 67–68
Eliyahu-Behar, Adi 262
Emanuel, Jeffrey 261

F

Faust, Avraham 69, 121, 122
Finkelstein, Israel 4, 14–15, 24–27, 34, 68, 128, 219, 235, 238
Fischer, Peter 86, 199
Flinders Petrie, W. M. 13, 70–71
Frank, Daniel 156
Frederick Jones Bliss 104
French, Elizabeth 180
Fugmann, Ejnar 116
Furumark, Arne 87

G

Garstang, John 13, 185–86, 193
Gates, Marie-Henriette 111
Gauss, Walter 79
Genz, Hermann 179, 283, 332
Georgiou, Artemis 199, 215, 217, 332, 344, 364
Gibson, Shimon 121

Gilboa, Ayelet 97, 330, 350, 366, 370
Gittlen, Barry 217
Godart, Louis 143, 145
Goetze, Albrecht 171
Goldman, Hetty 187–89
Gordon, Douglas H. 41
Gorny, Ronald 81
Grant, Elihu 99, 100
Gubel, Eric 226, 308, 338

H

Hadjisavvas, Sophocles 84–85
Halayqa, Issam 221
Hall, Harry Reginald 13
Hänsel, Bernhard 133–34
Hasel, Michael 47, 240, 254
Hauptmann, Harald 189–90
Heinz, Marlies 93
Hélène Sader 119
Herzog, Ze'ev 99, 120
Hinzen, Klaus-G. 150
Hooker, John 8, 168
Hruby, Julie 157

I

Iacovou, Maria 199, 217
Iakovidis, Spyros 138, 142, 144, 146, 167

J

Jannoray, Jean 76
Jensen, Eric 229–30
Jung, Reinhard 133, 155, 164
Jusseret, Simon 161

K

Kahn, Dan'el 255
Kaniewski, David 256, 273
Kanta, Athanasia 205, 315, 316, 343
Kaplan, Jacob 68–69, 69–70
Karacic, Steven 187
Karageorghis, Vassos 113–15, 206, 212–13, 273
Karakaya, Doğa 269, 283
Kassianidou, Vasiliki 217
Katzenstein, H. Jacob 92, 118
Kelm, George 120
Kelso, James 238

INDEX

Kilian, Klaus 9, 78, 131, 144, 154, 156, 164, 281
Kilani, Marwan 119
Kitchen, Kenneth 47
Knapp, Bernard 26, 61, 83, 91, 112, 123, 126–27, 199, 256, 262, 269, 271, 283
Knauf, Ernst Axel 13
Kochavi, Moshe 237
Kohlmeyer, Kay 87–88
Korfmann, Manfred 173–74, 309
Koşay, Hâmit Zübeyr 109–10
Kreimerman, Igor 43, 331, 337
Kurt Bittel 9, 9–10, 61–62, 109–10, 175–76, 272–73

L

LaFayette-Hogue, Shannon 157
Lagarce, Élisabeth 224
Lagarce, Jacques 224, 314, 320–21, 348
Lapp, Paul 122, 273
Lehmann, Gunner 111
Lehmann, Gustav 118
Lerat, Lucien 76
Lesko, Leonard H. 255
Liebowitz, Harold 232
Liverani, Mario 62–63, 254–55
Livieratou, Antonia 57
Lloyd, Seton 61–62
Loud, Gordon 235–36

M

Maeir, Aren 102–3
Maggidis, Christofilis 138
Magness, Jodi 284
Manning, Sturt 17, 26, 61, 91, 123, 126–27, 256, 269, 271, 283
Manuelli, Federico 62–63
Maran, Joseph 131, 155, 165, 167, 265
Margueron, Jean-Claude 88–89, 230–31, 353–54, 372–73
Martin, Mario 68–69, 235–36
Martino, Stefano de 197, 304, 322, 356, 362, 365
Maspero, Gaston 3, 8, 253
Mazar, Amihai 9, 73–74, 97, 120, 235
McClellan, Thomas 64–65, 88–89
McDonald, William 107
McGovern, Patrick 250

Mellaart, James 61–62
Merrillees, Robert 217
Meyer, Nathan 262
Middleton, Guy 78, 168
Milojcic, Vladimir 105
Mountjoy, Penelope 60–61, 78, 192–93
Müller-Karpe, Andreas 43, 181
Müller, Uwe 63–64, 255–56
Mumford, Gregory 101
Murray, Sarah 167

N

Negbi, Ora 244
Nelson, Michael 157
Niemeier, Wolf-Dietrich 60–61
Nowicki, Krzystof 58–59
Nur, Amos 5, 15, 56, 107, 115–16, 131, 133, 175, 199, 219, 252, 281–82

O

O'Connor, David 41
O'Connor, John 35
Ohata, Kiyoshi 98
Oliver Dickinson 8, 75
Omura, Sachihiro 111
Ortiz, Steven 239
Özgüç, Tahsin 180, 348
Özyar, Aslı 187, 359

P

Phythian-Adams, W. J. 123–24
Prausnitz, Moshe 94–95
Prince, Philip Alexander 7, 8, 14
Pritchard, James 256

R

Ramsay, W. M. 13
Rawson, Marion 157
Redsicker, David 35, 41
Ridder, André de 140–42
Riehl, Simone 269, 283
Rouge, Emmanuel de 8
Russell, Pamela 209, 318
Rutter, Jeremy 79, 106

S

Sacconi, Anna 143, 145

INDEX

Sackett, L. Hugh 58–59
Schaeffer, Claude F.-A. 200, 219–20, 252, 281
Schilardi, Demetrius 59–60
Schliemann, Heinrich 4, 7, 154, 173
Seeher, Jürgen 34, 177–79
Seton-Williams, Marjory Veronica 64–65
Shahack-Gross, Ruth 43, 335, 348
Sharon, Ilan 97, 332–33
Shelmerdine, Cynthia 11, 26, 77, 127, 166
Simon, Zsolt 44, 194
Simpson, R. Hope 8, 75
Singer-Avitz, Lily 238
Snodgrass, Anthony 34
Soennecken, Katja 100
Sommer, Klaus 221
South, Alisson 208–11
Spyropoulos, Theodoros 74, 143
Steel, Louise 205
Steen, Eveline van der 72
Stern, Ephraim 67–68, 93, 95, 97, 120
Strange, Jonathan 249
Sukenik, E. L. 98–99

T

Tappy, Ron 69–70
Tefnin, Roland 88–89
Theochares, Demtrios 137
Tsountas, Chrestos 146–47
Tubb, Jonathan 73–74
Tufnell, Olga 245

U

Usher, Bishop James 7
Ussishkin, David 44, 235, 245–46, 305, 308, 322, 328, 330, 352–53, 369, 373–74

V

Vanschoonwinkel, Jacques 131
Vermeule, Emily Townsend 168
Vidal, Jordi 221, 375
Vincent, L. H. 98
von der Osten, Hans Henning 81

W

Wace, Alan Lohn Bayard 146
Wagner-Durand, Elisabeth 93, 338
Ward, William Hayes 13
Weinberg, Saul 112
Welton, Lynn 260
Wolff, Samuel 239
Wood, Bryant 71
Woolley, Leonard 64–65, 115–16
Wright, G. Ernest 71

Y

Yağcı, Remzi 185, 359
Yahalom-Mack, Naama 262
Yalouris, Nicholas 107
Yasur-Landau, Assaf 96, 310, 348, 368
Yener, K. Aslihan 64–65
Yon, Marguerite 9, 221, 318, 348–50, 353
Younger, K. Lawson Jr. 61, 61–62, 259–60

Z

Zuckerman, Sharon 23–24, 46, 49, 165